The **Rough Guide** to

Mallorca and Menorca

written and researched by

Phil Lee

with additional research by

Gareth Rees, Jan Ogden, Gavin Thomas and

Yvonne McFarlane

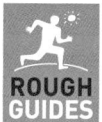

ROUGH
GUIDES

NEW YORK · LONDON · DELHI

www.roughguides.com

Contents

Architecture colour
section following p.160

Hiking colour
section following p.272

◀◀ Olive grove near Valldemossa ◀ Hotel Agriturismo Ca's Xorc

Introduction to

Mallorca and Menorca

No other Mediterranean holiday spot is as often and as unfairly maligned as Mallorca. The largest of the Balearic islands, an archipelago to the east of the Spanish mainland comprising four main islands – Mallorca, Menorca, Ibiza and Formentera – Mallorca is commonly perceived as little more than sun, sex, booze and high-rise hotels. Indeed, there's a long-standing Spanish joke about a mythical fifth Balearic island called "Majorca" (the English spelling), visited by an estimated eight million tourists a year – tourists who know little and care less about their island surroundings.

This negative image was spawned by the helter-skelter development of the 1960s, which submerged tracts of the coastline beneath hotels, villas and apartment blocks. In reality, however, the concrete sprawl is largely confined to the Bay of Palma and a handful of mega-resorts notching the east coast, and for the most part Mallorca remains – to the surprise of many first-time visitors – often beautiful and frequently fascinating, from the craggy mountains and medieval monasteries of its north coast through to the antique towns of the central plain. Indeed, there's a startling variety and physical beauty to the island, which, along with the mildness of the climate, has drawn well-heeled expatriates to settle here since the nineteenth century, from Habsburg dukes to artists, actors and writers of many descriptions, including Robert Graves, Michael Douglas and Roger McGough.

Straddling the sailing routes between the east and west Mediterranean, Mallorca was an important and prosperous trading station throughout the medieval period, but it was left behind in the Spanish dash to exploit the Americas from the early sixteenth century onwards. Neglected, Mallorca turned in on itself, becoming a deeply hierarchical and profoundly Catholic backwater dominated by a conservative landed gentry, who ruled the economic and political roost from their

▲ Robert Graves' house

large estates on the fertile central plain, Es Pla. Since the 1960s, however, **mass tourism** has literally stood things on its head. Agriculture, once the mainstay of the local economy, faded into the background, and the island's former poverty was all but washed away: Mallorca's population of 640,000 now enjoy the highest per capita level of disposable income in Spain.

To the east of Mallorca lies **Menorca**, the second largest and most agricultural island in the Balearic archipelago, with a population of just 66,000. Menorca's rolling fields, wooded ravines and humpy hills fill out the interior in between its two main – but still small – towns of Maó, the island's capital, and Ciutadella. Much of Menorca's landscape looks pretty much as it did at the turn of the twentieth century, though many of the fields are no longer cultivated, and only on the edge of the island (and

▼ Cala Major beach, Palma

5

then only in parts) have its rocky coves been colonized by sprawling villa complexes. Nor is the development likely to spread: the resorts have been kept at a discreet distance from the two main towns, and this is how the Menorcans like it. In addition, the islanders are also pushing ahead with a variety of environmental schemes, the most prominent being the creation of a chain of conservation areas that will eventually protect about half of the island, including the pristine coves that are one of its real delights.

Where to go

n **Mallorca**, the obvious place to begin a visit is **Palma**, the island capital, which arches around the shores of its bay just a few kilometres from Mallorca's busy international airport. Palma is the Balearics' one real city, a bustling, historic place whose grandee mansions and magnificent Gothic cathedral serve as a fine backdrop to an excellent café and restaurant

7

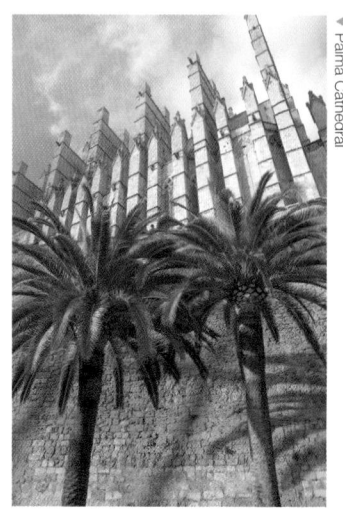

▼ Palma Cathedral

scene. Add to this lots of good hotels and you've got a city that deserves at least a couple of days. Indeed, many visitors spend their entire holiday here, day-tripping out into the rest of the island as the mood (and weather) takes them – an easy proposition given that it's only a couple of hours drive from one end of Mallorca to the other. To the east of Palma stretches **Es Pla**, an agricultural plain that fills out the centre of the island, sprinkled with ancient and seldom-visited country towns, the most interesting of which are **Binissalem**, **Sineu** and **Petra**. On either side of the plain are coastal mountains. To the north, the wild and wonderful **Serra de Tramuntana** rolls along the entire coastline, punctuated by deep sheltered valleys and beautiful cove **beaches**, notably Cala Deià and Platja de Formentor. Tucked away here too is **Sóller**, a delightful market town of old stone merchant houses that is best reached from Palma on the antique **railway**, an extraordinarily scenic journey. The mountains also hide a string of picturesque villages, most memorably **Banyalbufar**, **Deià**, the long-time haunt of Robert Graves, and **Fornalutx**, as well as a pair of intriguing monasteries at **Valldemossa**, where Chopin and George Sand famously wintered, and **Lluc**, home to a much-venerated statue of the Madonna. The range is also criss-crossed with footpaths and makes for ideal **hiking**, particularly in the cooler spring and autumn. Beyond

▲ Eating in Pollença

Lluc, the mountains roll down to a coastal plain that holds the lovely little town of **Pollença** and one of the island's most appealing medium-sized resorts, **Port de Pollença**, which is itself just along the bay from the sprawling but well-kept resort of **Port**

▲ Window shutters, Sant Elm

d'Alcúdia. In the north, Mallorca finishes with a final scenic flourish in the rearing cliffs of the **Península de Formentor**, where the cape draws hundreds of seabirds.

Mallorca's second mountain range, the gentler, greener **Serres de Llevant** shadows the coves of the east coast and culminates in the pine-clad headlands and medieval hill towns of the island's northeast corner. Many of the east-coast resorts are rather overblown, but the pick are **Cala Rajada**, close to several fine beaches, and **Porto Petro**. There are also a couple of easily visited cave systems – the most diverting is the **Coves del Drac** – and the comely hilltop town of **Artà**, close to the substantial prehistoric remains of **Ses Paisses**.

Smaller, flatter **Menorca**, the most easterly of the Balearics, boasts two attractive towns, the island capital of **Maó**, just 5km from the airport, and **Ciutadella**, 45km away to the west. Both towns have preserved much of their eighteenth- and early nineteenth-century appearance, though Ciutadella has the aesthetic edge, the mazy lanes and alleys of its antique centre shadowed by fine old mansions and monasteries,

Catalan and Castilian

A Romance language, stemming from Latin via medieval Provençal, Catalan (Català) is spoken by over six million people spread across the Balearics, parts of eastern Spain, Andorra and the French Pyrenees. Franco did his best to suppress Catalan, excluding it from the media and the schools, but, since his death in 1975, the Balearic islanders have reasserted the primacy of Catalan as their language of choice, the most obvious sign of this linguistic renaissance being the replacement of Castilian street names by their Catalan equivalents. Despite the resurgence of Catalan, however, the emigration of thousands of mainland Spaniards to the islands means that Castilian (Spanish) is now the dominant language in around forty percent of Balearic households.

9

Life's a beach

For all their diverse charms, the main Balearic activity – or lack of it – is sunbathing on the **beach**. At some resorts, like S'Arenal, this is a serious business with acres of roasting, glistening pecs and abs; at others, like Port de Pollença, it's a family affair, involving a bit of sandcastle-building here and a bit of swimming and pedalo-pedalling there.

On Mallorca, the finest sandy beaches are in the north fringing **Port d'Alcúdia**; at **Cala Millor** on the east coast; and, most fashionably – or, in terms of costume, most skimpily – on the **Platja de Palma**, just to the east of Palma at S'Arenal. All three of these beaches are flanked by a veritable army of hotels, whereas **Es Trenc**, another long sandy strand on the south coast, is comparatively undeveloped. The rockier northern coast, stretching from Port d'Alcúdia to Port d'Andratx, can't really compete, but it is home to a string of cove beaches, almost invariably made up of shingle and pebble – two of the most scenic being **Cala Deià** and **Cala Estellencs**. On Menorca, there are wide sandy beaches on the south coast at **Sant Jaume** and **Son Bou** and a battery of lovely sandy cove beaches, like those at **Cala Turqueta** and **Cala d'Algaiarens**.

plus a set of charming Gothic churches. Linking the two is the island's one and only main road, the **ME-1**, which slips across the rural interior, passing by the pleasant market towns of **Alaior**, **Es Mercadal** and **Ferreries**. A series of side roads connects the ME-1 with the island's **resorts**, the best

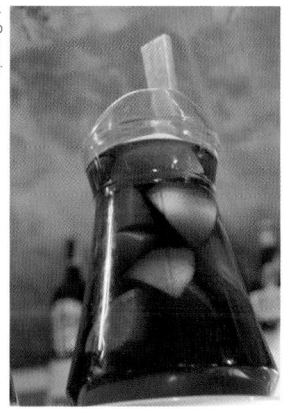

▶ Sangria

appointed of which are **Cala Santa Galdana** and the one-time fishing village of **Fornells**, as well as a string of wind-battered headlands and remote **cove beaches**, where there's not a concrete block in sight. The highway also squeezes past **Monte Toro**, Menorca's highest peak and the site of a quaint little convent, from where there are superlative island-wide views. Menorca's other claim to fame is its liberal smattering of prehistoric remains – two of the most important being **Talatí de Dalt**, outside Maó, and the **Naveta d'es Tudons**, near Ciutadella.

When to go

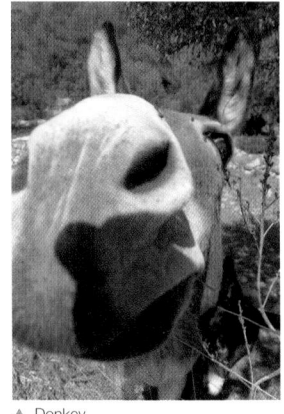
▲ Donkey

There's little difference between the **climates** of Mallorca and Menorca. Spring and autumn are the ideal times for a visit, when the weather is comfortably warm, with none of the oven-like temperatures that bake the islands in July and August. It's well worth considering a winter break too: even in January temperatures are usually high enough to sit out at a café in shirtsleeves. Both islands see occasional rain in winter, however, and the Serra de Tramuntana mountains, which protect the rest of Mallorca from inclement weather and the prevailing northerly winds, are often buffeted by storms, while Menorca, where there's no mountain barrier, can be irritatingly windy. Reflecting their agricultural past, the islanders have names for the four main winds that blow across their land – Tramuntana, Ponent, Migjorn and Llevant, respectively northerly, westerly, southerly and easterly.

Palma climate table

	Jan	Feb	Mar	Apr	May	Jun	Jul	Aug	Sep	Oct	Nov	Dec
Highest recorded temp – °C												
	22	23	24	26	31	37	39	37	35	31	26	24
Highest recorded temp – °F												
	72	73	75	79	88	99	102	99	95	88	79	75
Average daily max temp – °C												
	14	15	17	19	22	26	29	29	27	23	18	15
Average daily max temp – °F												
	57	59	63	66	72	79	84	84	81	73	64	69
Average daily min temp – °C												
	6	6	8	10	13	17	20	20	18	14	10	8
Average daily min temp – °F												
	43	43	46	50	55	63	68	68	64	57	50	46
Lowest recorded temp – °C												
	-3	-4	-1	1	5	8	12	11	4	1	1	-1
Lowest recorded temp – °F												
	27	25	30	34	41	46	54	52	39	34	34	30
Average hours of sunshine per day												
	5	6	6	7	9	10	11	11	8	6	5	4
Average number of days with rain												
	8	6	8	6	5	3	1	3	5	9	8	9

things not to miss

It's not possible to see everything that Mallorca & Menorca have to offer in one trip – and we don't suggest you try. What follows is a selective taste of the islands' highlights: gorgeous beaches and magnificent scenery, quaint towns and great places to eat and drink. They're arranged in five colour-coded categories, in no particular order, which you can browse through to find the very best things to see and experience. All highlights have a page reference to take you straight into the Guide, where you can find out more.

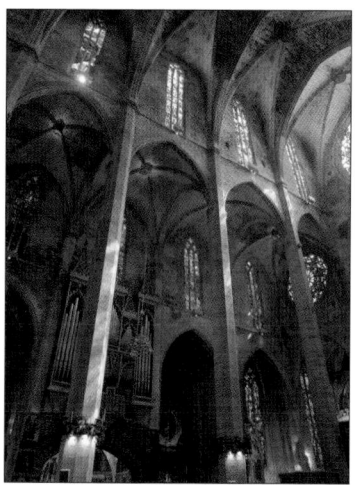

01 Palma Cathedral Page **70** • Dominating the waterfront, the monumental bulk of Palma's magnificent cathedral offers one of Spain's finest examples of the Gothic style, its interior flooded with kaleidoscopic shafts of light.

02 Valldemossa Page **135** • Sitting pretty in the hills, the ancient town of Valldemossa is home to a fascinating monastery whose echoing cloisters and shadowy cells once accommodated Chopin and George Sand.

03 Platja de Palma, S'Arenal Page **100** • Mallorca's most self-conscious beach, the Platja de Palma's miles of white sand are a magnet to the bronzed and the beautiful.

04 Talatí de Dalt Page **245** • In an attractive rural setting close to Maó, this extensive site is one of the most satisfying of Menorca's many prehistoric remains.

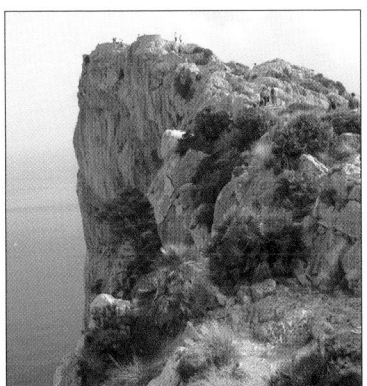

06 Península de Formentor Page **174** • The knobbly peaks and sheer cliffs of this spectacular peninsula backdrop one of Mallorca's best beaches and finest hotels.

05 Ciutadella Page **277** • The prettiest town on Menorca, with an antique centre full of mazy lanes shadowed by fine old mansions and monasteries, plus a charming set of Gothic churches.

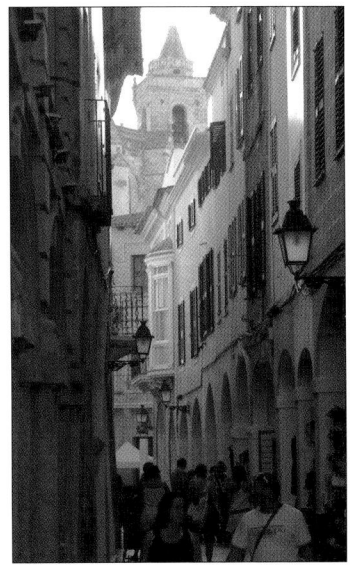

07 Cabrera island Page **225** • This austere, scrub-covered islet is home to a fourteenth-century castle, plentiful birdlife and the rare Lilford's wall lizard.

08 **Fornells** Page **259** • The attractive mini-resort of Fornells is famous for its gourmet *caldereta de llagosta* – lobster stew – which is on the menu at a string of enticing seafood restaurants.

09 **The Mallorcan Primitives** Page **72 & 78 & 82** • This medieval school of painters produced strikingly naive devotional works – Joan Desi being one of its most talented practitioners.

11 **Palma-Sóller train** Page **114** • The antique train that wends its way over the mountains from Palma to Sóller provides wonderful views and serves as a fine introduction to Mallorca's varied landscapes.

10 **Eating in Palma** Page **92** • Palma has the liveliest café and restaurant scene in the Balearics, with a hatful of excellent cafés and *tapas* bars, where you should be sure to try the islanders' favourite nibble, the spiralled flaky pastry known as an *ensaimada*.

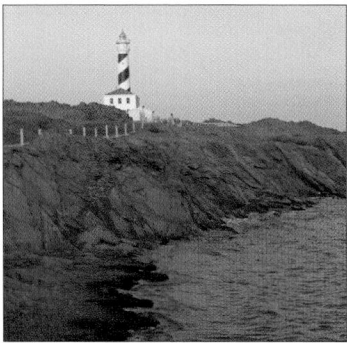

12 Cap de Favaritx Page **259** • This windswept cape, with its bare, lunar-like rocks, is a scenic highlight of Menorca's north coast.

14 Cala Turqueta Page **287** • Perhaps the finest of Menorca's many unspoilt cove beaches, this cala boasts a band of fine white sand set between wooded limestone cliffs and crystal-clear waters.

13 Maó Page **234** • Menorca's modest capital has an amiable small-town feel, its tiny centre graced by old stone houses that accommodate laid-back cafés and old-fashioned shops.

15 Sóller Page **114** • Tucked away in a handsome mountain setting, Sóller is an eminently appealing country town of old stone mansions that's just a quick tram ride from the seashore.

16 Artà Page **204** • The sun-bleached roofs of small-town Artà clamber up the steepest of hills to one of Mallorca's most important shrines, with the prehistoric village of Ses Païsses close at hand.

17 Deià
Page **126**
• The coastal village of Deià is an enchanting huddle of old stone buildings set against a handsome mountain backdrop – no wonder Robert Graves made his home here.

18 Hiking in the Serra de Tramuntana Page **141 & 162**
• Rolling along the west coast, this rugged mountain range holds scores of exhilarating hiking trails.

19 Monestir de Lluc Page **157**
• This rambling monastery holds the Balearics' most venerated icon, La Moreneta, and is also a great base for mountain hikes.

20 Jardins d'Alfábia Page **122** • The lush, oasis-like Jardins d'Alfábia are the finest gardens on Mallorca, their watered trellises and terraces dating back to the Moors.

Basics

Basics

Getting there

Literally hundreds of charter flights shuttle back and forth between Britain and Ireland and Mallorca and Menorca during the summer season and, although they are heavily booked by package-tour operators, there are almost always spare seats for the independent traveller, often at bargain-basement prices. There are also scores of scheduled flights to the islands from London and a string of regional UK airports, though for Menorca you often have to change, most conveniently at Barcelona or Palma. Visitors from North America, Australasia and South Africa will need to fly to London, Madrid or Barcelona – or another European hub – before catching an onward flight to the islands. It's also possible to reach Mallorca and Menorca by driving from the UK to Spain's east coast, from where there are ferries and catamarans over to the islands, but this takes two or three days in total.

Fares to Europe from North America, Australia, New Zealand and South Africa vary according to the time of year. They're most expensive around Easter and from June to September; fares drop during the "shoulder" seasons – October and the first half of May – and are cheapest during the low season from November to March (excluding Christmas and New Year, when prices are hiked up and seats are at a premium). Flying at weekends ordinarily adds a small premium to the fare. If you're flying to the islands from the UK or Ireland, the same general strictures apply, except on the UK to Palma route, where competition is so intense that prices can be slashed at any time of the year.

In some cases, you may actually find it cheaper to pick up a bargain **package deal** from one of the tour operators listed under "Agents and operators" on p.24.

Flights from the UK and Ireland

From the UK, Mallorca and Menorca are readily reached from London and a veritable raft of regional airports. There are loads of charter flights to both islands and frequent scheduled flights to Mallorca plus a more limited range of scheduled flights direct to Menorca – more if you opt to change planes at either Barcelona or Palma. Nonstop **flying times** from London to either island

are a little over two hours (or 2hr 45min from Manchester).

Fierce competition keeps fares cheap on **scheduled flights** on the London to Palma route, though from regional airports the price picture is much more variable. The least expensive flights are with the budget airlines – easyJet, for example, can charge as little as £30 for a return from London Gatwick or Stansted to Palma – whereas a standard, fully-flexible return from London Heathrow to Palma can cost up to £400, though £100–150 is more normal. Another option is Iberia's **open-jaw ticket**, whereby you fly to one Balearic island and return from another: London Heathrow–Palma and Menorca–London Heathrow can cost as little as £110 in low season, twice that, maybe more, in high season. Fares on **charter flights** vary enormously, but can sometimes represent a significant saving compared to scheduled flights. It's worth checking out charter fares either online (see "Online booking", p.22) or with the agents and operators listed on p.24.

From Ireland, charter flights are the cheapest and most obvious way to reach Mallorca and Menorca, though there's also a limited range of scheduled flights, mainly with Aer Lingus, British Airways and Iberia, and mostly via Barcelona. Summer charter flights direct to the islands are easy to pick up from either Dublin or Belfast. **Prices** are highest during August – reckon on around £200 return from

Belfast, €400 from Dublin – but drop a little in the months either side. Alternatively, you might save a few pounds/euros by taking a budget flight to London and then switching to a London–Palma flight. Low-cost carriers flying into London from Ireland include Ryanair, bmibaby and easyJet.

Flights from the USA and Canada

There are currently **no direct flights** from North America to Mallorca or Menorca. The nearest you'll get are the scheduled and charter flights from various North American cities to Madrid and Barcelona. Occasionally

– and especially if you're coming from Canada – you'll find it cheaper to travel to London (or another hub city) and pick up an inexpensive onward flight from there.

Iberia fly nonstop to Madrid from New York, Miami and Chicago, and have the advantage of connecting flights from Madrid direct to both Mallorca and Menorca. Alternatively, several **US airlines** fly direct from the east coast to Madrid, while Delta Airlines operates non-stop flights to Barcelona from New York and Atlanta. You may also find good deals on routings **via other European hub cities** – KLM via Amsterdam and British Airways via London are the obvious choices – but remember that you may be better off

---

Fly less – stay longer! Travel and climate change

Climate change is the single biggest issue facing our planet. It is caused by a build-up in the atmosphere of carbon dioxide and other greenhouse gases, which are emitted by many sources – including planes. Already, flights account for around 3–4 per cent of human-induced global warming: that figure may sound small, but it is rising year on year and threatens to counteract the progress made by reducing greenhouse emissions in other areas.

Rough Guides regard travel, overall, as a global benefit, and feel strongly that the advantages to developing economies are important, as are the opportunities for greater contact and awareness among peoples. But we all have a responsibility to limit our personal "carbon footprint". That means giving thought to how often we fly and what we can do to redress the harm that our trips create.

Flying and climate change

Pretty much every form of motorized travel generates CO_2, but planes are particularly bad offenders, releasing large volumes of greenhouse gases at altitudes where their impact is far more harmful. Flying also allows us to travel much further than we would contemplate doing by road or rail, so the emissions attributable to each passenger become truly shocking. For example, one person taking a return flight between Europe and California produces the equivalent impact of 2.5 tonnes of CO_2 – similar to the yearly output of the average UK car.

Less harmful planes may evolve but it will be decades before they replace the current fleet – which could be too late for avoiding climate chaos. In the meantime, there are limited options for concerned travellers: to reduce the amount we travel by air (take fewer trips, stay longer!), to avoid night flights (when plane contrails trap heat from Earth but can't reflect sunlight back to space), and to make the trips we do take "**climate neutral**" via a carbon offset scheme.

Carbon offset schemes

Offset schemes run by **climatecare.org**, **carbonneutral.com** and others allow you to "neutralize" the greenhouse gases that you are responsible for releasing. Their websites have simple calculators that let you work out the impact of any flight. Once that's done, you can pay to fund projects that will reduce future carbon emissions by an equivalent amount (such as the distribution of low-energy lightbulbs and cooking stoves in developing countries). Please take the time to visit our website and make your trip climate neutral.

www.roughguides.com/climatechange

continuing with a locally bought flight. Flying across the Atlantic, the widest range of deals is on the New York–London route, which is served by dozens of airlines. At the time of writing, a full-whack return fare with Iberia from New York to Mallorca via Madrid costs in the region of US$2700, but you can halve that – at least – by hunting down the best deals. **Flying time** is around seven hours from New York to Madrid.

There are no non-stop flights **from Canada** to Spain. However, you should be able to find a fairly convenient routing using a combination of airlines – most likely via another European capital – from any of Canada's major cities. At the time of writing, round-trip **fares** to Madrid start at around CDN$1500/1895 (low/high season) from Toronto and Montréal, and CDN$1890/2450 from Vancouver.

Flights from Australia, New Zealand and South Africa

There are **no direct flights** to Spain **from Australia**, and you'll need to change planes once or twice to reach Madrid or Barcelona, from where there are regular flights onto Mallorca and Menorca. Count on 24 hours via Asia or 30 hours via the USA, not including time spent on stopovers. The least expensive **scheduled flights** are usually via Asia with return tickets costing around A$2100/3300 low/high season from a number of airlines, including Japan Airlines, Thai Airways, Air France and Qantas. You may be able to save money by flying into London – or another European hub city – but this can often extend your journey by several hours.

There are no direct flights **from New Zealand** to Spain, and once again the less expensive itineraries are usually routed via Asia rather than the USA – to begin with try Thai Airways, Japan Airlines (JAL), and Singapore Airlines. Fares average around NZ$2700/3300 in low/high season. If you're flexible about which European city you fly into, then large savings can be made.

From **South Africa**'s two main international airports, Johannesburg and Cape Town, Spain is easy enough to reach by air, but this always involves **changing planes** in a European hub city such as Amsterdam or London (for onward flights from the UK to Mallorca and Menorca, see p.19). The **flying time** on a direct, nonstop flight from South Africa to London is just over eleven hours. **Fares** from South Africa to London start at around R5000 for a return trip in low season, sometimes less on charter flights and smaller airlines.

Flights from mainland Spain

Menorca and more especially Mallorca are easily reached by plane from mainland Spain with regular scheduled flights departing for the islands from a good number of Spanish cities, including Valencia, Barcelona and Madrid. **Journey times** are minimal (Barcelona to Palma takes just forty minutes) and **ticket prices** characteristically modest with the main carrier, Iberia, charging, for example, as little as €50 for the one-way flight from either Barcelona or Madrid to Palma. These sorts of price favour aircraft travel over the car ferries and catamarans that leave Barcelona, Valencia and Denia for

Flights between the Balearic Islands

Three of the **Balearic islands** have international airports – Ibiza, Mallorca and Menorca – and there are regular inter-island **flights** between Ibiza and Mallorca and Mallorca and Menorca; flights from Ibiza to Menorca are usually routed via Mallorca. The main carrier is Iberia, which operates between six and eight inter-island flights daily, though Air Berlin chips in with daily flights too. There's usually no problem with seat availability, but you need to book ahead during the height of the season and on public holidays. With Iberia, a one-way ticket between Ibiza and Menorca costs about €115; €85 between Menorca and Mallorca and Mallorca and Ibiza. The flying time between Ibiza and Mallorca and Mallorca and Menorca is forty minutes.

the islands unless, that is, you're in or near one of the departure ports anyway and/or taking your own vehicle over. For details of ferries and catamarans from the Spanish mainland to Mallorca and Menorca, see below; for details of ferries and catamarans between the Balearic islands, see p.26.

Trains

Travelling by **train** from London, it takes at least sixteen hours to reach **Barcelona**, from where there are regular ferries to Palma and Maó (see below). The first leg of the journey involves taking a **Eurostar** train from London Waterloo to Paris Gare du Nord. The easiest option on the second leg is the overnight **Talgo** service, which leaves Paris Gare d'Austerlitz daily for Barcelona's Estació-Sants. A standard return on the Talgo from Paris to Barcelona costs £100 and up per person in a four-person sleeper.

Buses

The main **bus route** between Britain and northeastern Spain connects London with Barcelona. Bus services from Britain are operated by **Eurolines**, with departures from London's Victoria Coach Station three times a week. The journey time is around 26 hours – long, but just about bearable if you take enough to eat, drink and read. The bus stops for twenty minutes or so every four to five hours, and the cross-Channel ferry, the price of which is included in the cost of a ticket, also relieves the tedium. A standard return fare costs £80–90, less if booked thirty days or more in advance.

Car and ferry

Clearly, if you intend to travel from the UK to either Mallorca or Menorca by car and ferry, you'll need lots of time – a couple of days, maybe more. The quickest way for you and your vehicle to cross the Channel is on the **Eurotunnel** shuttle service via the Channel Tunnel (see p.26 for contact details). Thereafter, it's a long drive across France and Spain to one of the ferry ports that serve the Balearic islands (see below). To save driving time – if not overall journey time – you could also take a **car ferry** direct from the UK to Spain. There are two options: Plymouth to

Santander with Brittany Ferries and Portsmouth to Bilbao with P&O Portsmouth (see p.26 for contact details).

Ferries and catamarans from mainland Spain

Three companies – **Acciona** Trasmediterranea, Iscomar and Balearia (see p.26 for contact details) – operate a dense network of **car ferry and catamaran** services between mainland Spain and the Balearic islands. All three apply a complex **fare** structure that takes into account the time of year, your length of stay, your accommodation on board and any accompanying vehicle. That said, all things being equal, the cost of a car ferry or catamaran ticket is roughly the same no matter which mainland ferry port you depart from and which island you sail to. Thus, it costs about the same to get from Valencia to Palma as it does to get from Barcelona to Maó. Setting aside special deals and packages, a return ticket is about twice as much as a single. As a **sample fare**, the price of a passenger ticket (without a cabin) from Barcelona to Maó or Palma with Balearia costs €60–130 on a car ferry and €80–170 on a catamaran; cars cost €160 and €280 respectively. As regards **sailing times**, a regular car ferry takes eight hours to get from Barcelona to Palma, just over half that on a catamaran; take away thirty minutes or so for Maó. **Note also that catamarans only operate in the high season, from April/May to September/October.**

In all cases, advance booking is recommended and is well-nigh essential if you're taking a vehicle or need a cabin. **Tickets** can be purchased at the port of embarkation or in advance by phone and online. In the UK, **Southern Ferries** (see p.26) is **Acciona** Trasmediterranea's official agent and is good for ferry bookings with other companies too.

Airlines, agents and operators

Online booking

ⓦ www.expedia.co.uk (in UK), ⓦ www .expedia.com (in US)

ⓦ www.expedia.ca (in Canada)

ⓦ www.lastminute.com (in UK)

ⓦ www.opodo.co.uk (in UK)
ⓦ www.orbitz.com (in US)
ⓦ www.travelocity.co.uk (in UK), ⓦ www
.travelocity.com (in US), ⓦ www.travelocity.ca
(in Canada) ⓦ www.zuji.com.au (in Australia),
ⓦ www.zuji.co.nz (in New Zealand)

Airlines

Aer Lingus US and Canada ☏ 1-800/IRISH-AIR, UK
☏ 0870/876 5000, Republic of Ireland ☏ 0818/365
000, ⓦ www.aerlingus.com. Dublin to Palma; Cork
and Dublin to Barcelona.
Air Berlin UK ☏ 0870/738 8880, ⓦ www.airberlin
.com. Manchester and London Stansted to Palma;
London Stansted to Maó; Palma to Maó. Also good
for flights from the Spanish mainland and a string
of German cities to both Mallorca and Menorca.
Air Europa US ☏ 1-800/238-7672, UK
☏ 0870/777 7709, ⓦ www.aireuropa.com. North
America to Europe.
Air France US ☏ 1-800/237-2747, Canada
☏ 1-800/667-2747, UK ☏ 0870/142 4343,
Australia ☏ 1300/390 190, SA ☏ 0861/340 340,
ⓦ www.airfrance.com. Worldwide.
Air New Zealand Australia ☏ 13 24 76, New
Zealand ☏ 0800/737 000, ⓦ www.airnz.co.nz. New
Zealand to Europe.
bmi US ☏ 1-800/788-0555, UK ☏ 0870/607 0555
or ☏ 0870/607 0222, Ireland ☏ 01/407 3036,
ⓦ www.flybmi.com. Aberdeen, Belfast, Dublin,
Durham Tees Valley, Glasgow, Leeds/Bradford,
London Heathrow, Manchester to Palma.
bmibaby UK ☏ 0871/224 0224, Republic of Ireland
☏ 1890/340 122, ⓦ www.bmibaby.com.
Birmingham, Cardiff, Durham Tees Valley, London
Heathrow, Manchester and Nottingham East
Midlands to Palma.
British Airways US and Canada ☏ 1-800/
AIRWAYS, UK ☏ 0870/850 9850, Republic of Ireland
☏ 1890/626 747, Australia ☏ 1300/767 177, New
Zealand ☏ 09/966 9777, ⓦ www.ba.com. London
Gatwick to Palma, Maó and Barcelona; Birmingham
to Barcelona.
Delta US and Canada ☏ 1-800/221-1212, UK
☏ 0845/600 0950, Republic of Ireland ☏ 1850/882
031 or 01/407 3165, Australia ☏ 1300/302 849,
New Zealand ☏ 09/379 3370, ⓦ www.delta.com.
North America to Europe.
easyJet UK ☏ 0905/821 0905, ⓦ www.easyjet.com.
Belfast, Bristol, Glasgow, Liverpool, London Gatwick,
London Stansted, Luton, Newcastle to Palma; Bristol,
Liverpool and London Gatwick to Maó.
Iberia US ☏ 1-800/772-4642, UK ☏ 0870/609
0500, Republic of Ireland ☏ 0818/462 000, SA
☏ 011/7831 102, ⓦ www.iberia.com. Dublin,

London Heathrow, and Manchester to Barcelona,
and onwards connections to Mallorca and Menorca.
JAL (Japan Airlines) US and Canada
☏ 1-800/525-3663, UK ☏ 0845/774 7700, Ireland
☏ 01/408 3757, Australia ☏ 02/9272 1111, New
Zealand ☏ 09/379 9906, ⓦ www.jal.com or
ⓦ www.japanair.com. Australasia to Europe via
Asia.
KLM (Royal Dutch Airlines) See also Northwest/
KLM. US ☏ 1-800/225-2525, UK ☏ 0870/507
4074, Republic of Ireland ☏ 1850/747 400,
Australia ☏ 1300/303 747, New Zealand ☏ 09/921
6040, SA ☏ 11/961 6767; ⓦ www.klm.com.
Barcelona to Palma and Maó.
Lufthansa US ☏ 1-800/645-3880, Canada
☏ 1-800/563-5954, UK ☏ 0870/837 7747,
Republic of Ireland ☏ 01/844 5544, Australia
☏ 1300/655 727, SA ☏ 0861/842 538, ⓦ www
.lufthansa.com. Barcelona, Madrid, Berlin and lots
of German cities to Palma. Stuttgart and Frankfurt
to Maó.
Monarch Scheduled UK ☏ 0870/040 5040,
ⓦ www.flymonarch.com. Manchester, Luton and
Birmingham to Palma and Maó.
MyTravel Airways UK ☏ 0870/241 5333, ⓦ www
.mytravel.com. London Gatwick and Manchester to
Palma and Maó.
Northwest/KLM US ☏ 1-800/225-2525, UK
☏ 0870/507 4074, Australia ☏ 1-300-767-310,
ⓦ www.nwa.com. North America to Europe.
Qantas Airways US and Canada ☏ 1-800/227-
4500, UK ☏ 0845/774 7767, Republic of Ireland
☏ 01/407 3278, Australia ☏ 13 13 13, New Zealand
☏ 0800/808 767 or 09/357 8900, SA ☏ 11/441
8550, ⓦ www.qantas.com. Australasia to Europe.
Ryanair UK ☏ 0871/246 0000, Republic of Ireland
☏ 0818/303 030, ⓦ www.ryanair.com. European
flights.
Singapore Airlines US ☏ 1-800/742-3333,
Canada ☏ 1-800/663-3046, UK ☏ 0844/800 2380,
Republic of Ireland ☏ 01/671 0722, Australia ☏ 13
10 11, New Zealand ☏ 0800/808 909, SA ☏ 11/880
8560 or 11/880 8566, ⓦ www.singaporeair.com.
Australasia to Europe via Asia.
South African Airways US and Canada
☏ 1-800/722-9675, UK ☏ 0870/747 1111,
Australia ☏ 1-800/221 699, New Zealand ☏ 09/977
2237, SA ☏ 11/978 1111, ⓦ www.flysaa.com.
South Africa to Europe.
Thai Airways US ☏ 1-212/949-8424, Canada
☏ 1-416/971-5181, UK ☏ 0870/606 0911, Australia
☏ 1300/651 960, New Zealand ☏ 09/377 3886;
ⓦ www.thaiair.com. Australasia to Europe via Asia.
Thomas Cook Airlines UK ☏ 0870/750 5711,
ⓦ www.thomascook.com. To Palma from Belfast,
Birmingham, Bournemouth, Bristol, Cardiff, Durham

Tees Valley, Edinburgh, Exeter, Glasgow, Humberside, Leeds, Liverpool, London Gatwick, London Stansted, Luton, Manchester, Newcastle, Norwich, Nottingham East Midlands. To Maó from Birmingham, Bristol, Edinburgh, Glasgow, London Gatwick, London Stansted, Manchester, Newcastle, Nottingham East Midlands.

Thomsonfly UK ☎0870/190 0737, ⓦwww .thomsonfly.com. To Palma from Aberdeen, Belfast, Birmingham, Bournemouth, Bristol, Cardiff, Coventry, Doncaster/Sheffield, Durham Tees Valley, Edinburgh, Exeter, Glasgow, Humberside, Inverness, Leeds, Liverpool, London Gatwick, London Stansted, Luton, Manchester, Newcastle, Norwich, Nottingham East Midlands, Southampton. To Maó from Birmingham, Bristol, Cardiff, Doncaster/Sheffield, Durham Tees Valley,.Edinburgh, Glasgow, Humberside, Leeds, Liverpool, London Gatwick, London Stansted, Luton, Manchester, Newcastle, Norwich, Nottingham East Midlands.

United Airlines US ☎1-800/UNITED-1, UK ☎0845/844 4777, Australia ☎13 17 77, ⓦwww .united.com. North America to Europe.

Virgin Atlantic US ☎1-800/821-5438, UK ☎0870/380 2007, Australia ☎1300/727 340, SA ☎11/340 3400, ⓦwww.virgin-atlantic.com. North America to Europe.

Agents and operators

ebookers UK ☎0800/082 3000, Republic of Ireland ☎01/488 3507, ⓦwww.ebookers.com. Low fares on an extensive selection of scheduled flights and package deals.

Freelance Holidays UK ☎01789/297705 ⓦwww .freelance-holidays.co.uk. A wide variety of Mallorcan self-catering accommodation in beautiful locations, including both the Serra de Tramuntana and the central plain, Es Pla – the least commercialized part of the island.

Headwater UK ☎08700/662650, ⓦwww .headwater.com. Well-regarded walking tour specialist providing guided hikes in the Serra de Tramuntana mountains. Their standard eight-day (seven-night) guided hike takes place from mid-September to May; it includes five guided walks, three-star hotel accommodation and flights and it costs £880–920 per person depending on the date.

Hidden Trails ☎1-604/323 1141, ⓦwww .hiddentrails.com. A Canadian operator which specialises in horse-riding holidays, including a week-long Mallorcan "Monastery Ride" holiday.

Ibertours Australia ☎03/9867 8833 or 1-800/500 016, ⓦwww.ibertours.com.au. Package tours to Mallorca and Menorca, with accommodation in top-range resort and country hotels.

Individual Traveller's Spain UK ☎08700/780 194, ⓦwww.indiv-travellers.com. Deluxe selection of Mallorcan farmhouses, villas, cottages and village houses, including several tasty offerings near Pollença and others in the small towns of the central plain, Es Pla.

Madrid and Beyond In Spain: ☎00 34/917 58 00 63, ⓦwww.madridandbeyond.com. Reputable, Madrid-based British operator with a small but enticing range of hotels in out-of-the-way places in Mallorca and Menorca. Also does tailor-made Balearic itineraries.

Mallorcan Walking Tours (MWT) Port de Pollença, Mallorca ☎609 70 08 26, ⓦwww .mallorcanwalkingtours.puertopollensa.com. Small, island-based company operating an outstanding range of hikes during spring and autumn. There is something to suit most levels of fitness and they cover the whole of the Serra de Tramuntana mountains as well as the hilly uplands north of Artà. Costs begin at about €25 per person per hike including transport to the trailhead where appropriate.

North South Travel UK ☎01245/608 291, ⓦwww.northsouthtravel.co.uk. Friendly, competitive travel agency, offering discounted fares worldwide. Profits are used to support projects in the developing world, especially the promotion of sustainable tourism.

Premier Travel Northern Ireland ☎028/7126 3333, ⓦwww.premiertravel.uk.com. Discount flight specialists.

Trailfinders UK ☎0845/058 5858, Republic of Ireland ☎01/677 7888, Australia ☎1300/780 212, ⓦwww.trailfinders.com. One of the best-informed and most efficient agents for independent travellers.

STA Travel US ☎1-800/781-4040, Canada ☎1-888/427-5639, UK ☎0870/1630 026, Australia ☎1300/733 035, New Zealand ☎0508/782 872, SA ☎0861/781 781. Worldwide specialists in independent travel; also student IDs, travel insurance, car rental, rail passes, and more. Good discounts for students and under-26s. ⓦwww .statravel.com.

Thomson UK ☎0870/165 0079, ⓦwww .thomson-holidays.com. One of the largest UK package-tour companies, offering all manner of Mallorcan and Menorcan holidays from city breaks to beach lazing. Something to match most budgets.

Tramuntana Tours c/Sa Lluna 72, Sóller, Mallorca ☎971 63 24 23, ⓦwww.tramuntanatours.com. Small but very recommendable company offering mountain-bike tours, fishing trips and an ambitious range of day-long guided walks with something to suit most aptitudes. Costs vary with the itinerary, but reckon on a minimum of €25 per trip per person. Transport is provided to and from the trailhead as/if required.

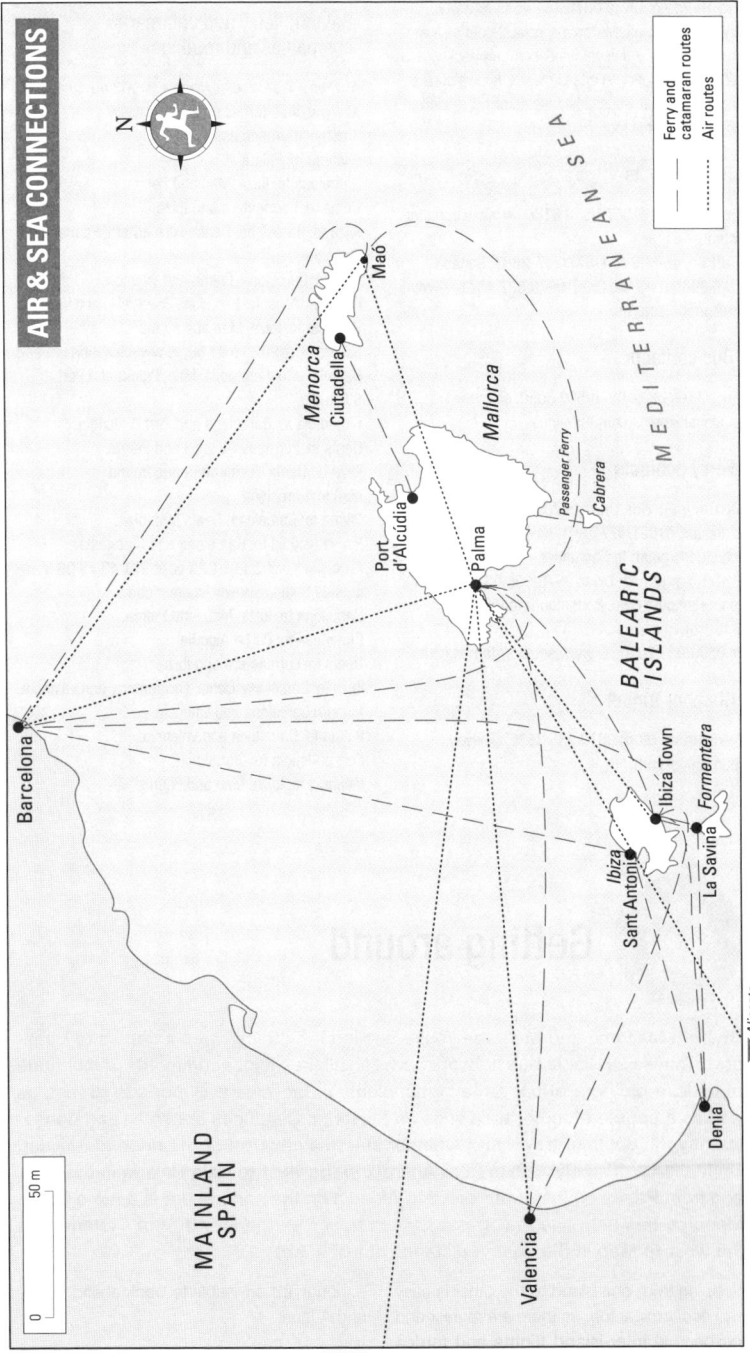

AIR & SEA CONNECTIONS

N

Ferry and
catamaran routes
Air routes

MEDITERRANEAN SEA

Menorca
Ciutadella
Maó

Mallorca

Port
d'Alcúdia
Palma

Passenger Ferry
Cabrera

BALEARIC
ISLANDS

Ibiza
Sant Antoni
Ibiza Town
Formentera
La Savina

Barcelona

MAINLAND
SPAIN

Valencia

Denia

▶ Alicante

▶ Madrid

50 m

0

Try Holidays UK ☎0870/754 4545 ⓦwww. tryholidays.co.uk. Mallorca specialist offering a wide-range of all-in and accommodation-only packages in all price brackets and often in lesser-known parts of the island. Their website has the details of guided hikes in Mallorca too.

Rail contacts

Eurostar UK ☎0870/518 6186, ⓦwww.eurostar .com.
Rail Europe US ☎1-877/257-2887, Canada ☎1-800/361-RAIL, UK ☎0870/837 1371, ⓦwww .raileurope.com/us.

Bus contacts

Eurolines UK ☎0870/580 8080, ⓦwww .nationalexpress.com/eurolines.

Ferry contacts

Brittany Ferries UK ☎08709/076 103, Republic of Ireland ☎021/4277 801, ⓦwww.brittanyferries .co.uk. Plymouth to Santander.
P&O Portsmouth UK ☎0870/598 0333, ⓦwww .poportsmouth.com. Portsmouth to Bilbao.
Southern Ferries
☎0800/082 2010, ⓦwww.southernferries.com.

Channel Tunnel

Eurotunnel UK ☎0870/535 3535, ⓦwww .eurotunnel.com.

Balearic ferry and catamaran companies and routings

Acciona Trasmediterranea ☎902 45 46 45, ⓦwww.directferries.co.uk or ⓦwww .trasmediterranea.es.
Alicante to: Palma.
Barcelona to: Ibiza, Maó and Palma.
Denia to: Formentera and Ibiza.
Ibiza to: Barcelona, Denia, Formentera, Palma and Valencia.
Maó to: Barcelona, Palma and Valencia.
Palma to: Alicante, Barcelona, Ibiza, Maó and Valencia
Valencia to: Ibiza, Maó and Palma.
Balearia ☎902 16 01 80, ⓦwww.balearia.net/eng.
Barcelona to: Ciutadella, Maó, Palma and Port d'Alcúdia.
Ciutadella to: Barcelona and Port d'Alcúdia.
Denia to: Formentera, Ibiza and Palma.
Ibiza to: Denia, Formentera and Palma.
Maó to: Barcelona.
Palma to: Barcelona, Denia and Ibiza.
Port d'Alcúdia to: Barcelona and Ciutadella.
Iscomar ☎902 11 91 28 or ☎971 43 75 00 from outside Spain, ⓦwww.iscomar.com.
Barcelona to: Ibiza, Maó, and Palma.
Ciutadella to: Port d'Alcúdia.
Denia to: Formentera and Ibiza.
Ibiza to: Barcelona, Denia, Formentera, and Valencia.
Maó to: Barcelona and Valencia.
Palma to: Barcelona and Valencia.
Port d'Alcúdia to: Ciutadella.
Valencia to: Ibiza, Maó and Palma.

Getting around

On both Mallorca and Menorca you're spoiled for choice when it comes to trans-port. There's a reliable bus network between all the major settlements, a multitude of taxis, a plethora of car rental firms, plenty of bicycles and mopeds to rent, as well as a couple of minor train lines on Mallorca. Distances are small and conse-quently the costs of travel low, whether in terms of petrol or the price of a ticket. On Mallorca, it's only 110km from Andratx in the west to Cala Rajada in the east, and from Palma on the south coast to Alcúdia on the north shore is a mere 60km. Menorca has only one major road, which traverses the island from Ciutadella in the west to Maó in the east, a distance of just 45km.

Hopping from one island to the other is easy and economical too, as there are regular and inexpensive **inter-island flights and ferries** – though it's advisable to book ahead in July and August.

Addresses are usually abbreviated to a standard format – "c/Bellver 7" translates as Bellver Street (*carrer*) no. 7. *Plaça* means square. "Plaça Rosari 5, 2è" means the second floor at no. 5. "Passeig d'es Born 15, 1–C" means suite C, first floor, at no. 15. "s/n" (*sense número*) indicates a building without a street number. In Franco's day, most avenues and boulevards were named after Fascist heroes and, although the vast majority were rechristened years ago, there's still some confusion in remoter spots. Another source of bafflement can be house numbers: some houses carry more than one number (the by-product of half-hearted reorganizations), and on many streets the sequence is absolutely impossible to fathom.

By bus

Both Menorca and Mallorca have an extensive network of reliable **bus services** linking the main towns – Palma, Maó and Ciutadella – with most of the villages and resorts of the coast and interior, though in the wintertime (Nov–March) buses to most resorts are scaled back and in Menorca some resorts have no bus services at all. These main bus routes are supplemented by more intermittent local services between smaller towns and between neighbouring resorts. **Ticket prices** are reasonable: the one-way fare from Palma to Port de Sóller, for instance, is just €2.50, from Maó to Ciutadella €5. In addition, Palma, the only large city here, has its own public transit system, with a multiplicity of bus services linking the centre with the suburbs and surrounding beach resorts – see p.62 and p.63 – while all the larger resorts have some form of local transport, either by bus or electric mini-train.

On all island bus services, **destinations** are marked on the front of the bus. Passengers enter the bus at the front and buy tickets from the driver; alternatively, tickets can be bought in advance at a bus station. Most **bus stops** are now clearly marked in bright yellow and red colours, but a few of the old (and hard to find) green bus stops have yet to be replaced. A confusing variety of bus

companies operate the various routes on Mallorca, but their efforts are coordinated by **tib** (Transports de les Illes Balears); most buses on Menorca are operated by **Transportes Menorca**. Island-wide **timetables** are readily available at major bus stations and local timetables are usually carried by tourist offices. The Catalan words to look out for on timetables are *diari* (daily), *feiners* (workdays, including Saturday), *diumenge* (Sunday) and *festius* (holidays). Remember that bus services are drastically reduced on **Sundays** and **holidays**, and it's best to not even consider travelling out into the sticks on these days. The official, multilingual website of tib (Transport de les Illes Baleares) Ⓦtib.caib.es, displays all of Mallorca's train and bus timetables; for Menorca services check Transportes Menorca's website Ⓦwww.transportesmenorca.net.

By train

Mallorca has its own, narrow-gauge **train network**. One line, which has old rolling stock and is especially popular with tourists, travels through magnificent mountain scenery on its way from Palma to Sóller (see p.114); the second, a modern line geared up for local use, shuttles across the flatlands of the interior from Palma to Inca, just beyond which it forks, with one branch nudging south to Sineu, Petra and Manacor, the other pushing on to Sa Pobla. At the time of writing, work is underway to extend the line from Sa Pobla to Alcúdia. Each line has its own train station in Palma (see p.63). The standard return fare from Palma to Sóller is €14, €9 one-way, whereas fares on the more modern line are trifling – it's just €2.50, for instance, from Palma to Inca. The stations on the modern line also serve as starting points for buses to the surrounding towns and villages.

By car

Getting around on public transport is easy enough, but you'll obviously have more freedom if you have **your own vehicle** – predictably, most of the more secluded beaches are only accessible under your own steam. Major and minor roads are very good, but country byroads are variable, ranging from middling dirt and gravel tracks to the most precarious of dirt trails that are particularly lethal after rain. Traffic is generally well-behaved, but noisy, especially in Palma, where the horn is used as a recreational tool as well as an instrument of warning. **Fuel** (*gasolina*) comes in three main grades. Different companies use different brand names, but generally *Super Plus* is 98-octane fuel, selling at about €1.07 per litre, and *Super* is 95-octane, selling at about €1.05 per litre; both are without lead (*sense plom/sin plomo*). Diesel (*gasoleo* or *gasoil*) costs about €0.91 per litre. Both Menorca and Mallorca are well supplied with petrol stations; a few are open 24 hours a day, seven days a week, though most close around 9pm or 10pm and on public holidays.

Most foreign **driving licences** are honoured in Spain, including all EU, US, Australasian and Canadian ones. If you're bringing your own car, you must have adequate insurance, preferably including coverage for legal costs, and it's advisable to have an appropriate **breakdown** policy from your home motoring organization too. In the UK, for example, the AA charge about £120 for a year's Europe-wide breakdown cover, with all the appropriate documentation. Note, however, that rates vary depending on the age of the vehicle and increase if you're towing anything.

Some rules of the road

Speed **limits** are posted throughout the Balearics: the maximum on main urban roads is 50kph, on other roads 90kph or 100kph, on motorways 120kph. Speed traps are fairly frequent on the main highways. If you're stopped for any violation, the Spanish police can (and usually will) levy a stiff on-the-spot fine of up to €1500 before letting you go on your way, their draconian instincts reinforced by the fact that few tourists are likely to appear in court to argue the case. Most **driving rules** and regulations are pretty standard: seat belts are compulsory, "Stop" signs mean exactly that, and drink-driving will land you in big trouble. A single, unbroken white line in the middle of the road means no overtaking, even if the rule is frequently ignored; note also that drivers often sound their horns

when overtaking. You yield to traffic coming from the right at all junctions, whether or not there's a give way sign; and be prepared for road signs that give very little, if any, warning of the turning you might require. On major trunk roads, turnings that take vehicles across oncoming traffic are being phased out and replaced by semicircular minor exits that lead round to traffic lights on the near side of the major road.

Finally, drivers do not have to stop (and usually don't) at **zebra crossings**, which merely indicate a suitable pedestrian crossing place: if you come to an abrupt stop at a crossing, as you might do in Britain, the pedestrians will be amazed and someone may well crash into your rear end.

Car rental

There are literally scores of companies offering **car rental** (still rendered in Castilian as *coches de alquiler*), with offices thronging the islands' resorts, larger towns and airports. All of the major international players have outlets, and there are also dozens of small companies. We have provided a small selection in the "Listings" sections for Palma, Maó and Ciutadella, but comprehensive lists of car rental companies are available from the islands' tourist offices. To rent a car, you'll have to be 21 or over (and have been driving for at least a year), and you'll probably need a credit card – though some places will accept a hefty deposit in cash and some smaller companies simply ignore all the normal regulations altogether. However, no car rental firm will allow you to transport their vehicles from one Balearic island to another. If you're planning to spend much time driving on rougher tracks, you'll probably be better off with a moped, or even a four-wheel drive vehicle (about thirty percent more expensive than the average car and available from larger rental agencies).

Rental charges vary enormously: out-of-season costs for a standard car can fall to as little as €25 per day with unlimited mileage; in July and August, by comparison, the same basic vehicle could set you back €60 a day (though weekly prices are slightly better value, and special rates operate at the weekend). The big companies all offer competitive rates, but you can often get a better deal through a local rental firm, but in this case you should proceed with care. In particular, check the policy for the excess applied to claims, and ensure that it includes CDW (collision damage waiver), applicable if an accident is your fault, and, in general, adequate levels of financial cover. **Fly-drive** deals are also well worth investigating. In Britain, for example, Iberia (see p.23) offers good car rental deals as long as you book your flight with them.

Car rental agencies

Alamo US ☎1-800/462-5266, ⊛www.alamo.com.
Apex New Zealand ☎0800/939 597 ⊛www .apexrentals.co.nz.
Auto Europe US and Canada ☎1-888/223-5555, ⊛www.autoeurope.com.
Avis US ☎1-800/230-4898, Canada ☎1-800/272-5871, UK ☎0870/606 0100, Republic of Ireland ☎021/428 1111, Australia ☎13 63 33 or 02/9353 9000, New Zealand ☎09/526 2847 or 0800/655 111, ⊛www.avis.com.
Budget US ☎1-800/527-0700, Canada ☎1-800/268-8900, UK ☎0870/156 5656, Australia ☎1300/362 848, New Zealand ☎0800/283 438, ⊛www.budget.com.
Dollar US ☎1-800/800-3665, ⊛www.dollar.com.
Enterprise Rent-a-Car US ☎1-800/261-7331, ⊛www.enterprise.com.
Europcar US & Canada ☎1-877/940 6900, UK ☎0870/607 5000, Republic of Ireland ☎01/614 2800, Australia ☎393/306 160, ⊛www.europcar .com.
Europe by Car US ☎1-800/223-1516, ⊛www .europebycar.com.
Hertz US & Canada ☎1-800/654-3131, UK ☎020/7026 0077, Republic of Ireland ☎01/870 5777, New Zealand ☎0800/654 321, ⊛www. hertz.com.
Holiday Autos UK ☎0870/400 4461, Republic of Ireland ☎01/872 9366, Australia ☎299/394 433, ⊛www.holidayautos.co.uk. Part of the lastminute .com group.
National US ☎1-800/CAR-RENT, UK ☎0870/400 4581, Australia ☎0870/600 6666, New Zealand ☎03/366 5574, ⊛www.nationalcar.com.
SIXT Republic of Ireland ☎1850/206 088, UK ☎0800/4747 4227, US ☎1-877/347-3227, ⊛www.irishcarrentals.ie.
Skycars UK ☎0870/789 7789, ⊛www.skycars .com.
Suncars UK ☎0870/500 5566, Republic of Ireland ☎1850/201 416, ⊛www.suncars.com.

Thrifty US and Canada ☎1-800/847-4389, UK ☎01494/751 540, Republic of Ireland ☎01/844 1950, Australia ☎1300/367 227, New Zealand ☎09/256 1405, ⊛www.thrifty.com.

Taxis

The excellence of the islands' bus and train services means it's rarely necessary to take a **taxi**, though they are a fast and easy way of reaching your resort from the airport and, perhaps more importantly, of getting back to your hotel after a day's hiking. In the latter case, you should fix a collection point before you set out – there's no point wandering round a tiny village hoping a taxi will show up. Throughout the Balearics, the taxis of each town and resort area have their own livery: Palma taxis, for example, are black with a cream-coloured roof and bonnet (hood). Local journeys are all metered, though there are supplementary charges for each piece of luggage and for travel at night and on Sundays. For longer journeys there are official prices, which should be displayed at the islands' airport and at some taxi stands and tourist offices. Naturally, you're well advised to check the price with the driver *before* you get going. Fares are reasonable, but not inexpensive: the journey from the airport to downtown Palma, a distance of around 11km, will cost you in the region of €20, while the fare from Palma airport to Port d'Andratx (37km) is about €50.

By moped

Mopeds (scooters) are a popular means of transport, especially for visiting remoter spots, and are widely available. Prices start at about €15 per day, including insurance and crash helmets, which must be worn. Be warned, however, that the insurance often excludes theft – always check with the company first. You will generally be asked to show some kind of driving licence (particularly for mopeds over 50cc) and to leave a deposit on your credit card, though most places will accept cash as an alternative. We've listed names and addresses of rental companies throughout the Guide where appropriate; tourist offices can provide comprehensive lists of suppliers.

For flights and ferries between Mallorca and Menorca, see p.21 and p.26.

Cycling

Cycling can be an enjoyable way of exploring the islands, though the quiet(er) roads of Menorca are a good deal more palatable than the busy roads of Mallorca – particularly as island bicycle lanes are well-nigh non-existent. Furthermore, Menorca is fairly easy going, whereas you have to be pretty fit to tackle the steep hills of northern Mallorca, if not the island's central plain. Even worse, although the Spanish are keen cycling fans this doesn't mean they will necessarily be obliging on the roads and neither is information readily forthcoming: the best you'll get is on the Internet, where the multilingual **Mallorca Cycling Tourist Guide** (⊛ www.baleares.com/tourist.guide/cycling) outlines eight circular cycle routes, from 95km to 320km. Bear in mind also that cyclists are not permitted into the Sóller tunnel at the end of the Palma-Sóller road.

More positively, bicycles are transported free on Palma-Inca-Manacor-Sa Pobla trains and either free or at minimal cost on ferries from the mainland (and between the Balearic islands); you can't, however, take bikes on the train to Sóller and, although some buses allow cycles, most do not.

Renting a bike costs anywhere between about €8 and €14 a day for an ordinary bike, or about thirty percent more for a mountain bike. Renting is straightforward: there are dozens of suppliers (there are usually several at every resort) and tourist offices can provide a list or advise you of the nearest outlet; we've also listed a few in the guide.

Getting **your own bike** to the islands should present few problems. Most airlines are happy to take them as ordinary baggage provided they come within your weight allowance (though it's sensible to check first; crowded charter flights may be less obliging). You'll have to deflate the tyres to avoid explosions in the unpressurized hold and turn the handlebars sideways. Bike **parts** can often be found at auto repair shops or garages – look for Michelin signs – and there are bike shops in the larger towns.

Accommodation

Package-tour operators have a stranglehold on thousands of hotel rooms, villas and apartments in both Mallorca and Menorca. Some good independent agencies rent villas (try www.villanet.co.uk for some great properties in Menorca) but prices can be high. That said, reasonably priced rooms are still available to the independent traveller, even if options can be limited at the height of the season. Off-season you should be able to get a simple, medium-sized double room with shower and sink for around €65, whereas in August the same room, if available, can set you back as much as €85 – though this still compares reasonably well with much of Europe. You can, however, easily spend €100 and upwards in hotels with three or more stars – some of them being very firmly in the super-luxury class.

Vacant rooms are at their scarcest from late June to early September, when **advance reservations** are strongly recommended. Most hoteliers speak or read at least a modicum of English, so visitors who don't speak Catalan or Spanish can usually book over the Internet or by phone, but in either case a confirmatory email is always a good idea. In Mallorca the easiest place to get a room is Palma, with Sóller and Pollença lagging not far behind, though you might also consider staying at the five island monasteries that offer accommodation (see p.32) as these are a good bet for vacancies even in high summer. In Menorca, accommodation is much thinner on the ground, with only Maó, Ciutadella and maybe Fornells likely to have high-season vacancies.

Outside of peak season – and especially at the large deluxe hotels – it's often worth **bargaining** over room prices since the posted tariff doesn't necessarily mean too much. Indeed, many hotels have rooms at different prices, and tend to offer the more expensive ones first. Many places also have rooms with three or four beds at not a great deal more than the price of a double room, which represents a real saving for small groups. On the other hand, people travelling alone invariably end up paying over the odds. We've detailed where to find places to stay in all the key destinations described in the guide, from the most basic of rooms to luxury hotels, and given a price range for each (see box below). We've also indicated where an establishment closes over the winter – a common occurrence in Menorca and frequent in Mallorca.

Fondas, casas de huéspedes, pensions, hostals and hotels

The one thing all travellers to the Balearics need to grasp is the diversity of types of places to stay – though in practice the various categories often overlap. The least expensive places are **fondas**, **casas de huéspedes** and **pensions** (*pensiones* in

Castilian), further categorized with either one or two stars. Establishments in these categories are few and far between in the Balearics, and the distinctions between them blurred, but in general you'll find food served at *fondas* and *pensions* (some rent rooms on a meals-inclusive basis only), while *casas de huéspedes* – literally "guest houses" – are often used as long-term lodgings. Confusingly, the name of many *pensions* does not follow their designation: lots of *pensions* call themselves *hostals* and vice versa. As a result, the name isn't always a reliable guide to the establishment's price, though the sign outside usually is (see box on p.32).

Slightly more expensive are **hostals** (*hostales* in Castilian) and **hostal-residencias**, categorized from one to three stars. A one-star *hostal* generally costs about the same as a *pension*. Many *hostals* offer good, functional rooms, often with a private shower. The *residencia* designation means that no meals other than breakfast are served.

Moving up the scale, **hotels** are also graded with from one to five stars. One-star hotels cost no more than three-star *hostals* (sometimes less), but three-star hotels cost a lot more, and at four or five stars you're in the luxury class with prices to match. There are also a handful of *hotel-residencias*, where the only meal provided is breakfast, and an increasing number of (un-starred) **hotels d'interior**, mostly bijou family-run hotels away from the coast (hence "interior").

It's safe to assume that bedrooms will be adequately clean and furnished in all the higher categories of accommodation, but down amongst the budget rooms you'd be

Accommodation price codes

All the **accommodation** detailed in this guide has been graded according to the nine price categories listed below. These represent how much you can expect to pay in each establishment for the **least expensive double room in high season** excluding special deals and discounts; for a single room, expect to pay around two-thirds the price of a double. Our categories are simply a guide to prices and do not give an indication of the facilities you might expect; as such they differ from the star-system applied by the tourist authorities. Note that in the more upmarket *hostals* and *pensions*, and in anything calling itself a hotel, you'll pay a **tax** (IVA) of seven percent on top of the room price.

❶ Under €40	❹ €65–80	❼ €150–200
❷ €40–50	❺ €80–100	❽ €200–250
❸ €50–65	❻ €100–150	❾ over €250

well advised to ask to see where you'll be sleeping before you part with any money: standards vary greatly (even between rooms in the same place) and it does no harm to check that there's hot water if there's supposed to be, or that you're not being stuck at the back in an airless box. Note that bathrooms in many *pensions* and *hostals* (some hotels too) will have only showers, not bath tubs.

By law, each establishment must display its room rates, and there should be a card on the room door showing the prices for the various seasons. If you think you're being overcharged, complain there and then.

Monasteries

Mallorca's monasteries have run out of monks, so five of them have given up the monastic ghost and now let out empty cells to visitors of both sexes. All occupy delightful settings in the hills or on hilltops, and the majority are dotted across the interior of the island. The **five are**: the Santuari de Sant Salvador near Felanitx (see p.216); the Ermita de Nostra Senyora de Bonany near Petra (see p.199); the Ermita de Nostra Senyora del Puig outside Pollença (see p.166); the Monestir de Lluc (see p.157); and the Santuari de Nostra Senyora de Cura, on Puig Randa near Algaida (see p.201). There's an increasing demand for this simple, cheap form of accommodation so, although it's possible just to turn up and ask for a room, you'd be well advised to either phone ahead or, if your Spanish isn't good enough, get the local tourist office to make a reservation on your behalf. For a double room, the more rough and ready monasteries **charge** around €20 per double per night, rising to about €30 at Sant Salvador and Lluc and €60 at Cura, all three of which have been remodelled and refitted; easily the most popular of the five is Lluc. Reasonably priced food is usually available at

all these monasteries, but check arrangements when you book. In the same vein, the former **monastic lodgings** above the Ermita de la Victòria (see p.181) have been turned into a small hotel with doubles at €66, making another excellent budget choice.

Mountain refuges

Mallorca's governing council is in the process of developing a string of mountain **refugis** (refuges) to cater for the island's hikers and walkers. There are just eleven at present, but more are planned, and they offer simple but perfectly adequate lodgings and food at inexpensive prices (**❶**). All are sited in old stone buildings of one description or another and, although four can be reached by car, the rest can only be reached on foot. Each is restricted to a maximum of thirty beds and **reservations** at least five days in advance are essential on ☏971 17 37 00 or ☏971 51 70 70; more details are available online at ⓦwww.conselldemallorca.net/mediambient/pedra. Handy locations include La Muleta, near the lighthouse at Port de Sóller (see p.119); two just off the MA-10 in the Gorg Blau (see p.156); La Trapa near Sant Elm (see pp.146–147); and the Castell d'Alaró (see p.123).

Agrotourism – fincas

Many of **Mallorca's** old stone **fincas** (farmhouses) have been snaffled up for use as holiday homes and scores of them are now leased by their owners to package-tour operators for the whole or part of the season. Others, however, can be booked direct or through the government agency responsible for developing rural tourism, the **Associació Agroturisme Balear**, Avgda Gabriel Alomar i Villalonga 8a–2a, 07006 Palma (☏971 72 15 08, ⓦwww.agroturismo-balear.com). Some of these fincas are modest affairs and still a

---

Accommodation signage

Although the practice is on the wane, every place offering accommodation in the Balearics has traditionally sported a **square blue sign** on the outside, inscribed with its category and number of stars. These are as follows:

F	CH	P	H^S	$\overset{S}{HR}$	H
fonda	casa de huéspedes	pensió	hostal	hostal-residencia	hotel

part of working farms, but the majority are comparatively luxurious and many are situated in remote and beautiful spots. They are not, however, cheap: prices range from €80 to €200 per person per night, and a minimum length of stay of anything between two nights and two weeks is often stipulated.

HI Hostels

There are no **youth hostels** (*albergues juveniles*) on Menorca and only two on Mallorca – one near Palma (see p.101), the other outside Alcúdia (see p.181). The former is open from February to October, the latter from February to November. Both tend to be block-booked by school groups, so unless you reserve well in advance you shouldn't rely on either as a viable source of inexpensive accommodation. At both, the price of a bed is about €14 and you'll need a sheet or sleeping bag. Both hostels are affiliated to Hostelling International (HI) and they expect you to have a HI membership card, available either from your home hostelling organization or buyable on the spot at minimal cost. Specific details of both hostels are given in the guide.

Camping

Menorca possesses two official campsites: the well-appointed **Son Bou** (see p.267), just outside the south-coast resort of Son Bou, and the plainer but very pleasant **S'Atalaia** (see p.272), near the resort of Cala Santa Galdana. The Son Bou can accommodate about four hundred campers, the S'Atalaia just one hundred – and both take tents, trailer caravans and motor caravans. Although neither has a seashore location, they're both very popular, and in the summer it's best to make a reservation well ahead of time. Prices and specific details of each site are given in the relevant chapters. There are currently no official campsites on **Mallorca**.

Camping rough is legal, but not encouraged, and has various restrictions attached: you're not allowed to camp in urban areas, military zones, parks and tourist resorts. Neither are you allowed to camp on beaches – though there is some latitude if you're discreet – and if you want to camp out in the countryside you'll need to ask locally and/or get permission from the landowner.

Food and drink

Traditional Balearic food, which has much in common with Catalan food, is far from delicate, but its hearty soups and stews, seafood dishes and spiced meats can be delicious. In common with other areas of Spain, this regional cuisine has, after many years of neglect, experienced something of a renaissance, and nowadays restaurants offering Cuina Mallorquína (and to a lesser extent Cuina Menorquína) are comparatively commonplace and should not be missed. Neither should a visit to one of the islands' many pastry shops (pastisserias), where you'll find the sweetest of confections and the Balearics' gastronomic pride and joy – ensaimadas (spiralled flaky pastries).

While scores of touristy restaurants dish up bland and over-priced pizza, burgers and pasta, or sanitized versions of local favourites, such as omelettes and grilled meats, there are still plenty of places where the food is more distinctive and flavoursome. Fresh

fish and seafood can be excellent, though it's almost always expensive, partly because much of it is imported – despite the best efforts of the local fishing industry. Nevertheless, you're able to get hake, cod (often salted) and squid at very reasonable prices, while fish stews and soups are often truly memorable, as is the lobster stew – *caldereta de llagosta* – that turns up in many restaurants in Menorca. **Meat** can be outstanding too, usually either grilled and served with a few fried potatoes or salad, or – like ham – cured or dried and served as a starter or in sandwiches. Veal is common, served in large stews, while poultry is often mixed with seafood (chicken and prawns) or fruit (chicken/duck with prunes/pears).

Vegetables rarely amount to more than a few chips or boiled potatoes with the main dish, though there are some splendid vegetable concoctions to watch out for, such as *tumbet*, a pepper, potato, pumpkin and aubergine (eggplant) stew with tomato purée. It's usual to start your meal with a **salad**, either a standard green or mixed affair, or one of the islands' own salad mixtures, which come garnished with various vegetables, meats and cheeses. **Dessert** in the cheaper places is nearly always fresh **fruit** or *flam*, the local version of *crème caramel*; look out also for *crema catalana*, with a caramelized sugar coating (the Catalan version of *crème brûlée*), and *músic*, dried fruit-and-nut cake.

Opening hours vary considerably. As a general rule cafés open from around 9am until at least early in the evening, and many remain open till late at night. Restaurants open from around noon until sometime between 2pm and 4pm, before reopening in the evening from around 6/7/8pm until 10/11pm. Those restaurants with their eye on the tourist trade often stay open all day and can be relied upon on Sundays, when many local spots close.

There are lots of websites recommending island restaurants, but the pick of the lot is Ⓦ www.mallorca-restaurants-121.com.

Breakfast, snacks and sandwiches

For **breakfast** you're best off in a café or café-bar. Some *hostals* and most hotels will

> For a glossary of **Catalan and Castilian food and drink terms** and a list of popular Balearic dishes, see pp.344–348.

serve a basic continental breakfast, but it's generally less expensive and more enjoyable to go out. A traditional Balearic breakfast (or lunch) dish is *pa amb tomàquet* (*pan con tomate* in Castilian) – a massive slice of bread rubbed with tomato, olive oil and garlic, which you can also have topped with ham – washed down with a flagon of wine. *Pa amb oli* (bread rubbed with olive oil) arrives in similar style, but dispenses with the tomato. If that sounds like gastronomic madness, other breakfast standbys include *torradas* (*tostadas*; toasted rolls) with oil or butter and jam, and *xocolata amb xurros* (*chocolate con churros*) – long, fried tubular doughnuts that you dip into thick drinking chocolate. Most places also serve *ou ferrat* (*huevo frito*; fried egg) and cold *truita* (*tortilla*; omelette), both of which make a fortifying breakfast.

Coffee (see p.38) and **pastries** (*pastas*), particularly croissants and doughnuts, are available at some bars and cafés; for a wider selection of cakes, head for a *pastisseria* (pastry shop) or *forn* (bakery). These often sell a wide array of appetizing baked goods besides the obvious bread, croissants and *ensaimadas*. Some bars specialize in **sandwiches** (*bocadillos*), usually outsize affairs in French bread served either hot or cold, or you can get them prepared – or buy the materials to do so – at grocery shops. **Menorcan cheese** (*formatge*), commonly known as *queso Mahón*, is a popular filling – the best is hard and has a rind.

Tapas and racions

Tapas are small snacks of three or four chunks of fish, meat or vegetables, cooked in a sauce or served with a dollop of salad, which traditionally used to be provided free with a drink. These days you have to pay for anything more than a few olives, but a single helping rarely costs more than €8 unless you're somewhere very flashy. **Racions** (*raciones* in Castilian) are bigger portions of the same, served with bread and usually enough in themselves to make a light meal; they cost around €10. The more people you're with, of course, the better: half-a-dozen or so different dishes can make a varied and filling meal for three or four people.

One of the advantages of eating *tapas* in bars is that you are able to experiment. Most places have food laid out on the counter, so you can see what's available and order by pointing without necessarily knowing the names; others have blackboards.

Full meals

Meals are usually eaten in a **café** or **restaurant**, though the distinction between the two, particularly at the cheaper end of the market, is often very blurred. In similar fashion, cafés blend seamlessly into cafeterias, café-bars and bars, almost all of which serve at least some food. That said, the average price of an average meal in an average establishment does slide down the scale from restaurant to café to bar. At a café, something like egg and steak, chicken and chips, or *calamars* and salad will generally cost in the region of €8, excluding drink, whereas the price of a main course at a good-quality restaurant averages about €17. Restaurants run from simple affairs with formica tables and checked tablecloths to expense-account palaces. Many have a daily set menu – the **menú del día** – in addition to an à la carte menu, though some of the more basic places only serve a *menú del día*. This consists of two, three or four courses, including bread, wine and service, and usually costs €10–15, quite a bit more in glitzy restaurants and at seaside resorts.

In all but the most rock-bottom establishments it's customary to leave a small **tip**; ten to fifteen percent is generally regarded as sufficient. The other thing to take account of is **IVA**, a sales tax of seven percent, which is either included in the prices (in which case it should say so on the menu) or added to your bill at the end.

Vegetarian and vegan

Palma has a couple of **vegetarian** restaurants and most of the resorts are accustomed to having vegetarian guests, but elsewhere the choice isn't so great and is essentially confined to large salads, fried eggs and chips or omelettes. If you eat fish, however, you'll find seafood almost everywhere.

If you're a **vegan**, you'll no doubt come prepared to cook your own food at least

> If you're a **vegetarian**, try in Catalan *"Sóc vegetarià/ana – es pot menjar alguna cosa sense carn?"* (I'm a vegetarian – is there anything without meat?). In Castilian, that's *"Soy vegetariano/a – hay algo sin carne?"* Alternatively, you may be better understood if you simply resort to the Catalan *"No puc menjar carn"* (I can't eat meat).

some of the time. That said, some restaurant salads and vegetable dishes are vegan – like *espinacs a la Catalana* (spinach, pine nuts and raisins) and *escalivada* (aubergine/ eggplant and peppers) – but they're few and far between. Fruit and nuts are widely available, and most pizza restaurants will serve you a vegetarian pizza without cheese: ask for *vegetal sense formatge* (in Castilian, *vegetal sin queso*).

For vegetarian and vegan **shopping**, use the markets – where you can buy ready-cooked lentils and beans, and pasta – or look out for shops marked *Aliments regim* (*dietética* in Castilian), which sell wholefoods, soya milk and desserts, and so on.

Drinking and drinks

You'll do most of your everyday **drinking** – from morning coffee to a nightcap – in a **bar** or **café**. Bars situated in old wine cellars are sometimes called *cellers* or *tavernas*; a *bodega* traditionally specializes in wine. In Palma you also have the choice of drinking in rather more salubrious surroundings in the so-called *bars modernos* – designer bars, for want of a better description. Some of these are extraordinarily chic and stylish, sights in their own right, but their drinks are invariably expensive. Locals hang out here for hours whilst managing to imbibe very little.

Bar **opening hours** are difficult to pin down, but you should have little trouble in getting a drink somewhere in Palma between noon and 2am or even 3am. Elsewhere you're OK until at least 11pm, sometimes midnight. The islands' nightclubs tend to close by 3am or 4am. Some bars close on Sundays, and don't expect much to be happening in the resorts out of season.

Wine

Wine (*vi* in Catalan, *vino* in Castilian) is the invariable accompaniment to every meal and is, as a rule, inexpensive whether it be red (*negre/tinto*), white (*blanc/blanco*) or rosé (*rosada/rosado*). In a bar, a small glass will generally cost anything from €0.50 to €0.80; in a restaurant, prices start at around €1.80, and even in the poshest of places you'll be able to get a bottle of house wine for under €15. If you're having the *menú del día*, house wine will be included in the price – you'll get a third- to a half-litre per person.

On both islands, all the more expensive restaurants, supermarkets, and some of the cheaper cafés and restaurants carry a good selection of Spanish wines. The thing to check for is the appellation **Denominació d'Origen (DO)**, which indicates the wine has been passed as being of sufficiently high quality by the industry's watchdog, the Instítuto Nacional de Denominaciónes d'Origen (INDO). Over forty regions of Spain currently carry DO status, including the north central region that produces Spain's most famous and widely distributed red wine, **Rioja**, which is hard to match for reliability and finesse. The Rioja wines are generally made of the *tempranillo* and *garnacha* grapes and are classified according to their age. At one end of the scale, *joven* indicates a young, inexpensive, straightforward wine, which has spent no time in wood. Wines labelled *con crianza* (with breeding) or *reserva* have received respectively moderate and generous ageing in oak casks and in the bottle. At the top of the scale, in both price and quality, are the *gran reserva* wines, which are only produced in the best years and which have to spend at least two years in the cask followed by three in the bottle before being offered for sale. The names to look for in red Rioja include **Martínez-Bujanda**, **Tondonia** and **Monte Real**. The region of **Navarra** also produces excellent wine using similar techniques and grape varieties at a fraction of the price of Rioja. The labels to watch for here are **Chivite** and **Señorío de Sarría**. Around Barcelona, the region of **Penedès** is noted for the wines of **Torres** and **Masía Bach**, whilst the reds of the **Ribera del Duero** region, 120km north of Madrid, include **Protos, Viña Pedrosa** and **Pesquera**, all three of which offer the smooth integration of fruit and oak that is the hallmark of good Spanish wine.

Spain's **white wines** have not enjoyed the same reputation as the reds. Traditionally, they tended to be highly alcoholic and over-oaked. Spain's best white, the **Rioja Blanca** made by **Marqués de Murrieta**, descends from this tradition, but offers a smooth-tasting marriage of oak and lemony fruit. Spain's excellent reputation for **sparkling wine** has been built on the performance of two producers, Freixenet and Codorniú, which hail from a small area west of Barcelona. Local grape varieties are used and the best examples, known as **cava**, are made by the same double-fermentation process as is used in champagne production.

For a smashing introduction to the wines of Spain with precise definitions of all the various Denominaciónes d'Origen (DOs, see p.37), including Mallorca's two DOs, Pla i Llevant and Binissalem, check out ⓦwww.winesfromspain.com.

Sherry, brandy, gin and beer

Fortified wines and spirits in the Balearics are the same as those found throughout Spain. The classic Andalucian wine, **sherry** – *vino de Jerez* – is served chilled or at room temperature, a perfect drink to wash down *tapas*. The main distinctions are between *fino* or *jerez seco* (dry sherry), *amontillado* (medium), and *oloroso* or *jerez dulce* (sweet); these are the terms you should use to order. In mid-afternoon – or even at breakfast – many islanders take a *copa* of **liqueur** with their coffee. The best – certainly to put *in* your coffee – is **coñac**, excellent Spanish brandy, mostly from the south and often deceptively smooth. If you want a brandy from Mallorca, try the mellow but hard-hitting Suau, or look for Torres, from Catalunya. Other good brands include Magno, Veterano and Soberano. Most other spirits are ordered by brand name, too, since there are generally cheaper Spanish equivalents for standard imports. Larios **gin** from Málaga, for instance, is about half the price of Gordons, but around two-thirds the strength and a good deal rougher. The Menorcans, who learnt the art of gin-making from the British,

Mallorcan wine

Wine production flourished in the Balearics in classical times, but it was the Moors who finessed the sweet "Malvasia" wine – akin to Madeira – that was long one of the islands' main exports. This all ended in the late nineteenth century when the vineyards were devastated by **phylloxera**, whose root-eating activities changed the course of Spanish wine history. The small yellow phylloxera aphid, about 1mm long, was indigenous to eastern North America. It first appeared in Spain in 1878, carried either in soil or on agricultural tools and footwear, and in the space of twenty years it destroyed Spain's existing vine stock and made thousands bankrupt. Indeed, vine cultivation never re-established itself on Ibiza or Menorca, and, with the best will in the world, Mallorcan wines, produced from newly imported vines, were long regarded as being of only average quality.

During the late 1980s, however, a concerted effort was made to raise the standard of Mallorcan wine-making, driven on one side by the tourist industry and on the other by local producers who realized that they could prosper by producing wine of international quality. This meant new methods and new equipment, and the investment began in earnest, especially in and around **Binissalem**, a small town northeast of Palma. The results were encouraging and, following vigorous local campaigning, Binissalem was justifiably awarded its Denominació d'Origen credentials in 1991. Binissalem remains Mallorca's leading wine, but its success has inspired others and in 2000 a second Denominació d'Origen was granted, **Pla i Llevant**, covering the central and eastern part of the island from Algaida to Felanitx.

Widely available throughout Mallorca, **red Binissalem** is a robust and aromatic wine made predominantly of the local *mantonegro* grape. It is not unlike Rioja, but it has a distinctly local character, suggesting cocoa and strawberries. The best producer of the wine is **Franja Roja**, who make the **José Ferrer** brand – well worth looking out for, with prices starting at around €5 per bottle, or €15 for the superior varieties; you can also visit their Binissalem winery (see p.194). **White and rosé Binissalem** struggle to reach the same standard as the red, but the **Binissalem Blanco** made by **Herederos de Ribas** is a lively and fruity white that goes well with fish. Names to look out for with the **Pla i Llevant** designation include the white wines of **Miquel Oliver**, whose Petra winery is open to the public (see p.198), and the whites and reds of **Miquel Gelabert** and **Toni Gelabert** from Manacor. Also around the island are various country wineries making inexpensive and unpretentious wine predominantly for local consumption. The best places to sample these local, coarser wines is in the *cellers* and bars of the country towns of the interior – and the best of them carry the label **Vin de la Terra**.

If you're visiting in late September, you can catch Binissalem's **Festival of the Grape Harvest** (Festa d'es Verema), which takes place during the week leading up to the last Sunday of the month. Saturday is the best day, with a procession of decorated floats and a good deal of free wine. On a more sedate level, Palma's **Food Week** (Setmana de Cuina Mallorquína) takes place in the middle of May all over the centre of town, with stalls featuring the cuisine and wine of the island.

still produce their own versions, in particular the waspish Xoriguer. Always specify *nacional* to avoid getting an expensive foreign brand.

Almost any **mixed drink** seems to be collectively known as a *Cuba libre* or *cubata*, though strictly speaking this should refer only to rum and Coke. For mixers, ask for orange juice (*suc de taronja* in Catalan), lemon (*llimona*) or tonic (*tònica*).

Pilsner-type beer, **cervesa** (more usually seen in Castilian as *cerveza*), is generally pretty good, though more expensive than wine. The two main brands you'll see everywhere are San Miguel and Estrella. In Palma, keep an eye out for draught *cerveza negra*

– black fizzy beer with a bitter taste. Beer generally comes in 300ml bottles or, for a little bit less, on tap: a small glass of draught beer is a *cana*, a larger glass a *cana gran*. Equally refreshing, though often deceptively strong, is **sangría**, a wine-and-fruit punch which you'll come across at *festas* and in tourist resorts.

Soft drinks

Soft drinks are much the same as anywhere in the world, but one local favourite to try is *orxata* (*horchata* in Castilian) – a cold milky drink made from tiger nuts. Also, be sure to try a *granissat*, or iced fruit-squash; popular flavours are *granissat de llimona* or *granissat de café*. You can get these drinks from **orxaterias** and **gelaterias** (ice cream parlours; *heladerías* in Castilian).

Although you can drink the **water** almost everywhere, bottled water – *aigua mineral* – is ubiquitous, either sparkling (*amb gas*) or still (*sense gas*).

Coffee and tea

Coffee is invariably espresso, slightly bitter and, unless you specify otherwise, served black (*café sol*). A slightly weaker large black coffee is called a *café americano*. If you want it white ask for *café cortado* (small cup with a drop of milk) or *café amb llet* (*café con leche* in Castilian) made with hot milk. For a large cup ask for a *gran*. Black coffee is also frequently mixed with brandy, cognac or whisky, all such concoctions termed *carajillo*; a liqueur mixed with white coffee is a *trifásico*. **Decaffeinated** coffee (*descafeinat*) is increasingly available, though in fairly undistinguished sachet form.

Tea (*te*) comes without milk unless you ask for it, and is often weak and insipid. If you do ask for milk, chances are it'll be hot and UHT, so your tea isn't going to taste much like the real thing. Better are the **infusions** that you can get in most bars, such as mint (*menta*), camomile (*camamilla*) and lime (*tiller*).

The media

English-language newspapers and magazines are widely available in both Mallorca and Menorca, and most hotel (if not hostal) rooms have satellite TV.

Newspapers and magazines

British and other European newspapers, as well as *USA Today* and the *International Herald Tribune*, are all widely available in the resort areas and larger towns of Mallorca and Menorca. These are supplemented by a hotchpotch of locally produced English papers and journals, easily the most informative of which is the enjoyably chatty *Majorca Daily Bulletin*. The online edition is available at ⓦwww.majorcadailybulletin.es.

Of the **Spanish newspapers**, the best are the centre-left *El País* and the centre-right *El Mundo*, both of which have good arts and foreign news coverage. Other national papers include the solidly elitist *ABC* and the equally conservative *La Vanguardia*. Printed in Catalan, *Avui* is the chief nationalist paper, but its main competitor, the *El Diari de Barcelona,* is more liberal. On the Balearics, there are several rather modest local papers, of which *Ultima Hora*, *Menorca Diario Insular* and *Diario de Mallorca* are the most substantial.

Spain is awash with glossy **magazines**, both native to the country and Spanish versions of international periodicals. And, of course, Spain is the home of *Hola* – the original of *Hello*, heaven help us.

Television and radio

Spaniards love their **television**, and consequently you'll catch more of it than you might expect sitting in bars and cafés. On the whole it's hardly riveting stuff, the bulk being a mildly entertaining mixture of kitsch game shows and foreign-language films and TV series dubbed into Spanish. Soaps are a particular speciality, either South American *culebrones* ("serpents" – they go on and on), which take up most of the daytime programming, or well-travelled British or Australian exports, like *EastEnders* (*Gent del Barri*). Sports fans are well catered for, with regular live coverage of football (soccer) and basketball matches; in the football season, you can watch one or two live matches a week in many bars. The number of TV stations is increasing all the time, but the two main national channels are TVE1 and TVE2, and you'll probably also spot the Catalan TVE3 and Canal 33. Most Balearic hotel rooms have **satellite TV**, which gives access to some or all of the international channels – CNN and so forth.

The *Majorca Daily Bulletin* and other local English-language newspapers detail the **BBC World Service radio**'s frequencies and broadcasting schedules; alternatively, consult ⓦwww.bbc.co.uk/worldservice. For **Radio Canada** go to ⓦwww.rcinet.ca; for **Voice of America**, ⓦwww.voa.gov.

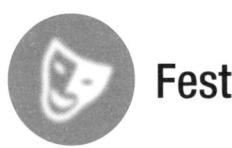

Festivals

Everywhere in Mallorca and Menorca takes at least one day off a year to devote to a festival. Usually it's the local saint's day, but there are celebrations, too, of harvests, deliverance from the Moors, of safe return from the sea – any excuse will do. Each festival is different, with a particular local emphasis, but there is always music, dancing, traditional costume and an immense spirit of enjoyment. The main event of most festas is a parade, either behind a revered holy image or a more celebratory affair with fancy costumes and gigantones, giant carnival figures that rumble down the streets to the delight, or terror, of children.

Although these *festas* take place throughout the year – and it's often the obscure and unexpected event which proves to be most fun – Easter **Holy Week** (*Setmana Santa*) stands out, its passing celebrated in many places with magnificent processions.

The list below gives the highlights of the festival year. For information about less prominent festivals, try local tourist offices. Remember that although outsiders are nearly always welcome at a *festa*, you shouldn't turn up expecting to find somewhere to stay on spec – every room in town will almost certainly have gone. For public holidays, see box p.50.

January

16: Revetla de Sant Antoni Abat (Eve of St Antony's Day) is celebrated by the lighting of bonfires (*foguerons*) in Palma and several of Mallorca's villages, especially Sa Pobla and Muro. In these two villages, the inhabitants move from fire to fire, dancing round in fancy dress and eating *espinagades*, traditional eel and vegetable patties. Also takes place in Sant Lluís on Menorca.

17: Beneïdes de Sant Antoni (Blessing of St Antony). St Antony's feast day is marked by processions in many of Mallorca's country towns, notably Sa Pobla and Artà, with farmyard animals herded through the streets to receive the saint's blessing and protection against disease.

17: Processó d'els Tres Tocs (Procession of the Three Knocks). Held in Ciutadella, Menorca, this procession commemorates the victory of Alfonso III over the Muslims here on January 17, 1287. There's a mass in the cathedral first and then three horsemen lead the way to the old city walls, where the eldest of the trio knocks three times with his flagstaff at the exact spot the Catalans first breached the walls.

19: Revetla de Sant Sebastià Palma has bonfires, singing and dancing for St Sebastian.

20: Festa de Sant Sebastià This feast day is celebrated in Pollença with a procession led by a holy banner (*estenard*) picturing the saint. It's accompanied by *cavallets* (literally "merry-go-rounds"), two young dancers each wearing a cardboard horse and imitating the animal's walk. You'll see *cavallets*, which are of medieval origin, at many of the island's festivals.

February

Carnaval Towns and villages throughout the islands live it up during the week before Lent with marches and fancy dress parades. The biggest and liveliest is in Palma, where the shindig is known as *Sa Rua* (the Cavalcade).

March/April

Setmana Santa (Holy Week) is as keenly observed in the Balearics as it is everywhere else in Spain. On **Maundy Thursday** in Palma, a much venerated icon of the crucified Christ, *La Sang*, is taken from the eponymous church on the Plaça del Hospital (off Passeig de la Rambla) and paraded through the city streets. There are also solemn **Good Friday** (*Divendres Sant*) processions in many towns and villages, with the more important taking place in Palma and Sineu. Most holy of all, however, is the Good Friday **Davallament** (The Lowering), the culmination of Holy Week in Pollença. Here, in total silence and by torchlight, the inhabitants lower a figure of Christ down from the hilltop Oratori to the church of Nostra Senyora dels Àngels.

During Holy Week there are also many **romerias** (pilgrimages) to the island's holy places, with one of the most popular being the climb up to the Ermita Santa Magdalena, near Inca. The Monestir de Lluc, which possesses Mallorca's most venerated shrine, is another religious focus during this time,

with the penitential trudging round its Camí dels Misteris del Rosari (The Way of the Mysteries of the Rosary).

In Menorca's Ciutadella, there's also the **Matança dels bruixots** (the Slaughter of the Wizards), in which puppets representing well-known personalities are hung in the streets.

May

8: Festa de la Verge del Toro (The Festival of the Virgin of the Bull). The day of the patron saint of Menorca begins with a special mass at the hilltop shrine of Monte Toro and continues with a shindig down in the little town of Es Mercadal.

Mid-May: Sa Fira i Es Firó in Port de Sóller and Sóller features mock battles between Christians and infidels in commemoration of the thrashing of a band of Arab pirates in 1561. Lots of booze and firing of antique rifles (into the air).

June

Early to mid-June: Corpus Christi At noon in the main square of Pollença an ancient and curious dance of uncertain provenance takes place – the *Ball de les Àguiles* (Dance of the Eagles) – followed by a religious procession.

23–25: Festa de Sant Joan This midsummer festival has been celebrated in Ciutadella since the fourteenth century. There are jousting competitions, folk music, dancing and processions following a special mass held in the cathedral on the 24th. Another highlight is on the Sunday before the 24th, when the *S'Homo d'es Bé* (the Man of the Lamb) leads a party of horsemen through the town. Clad in animal skins and carrying a lamb in honour of St John, he invites everyone to the forthcoming knees-up.

July

15–16: Día de Virgen de Carmen The day of the patron saint of seafarers and fishermen is celebrated in many coastal settlements – principally Palma, Maó, Port de Sóller, Colònia de Sant Pere, Porto Colom and Cala Rajada – with parades and the blessing of boats.

Third Sunday: Festa de Sant Martí in Es Mercadal, Menorca, celebrates the feast day of St Martin with a popular religious procession followed by dancing and all sorts of fun and games.

Last Sunday: Festa de Sant Jaume This festival in Alcúdia and Menorca's Es Castell celebrates the feast day of St James with a popular religious procession followed by folk dances, fireworks and the like.

August

2: Mare de Déu dels Àngels Moors and Christians battle it out again, this time in Pollença.

Second weekend: Festa de Sant Llorenç High jinks on horseback through the streets of Alaior, Menorca.

20: Cavallet (see p.40) dances in Felanitx.

Last week: Festa de Sant Bartomeu Three days of festivities in Ferreries, Menorca.

September

7–9: Festa de la Mare de Déu de Gràcia This three-day festival in Maó, celebrates the Virgin of Grace, the city's patron saint, and begins with a pilgrimage to the chapel of the Virgin. Thereafter, there are processions and parades along with horseback games in which the horses are trained to rear up on their hind legs.

Second week: Nativitat de Nostra Senyora (Nativity of the Virgin) In Alaró, honouring the Virgin with a pilgrimage to a hilltop shrine near the Castell d'Alaró.

October

Third Sunday Festa d'es Butifarra (Sausage Festival). Of recent origins, this festival follows on from tractor and automobile contests held in the village of Sant Joan. It features folk dancing and traditional music as well as the eating of specially prepared vegetable pies (*coca amb trampó*) and sausages (*berenada de butifarra*).

December

Christmas (*Nadal*) is especially picturesque in Palma and Ciutadella, where there are Nativity plays in the days leading up to the 25th.

Outdoor activities

During the day at least, tourist life on Mallorca and Menorca is centred on the **beach**. There are long and generous strands at several of the major resorts – primarily Port d'Alcúdia, Port de Pollença, S'Arenal and Son Bou – and several dozen smaller cove beaches. At all the larger resorts, a veritable army of companies offer equipment for hire for a wide range of **beach sports and activities**, from sailing and pedalo pedalling through to jet skiing, water boarding, **windsurfing** and **scuba diving**, not to mention sandcastle-building competitions.

Away from the coast, cycling (see p.30) is a popular pastime as is **horse and pony riding** with a clutch of stables and many kilometres of bridle path. The most popular riding areas on Mallorca are the low hills of the Serres de Llevant in the east and the foothills of the Serra de Tramuntana, whilst Menorca's stables are mostly inland close to the (one) main road. For a list of outlets, see ⓦ www.mallorcaonline.com/sport/equitau.htm and ⓦ www.menorca-info.com.

Golfers can thrash away at no less than fourteen **golf courses on Mallorca**, all of which are listed on ⓦ www.allspaingolf.com.

Parks – regional and national

There are four protected **Parcs Natural** (Natural Parks) on the islands – three on Mallorca and one on Menorca. Menorca's is S'Albufera des Grau (see p.258); the other three are Mondragó on Mallorca's east coast (see p.219); Sa Dragonera (see p.147); and S'Albufera (see p.185). Cabrera island (see p.225) and its surrounding waters are a **national park**. The whole of Menorca is classed as a 'Biosphere Reserve' by UNESCO.

Hiking

Hiking is a popular outdoor activity on both islands, with hundreds of hikers arriving here in the spring and autumn, necessarily away from the heat of the summer sun. On Mallorca, the prime hiking area is the Serra de Tramuntana mountain range that bands the northern coast, whereas Menorca is sufficiently rural to offer pleasing walks almost everywhere, though it's the island's northern coast that offers the most dramatic scenery. It is also encouraging to note that the islands' hiking trails, which were once notorious for their poor signage, are in the process of being re-signed. We have described a number of **day-long hikes** on both Mallorca and Menorca (see p.132, p.140, p.162, p.172, p.180, p.246, p.256, p.270, p.274) and recommended two Mallorcan companies that organize **guided hikes** – Mallorcan Walking Tours (see p.24) and Tramuntana Tours (see p.24).

Windsurfing

Windsurfing is common to lots of resorts on both islands, but the prime spot – or at least one of the prime spots – is the windswept coast and wide, wave-less bay of Fornells, on the north side of Menorca. Fornells is home to one of the best windsurfing companies in the Balearics, *Windsurf Fornells* (☎971 18 81 50, ⊛www.excellence.es/fornells), who – amongst several courses – offer a four-day training course (two hours per day) for €150/180 low/high season.

Scuba diving

By and large, **scuba diving** off Mallorca is something of an anticlimax: there may be lots of companies offering this service, but the island's underwater world lacks colour and clarity with the exception of the clear and reefy waters around the island of Sa Dragonera. Menorca, on the other hand, offers first-rate diving with visibility averaging around 30m, lots of reefs and a scattering of shipwrecks. Some divers swear by Menorca's north coast, but others prefer the west. An initial dive – a try dive – costs about €60–70, an ordinary boat dive about €45–55.

Scuba diving contacts

Diving Center Fornells Fornells, Menorca ☎971 37 64 31, ⊛www .divingfornells.com.
Diving Centre Poseidon Cala Santandria, Menorca ☎971 38 26 44, ⊛www.bahia-poseidon.de.
Scuba Activa Sant Elm, Mallorca ☎971 23 91 02, ⊛www.scuba-activa .de.
Ulmo Diving Port d'Addaia, Menorca ☎971 35 90 05, ⊛www.ulmodiving .com.

Sports

Spain may be associated with bullfighting more than any other spectator sport, but it's football that really ignites the nation.

Football

The Spanish love their **fútbol** (football/soccer) and the country's two dominant teams, Real Madrid and FC Barcelona, attract a desperately loyal following. Both are in Division 1 (*La Primera Liga*) of the Spanish football league as is Mallorca's Real Club Deportivo Mallorca, or **Real Mallorca** (⊛www.rcdmallorca.es), which has had considerable success itself. Real Mallorca plays in the Estadio Son Moix stadium on the north side of Palma and the season runs from early September to April with a short Christmas break; most matches are on Sunday afternoons and tickets, which are available at the turnstiles, cost €35–80. For fixture details, go the club website or ask at the nearest tourist office.

Bullfighting

In recent years the popularity of the **bullfight** has declined across Spain, though it was never as big a deal in Catalunya and the Balearics as elsewhere. Mallorca has two main rings – one in Palma, the other in Muro – and both still attract large crowds. The spectators turn up to see the *matadores* dispatch the bulls cleanly and with "artistic merit", which they reward with thunderous applause and the waving of handkerchiefs. A prolonged and messy kill will get the audience whistling in derision. Many Spaniards do, of course, object to the whole spectacle, and at the time of writing there are political moves afoot to have it banned in Catalunya, but when Spaniards tell you that bullfighting is controversial, they are likely to be referring to new refinements to the "sport", especially the allegedly widespread but illegal shaving down of bulls' horns. The horns are as sensitive as fingernails a few millimetres in, and paring them down deters the animals from charging and affects their balance, thereby reducing the danger to the *matador*. Many neutrals are particularly offended by the use of **horses**: padded up for protection, the horses are repeatedly charged by the bulls, which clearly terrifies them – though they can't make their feelings heard as their vocal chords have been cut.

If you spend any time in Mallorca and Menorca during the season (there are eight or nine bullfights between March and October), you may well encounter *los toros* on a bar TV. It may be worth watching one of these before deciding whether to attend a live *corrida* or not.

The corrida

Highly stylized, each bullfighting programme, or **corrida**, begins with a procession to the accompaniment of a *paso doble* by the band. Leading the procession are two *algauziles* or "constables", on horseback and in traditional costume, followed by the three *matadores*, who will each fight two bulls, and their personal teams, each comprising two mounted assistants – *picadores* – and three *banderilleros*. At the back are the mule teams who will drag off the dead bulls. The *picadores* stab pikes into the beast's withers to soften it up and the process is continued by the *banderilleros*, who stick beribboned and sharpened sticks into the bull in preparation for the *matador*, who kills the animal off.

Tickets and seating

Tickets for *corridas* cost €20 and up – much more for the prime seats and prestigious fights. The cheapest seats are *gradas*, the highest rows at the back, from where you can see everything that happens without too much of the detail; the front rows are known as the *barreras*. Seats are also divided into *sol* (sun), *sombra* (shade) and *sol y sombra* (shaded after a while), though these distinctions have become less relevant as more and more bullfights start later in the day, at 6pm or 7pm, rather than the traditional 5pm. The *sombra* seats are more expensive, not so much for the spectators' personal comfort as for the fact that most of the action takes place in the shade. On the way in, you can rent **cushions**: two hours sitting on concrete is not much fun. Beer and soft drinks are sold inside.

Shopping

Big-city Palma has its full share of chain and department stores (see p.96) as well as lots of specialist food and drink shops (see box, p.96), but everywhere else – on both Mallorca and Menorca – is much too small to offer much of a shopping "scene". That said, open-air **markets** (see box below), mostly selling fresh fruit and vegetables, but some also selling every tourist trinket known on earth, are extremely popular with tourists and lots of towns have one, once or twice weekly; go early – at about 8am – to get the best deals. As for **local specialities**, look out for artificial pearls from Manacor;

Camper shoes; fancy green-tinted glass chandeliers; and *siurells*, white clay whistles flecked with red and green paint and shaped to depict a figure, an animal or rural scene – they are almost always mass-produced today, but have a long island pedigree as tokens of friendship. In addition, Mallorcan wine (see box, p.37) and Menorcan cheese, gin and honey come highly recommended; you shouldn't leave the Balearics without having at least one *ensaimada* (spiralled flaky pastry); and, amongst a whole battery of gastronomic treats (see p.33), summon up some

Principal open-air markets (mercats)

Mondays	Santanyí	Ciutadella
Calvià	Sineu	Esporles
Manacor		Lloseta
Montuiri	**Thursdays**	Manacor
	Alaior	Maó
Tuesdays	Campos	Santanyí
Alcúdia	Inca	Sóller
Artà		
Maó	**Fridays**	**Sundays**
Puigpunyent	Algaida	Alcúdia
	Binissalem	Binissalem
Wednesdays	Ciutadella	Es Mercadal
Andratx	Inca	Felanitx
Bunyola	Llucmajor	Inca
Capdepera		Llucmajor
Llucmajor	**Saturdays**	Muro
Petra	Alaró	Pollença
Port de Pollença	Bunyola	Sa Pobla
Pollença	Campos	Valldemossa

For markets in Palma, see p.98.

courage and try a **sausage** (*sobrasada*), preferably one made from the island's own breed of black pig and bearing the label *Sobrasada de Mallorca de Cerdo Negro*.

Shopping hours are normally Monday to Friday 9.30/10am to 1.30/2pm and 5–7/8pm, plus Saturday morning 9.30/10am to 1.30/2pm, though big department stores operate longer hours, typically Monday to Saturday 9.30am–9.30pm. In the resorts, many shops and stores are open daily from 9.30am till late.

Clothing and shoe sizes

Women's dresses and skirts

American	4	6	8	10	12	14	16	18
British	8	10	12	14	16	18	20	22
Continental	38	40	42	44	46	48	50	52

Women's blouses and sweaters

American	6	8	10	12	14	16	18
British	30	32	34	36	38	40	42
Continental	40	42	44	46	48	50	52

Women's shoes

American	5	6	7	8	9	10	11
British	3	4	5	6	7	8	9
Continental	36	37	38	39	41	42	43

Men's suits

American	34	36	38	40	42	44	46	48
British	34	36	38	40	42	44	46	48
Continental	44	46	48	50	52	54	56	58

Men's shirts

American	14	15	15.5	16	16.5	17	17.5	18
British	14	15	15.5	16	16.5	17	17.5	18
Continental	36	38	39	41	42	43	44	45

Men's shoes

American	7	7.5	8	8.5	9.5	10	10.5	11	11.5
British	6	7	7.5	8	9	9.5	10	11	12
Continental	39	41	41	42	43	44	44	45	46

Travel essentials

Travelling with children

Most Balearic *hostals*, pensions and hotels welcome children and many offer rooms with three or four beds. Restaurants and cafés almost always encourage families too. Many package holidays have child-minding facilities as part of the deal and many more organize a programme of kids' activities. Younger children will, of course, be quite happy to play around on the beach, but pre- and early teens may well want a bit more crash, bang and wallop, which is available on Mallorca at four water/theme parks: Hidropark in Port d'Alcúdia (see p.185); Aqualand and Western Water Park in Magaluf (see p.105); and Aqualand in S'Arenal (see p.101). Concessionary rates for children under 14/15 years are commonplace and infants go free. For babies, eating out seems to work quite well (some places will prepare food specially) though you might want to bring powdered milk – babies, like most Spaniards, are pretty contemptuous of the UHT stuff generally available. Disposable nappies and other basic supplies are widely available in the resort areas and the larger towns.

Costs

In terms of transport, food and wine, Mallorca and Menorca remain budget destinations for northern Europeans, North Americans, Australians and New Zealanders, but hotel prices are now on a par with most of Europe. On **average**, if you're prepared to buy your own picnic lunch, stay in inexpensive *hostals* and hotels, and stick to the cheaper bars and restaurants, you could get by on around €50/£33/US$63 per person per day, assuming you're sharing a room. If you intend to stay in three-star hotels and eat at quality restaurants, you'll need more like €100/£67/US$126 a day per person, with the main variable being the cost of your room – and bear in mind that room prices rise steeply as the season

progresses. On €150/£100/US$190 a day and upwards, you'll be limited only by your energy reserves, unless you're planning to stay in a five-star hotel, in which case this figure won't even cover your bed. One additional cost is **IVA**, a seven percent sales tax levied on most goods and services. Check in advance to see if IVA is included in the price of your bigger purchases; otherwise, especially in more expensive hotels and restaurants, you may be in for a bit of a shock. As for **tipping**, taxi drivers, restaurant and bar staff anticipate a tip of between ten and fifteen percent.

Crime and personal safety

Many expatriates love Mallorca and Menorca for their lack of **crime** – and with good reason. In the islands' villages and small towns petty crime is unusual, and serious offences, from burglary to assault and beyond, extremely rare. Of the three larger towns, only Palma presents any problems, mostly low-key stuff such as the occasional fight and minor theft, and commonsense precautions are normally enough to keep you out of any trouble. Nevertheless, you should be aware that noisy and aggressive males commonly colonize some of the late-night bars at the seedier resorts – S'Arenal and Magaluf have the worst reputations, though it's more a question of which bar you're in, rather than the resort you're staying at – and that **theft from parked cars** (as distinct from car theft) is on the increase, especially at major tourist attractions: whatever you do, don't leave anything in view when you park. If you are a **victim of crime**, you'll need to go to the **police** (see p.52) to report it, not least because your insurance company will require a police report or number. In dealing with the police, remember that, although they are polite enough in the normal course of events, they can be extremely unpleasant if you get on the wrong side of them. At all times, keep your cool and remember, especially if you are British, just how unpleasant some of your compatriots can be when they are tanked up.

Travellers with disabilities

Despite their popularity as holiday destinations, facilities for **travellers with disabilities** on both Mallorca and Menorca lag some way behind most of the EU. That said, things are improving. Hotels with wheelchair access and other appropriate facilities are increasingly common and, by law, all new public buildings in Spain are required to be fully accessible. On the other hand, toilet facilities for people with disabilities are rare; car rental firms are very ill-stocked with adapted vehicles, even though there are designated disability parking bays; and, although most EMT buses in Palma have low-floor access, some don't and none do elsewhere on the island. More positively, **flying** to the islands should pose few problems as all the scheduled airlines concerned are more than willing to assist.

Electricity

The current is 220 volts AC, with standard European-style two-pin plugs. Brits will need an adaptor to connect their appliances, North Americans both an adaptor and a transformer.

Entry requirements

Citizens of all EU and EEA countries only need a valid **passport or national identity** card to enter Spain, where – with some limitations – they also have the right to work, live and study. US, Australian, Canadian and New Zealand citizens need only a valid passport for visits of up to **ninety days**, but are not allowed to work. Non-EU citizens who wish to visit Spain for longer than ninety days must get a special **visa** from a Spanish consulate or embassy before departure (see below for addresses). Visa requirements do change and it is always advisable to check the current situation before leaving home.

Gay and lesbian travellers

Gay and lesbian life in the Balearics has come a long way in the twenty-five years or so since Franco's death, and island attitudes have changed dramatically as they have in the rest of the country. Indeed, in 2005 Spain became the fourth country (after Canada, the Netherlands and Belgium) to legalize **gay marriage** and there is now a battery of laws against discrimination on the grounds of sexual preference. The **gay scene** in Mallorca and Menorca is fairly low-key – especially compared with neighbouring Ibiza – but Palma has quite enough action to be going on with.

Health

Under reciprocal health care arrangements, all citizens of the EU (European Union) and EEA (European Economic Area) are entitled to **free**

Spanish embassies and consulates

Australia Embassy: 15 Arkana St, Yarralumla, Canberra, ACT 2600 ℡02/6273 3555, ⓦwww.mae.es/embajadas/canberra/en/home.

Canada Embassy: 74 Stanley Avenue, Ottawa, Ontario K1M 1P4 ℡1-613/747 2252, ⓦwww.embaspain.ca. Also consulates in Edmonton, Halifax, Montréal, Québec, St John's, Toronto, Vancouver and Winnipeg.

Ireland Embassy 17A Merlyn Park, Ballsbridge, Dublin 4 ℡01/269 1640, ⓦwww .mae.es/embajadas/dublin/en/home.

New Zealand See Australia.

UK Embassy: 20 Draycott Place, London SW3 2RZ ℡0207/589 8989, ⓦwww .conspalon.org. Consulates in Edinburgh and Manchester.

USA Embassy: 2375 Pennsylvania Ave NW, Washington DC 20037 ℡1-202/452-0100, ⓦwww.mae.es/embajadas/washington/en/home. Also consulates in Boston, Chicago, Houston, Los Angeles, Miami, New Orleans, New York, and San Francisco.

medical **treatment** within Spain's public health care system. Non-EU/EEA nationals are not entitled to free treatment and should, therefore, take out their own medical insurance. EU/EEA citizens may, however, also want to consider private health insurance, both to cover the cost of items not within the EU/EEA scheme, such as dental treatment and repatriation on medical grounds, and to enable them to seek treatment within the private sector. Note also that the more worthwhile insurance policies promise to sort matters out before you pay (rather than after) in the case of major expense; if you do, however, have to pay upfront, get and keep the receipts. For more on insurance, see next listing. No **inoculations** are currently required for Mallorca or Menorca.

The **public health care system** in the Balearics is of a good standard and widely available with clinics and hospitals in all the larger towns. If you're seeking treatment **under EU/EEA reciprocal health arrangements**, it may be prudent to double check that the medic is working within (and seeing you as a patient of) the public system. That being the case, you'll receive free treatment just as the locals do. Sometimes you will be asked to produce documentation to prove that you are eligible for EU/EEA health care, sometimes no one bothers, but technically you should have your passport and your **European Health Insurance Card (EHIC)** to hand. If, on the other hand, you have a travel insurance policy covering medical expenses, you can seek treatment in either the public or **private health sectors**, the main issue being whether – at least in major cases – you have to pay the costs upfront and then wait for reimbursement or not. Note that in the larger resorts your hotel will probably be able to arrange an appointment with an English-speaking doctor, who will almost certainly see you as a private patient; elsewhere, you'll be lucky if the medic speaks English.

Minor complaints can often be remedied at a **pharmacy** (*farmàcia*): pharmacists are highly trained, willing to give advice (often in English), and able to dispense many drugs which would only be available on prescription in many other countries. Pharmacies are ubiquitous and are listed in the Yellow Pages. **Condoms** are available from most *farmàcias* and from all sorts of outlets in the resorts, such as bars and vending machines. It's a good job: a recent survey of 18- to 30-year-old visitors found that the average time between arrival and first sexual contact was 3hr 42min.

Insurance

Prior to travelling, you'd do well to take out an **insurance policy** to cover against theft, loss and illness or injury. Before paying for a new policy, however, it's worth checking whether you already have some degree of cover: for instance, EU health care privileges apply in both Mallorca and Menorca (see p.47), some all-risks home insurance policies may cover your possessions when overseas, and many private medical schemes include cover when abroad.

After exhausting the possibilities above, you might want to contact a **specialist travel insurance company**. A typical travel insurance policy usually provides cover for loss of baggage, tickets and – up to a certain limit – cash or cheques, as well as cancellation or curtailment of your journey and medical costs. Most of them exclude so-called **dangerous sports** – climbing, horse-riding, windsurfing and so forth – unless an extra premium is paid. Many policies can be chopped and changed to exclude coverage you don't need – for example, sickness and accident benefits can often be excluded or included at will. If you do take medical coverage, ascertain whether benefits will be paid as treatment proceeds or only after your return home, and whether there is a 24-hour medical emergency number. When securing baggage cover, make sure that the per-article limit will cover your most valuable possessions. If you need to make a claim, keep **receipts** for medicines and medical treatment. In the event you have anything stolen, you must obtain a **crime report** statement or number.

Emergency phone number

For medical, fire and police emergencies, call ☏112.

Rough Guides travel insurance

Rough Guides has teamed up with Columbus Direct to offer you **travel insurance** that can be tailored to suit your needs. Products include a low-cost **backpacker** option for long stays, a **short break** option for city getaways, and a typical **holiday package** option. There are also annual **multi-trip** policies for those who travel regularly. Different sports and activities (trekking, skiing, etc) can usually be covered if required as well. See our website (℗www.roughguidesinsurance.com) for eligibility and purchasing options. Alternatively, UK residents should call ℡0870/033 9988; Australians should call ℡1300/669 999 and New Zealanders should call ℡0800/55 9911. All other nationalities should call ℡+44 870/890 2843.

Internet and email

There are Internet cafés in the three main towns on Mallorca and Menorca – Maó, Ciutadella and Palma – and many hotels and some *hostals* provide Internet access for their guests either free or at minimal charge. We've given addresses of Internet cafés in the guide where appropriate.

Laundry

As you would expect, most hotels – and a few *hostals* – operate a full laundry service and there are a couple of self-service launderettes (usually rendered in Castilian as *lavandería automática*) in Palma and Maó.

Mail

There is a **post office** (*correu*) in every town and most of the larger villages, the majority handily located on or near the main square. Opening hours are usually Monday to Friday 9am to 2pm, though the post offices in Palma, Maó and Ciutadella are open much longer (Mon–Fri 8.30am–8.30pm, Sat 9.30am–1pm). All post offices close on public holidays. **Outbound post** is slow but reasonably reliable, with letters or cards taking about a week to reach Britain and Ireland, up to two weeks to North America and Australasia. You can buy **stamps** (*segells*) at tobacconists (look for the brown and yellow *tabac* or *tabacos* sign) and at scores of souvenir shops as well as at post offices. **Post boxes** are yellow; where you have a choice of slots, pick the flap marked *províncies i estranger* or *altres destinos*. Postal rates are inexpensive, with postcards and small letters attracting two tariffs: one to anywhere in Europe, the other worldwide. **Inbound post** is reasonably reliable too.

Maps

Detailed **road maps** of Mallorca and/or Menorca are widely available from island newsagents, petrol stations, souvenir shops and bookshops. There are several different types on offer, but the ones recommended below shouldn't cost more than €7. Before you buy a map, there are two things to check out: firstly, it's important that the map is in the local language, **Catalan**; Castilian (Spanish) maps are either obsolete or impossibly confusing to use. To ensure you're buying a Catalan map of Mallorca, check out the spelling of Port de Pollença on the north coast – if it reads "Puerto de Pollensa", you've got a Castilian map; similarly, on Menorca, check the capital is marked Maó, not the Castilian "Mahón". Just to confuse matters, however, some maps do switch between the two languages for no apparent reason. The second caution is that all Balearic **road numbers** were changed in 2006, so – for example – the main road running along Mallorca's north coast was the C710, but is now the MA-10 and Menorca's one and only main road is now the ME-1 (not the C721).

Currently, the most up-to-date road maps are produced by **Triangle Postals** (℗www .trianglepostals.com), who publish *Mallorca* (1:130,000) and *Menorca* (1:60,000). These two maps accurately portray the islands' highways and principal byways along with topographical details, but neither has an index and both are hard to find on the islands themselves – best to get copies before you go. The *Rough Guide Map to Mallorca* (1:80,000) is equally difficult to locate on the islands, but it does have an index and, although the road numbers are the old ones, it is more detailed than all of its main rivals. More readily available in the Balearics is GeoCenter's clear and easy-to-use *Leisure Map Mallorca* (1:120,000) and the *Berlitz Holiday Map Menorca* (1:55,000). Both of these usefully indicate distances between settlements and mark salient geographical features, but neither has an index and both have the old road numbers. The best **town and resort maps** are produced by Distrimapas Telstar (🌐www.distrimapas-telstar.es) at the 1:10,000 to 1:15,000 scales; they cost about €5–7 each and are widely available.

Of the several **Mallorca hiking maps** on the market, the classiest are those published by a German company, Reise Know-How (🌐www.reise-know-how.de), whose products are available direct from the company or internationally at leading bookstores at about £9/€15 – but not in the Balearics themselves. They publish four large topographical maps of Mallorca (1:40,000) – North, East, South and West – each of which is marked with all the main hiking trails and bicycle routes. Their only serious competitor is Editorial Alpina (🌐www.editorialalpina.com), a Spanish company who publish three multilingual *Map & Hiking Guides* to the Tramuntana mountains – one each for the North, Centre and South. The guide books give the low-down on a variety of hikes in reasonable detail and the maps (at 1:25,000) are the most detailed on the market. All maps and guides cost €9 each and are widely available across Mallorca – at, for example, Sóller tourist office (see p.114). **Menorca hiking maps** are much thinner on the ground and the best you'll do is the very competent *Menorca Tour & Trail Map* (1:40,000) produced by **Discovery Walking Guides** (🌐www.walking.demon.co.uk) and costing £8; the same company also offers the *Walk! Menorca* hiking guide and maps (1:40,000) for £12; neither publication is available on the island.

Money and exchange

Spain's currency is the **euro** (€). Each euro is made up of 100 cents. Euro notes and coins feature a common EU design on one face, but different country-specific designs on the other. The **exchange rate** for the euro at time of writing was 0.67 to the British pound, 1.26

to the US dollar, 1.41 to the Canadian dollar, 1.68 to the Australian dollar and 1.98 to the NZ dollar. All well-known brands of **traveller's cheque** in all major currencies are widely accepted in Mallorca and Menorca, and you can change them as well as foreign currency into euros at most Balearic **banks** and **savings banks**, which are ubiquitous; **banking hours** are usually Monday to Friday from 9am to 2pm, with many banks opening on Saturday mornings from 9am to 1pm from October to April. Most visitors, however, now resort to **ATMs** and these are commonplace in Palma, Maó, Ciutadella and all the larger resorts. Most ATMs give instructions in a variety of languages, and accept a host of **debit cards** without charging a transaction fee. **Credit cards** can be used in ATMs too, but in this case transactions are treated as loans, with interest accruing daily from the date of withdrawal. All major credit cards, including American Express, Visa and Mastercard, are widely accepted.

Opening hours and public holidays

Although there's been some movement towards a northern European **working day**

Public holidays

January 1 New Year's Day (Cap d'Any)

January 6 Epiphany (Reyes Magos)

Maundy Thursday (Dijous Sant)

Good Friday (Divendres Sant)

May 1 Labour Day (Día del Treball)

August 15 Assumption of the Virgin (Assumpció)

October 12 Spanish National Day (Día de la Hispanidad)

November 1 All Saints (Tots Sants)

December 6 Constitution Day (Día de la Constitució)

December 8 Immaculate Conception (Inmaculada Concepción)

December 24 Christmas Eve

December 25 Christmas Day (Nadal; Navidad in Castilian)

December 26 Boxing Day/St Stephen's Day (Dia de Sant Esteban) in Menorca and Mallorca – especially in Palma and the major tourist resorts – most shops and offices still close for a **siesta** of at least two hours in the hottest part of the afternoon. There's a lot of variability, but basic working hours are typically Monday to Friday 9am to 1pm & 4pm to 7pm, Saturday 9am to 1pm; notable exceptions are the extended hours operated by the largest department stores, some important tourist attractions and most tourist and souvenir shops. Government offices are not open on Saturdays. In winter (Nov–March), Menorca's tourist industry pretty much shuts up shop and although things aren't so clear cut in Mallorca most of the resorts scale right down.

Local festivals (see pp.39–41) are a prominent feature of island life and they work in tandem with **public holidays**, whose precise dates and details are fixed annually – so there may be some (minor) variations to the list in the box on p.50. The island's resorts are generally oblivious to public holidays as are hotels and most restaurants, but almost all businesses and shops close and public transport is reduced to a skeleton service.

Phones

On both Mallorca and Menorca, all the larger towns and villages and most of the countryside is on the **mobile phone (cell phone)** network at **GSM900/1800**, the band common to the rest of Europe, Australia and New Zealand. This means that the vast majority of mobile phones from these countries will work here though, if you haven't used your mobile abroad before, you should check with your phone company: some mobiles are, for example, barred from international use. It's also a good idea to check **call charges** as costs can be excruciating – particularly irritating is the supplementary charge that you pay on incoming calls. International **texting** (SMS) via the GSM band is – or can be – dead easy too. Depending on the mobile, there's often no need to tap in international codes, you just send the message as you would back home. Again, your phone company will, if necessary, offer advice and details of charges. Things are a tad more complicated for Canadians and Americans. The **North American mobile network** is not compatible with the GSM band, so you'll need a

Phoning home from the Balearics

Note that the initial zero is omitted from the area code when dialing the UK, Ireland, Australia and New Zealand from abroad. Dial the international access code ☎00 followed by:

Australia: ☎61, then the area code, then the number.
Canada: ☎1, then the area code, then the number.
Republic of Ireland: ☎353, then the area code, then the number.
New Zealand: ☎64, then the area code, then the number.
South Africa ☎27, then the area code, then the number.
UK: ☎44, then the area code, then the number.
US: ☎1, then the area code, then the number.

Phoning the Balearics from abroad
Dial your international access code, followed by ☎34 for Spain and then the nine-digit local number. Note that all Balearic phone numbers begin with ☎971, but this is an integral part of the number, not an (optional) area code.

Useful telephone numbers:
Directory enquiries (national) ☎11888
Directory enquiries (international) ☎11886
Emergencies ☎112
Operator Services ☎1009

tri-band phone, which is able to switch from one band to the other.

As regards **ordinary phones**, you'll find that international and domestic calls are slightly cheaper after 10pm and before 8am, and after 2pm on Saturday and all day Sunday. Almost every hotel room has a phone, but there is almost always an exorbitant surcharge for their use. To reduce costs, contact your phone company back home about a **telephone charge card**. Using a PIN number, these cards allow you to make calls from most public, private and hotel phones abroad with the costs charged to your home account.

The police

Franco created a **police force** of labyrinthine complexity and since his death political parties of all persuasions have dodged the fundamental reorganization that is really needed. The reason is simple: no one wants to stir things up. There are three main types of police in Spain: the Guardia Civil, the Policía Nacional and the Policía Municipal, all of them armed. Dressed in green uniforms, the **Guardia Civil** police the highways and the countryside, but they are generally regarded as being officious and best avoided. Even now, many Spaniards are deeply suspicious of them, remembering their enthusiastic support of Franco and the unsuccessful coup led by one of their colonels, Tejero, when he held the Spanish parliament hostage in February 1981. They have, however, had their sails trimmed in recent years – improbably, they've even assumed some environmental responsibilities – and the loathed tricorn hat has been abandoned except for ceremonial occasions. In fairness, the Guardia Civil has attempted to improve its image, launching what (almost) amounts to a charm offensive and recent tourists' reports of their attitude have been favourable. A second police force, the brown-uniformed **Policía Nacional**, have made a better fist of the transition to democracy despite their disagreeable origins as Franco's brutal security police, the Policía Armada; they were even instrumental in Tejero's failure. They are mainly seen in Palma, armed with submachine guns and guarding key installations or personnel. They are also used to control crowds and demonstrations and – despite their democratic credentials – are not known for their sensitivity. Consequently, if you do need the police, and above all if you're reporting a (serious) crime, you're usually better off seeking out the more sympathetic **Policía Municipal**, who wear blue uniforms. The problem is that this force only operates in the towns, and so in the countryside you'll usually have no choice but to throw yourself on the tender mercies of the Guardia Civil, who are inclined to resent the suggestion that any crime exists on their turf. Indeed, you may end up feeling as if you're the one who stands accused. Many police officers **speak English**, especially in the towns and resort areas, but you can't bank on it.

Smoking

On January 1, 2006, new anti-smoking legislation was passed in Spain, making **smoking illegal** in all theatres, bars and restaurants as well as on public transport, though the positive effects of this ban have been partly negated by local exemptions allowing smoking in scores of restaurants and bars. Owners of these establishments must display their exemption certificate.

Time

Spain is one hour ahead of Greenwich Mean Time, six hours ahead of US Eastern Standard Time, nine hours ahead of US Pacific Standard Time, nine hours behind Australian Eastern Standard Time and eleven hours behind New Zealand – except for periods during the changeovers made in the respective countries to and from daylight saving. In Spain, the clocks go forward an hour on the last Sunday of March and back an hour on the last Sunday of October.

Toilets

Public toilets are rare but averagely clean, though they almost never have any paper. They're commonly referred to as *los servicios* or *el lavabo*. The usual signs are, for "Ladies", *Dones* or the Castilian *Damas* and, for "Gentlemen", *Homes* or the Castilian *Caballeros*. You may also see the potentially confusing *Señoras* (Women) and *Señores* (Men).

Tourist information

There are scores of **websites** devoted to the Balearics, but most of them have something to sell and impartial information, never mind facts and figures, can be surprisingly hard to track down. That said, there are a handful of useful websites organized by the Spanish National Tourist Office (the SNTO) and the Balearic government (see below).

In **Mallorca**, there's a helpful provincial tourist office at the airport (see p.61) and another in the centre of Palma (see p.63). Both will provide free road maps of the island and leaflets detailing all sorts of island-wide practicalities – from bus and train timetables to lists of car rental firms, ferry schedules and boat excursion organizers. In addition, most towns and almost every resort has its own **tourist office**, whose opening times and addresses are given in the Guide. These vary enormously in quality, and while they are generally extremely useful for local information, they cannot be relied on to know anything about what goes on outside their patch. In **Menorca**, there are efficient year-round tourist offices in the two main towns, Maó and Ciutadella, and a tourist information desk at the airport.

Useful websites

ⓦ **www.conselldemallorca.net** Well-presented website emanating from Mallorca's parliamentary council. Particularly good for local news and current affairs.

ⓦ **www.digame-online.com.** Lively online guide as to what to do and where to go in Mallorca. Strong on theatre, festivals, dance and music.

ⓦ **www.mallorcaweb.com** and ⓦ **www.menorcaweb.com** Compendious websites dedicated to the islands, covering everything from art and culture through to restaurants, politics and economics.

ⓦ **www.menorca-info.com** Comprehensive and clearly laid out guide to the island with oodles of practical information on everything from ferries to food, car rental to camping.

ⓦ **www.menorcavirtual.com** This well-organized portal will link you to many of Menorca's businesses. The emphasis is on car rental, accommodation and water sports. Most listings are in English.

ⓦ **www.okspain.org** Official site of the USA's SNTO.

ⓦ **www.spain.info.** The official website of the Spanish National Tourist Office (SNTO) provides an excellent general introduction to the country as a whole, and its myriad synopses – on everything from national parks to accommodation – are concise and clearly, even temptingly written.

ⓦ **www.tourspain.co.uk.** Official site of the UK's SNTO.

ⓦ **www.tourspain.toronto.on.ca.** Official site of the Canadian SNTO.

ⓦ **www.visitbalears.com** The Balearic government's official, English-language tourist site with separate sections for all of the islands. Covers a wide range of topics – from shopping through to nature – but many of the synopses are more than a little terse. Clearly laid out; a useful introduction.

Guide

Guide

① Palma and around

Mallorca

Menorca

0   20 km

N

CHAPTER 1 # Highlights

✳ **Palma Cathedral** The city's outstanding attraction, and one of Spain's finest Gothic cathedrals, whose honey-coloured walls and buttresses dominate the waterfront from the crest of a hill. See p.70

✳ **Mallorcan Primitives** The Museu de la Catedral is home to a fascinating selection of works by the distinctive school of medieval island painters known as the Mallorcan Primitives. See p.72

✳ **The Old Town, Palma** Recently restored, Palma's old town is the most intriguing part of the city, its narrow lanes and alleys intercepted by attractive little piazzas and flanked by a handsome medley of Gothic churches and Renaissance mansions. See p.77

✳ **Eating in Palma** Palma has the island's widest and liveliest selection of cafés, restaurants and *tapas* bars, ranging from informal local joints to Michelin-starred palaces offering the latest in international culinary chic. See p.92

✳ **Platja de Palma, S'Arenal** Perhaps the most self–conscious beach in Mallorca, awash with preening sunbathers who come to enjoy the fine white sands which extend for some 4km around the Bay of Palma. See p.100

✳ **Miró Foundation, Cala Major** The artist Joan Miró hunkered down in Mallorca to avoid the attentions of General Franco and his chums, creating some of his finest paintings during his long exile, on display here in this modern gallery. See p.101

△ Palma Cathedral

Palma and around

ALMA is an ambitious city. In 1983 it became the capital of one of Spain's newly established autonomous regions, the **Balearic islands**, and since then it has shed the dusty provincialism of yesteryear, developing into a go-ahead and cosmopolitan commercial hub of over 300,000 people. The new self-confidence is plain to see in the city centre, a vibrant and urbane place of careful coiffures and well-cut suits, which is akin to the big cities of the Spanish mainland and a world away from the heaving tourist enclaves of the surrounding bay. There's still a long way to go – much of suburban Palma remains obdurately dull and somewhat dilapidated – but the centre now presents a splendid ensemble of lively shopping areas and refurbished old buildings, mazy lanes, fountains, gardens and sculpture, all enclosed by what remains of the old city walls and their replacement boulevards.

This geography encourages downtown Palma to look into itself and away from the sea, even though its harbour – now quarantined by the main highway – has always been the city's economic lifeline. The Romans were the first to recognize the site's strategic value, establishing a military post here known as Palmaria, but real development came with the Moors, who made their **Medina Mayurka** a major seaport protected by no fewer than three concentric walls. Jaume I of Aragón captured the Moorish stronghold in 1229 and promptly started work on the **cathedral**, whose mellow sandstone still towers above the waterfront, presenting from its seaward side – in the sheer beauty of its massive proportions – one of Spain's most stunning sights.

As a major port of call between Europe and North Africa, Palma boomed under both Moorish and medieval Christian control, but its wealth and prominence came to a sudden end with the Spanish exploitation of the New World: from the early sixteenth century, Madrid looked west across the Atlantic and Palma slipped into Mediterranean obscurity. One result of its abrupt decline has been the preservation of much of the **old town**, with its beguiling tangle of narrow, labyrinthine streets and high-storeyed houses. The pick of Palma's other historic attractions are the fourteenth-century **Castell de Bellver** and the heavyweight Baroque **Basílica de Sant Francesc**.

Yet for most visitors, Palma's main appeal is its sheer vitality: at night scores of excellent **restaurants** offer the best of Spanish, Catalan and Mallorcan cuisine, while the city's **cafés** buzz with purposeful chatter. Palma also boasts **accommodation** to match most budgets, making it a splendid base from which to explore the island. In this respect, the city is far preferable, at least for independent travellers, to the string of resorts along the neighbouring **Badía de Palma** (Bay of Palma), where nearly all the accommodation is block-booked by tour operators. If you are tempted by a cheap package, however, it's

PALMA & AROUND

Manacor
Llucmajor
Llucmajor
Inca
Inca
Sóller
Puigpunyent & La Granja
Estellencs
Port d'Andratx
Port d'Andratx

N

5 km
0

MA-15
MA-13A
MA-19
PM19
S'Arenal
Platja de Palma
Sometimes
Ses Maravelles
Cala Blava
Cap Enderrocat
Ca'n Pastilla
MA-15
MA-13A
MA-13
MA-11
VIA CINTURA MA-20
PALMA
Catedral
Es Portixol
Es Molinar
Cala Gamba
Cala Major
Fundació Pilar
i Joan Miró
Ferry Port
Castell de
Bellver
Gènova
Illetes
Bendinat
Badia de Palma
VIA CINTURA
MA-20
MA-1
MA1C
Portals
Nous
Palma
Nova
Torrenova
Magaluf
Cala Mago
Portals Vells
MILITARY ZONE
Cap de Cala Figuera
MA1C
Calvià
MA-1
Galilea
MA-1031
Capdellà
MA-1031
Andratx
MA-10
Peguera
Cala
Fornells
Camp
de Mar
Santa Ponça

as well to bear in mind that the more agreeable of the resorts lie to the west of the city, where a hilly coastline of rocky cliffs and tiny coves is punctuated by small, sandy beaches. Development is ubiquitous, but **Cala Major** is of interest as the site of the former home and studio of Joan Miró; well-to-do **Illetes** has several excellent hotels and a couple of lovely cove beaches; and pint-sized **Cala Fornells** has a fine seashore setting and several good hotels, and is also within easy reach of the spacious sandy shorelines of family-oriented **Santa Ponça** and **Peguera**. Places to avoid include lager-swilling **Magaluf** and all the resorts to the east of Palma, where the pancake-flat shoreline is burdened by a seamless band of skyscrapers stretching from **Ca'n Pastilla** to **S'Arenal** – behind what is, admittedly, one of the island's longest and most impressive beaches, the **Platja de Palma**.

Arrival

Mallorca's international **airport** is 11km east of downtown Palma, immediately behind the resort of Ca'n Pastilla. It consists of one enormous terminal, which handles both scheduled and charter flights, with separate floors for arrivals (downstairs) and departures (upstairs). Both floors have airport **information desks** – a good job, as the airport can be very confusing. On the arrivals floor, a flotilla of **car rental** outlets jostle for position by the luggage carousels. Beyond, through the glass doors, is the main **arrivals hall**, which has 24-hour **ATMs** and **currency exchange** facilities, dozens of package-tour agents plus a **provincial tourist office** (Mon–Sat 9am–6.30pm, Sun 9am–1.30pm) with a wide range of brochures, key public transport timetables, maps, and lists of hotels and *hostals*; it's beside Exit 4. The tourist office will not, however, help arrange **accommodation** and neither will most of the package-tour travel agents. An exception is the extremely helpful Prima Travel (℡971 26 01 43, ⓦ www.prima-travel.com), who have a good selection of hotels, apartments and villas in all price ranges, plus English-speaking staff.

The airport is linked to the city and the Bay of Palma resorts by a busy highway (*autopista*), which shadows the shoreline from S'Arenal in the east to Palma Nova and Magaluf in the west. The least expensive way to reach Palma from the airport is by **EMT bus #1** (daily every 15min from 6am to 2.30am; €1.85), which leaves from the main entrance of the terminal building, just behind the taxi rank. They reach the city's inner ring road near the foot of Avinguda Gabriel Alomar i Villalonga, at the c/Joan Maragall junction, then head on to Plaça Espanya, on the north side of the centre, before continuing west to the Passeig Mallorca and then south to the top of Avinguda Jaume III and the ferry terminal. There are frequent stops along the way. A **taxi** from the airport to the city centre will set you back about €20; taxi rates are controlled and a list of island-wide fares should be available from the provincial tourist office in the arrivals hall.

By ferry

The Palma **ferry terminal** is about 4km west of the city centre. Trasmediterranea and Iscomar ferries arrive at Terminal 2; Balearia ferries at Terminal 3, about 150m away. **EMT bus #1** (daily every 15min from 6am to 2.30am; €1.10) leaves every fifteen minutes from outside Terminal 2 to the Plaça Espanya. There are also **taxi** ranks outside both terminal buildings; the fare to the city centre is about €10.

Orientation

Almost everything of interest in Palma is located in the city centre, a roughly circular affair whose southern perimeter is defined by the cathedral and the remains of the old city walls, which in turn abut the coastal motorway and the harbour. The city centre's landward limits are determined by a zigzag of wide boulevards built beside or in place of the old town walls – **Avinguda de la Argentina** and **Avinguda Gabriel Alomar i Villalonga** connect with the coastal motorway, thereby completing the circle. The **Via Cintura (MA-20)**, the ring road around the suburbs, loops off from the coastal motorway to create a much larger, outer circle.

The city centre itself is crossed by four interconnected avenues: **Passeig d'es Born**, **Avinguda Jaume III**, **c/Unió** (which becomes **c/Riera** at its eastern end) and **Passeig de la Rambla**. Your best bet is to use these four thoroughfares to guide yourself round the centre – Palma's jigsaw-like side streets and squares can be very confusing. Central Palma is about 2km in diameter, roughly thirty minutes' walk from one side to the other. If you're in a hurry, **taxi** fares are reasonable. There are ranks outside all the major hotels; alternatively, phone Taxi Radio Palma (☎971 40 14 14) or Radio Taxi (☎971 75 54 40).

City transport

To reach the city's outskirts, take the **bus**. City buses are operated by **EMT** (Empresa Municipal de Transports) and almost all their services, which combine to link the centre with the suburbs and the nearer tourist resorts, pass through **Plaça Espanya**; several of the more useful services also pass through Placa de la Reina. In the city centre, each EMT bus stop displays a schematic plan showing the route followed by – and the timetable of – those buses that halt at that particular stop; in addition, an electronic display shows when the next bus or buses will arrive. **Tickets** are available from the driver and cost €1.10 per journey within the city limits. You can buy a **carnet** of ten at a discount (€7.50) from most *tabacs* (tobacconists) and some newsagents. EMT also has an **enquiry telephone line** in Spanish and Catalan on ☎971 21 44 44, or visit their website at ⓦwww.emtpalma.es.

Parking in Palma

Trying to find a **car parking space** in downtown Palma can be a nightmare – and you're well advised to leave your vehicle on the city's outskirts, especially for visits of more than an hour or two. If you're staying downtown, choose a hotel which either has its own car park or has an arrangement with a local one (some hotels offer discounts or will reimburse part of the cost). Parking in the city centre requires an **ORA ticket** during busy periods (Mon–Fri 9.30am–2pm & 4.30–8pm, Sat 9.30am–2pm). At other times – when the centre is much less congested – parking is free. Tickets are readily available from ORA parking meters but, although the cost is minimal (around €1.30 per hour), the longest-lasting ticket only provides two hour's parking – and fines are immediate and steep. Note also that if the time allowed overlaps into a free period, your ORA ticket is still valid when restricted time begins again. As for **car parks**, the Parc de la Mar near the cathedral often has spaces when the others do not.

Island-wide bus services are operated by several companies under the auspices of **tib** (Transportes de les Illes Baleares). All services depart from the **bus station** about 400m north of Plaça Espanya, along c/Eusebi Estada. For timetable information, tib has a Spanish/Catalan information line on ℡971 17 77 77, maintains a website on ⓦhttp://tib.caib.es and operates a very helpful **bus station information desk** (daily 6am–10pm), where most of the staff speak at least some English. The information desk provides train information too.

Mallorca has **two train lines**: one, the modern line, links Palma with most of the larger towns of the central plain, including Binissalem, Inca, Sineu, Manacor and Sa Pobla; the second is the delightful antique train line running from Palma to Sóller (see p.114). At present, the train station of the modern line is next door to the bus station, but – in a burst of what many islanders consider insane extravagance – it will soon be underground on the north side of Plaça Espanya. The Sóller train station is also on the north side of Plaça Espanya. There are ticket offices at both stations.

Alternatively, **Citysightseeing** (℡971 22 04 28, ⓦwww.city-sightseeing.com) operates double-deck, hop-off, hop-on bus trips around the major sights throughout the year (May–Sept daily 9.30am–8pm & Oct–April daily 9.30am–7pm; every 20–30min). Their buses head round the city centre's enclosing boulevards and venture west as far as the ferry terminal, but frankly EMT's buses are a better bet with one exception: EMT does not provide a bus service from the city centre to either the Poble Espanyol (see p.90) or the Castell de Bellver (see p.90), whereas Citysightseeing does. Citysightseeing **tickets**, which are available on board the bus, cost €13 and are valid for 24 hours. The most popular departure point is Plaça de la Reina, metres from the cathedral. Finally, a more sedate way of seeing Palma is to take a traditional **horse-and-carriage ride** – they hang around next to the cathedral; count on around €40 for half an hour.

Information

There's a **provincial tourist office** just off Passeig d'es Born at Plaça de la Reina 2 (Mon–Fri 9am–8pm, Sat 9am–2.30; ℡971 71 22 16). The main **municipal office** is on the north side of Plaça Espanya (daily 9am–8pm; ⓦwww.a-palma.es) and there's another, much smaller municipal office inside Can Solleric, at Passeig d'es Born 27 (Mon–Fri 9am–8pm, Sat 9am–1.30pm). The first two provide city- and island-wide information, dispensing free maps, accommodation lists, bus schedules, ferry timetables, lists of car rental firms and all sorts of special-interest leaflets, including the useful *Palma: Best Mediterranean Shopping* brochure, which details many of the city's most distinctive shops. The third office only has a limited range of city information. Palma's official website, ⓦwww.a-palma.es, is multilingual and has a battery of information, including "where to go" and "what's on" sections.

Accommodation

There are several dozen **hostals and hotels** dotted around Palma, but nonetheless demand can still outstrip supply in peak periods, most notably in June, early

PALMA

0 _____ 400 m

- - - ORA (Restricted
Parking Area)

CLUBS
Pacha 8
Tito's 7

SHOPS
Colmado Manresa aa
La Favorita bb

RESTAURANTS
Casa Eduardo 6
Koldo Royo 4
Mangiafuoco 2
Museu 3

CAFÉS & TAPAS BARS
Diner 1
Mollet 5

ACCOMMODATION
AC Ciutat de Palma A
Araxa B
Catalonia Majórica H
Costa Azul C
Melià Palas Atenea E
Mirador D
Portixol F
Rosamar G

Poble
Espanyol

Auditorium

Badia de Palma

Castell
de Bellver

Plaça Gomila ▼   ▼ G & H   ▼ 8, Parc Quarentena (150m), ferry port & Andratx

July and September, when you really need to book ahead of time. Perhaps surprisingly, things are not usually as tight from the middle of July to late August, when many Spaniards try to avoid the searing heat of this and every other Spanish city, but vacant rooms can still get mighty thin on the ground. Note also that in periods of high demand, some places insist on a minimum stay of two or three nights. If you need assistance, contact Prima Travel (☎971 26 01 43, ⓦwww.prima-travel.com), who specialize in last-minute accommodation and have an office at the airport.

Many of Palma's more enticing hotels and *hostals* are in the centre, which is a good job given that this is by far the most engaging part of the city. In particular, there's a cluster of **budget** places along the narrow, cobbled side streets off the Passeig d'es Born and a number of more modern **mid-range hotels** on the Passeig Mallorca, a particularly attractive portion of the inner ring road, where two sections of old city wall run down the middle of the boulevard on either side of a deep watercourse-cum-moat. There's another cluster of modern high-rises, including some quite plush places, to the west of the centre, overlooking the waterfront along Avinguda Gabriel Roca (also known as the Passeig Marítim), but the city's most **distinctive hotels** – and not necessarily the most expensive – are concentrated in the old town, in a string of beautifully converted old mansions.

One final word of caution: many hotels and hostals, especially at the bottom end of the market, have some pretty ropey rooms as well as some good ones. If you are not satisfied, ask for a transfer.

Inexpensive

Hostal Apuntadores c/Apuntadors 8 ☏971 71 34 91, ⓦ www.palma-hostales.com. Simple, straightforward rooms in an old house with a central location just off Passeig d'es Born. Some rooms are en suite, others have shared facilities. A long-established *hostal* but light sleepers should bag a room at the back as c/Apuntadors can get very noisy at night. Breakfast is served in the café in the reception area. ❷

Hostal Brondo c/Ca'n Brondo 1 ☏971 71 90 43, ⓦ www.hostalbrondo.net. In a central but quiet street, this stylish little place

occupies a sympathetically modernised old house complete with ancient stone arches and traditional whitewashed plasterwork. The guest rooms are decorated in plain but pleasant modern style and are both en suite and with shared facilities. Shared bath ❷, en suite ❸

Hostal-residencia Regina c/Sant Miquel 77 ☏971 71 37 03, ⓦ www.hostalreginapalma.com. Small, family-run hotel in an unusual, long and low-slung 1920s building. The interior has recently been refurbished in (a vaguely) retro style and the twelve guest rooms, all of which are on the first floor, are en suite and air-conditioned. A

65

three-minute walk from Plaça Espanya. There's a roof terrace, but no breakfast. ❸

Hostal Ritzi c/Apuntadors 6 ☎971 71 46 10, 🖥www.hostalritzi.com. Well-regarded and long-established one-star *hostal* in the centre of the city, just off Passeig d'es Born. Occupies an ancient but well-kept five-storey house and although the rooms, both en suite and with shared facilities, could hardly be described as super comfortable, they are perfectly adequate. Shared bath ❷, en suite ❸

Hotel Rosamar Avgda Joan Miró 74 ☎971 73 27 23. A gay-friendly gathering place for an international crew of men and a few women, the Rosamar occupies a well-kept, modern block with forty guest rooms. Has no less than three sun terraces with views out over the bay. Ask for a room with a sea view. Situated 3km west of the centre, at the junction of c/Patrimoni and Avgda Joan Miró, and reachable on EMT bus #3 from several points in the city, including Plaça Joan Carles I (every 15min). ❸

Hostal Terminus Eusebi Estada 5 ☎971 75 00 14, 📧terminus@mail.cinet.es. Fetching two-star establishment with a quirkily old-fashioned foyer and fairly large and frugal but still comfortable rooms. Very handy for the Sóller train station – which is a plus – but also within earshot of construction works until late 2007. ❸

Moderate

AC Ciutat de Palma Plaça Pont 3 ☎971 22 23 00, 🖥www.ac-hotels.com. Gleamingly new chain hotel in a stylishly revamped, six-storey high-rise on the edge of the groovy Santa Catalina quarter. The interior is resolutely modern, all angular lines and big vases, but the bedrooms, of which there are 85, are very comfortable. Catch EMT bus #6 from several places in the centre, including Plaça de la Reina. Rack rate ❻, but discount deals are commonplace.

Hotel Almudaina Avgda Jaume III, 9 ☎971 72 73 40, 🖥www.hotelalmudaina.com. Dapper modern rooms in one of the attractive 1940s blocks overlooking the city's premier shopping street. Popular with Spanish business folk. ❺

Hotel Araxa c/Alférez Cerdá 22 ☎971 73 16 40, 🖥www.hotelaraxa.com. Attractive four-storey modern hotel with pleasant gardens and an outdoor swimming pool. Most rooms have balconies. It's in a quiet residential area about 2km west of the centre, not far from the Castell de Bellver. To get there by public transport, take EMT bus #6 and get off at c/Marquès de la Sènia, just before the start of Avgda Joan Miró; it's a five- to ten-minute walk from the bus stop. ❻

Hotel Born c/Sant Jaume 3 ☎971 71 29 42, 🖥www.hotelborn.com. Delightful hotel in an excellent downtown location, set in a refurbished mansion with big wooden doors and a lovely courtyard, where you can have breakfast under the palm trees. The rooms, most of which face onto the courtyard, are comfortable if a little plain, and all have a/c. It's a popular spot, so book early in high season. ❻

Hotel Catalonia Majórica c/Garita 3 ☎971 40 02 61, 🖥www.hoteles-catalonia.com. Big and modern four-star hotel overlooking the coast from near the ferry port about 4km west of the centre. Some 170 rooms kitted out in brisk and efficient chain-hotel style. Ask for a room with a sea view. Competitively priced from ❹

Hotel Costa Azul Passeig Marítim (Avgda Gabriel Roca) 7 ☎971 73 19 40, 🖥www .esperanzahoteles.com. Recently remodelled, this standard high-rise has balconied rooms overlooking the bay and a heated indoor swimming pool. Breakfast included. ❻

Hotel Dalt Murada c/Almudaina 6 ☎971 42 53 00, 🖥www.daltmurada.co.uk. One of the most delightful hotels in the city, this family-run place occupies a splendid old mansion that comes complete with many of its eighteenth-century – and even earlier – features. Each of the guest rooms has its own character, but they are all large and extremely well-appointed and most hold antique furnishings; the exception is the immaculately modern penthouse suite. Breakfast is served in the garden, weather permitting. Great location too – down an old cobbled alley metres from Plaça Cort. The family also own the small and much plainer, six-room *Hotel Casa Padrina*, which occupies a late nineteenth-century townhouse in somewhat gloomy surroundings at the corner of c/Missió and c/Tereses. Rates: Dalt Murada ❻–❼, Casa Padrina ❻

Hotel H M Jaime III Passeig Mallorca 14 ☎971 72 59 43, 🖥www.hmhotels.net. Agreeable four-star hotel with smart modern rooms, mostly with balconies, and a newly kitted out foyer decorated in crisp, minimalist style. Front rooms overlook the Passeig Mallorca, which can make them a tad noisy, and there's chic shopping just around the corner. ❻

Hotel Mirador Passeig Marítim (Avgda Gabriel Roca) 10 ☎971 73 20 46, 🖥www.hotelmirador.es. Down by the waterfront, ten minutes' walk to the west of the city centre, this unassuming, four-star high-rise hotel is popular with visiting Spaniards. Considering its bayside location, room rates are very reasonable. ❻

Hotel Palau Sa Font c/Apuntadors 38 ☎ 971 71
22 77, 🌐 www.palausafont.com. This smooth and
polished, four-star hotel, decorated in warm Italian
colours and graced by sculptures and other modern
works of art, manages to be both stylish and
welcoming. There's a small pool on the roof
terrace, and some rooms enjoy inspiring views of
the cathedral. Breakfast included. ⑤, but discounts
are frequent, though note that cards are not
accepted on special deals.
Hotel Palladium Passeig Mallorca 40 ☎ 971 71
28 41, 🌐 www.hotelpalladium.com. Proficient
three-star hotel offering spick-and-span accommodation in a modern tower block overlooking the
handsome Passeig Mallorca. ⑤
Hotel San Lorenzo c/Sant Llorenç 14 ☎ 971 72
82 00, 🌐 www.hotelsanlorenzo.com. Amongst the
narrow lanes of what was once the fishermen's
quarter of Sant Pere, this chi-chi, four-star hotel
has been cleverly shoehorned into an old seventeenth-century mansion. The antique details have
been lovingly preserved, while modern facilities,
such as the swimming pool in the garden, have
been tastefully added. Every mod con. ⑥
Hotel Saratoga Passeig Mallorca 6 ☎ 971 72 72
40, 🌐 www.hotelsaratoga.es. Bright, modern,
centrally located hotel in a smart seven-storey block
complete with a rooftop café and garden swimming
pool. Rooms are neat and trim, with marble floors
and balconies either overlooking the boulevard
(which can be noisy) or an interior courtyard (much
quieter). Substantial banquet-breakfast included. ⑥

Expensive

Hotel Convent de la Missió c/de la Missió 7A
☎ 971 22 73 47, 🌐 www.conventdelamissio.com.
Über cool, fourteen-room hotel, whose slick
minimalism has been intelligently intruded into the
wide spaces of a former convent. The location is,
however, really rather drab – on a dull side street
off c/Sant Miquel. ⑧
Hotel Melià Palas Atenea Passeig Marítim (Avgda
Gabriel Roca) 29 ☎ 971 28 14 00, 🌐 www
.solmelia.com. A vast, classy 1960s-style foyer

leads to attractively furnished, comfortable rooms
with balconies overlooking the bay. There's also an
inviting bar. ⑦
Hotel-residencia Palacio Ca Sa Galesa
c/Miramar 8 ☎ 971 71 54 00, 🌐 www
.palaciocasagalesa.com. Charmingly renovated
seventeenth-century mansion set amongst the
narrow alleys of the oldest part of town, with just
twelve luxurious and tastefully furnished rooms and
suites. There's an indoor heated swimming pool
(set in a renovated ancient Roman bath) and fine
views of the city from the roof terrace. Opened in
the early 1990s, this was one of the first deluxe
hotels to occupy an old island mansion and its
success has set something of a trend. ⑨
Hotel Portixol c/Sirena 27 ☎ 971 27 18 00,
🌐 www.portixol.com. Es Portixol, just a couple of
kilometres east of Palma Cathedral, was once the
preserve of local fishermen, who docked their
boats at either of its sheltered coves. The district
hit the skids in the 1960s, but it's now championed
as an exemplar of urban renewal, its terrace
houses all cleaned and dusted, one cove turned
into a marina, the other into a tiny beach resort.
Leading the aesthetic charge is this high-rise,
seafront hotel, a very urban and urbane spot with
all sorts of finessed details, from creative
backlighting through to guest room TV cabinets
that look like mini beach huts. It's all good fun, but
note that it's worth paying extra for a room with a
sea view. There's an outside swimming pool and a
first-rate restaurant, where you can dine either
inside or outside looking out over the ocean. ⑦,
sea view ⑧
Hotel Puro Montenegro 12 ☎ 971 42 54 50,
🌐 www.purohotel.com/page. Self-conscious
designer hotel much admired by the likes of Condé
Nast. Aimed at the 'hip' city dweller, there are rugs
on the ceiling, cushions on the floor, and a sort of
erotic charge to the public areas aided and abetted
by the house music. As you might expect, the guest
rooms are similarly slick and á la mode. The hotel
is in an old house amongst the narrow side streets
west of the Passeig d'es Born. ⑧

The City

There's not much argument as to where to start a tour of Palma – it's got to be
the **cathedral**, which dominates the waterfront from the crest of a hill. Central
Palma's other landmark is the **Palau de l'Almudaina** next door, an important
royal residence from Moorish times and now the repository of a mildly engaging assortment of municipal baubles, though successive modifications have
robbed the building of much of its character. Spreading northeast behind the
cathedral are the narrow lanes and ageing mansions of the most intriguing part

CENTRAL PALMA

PALMA AND AROUND

Bus Station & Inca Train Station (400m)

Future site of Inca Train Station

Soller Train Station

PLAÇA ESPANYA

MARIE CURIE

Mercat de l'Olivar

Sant Miquel

Museu d'Art Espanyol Contemporani

Teatre Principal

L'Aguila

Can Rei

Gran Hotel

PASSEIG DE LA RAMBLA

VIA ROMA

Hospital General

Can Balaguer

Can Solleric

Teatre Municipal

Can Pavesi

Can Moner

EL PUIG DE SANT PERE

PASSEIG MALLORCA

AVINGUDA JAUME III

Es Baluard & 10 (20m)

N

ACCOMMODATION

Almudaina	H
Apuntadores	N
Born	G
Brondo	J
Casa Padrina	E
Convent de la Missió	D
Dalt Murada	P
H M Jaime III	F
Palacio Ca Sa Galesa	Q
Palau Sa Font	K
Palladium	C
Puro	M
Regina	B
Ritzi	O
San Lorenzo	L
Saratoga	I
Terminus	A

RESTAURANTS

Aramis	11
Asador Tierra Aranda	4
Caballito del Mar	29
Ca'n Carlos	3
Celler Pagès	14
Forn de Sant Joan	17
Museu	10
S'Olivera	25

LATE-NIGHT BARS

Abaco	18
Escape	16
Gotic	27
La Lonja	24
Latitude 39	15

CAFÉS & TAPAS BARS

Bosch	7
Bon Lloc	12
Ca'n Joan de S'Aigo	13
Cappuccino	19
El Pilon	9
Gran	6
Jaime III	1
La Bodeguita Mesón	
Salamanca	5
La Bóveda	26
La Taberna del Caracol	30
Lirico	21
Lizarran	8
Minimal	22
Orient Express	2
Plaça	20
Port Pesquer	28
Sa Imprenta	23

SHOPS

Camper	cc
Camper	gg
Casa del Mapa	nn
Colmado Santo Domingo	mm
El Corte Inglés	ee
Especias Crespi	ff
Fet a Mà	aa
Forn des Teatre	ii
Forn Fondo	kk
Frasquet	ll
La Concha	bb
La Favorita	dd
Librería Fondevila	jj
Majorica	hh
Vidrias Gordiola	oo

69

of the **old town**. A stroll here is a pleasure in itself, and tucked away among the side streets are two good diversions: the **Museu de Mallorca**, the island's most extensive museum, and the Baroque **Basílica de Sant Francesc**.

North of the old town lies the heart of the early twentieth-century city, where the high-sided tenements are graced by a sequence of flamboyant buildings in the *Modernista* style (the Spanish, and especially Catalan, form of Art Nouveau), particularly on and around **Plaça Weyler**.

West of the city centre, you should consider a visit to the **Castell de Bellver**, an impressive hilltop castle, and perhaps also to the much less interesting **Poble Espanyol**, which comprises detailed, scaled-down reproductions of character-istic buildings from every region of Spain.

The cathedral

Legend has it that when the invasion force of Jaume I of Aragón and Catalunya stood off Mallorca in 1229, a fierce gale threatened to sink the fleet. The desper-ate king promised to build a church dedicated to the Virgin Mary if the expedi-tion against the Moors was successful. It was, and Jaume fulfilled his promise, starting construction work the next year. The king had a political point to make too – he built his cathedral, a gigantic affair of golden sandstone, bang on top of the Great Mosque inside the Almudaina, the old Moorish citadel. The Reconquista – the expulsion of the Moors by the Christians – was to be no temporary matter.

As it turned out, the **cathedral** ("La Seu" in Catalan) was five hundred years in the making. Nonetheless, although there are architectural bits and bobs from several different eras, the church remains essentially Gothic, with massive exterior buttresses – its most distinctive feature – taking the weight off the pillars within. The whole structure derives its effect from its sheer height, impressive from any angle, but startling when viewed from the waterside esplanade.

The doors and bell tower

The finest of the cathedral's three doors is the **Portal del Mirador** ("Lookout Door"), which overlooks the Bay of Palma from the south facade. Dating from the late fourteenth century, the newly buffed and scrubbed Mirador features a host of Flemish-style ecclesiastical figurines set around a tympanum where heavily bearded disciples sit at a Last Supper. In contrast, the west-facing **Portal Major** ("Great Door"), across from the Almudaina, is a neo-Gothic disaster, an ugly reworking – along with the sixty-metre-high flanking turrets – of a far simpler predecessor that was badly damaged by an earthquake in 1851.

On the north side is a third door, the **Portal de l'Almoina**, decorated in a simple Gothic design of 1498. Above rises the solid squareness of the **bell tower** (closed to the public), an incongruous, fortress-like structure that clearly did not form part of the original design. When the largest of the bells, the 5700-kilo N'Eloi, was tolled in 1857, it shattered most of the cathedral's windows.

The interior

You **enter** the cathedral (April, May & Oct Mon–Fri 10am–5.15pm, Sat 10am–2.15pm; June–Sept 10am–6.15pm, Sat 10am–2.15pm; Nov–March Mon–Fri 10am–3.15pm, Sat 10am–2.15pm; €4.50) on the north side through the museum (see p.72). The majestic proportions of the **interior** are seen to best advantage from the western end, from the Portal Major. In the central **nave**, fourteen beautifully aligned, pencil-thin pillars rise to 21m before their ribs branch out, like fronded palm trees, to support the single-span, vaulted roof. The nave, at 44m high, is one of the tallest Gothic structures in Europe, and its 121-metre length is of matching grandeur. This open, hangar-like construction, typical of Catalan Gothic architecture, was designed to make the high altar visible to the entire congregation and to express the mystery of the Christian faith, with kaleidoscopic floods of light filtered in through the **stained-glass windows**. Most of the original glass was lost long ago, but recent refurbishment has returned several windows to their former glory and, now that many others have been un-bricked, the cathedral has re-emerged from the gloom imposed by Renaissance, Baroque and neo-Gothic architects. There are seven rose windows, the largest of which crowns the triumphal arch of the apse at the east end and boasts over 1200 individual pieces of glass; providing the sun is out, it showers the nave with a wonderful, dappled light in the morning. The cathedral's designers also incorporated a specific, carefully orchestrated artifice: twice a year, at 6.30am on Candlemas and St Martin's Day, the sun shines through the stained glass of the eastern window onto the wall immediately below the rose window on the main, western facade.

Gaudí's restoration

The first attempt to return the church to something like its original Gothic splendour was made at the beginning of the twentieth century when an inspired local bishop commissioned the *Modernista* Catalan architect **Antoni Gaudí** (1852–1926) to direct a full-blown restoration. At the time, Gaudí was renowned for his fancifully embellished metalwork, and his functionalist extrapolation of Gothic design was still evolving. This experimentation led ultimately to his most famous and extravagant opus, the church of the Sagrada Familia in Barcelona, but here in Palma his work was relatively restrained – though still deeply controversial. Indeed, certain Catholic dignitaries took the aesthetic hump over the revamp and when, in 1926, a Barcelona tram flattened Gaudí they must have thought their prayers had been answered.

Gaudí worked on Palma's cathedral intermittently between 1904 and 1914, during which time he removed the High Baroque altar and shifted the ornate choir stalls from the centre to the side of the cathedral, placing them flat against the walls of the presbytery. The new high altar, a medieval alabaster table of plain design, was then located beneath a phantasmagorical **baldachin**, a giant canopy, enhanced by hanging lanterns, which was supposed to symbolize the Crown of Thorns. It's not a great success, though to be fair Gaudí never had time to complete it – he wanted it to be made of wrought iron, but what you see today is in fact a trial piece fashioned from cork, cardboard and brocade.

Other examples of Gaudí's distinctive workmanship are dotted around the cathedral. The **railings** in front of the high altar are twisted into shapes inspired by Mallorcan window grilles, while the wall on either side of the **Bishop's Throne**, at the east end of the church, sports ceramic inlays with brightly painted floral designs. Yet Gaudí's main concern was to revive the Gothic tradition by allowing extra light. To this end he introduced **electric lighting**, bathing the apse in bright artificial light and placing lamps and candelabra throughout the church. This was all very innovative: at the time, no choir had ever before been removed in Spain and electric lighting was a real novelty. The artistic success of the whole project, though, was undeniable, and it was immediately popular with the congregation. Like the rest of his work, however, it did not bring Gaudí much international acclaim: it was only in the 1960s that his techniques were championed and copied across western Europe, and that his crucial role in the development of modernism was finally acknowledged.

The chapels

The aisles on either side of the central nave are flanked by a long sequence of **chapels**, dull affairs for the most part, dominated by dusty Baroque altars of gargantuan proportions and little artistic merit. The exception, and the cathedral's one outstanding example of the Baroque, is the **Capella del Corpus Christi**, at the head of the aisle to the left of the high altar. Begun in the sixteenth century, the chapel's tiered and columned altarpiece features three religious scenes, cramped and intense sculptural tableaux showing – from top to bottom – the temptations of St Anthony, the presentation of Jesus in the temple, and the Last Supper. Just in front and across from the chapel is a massive stone **pulpit** that was moved here by Gaudí, a makeshift location for this excellent illustration of the Plateresque style. Dated to 1531, the pulpit's intricate floral patterns and bustling Biblical scenes cover a clumsy structure, the upper portion of which is carried by telamons, male counterparts of the more usual caryatids.

Though you can't now reach the **Capella de la Trinitat** (Trinity Chapel) – it's at the east end of the church directly behind the high altar – this tiny chapel is also of interest. Completed in 1329, it accommodates the remains of Jaume II and Jaume III, two notable medieval kings of Mallorca (for more on whom, see pp.298–300). Initially, the bodies were stored in a tomb that operated rather like a filing cabinet, allowing the corpses to be venerated by the devout. They were viewed in 1809 by the first British traveller to write an account of a visit to Mallorca, the unflappable Sir John Carr, who calmly observed that, "considering the monarchs had been dead for five hundred years ... they were in a state of extraordinary preservation". This gruesome practice was finally discontinued during the nineteenth century, and alabaster sarcophagi now enclose the royal bones.

Visitors exit the cathedral via the cloisters, from where they can regain the museum.

The Museu de la Catedral

The ground floor of the bell tower and two adjoining chapterhouses have been turned into the **Museu de la Catedral** (same times and ticket as the cathedral), which holds an eclectic assortment of ecclesiastical treasures. The first room's most valuable exhibit, in the glass case in the middle, is a gilded silver monstrance of extraordinary delicacy, its fairy-tale decoration dating from the late sixteenth century. On display around the walls is a hotchpotch of chalices and reliquaries and a real curiosity, the portable altar of Jaume I, a wood and silver chessboard with each square containing a bag of relics.

The second room is mainly devoted to the Gothic works of the **Mallorcan Primitives**, a school of painters that flourished on the island in the fourteenth and fifteenth centuries, producing strikingly naive devotional works of bold colours and cartoon-like detail. The work of two of the school's leading fourteenth-century practitioners is displayed here, beginning with the so-called **Master of the Privileges**, whose love of warm colours and minute detail is shown to good advantage in a large (though unlabelled) panel painting of *The Life of St Eulalia*, whose martyrdom fascinated and excited scores of medieval Mallorcan artists. A Catalan girl-saint, Eulalia defied the Roman emperor Diocletian by sticking to her Christian faith despite all sorts of ferocious tortures, which are depicted here in ecstatic detail. She was eventually burnt at the stake and at the moment of her death, white doves flew from her mouth. The Master of the Privileges was greatly influenced by Italian painters, but his contemporary, the **Master of Montesión**, looked to his Catalan contemporaries for his sense of movement and tight draughtsmanship as in two panels displayed here, one of the *Crucifixion*, the other of the *Virgin Mary*. Later, the work of the Mallorcan Primitives shaded into the new realism of the Flemish style, which was to dominate Mallorcan painting throughout the sixteenth century. **Joan Desi**'s (unlabelled) *Panel of La Almoina* (*c.* 1500) illustrates the transition – it's the large panel showing St Francis, complete with stigmata, at the side of Christ.

The third and final room, the **Baroque chapterhouse**, is entered through a playful Churrigueresque doorway, above which a delicate Madonna is overwhelmed by lively cherubic angels. Inside, pride of place goes to the High Baroque **altar**, a gaudy, gilded affair surmounted by the Sacred Heart, a gory representation of the heart of Jesus that was very much in vogue during the eighteenth century. Some imagination went into the designation of the reliquaries displayed round the room: there's a piece of Christ's flogging post, three thorns from Christ's crown and even a piece of the gall and vinegared sponge that was offered to the crucified Jesus. Of more appeal are a pair of finely carved, Baroque crucifixes, each Christ a study in perfect muscularity swathed in the flowing folds of a loincloth.

The Palau de l'Almudaina

Opposite the cathedral entrance stands the **Palau de l'Almudaina**, originally the palace of the Moorish *walis* (governors), and later of the Mallorcan kings (April–Sept Mon–Fri 10am–5.45pm, Sat 10am–1pm; Oct–March Mon–Fri 10am–1pm & 4–5pm, Sat 10am–1pm; €4 with audioguide, otherwise €3.20; free on Wed to EU citizens showing their passport). The present structure, built around a central courtyard, owes much of its appearance to Jaume II (1276–1311), who spent the last twelve years of his life in residence here. Jaume converted the old fortress into a lavish palace that incorporated both Gothic and Moorish features, an uneasy mixture of styles conceived by the Mallorcan Pedro Selva, the king's favourite architect. The two most prominent "Moorish" attributes are the fragile-looking outside walls, with their square turrets and dainty crenellations, and the delicate arcades of the main loggia, which can be seen from the waterside esplanade below.

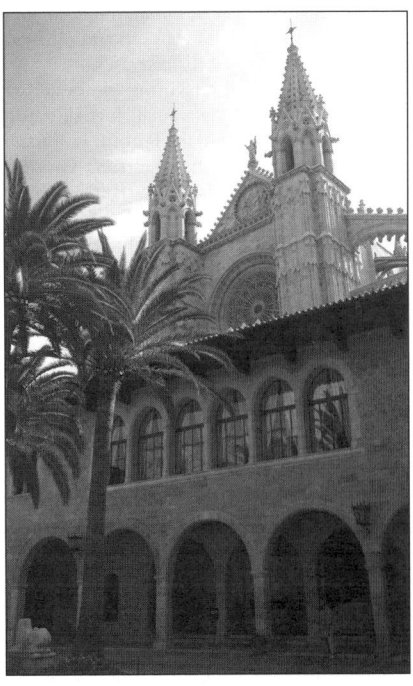

△ Palau de l'Almudaina

Once Mallorca was incorporated within the Aragonese kingdom, the Palau de l'Almudaina became surplus to requirements, though it did achieve local notoriety when the eccentric Aragonese king Juan I (1387–1395) installed an alchemist in the royal apartments, hoping he would replenish the treasury by turning base metal into gold. He didn't succeed. Today the palace serves a variety of official functions, has a small garrison to protect it, and holds a series of state apartments kept in readiness for visiting dignitaries and the king, which is presumably why those exhibits that are labelled carry Castilian inscriptions. When the king or some other bigwig is in residence, parts of the palace are usually cordoned off.

At the **reception**, pick up an audioguide or a plan, but note that the room numbers on the plan are not currently displayed in the rooms themselves – not that this is too much of a problem as the palace is not that big.

The interior

A visit begins with a series of medieval corridors and rooms whose rough stonework is almost entirely devoid of ornamentation, but things pick up in the **Salón de Consejos** (Hall of Councils; Room 4), where the walls sport a group of admirable Flemish tapestries, fifteenth- and sixteenth-century imports devoted to classical themes. Amongst them is a Roman Triumph, a blood-curdling war scene, and, best of the lot, the suicide of Cleopatra, showing a particularly wan-looking queen with the guilty asp slithering discreetly away. Moving on, the **Comedor de Oficiales** (Officers' Mess; Room 5) possesses a handful of Flemish genre paintings, fine still-life studies including one by the seventeenth-century Antwerp-based artist Frans Snyders – there's no label, but it's the painting with the man, the woman, the cat and several carcasses. Snyders was a contemporary of Rubens and odd-jobbed for him, painting in the flowers and fruit on many of his canvases.

Beyond, there are charming views across the city from the outside **terraza** (terrace), which holds a small formal garden, and then it's inside again for the **Sala de Guardia** (Guard Room; Room 9), where there are several dire eight-eenth-century Spanish tapestries. Crude and inexact, these are in striking contrast to the Flemish tapestries exhibited elsewhere, but by then Spain had lost control of the Netherlands and the Spanish court could no longer acquire pieces from its traditional suppliers. In 1725, the Spanish king founded a tapes-try factory in Madrid, but its products – as demonstrated here – were poor, and there must have been some aesthetic gnashing of teeth when the Spanish court took delivery. Nearby, the **Baños Árabes** (Arab Baths; Room 10) are a rare survivor from Moorish times, comprising three stone-vaulted chambers, one each for cold, tepid and hot baths. Enough remains to see how this sophisticated set-up worked and why the Christian kings who supplanted the Moors adopted them lock, stock and barrel.

After the Arab Baths, you move into the central courtyard, from where the **Escalera Real** (Royal Staircase), installed by Philip II, leads up to the **state apartments** that fill out the palace's upper level. These apartments are really rather sterile, but there are several splendidly ornate Mudéjar wooden ceilings and one magnificent seventeenth-century tapestry, *The Siege of Carthage*, which covers the back wall of the **Salón Mayor** (Main Hall; Room 19). The last room here is the **Despacho de Su Majestad el Rey** (Office of the King; Room 20), which has an attractive Gothic gallery and was where the Moors surren-dered to Jaume I in 1229.

Afterwards, it's back into the courtyard for the **Capella de Santa Ana** (Chapel of St Anne; Room 21), a largely fourteenth-century Gothic structure that is still used for army officers' masses and weddings. The interior, with its fine vaulted and embossed ceiling, is decidedly intimate, almost cosy, a suitable home for the **Capella de St Praxedis**, which, with its medieval effigy and reliquary, is devoted to a much venerated saint. A fourth-century figure, Praxedis survived the massacre of her Christian companions and had the presence of mind to mop up their blood with a sponge and preserve it for later worship; Jaume III brought the reliquary back with him from Rome. Incidentally, the delicate marble carving above the chapel entrance is carved in the Romanesque style, a deliberate use of what was by then an archaic tradition. The three figures above the door depict the Virgin Mary with saints Anne and Joachim to either side.

The Palau March

Just along c/Palau Reial from the Almudaina, across the top of the wide flight of stone steps that leads up from Plaça de la Reina, is the **Palau March** (April–Oct Mon–Fri 10am–6pm, Sat 10am–2pm; Nov–Mar Mon–Fri 10am–5pm, Sat 10am–2pm; €3.60; ⓦwww.fundbmarch.es), whose arcaded galleries, chunky columns and large stone blocks fill out the entire block between c/Palau Reial and c/Conquistador. The palace was built between 1939 and 1945 in the general style of the city's earlier Renaissance mansions on behalf of **Joan March**, long the island's most powerful inhabitant (see box below). A visit begins with the palace's most enjoyable feature, its splendid **Italianate courtyard**, which offers

Joan March

One of the most controversial figures in Mallorca's recent history, **Joan March** (1880–1962) was born a peasant's son in the small town of Santa Margalida on the east side of the island. At school, he showed his entrepreneurial flair by loaning money to his classmates at a high rate of interest and deciding, so the story goes, to start a trade in cigarettes, charging by the puff. March's father was a pig herder and at the age of 20 Joan negotiated the first of his major business deals, supplying meat direct to a sausage factory in Barcelona. In the next few years he allegedly established a dominant position in the **tobacco smuggling** trade with Algeria, displaying a ruthlessness that made him feared and loathed in equal measure.

March made more money in World War I, when both the British and the Germans paid him for his services, and took advantage of the difficulties experienced by the island's landed aristocracy to make yet more. For a variety of reasons, including the phylloxera infestation of the vineyards (see box, p.37), many of Mallorca's large estates had become uneconomic. March bought them up for a song and then sold them back to the farm hands who had previously worked them. The profit on each transaction was small, but there was the economy of scale: March sold no less than forty thousand land titles, an enormous number for a small island, and by these means transformed the structure of Mallorcan society as an accidental corollary to his greed.

During the Spanish Civil War, it seems likely that March loaned Franco money on generous terms and helped the Fascists with military supplies. Whatever the truth, March did become the richest man in Franco's Spain and was much favoured by the regime. In 1955, for reasons that remain obscure, he decided to reinvent himself, becoming a **patron of the arts**, buying up dozens of sculptures and paintings and giving millions of pesetas to a new charitable foundation, the **Fundació Joan March**. In Palma, the fundació runs the Museu d'Art Espanyol Contemporani (see p.87) and March's old house, the Palau March (see above) is open to the public. However, the man is mainly recalled by the bank he set up in 1926, the **Banca March**, which now has branches right across the island.

attractive views over the city centre and displays a potpourri of modern **sculpture** drawn from the March collection. Amongst the twenty or so pieces exhibited, there are two Henry Moores, a Rodin torso and a fetchingly eccentric *Orgue del Mar* (Organ of the Sea) by Xavier Corberó (b.1935).

After the courtyard, the interior of the *palau* is a distinct anti-climax, its cold marble walls displaying an odd and unsatisfying mix of curios with almost no labelling at all. The book room is of some mild interest with its collection of idiosyncratic collection of old volumes, including the Mallorcan Bakers' Association Rule Book of 1415, but it's difficult to know quite what to make of the Neapolitan Nativity Scene, where an army of kitsch eighteenth-century models fill up an entire room. Things get even worse on the first floor, where the March family's one-time music room is decorated with racist murals depicting New Orleans jazz scenes of frolicking "Negroes"; the murals are by the Spanish painter Josep Maria Sert (1874–1945), who did much better elsewhere.

The city walls and Parc de la Mar

A wide flight of steps leads down from between the cathedral and the Palau de l'Almudaina to a handsomely restored section of the **Renaissance city walls**, whose mighty zigzag of bastions, bridges, gates and dry moats once encased the whole city. These replaced the city's **medieval walls**, portions of which also survive – look back up from the foot of the steps and a large chunk is clearly visible beneath the east side of the cathedral. Constructed of sandstone blocks and adobe, the earlier fortifications depended for their efficacy on their height, with a gallery running along the top from which the defenders could fire at the enemy. By the middle of the fifteenth century, however, the development of more effective artillery had shifted the military balance in favour of offence, with cannons now able to breach medieval city walls with comparative ease. The military architects of the day soon evolved a new design in which walls were built much lower and thicker to absorb cannon shot, while four-faced bastions – equipped with artillery platforms – projected from the line of the walls, providing the defenders with a variety of firing lines. The whole caboodle was protected by a water-filled **moat** with deep, sheer sides. The costs of re-fortifying the major cities of western Europe were astronomical, but every country joined in the rush. In Palma, the Habsburgs ordered work to start on the new (Renaissance) design in the 1560s, though the chain of bastions was only completed in 1801.

From the foot of the steps below the cathedral, a wide and pleasant **walkway** travels along the top of the Renaissance walls, providing delightful views of the city and harbour plus an insight into the tremendous strength of the fortifications. Heading west, the walkway leads to the **tiered gardens** of a lush Moorish-style park, which tumble down to and run along beside Avinguda d'Antoni Maura, an extension of the tree-lined Passeig d'es Born (see p.83). In the opposite direction – east from the steps below the cathedral – the walkway passes above the planted trees, concrete terraces and ornamental lagoon of the **Parc de la Mar**, an imaginative and popular redevelopment of the disused land that once lay between the walls and the coastal motorway. Indeed, it has proved so popular that the municipality are considering shoving the road underground so that they can extend the park to the seashore.

Wall and walkway zigzag along the south side of old Palma before eventually fizzling out at Plaça Llorenç Villalonga, but long before that – just a couple of minutes from the cathedral – you reach the double **Portella gateway**, the outer portal of which carries the Bourbon coat of arms above its arch; you can come off the walkway here, going down one of the wide stone ramps to reach the foot of c/Portella.

The old town

The medina-like maze of streets at the back of the cathedral constitutes the heart of the **old town**, which extends north to Plaça Cort and east to Avinguda Gabriel Alomar i Villalonga. Long a neglected corner of the city, most of the district has now been refurbished in an ambitious and massively expensive project that has restored much of its antique charm. The area's general appearance is its main appeal, rather than any specific sights, and you can spend hour after hour wandering down narrow lanes and alleys, loitering in the squares, gazing at Renaissance mansions and peering at imposing Baroque and Gothic churches. Nonetheless, there are a couple of obvious targets, namely the district's two finest churches – the **Església de Santa Eulalia** and the **Basílica de Sant Francesc** – plus the city's most extensive museum, the **Museu de Mallorca**.

The Banys Àrabs

Leaving the city walls at the Portella gate (see p.76), you'll find yourself on the edge of the old town at the foot of c/Portella. North of the gate, take the first turning on the right for the **Banys Àrabs** (Arab Baths), at c/Can Serra 7 (daily: June–Sept 9am–8pm; Oct–May 9am–6pm; €1.50). One of the few genuine reminders of the Moorish presence, this tenth-century brick *hammam* (bath house) consists of a small horseshoe-arched and domed chamber that was once heated through the floor. The arches rest on stone pillars, an irregular bunch thought to have been looted from the remains of the island's Roman buildings. The baths are reasonably well preserved, but if you've been to the baths in Girona or Granada, or even the Baños Árabes in the Palau de l'Almudaina (see p.74), these are really rather anticlimactic. The lush garden outside, with tables where you can picnic, is perhaps nicer.

Casa Museu J. Torrents Lladó

Close to the Banys Àrabs, at c/Portella 9, the old house and studio of the Catalan artist J. Torrents Lladó (1946–93) has been pleasantly converted into a small museum, the **Casa Museu J. Torrents Lladó** (mid–June to mid–Sept Tues–Fri 11am–7pm & Sat 10am–2pm; mid–Sept to mid–June Tues–Fri 10am–6pm, Sat 10am–2pm; €3), celebrating his life and work. Lladó trained in Barcelona but, after some initial dabblings, he rejected Modernism in the late 1960s, moving to Mallorca in 1968. Here, he became well known as a society portraitist, painting pictures of the rich and famous in a dark and broody Baroque style, examples of which hang alongside a number of landscapes, both watercolours and sticky oils.

The Museu de Mallorca

From the Lladó museum, it's a few metres north up along c/Portella to the expansive **Museu de Mallorca** (Tues–Sat 10am–7pm, Sun 10am–2pm; €3), which occupies **Can Aiamans**, a rambling Renaissance mansion whose high-ceilinged rooms make a delightful setting for an enjoyable medley of Mallorcan artefacts. The earliest items date from prehistoric times, but there's also a superb assortment of Gothic paintings and some excellent examples of *Modernista* fittings and furnishings. The labelling of the exhibits is, however, very patchy.

The collection begins in the **basement**, on the right hand side of the entrance courtyard, with a series of rooms that track through the island's early history with a ragbag of archeological finds and displays on the *navetas* and *talayots* typical of Mallorca's prehistoric talayotic culture (for more on which, see p.293). Archeologists have been arguing for decades about exactly when the island was first settled, an arcane dispute focused on a confusing series of finds made in the scattering of caves where the earliest islanders took shelter: the museum plays it safe by hedging its chronological bets.

By comparison, the **Late Talayotic Period** (500/400 BC–123 AD) is much more clearly defined and it's then that the islanders either made – or possibly imported – the finely detailed and extremely bellicose statuettes which now have a whole room to themselves. Of the dozen or so statuettes on display, most are of nude men, helmeted and armed, aggressive figurines clearly representative of a warlike culture: indeed, such was the islanders' reputation as warriors, that the Carthaginians recruited hundreds of them to fight in their armies during the Punic Wars against Rome in the third century BC. Equally striking, and in the same room, is the **Bou de Talapí**, an angular carving of a bull's head that exudes a brutish strength of almost disconcerting proportions.

After the talayotic section, there is a modest display on **Roman** Mallorca, including a number of finely worked funerary tablets, and another on the **Moorish** period, where the highlights are some ornate Mudéjar wooden panelling and an exquisite selection of Arab and Moorish jewellery, though at the time of writing the jewellery had been (temporarily) removed from view.

The Moorish section leads back to the main courtyard, which you cross to reach the rest of the collection.

The museum's Mallorcan Primitives

On the left hand side of the entrance courtyard, an old stone stairway leads up to the first of a couple of rooms devoted to the **Mallorcan Primitive painters** (for more on whom, see p.72). On display in this first room are works by the Masters of Bishop Galiana, Montesión and Castellitx and, best of the lot, a panel painting entitled *Santa Quiteria*, whose lifelike, precisely executed figures – right down to the king's wispy beard – are typical of the gifted **Master of the Privileges**. In the same room there's also a curious thirteenth-century work of unknown authorship dedicated to St Bernard, with the saint on his knees devotedly drinking the milk of the Virgin Mary.

Beyond is a room of religious statues and carved capitals and then a second room of Gothic paintings, which is distinguished by a sequence of works by **Francesc Comes** (1379–1415), whose skill in catching subtle skin textures matches his Flemish contemporaries and represents a softening of the early Mallorcan Primitives' crudeness. In his striking *St George*, the saint – girl-like, with typically full lips – impales a lime-green dragon with more horns than could possibly be useful. One of the last talented exponents of Mallorcan Gothic, the **Master of the Predellas** – probably a certain Joan Rosató – is represented by his Bosch-like triptych of the *Life of Santa Margalida*, with each group of onlookers a sea of ugly, deformed faces and merciless eyes. The work outlines the life of Margaret of Antioch, one of the most venerated saints in medieval Christendom. During the reign of the Roman emperor Diocletian (284–305 AD) she refused to marry a pagan prefect and was consequently executed after being tortured with extravagant gusto. As if this weren't enough, she also had to resist more metaphysical trials: Satan, disguised as a dragon, swallowed her, but couldn't digest her holiness, so his stomach opened up and out she popped unharmed. This particular tribulation made Margaret the patron saint of pregnant women.

The ensuing rooms display the stodgy art of the Counter-Reformation, though Palma's own Miquel Bestard makes a successful appearance in his whopping *Feeding of the Five Thousand*. Miraculously, Jesus feeds the hungry crowd from a meagre supply of loaves and fishes, but the subtext is much more revealing: Bestard's crowds are well behaved and respectful of authority – just what the Catholic hierarchy had in mind.

The museum's modern art

Up above the Mallorcan Primitives, the museum's **top floor** holds a mildly engaging assortment of nineteenth- and early twentieth-century paintings by both native artists and foreign artists once resident in Mallorca. This includes a neat sample of works by Mallorca's own **Juli Ramis** (1909–90), whose striking style is illustrated by his oil-on-fabric *Tres Cavalls* (Three Horses) and the radiant blues of *Tardor en blau* (Blue Autumn). A native of Sóller, Ramis left the island when he was nineteen to spend the next sixty years abroad, travelling widely and becoming acquainted with some of the leading artistic lights of his day, notably Picasso and his chums. Ramis mixed his styles, but was essentially an Expressionist with Surrealistic leanings. He returned to Mallorca in the last years of his life and died in Palma.

Also on this floor are two rooms of **Modernista** fittings and furnishings, mostly retrieved from shops and houses that have since been demolished. Of particular interest are the charming wall tiles manufactured at the island's **La Roqueta** works. The pottery was in production for just twenty years (1897–1918), but this coincided with the vogue for the Modernista pieces in which La Roqueta excelled. For once, the labelling is quite good.

North to Can Marquès

Continuing on up the hill from the Museu de Mallorca, c/Portella leads into c/Morey where, at no. 9, you'll find **Can Oleza** (no public access), a sixteenth-century mansion with an elegant shaded courtyard embellished by a handsome balustrade and a set of Ionic columns. Close by, turn left up c/Almudaina for a peek at the chunky remains of the old east gate, the **Arc de L'Almudaina** – a remnant of the Moorish fortifications topped with medieval barbicans – and to see **Can Bordils**, at no. 9, one of the city's oldest private mansions (it's now a municipal office building).

Opposite Can Bordils, just along the street at c/Zanglada 2A, is **Can Marquès** (Mon–Fri 10am–3pm & Sat 11am–2pm; €6), one of the few old mansions to be open to the public, which sounds really promising, but the interior is disappointingly dull. Visitors slope round half a dozen rooms equipped with an insipid assortment of mostly late nineteenth- and early twentieth-century furniture, the only highlight being several superb chandeliers – long an island speciality.

Santa Eulalia and Can Vivot

Overshadowing the square at the top of c/Morey is the **Església de Santa Eulalia** (Mon–Fri 7am–12.30pm & 5.45–8.30pm, Sat 7am–1pm & 4.30–8.45pm, Sun 8am–1pm & 6.30–8.30pm; free), which was built on the site of a mosque in the mid-thirteenth century. It took just 25 years to complete and consequently possesses an architectural homogeneity that's unusual for ecclesiastical Palma, though there was some later medieval tinkering, and nineteenth-century renovators added the belfry and remodelled the main (south) facade.

Mansions in Palma

Most of medieval Palma was destroyed by fire, so the patrician **mansions** that characterize the old town today generally date from the reconstruction programme of the late seventeenth and early eighteenth centuries. Consequently they were built in the fashionable Renaissance style, with columns and capitals, loggias and arcades tucked away behind outside walls of plain stone three or four storeys high, and are surprisingly uniform in layout. Entry to almost all of these mansions was through a great arched **gateway**, which gave onto a rectangular courtyard around which the house was built. Originally, the **courtyard** would have been cheered by exotic trees and flowering shrubs, and equipped with a fancy stone and ironwork well-head, where visitors could water their horses. From the courtyard, a stone **exterior staircase** led up to the main public rooms – with the servants' quarters below and the family's private apartments up above.

Very few of these mansions are open to the public, and all you'll see for the most part is the view from the gateway – the municipality actually pays people to leave their big wooden gates open. Several have, however, passed into the public domain, the Can Aiamans, now the home of the Museu de Mallorca (see p.77), being the prime example. Others meriting a quick gander are Can Bordils (p.79), Can Oleza (p.79), Can Vivot (below), Can Marquès (see p.79) and Can Solleric (p.84), but only the last two of these are open to the public.

The church is typically Gothic in construction, with a yawning nave originally designed – as in the cathedral – to give the entire congregation a view of the high altar. The bricked-up windows of today – as well as the darkness of the stained glass – keep out much of the light and spoil the effect, but suggestions that they be cleared have always been ignored. Framing the nave, the aisles accommodate twelve shallow **chapels**, one of which (the first on the right) sports a delightful Gothic panel-painting in finely observed Flemish style. In kitsch contrast, the other chapels are standard-issue Baroque, though they pale into insignificance when compared with the hourglass-shaped **high altarpiece**, a flashy Baroque extravagance of colossal proportions. This holy ground witnessed one of the more disgraceful episodes of Mallorcan history. During Easter week, 1435, a rumour went round that Jewish townsfolk had enacted a blasphemous mock-up of the Crucifixion. There was no proof, but the Jews were promptly robbed of their possessions and condemned to be burnt at the stake unless they adopted Christianity. The ensuing mass baptism was held here at Santa Eulalia.

Just west of the Plaça Santa Eulalia lies the fetching Plaça Cort (see p.83), whilst around the back of the church, at c/Can Savella 4, is **Can Vivot**, an especially opulent early eighteenth-century mansion, whose spacious main courtyard, with its handsome columns and arches, is distinguished by a lovely staircase. Built on top of a Moorish palace, the interior of the mansion is decorated in fine Neoclassical style, especially the sumptuous library, which is filled with scientific instruments of the age, though the house and library are only occasionally open to the public.

The Basílica de Sant Francesc

A short walk east of the Plaça Santa Eulalia along c/Convent de Sant Francesc is the **Basílica de Sant Francesc** (daily 9.30am–12.30pm & 3.30–6pm; closed Sun afternoon; €1), a domineering pile that occupies the site of the old Moorish soap factory. Built for the Franciscans towards the end of the thirteenth century, the original church was a vast Gothic edifice that benefited from royal patronage after King Jaume II's son, also named Jaume, became a member of the order in 1300. Subsequent medieval remodellings replaced the initial wooden ceiling with a single-span, vaulted stone roof of imposing dimensions and added stately chapels to the nave and apse. The Basílica became the most fashionable church in medieval Palma and its friars received handsome kickbacks for entombing the local nobility within its precincts. Increasingly eager to enrich themselves, the priests came to compete for possession of the corpses, while the various aristocratic clans vied with each other in the magnificence of their sarcophagi. These tensions exploded when a certain Jaume Armadams had a jug of water emptied over his head on All Saints' Day, 1490. The congregation went berserk and over three hundred noblemen fought it out in the nave before the priests finally restored order. The scandal caused the Basílica to be closed by decree for several decades.

In the seventeenth century the church was badly damaged by lightning, prompting a thoroughgoing reconstruction, which accounts for most of its present-day appearance. The main **facade**, which dates from this period, displays a stunning severity of style, with its great rectangular sheet of dressed sandstone stretching up to an arcaded and balustraded balcony. The facade is pierced by a gigantic rose window of Plateresque intricacy and embellished by a **Baroque doorway**, the tympanum of which features a triumphant Virgin Mary engulfed by a wriggling mass of sculptured decoration. Above the Madonna is the figure of St George, and to either side and below are assorted saints – look out for the scholar and missionary Ramon Llull, shown reading a book. The strange statue in front of the doorway of a Franciscan monk and a young Native American celebrates the missionary work of **Junipero Serra** (see p.198), a Mallorcan priest despatched to California in 1768, who subsequently founded the cities of San Diego, Los Angeles and San Francisco.

The church's **interior**, approached through a neat and trim Gothic cloister, is distinguished by its monumental **high altar**, a gaudy Baroque affair featuring balustrades, lattice-work and clichéd figurines beneath a painted wooden statue of *St George and the Dragon*. It's heady stuff as are the rolling scrolls and trumpeter-angel of the eighteenth-century **pulpit** on the wall of the nave, and the ornate Gothic-Baroque frontispiece of the **organ** just opposite. Close by, recessed chapels enclose the ambulatory and the first one on the left holds the **tomb of Ramon Llull**, whose bones were brought back to Palma after his martyrdom in Algeria in 1315. Considering the sanctity of the man's remains, it's an odd and insignificant-looking memorial, with Llull's alabaster effigy set high up on the wall to the right of the chapel altarpiece at a disconcertingly precarious angle.

The Templar chapel

Follow c/Ramon Llull east from the basilica and you'll soon spy the large and distinctive fortified **gateway** at the end of the street. Dating from the thirteenth century, the gateway once marked the entrance to the castle-like compound of the **Knights Templar**, a military order founded to support the Crusades. The knights established bases right across the Mediterranean and this was one of the more important – though they were soon to be dispossessed. The order was rich and secretive, its independence resented by the papacy and just about every secular ruler in Europe. In 1312, following trumped-up charges of heresy, sorcery and bestiality, the pope disbanded the order and their Palma compound passed into the hands of the Hospitallers of St John, a rival knightly order. The Knights Hospitallers survived until 1802, when the Spanish king disbanded them and confiscated their property.

Ramon Llull

The life of **Ramon Llull** (1235–1315) – a figure beloved of Catholic propagandists – was an exercise in redemption through carnal excess. As a young man, Llull was an ebullient rake in the retinue of the future Jaume II. His sexual adventures were not impeded in the least by his marriage, but they ground to a dramatic halt when a certain Ambrosia de Castillo, his latest amatory target, whom he had pursued into the church of Santa Eulalia on horseback, revealed to him her diseased breasts. A deeply shocked Llull devoted the rest of his life to the Catholic faith, becoming a fearless missionary and dedicated scholar of theology, philosophy and alchemy. Exemplifying the cosmopolitan outlook of thirteenth-century Mallorca, Llull learnt to read, write and speak several languages including Arabic, and travelled to France, much of Spain and North Africa. He also founded a monastery and missionary school on **Puig Randa** (see p.201), 35km east of Palma, where he spent ten years in seclusion, writing no fewer than 250 books and treatises. It was Llull's scholarship that attracted the attention of his old friend Jaume II, who summoned him to court in 1282. With royal patronage, Llull then established a monastic school of Oriental languages near Valldemossa, where he trained his future missionary companions. Llull was killed on his third evangelical excursion to Algeria in 1315, his martyrdom ensuring his subsequent beatification.

An alley leads through the gateway to the only other surviving part of the military compound, the **Templar chapel** (in theory open Mon–Fri 9.30am–1pm & 3.30–7pm, Sat 9.30am–1pm), whose Gothic and Romanesque features were extensively remodelled in the 1880s. Inside, the gloomy nave is divided into three bays with ribbed vaulting and a wooden ceiling over the atrium. The Romanesque side-chapels in the entrance area are perhaps the church's most diverting feature, all slender columns, rounded arches and intense foliate and geometric decoration.

Plaça Sant Jeroni

From the Templar gateway, head south along c/Temple for a couple of minutes to reach **Plaça Sant Jeroni**, a pretty little piazza set around a diminutive water fountain. The severe stone walls of a former convent, now a college, dominate one side of the square, while the **Església de Sant Jeroni** fills out another. The church facade is mostly a plain stone wall, but it is broken up by two doorways, the one on the left displaying a swirl of carved foliage and garlands of fruit. The door's tympanum portrays the well-known story of Saint Jerome in the desert, during which the saint endures all sorts of tribulations and temptations, but still sticks true to the faith; above, two heraldic lions stand rampant. The **interior**, with its heavy stone vaulting and over-sized organ, is mostly seventeenth-century, but it's rarely open to the public – a shame given that the church holds several paintings by the Mallorcan Primitives including Pere Terrencs' striking *Sant Jeroni*.

The Museu Diocesà

The **Museu Diocesà** (Diocesan Museum; Mon–Fri 10am–1pm & 4–7pm, but times may vary; €3) is housed in the plain nineteenth-century chapel of a former seminary just off Plaça Sant Jeroni at c/Calders 2. The premises may be uninspiring, but the museum does hold an excellent collection of Mallorcan Primitives, including an intriguing *St Paul* by the Master of Bishop Galiana, whose tight lines are very much in the Catalan tradition. This particular panel painting is a didactic cartoon-strip illustrating the life of St Paul, who is shown with his Bible open and sword in hand, a view of the Church militant that must have accorded well with the preoccupations of the powerful bishops of Mallorca. Look out also for the way Galiana portrays the Conversion on the road to Damascus, with Saul-Paul struck by a laser-like beam of light.

A second high point is the *Passion of Christ* by an unknown artist dubbed the Master of the Passion of Mallorca. Dated to the end of the thirteenth century, the painting follows a standard format, with a series of small vignettes outlining the story of Christ, but the artistry is in the warm and gentle detail: the Palm Sunday donkey leans forward pushing his nose towards a child; one of the disciples reaches out across the Last Supper table for the fish; and two of Jesus' disciples slip their sandals off in eager anticipation during the Washing of the Feet. By contrast, Alonso de Sedano's sixteenth-century *Crucifixion* is a sophisticated work of strong, deep colours within a triangulated structure. Above is the blood-spattered, pale-white body of Christ, while down below – divided by the Cross – are two groups, one of hooded mourners, the other a trio of nonchalant Roman soldiers in contemporary Spanish dress. Also noteworthy is a large and dramatic *St George and the Dragon*, a panel painting of the late fifteenth century attributed to Pere Niçard with the stern fortifications of Palma in the background.

Monti-Sion

Back on Plaça Sant Jeroni, c/Seminari and then c/Monti-Sion run west through the depths of the old town past the **Església de Monti-Sion** (most likely to be open Mon–Fri 7–8.30am), whose thundering facade is a hectic heap of angels and saints, coats of arms and wriggling foliage. Below the figure of the Virgin, look out for a strangely inconclusive representation of the Devil – half-sheep, half-dragon. Beyond the church, c/Monti-Sion leads to a crossroads: turn right along c/Pare Nadal to reach the Basílica de Sant Francesc (see p.80) or keep dead ahead and the twisting side streets will deliver you onto Plaça Santa Eulalia, footsteps from Plaça Cort.

Plaça Cort

Bustling **Plaça Cort**, with its elegant nineteenth-century facades and grizzled olive tree, was named after the various legal bodies – both secular and religious – which were once concentrated here. Along with much of the rest of Spain, Mallorca possessed a truly Byzantine legal system until the whole caboodle was swept away and rationalized during the Napoleonic occupation. Today, one side of the square is dominated by the **Ajuntament** (Town Hall), a debonair example of the late Renaissance style: pop in for a look at the grand and self-assured foyer, which mostly dates from the nineteenth century, and the six folkloric *gigantones* (giant carnival figures) stored here – four in a corner, the other two tucked against the staircase.

From Plaça Cort, it's a pleasant five-minute stroll to the Passeig d'es Born via c/Sant Domingo, which weaves downhill lined by attractive nineteenth-century town houses with wrought-iron grilles and stone balconies. Alternatively, it's a short walk from Plaça Cort along c/Palau Reial to Palau March and the cathedral.

Passeig d'es Born and Plaça de la Reina

Distinguished by the stone sphinxes at its top and bottom, the **Passeig d'es Born** has been the city's principal promenade since the early fifteenth century, when the stream that ran here was diverted following a disastrous flash flood. Nowadays, this leafy avenue is a little too traffic-congested to be endearing, though it's not nearly as choked as it used to be, but it is still at the heart of the city, and close to some of Palma's most fashionable bars and restaurants.

At no. 27, overlooking the *passeig*, is the fine Italianate loggia of **Can Solleric** (Tues–Sat 10am–2pm & 5–9pm, Sun 10am–1.30pm; free), a lavish mansion of heavy wooden doors, marble columns and vaulted ceilings built for a family of cattle and olive oil merchants in 1763. Recently restored, the house now displays temporary exhibitions of modern art and has a small tourist information desk.

At the foot of the Passeig d'es Born is tiny, leafy **Plaça de la Reina**, from where a wide and elegant flight of steps, the **Costa de la Seu**, leads up beneath the spiky walls of the Palau de l'Almudaina to the cathedral (see p.70) and the Palau March (see p.75); the *palau* originally extended right down to c/Conquistador, incorporating what is now the *Cappuccino* café (see p.93) as well as the tiny Biblioteca March Servera (library).

El Puig de Sant Pere

The ancient neighbourhood of **El Puig de Sant Pere** (St Peter's Mount) covers the area west of the Passeig d'es Born and north to Avinguda Jaume III. Here, a cobweb of narrow lanes and alleys shelter another sprinkling of patrician mansions, though most of the old houses were divided up into apartments years ago to cater for the district's sailors, dockers and fishermen. Again, it's the general flavour of the area that appeals rather than specific sights, but it's still worth seeking out two late Renaissance facades on c/Sant Feliu, which runs off Passeig d'es Born. At no. 8 is **Can Moner**, whose ornate doorway sports telamons, cherubs and cornucopia, whilst no. 10, **Can Pavesi**, offers a mythical beast with its tongue stuck right out.

There's a gruesome story behind the name of a lane off nearby c/Estanc. **Mà del Moro**, "The Hand of the Moor", harks back to Ahmed, an eighteenth-century slave who murdered his master in a house on this alley. Ahmed was executed for the crime, and his hand was chopped off and stuck above the doorway of the house where the murder was committed – "pour encourager les autres" as Voltaire would have it.

Avinguda d'Antoni Maura

South of Plaça de la Reina, **Avinguda d'Antoni Maura** runs down to the wide breakwater that marks the start of Palma harbour (see p.89). The avenue takes its name from **Antoni Maura** (1853–1925), a Mallorcan who served as prime minister of Spain four times between 1903 and 1921. An outstanding orator and extraordinarily forceful personality, Maura was a conservative who saw universal suffrage as "the politics of the mob", preferring a limited franchise and a constitution which gave power to the middle classes, as long as they marched to the tune of the Church and the Crown. To give the man some credit, his conservatism with regard to universal suffrage – which was in place from 1887 – was prompted by Spain's particular circumstances. In a backward, largely agrarian society, most Spaniards were largely indifferent to national issues and power was concentrated in the hands of district bosses, or *caciques*, who would bring out the vote for any candidate provided they were guaranteed control of political patronage. Some bosses ruled by intimidation, others by bribery, but the end result was a dense mixture of charity and jobbery, dubbed *caciquismo*, which made national government well-nigh impossible. Maura struggled against this chicanery, and his assertive nationalism was quite enough for Franco to have this avenue named after him; no one has bothered to change it since.

From Passeig d'es Born to Avinguda Jaume III and Es Baluard

Avinguda Jaume III, which marches west from the top of Passeig d'es Born, is lined by the stone arcades of the sturdy shops and office blocks that were erected in the 1940s. This is Francoista architecture at its most appealing – very symmetrical and self-consciously Spanish – and it's here today you'll find some of the island's chicest clothes shops, as well as downtown's biggest department store, **El Corte Inglés** (Mon–Sat 9.30am–9.30pm). There's something very engaging about the airs and graces of the avenue, with its jostle of beshorted tourists and besuited Spaniards, and the web of ancient alleys immediately to the north is another attractive corner of the city, all high stone walls and dignified old mansions focused on **c/Concepció**.

At the top of the avenue, the **Passeig Mallorca** is bisected by the deep, walled watercourse which once served as the city moat and is now an especially handsome feature of the city. Turn left here, on this side of the *passeig*, and you soon reach the mammoth **bastion** which long anchored the southwest corner of the Renaissance city wall and now holds the much lauded **Es Baluard museu d'art modern i contemporani**, on Plaça Porta Santa Catalina (Modern & Contemporary Art Museum; June–Sept Tues–Sun 10am–11pm; Oct–May Tues–Sun 10am–8pm; €6; ⓦ www.esbaluard.org). The museum has three floors – the top two floors for the permanent collection, the other for temporary exhibitions – sub-divided into themed areas such as "Mediterranean Landscapes" and the grandly named "Figurative renovation during the first half of the twentieth century". However, at the risk of sounding churlish, the most striking feature is just how few paintings there are on display and, given the lavishness of the setting, the small extent of the permanent collection. That said, there are a handful of Mirós, including one of his few attempts at landscape painting, and a rare and unusual sample of Picasso ceramics, most memorably a striking, white, ochre and black vase-like piece entitled *Big Bird Corrida*. Much more successful are the large, geometric **sculptures** that are carefully positioned outside the museum across the top of the bastion in a perfect match of style and setting. In particular, look out for the irregular, rusting cubes of Gerardo Rueda's (1926–96) *Almagra* and the plaque-like severity of *Triplico* by José Luís Sanchez (b.1926). There are also grand views out over the coast from the bastion and an outstanding restaurant (see p.94).

Doubling back from Es Baluard, cross the footbridge that spans the Passeig Mallorca to reach **La Feixina**, a pleasant terraced **park**, whose trees, lawns, flower beds and fountains step south to the foot of **Avinguda Argentina** across from the jetties where the fishing boats come in. The only scenic blot in the park is the whopping **column** erected by Franco to honour those Balearic sailors who were loyal to the Fascist cause.

From Passeig d'es Born to Passeig de la Rambla

Eastwards from the top of the Passeig d'es Born runs **c/Unió**, a new if rather unimaginative appellation – it means "unity" – for a street Franco had previously named after General Mola, one of the prime movers of the Nationalist rebellion of 1936. Mola was killed in a plane accident during the Civil War, possibly to Franco's relief. Hitler, for one, thought that Mola was the more competent, remarking that his death meant that "Franco came to the top like Pontius Pilate in the Creed."

Near the start of c/Unio, at no.3, **Can Balaguer** is a sprawling Renaissance mansion with imposing doors and a grand cobbled courtyard. A mouldy sort of place, in need of a lick of paint, it's now home to the antiquated offices of the city's art society, the Círculo de Bellas Artes (no admission).

A few metres further east along c/Unió is tiny **Plaça Mercat**, the site of two identical *Modernista* buildings commissioned by a wealthy baker, Josep Casasayas, in 1908. Each is a masterpiece of flowing, organic lines tempered by graceful balconies and decorated with fern-leaf and butterfly motifs. Just

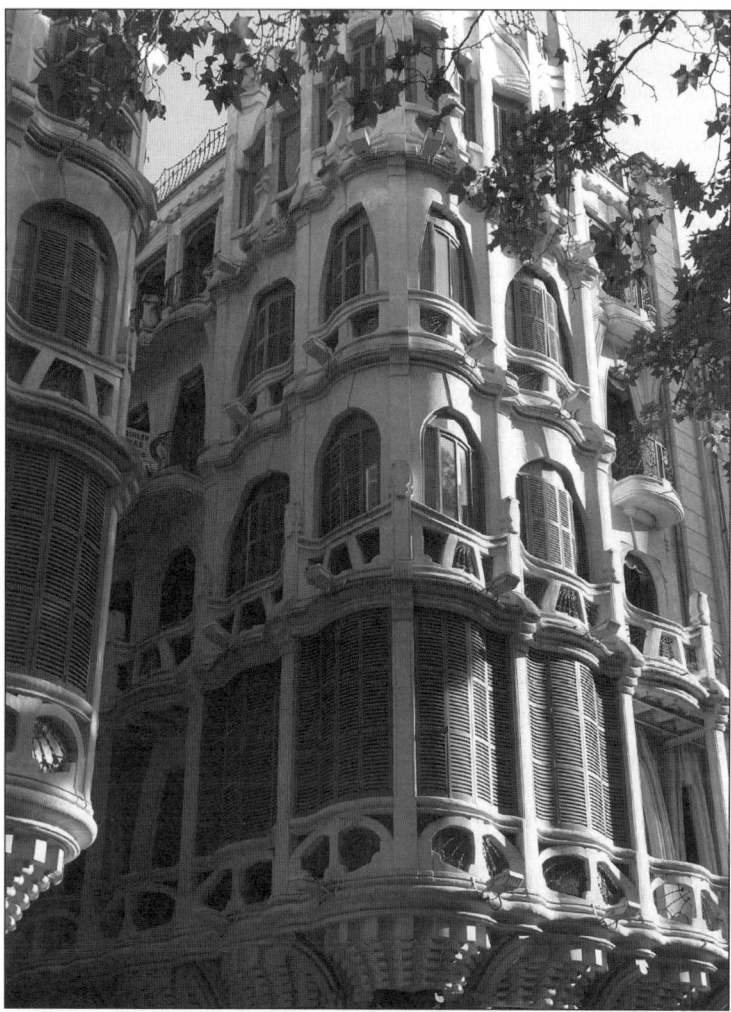

△ *Modernista* facade

down the street, on **Plaça Weyler**, stands a further *Modernista* extravagance, the magnificent **Gran Hotel** of 1903. Recently scrubbed and polished, the facade boasts a playful turret-tower, balconies, columns and bay windows enlivened with intricate floral trimmings and brilliant polychrome ceramics inspired by Hispano-Arabic designs. The interior houses a café-bar (see p.93), a good art bookshop and the spacious **Fundació La Caixa** art gallery (Tues–Sat 10am–9pm, Sun 10am–2pm; free), which organizes an excellent and wide-ranging programme of temporary exhibitions. The permanent collection is essentially confined to a large sample of work by the Catalan impressionist-expressionist **Hermen Anglada–Camarasa** (1871–1959), who is best known for the evocative Mallorcan land- and seascapes he produced during his sojourn on the island from 1914 to 1936. Unfortunately, the gallery only has a few of these and Camarasa is ill-represented by two huge and drearily folkloric canvases entitled *Valencia* and *El Tango de la Corona*, though a couple of sombre women's portraits do leaven the artistic loaf.

There's another excellent example of *Modernista* across the street from the Gran Hotel in the floral motifs and gaily painted wooden doorway of the **Forn des Teatre** (theatre bakery) at Plaça Weyler 9. From here, it's a few paces more to the Neoclassical frontage of the **Teatre Principal**, whose tympanum sports a fanciful relief dedicated to the nine Muses of Greek mythology. The theatre has long been the city's main auditorium for classical music, ballet and opera and will be again once the present refurbishment is completed.

At the theatre, the main street – now c/Riera – does a quick about-face to join the **Passeig de la Rambla**, whose plane trees shelter Palma's main flower market. The two statues at the foot of the boulevard, representing Roman emperors, were placed here in 1937 in honour of Mussolini's Italy – one set of Fascists tipping their municipal hats to another, though currently one of the statues has gone walkabout.

Plaça Major and around

On both sides of the Teatre Principal, steep flights of steps lead up to **Plaça Major**, a large pedestrianized square built on the site of the former headquarters of the **Inquisition** (see box p.88). The square, a rather plain affair with a symmetrical portico running around its perimeter, once housed the fish and vegetable market, but nowadays it's mainly popular for its pavement cafés. On the south side of Plaça Major lies the much smaller **Plaça Marquès del Palmer**, a cramped setting for two fascinating *Modernista* edifices. The more dramatic is **Can Rei**, a five-storey apartment building splattered with polychrome ceramics and floral decoration, its centrepiece a gargoyle-like face set between a pair of winged dragons. The facade of the adjacent **L'Àguila** building is of similar ilk, though there's greater emphasis on window space, reflecting its original function as a department store.

To the south, the shopping area between Plaça Marquès del Palmer and Plaça Cort retains an agreeably old-fashioned air, with three- and four-storey buildings flanking its main streets – principally pedestrianized **c/Jaume II** – and embellished with an abundance of fancy iron-grilled balconies.

The Museu d'Art Espanyol Contemporani and Església Sant Miquel

Running north from Plaça Major, **c/Sant Miquel** is another popular and pleasant shopping street. Here, at no. 11, the **Banca March** occupies a fine

The Spanish Inquisition

In 1478, mindful of his need for their military support, the **pope** granted Spain's Isabella I and Fernando V the right to establish their own **Inquisition**. It was much appreciated. The dual monarchs had realised that the Catholic faith was the most powerful force binding a fragmented Spain together, and were sure the Inquisition would both consolidate the Church's position and buttress their own. Installed in Castile in 1480 and in Aragón and Catalunya – including the Balearics – seven years later, the Inquisition began its work with the **Jews**. During the Middle Ages, the Jews had played a leading role in Spain's cultural and economic life and were generally treated with tolerance. This began to change in the late fourteenth century, when many Spaniards became increasingly resentful of the Jews' commercial clout and their role as rent collectors for the big landowners. In 1391, anti-Semitic riots broke out across much of Spain – including Mallorca – and many Jews, in fear for their lives, hastily submitted to baptism. These new Christians were subsequently called **conversos**, but in the event baptism merely staved off disaster. The riots continued – like the disturbance in Palma in 1435 (see p.80) – and matters came to a head after the capture of Spain's last Moorish kingdom, Granada, in 1492. Flush with military success but short of cash, Fernando and Isabella **expelled** from Spain all those Jews who had not turned Christian – about 120,000 – and confiscated their property, leaving the remaining conversos isolated and vulnerable.

Following the Reformation, the Inquisition turned its gaze onto the **Protestants**, though in truth there were very few of them in Iberia – only two thousand were indicted in Spain in the whole of the sixteenth century. Nevertheless, despite the limited nature of the Protestant threat, the Inquisition was profoundly influential. Most Spaniards regarded it as a bastion against heresy and, acting in this spirit, the Inquisitors kept all progressive thought at bay. Thus, whereas much of Europe was convulsed by disputation, Spain sank into ritual and dogma with the threat of the Inquisition in the background: in Palma few potential heretics could ignore the louring presence of its headquarters, plonked on a hill overlooking the city (now occupied by Plaça Major). Furthermore, by its very processes the Inquisition created an atmosphere of fear and mistrust. The Inquisitors acted on charges of heresy brought to them by the public, but these accusations were often frivolous or motivated by personal enmity. Worse still, even the most orthodox Catholic could not be sure of acquittal. The Inquisitor's examinations were often so theologically complex and long-winded that the danger of self-condemnation was ever-present – and under torture, many would confess to anything and everything.

Opposed by reforming clerics in the eighteenth century and increasingly ignored by the state, the Inquisition gradually lost influence. It was finally **abolished** during the Napoleonic occupation of Spain in 1808. Fifteen years later, in 1823, the headquarters of the Inquisition in Palma was demolished.

Renaissance mansion whose *Modernista* flourishes date from a tasteful refurbishment in 1917. The building has two entrances, one to the bank, the other to the upper-floor **Museu d'Art Espanyol Contemporani** (Mon–Fri 10am–6.30pm, Sat 10am–2pm; free), which showcases a prime sample of contemporary art drawn from the collection of the March family (for more on Joan March, see p.75). The collection features seventy works by 52 twentieth-century Spanish artists, the intention being to survey the Spanish contribution to modern art – a theme which is further developed by temporary exhibitions. The earliest piece, Picasso's *Tête de Femme* (1907), is of particular interest, being one of the first of the artist's works to be influenced by the primitive forms that were to propel him, over the following decade, from the re-creation of natural appearances into abstract art. Miró and Dalí are also represented, and there's one still life by the Spanish Cubist Juan Gris, as well as a number of harsh abstractions by the leading contemporary Catalan artist Antoni Tàpies (b.1923). Rather harder to negotiate are the allegedly "vigorous" abstractions of both the El Paso (Millares, Feito, Canogar) and the Parpalló (Sempere, Alfaro) groupings of the late 1950s.

From the museum, it's a brief hoof north along c/Sant Miquel to the **Església Sant Miquel** (Mon–Sat 8am–1.30pm & 5–7.30pm, Sun 10am–1pm & 6–7.30pm; free), whose sturdy exterior is the result of all sorts of architectural meddlings. Inside, the barrel-vaulted nave is almost entirely windowless, a dark and gloomy space where the one highlight is the high altarpiece, a Baroque classic with a central image celebrating St Michael in smiting mode. The altarpiece is a good example of the intricate work of Francesc Herrara (1590–1656), a much-travelled Spanish painter of religious and genre subjects known for his purposeful compositions and tangy realism.

West along the harbourfront

The various marinas, shipyards, fish docks and ferry and cargo terminals that make up Palma's **harbourfront** extend west for several kilometres from the bottom of Avinguda d'Antoni Maura to the edge of Cala Major (see p.101). The harbour is at its prettiest at this eastern end, where a cycling and walking path skirts the seashore, with boats to one side and bars, restaurants, apartment blocks and the smart hotels of the **Avinguda Gabriel Roca** – often dubbed the Passeig Marítim – across the main road on the other.

Sa Llotja

The first harbourfront landmark is the fifteenth-century **Sa Llotja**, the city's former stock exchange (open for exhibitions: Tues–Sat 11am–1.30pm & 5–8.30pm, Sun 11am–2pm; free). This carefully composed late-Gothic structure is one of the masterpieces of Mallorca's own **Guillermo Sagrera**, one of the most original European architects of his day, and it is distinguished by its four octagonal turrets, slender, spiralling columns and tall windows. The building now hosts frequent, and occasionally excellent, exhibitions (some of which you'll have to pay to get into). It also boasts a series of fierce-looking gargoyles and a muscular angel – appropriately the Guardian Angel of Commerce – above the front door.

Next door, the dignified **Consolat de Mar** was built in the 1660s to accommodate the Habsburg officials who supervised maritime affairs in this part of the empire. Today, as the home of the president of the Balearic islands, it's closed to the public, but the outside is worth a second look for its pair of crusty old cannons and elegant Renaissance gallery. The forlorn-looking gate between the two buildings – the **Porta Vella del Moll** – originally stood at the end of Avinguda d'Antoni Maura, where it was the main entrance into the city from the sea; it was moved here when portions of the town wall were demolished in the 1870s.

To the Parc Quarentena

From the Consolat, it's just a few minutes' walk west to the foot of **Avinguda Argentina**, where the fishing boat jetties are on one side and a pleasant terraced park leading up towards Es Baluard is on the other. Pressing on, it's a further fifteen or twenty minutes' stroll along the hotel- and palm-lined esplanade to the next worthwhile objective, the delightful **Parc Quarentena**, a leafy little park whose cool and shaded terraces, with their aromatic trees and shrubs, clamber up the hillside from the harbourfront. If you do thread your way up through the park, you can exit on c/Patrimoni, metres from the dreary modernity of Plaça Gomila and Avinguda Joan Miró.

Northwest of the centre: the Poble Espanyol

The kitsch **Poble Espanyol** (Spanish Village; April–Nov Mon 9am–8pm, Tues–Thurs 9am–2am, Fri & Sat 9am–4am & Sun 9am–midnight; Dec–March Mon–Thurs 9am–8pm, Fri & Sat 9am–4am & Sun 9am–midnight; €7.50; ⓦwww.poble-espanyol.com) was constructed between 1965 and 1967, its Francoist intentions apparent in its celebration of everything Spanish. Walled like a medieval city, the "village" contains accurate, scaled-down reproductions of about twenty old and important buildings, such as Barcelona's Palau de la Generalitat, Seville's Torre del Oro, a segment of Granada's Alhambra, El Greco's house in Toledo, and the Ermita de San Antonio in Madrid. These are dotted round the village's streets and squares, where you'll also find souvenir shops, restaurants and bars. It's all a bit daft – and school parties swamp the place during the day – but it's one way of introducing yourself to Spanish architecture.

The Poble Espanyol is about 2.5km northwest of the city centre, and reachable direct on Citysightseeing double-decker buses (see p.63). By regular **bus**, the nearest you'll get is Avinguda Andrea Doria, about ten minutes' walk from the 'village' – take EMT bus #4 from Plaça Espanya.

West of the centre: the Castell de Bellver

Boasting superb views of Palma and its harbour from a wooded hilltop some 3km west of the city centre, the **Castell de Bellver** (April–Sept Mon–Sat 8.30am–8.30pm, Sun 10am–6.30pm; Oct–March Mon–Sat 8.30am–7pm, Sun 10am–5pm; €2, but free on Sun, when the castle museum is closed) is a handsome, strikingly well-preserved fortress built for Jaume II at the beginning of the fourteenth century. Of canny circular design, the castle's immensely thick walls and steep ditches encircle a central **keep** that incorporates three imposing towers. In addition, an overhead, single-span **stone arch** connects the keep to a massive, freestanding tower, built as a final refuge. To enhance defence, the walls curve and bend and the interconnecting footbridges are set at oblique angles to each other. It's all very impressive – and looks well-nigh impregnable – but the castle was also intended to serve as a royal retreat from the summer heat, and so the austere outside walls hide a commodious, genteel-looking **circular courtyard**, surrounded by two tiers of inward-facing arcades that once belonged to the residential suites. The whole construction is ingenious, incorporating many skilful touches: the flat roof, for example, was designed to channel every drop of rainwater into a huge underground cistern.

Soon after its construction, improvements in artillery rendered the original fortress obsolete and although modifications were made, they were never very convincing. Neither did it last long as a royal residence. As early as the 1350s the

---

Raixa, the old country home of Cardinal Despuig, has also passed into public ownership and its terraced gardens are a delight – or at least they will be when they have been revamped as part of a project that looks like extending into 2009. Raixa is in between Palma and Sóller (see p.122).

keep was in use as a prison, a function it performed until 1915. More recently, the castle interior has been turned into a **museum** with a plodding history of the city on the ground floor and a small but delightful collection of **Roman statuary** up above. A local antiquarian and ecclesiastical bigwig by the name of **Cardinal Antonio Despuig** (1745–1817) gathered together these classical

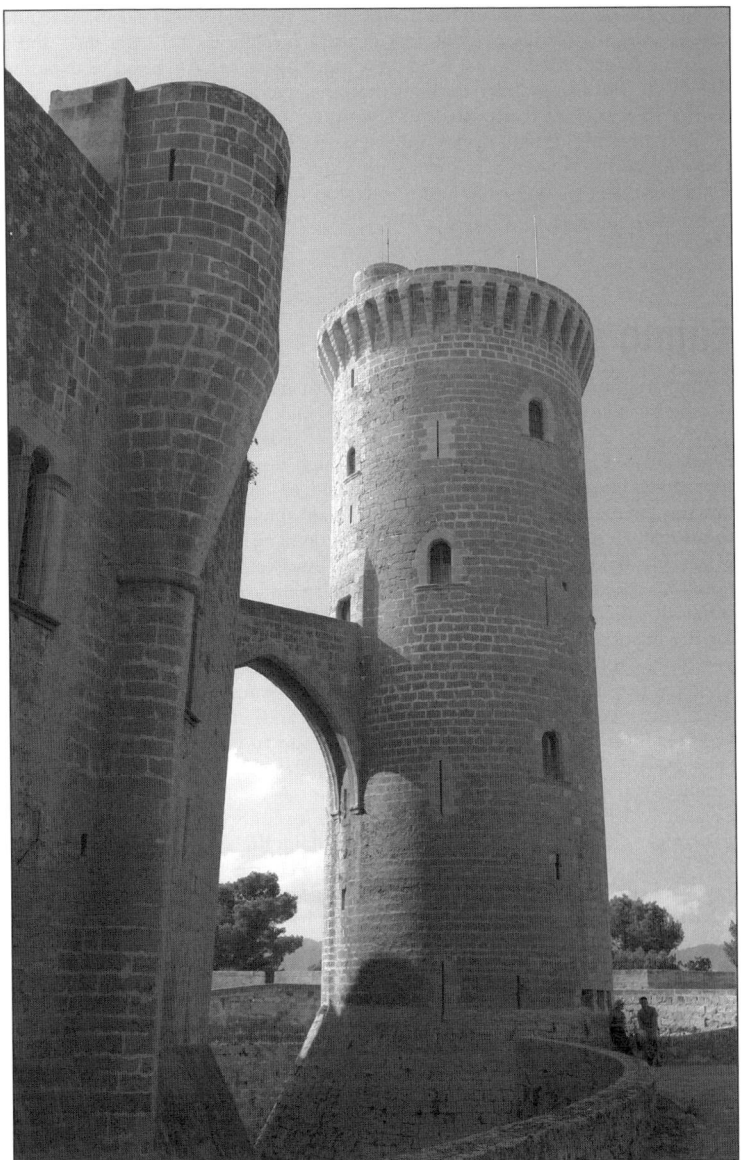

△ Castell de Bellver

pieces and bequeathed the whole lot to the city on his death. The only problem is that there's absolutely no labelling, so unless you're a classical expert it's impossible to know quite what you're looking at. That said, amongst the miscellany of busts and effigies, there's no mistaking a rare and perfectly preserved column of strikingly patterned *cippolino* marble and, most extraordinary of all, a small and exquisite alabaster of a sleeping hermaphrodite, apparently troubled by a confusing dream, half-in but mainly out of her toga. Other exhibits include carved seals, marble inscriptions, first-century medallions, a funeral stele, and a fearsome bust of Medusa, her head crawling with snakes. After you've explored the castle, you can wander through the pine-scented woods that surround it: there's a network of **footpaths**, but few signs.

Citysightseeing double-decker buses (see p.63) link the city centre with the Castell, but otherwise you're stuck with a stiff, thirty-minute walk uphill from Plaça Gomila, the site of the nearest bus stop (EMT bus #6). If you're driving, follow the signs from Avinguda Joan Miró (one-way west from the centre to Plaça Gomila).

Eating and drinking

Eating well in Palma can be less pricey than anywhere else in Mallorca. Inexpensive **cafés** and **tapas bars** are liberally distributed around the city centre, with a particular concentration in the side streets off the Passeig d'es Born and Avinguda d'Antoni Maura – though note that those on c/Apuntadors, at the heart of the city's nightlife, tend to charge over the odds. Some downtown cafés are up and running by 9am, but with most visitors taking **breakfast** at their hotel there's not much demand for early-morning eating places. For light **lunches** and snacks (*tapas*), however, you're spoiled for choice. You can chomp away in chic modernist surroundings or join the crowds in simple formica-and-wallpaper-diners where the food more than compensates for the decor – and then there's everything in between. *Tapas* can cost as little as €3 per dish and should never cost more than €10.

There's not much distinction between *tapas* bars and **restaurants**, as many of the former serve full meals as well as snacks – and, of course, put a couple of *tapas* together and you've got a full meal anyway. In fact, the differences often have more to do with appearance than food: if you've got a tablecloth, for instance, you're almost certainly in a restaurant. Most Palma restaurants have a Catalan – or Mallorcan – menu, but there are lots of Spanish places too, as well as a couple of vegetarian café-restaurants. At all but the most expensive of places, €20 should cover the cost of a starter and main course. In addition, most of the city's restaurants offer excellent-value *menús del día* at lunchtime.

Many of Palma's cafés, restaurants and *tapas* bars are geared up for the tourist trade, especially those along the harbourfront and on c/Apuntadors, and **multilingual menus** (in English, German, Catalan and Castilian) are commonplace. It's foolish to be snooty about them as some serve delicious food, but more exclusively local haunts are easy to find too, most memorably in and around the old town. The following are marked on the map on pp.68–69 unless otherwise stated.

Cafés and tapas bars

Bar Bosch Plaça Rei Joan Carles I. One of the most popular and inexpensive *tapas* bars in town, the traditional haunt of the city's intellectuals and usually humming with conversation. At peak times you'll need to be assertive to get served. Daily 8am–2am.

Bar Mollet c/Contramoll Mollet 2 (see map pp.64–65) ☎971 71 98 71. Located just across from the fish market, this place has some of the freshest fish in town. The first-rate *menú del día* (Mon–Fri €10, Sat €15) includes wine and dessert. Mon–Sat 6am–4.30pm.

La Bodeguita Mesón Salamanca c/Sant Jaume 3. In a glossily refurbished old town house just off Avgda Jaume III, this establishment has a ground-floor wine bar offering tasty *tapas* from €8 and up. Mon–Sat 1–11.30pm.

Bon Lloc c/Sant Feliu 7. One of the few vegetarian café-restaurants on the island, with good food at low prices and an informal, homely atmosphere in pleasant premises; the set menu goes for under €20. Open Mon–Sat 1–4pm.

La Bóveda c/Boteria 3, off Plaça Llotja. Classy, fashionable *tapas* bar, one of several on this short alley, with long, wide windows and wine stacked high along the back wall – come early or be prepared to queue to get in. Mon–Sat 1.30–4pm & 8.30pm–12.30am.

Café del Gran Hotel Plaça Weyler 3. Smart, modern café that makes a good spot for lunch, with tables inside or out on a pleasant, little square. The *menú del día* is excellent value at €15.

Café Lirico Avgda d'Antoni Maura 6. Most of Palma's downtown cafés have been modernized, but not this one – its large mirrors, imitation marble and weatherbeaten clientele are reminiscent of Spanish cafés of yesteryear. Not much in the way of choice, but certainly good fun. Snacks from €4. Mon–Sat 7am till late.

Café Plaça Plaça Santa Eulalia s/n. Popular café on this busy square offering a wide range of *tapas* and crêpes (from €6), pastries and cappuccinos heaped with whipped cream.

Café Port Pesquer Avgda Gabriel Roca s/n. Also known as El Pesquero, this bright and breezy café-restaurant, with its expansive open-air terrace, occupies a distinctly nautical, chalet-like structure right on the bayshore, overlooking the fishing jetties a couple of minutes' walk east of Avgda Argentina. Serves up a good range of *tapas* (€7–10), a filling version of *pa amb oli* with cheese or ham (€12), and a range of fresh fish dishes for €14 and up. Note, however, that at busy times the service can be a tad tardy. Daily from 10am till late.

Cafeteria Jaime III Avgda Jaume III, 20. Popular with office workers and shoppers, this brisk modern café serves up a good line in snacks – try their *pa amb oli* with smoked ham. Mon–Sat 8am–10pm.

🏃 **Ca'n Joan de S'Aigo** c/Can Sanç 10. A long-established coffee house with wonderful,

freshly baked *ensaimadas* (spiral pastry buns) and fruit-flavoured mousses to die for. Charming decor too, from the kitschy water fountain to the traditional Mallorcan green-tinted chandeliers. It's on a tiny alley near Plaça Santa Eulalia – take c/Sant Crist and its continuation c/Canisseria then turn right. Daily (except Tues) 8am–9pm.

Cappuccino c/Conquistador. Attractive terrace café occupying the lower part of the Palau March. The inexpensive food is uninspiring, but the setting is great.

Diner c/Sant Magi 23, Santa Catalina (see map pp.64–65) ☎971 73 62 22. A little slice of Americana, serving hamburgers, milkshakes, hash browns, pancakes, BLTs and Dixie fried chicken – all homemade and using only the best ingredients, and at moderate prices too. Open daily, 24hr.

Lizarran c/Ca'n Brondo 6. Despite the clumsy decor, this is a popular spot dishing up Basque-style *tapas* – things like smoked salmon with chopped onions, and artichoke hearts with pepper and bacon, all served on a small slice of French bread. *Tapas* from €6. Mon–Sat noon–midnight.

Minimal Passeig Mallorca 10. Slick, modern café in a pleasant setting in the stone arcade bordering (an almost traffic–free part of) the *passeig*. Illy coffee and a delicious range of salads from €8–12. Mon–Sat 11am–11pm.

Orient Express c/Llotja de Mar 6. Beside Sa Llotja, this idiosyncratic café-restaurant has an interior like the inside of a railway carriage. Crêpes are the speciality; you may well have to wait for a seat at lunchtime. Mon–Fri 1.30–4pm & 8pm–midnight, Sat 8pm–midnight.

El Pilon c/Can Cifre 4. Vibrant, cramped and crowded *tapas* bar in stone-vaulted, cave-like premises on a side street off the north end of Passeig d'es Born. The kitchen is open – so you can watch your order being prepared – and although the quality of the food can vary, there's no disputing the variety of *tapas* (and full meals) on offer. *Tapas* from €5. Popular with tourists. Mon–Sat 1pm till late.

Sa Impremta c/Morey 4. Amiable neighbourhood café-restaurant with medieval-looking wood-beam ceilings and traditional shuttered windows. A tasty range of Italian dishes plus great salads for €7–10. Daily noon–4.30pm & 6.30pm–midnight.

🏃 **La Taberna del Caracol** c/Sant Alonso 2 ☎971 71 49 08. Deep in the depths of the old town, this smashing *tapas* bar occupies charming old premises, all wooden beams and ancient arches. A first-rate range of *tapas* begin at just €6. Mon–Sat 1–3.30pm & 7.30–11.30pm. Reservations advised at peak times.

Restaurants

Aramís c/Montenegro 1 ☏ 971 72 52 32. Set in a sympathetically refurbished old stone mansion on a side street off Passeig d'es Born, this superb restaurant has an imaginative menu with an international range of dishes – ravioli and pumpkin, wild mushrooms en croute for example – and there's an unbeatable *menú del día* (€14) plus a wonderful house red. Mains average €25. Reservations recommended. Mon–Fri 1–3.30pm & 8–11pm, Sat 8–11pm.

Asador Tierra Aranda c/Concepció 4 ☏ 971 71 42 56. A smart and fairly formal carnivore's paradise in an old mansion off Avgda Jaume III: meats either grilled over open fires or roasted in wood-fired ovens, with suckling pig and lamb house specialities. Weather permitting, you can also eat in the garden. Mains average €20–25. Tues–Sat 1–4pm & 8–11pm, Sun & Mon 1–4pm only; closed annual holidays in July. Reservations advised.

Caballito del Mar Passeig Sagrera 5 ☏ 971 72 10 74. Smooth and polished restaurant that has long been a favourite with well-heeled British holidaymakers. There was a time when this was undoubtedly the best seafood restaurant in town and although this probably isn't the case today, it does excel with its house speciality – the *daurada amb sal al forn* (sea bream oven-baked in salt). Across from Sa Llotja, it faces out onto busy Avgda Gabriel Roca and the harbourfront. Main courses average €20–25, but the extras soon mount up. Reservations well-nigh essential. Tues–Sun 12.30–4pm & 8–11.30pm.

Ca'n Carlos c/Aigua 5 ☏ 971 71 38 69. Charming, family-run restaurant featuring first-class Mallorcan cuisine that takes in such delights as cuttlefish and snails. The menu isn't extensive, but everything is carefully prepared and there's a daily special as well as a fish of the day. Good dishes to sample are *fava parada* (dried-bean stew) and *caragols de la mallorquina* (snails). Main courses average around €15. Mon–Sat 1–4pm & 8–11pm.

Casa Eduardo Contramoll Mollet 4 (see map on pp.64–65) ☏ 971 71 65 74. Spick-and-span restaurant located upstairs in one of the plain modern buildings beside the fish dock. There's an enjoyable view of the harbour, but the real treat is the fresh fish – a wonderful range, all simply prepared, though grilled is best. It's located just across from – and east of – the foot of Avgda Argentina. Main courses average €16. Tues–Sat 1–3.30pm & 8–11pm.

Celler Pagès c/Felip Bauza 2, off c/Apuntadors at ☏ 971 72 60 36. Tiny, inexpensive restaurant with an easy-going family atmosphere serving traditional Mallorcan food – try the stuffed marrows with home-made mayonnaise on the side or the delicious roast leg of duck with dried plums and grilled vegetables. Reserve at weekends. Mon–Sat 1–3.30pm & 8–11pm.

Forn de Sant Joan c/Sant Joan 4 ☏ 971 72 84 22. Set in an old bakery, this smart and extremely popular Catalan restaurant offers a first-rate range of seafood dishes (€15–20) and does an excellent line in *tapas* (from €10) – try the red peppers stuffed with shellfish, followed by the lemon and cinnamon mousse. The location, bang in the centre of the city's nightlife, pumps up the prices here, but it's still very bearable. Daily 7pm to midnight.

Koldo Royo Avgda Gabriel Roca 3 (see map on pp.64–65) ☏ 971 73 24 35. Very expensive restaurant (count on €70 and up for a three-course meal), but worth it if you're after experiencing the outstanding modern Mediterranean creations of a Michelin-starred Basque chef – strawberry gazpacho, chestnut risotto with wild mushrooms, white asparagus with black truffles, and so on. Reservations essential. Mon–Fri 1.30–3.30pm & 8.30–11.30pm, Sat 8.30–11.30pm.

Mangiafuoco Plaça Vapor 4, Santa Catalina (see map on pp.64–65) ☏ 971 45 10 72. Tuscan-owned restaurant-cum-wine-bar offering top-notch Italian food and specializing in dishes featuring truffles, which are flown in weekly from Tuscany. Try the *pappardelle al tartuffo* and prepare to be wowed, especially when it's washed down with one of the superb house wines. Attractive setting too – metres from the top of the low ridge that overlooks the harbourfront. Mains average €20–25. Daily except Tues 1.30–3.30pm & 8–11pm.

Restaurant del Museu Es Baluard Museu, Plaça Porta Santa Catalina s/n ☏ 971 90 81 99. Adjacent to the Es Baluard gallery (see p.85), this excellent restaurant occupies two modernist glass cubes with views out across the bay. The menu is based on Mallorcan cuisine, but there are all sorts of international flourishes – try the lamb. Main courses cost around €16 in the evening, slightly less during the day. Tues–Sun noon–3.30pm & 8–11pm.

S'Olivera c/Morey 5 ☏ 971 72 95 81. Appealing restaurant, with antique bric-a-brac and paintings dotted round the walls. Food includes a first-rate range of *tapas* (around €6 per portion), plus quality Spanish cuisine and a good-value lunchtime *menú del día* (€10). Mon–Sat 1.30–3.30pm & 8–11pm.

Nightlife and entertainment

Most of the cafés and *tapas* bars listed above are quite happy just to ply you with drink until midnight or beyond. In addition, there is a cluster of lively **late-night bars** – mostly with music as the backdrop rather than the main event – amongst the narrow and ancient side streets backing onto **Plaça Llotja**. Alternatively, a number of more modish bars can be found strung out along **Avinguda Gabriel Roca** in the vicinity of the Jardins La Quarentena, an area of ritzy hotels and apartment blocks which hums at night with fashionable locals, dressed to the nines, hopping from bar to bar.

Clubs (*discotecas*) are not Palma's forte, but there are a couple of decent ones on Avinguda Gabriel Roca. They're rarely worth investigating until around 1am and entry charges will cost you anything up to €20, depending on the night and what's happening (although entry is sometimes free). The door staff usually operate an informal dress code of one sort or another – if you want to get in, avoid beach gear and (heaven forbid) white trainers.

Traditionally, Palma has had little to offer in terms of **performing arts**, but matters are on the mend. The grand nineteenth-century Teatre Principal, Plaça Weyler 16 (℡971 71 33 46, ⓦwww.teatreprincipal.com), is currently being revamped and will feature classical music and opera, whilst the Teatre Municipal, Passeig Mallorca 9B (℡971 73 91 48, ⓦwwwpalmademallorca.es), offers a varied programme of contemporary drama, classic films, dance and ballet. In summer, there's almost always something going on at the open-air Parc de la Mar, just below the cathedral, and other summer venues for music and dance include Can Solleric, at Passeig d'es Born 27 (see p.84), the Castell de Bellver (see p.90), the Fundació Miró in Cala Major (see p.101) and the Auditorium, Avgda Gabriel Roça 18, ℡971 73 53 28, ⓦwww.auditoriumdepalma.com). Ask at the tourist office (see p.63) for a complete listing of upcoming events. The following are marked on the map on pp.68–69 unless otherwise stated.

Late-night bars

Abaco c/Sant Joan 1 ℡971 71 49 39. Set in a charming old mansion, this is easily Palma's most unusual bar, with an interior straight out of a Busby Berkeley musical: fruits cascading down its stairway, caged birds hidden amid patio foliage, elegant music and a daily flower bill you could live on for a month. Drinks, as you might imagine, are extremely expensive (cocktails cost as much as €15) but you're never hurried into buying one. It is, however, rather too sedate to be much fun if you're up for a big night. Located in the city centre, just off c/Apuntadors. Daily 9pm–2am, but closed for most of Jan.

Escape Plaça Draçana 13. Friendly little place, and always lively, set just off a square that gets busier if not exactly prettier every year. Close to the harbourfront too.

Gotic Plaça Llotja 2. Tiny bar and café with a candlelit patio and pavement tables that nudge out across the square, adding a touch of romance.

Latitude 39 c/Felip Bauza 8, off c/Apuntadors. Tiny, upbeat bar, playing jazz, blues and sometimes classical music.

La Lonja c/Llotja de Mar 2. A popular, well-established haunt, with revolving doors and pleasantly old-fashioned decor; the background music caters for (almost) all tastes. There's *tapas* as well, and you can sit out in the square right in front of Sa Llotja.

Clubs

Pacha Avgda Gabriel Roca 42 (see map on pp.64–65) ℡971 45 59 08, ⓦwww .pachamallorca.com. Loud, popular and raucously housey disco with a gyrating dance floor and a couple of bars inside and another bar outside in the garden. A ten-minute walk west of the Jardins La Quarentena, and 800m east of the ferry terminal. Dress up to get in – no dullards. There's generally a gay night, "Pacha Loca", at least once a week, mostly on Sunday. Entrance (usually) €15. June–Sept daily 11pm–6am, Oct–May Thurs–Sun 11pm–6am.

Tito's Plaça Gomila 3 (See map on pp.64–65) ℡971 73 00 17, ⓦwww.titosmallorca.com. With its stainless steel and glass exterior, this long-established nightspot looks a bit like something from a sci-fi film. Outdoor lifts carry you up from

Avgda Gabriel Roca (the back entrance) to the dance floor, which pulls in huge crowds from many countries – or you can go in through the front entrance on Plaça Gomila. The music (anything from house to mainstream pop) lacks conviction, but it's certainly loud. The Avgda Gabriel Roca entrance is just on the city-centre side of the Jardins La Quarentena. Admission about €20. June to early Sept daily 11pm–5am, Oct–May Fri–Sun 11pm–5am.

Shopping

Like every other big city in Spain, Palma has its share of multinational stores, but although some of them have extended **opening hours**, most still stick to the traditional norm – Monday to Friday 9/10am to 1.30pm or 2pm, Saturday 9/10am to 1/2pm. As for the specifics, there's a particular concentration of up-market and/or designer **clothes shops** on and around Avgda Jaume III. Here, on Plaça Rei Joan Carles I, there are two Zara stores – one for men and for women – an M&M, and a Loewe, both chainstores, at Avgda Jaume III, 1. **Camper shoes** are made on the island and they have two stores in Palma – one

Specialist food and drink shops

Amongst the city's specialist food shops, **Colmado Santo Domingo**, c/Sant Domingo 1 (Mon–Fri 10am–1.30pm & 5–7.30pm, Sat 10am–1pm), is a tiny, cave-like, old-fashioned store packed with hanging sausages and local fruit and veg; it's right in the centre, metres from Plaça Cort. The sausages you should try carry the 'Sobrasada de Mallorca de Cerdo Negro' label, which guarantees they are made from the island's own indigenous black pig. To the north of the centre, Palma's main covered market, the **Mercat de l'Olivar**, on Plaça Olivar (Mon–Sat 7am–2pm; for more on markets, see p.98), has dozens of fresh food and seafood stalls and one to look out for, on its eastern side, is **Molt Bó**, which specializes in locally made dairy products and pastas, whilst **La Montana** does a great line in *sobrasadas*. Near the market, the cheerily painted **La Favorita**, c/Sant Miquel 38 (Mon–Fri 9.30am–1.30pm & 5–7.30pm, Sat 10am–1pm), is one of the city's best delis, with all sorts of Spanish and Italian treats and a superb range of oils. There's another branch of **La Favorita** at c/Pou 33, in Santa Catalina, a groovy part of the city immediately to the west of Avinguda Argentina (see map on pp.64–65). Close by, also in Santa Catalina, is **Colmado Manresa**, c/Fábrica 19 (Tues–Fri 9am–2pm & 5–8.30pm, Sat 9am–2pm; see map on pp.64–65), founded in 1949 and stuffed with all manner of island delicacies, including premium, black-pig *sobrasadas* and rice from Sa Pobla.

Palma has a platoon of good cake and pastry shops (*pastelerías*), including **Forn des Teatre**, Plaça Weyler 9 (Mon–Sat 9am–12.30pm & 4.30–7.30pm), and the excellent **Forn Fondo**, c/Unió 15 (Mon–Sat 8am–8.30pm & Sun 8am–2pm), where the fig cake (*higos* in Castilian) is especially delicious. Both sell the freshly baked *ensaima- das* (spiral pastry buns) that are so much a feature of island life, but the best – though this is the subject of much argument – come from *Ca'n Joan de S'Aigo*, a charming coffee house near Plaça Santa Eulalia (see p.93). The pick of the city's several spice shops is **Especias Crespi**, to the southeast of Plaça Espanya at c/Sindicat 64 (Mon–Fri 10am–1.30pm & 5–7pm, Sat 10am–1pm) and there's a first-class chocolatier, **Frasquet**, just off Plaça Mercat at c/Orfila 4 (Mon–Fri 9am–1.30pm & 5–8pm, Sat 10am–1pm) – try the *torrons*, almond-paste balls doused in roasted pine nuts.

Many Palma shops and most supermarkets stock a reasonable range of Spanish wines, and a goodly proportion also carry Balearic vintages. The biggest department store in the city centre, **El Corte Inglés**, Avgda Jaume III, 15 (Mon–Sat 9.30am–9.30pm), has an especially wide selection of both Spanish and Mallorcan wine in its basement, all at competitive prices.

at Avgda Jaume III, 16, the other at c/Sant Miquel 17 (both Mon–Sat 10am–8.30pm) – and so are **artificial pearls** (see p.203): the largest pearl manufacturer is Majorica, who have dozens of official agents in Palma as well as their own outlet at Avgda Jaume III, 11 (Mon–Fri 9.30am–1.30pm & 4.30–8pm, Sat 9.30am–1.30pm). **Glass-making** is a traditional island craft; Vidrias Gordiola, near the Ajuntament at c/Victoria 2 (Mon–Fri 10.15am–2pm & 4.30–8pm, Sat 10.15am–2pm), has a fine range of clear and tinted glassware, from bowls, vases and lanterns through to some wonderfully intricate chandeliers. For **pottery** and other handmade wares, including olive wood products, try Fet a Mà, c/Sant Miquel 52 (Mon–Fri 10am–1.30pm & 4.30–8pm, Sat 9.30am–1.30pm) or the delightfully old-fashioned La Concha, c/Jaume II, 19 (Mon–Fri 10am–1.30pm & 5–8pm, Sat 9.30am–1pm), which also stocks cheap and cheerful **souvenirs** such as brightly coloured Spanish fans, garish Spanish plates, model cherubs and mini-*gigantones* (carnival figures). Both sell **siurells**, white clay whistles flecked with red and green paint and shaped to depict a figure, an animal or a scene (a man sitting on a donkey, for instance); *siurells* have been given as tokens of friendship in Mallorca for hundreds of years.

For **books and maps**, El Corte Inglés, Avgda Jaume III, 15 (Mon–Sat 9.30am–9.30pm), sells a small and rather eccentric assortment of English-language novels from Ken Follett to Anne Frank, and also has a modest selection of Mallorca guidebooks and maps. Librería Fondevila, near the Teatre Principal at Costa de Sa Pols 18 (Mon–Fri 9.30am–1.30pm & 5–7.30pm, Sat 9.30am–1pm), has a rather better selection of general maps of Mallorca, but easily the best **map** shop in town is the Casa del Mapa, c/Sant Domingo 11 (Mon–Fri 10am–1.30pm & 5–7.30pm, Sat 10am–1pm).

For specialist food and drink shops, see box opposite.

Listings

Airlines Air Europa ☎902 401 501; British Airways ☎902 111 333; bmibaby ☎902 999 262; easyJet ☎902 299 992; Iberia ☎971 78 99 76; Spanair ☎902 131 415. For a full list of airlines, consult the Yellow Pages under *Linies aèries* (*Lineas aéreas* in Spanish).

Airport information ☎971 78 90 99.

Banks and exchange There are plenty of banks on and around the Passeig d'es Born and Avgda Jaume III. ATMs are commonplace too.

Beaches The closest beach to the city centre is the narrow strip of sand next to the *autopista* just east of Avgda Gabriel Alomar i Villalonga. Swimming is not, however, recommended here as the water is too polluted. Instead most locals make the half-hour trip on EMT bus #15 east to the Platja de Palma (see p.100).

Bike rental Palma on Bike, just southeast of Plaça Major at Plaça Salvador Coll 8 (☎971 71 80 62, wwww.palmaonbike.com) rents out city and mountain bikes from just €12 per day. Advance reservations, at least 24hrs ahead of time, are advised. They also do bike tours.

Bullfights Palma's bullfighting ring, the Plaça de Toros (☎971 75 16 39), is a few blocks northeast of the Plaça Espanya along c/Reina Maria Cristina in El Coliseo Balear, on c/Arquitecte Gaspar Bennàzar. You can get tickets and details from travel agents and hotel receptions. For more on bullfighting, see "Basics" p.43.

Buses Details of all island bus services are available from the information desk (daily 6am–10pm) at Palma bus station, about 400m north of Plaça Espanya, along c/Eusebi Estada. The city's two main tourist offices (see p.63) supply bus timetables too. Alternatively, call ☎971 17 77 77 for information on island-wide bus services, or ☎971 21 44 44 for details of EMT city buses – though in both cases, you'll need to speak either Spanish or Catalan to get anywhere.

Car rental Mallorca's airport heaves with car rental companies, as does Palma – there's a concentration of both large and small companies along Avgda Gabriel Roca. Amongst the big companies there are branches of Atesa at Avgda Gabriel Roca 25 ☎971 45 66 02; Betacar-Europcar, Avgda

Gabriel Roca 19 ☎971 73 77 58 (airport ☎971 78 91 35); Hertz, Avgda Gabriel Roca 13 ☎971 73 47 37 (airport ☎971 78 96 70); and Centauro, at the airport ☎971 78 93 60. The city's two main tourist offices (see p.63) can supply a complete list.

Consulates Ireland, c/Sant Miquel 68A ☎971 71 92 44; UK, Plaça Major 3D ☎971 71 24 45. For a complete list, look under *consolats* (Castilian *consulados*) in the Yellow Pages.

Doctors and dentists In the resort areas and in Palma most hotel receptions will be able to find an English-speaking doctor or dentist. For complete lists look under *metges* (Castilian *médicos*) or *clíniques dentals* (*clínicas dentales*) in the Yellow Pages.

Email and Internet The best Internet café in town is *Xpace*, just off Passeig d'es Born at c/Sant Gaietà 4 (Mon–Sat 11am–11pm & Sun noon–11pm).

Emergencies ☎112.

Ferries and catamarans Palma's two main tourist offices have ferry and catamaran schedules and tariffs. Tickets can be purchased either at travel agents (see below) or direct from the three ferry companies concerned. These are Trasmediterranea (☎902 45 46 45, ⊛www.trasmediterranea.es); Balearia (☎902 16 01 80, ⊛www.balearia.net /eng); and Iscomar (☎902 11 91 28, ⊛www .iscomar.com). All three have offices down at the ferry port, about 3.5km west of the city centre along Avgda Gabriel Roca. For details of ferry services to Mallorca from mainland Spain, Menorca and Ibiza, see p.21 and p.26.

Football Mallorca's premier team is Real Club Deportivo Mallorca (⊛www.rcdmallorca.es), who play at the Estadio Son Moix stadium on the north side of town. Fixture details either direct or from the tourist office; tickets cost €35–80.

Gay and lesbian scene The suburb of El Terreny, about 3km west of the centre below the Castell de Bellver, is the focus of the city's gay life, with a rainbow-flagged hotel, the *Rosamar* (see p.66), and

a decent selection of gay and lesbian bars. For general information, venues and events, contact Ben Amics ("Good Friends"), which operates a website (Spanish only, ⊛www.benamics.com) and an info line (971 71 56 70; 6pm–9pm). *Pacha* nightclub (see p.95) usually has a gay night once a week.

Libraries There's a quaint old municipal library inside the Ajuntament (Town Hall) on Plaça Cort (Mon–Fri 8.30am–8.30pm & Sat 9am–1pm).

Maps See "Shopping" p.96.

Markets Palma's big Rastrillo (flea market) is held every Saturday morning (8am–2pm) on Avgda Gabriel Alomar i Villalonga, between Plaça Porta d'es Camp and c/Manacor. There's a fresh fruit and vegetable market on Plaça Navegació, just west of Avgda Argentina (Mon–Sat 7am–2pm); and a daily flower market on Passeig de la Rambla. Mercat Olivar, the city's main covered market, is on Plaça Olivar (Mon–Sat 7am–2pm).

Pharmacies Central pharmacies include Farmacia Castañer, Plaça Rei Joan Carles I, 3; and Farmacia Muret, Plaça Weyler 10. A full list of pharmacies is in the Yellow Pages under *farmàcies* (Castilian *farmacias*).

Post office The central *correos/correu* is at c/ Constitució 5 (Mon–Fri 8.30am–8.30pm, Sat 9.30am–2pm).

Trains Both main tourist offices (see p.63) as well as the information desk at the bus station (see p.63) have train timetables. Or you can phone direct: Palma to Inca, Manacor and points east on ☎971 17 77 77, (⊛tib.caib.es); Palma to Sóller on ☎971 75 20 51, (⊛www.trendesoller.com).

Travel agencies There are dozens of travel agencies in Palma, listed in full in the Yellow Pages under *agències de viatges* (Castilian, *agencias de viajes*). One helpful downtown choice is Viajes Iberia, Passeig d'es Born 14 (☎971 72 67 43). There's also a recommendable travel agent at El Corte Inglés department store, on Avinguda Jaume III (see p.96).

Around Palma

Strewn around the sheltered waters of the **Badía de Palma** are the package tourist resorts that have made Mallorca synonymous with the cheap and tacky. In recent years the Balearic government have done their best to improve matters – greening resorts, restricting high-rise construction and redirecting traffic away from the coast – but their inherited problems remain. In the 1960s and 1970s, the bay experienced a building boom of almost unimaginable proportions as miles of pristine shoreline sprouted concrete and glass hotel towers, overwhelming the area's farms and fishing villages. There were few planning controls, if any, and the legacy is the mammoth sprawl of development that now extends, almost without interruption, from **S'Arenal** in the east to **Magaluf** in the west – with Palma roughly in the middle. To make matters worse, it is also debatable as to whether the recent move away from high-rise construction is well-conceived. The new villa complexes that are now the fashion gobble up the land at an alarming rate and multiply traffic. Furthermore, although the new villas are rarely more than three storeys high and built in a sort of pan-Mediterranean style – some with Neoclassical features, others more reminiscent of Spanish design – they end up looking terribly, remorselessly suburban. As a consequence, although the thirty-kilometre-long stretch of coast between S'Arenal and Magaluf is divided into a **score or more resorts**, it's often impossible to pick out where one ends and the next begins. That said, most of the resorts have evolved their own identities, either in terms of the nationalities they attract, the income group they appeal to, or the age range they cater for.

East of Palma lies **S'Arenal**, mainly geared up for young German tourists, with dozens of pounding bars and all-night clubs. S'Arenal also fringes one of Mallorca's best **beaches**, the **Platja de Palma**, which stretches from S'Arenal round to **Ca'n Pastilla**, but although the beach is superb, the flat shoreline behind it accommodates an unprepossessing, seemingly endless strip of restaurants, bars and souvenir shops.

West of Palma, the coast bubbles up into the low, rocky hills and sharp coves that prefigure the mountains further west. The sandy beaches here are far smaller – and some are actually artificial – but the terrain makes the tourist development seem less oppressive. **Cala Major**, the first stop, was once the playground of the jetset. It's hit grittier times, but some of the grand old buildings have survived and the **Fundació Pilar i Joan Miró**, which exhibits a fine selection of Miró's work in what was once his home and studio, makes an enjoyable detour. The neighbouring resort of **Illetes** is a good deal more polished, boasting comfortable hotels and attractive cove beaches, and is perhaps the best place to stay hereabouts, though you might also consider neighbouring **Portals Nous**, which has an affluent and exclusive air born of its swanky marina. Next up comes British-dominated **Palma Nova**, a major package holiday destination popular with all ages, and the adjacent **Magaluf**, where modern high-rise hotels, thumping nightlife and a substantial sandy beach cater to a youthful and very British crowd. South of Magaluf, the charming cove beach of **Portals Vells** is a real surprise, sheltered by an undeveloped, pine-studded peninsula. West of Magaluf, the coastal highway leaves the Badia de Palma for large and sprawling **Santa Ponça** before pushing on to **Peguera**, a large, rambling resort with attractive sandy beaches and a relaxed family atmosphere. Next door – and much more endearing – is tiny **Cala Fornells**, where pretty villas thread along the coastal hills and a trio of first-rate hotels overlook a wooded cove – and concrete-slab beaches, which are not as bad as they sound; the development is fairly restrained here and, if you're after a straightforward resort holiday, this is as good as it gets on the Badía de Palma. From Cala Fornells, it's another short hop to the good-looking bay which encloses the burgeoning resort of **Camp de Mar**.

Practicalities

Although the Badía de Palma resorts boast hundreds of **hotels**, *hostals* and apartment buildings, the bulk are block-booked by the package tourist industry from May or June through to September or October, with frugal pickings for the independent traveller; out of season, many places simply close down. We've selected several of the more interesting and enjoyable package hotels, as well as picking out several relatively inexpensive places where there's a reasonable chance of finding a vacancy independently in high season, but left it at that. Neither have we have described resort **nightlife** since the liveliest discos and clubs are, as a general rule, concentrated in the tackier spots. This stretch of coast also has hundreds of **restaurants** and cafés, but the choice is not as diverse as you might expect, and for the most part standards are not very high: the vast majority of places serve either low-price pizzas and pastas or a sort of pan-European tourist menu.

Transport

Buses along the Badía de Palma coast are fast and efficient. The resorts in the immediate vicinity of Palma are served by **EMT** (Spanish and Catalan information line ☏971 21 44 44, ⓦwww.emtpalma.es), all of whose buses pass through Plaça Espanya; most EMT buses also have several other city-centre stops. Principal EMT services include bus #3, heading west to Cala Major & Illetes; bus #15 running through Ca'n Pastilla to S'Arenal; and bus #17, which travels the old coastal road east through Es Portixol to Ca'n Pastilla. Further afield, the remaining Badía de Palma resorts, including Portals Nous, Magaluf and Peguera, plus the likes of Port Andratx (see p.147) and Sant Elm (see p.146), are served by **TransaBús** (Spanish/Catalan information line ☏971 17 77 77, ⓦtib.caib.es); all TransaBús leave from the bus station on c/ Eusebi Estada. **Ticket prices** are incredibly low – the 25-minute journey to S'Arenal, for instance, costs just €1.15; for frequencies and journey times, see p.107.

Driving is straightforward: the *autopista* (motorway) shoots along the coast from S'Arenal right round to Palma Nova and then slices across a narrow peninsula to reach Santa Ponça and Peguera. Alternatively, you can choose to take the old coastal road through most of the resorts, heading east from Palma to Es Portixol and ultimately S'Arenal, or west from Cala Major to Magaluf.

East of Palma

The *autopista* rushes **east** out of Palma with tourist resorts on one side and the **airport** on the other. The flatlands backing onto the coast were once prime agricultural land, hence the ruined **windmills**, built to pump water out of the marshy topsoil and now gaunt reminders of earlier, more pastoral times. The alternative route, along the old coastal road, is a bit more interesting and a lot slower; take the turning off the *autopista* just beyond the city walls (signposted to Ca'n Pastilla) and follow the road as it tracks through a series of resorts, beginning with **ES PORTIXOL**, an intelligently revamped old quarter with its own small beach and top-ranking *Hotel Portixol* (see p.67). Pushing on, you soon reach **CALA GAMBA**, an unassuming little place with a pleasant horse-shoe-shaped harbour, and then **CA'N PASTILLA**, the first substantial tourist resort on this part of the coast, its fifty-odd hotels and apartment buildings set in a rough rectangle of land pushed tight against the seashore. The place is short on charm and certainly too close to the airport for sonic comfort, but it does herald the start of the fine Platja de Palma beach.

Sometimes, Ses Maravelles and S'Arenal

The **Platja de Palma**, the four-kilometre stretch of sandy beach that defines the three coterminous (and indistinguishable) resorts of **SOMETIMES**, **SES MARAVELLES** and **S'ARENAL**, is crowded with serious sun-seekers, a sweating throng of bronzed and oiled bodies slowly roasting in the heat. The beach is also a busy pick-up place, the spot for a touch of verbal foreplay before the night-time bingeing begins. It is, as they say, fine if you like that sort of thing – though older visitors can't but help look marooned. A wide and pleasant walkway lined with palm trees runs behind the beach and this, in turn, is edged by a long sequence of bars, restaurants and souvenir shops. A toy-town tourist "train" shuttles up and down the walkway, but there's so little to distinguish one part of the beach from another that it's easy to become disoriented. To maintain your bearings, keep an eye out for the series of smart, stainless-steel beach bars, each numbered and labelled, in Castilian, "*balneario*", strung along the shore: Balneario no. 15 is by the Ca'n Pastilla marina, while no. 1 is near S'Arenal harbour.

Singling out any part of this massive complex is a pretty pointless exercise, but the area around **S'Arenal harbour** does at least have a concentration of **facilities**. There's car rental, currency exchange, boat trips and nightclubs, and you can eat well at the lively terrace bar of the harbourside *Club Nàutico*. S'Arenal also boasts **Aqualand** (mid–May to Sept daily 10am–5/6pm; €21, children €15; ⓦwww.aqualand.es), a huge leisure complex of swimming pools, water flumes and kiddies' playgrounds. It's between the *autopista* and the eastern edge of the resort, about 15km east of Palma, and reachable on EMT bus #15.

Accommodation

All three resorts extend a few blocks inland and encompass dozens of **places to stay**. The cheapest accommodation is provided by the **HI hostel**, the *Albergue Platja de Palma*, at c/Costa Brava 13 in Sometimes (☏971 26 08 92; €15–20 per person), which has nine two- to four-bed dorms with en-suite bathrooms; advance booking is well-nigh essential as the hostel is popular with school groups. The hostel is a 25-minute journey on EMT bus #15 from Palma's Plaça Reina or Plaça Espanya; ask to be put off at the giant *Hotel Iberostar Royal Cristina* on the main road. The hostel is a couple of hundred metres further along the road on the left – and a couple of minutes' walk from Balneario no. 9. It should be open all year, but sometimes closes for a month or two in the winter.

At the other end of the market, the four-star **hotel** *Iberostar Royal Cristina*, on Arenas de Bilbao (☏971 49 22 11, ⓦwww.iberostar.com; ❻), offers luxury rooms and apartments, although it doesn't overlook the beach. Another mid-range option is the three-star *Iberostar Royal Cupido*, a bright, modern 200-room hotel which backs onto the beach a couple of minutes' walk west of the *Royal Cristina* at c/Marbella 32 (☏971 26 43 00, ⓦwww.iberostar.com; ❼).

West of Palma

Just a couple of kilometres to the **west** of Palma's ferry port, cramped and crowded **CALA MAJOR** snakes its way along a hilly stretch of coastline bisected by its main street (the MA-1C). This modest, modern pile-up is brightened by the occasional *Modernista* building, reminders of halcyon days when the resort was a byword for elegance and exemplified by the five-star *Hotel Nixe Palace* (☏971 70 08 88, ⓦwww.nixepalace.com; ❼), a large and attractive structure which hogs the shoreline beside the main road. There's also the small matter of a royal palace, the **Palacio de Marivent**, and although you can't go in, you can glimpse it from the main street – it's close to the *autopista* (motorway) at the east end of the resort.

Cala Major's Fundació Pilar i Joan Miró

Opposite the Palacio de Marivent, the signposted road to Gènova dog legs up the hill for 500m to run past the **Fundació Pilar i Joan Miró**, c/Joan de

Saridakis 29 (mid–June to mid–Sept Tues–Sat 10am–7pm, Sun 10am–3pm; mid–Sept to mid–May Tues–Sat 10am–6pm, Sun 10am–3pm; €5), where the painter **Joan Miró** (1893–1983) lived and worked for much of the 1950s, 1960s and 1970s; EMT bus #6 (every 30min, hourly on the weekend) from central Palma stops 100m below the entrance en route to La Bonanova.

Initially – from 1920 – the young Miró was involved with the **Surrealists** in Paris and contributed to all their major exhibitions: his wild squiggles, super-charged with bright colours, prompted André Breton, the leading theorist of the movement, to describe Miró as "the most Surrealist of us all". In the 1930s he adopted a simpler style, abandoning the decorative complexity of his earlier work for a more minimalist use of symbols, though the highly coloured forms remained. Miró **returned to Barcelona**, the city of his birth, in 1940, where he continued to work in the Surrealist tradition, though as an avowed opponent of Franco his position was uneasy. In 1957 he **moved to Mallorca**, its relative isolation offering a degree of safety. His wife and mother were both Mallorcan, which must have influenced his decision, as did the chance to work in his own purpose-built studio with its view of the coast. Even from the relative isolation of Franco's Spain he remained an influential figure, prepared to experiment with all kinds of media, right up until his death here in Cala Major in 1983.

The expansive hillside premises of the Fundació include Miró's old **studio**, an unassuming affair that has been left pretty much as it was at the time of his death. It's worth a quick gander for a flavour of how the man worked – tackling a dozen or so canvases at the same time – but unfortunately you're only allowed to peer through the windows. Opposite are the angular lines of the bright-white art gallery, the **Edificio Estrella**, which displays a rotating and representative sample of the prolific artist's work. Miró was nothing if not productive, and the Fundació owns 134 paintings, 300 engravings and 105 drawings, as well as sculptures, gouaches and preliminary sketches – more than six thousand works in all. There are no guarantees as to what will be on display, but you're likely to see a decent selection of his paintings, the familiar dream-like squiggles and half-recognizable shapes that are intended to conjure up the unconscious, with free play often given to erotic associations. The gallery also stores a comprehensive collection of Miró documents and occasionally hosts exhibitions.

Illetes

Prosperous **ILLETES** (sometimes written Illetas), just off the MA-1C coastal road immediately to the west of Cala Major – and 7km from Palma – comprises a ribbon of restaurants, hotels and apartment buildings which bestride the steep hills that rise high above a rocky shoreline. There's precious little space left, but at least the generally low-rise buildings are of manageable proportions. A string of tiny cove beaches punctuates the coast, the most attractive being the pine-shaded **Platja Cala Comtesa**, at the southern end of the resort, alongside a military zone.

The long main street, Passeig d'Illetes, runs past several top-notch **hotels**. The most enjoyable is the *Bon Sol*, about halfway along (☎971 40 21 11, ⊛www .ila-chateau.com/bonsol; ❼), which tumbles down the cliffs to the seashore and its own artificial beach. A family-run concern, the hotel has all the conveniences you could want and the better rooms have fine views out over the bay. A second good choice is the *Hotel Albatros*, a chain hotel located near the north end of Passeig d'Illetes (☎971 40 22 11, ⊛www.barceloalbatros.com; ❻); rooms here have balconies and there's a swimming pool and private beach. The *Albatros* is just to the south of the luxurious, five-star *Hotel Melià de Mar* (☎971 40 25 11,

△ Illetes beach

ⓦ www.solmelia.com; ⑧), which occupies a standard-issue high-rise perched right on the coast.

Most visitors eat in their hotels, but there is a smattering of smart **cafés and restaurants** on the main drag, including *Es Parral* towards the south end of the resort at Passeig d'Illetes 75 (daily: 10am–midnight, kitchen 12.30–4pm & 6–10pm; ⓣ971 70 11 27), where they serve a Mallorcan-Spanish menu with mains hovering around €18. Even better, with a more international menu and much groovier, is *Virtual Club*, a combined restaurant, bistro, cocktail bar and nightclub whose various buildings – including a clutch of palm-thatched huts – press against the seashore beside Passeig d'Illetes (ⓣ971 70 32 35, ⓦ www.virtualclub.es).

Bendinat and Portals Nous

Beyond the two Illetes turnings, the MA-1C coastal road cuts through the peripheries of **BENDINAT**, whose older, leafier streets meander down to the seashore lined by the villas of the well-to-do. It's a pretty spot, and tucked away on a quiet, rocky cove is the charming *Hotel Bendinat*, Avgda Bendinat (mid–Feb to Oct; ⓣ971 67 57 25, ⓦ www.hotelbendinat.es; ⑨), dating from the 1950s and built in the traditional *hacienda* style, with a beautiful arcaded terrace overlooking the sea. You can stay either in the main building, where most of the bedrooms have balconies, or in one of the trim, whitewashed bungalows that dot the gardens; at peak times, there is a minimum three-night stay.

On its west side, Bendinat merges with **PORTALS NOUS**, another ritzy settlement where polished mansions fill out the green and hilly terrain between the coast and the dull and drab main street (MA-1C). There's a tiny **beach** too, set beneath the cliffs and reached via a flight of steps at the foot of c/Passatge del Mar, but the big deal is the **marina**, one of Mallorca's most exclusive, where the boats look more like ocean liners than pleasure yachts. What you make of all this glitz and the flock of celebrities that it attracts is very much a matter of taste (and politics), but the marina is certainly a lively spot. The most hyped of its many **bars and restaurants** is the Michelin-starred *Restaurant Tristán* (T 971 67 55 47), where you can expect to pay an arm and a leg for the nouvelle cuisine – count on around €100 per person; much more affordable is *Wellies*, a waterfront café-bar with a tasty range of international dishes. In striking contrast, **Marineland**, just south along the seashore from the marina, is one of the tackiest attractions on the island, with shark tanks and a tropical fish aquarium, as well as dolphin and sea-lion shows (daily: July–Aug 9.30am–6pm; Feb–June & Sept to mid–Dec 9.30am–5pm; €17; W www.marineland.es). Young children love the place; adults mostly suffer in silence.

Portals Nous has precious few **hotels** – much of the shoreline is occupied by private villas and apartments – and the best local accommodation is about 3km to the west of the marina in the next resort along, **COSTA D'EN BLANES**, at the four-star *Hotel Punta Negra Resort* (T 971 68 07 62, W www.h10hotels .com; ❸), beside the MA-1C old coastal road and set on two rugged, unspoilt coves with crystal clear water.

Palma Nova and Calvià

Old Mallorca hands claim that **PALMA NOVA**, 4km west of Portals Nous, was once a beauty spot, and certainly its wide and shallow bay, with good beaches set among a string of bumpy headlands, still has its moments. But for the most part, the bay has been engulfed by a broad, congested sweep of tourist facilities. With the development comes a vigorous nightlife and a platoon of hotels on or near the seashore – though, as elsewhere, most are block-booked by tour operators throughout the season.

Some 6km north of Palma Nova, tucked away in the hills behind the coast, is the tiny town of **CALVIÀ**, the region's administrative centre – hence the oversized town hall, paid for by the profits of the tourist industry. The parish church of **Sant Joan Baptista** (Mon–Sat 10am–1pm), dating from 1245, dominates the town, though the building's Gothic subtleties mostly disappeared during a nineteenth-century refurbishment that left a crude bas-relief carving of the Garden of Gethsemane above the main door. There are pleasant views across the surrounding countryside from outside the church, and the adjacent square is home to a modern mural showing a rather neat depiction of the island's history. Calvià also possesses a very good **restaurant**, the *Méson Ca'n Torrat* (T 971 67 06 82; daily except Tues from 8pm), located just down the hill from the main square and specializing in shoulder of lamb and suckling pig; main courses average around €17.

TransaBús **bus** #L111 runs from Palma through Palma Nova to Calvià seven times daily Monday through Saturday, four times on Sunday. From Calvià, it's a short drive west to **Es Capdellà** and the **Serra de Tramuntana**, covered in Chapter 2.

Magaluf

TORRENOVA, on the chunky headland at the far end of Palma Nova, is a cramped and untidy development that slides into **MAGALUF**, whose high-rise towers march across the next bay down the coast. For years a bargain-basement package holiday destination, Magaluf finally lost patience with its youthful British visitors in 1996. The local authorities won a court order allowing them to demolish twenty downmarket hotels in an attempt to end – or at least control – the annual binge of "violence, drunkenness and open-air sex" that, they argued, characterized the resort. The high-rise hotels were duly dynamited and an extensive clean-up programme subsequently freshened up the resort's appearance. However, short of demolishing the whole lot, there's not too much anyone can do with the deadening concrete of the modern town centre – and the demolished blocks will anyway be replaced, albeit by more upmarket hotels. These draconian measures have brought some improvement, but the resort's British visitors remain steadfastly determined to create, or at least patronize, a bizarre caricature of their homeland: it's all here, from beans-on-toast with Marmite to pubs like *Tom Brown's Chicken & Steak Inn*.

Stuck on the western edge of Magaluf, **Aqualand** (daily: May, June, Sept & Oct 10am–5pm; July & Aug 10am–6pm; €18.50, children 3–12 years €12.30; ⓦ www.aqualand.es) is a giant-sized water park with swimming pools, water chutes and flumes which rivals Aqualand in S'Arenal; like its sister, it's immensely popular, drawing kids in their hundreds. Across the road is a second theme park, **Western Water Park** (May–Oct daily 10am–5/6pm; €18.50, children 3–12 years €12.50; ⓦ www.western-park.com). The main event here is a replica Wild West town – one of the most incongruous sights in Spain – as well as a waterpark, with all the Wild West clichés.

In the unlikely event that you want to find a room in Magaluf, you can get a free map giving the location of all the resort's hotels at the **tourist office**, on the square one block back from the beach at Avinguda Pere Vaquer Ramis 1 (daily 9am–6pm; ⓣ 971 13 11 26, ⓦ www.visitcalvia.com).

South to Portals Vells

Things pick up on the edge of Magaluf with the spatulate **peninsula** that extends to the south of the resort, poking its knobbly head out into the ocean. The west side of the peninsula has been extensively developed, but the east side has been barely touched, its pine-clad coves bumping down to Portals Vells and ultimately the Cap de Cala Figuera lighthouse – but note that there is no public transport. The clearly signposted **road to Portals Vells** begins where the MA-1 *autopista* merges with the MA-1C just to the north of Magaluf. From here, the road cuts south, running past the Aqualand theme park and keeping straight at a fork where the road to Santa Ponça curves off to the right. South of the fork, the road narrows into a country lane, passing a golf course before heading off into the woods. After about 4km, a steep turning on the left leads down 1km to **Cala Mago** (still signposted in Castilian as Playa El Mago), where a rocky little headland with a shattered guard house has lovely beaches to either side. Park and walk down to whichever cove takes your fancy: the nudist beach on the right with its café-restaurant, or the delightful pine-shaded strand on the left with its beach bar, tiny port and sprinkling of villas. Both provide sunloungers and showers.

Continuing a further 600m past the Cala Mago turning, a second side road cuts for a kilometre down to the cove beach of **PORTALS VELLS**. Despite a bar-restaurant and a handful of villas, this remains a pleasant, pine-scented spot of glistening sand, rocky cliffs and clear blue water, especially appealing early in the morning before it gets crowded. Clearly visible from the beach are the **caves** of the headland on the south side of the cove. A footpath leads to the most interesting, an old cave church where the holy-water stoup and altar have been cut out of the solid rock – the work of shipwrecked Genoese seamen, according to local legend.

Beyond the Portals Vells turning, the road continues south for 1.5km until it reaches a broken-down barbed-wire fence at the start of a disused military zone. You can't drive any further and you're not supposed to walk beyond the fence either, but some people do, braving the no-entry signs to scramble through the pine woods and out along the headland for about 1.5km to reach the solitary **Cap de Cala Figuera lighthouse**.

Santa Ponça

West of Magaluf, the MA-1 motorway trims the outskirts of **SANTA PONÇA**, one of the less endearing of the resorts that punctuate this stretch of coast. Mostly a product of the 1980s, this sprawling conurbation has abandoned the concrete high-rises of yesteryear for a pseudo-vernacular architecture that's littered the hills with scores of tedious villas. More positively, the setting is attractive, with rolling hills flanking a broad bay, the resort's white sandy beaches offer safe bathing, and there's **diving** for all levels of experience as well as novices with Zoea Mallorca, at the Club Náutico (℡971 69 14 44, Wwww .zoeamallorca.com).

Peguera

Sprawling **PEGUERA**, about 6km north of Santa Ponça, is strung out along a lengthy, partly pedestrianized main street – the Avinguda Peguera – immediately behind several generous sandy beaches. There's nothing remarkable about the place, but it does have an easy-going air and is a favourite with families and older visitors. The MA1 loops right round Peguera and the easiest approach, if you're just after the **beach**, is from the south. Head into the resort along the main street and park anywhere you can before you reach the pedestrianized part of the Avinguda de Peguera, where the town's baffling one-way system sends you weaving through the resort's side streets – best avoided, if you can.

Cala Fornells

Next door to Peguera is the much prettier – and much smaller – resort of **CALA FORNELLS**, which is reached via either of two signed turnings on the Avinguda Peguera to the west of the pedestrianised centre. Take the more easterly turning and the road climbs up to a string of chic, *pueblo*-style houses that perch on the sea cliffs and trail round to the tiny centre of the resort, where a wooded cove is set around a minuscule beach and concreted sunbathing slabs. Although Cala Fornells tends to be overcrowded during the daytime, at night the tranquillity returns, and it makes a good base for a holiday. You can also stroll out into the surrounding woods along a wide, dirt track which runs up behind the hotels, cutting across the pine-scented hills towards the stony cove beach of **Caló d'es Monjo**, 1km to the west.

Cala Fornells has two fetching **hotels**, both behind the beach at the end of the access roads: the sprucely modern, four-star *Coronado* (℡971 68 68 00, Wwww.hotelcoronado.com; ❻), where all 140 bedrooms have sea views and balconies; and the more sympathetic, green-shuttered and white-painted *Cala Fornells* (℡971 68 69 50, Wwww.calafornells.com; ❻). If your wallet won't stretch to either of these, Peguera has plenty of bargain-basement *hostals* (❷–❸) in the characterless side streets sloping up from its seafront. Peguera's seasonal **tourist office**, just off the main drag at the east end of the resort (Mon–Sat 9am–5pm; ℡971 68 70 83), issues comprehensive accommodation lists as well as local maps giving the location of all the resort's hotels.

Peguera has dozens of bright, inexpensive **cafés** and **restaurants**, from pizza joints through to seafood places. The best spot in town is *La Gran Tortuga* (☎971 68 60 23; closed Mon), which overlooks the seashore on the more easterly of the two roads into the resort. It serves superb seafood, has a terrace bar and even boasts its own swimming pool. A three-course evening meal will set you back about €40, but you can enjoy its excellent lunches for much less.

Camp de Mar

Tucked away among the hills 3km west of Peguera, **CAMP DE MAR** has an expansive beach and fine bathing, though the scene is marred by the presence of two thumping great **hotels** dropped right on the seashore – the *Hotel Playa Camp de Mar*, a British favourite, and the smarter, four-star *Hotel Riu Camp de Mar*, which caters mainly to Germans. Both are modern high-rises equipped with spacious, balconied bedrooms, and both can be booked only through packaging agents – which gives you a clear idea of what this resort is like. Camp de Mar and its surroundings are also in the middle of a massive expansion, with brand-new villa complexes trailing back from the beach in an all-too-familiar semi-suburban sprawl. All the same, the **beach** is an amiable spot to soak up the sun, and it's hard to resist the eccentric café stuck out in the bay and approached via a rickety walkway on stilts; or try the *Bar La Siesta*, overlooking the beach, for romantic sunsets and wonderful paellas.

A minor road twists west from Camp de Mar over wooded hills to **Port d'Andratx** (see p.147).

Travel details

City buses

Palma to: the airport (#1; every 15min; 25min); Cala Major (#3; every 10min; 15min); Gènova (#4; every 20min; 30min); Illetes (#3; every 10min; 20min); S'Arenal (#15; every 10min; 30min). Note: EMT buses stop all over the city centre, but almost all services are routed through Plaça Espanya. For information, call ☎971 21 44 44, or consult ⓦwww.emtpalma.es.

TransaBús services in the Palma area
Palma to: Andratx (hourly; 1hr); Calvià (4–7 daily; 45min); Camp de Mar (hourly; 45min); Magaluf (hourly; 25min); Palma Nova (hourly; 20min); Peguera (hourly; 35min); Port d'Andratx (hourly; 1hr 15min). Note: all TransaBús services depart from the main bus station on c/Eusebi Estada, but most also stop at other points in the city centre. For further details, call ☎971 17 77 77, or check out ⓦtib.caib.es

Island-wide buses

Palma to: Alaró (Mon–Fri 1 daily; 30min); Alcúdia (Mon–Sat every 30min to 1hr, 5 on Sun; 1hr); Artà (Mon–Sat 4 daily, 2 on Sun; 1hr 20min); Banyalbufar (Mon–Sat hourly, 3 on Sun; 1hr); Binissalem (3–6 daily; 20min); Bunyola (Mon–Fri hourly, Sat & Sun every 1–2hr; 20min); Cala d'Or (Mon–Sat 6 daily, 3 on Sun; 1hr 10min); Cala Figuera (Mon–Sat 1–2 daily; 1hr 30min); Cala Millor (Mon–Sat 10 daily, 3 on Sun; 1hr 15min); Cala Rajada (2–6 daily; 1hr 35min); Ca'n Picafort (2–4 daily; 1hr 30min); Colònia de Sant Jordi (Mon–Sat 6 daily, 3 on Sun; 1hr); Coves del Drac (Mon–Sat 4 daily, 1 on Sun; 1hr); Deià (3–5 daily; 45min); Esporles (Mon–Sat hourly, 4 on Sun; 30min); Estellencs (Mon–Sat hourly, 3 on Sun; 1hr 20min); Felanitx (Mon–Sat every 1–2hr, 5 on Sun; 1hr); Formentor (Mon–Sat 1 daily; 1hr 30min); Inca (Mon–Sat hourly, Sat & Sun 3–5 daily; 30min); Galilea (2–4 daily; 45min); La Granja (Mon–Sat hourly, 4 on Sun; 35min); Lluc: train to Inca (see below), then bus from Inca to Lluc (Mon–Fri every 1–2 hours, 1 on Sat & Sun; bus takes 35min); Manacor (Mon–Sat 10 daily, 5 on Sun; 45min); Montuiri (Mon–Sat every 1–2hr, 5 on Sun; 35min); Pollença (Mon–Fri 5 daily, 3 on Sat, 2 on Sun; 1hr 10min); Port d'Alcúdia (Mon–Sat every 30min to 1hr, 5 on Sun; 1hr 15min); Port de Pollença (Mon–Fri 5 daily, 3 on Sat, 2 on Sun; 1hr 15min); Port de Sóller (via the tunnel: Mon–Fri hourly, Sat & Sun every 1–2hr; 35min; via Valldemossa: 3–5 daily; 1hr 30min); Porto Colom (Mon–Sat every 1–2hr, 3 on Sun; 1hr 30min); Porto Cristo (Mon–Sat 9 daily, 3 on Sun; 1hr 10min); Porto Petro

(Mon–Sat 6 daily, 3 on Sun; 1hr 35min); Santanyí (Mon–Sat 6 daily, 3 on Sun; 1hr); Sineu (2–4 daily; 1hr); Sóller ((via the tunnel: Mon–Fri hourly, Sat & Sun every 1–2hr; 30min; via Valldemossa: 3–5 daily; 1hr 15min); Valldemossa (Mon–Fri every 1–2hr, Sat 6 daily, Sun 4 daily; 30min).

Peguera to: Andratx (every 30min; 20min); Banyalbufar (1 weekly; 1hr 15min); Estellencs (1 weekly; 1hr); Port d'Andratx (every 30min; 30min); Valldemossa (1 weekly; 2hr).

Note: all island-wide buses depart from the main bus station on c/Eusebi Estada. For further details, call ☎971 17 77 77, or check out ⊛tib.caib.es.

Trains

Palma to: Binissalem (every 30–40min; 30min); Inca (every 30–40min; 40min); Lloseta (every 30–40min; 35min); Manacor (hourly; 1hr); Muro (hourly; 50min); Petra (hourly; 55min); Sa Pobla (hourly; 1hr); Sineu (hourly; 50min).
Note: For further information, call ☎971 17 77 77, or check out ⊛tib.caib.es.
Palma to: Sóller (7 daily; 1hr).
Note: For further information, call ☎971 75 20 51, ⊛www.trendesoller.com.

2

Western Mallorca

CHAPTER 2 # Highlights

✳ **Sóller** This delightful town boasts handsome stone mansions, a dinky main square and an exquisite setting tucked away amidst craggy mountains – but it's still handy for the odd sandy beach or two. See p.114

✳ **Jardins d'Alfábia** First established by the Moors, these are the finest gardens in Mallorca, with lush trellises and verdant terraces leading to the sweetest of lily-choked pools. See p.122

✳ **Deià** One of Mallorca's most beguiling villages, where a huddle of ancient stone houses are set against a spectacular mountain backdrop. See p.126

✳ **Hiking in the Serra de Tramuntana** Criss-crossed by scores of exhilarating trails, the rugged mountains that range along the length of the island's northwest shore offer the finest hiking in the Balearics. See pp.132–133 and pp.140–141

✳ **Valldemossa Monastery** On the edge of the mountains, the old stone town of Valldemossa zeroes in on its splendid medieval monastery, whose echoing cloisters once sheltered George Sand and Frédéric Chopin. See p.136

✳ **Palma-Sóller train** Ride the antique train over the mountains from Palma to Sóller for a wonderful introduction to the island's varied topographical charms. See p.144

△ Valldemossa

Western Mallorca

Mallorca is at its scenic best in the gnarled ridge of the **Serra de Tramuntana**, the imposing mountain range which stretches the length of the island's northwestern shore, its rearing peaks and plunging seacliffs intermittently punctuated by valleys of olive and citrus groves. Midway along and cramped by the mountains is **Sóller**, an antiquated merchants' town that serves as a charming introduction to the region, especially when reached on the scenic narrow-gauge **train line** from Palma. From Sóller, it's a short hop down to the coast to **Port de Sóller**, a one-time port and fishing village that has become a popular resort set around a deep and handsome bay: this geographical arrangement – the town located a few kilometres inland from its port – is repeated across Mallorca, a reminder of more troubled days when marauding corsairs forced the islanders to live away from the coast. Nearby, the mountain valleys in the vicinity of Sóller were once remote and isolated, but today they shelter the bucolic stone-built villages of **Biniaraix**, **Fornalutx** and **Orient**, from where it's a short haul down to Binissalem (see Chapter 4), perhaps the most interesting town on the island's central plain, Es Pla. Also within easy reach of Sóller are two appealing gardens: the oasis-like **Jardins d'Alfàbia** and the Italianate terraces of **Raixa**, though the latter is closed for a revamp at the time of writing.

Southwest of Sóller, the principal coastal road, the **MA-10**, threads up through the mountains to reach the beguiling village of **Deià**, tucked at the base of formidable cliffs and famous as the former home of Robert Graves. Beyond lies the magnificent Carthusian monastery of **Valldemossa**, whose echoing cloisters briefly accommodated George Sand and Frédéric Chopin during the 1830s, and the *hacienda* of **La Granja**, another compelling if over-visited stop. Continuing southwest, the MA-10 wriggles high above the shoreline, slipping through a sequence of mountain hamlets, of which **Banyalbufar** and **Estellencs** are the most picturesque, their tightly terraced fields tumbling down the coastal cliffs. A few kilometres further and you leave the coast behind, drifting inland out of the mountains and into the foothills that precede the

---

The best Mallorcan **hiking guides** are produced by Editorial Alpina (✆www.editorial alpina.com), who publish three guides at €9 that together cover the whole of the northwest coast – "Mallorca Tramuntana Sud", "Mallorca Tramuntana Central" and "Mallorca Tramuntana Norte". The English-language editions of all three are clearly written and the **maps** (at 1:25,000) are well presented and very detailed, the only problem being one of availability: Sóller tourist office may have copies as may one of the town's bookshops, but it's probably best to get a copy before you leave home.

WESTERN MALLORCA

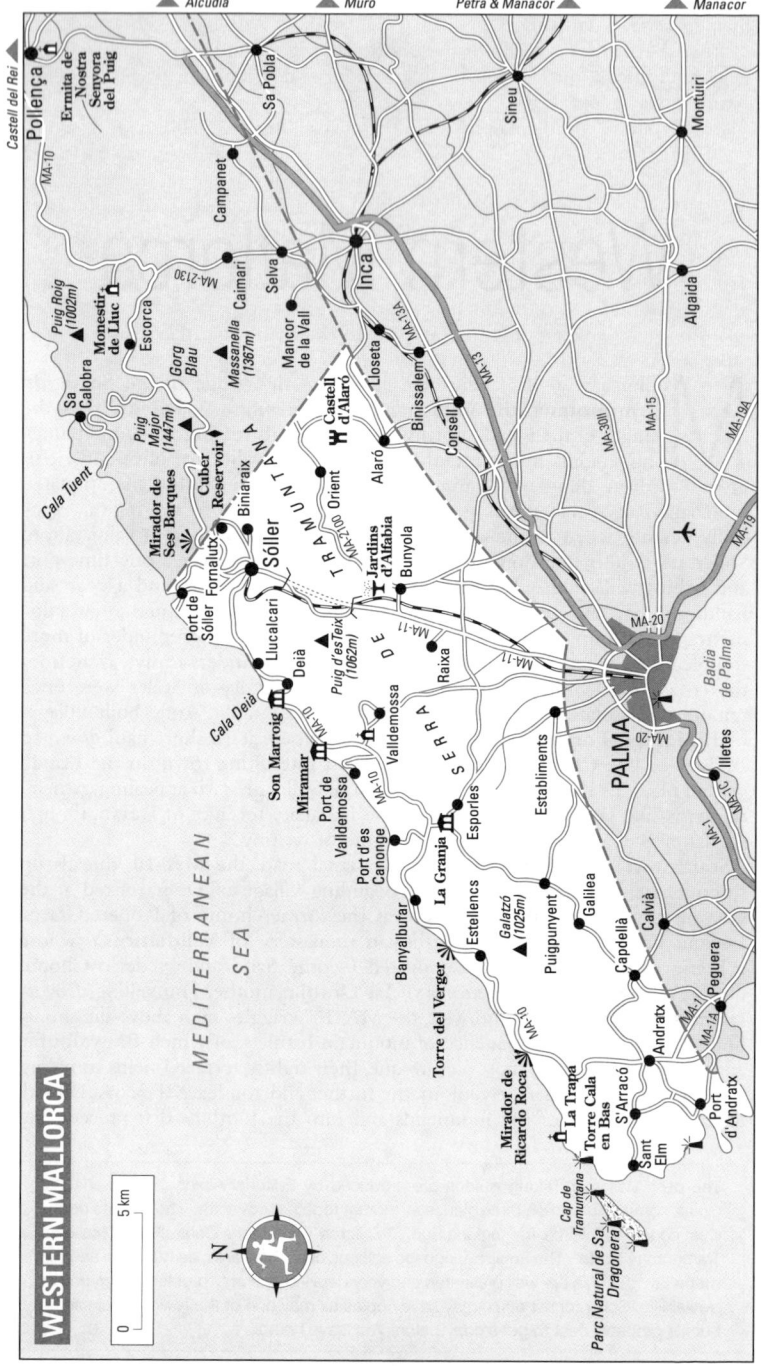

0   5 km

N

Alcúdia   *Muro*   *Petra & Manacor*   *Manacor*

Castell del Rei

Pollença
Ermita de
Nostra
Senyora
del Puig

MA-10

Sa Pobla

Sineu

Montuïri

Campanet

Inca

Algaida

*Puig Roig
(1002m)*

Monestir
de Lluc

Caimari

Selva

MA-2130

Sa
Calobra

Escorca

MA-13A

Mancor
de la Vall

Lloseta

Binissalem

MA-15

MA-3011

*Gorg
Blau*

*Massanella
(1367m)*

Cala Tuent

*Puig
Major
(1447m)*

Cuber
Reservoir

Biniaraix

Castell
d'Alaró

Alaró

Consell

MA-13

MA-19A

Mirador de
Ses Barques

Fornalutx

Sóller

Orient

Jardins
d'Alfàbia

Bunyola

MA-2100

T R A M U N T A N A

Port de
Sóller

Llucalcari

MA-11

MA-11

Badia
de Palma

Deià

*Puig d'es Teix
(1062m)*

Raixa

MA-20

Illetes

Cala Deià

D E

PALMA

MA-20

MA-1C

MA-19

Son Marroig

Miramar

Valldemossa

S E R R A

Establiments

Port de
Valldemossa

MA-10

MA-1

Port d'es
Canonge

La Granja

Esporles

M E D I T E R R A N E A N
S E A

Estellencs

*Galatzó
(1025m)*

Puigpunyent

Galilea

Calvià

Banyalbufar

Capdellà

MA-1A

Peguera

Torre del Verger

MA-10

Andratx

Port
d'Andratx

Mirador de
Ricardo Roca

La Trapa

Torre Cala
en Bas

S'Arracó

Sant
Elm

*Cap de
Tramuntana*

*Parc Natural de Sa
Dragonera*

market town of **Andratx**. Beyond, on Mallorca's western tip, lie the safe waters of **Port d'Andratx**, a medium-sized resort draped around a handsome inlet, its villas announcing the start of the intense tourist development that eats up the coast eastwards to Palma.

The Serra de Tramuntana provides the best walking on Mallorca, with scores of **hiking trails** latticing the mountains. There are trails to suit all aptitudes and all levels of enthusiasm, from the easiest of strolls to the most gruelling of long-distance treks, and generally speaking paths are well marked, though apt to be clogged with thorn bushes. Details of several walks are given in the text, and two day-long hikes, beginning in Valldemossa and Deià, are described in depth. Spring and autumn are the best times to embark on the longer trails; in mid-summer the heat can be enervating and you'll have to haul a large quantity of water around with you. Bear in mind also that the mountains are prone to mists, though they usually lift at some point in the day. For obvious safety reasons, lone mountain walking is not recommended: the dangers are very real at any time of year, and fatalities are not unheard of, often caused by – or related to – heat stroke or dehydration. See the box on p.111 for information on hiking guides.

If you're looking for **beaches**, on the other hand, Port de Sóller has a pleasant sandy strip, but otherwise it's all rock and pebble, though there is compensation in the scenery, wild and wonderful at both **Cala Estellencs** and **Cala Deià**.

Port d'Andratx, Sóller and Port de Sóller have the widest range of **accommodation**, but all the villages in the region have at least a couple of places to stay. Nevertheless, from June to early September (and sometimes beyond), vacancies are extremely thin on the ground and advance reservations are strongly advised. To compensate, distances are small – from Andratx to Sóller via the MA-10 is only about 70km – the roads are good and the **bus** network is adequate to good for most destinations. **Taxis** can work out as a reasonable deal too, especially if you're travelling in a group: the fare for the seventy-kilometre trip from Sóller to Andratx, for instance, is about €60, central Palma to Sóller €30. Take note if you have your own vehicle, that although all the villages along the coast have small car parks, in summer finding a spare lot between about 10am or 11am and 5pm can be problematic, and very frustrating.

Sóller and around

At the end of the train line from Palma lies **Sóller**, one of the most laid-back and enjoyable towns on Mallorca, and an ideal and inexpensive base for exploring the surrounding mountains. Most visitors, though, stick religiously to the coast, taking the rumbling tram on from Sóller down to the popular and amenable seaside resort of **Port de Sóller**, which has the nicest **beach** hereabouts, a horseshoe of sand at the back of the bay, as well as a clutch of good restaurants and budget hotels. However, the best of the region lies just inland. To the northeast, Sóller's mellow mansions fade seamlessly into the orchards and farmland that precede the charming hamlets of **Biniaraix** and **Fornalutx**, both within easy walking distance of town. Further afield, on the landward side of the Serra de Tramuntana, spread the verdant gardens of the **Jardins d'Alfàbia** and the hamlet of **Orient**, on the road to the remote ruins of the **Castell d'Alaró**. Beyond the castle are the attractive little towns of **Alaró** and Binissalem (see p.193), the centre of Mallorca's wine industry and a station on the Palma to Inca and points east train line.

Getting to Sóller and Port de Sóller

Fast and straight, the **MA-11** cuts straight across the island from Palma to Sóller, tunnelling straight through the mountains as it approaches its destination. The twenty-kilometre journey takes about thirty minutes to drive and the **tunnel**, which is 2.7km long, costs €4.15 per car. You can avoid the tunnel – and the toll – by driving over the mountains along a zigzagging minor road, an enjoyable detour with smashing views that adds 7km to the trip. **Cyclists** are not allowed in the tunnel because of vehicle fumes.

There's a frequent direct **bus** service from Palma to Sóller and Port de Sóller via the tunnel; other buses are routed via Valldemossa and Deià. More intermittent bus services run along the main coastal road, the MA-10, from Andratx to Valldemossa, Sóller and Port de Sóller.

The **trains** from Palma to Sóller (see box below) link with the clanking old **trams** that roll their way down to the coast at Port de Sóller, 5km away. The trams, some of which date back to 1912, depart every hour on the hour daily from 7am to 7pm, sometimes later; the fifteen-minute journey costs €3 each way.

Sóller

Rather than any specific sight, it's the general flavour of **SÓLLER** that appeals, with the town's narrow, sloping lanes cramped by eighteenth- and nineteenth-century **stone houses** adorned with fancy grilles and big wooden doors – the former dwellings of the region's rich fruit merchants. A couple of low-key attractions fill out a wander around town, while the picturesque villages of **Biniaraix** and **Fornalutx** are within comfortable walking distance.

Arrival and information

Buses to Sóller pull in beside Plaça Amèrica, on the north side of the town centre, about five minutes' walk from the main square, Plaça Constitució. The **train station** and adjacent **tram terminus** are immediately to the south of the main square. Next to the tram terminus is Sóller **tourist office** (Mon–Fri 9.30am–2pm & 3–5pm, Sat 9.15am–1pm; ☏971 63 80 08, ⓦwww.sollernet .com), which occupies an old train carriage plonked in the middle of Plaça

The train from Palma to Sóller

The 28-kilometre **train** journey from Palma to Sóller is a delight, dipping and cutting through the mountains and fertile valleys of the **Serra de Tramuntana**. The line was completed in 1911 on the profits of the orange and lemon trade: the railway was built to transport the fruit to Palma, at a time when it took a full day to make the trip by road. The rolling stock is tremendously atmospheric too, with narrow carriages – the gauge is only 914mm – that look like they've come out of an Agatha Christie novel.

First the train has to clear the scratchy suburbs of Palma, but within about fifteen minutes it's running across pancake-flat farmland with the impenetrable-looking peaks of the Serra de Tramuntana dead ahead. After clunking through the outskirts of **Bunyola**, the train threads upwards to spend five minutes tunnelling through the mountains, where the noisy engine and dimly lit carriages give the feel of a roller-coaster ride. Beyond, out in the bright mountain air, are the steep valleys and craggy thousand-metre peaks at the heart of the Serra de Tramuntana, and everywhere there are almond groves, vivid with blossom in January and February.

There are six **departures** daily from Palma station throughout the year and the whole ride takes just under an hour. An ordinary one-way **ticket** costs €9, a return €14.

d'Espanya. They issue free town maps, have a comprehensive list of accommodation, and sell a local **hiking guide** entitled "Walking between the Sea and the Mountains" (€8). Note, however, that the maps in the guide aren't very good and, although many of the more popular hikes are well signposted and the text is very detailed, you'd be as well to opt for an Editorial Alpina hiking guide (see p.111) instead: the Sóller tourist office should have copies, but if not you can take pot luck at Libreria Calabruix, a bookshop just off the main square at c/Sa Lluna 7.

Bike rental is also possible in Sóller with *Vivas*, c/Sant Teresa 20 (☎971 63 02 34, ⓦwww.rentabikevivas.com), who charge €9 per day for their more basic mountain bikes, up to €20 for a Racing Alpinestar. A comparable service is provided by *Tramuntana Tours*, c/Sa Lluna 72 (☎971 63 24 23, ⓦwww.tramuntanatours.com), though their main preoccupation is an extensive programme of tours and excursions. They offer mountain-bike tours, fishing trips and an ambitious range of day-long **guided walks** with something to suit most aptitudes. There are, for example, medium-to-difficult guided walks to Alaró Castle (14km) and Valldemossa (16km) and up the Barranc de Biniaraix (16km); a difficult clamber down the Torrent de Pareis gorge (8km); and an easy jaunt round the Sóller valley (11km). Costs vary considerably, but reckon on a minimum of €25 per trip per person. Transport is provided to and from the trailhead as required and the operators will, within reason, collect hikers from where they are staying. If you want a **taxi**, call ☎971 63 84 84.

Leaving Sóller, buses heading both east and west along the coast are often full. To make sure of a seat, you'll need to go down to Port de Sóller, where these services usually originate.

Accommodation

Until a few years ago, there was hardly anywhere to stay in Sóller, but recently the town has mushroomed **hotels** as if there was no tomorrow. Even better, standards are generally high, there's a good chance of finding a vacant room here in high season and prices are very competitive.

Casa Bougainvillea c/Sa Mar 81 ☎971 63 31 04, ⊛www.casa-bougainvillea.com. This enjoyable B&B occupies an old, sympathetically modernized three-storey town house a short walk from Plaça Constitució. There are eight guest rooms here, all en suite, and each is decorated in a pleasingly unfussy style. Weather permitting, breakfast is served in the garden, where guests can idle away their time reading and relaxing. Very competitively priced too, with doubles and twins at €90. ⑤

Casa Margarita c/Reial 3 ☎971 63 42 14, ⊛www.sollernet.com/casamargarita. Pleasant, traditional rooms in an attractive old terraced house close to the train station. Stay at the back (away from the road) if you're a light sleeper. ②

Gran Hotel Sóller c/Romaguera 18 ☎971 63 86 86, ⊛www.granhotelsoller.com. There are four good things about this five-star hotel: the central location, the rooftop café, pool and breakfast bar, the garden, and the building, a grand structure whose *Modernista* flourishes date back to the 1880s – amazingly enough, considering its size, the building started out as a private house. Unfortunately, the interior has been kitted out in a plush but pedestrian modern style and although the guest rooms have every convenience, they hardly stir the imagination. And it is very expensive. ⑨

Hostal S'Ardeviu c/Vives 14 ☎971 63 83 26, ⊛www.sollernet.com/sardeviu. Down a narrow alley, just a stone's throw away from the main square, the S'Ardeviu is a small, family-run *hostal* in an intelligently revamped old mansion. Many of the house's original features have been maintained and the bedrooms are neat and trim. Small double ⑤, large ⑥

🚶 **Hotel Ca'l Bisbe** Bisbe Nadal 10 ☎971 63 12 28, ⊛www.hotelcalbisbe.com. This appealing four-star hotel occupies a sensitively refurbished former bishop's palace, complete with beamed ceilings, pool and garden. Each of the guest rooms is generously appointed with every mod con. ⑥

🚶 **Hotel Ca's Xorc** Ctra Sóller–Deià (MA-10) Km 56.1 ☎971 63 82 80, ⊛www.casxorc. com. Located high in the hills, about 5km west of Sóller along the MA-10, this superb hotel occupies a renovated old olive mill in which each guest room has been decorated in sleek modern style. There's an outside pool and handsome terraced gardens, and the food is simply fabulous, featuring local ingredients and variations on traditional Mallorcan dishes. Reservations essential; closed mid–Nov to Feb. ⑦

🚶 **Hotel El Guía** c/Castanyer 2 ☎971 63 02 27, ⊛www.sollernet.com/elguia. There may be several glossy new hotels in Sóller, but this long-established, two-star, family-run place is hard to beat. Set behind a pretty little courtyard, the hotel's layout and decor are very traditional and although the guest rooms are a tad spartan, they are perfectly adequate. To get there, walk down the steps from the train station platform and turn right. Closed Dec–Feb. ④

Hotel Salvia c/Palma 18 ☎971 63 49 36, ⊛www.hotelsalvia.com. "Leave the madness behind", says the hotel's website rather opaquely, but there's no gainsaying the stately charms of the big old mansion that now accommodates this ritzy, six-room hotel. Each of the bedrooms is large and well appointed, has valley views and is kitted out with antique furniture. No facilities for children under 14. Situated in a quiet side street a five- to ten-minute walk from the train station. April–Oct. ⑧

The Town

All streets lead to the main square, **Plaça Constitució**, an informal, pint-sized affair of big old plane trees, crowded cafés and grouchy mopeds just down the hill from the train station. The square is dominated by the hulking mass of the church of **St Bartomeu** (Mon–Thurs 10.30am–1pm & 2.45–5.15pm, Fri & Sat 10.30am–1pm), a crude but somehow rather fetching neo-Gothic remodelling of a medieval original. Its most appealing features are the enormous and precisely carved rose window stuck high in the main facade and the enormous and apparently pointless balustrade above it. Inside, the cavernous nave is suitably dark and gloomy, the penitential home of a string of gaudy Baroque altarpieces. Next door, the **Banco de Sóller** is a *Modernista* extravagance, sheathed in a coat of roughly dressed stone and adorned by miniature balconies and wrought iron grilles, all the work of Joan Rubiò, a Gaudí acolyte. Rubiò was also responsible for a couple of *Modernista* touches on St Bartomeu and for the flamboyant design of **Can Prunera**, just east of the square at c/Sa Lluna 90. At no. 16 is **Can Prohom**, a grand eighteenth-century mansion where the district's landed gentry used to stay when they came into town. Head down c/Sa Lluna to get to the pretty village of Biniaraix (see below), 2km away to the east.

Back on Plaça Constitució, take c/Bauçà for the five-minute walk west to the house and gardens that comprise the **Museu Balear de Ciències Naturals** (Balearic Museum of Natural Sciences; Tues–Sat 10am–6pm, Sun 10am–2pm; €5; Ⓦ www.jardibotanicdesoller.org). The house, an old merchant's mansion stuck beside the main Palma–Sóller road, has been stripped out to accommodate a series of modest displays with temporary exhibitions on the top floor and the permanent collection on the two floors down below. This **permanent collection** begins with a fairly good section on the leading botanists of yesteryear, including Archduke Ludwig Salvator (see p.134), and continues with an assortment of island fossils and rocks. The labelling is in Catalan, but English leaflets are available at the house's reception desk. Outside, the neat and trim **Jardí Botànic** (same hours) rolls down the hillside divided into thirteen small areas, half of which (M1–M6) are dedicated to Balearic species, including dune and sea-cliff species in M2, shade-loving plants in M4, and mountain plants in M5. A free English-language brochure identifying and illustrating many of the plants is issued at the main gate (for both the house and the gardens).

Eating and drinking

Sóller's main square and its immediate surroundings heave with **cafés** and **café-bars**, but although prices are very reasonable, the quality of the food on offer – with one or two exceptions – is very disappointing. The **restaurant** scene is similarly constrained and although there is one good spot, you may decide to pop down to Port de Sóller (see p.119) for a bite to eat instead.

 Àtico c/Romaguera 18. The rooftop café of the Gran Hotel offers great views over the town centre as well as tasty snacks (€12 and up) from a lively Spanish menu. The *menú del día* is a particularly good deal here at just €17.

Bar Es Firo Plaça Constitució 10B. Small and old-fashioned locals' café-bar that's at its most authentic early in the morning.

Bar Turismo Avgda d'es Born 8. By the tram lines just up from Plaça Constitució, this convivial little bar is an amenable spot to nurse a drink – and a good place for a freshly baked *ensaimada* early in the morning.

 Don Cipriani Gran Via 43 ☎971 63 30 49. Arguably the best restaurant in town, this attractively decorated Italian place specialises in home-made pastas and pizzas with main courses averaging around €16. Tues–Sun noon–3.30pm & 7.30–11pm.

Restaurant El Guía c/Castanyer 2 ☎971 63 02 27. In the hotel of the same name, this trim little restaurant sticks to Mallorcan dishes, which it does very well. Mains from around €15. Closed Mondays, plus limited opening hours Nov–March.

Sa Cova Plaça Constitució 7. Squeezed into a corner of the main square, this easygoing café-restaurant offers a wide variety of tapas and full meals, with main courses from €12. Closed Sun eve.

East of Sóller: Biniaraix and Fornalutx

Following c/Sa Lluna east from Sóller's main square, it takes about half-an-hour to stroll to the village of **BINIARAIX**, passing orchards and farmland criss-crossed with ancient irrigation channels and dry-stone walls. The village, nestled in the foothills of the Serra de Tramuntana, is tiny – just a cluster of old stone houses surrounding a dilapidated church and the smallest of central squares – but it is extraordinarily pretty. It is also a useful starting point for **hiking** into the surrounding mountains, the most popular route being the stiff but particularly scenic, two-hour haul up to the L'Ofre farmhouse at the top of the **Barranc de Biniaraix**, a beautiful ravine of terraced citrus groves set in the shadow of the mountains. To get to the Biniaraix **trailhead**, walk uphill from the square along c/Sant Josep. After about 200m you'll reach a spring and cattle trough, where a sign offers a choice of hiking trails, including the one up the *barranc*.

Sections of the trail up the *barranc* use the old **cobbled roadway** that was once part of the pilgrims' route between Sóller and the monastery at Lluc (see p.157). Built in the fifteenth century, the roadway's maintenance proved a real headache for a long line of bishops: sometimes they had to threaten the peasantry with fines to keep the road in good order, sometimes they offered indulgences, but the snail hunters who regularly broke down the retaining walls to collect the gastropods for eating, proved indifferent to both. At the top of the ravine, you can extend your walk by clambering west up to the **Es Cornadors** viewpoint – allow 45 minutes each way – or by heading northeast to the Cúber reservoir (see p.156), a comparatively easy walk across even ground – allow about two hours. Otherwise, you'll have to return the way you came.

Fornalutx

Good-looking **FORNALUTX**, a couple of kilometres northeast of Biniaraix along a narrow, signposted country lane, is often touted as the most attractive village on Mallorca, and it certainly has a superb location. Orange and lemon groves scent the valley as it tapers up towards the settlement, whose honey-coloured stone houses huddle against a mountainous backdrop. Matching its setting, the quaint centre of Fornalutx fans out from the minuscule main square, its narrow cobbled streets stepped to facilitate mule traffic, though nowadays you're more likely to be hit by a Mercedes than obstructed by a mule: foreigners love the place and own about half of the village's four hundred houses. This sizeable expatriate community sustains several **restaurants**, most memorably the homely *Es Turó* (☎971 63 08 08; closed Thurs), which offers good-quality Mallorcan cuisine at very reasonable prices – a full meal, including wine, costs about €20. The restaurant has a pleasant outside terrace with valley views and is located just a couple of minutes' walk uphill from the main square (and away from Sóller). It's fine just to have a drink here too, and there are also a couple of small cafés on the main square.

As for **accommodation**, Fornalutx has three smart and appealing hotels, kicking off with the charming *Fornalutx Petit Hotel*, c/Alba 22 (☎971 63 19 97, ⓦwww.fornalutxpetithotel.com; ❻), which occupies an attractively furnished and spotlessly clean old stone house with a terraced garden and pool overlooking the orchards behind. Reservations are essential here and at the neighbouring – and very similar – *Ca'n Reus*, c/Alba 26 (☎971 63 1174, ⓦwww.canreushotel.com; ❻), though the chic-rustic decor here is a tad more self-conscious. To get to c/Alba, walk down the main street from the square (back towards Sóller) and take the first left just beyond the conspicuous railings – a minute's stroll. The third hotel, the *C'an Verdera*, at c/des Toros 1 (☎971 63 82 03, ⓦwww.canverdera.com; ❼), is the plushest of the lot, its stylish modernity shoehorned into an old stone building amongst the side streets immediately to the west of the main square; the hotel is small, but it does have a garden, terrace and outside pool.

If you're heading back to Sóller, there's a limited **bus** service from Fornalutx and Biniaraix (Mon–Sat 4 daily, Sun 2 daily; 10min/5min) or you can take a

taxi – the fare from Fornalutx to Sóller is about €10. If you can't see one hanging around, call ☎971 63 84 84.

Port de Sóller

PORT DE SÓLLER is one of the most popular spots on the west coast, and its handsome, horseshoe-shaped bay, ringed by forested hills, must be one of the most photographed places on the island after the package resorts around Palma. The high jinks of the Badía de Palma are, however, a world away from this low-key, family-oriented resort, grafted onto an old fishing port and naval base. Attractions here include two pleasant strips of **beach** with generally clean and clear water, plus a wide selection of restaurants. It's also worth making the enjoyable hour-long hike west to the **lighthouse** (*far*) guarding the cliffs of Cap Gros above the entrance to its inlet. From here, the views out over the wild and rocky coast and back across the harbour are truly magnificent, especially at sunset. There's a surfaced road all the way: from the tram terminus, walk round the southern side of the bay past Platja d'en Repic and keep going, following the signs.

Arrival and information

Trams from Sóller shadow the main road and clank to a stop beside the jetties bang in the centre of town. From here, it's a couple of minutes' walk east to the **tourist office**, located beside the church on c/Canonge Oliver 10 (Mon–Fri 9.30am–1pm & 3–6.30pm, Sat 10am–1pm; ☎971 63 30 42, Ⓦwww.sollernet .com). They carry a reasonable range of local information, including restaurant and accommodation lists, maps and boat-trip details. **Buses** stop outside the tourist office.

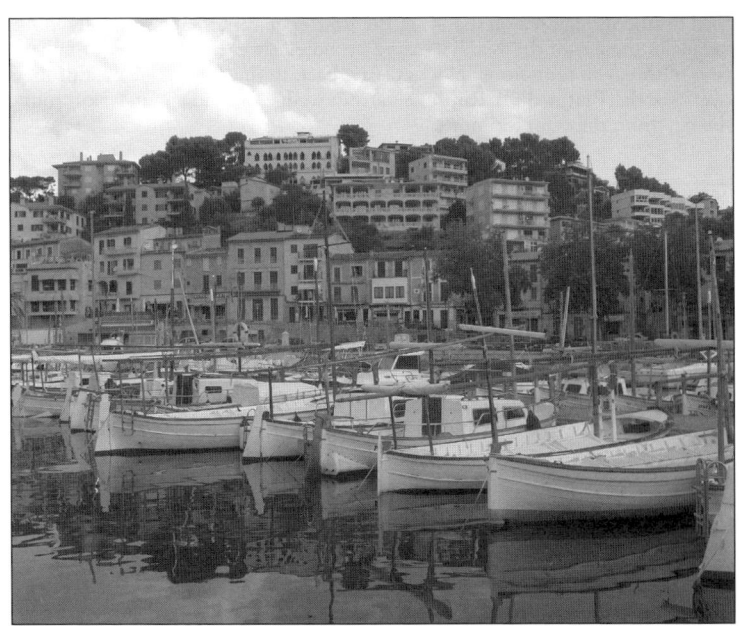

△ Port de Sóller

Sa Fira i Es Firó

If you're around Sóller and Port de Sóller in the second week of May, be sure to catch the **Sa Fira i Es Firó**, which commemorates the events of May 1561 when a large force of Arab pirates came to a sticky end after sacking Sóller. The Mallorcans had been taken by surprise, but they ambushed and massacred the Arabs as they returned to their ships and took grisly revenge by planting the raiders' heads on stakes. The story – bar decapitations – is played out in chaotic, alcoholic fashion every year at the festival. The re-enactment begins with the arrival of the pirates by boat, and continues with fancy-dress Christians and Arabs battling it out through the streets of the port, to the sound of blanks being fired in the air from antique rifles. On the days preceding this knees-up, there are also sporting and cultural events as well as a large, open-air market. The tourist office can give you a rough idea of the schedule of events, plus details of the dances and parties that follow.

In summer, **boats** leave the dock by the tram terminus for day trips along the coast. The two main operators are Barcos Azules (☎971 63 01 70, ⌨www.barcosazules.com) and Tramontana Cruceros (☎971 63 31 09, ⌨www.tramontanacruceros.com), whose boats travel **northeast** to Cala Tuent (May–June & Sept–Oct Mon–Fri 1 daily; €11), Sa Calobra (May–Oct 3 daily; €20) and Formentor (June–Aug 1 weekly; €18); and **southwest** to Sa Foradada (May–Oct 1 weekly; €10) and Sant Elm (May–Oct 1 weekly; €20). Cala Tuent (see p.156) is the most diverting of these destinations, though each trip is in itself a good way of seeing a chunk of coast.

Accommodation

Most of the port's hotels and *hostals* overlook the bay and although **rooms** are hard to find in high season thanks to the tour operators, there are usually lots of vacancies the rest of the year. There are no hotel tower blocks here, but rather a ring of three- to four-storey blocks dating back to the 1960s. The pick of these overlook the **Platja d'en Repic**, a narrow wedge of sand about 1.5km round the bay from the tram terminus.

Hotel Eden c/Lepanto 2 ☎971 63 16 00, ⓦwww.
hoteleden.com. Mainstream, family-oriented
hotel in two adjacent blocks, with large pools and
comfortable facilities. ⑤

🏃 **Hotel Es Port** c/Antoni Montis s/n ☎971
63 16 50, ⓦwww.hotelesport.com. Arguably the best and certainly the most distinctive
hotel in the port, this three-star establishment
occupies a fortified country house that dates back
to the seventeenth century. The interior displays
many original features and the guest rooms are
generally commodious and well appointed with
traditional furnishings and fittings, though some
are in the modern – and less appealing – annexe.
The hotel sits in its own lush gardens at the back
of the port, a few minutes' walk from the waterfront, and there's an expansive outside swimming
pool. ⑤

Hotel Generoso c/Marina 4 ☎971 63 14 50,
ⓦwww.hotelgeneroso.com. Routine modern block
near the tram terminus with a hundred or so
recently revamped guest rooms kitted out in brisk
modern style. ⑤

Hotel Los Geranios Passeig de Sa Platja 15
☎971 63 14 40, ⓦwww.hotel-losgeranios.com.
Straightforward one-star seafront hotel overlooking
the Platja d'en Repic, with twenty-odd rooms on
four floors, mostly with sea views. ⑥

Hotel Marina Passeig de Sa Platja 3 ☎971 63
14 61, ⓦwww.hotelmarinasoller.com. Pleasant
two-star hotel overlooking the Platja d'en Repic.
The rooms are pretty characterless, decorated in
plain chain style, but they are perfectly adequate,
competitively priced and most have bayside balconies. Closed mid-Nov to mid-Jan. ④

Hotel Miramar c/Marina 12 ☎971 63 13 50,
ⓦwww.solleronline.com/hotelmiramar. A standard-
issue modern block overlooking the bay from near
the tram terminus and with just thirty functional
rooms. ④

Eating and drinking

Port de Sóller heaves with **cafés** and **restaurants**, but standards are very variable: some serve up mediocre food with the package tourist in mind, others
are more authentically *Mallorquín* – or at least Spanish. The majority are dotted
along the bayshore, though there are a few more amongst the port's side streets
and a couple of excellent places behind the Platja d'en Repic.

Restaurant-bar Agapanto Camí Far 2 ☎971 63
38 60, ⓦwww.agapanto.com. At the west end of
Platja d'en Repic, beside the seashore at the start
of the road up to the lighthouse, the *Agapanto* is
a flashy, shaded, very modish bar and restaurant
dabbling in fusion food with "ambient" sounds to
match. Vegetarian main courses, of which there is
a good range, start at €13, a few euros more for
the meat and fish. Also offers live music from salsa
through to jazz. Daily except Wed noon–4.30pm &
6.30pm–midnight.

Restaurant Embat c/Església 8 ☎971 63 49
71. This quiet, low-key restaurant, tucked away
on a side street just off the waterfront, focuses
on seafood with carefully prepared main courses
averaging about €12. Daily except Wed & Sun
12.30–4pm & 7.30–9.30pm.

Restaurant Es Canyís Passeig de Sa Platja 32
☎971 63 14 06. Bright and cheerful bistro-style
restaurant offering a good range of Spanish dishes
from its bayshore premises behind the Platja
d'en Repic. The snails are a house speciality.
Main courses average €14. Tues–Sun 1–4pm &
8–11pm.

🏃 **Restaurant Es Faro** Cap Gros ☎971 63 37
52. Set in a wonderful location, high up on
the cliffs at the entrance to the harbour, this well-
known restaurant offers spectacular views from its
outside terrace. During the day, the *Es Faro* serves
up coffees, light meals and an excellent *menú del
día* and at night it's à la carte with the seafood
being much favoured. Mains from €20. An easy
1.7km drive – or stiff walk – up from Platja d'en
Repic. Reservations strongly recommended in the
evening. Open March–Sept daily 11am to midnight,
Oct–Feb daily 10am–5pm & 7–10pm, though out of
season they sometimes close on one day a week.

🏃 **S'Àtic** On the top floor of the *Hotel Los
Geranios*, Passeig de Sa Platja 15 ☎971
63 81 13. Elegantly understated establishment,
with views over the bay and outstanding nouvelle
Mediterranean-meets-Mallorcan cuisine. Mains
from €20. Tues 7.30–10.30pm & Wed–Sun
1.30–3.30pm & 7.30–10.30pm.

South of Sóller: to the Jardins d'Alfàbia and Raixa

Heading south from Sóller, the main road to Palma tunnels through the Serra de
Tramuntana, but there is an alternative, much more scenic route along a minor

road that hairpins up and over the mountains, threading its way past the **Coll de Sóller**, a rocky pass with a lookout point offering splendid views out over the coast. Whichever route you choose, be sure to drop by the **Jardins d'Alfàbia**, lush and beautiful terraced gardens to be found a few metres from the south end of the tunnel (April–Sept Mon–Sat 9.30am–6.30pm; Oct–March Mon–Fri 9.30am–5pm & Sat 9.30am–1pm; €4.50). Shortly after the Reconquista, Jaume I granted the estate of Alfàbia to a prominent Moor by the name of Benhabet. Seeing which way the historical wind was blowing, Benhabet, as governor of Pollença, had given his support to Jaume, provisioning the Catalan army during the invasion. There was no way Jaume I could leave his Moorish ally in charge of Pollença (and anyway it was already pledged to a Catalan noble), but he was able to reward him with this generous portion of land. Benhabet planned his new estate in the Moorish manner, channelling water from the surrounding mountains to irrigate the fields and fashion oasis-like gardens. Generations of island gentry added to the estate without marring the integrity of Benhabet's original design, thus creating the lovely gardens of today.

From the roadside, you follow a stately avenue of plane trees towards the gatehouse. In front of the gatehouse is the ticket office and a sign that directs visitors up a wide flight of stone steps and into the **gardens**, where the footpath leads past ancient stone walls, ivy-covered columns, gurgling watercourses and brightly coloured flowers cascading over narrow terraces. Trellises of jasmine and wisteria create patterns of light and shade and there's even a visitor-operated water feature – press the button and retire. At the end of the path is a verdant jungle of palm trees, bamboo and bullrushes tangling a tiny pool choked with water lilies. It's an enchanting spot, especially on a hot summer's day, and an outdoor **bar** (usually) sells big glasses of freshly squeezed orange juice – a snip at just €2.

A few paces away is the **house**, a rather routine, veranda'd *hacienda* whose handful of rooms contain an eccentric mix of antiques and curios. Pride of place goes to a superb **oak chair** adorned with delightful bas-relief scenes depicting the story of Tristan and Isolde. There were several versions of this well-known medieval tale, but the one on the chair is all about jealousy: on the front the two protagonists are shown playing chess, an innocent enough pastime, but one that stirs the jealousy of Isolde's husband the king, whose head appears in the tree on the back of the chair peering down at the two of them as they walk in the garden. The chair has been in the house for centuries and local legend asserts that the uncrowned Jaume IV ordered it, but never had the chance to take possession. Jaume was captured – and his father, King Jaume III, killed – by the Aragonese at the battle of Llucmajor in 1349, and the younger Jaume spent the rest of his days in exile. Unfortunately, it's all poppycock as the chair was actually made in the fifteenth century in Flanders.

At the front of the house, the cobbled **courtyard** is shaded by a giant plane tree and surrounded by good-looking, rustic outbuildings. Beyond lies the **gatehouse**, an imposing structure sheltering a fine coffered ceiling of Mudéjar design, with an inscription praising Allah.

Raixa

Pressing on south from the Jardins d'Alfàbia, along the MA-11, it's about 5km to the short gravel lane that leads west to **Raixa**, the one-time country estate of the eighteenth-century antiquarian Cardinal Antonio Despuig (whose collection of classical sculpture can be seen in Palma – see pp.90–91). The cardinal carved a sequence of terraced **gardens** out of the hill beside his country home and then proceeded to decorate them with Neoclassical statues, water fountains and even bits of old masonry recovered from medieval buildings in Palma – all in the fashionable Italian style of his day. Despuig saw himself as a leading light of the Enlightenment, but underneath the cultured cassock was a medieval piety: he died in Italy and on his deathbed he left instructions for his heart to be cut out and buried close to the body of Mallorca's favourite saint, Catalina Thomàs (see p.139). At the time of writing, the manor house and the gardens are being refurbished, but should be open again in 2008.

The sign to Raixa is easy to miss: travelling south from Sóller, if you reach the traffic island at the junction of the MA-11 and the MA-1140/MA2030, you've gone too far. Double back and the Raixa turning is about 500m to the north.

Southeast of Sóller: to Orient and Alaró

In between Alfàbia and Raixa, a country road (the MA-2010 and then the MA-2100) forks east off the MA-11, looping past the sun-bleached walls of the unremarkable market town of **BUNYOLA** before snaking across the forested foothills of the Serra de Tramuntana. It's a beautiful drive (though some of the bends are nerve-jangling), and after about 12km you reach **ORIENT**, a tiny hamlet of ancient houses scattered along the edge of the Vall d'Orient, a valley where hills crimp and crowd olive and almond groves. The main part of the village slopes up the hill from the road and at the top is a dinky little parish **church** named in honour of Sant Jordi (St George), whose effigy cuts a striking pose on the high altar. For most of its history, Orient was as poor as it was remote, but tourism has transformed the place and now the locals, who only number about thirty, share their bucolic retreat with second-home owners and no less than three smart, rural-chic hotels.

The most engaging **hotel** in Orient is the four-star *Hotel Muntanya* (T971 61 53 73, Wwww.daltmuntanya.net; ⑥; closed Nov–Jan), which occupies a sympathetically remodelled old house with eighteen individually styled bedrooms, many of which have mountain views. Its two rivals are the recently renovated *Agroturismo Son Palou*, in the big old mansion next to the church (T971 14 82 82 Wwww.sonpalou.com; ⑥), and *Hotel L'Hermitage*, located about 1km east of Orient on the MA-2100 (T971 18 03 03, Wwww.hermitage-hotel.com; closed Dec to mid–Feb; ⑦); *L'Hermitage* has 24 immaculate rooms – four in the original medieval monastery and twenty in the surrounding chalets. As you would expect, all three hotels have a full range of facilities, including gardens and outside pools and two of them – the *Muntanya* and *L'Hermitage* – have their own **restaurants**. The restaurant at the *L'Hermitage* is generally reckoned to be the more accomplished of the two, a fairly formal affair with a mammoth antique olive press as its centrepiece; the menu, which features local ingredients, is international with a predisposition to Mediterranean dishes and main courses start at around €20. The *Muntanya* restaurant is much more relaxed, spreading out over an outside terrace and concentrating on traditional Mallorcan cuisine – try the rabbit.

There are two **buses** daily from Bunyola to Orient and the journey takes thirty minutes, but there are no buses between Orient and Alaró (see p.124).

The Castell d'Alaró

Beyond Orient, the MA-2100 edges along the narrow valley of the Torrent d'en Paragon for around 3km, before veering south to slip between a pair of molar-like hills whose bare rocky flanks tower above the surrounding forest and scrub. The more westerly of the two sports the sparse ruins of the **Castell**

d'Alaró, originally a Moorish stronghold but rebuilt by Jaume I. Visible for miles around, the castle looks impregnable on its lofty perch, and it certainly impeded the Aragonese invasion of 1285; when an Aragonese messenger suggested terms for surrender, the garrison's dual commanders responded by calling the Aragonese king Alfonso III "fish-face", punning on his name in Catalan (*anfos* means "perch"). When the castle finally fell, Alfonso had the two roasted alive – goodness knows what he'd have done if they'd called him something really rude.

Access to the castle is from the south: coming from Orient, watch for the signposted right turn just beyond the Kilometre 18 stone marker. The first 3km of this side road are bumpy and narrow but reasonably easy, whereas the last 1.3km is gravel and dirt, with a perilously tight series of hairpins negotiating a very steep hillside – especially hazardous after rain. The road emerges at a car park and an old ramshackle farmstead, whose barn now holds the *Es Verger* **restaurant** (closed Mon, but otherwise opening hours vary – best to check on ☎971 18 21 26). It's tempting to linger here: the views down over the plain are sumptuous and the food delicious, particularly the house speciality, oven-baked lamb. From the restaurant, you can also spy the ruins of the castle above, about an hour and a half's walk away along a clearly marked track. The trail leads to the castle's stone gateway, beyond which lies an expansive wooded plateau accommodating the fragmentary ruins of the fortress, plus the tiny pilgrims' church of **Mare de Déu del Refugi**. There's a simple restaurant and bar up here too, serving traditional Mallorcan food: the *pa amb oli* is a snip at under €5.

Alaró

Back on the MA-2100, it's about 1.5km south from the castle turn-off to the town of **ALARÓ**, a sleepy little place of old stone houses fanning out from an attractive main square, **Plaça Vila**. A long and elegant arcaded gallery flanks one side of the square, and a second is shadowed by the **church**, a fortress-like, medieval affair whose honey-coloured sandstone is embellished with Baroque details. The town was once at the centre of the trade between the mountains and the plain, with farm produce going one way, animal skins and charcoal the other, but it really hit the headlines in 1901 when it became the first place on the island to install electric street lighting – even ahead of Palma, much to the chagrin of that city's ruling council.

Nowadays, Alaró's main square holds several cafés and **restaurants**, where local families gather on the weekend. The pick of the bunch is *Es Traffic*, at no. 8 (☎971 87 91 17; closed Tues), which serves up Mallorcan specialities – notably casseroles – in a pleasantly renovated old mansion with a wood-beamed ceiling or in the spacious garden out the back. There's no overly compelling reason to overnight here, but the town does have a good-quality **hotel**, the *Can Xim* (☎971 87 91 17, ⓦwww.canxim.com; ⊚), in an old stone building on the main square and with eight pleasantly modern double rooms.

Just south of Alaró, you leave the foothills of the Serra de Tramuntana behind and slip down onto the central plain, Es Pla, where the nearest target is **Binissalem** (see p.193), an intriguing country town at the centre of the island's wine industry and home to *Scott's* (see p.196), arguably the island's most enjoyable hotel.

On weekdays, there is one **bus** daily direct from Palma to Alaró, though you can also take the train from Palma to Binissalem and get a taxi on from there, about a ten-minute drive.

Deià to Port d'Andratx

The western reaches of the **Serra de Tramuntana** rise out of the flatlands around Palma, with the range's forested foothills and sheltered valleys soon giving way to the craggy, wooded mountains that crimp most of the **southwest coast**. Several fast roads link Palma with the coast – the prettiest runs to Valldemossa – and a delightful network of country roads pattern the foothills, but the key sights and the best scenery are most readily reached along the main coastal road, the **MA-10**.

West of Sóller, the MA-10 skirts the broad and wooded slopes of the Puig d'es Teix to reach **Deià**, an ancient mountain village which perches on the steep terraced slopes above the seashore, clinging to the fame brought by its association with the writer **Robert Graves**, whose former house has recently been opened to the public. The next 20km of coastline boasts four of Mallorca's star attractions, allied to some of its finest coastal scenery: **Son Marroig** and **Miramar**, two complementary mansions once owned by a Mallorca-loving Habsburg, Archduke Ludwig Salvator; the hilltop monastery of **Valldemossa**, complete with its echoing cloisters and choice examples of modern art; and the old grandee's mansion and estate of **La Granja**. This captivating quartet is hard to beat, although the tiered hamlets that decorate the coast further down the road are also instantly beguiling. Of these, both **Banyalbufar** and **Estellencs** occupy fine sites and are well worth at least a fleeting visit, probably more. Alternatively, you can travel inland from La Granja, climbing the slopes of the leafy foothills and rambling through secluded valleys of almond, olive and carob trees to reach the charming village of **Galilea**. Both the Galilea route and the MA-10 coast road emerge from the Serra de Tramuntana at **Andratx**, a crossroads town with easy access to the tiny port and often underestimated mini-resort of **Sant Elm**, where you can hike out into the mountains or catch the passenger boat over to the **Sa Dragonera**, the humpy island nature reserve that lies just offshore. Andratx is also within easy striking distance of the more commercialized harbour-cum-resort of **Port d'Andratx**, long a popular holiday spot for Germans and Brits alike.

Beach lovers have meagre pickings in this part of the island. There's a good sandy beach with safe swimming at Sant Elm, but further up the coast, shingle strips will have to suffice. The most impressive of these is **Cala Deià**, set beneath the mountains at the end of a narrow ravine. **Accommodation** can be hard to find, too. Each of the destinations mentioned above has at least a couple of places to stay, but you're strongly advised to book well ahead if you're visiting between June and September or even October. Deià and Port d'Andratx have the widest choice of hotels and *hostals*, and so represent the best bets for a last-minute vacancy, with Sant Elm, Valldemossa and Banyalbufar the runners up.

Getting around

There is a regular **bus** service from Palma to Port de Sóller via Valldemossa, Miramar, Son Marroig, Deià and Sóller, and another from Palma to Esporles, La Granja, Banyalbufar and Estellencs. There are also fast and frequent buses from Palma to Andratx and Port d'Andratx, a regular service from Andratx to Sant Elm and a daily if more infrequent bus service from Palma to Galilea. The only major gap is along the MA-10 coast road between Estellencs and Andratx, where you're limited to the once weekly bus linking Peguera, Andratx, Estellencs, Banyalbufar and Valldemossa. For frequencies and journey times, see p.149.

Distances between destinations are short, so **taxis** can work out a reasonable proposition if you're in a group: the fare for the thirteen-kilometre trip from Port de Sóller to Deià, for example, is just €20.

Deià

DEIÀ, 10km west of Sóller, is beautiful. The mighty Puig d'es Teix (1062m) meets the coast here, and, although the mountain's lower slopes are gentrified by the villas of the well-heeled and well-to-do, it retains a formidable, almost mysterious presence, especially in the shadows of a moonlit night. Deià's long main street, Arxiduc Lluis Salvador, which doubles as the coastal highway (MA-10), skirts the base of the Teix and shows off the bulk of the village's hotels and restaurants to fine advantage.

At times, Deià's main drag is too congested to be much fun, but the tiny heart of the village, tumbling over a high and narrow ridge on the seaward side of the road, still retains a surprising tranquillity. Labyrinthine alleys of old peasant houses curl up to a pretty **parish church**, in the precincts of which is buried **Robert Graves**, the village's most famous resident – his headstone marked simply "Robert Graves: Poeta, E.P.D." (*En Paz Descanse*, "Rest In Peace"). From the graveyard, there are memorable views out over the coast and of the Teix, with banks of carefully terraced fields tumbling down from the mountain towards the sea. The church itself is unremarkable, but one of its outbuildings does hold a modest **museum** (Sat 9am–7pm; €2), which possesses a folksy assortment of religious bric-a-brac.

Arrival, and information

Buses from points east and west along the coast scoot through Deià at regular intervals, travelling along the main drag, which doubles as the coastal highway, the MA-10. The main **bus stop** is towards the east end of the village. There's no tourist information office as such, but most if not all of the hotels and pensions will gladly provide advice on local walks, have bus timetables and will supply a free copy of the locally produced *Deià Pocket Guide*, which details almost everything you could possibly want to know; there are also two useful websites, ⓦdeia.info and ⓦwww.deia-mallorca.com. For a **taxi**, call ☎609 38 61 68. It takes about fifteen minutes to walk from one end of the village to the other along the main street.

Deià is the haunt of long-term expatriates, including a small army of writers and artists, who help give credibility to a several prestigious festivals, most notably the **Festival de Deià** (☎971 63 91 78, ⓦwww.soundpost.org) whose classical music concerts begin in April and end in September.

Accommodation

Deià boasts two of the most luxurious **hotels** on the island as well as a handful of delightful, less expensive places. There's a reasonable chance of finding a room on spec at any time of the year, but you're really much better off making a reservation at least a day or two in advance.

Hostal Villa Verde c/Ramón Llull 19 ☎971 63 90 37, ⓦwwww.hostalvillaverde.com. Perhaps not the friendliest of places, this ten-room *hostal* does have a great location, glued to the side of a hill in between the main road and the church. The rooms are clean and simple and guests gather on the shaded terrace facing Puig d'es Teix. ❹

Hotel Costa d'Or 2km east along the MA-10 coast road at the hamlet of Llucalcari ☎971 63 90 25, ⓦwww.hoposa.es. This splendid four-star hotel occupies a wonderful setting, overlooking an undeveloped slice of coast and surrounded by pine groves and olive terraces. There's a shaded terrace bar and a splendid outdoor swimming pool. The rooms are kitted out in slick, modern style and the best look out over the ocean. Closed Nov–March. ❼

Hotel Es Molí Carretera Deià-Valldemossa s/n ☎971 63 90 00, ⓦwww.esmoli.com. This long-established, four-star hotel has an excellent reputation which is fully deserved. The main building is graced by arcaded galleries in the Spanish style. Inside, the public areas are smart, modern and roomy and are used to exhibit the work of local artists. All ninety well-appointed, air-conditioned bedrooms are tastefully decorated; most have a balcony and many have wide coastal views. Amenities include gorgeous terraced gardens, an outside pool, charming breakfast terrace and a minibus to take guests to the hotel's own (rocky) beach, a twenty-minute drive to the east. Closed Nov to March. ❽

Hotel d'es Puig c/Es Puig 4 ☎971 63 94 09, ⓦwww.hoteldespuig.com. A smart and tastefully furnished hotel with eight bedrooms in an elegantly converted, four-storey old stone house located in the centre of the village, between the MA-10 and the church. Pay a few euros more for a room with a balcony. Closed Jan. ❻

Hotel La Residencia c/Son Canais s/n ☎971 63 90 11, ⓦwww.hotel-laresidencia.com. Models and nannies, big cars and flash clothes are the order of the day here in what must be Mallorca's most self-conscious hotel. The decor is minimalist-meets-rustic Mallorca and the hotel itself is an extrapolation of two old stone manor houses. It overlooks the main drag at the east end of the village. Facilities abound – pools, bars, restaurants, tennis court, a spa and so on and so forth. ❾

Hotel Sa Pedrissa Carretera Deià-Valldemossa s/n ☎971 63 91 11, ⓦwww.sapedrissa.com. This new hotel, about 2km west of Deià on the MA-10 coastal road, occupies an immaculately revamped old stone farmhouse which, along with its assorted outhouses, perches high above – and has wide views over – the coast. Stone and marble floors, exposed wooden beams and oodles of white paint set the tone, there's a terrace pool and each of the nine bedrooms is impeccably turned out. ❽ or ❾

Pensión Miramar c/Ca'n Oliver s/n ☎971 63 90 84, ⓦwww.pensionmiramar.com. You don't get many good deals in Deià, but this is one of them – a family-run pension in an old and traditional stone finca perched high above (and signposted from) the main road about halfway through the village. There are nine spartan but entirely adequate rooms here – some en suite, some with shared facilities – and the views over the village from the courtyard in front of the house are absolutely stunning. On foot, it takes about ten minutes to walk up from the main road. Closed Dec–Feb. ❹

The Robert Graves house – Ca N'Alluny

Graves put Deià on the international map and his old home, **Ca N' Alluny** (Tues–Sun 10am–5pm; €5; timed visits by advance reservation on

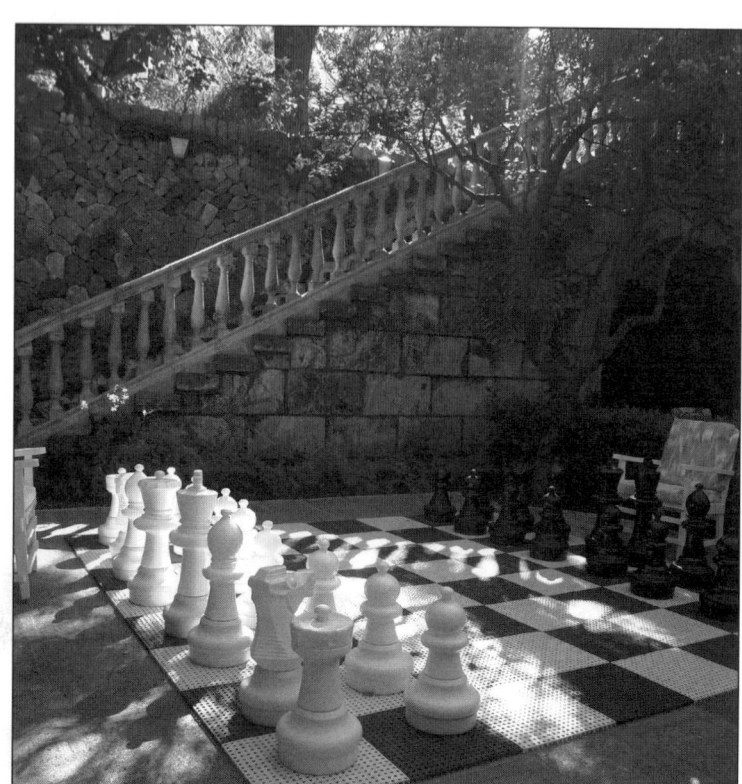

△ *Hotel Es Molí* gardens

☎971 63 61 85, Ⓦwww.fundaciorobertgraves.com), a substantial stone building beside the main road about 500m east of the village, was opened to the public in 2006. For the most part, the house has been returned to its 1940s appearance and is adorned with Graves's own furnishings and fittings. A visit begins with a short film on the author's life and times and then come the period rooms. The study, where Graves produced much of his finest work, is of particular interest. Beyond is an exhibition room, with yet more biographical information and old photographs and manuscripts, and then it's on into the garden, where there are olive, carob, fruit and almond trees plus a small open-air theatre, where Graves and his chums were wont to read their poetry. For more information on Robert Graves see the box on p.129.

Deià Archeological Museum

Deià's other specific sight, its **Archeological Museum** (Tues, Thurs & Sun 4–6pm; free; times may vary, confirm on ☎971 63 90 01), is hidden away in the wooded ravine below and between the old centre of the village and the *Hotel Es Molí* up on the main road. The archeologists William and Jacqueline Waldren founded the museum in 1962 to display the items they had retrieved from a number of local prehistoric sites. In particular, the couple had just hit the archeological headlines with their investigations into a prehistoric cave dwelling near Deià. Here they found a great hoard of bones, the remains of a veritable herd of *Myotragus balearicus*, a goat-like animal unique to the Balearics that seems to have been the nutritional mainstay here in prehistoric times. More importantly, the bones were found at a level in the subsoil that pushed back the date at which the earliest islanders were thought to have lived here by several

Robert Graves in Deià

The English poet, novelist and classical scholar **Robert Graves** (1895–1985) spent two periods living in Deià, the first in the 1930s, and the second from the end of World War II until his death. During his first stay he shared a house at the edge of the village with **Laura Riding**, an American poet and dabbler in the mystical. Riding had arrived in England in 1926 and, after she became Graves's secretary and collaborator, the two of them began an affair that was to break up both of their marriages. The tumultuous course of their relationship created such a furore that they decided to leave England, settling in Mallorca on the advice of Gertrude Stein in 1930. The fuss was not simply a matter of morality – many of their friends were indifferent to adultery – but more to do with the self-styled "**Holy Circle**" they had founded, a cabalistic and intensely self-preoccupied literary-mystic group. The last straw came when Riding, in her attempt to control the group, jumped out of a window, saying "Goodbye, chaps", and the besotted Graves leapt after her. No wonder his mate T.E. Lawrence ("of Arabia") wrote of "madhouse minds" and of Graves "drowning in a quagmire".

Both recovered, but the dottiness continued once they'd moved to Deià, with Graves acting as doting servant to Riding, whom he reinvented as a sort of all-knowing matriarch and muse. Simultaneously, Graves thumped away at his prose: he had already produced *Goodbye to All That* (1929), his bleak and painful memoirs of army service in the World War I trenches, but now came his other best-remembered books, **I, Claudius** (1934) and its sequel **Claudius the God** (1935), historical novels detailing the life and times of the Roman emperor. Nonetheless, to Graves these "potboilers", as he styled them, were secondary to his poetry – usually carefully crafted love poems of melancholic tenderness in praise of Riding – which were well received by the critics of the time.

At the onset of the Spanish Civil War, Graves and Riding left Mallorca, not out of sympathy for the Republicans – Graves was far too reactionary for that – but to keep contact with friends and family. During their exile Graves was ditched by Riding, and he subsequently took up with a mutual friend, **Beryl Hodge**. After Graves had returned to Deià in 1946, he worked on *The White Goddess*, a controversial study of prehistoric and classical myth that argued the existence of an all-pervasive, primordial religion based on the worship of a poet-goddess. Hodge joined him in the midst of his labours (the book was published in 1948), and in 1950 they were married in Palma. They were not, however, to live happily ever after. Graves had a predilection for young women, claiming he needed female muses for poetic inspiration, and although his wife outwardly accepted this waywardness, she did so without much enthusiasm. Meanwhile, although Graves's novels became increasingly well known and profitable, his poetry, with its preoccupation with romantic love, fell out of fashion, and his last anthology, *Poems 1965–1968*, was widely criticized by the literary establishment.

Nevertheless, Graves's international reputation as a writer attracted a steady stream of visitors to Deià from the ranks of the literati, with the occasional film star dropping by to add to the self-regarding stew. By the middle of the 1970s, however, just as an acclaimed BBC TV production of *I, Claudius* was bringing his books to a wider public in his native country, Graves had begun to lose his mind, and ended his days in sad senility. The house where Graves lived in Deià from 1946 onwards was opened to the public in 2006 (see p.127).

hundreds years – to 4000 or even 5000 BC. The Waldrens have carried on with their archeological explorations ever since, and the museum displays many of the key finds from over forty years of work.

Cala Deià

Much loved by Graves, **Cala Deià**, is the nearest thing the village has to a beach, comprising some 200m of shingle at the back of a handsome rocky cove of jagged cliffs, boulders and white-crested surf. It's a great place for a swim, the water is clean, deep and cool, and there's a ramshackle beach bar (summer daily 12.30–5pm) to keep the swimmers happy. Most of the time, the cove is quiet and peaceful, but parties of day-trippers do sometimes stir things up. There are two ways to get there **on foot**. The more obvious route is signed from the bend in the road 80m or so northeast of the bus stop; it leads down a wooded ravine and takes about thirty minutes to complete – and directions are given in the first part of the "Coastal Walk" route to Port de Sóller described on p.132. Even more bucolic, however, is the path that threads its way through the wooded and terraced gulch in between the old centre of the village and the *Hotel Es Molí*; this takes about forty minutes. To **drive** there, head northeast along the main road out of Deià and watch for the sign about 700m beyond the *Hotel La Residencia*.

Eating and drinking

As far as eating and drinking are concerned in Deià, you're spoiled for choice. Dotted along the main street – c/Arxiduc Lluís Salvador (the MA-10) – are several smart and polished **restaurants** plus a number of more modest **café-bars**, ideal for nursing a drink and, especially in the off-season, checking out the expat scene. The village also has an excellent **grocery-store-cum-bakery**, *Forn Deià*, about 200m west of the main bus stop.

Patricia's Bar c/Felip Bauçá s/n. Lively, little bar just off the main street at the west end of the village. Snacks and light meals plus occasional live music, usually in the wintertime. Daily except Wed noon–midnight.

Restaurant Ca'n Quet Carretera Deià-Valldemossa s/n ☎971 63 91 96. Operated by – and situated just a couple of hundred metres west of – the *Hotel Es Molí*, this smart restaurant serves up a creative menu featuring the very best of local ingredients, from island fish through to homegrown vegetables. The service is impeccable as are the views from the restaurant's wide, elevated terrace. Main courses €20 and up. Tues–Sun 1–4pm & 8–11pm. Closed Nov–March.

Restaurant Deià c/Arxiduc Lluís Salvador s/n ☎971 63 92 65. Pleasant restaurant with a lively menu offering a mix of Mediterranean and Mallorcan dishes with main courses at around €15. Occupies an attractive location, footsteps off the main street at the west end of the village with an outdoor terrace overlooking a wooded gulch. Daily noon–4pm & 7–11pm.

Restaurant Es Racó d'es Teix c/Vinya Vella 6 ☎971 63 95 01. Delightful Michelin-starred restaurant in an old stone house with an exquisite shaded terrace, located a steep 30m or so above the main road, about halfway into the village – watch for the sign. The Mediterranean fusion cuisine is memorable, as are the prices (up to €120 for a three-course meal including wine, main courses from €30). Reservations well-nigh essential. Daily except Tues 1–3pm & 8–11pm.

Restaurant Jaime c/Arxiduc Lluís Salvador 22 ☎971 63 90 29. First-rate, terraced restaurant, on the main drag about halfway into the village, specializing in traditional Mallorcan cuisine – try the pork in cabbage leaves. Main courses hover around €20. Daily except Mon 1–3pm & 7.30–11pm.

Restaurant Sa Dorada c/Arxiduc Lluís Salvador 24 ☎971 63 95 09. One of the best places in town for fish, with main courses from around €15. It's located about halfway into the village on the main road – and you can eat either inside or on the terrace out at the back. Daily except Mon 1–4pm & 6.30–11.30pm. Opens at 7pm in winter.

A COASTAL WALK FROM DEIÀ TO PORT DE SÓLLER

Port de Sóller

Sóller

Sóller

MULETA GRAN

N

Rocamar ⦿

Muleta
(222m) ▲

Bens
d'Avall ■ Alconassar

C710

Can
Prohom Castell

Cala
Deià Llucalcari ●

● Son Coll

Valldemossa

KEY TO WALKS:
▶▶ ▶▶ Hiking Route

0   1 km

C710

Hotel La
Residencia ⦿

Deià ★ Bus Stop

Es Molí ⦿

Son Marroig

Beyond Deià, the MA-10 snakes its way along the coast for 3km to reach **Son Marroig**, an imposing L-shaped mansion perched high above the seashore (and just below the road). The house dates from late medieval times, but was refashioned in the nineteenth century to become the favourite residence of the Habsburg archduke **Ludwig Salvator** (see box, p.134). Dynastically insignificant but extremely rich, the Austrian aristocrat was a man in search of a hobby – and he found it in Mallorca. He first visited the island at the tender age of 19, fell head-over-heels in love with the place, and returned to buy Son Marroig along with a sizeable slice of the west coast between Deià and Port de Valldemossa.

The Son Marroig estate (Mon–Sat 9.30am–6pm; €3) comprises the house, its gardens and the headland down below. Despite its setting and long history, the **house** actually conspires to be rather dull with all its key exhibits piled

12km; 4hr–4hr 30min. Mainly easy; difficult in parts.

This delightful **walk** starts in **Deià** village and ends in **Port de Sóller**. There's a fairly regular bus service between the two places (see p.149), which makes the round trip relatively straightforward, but be sure to confirm bus times before you set out. The coast north of Deià is dotted with pine trees and abandoned olive terraces, and slopes steeply down to the sea from the high massif of Sa Galera. On such steep terrain, run-off water plays havoc with terrace walls and paths, so although this walk is mainly easy, care is needed where erosion has occurred. All the way the views are superlative, beginning with the panorama of the blue-green waters of **Cala Deià** (see p.130). The views from the bus on your return journey are equally outstanding: notice especially the picturesque hamlet of **Llucalcari** (see Hotel Costa d'Or, p.127), which cannot be seen from the coastal path below. The walking route, which sometimes drops almost to sea-level and at other times rises to avoid difficult ground, is partially waymarked with red paint and cairns, although a certain amount of route-finding is required due to gully erosion and fallen trees. There are stiles at all the boundary fences the path crosses.

The route

From the **bus stop** in Deià, walk in the Sóller direction and turn left down c/Vinyeta, which is signed "Sóller 2hr 30 min". After five minutes, where the road ends, cross a makeshift stile and take the path through an olive grove. Continue on downhill following the path, which crosses another stile, criss-crosses a road several times and then joins this same road. Continue along it to reach picturesque **Cala Deià** with its beach bars, beached boats and rumbling surf.

To access the **coastal path** retrace your steps from the beach to find a flight of steps located some 50m back from where the road ends. (There is another flight of steps closer to the beach, but this just leads to a public toilet.) Ascend the steps and you're on the coastal path. After about five minutes you will see a path to the left, ignore this and continue on. After a further two minutes a stone path swings right off the main path. Again, ignore this and continue on along the unsurfaced track marked with a line of **red painted stones**. This track bears left then turns right before crossing a low wall. After bearing right again, it then turns sharp left downhill beside the wall. One minute later turn right again and continue straight on, passing a *mirador* (viewpoint) with a private path descending to it from an unseen house above. Continue, ascending around a big boulder on your right and you will now be walking along an attractive headland through pine trees overlooking the sea and the rocks at Cala Deià.

After a further five to ten minutes you will reach a clearing with a **small stone circular table** and log seats. Pass through the clearing and bear right, keeping close to a stone wall. Stay well to the right as there is a steep drop to the left. After about one

into two large and gloomy first-floor rooms. Here you'll find a small sample of Hispano-Arabic pottery, a display featuring some of the archduke's manuscripts and pamphlets, and several ducal photographs: whatever else he did on the island, the duke certainly must have enjoyed his food, ballooning up from a regular-sized young man to quite a heavyweight. There are also photographs of the duke's two other Mallorcan houses, Miramar (see p.134) and **S'Estaca** (no public access), down near Port de Valldemossa and now a home of Michael Douglas. These distractions won't detain you for long however, and you'll soon want to head out to the **garden**, whose terraces are graced by a Neoclassical belvedere of Tuscan Carrara marble. The views west along the jagged, forested coast are simply gorgeous.

minute negotiate a stile and continue through pine woods. Further on you will cross another stile. Beyond this the path bears left, crosses a wall and drops down to a clearing. (Take care not to go wrong here as there are some private paths to houses and also fallen trees obscuring your way.)

Your route continues alongside the coast and you will soon reach a **large circular stone table** with log seats. At this point the path forks left downhill and leads you via a gap in a wall and after a few minutes towards a stone enclosure. Pass below this and along the left side of a wall where the ground rises steeply inland. A minute or so further on you will pass a house on the right. Beyond this the path zigzags towards the sea and then reaches a clearing with a view of a rocky cove. Negotiate an eroded gully and continue on passing walled terraces and then a house, both to your right. The path then crosses a stile and then ascends inland. Look out for a stone marker on the path which looks like a small **Z** and at this point go right uphill and then immediately left under a pine tree. You will now be on a terrace. Ahead of you will be fallen trees, so bear sharp right, then left while climbing upwards to reach a small clearing in the pine trees. Bear left along the lowest terrace and then downhill to reach the next gully. Cross it, negotiating fallen trees and go up the other side towards the next gully which is heavily eroded, cross it and climb steeply out.

Continue on, via a gap in a wall to reach the headland at the top. On reaching a **barbed wire fence** turn left and walk steeply downhill towards the sea with the fence on your right. Follow the fence until you reach a stile. Beyond the stile the path is well waymarked. It crosses a stone wall, descends to an olive grove and pine trees with large boulders to either side. Follow the path as It ascends to another stile. Cross this, pass a stone shack and further on, near a barbed wire gate, go over a further stile. Continue on, and upon reaching a recently constructed stone wall climb the steps towards its end. Follow the path through tall trees and descend to a concreted road. Turn right on to this and follow it uphill, passing houses on the left until you reach the rear of the **Restaurant Ben d'Avall**.

The path swings right at this point. Immediately to your left is a canalized stream – usually dried up in summer – and beyond it the access road to the Ben d'Avall. You need to cross over the streambed to get to the road. Continue up the path from the right turn and look very carefully for a gap in the top of the streambed wall. This marks the point below which are a series of **metal pegs** that allow you to climb down the side of the streambed and up the other side. Having crossed the stream turn right and follow the road uphill for 1.5 km to reach the Muleta road junction. At this point turn left along the unsurfaced road, then right by a small electricity substation. After five minutes turn left and continue straight on following signs to **Port de Sóller**. The route is clearly signed from this point and leads directly to the now derelict **Rocamar Hostal**. Below the *Rocamar*, turn left for the Platja d'en Repic, Port de Sóller's largest beach (see p.120), or right for the main road to Sóller (see p.114).

Down below the garden is a slender promontory known as **Sa Foradada**, "the rock pierced by a hole", where the archduke used to park his yacht. The hole in question is a strange circular affair sited high up in the rock face at the end of the promontory. It takes about forty minutes to **walk** the 3km down to this rock, a straightforward excursion to a delightfully scenic spot, though the estate itself is a little scruffy and ill-kempt. There should be few problems with direction-finding on the walk, which begins at the gate just up the slope and to the left of the house. A sign on the gate insists you need to get permission at Son Marroig before setting out, but this is just to make sure you pay the admission fee. Walkers usually have to clamber over the gate's stile – though sometimes the gate is left open – and then, about 100m further on, need to

The Archduke Ludwig Salvator

Cousin to the Habsburg Emperor Franz Josef of Austria no less, the young **Ludwig Salvator** (1847–1915) was supposed to join the imperial army, but he cleared off and took his sea captain's certificate instead. Mightily miffed at this insubordination, the emperor decided a carrot was better than a stick and appointed him the Governor of Bohemia hoping that this would settle him down. It might have worked too, but for a freak accident: Salvator's young wife, **Mathilde**, was watching the archduke inspect his soldiers from a balcony until, bored out of her brain, she decided to have a furtive cigarette. It was a bad decision. The cigarette set her dress on fire and she burnt to death in double quick time. Out of sympathy, his family was now inclined to indulge Salvator's wanderlust and the archduke headed south to the Mediterranean in 1866. It was on his travels that the archduke first visited Mallorca and it made such an impression on him that he returned to live here, buying a chunk of the west coast and building (or at least adopting) no less than **three homes** – Son Marroig (see p.131), Miramar (see below) and S'Estaca, now the home of Michael Douglas.

Once in residence, Ludwig immersed himself in all things *Mallorquín*, learning the dialect and chronicling the island's topography, archeology, history and folklore in astounding detail. He churned out no fewer than **seven volumes** on the Balearics and, perhaps more importantly, played a leading role as a proto-environmentalist, conserving the coastline of his estates and, amongst many projects, paying for a team of geologists to chart the Coves del Drac (see p.214).

Salvator may have been hard working, but he also squeezed in a lot of R&R, allegedly sleeping with a platoon of local women and fathering a merry band of children. Back at Habsburg HQ, rumours of Salvator's endeavours – both in and out of the sack – went down badly: it was not so much that "Don Baleario", as he was nick-named, slept with peasant girls, but more that he recognized them and their (his) children, giving them money and land. To add grist to the mill, Salvator even brought one of his women – **Catalina Homar** – back to the Habsburg court in Vienna and, after her untimely death, publicly dedicated one of his books to her. It was, however, World War I that brought a sudden end to the archduke's stint in Mallorca rather than Vienna's disapproval. In 1914, at the outbreak of war, Salvator was summoned back to the Austro-Hungarian Empire to do his royal duty; he died within a year.

keep right at the fork in the track; as you approach the tip of the promontory, think carefully before deciding to attempt the precarious climb beyond the old jetties. On your return, you can slake your thirst at the **café-bar** (or for that matter the restaurant) overlooking the coast from beside the car park near the house, though you can expect to pay over the odds here.

Miramar

From Son Marroig, it's just 2km west along the coast to **Miramar** (Tues–Sun 9.30am–6pm; €3), once the site of a medieval monastery – hence the signs for the '**Monestir de Miramar**' – and the last of the three houses bought by the Archduke Salvator during his long sojourn on the island. Only recently opened to the public, the house and its grounds hold an improbable assortment of remains and memorials, beginning with a line of thirteenth-century **stone pillars**, all that is left of the original monastery built for the scholar-missionaries of Ramon Llull (see p.81 & p.82). Beyond the pillars is the **house**, which holds a mock-up of part of the archduke's yacht, the *Nixe II*, two rooms devoted to Ramon Llull and a horridly romantic stone memorial to the archduke's first secretary, a certain Vratislav Vyborny. Outside, the **grounds** offer tremendous views along the coast – so you don't really need to pay much attention to the geometric shapes that were originally – and allegedly – laid out by Llull or to the stone shrine the archduke built in Llull's honour.

Valldemossa and around

South of Miramar, the MA-10 stays high above the coast, twisting through what was once the archducal estate en route to the intriguing hill-town of **VALL-DEMOSSA**. Approaching from Deià, the town at first appears disappointing, as the MA-10 cuts through the drab western outskirts, but the approach from the south – from Palma – reveals the town to much better advantage. Here, with the mountains closing in, the road squeezes through a narrow, wooded defile before entering a lovely valley, whose tiered and terraced fields ascend to the town, a sloping jumble of rusticated houses and monastic buildings backclothed by the mountains.

The origins of Valldemossa date to the early fourteenth century, when the asthmatic **King Sancho** built a royal palace here in the hills where the air was easier to breathe. Later, in 1399, the palace was gifted to Carthusian monks from Tarragona, who converted and extended the original buildings into a **monastery**, now Mallorca's most visited building after Palma Cathedral. An enjoyable place to spend the night, Valldemossa has three appealing hotels as well as a couple of good restaurants and it's also within striking distance of its old seaport, tiny **Port de Valldemossa**, whose gaggle of modern villas and micro-beach of churning surf are reached along the dramatic hairpins of a narrow country road.

Arrival, information and accommodation

There is a good daily **bus service** to Valldemossa from Palma and Esporles as well as points along the coast between Port de Sóller and Estellencs. The main **bus stop** is beside the most westerly of the car parks that flank the modern bypass as it skirts the town centre to the north. From here, it's a couple of minutes' walk to the monastery and about the same to the **tourist office**, back along the bypass towards Palma (Mon–Fri 9am–1.30pm & 3–5pm, Sat 10am–1pm; ☏971 61 20 19).

Valldemossa has three recommendable **hotels**, kicking off with *Ca'n Mario*, c/Uetam 8 (☏971 61 21 22, ⓦwww.hostalcanmario.net; ❸), an attractive little one-star *hostal* with an elegant, antique-cluttered foyer and eight comfortably old-fashioned rooms. The *hostal* has been in business since 1890 and is a popular spot, so reservations are pretty much essential. It's situated just a minute's walk from the monastery: from the pedestrianized area between the cloisters and the palace, go down the slope and take the first turning on the right. Even more appealing is the ⚹ *Es Petit Hotel*, which occupies a tastefully renovated old stone house just along the street c/Uetam 1 (☏971 61 24 79, ⓦwww.espetithotel-valldemossa.com; ❸). There are eight, en suite guest rooms here, each decorated in a pleasant unfussy style and several have smashing views down the valley. A third and much more lavish option is the *Hotel Valldemossa*, Ctra Vieja de Valldemossa s/n (☏971 61 26 26, ⓦwww.valldemossahotel.com; ❾), where a grand Italianate stairway climbs up to what was originally a pair of nineteenth-century, hilltop farmhouses, but is now a sleek, rural-chic hotel. There is a heated indoor pool, a restaurant and an expansive terrace above lush gardens that tumble down the hillside; the hotel has just twelve rooms – three doubles and nine suites – and, as you might expect from the price, they have every mod con. It's all very chi-chi. The hotel is about five minutes' walk south from the monastery along the old Palma road.

Valldemossa monastery

Remodelled and restructured on several occasions, most of Valldemossa's **Real Cartuja de Jesús de Nazaret** (Royal Carthusian Monastery of Jesus of Nazareth; March–May & Oct Mon–Sat 9.30am–5.30pm, Sun 10am–1pm; June & July Mon–Sat 9.30am–6.30pm, Sun 10am–1pm; Nov–Feb Mon–Sat 9.30am–4pm, Sun 10am–1pm; €7.50) is of seventeenth- and eighteenth-century construction. It owes its present notoriety almost entirely to the novelist and republican polemicist **George Sand** (1804–76), who, with her companion, the composer **Frédéric Chopin** (1810–49), lived here for four months in 1838–39. They arrived just three years after the last monks had been evicted during the liberal-inspired suppression of the monasteries, and so were able to rent a commodious set of vacant cells. Their stay is commemorated in Sand's *A Winter in Majorca*, a sharp-tongued and sharp-eyed epistle that is available hereabouts in just about every European language (an extract is given on p.322). Reading the book today, what comes through strongly is Sand's frustration with the ossified

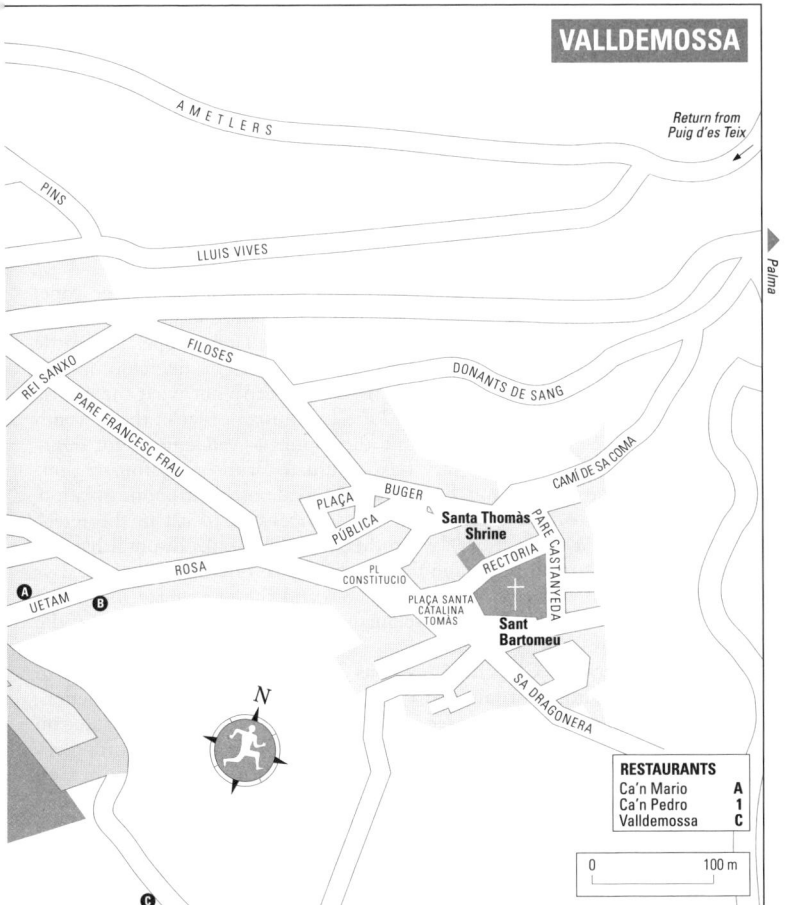

Return from
Puig d'es Teix

Palma

AMETLERS

PINS

LLUIS VIVES

FILOSES

REI SANXO

PARE FRANCESC FRAU

DONANTS DE SANG

CAMÍ DE SA COMA

PLAÇA
PÚBLICA

BUGER

ROSA

PL
CONSTITUCIO

PLAÇA SANTA
CATALINA
TOMÀS

UETAM

Santa Thomàs
Shrine

RECTORIA

PARE CASTANYEDA

Sant
Bartomeu

SA DRAGONERA

N

RESTAURANTS
Ca'n Mario   **A**
Ca'n Pedro   **1**
Valldemossa   **C**

0   100 m

social structures on the island, though her diatribes against reaction sometimes merge into a mean-spirited contempt for her Spanish neighbours. Ungraciously, Sand explains that her nickname for Mallorca, "Monkey Island", was coined for its "crafty, thieving and yet innocent" inhabitants, who, she asserts, are "heartless, selfish and impertinent". Quite what the islanders made of Sand is unknown, but her trouser-wearing, cigar-smoking image – along with her "living in sin" – could hardly have made the woman popular in rural Mallorca.

There's an obvious, though limited curiosity in looking around Sand and Chopin's old quarters, but the monastery boasts far more interesting diversions, and it's easy to follow the signs around the place. A visit begins in the gloomy, aisle-less **church**, a square and heavy construction that is distinguished by its late Baroque ceiling paintings and barrel vaulting, though the lines of the nave are spoiled by the clumsy wooden stalls of the choir. It also possesses a kitsch high altar and a fanciful bishop's throne, which somehow manages to look a little self-conscious. Beyond the church lie the shadowy **cloisters**, where the first port of call is the **pharmacy**, which survived the expulsion of the monks to serve the town's medicinal needs well into the twentieth century. Its shelves are crammed with a host of beautifully decorated majolica jars, antique glass receptacles and painted wood boxes, each carefully inscribed with the name of a potion or drug.

The nearby **prior's cell** is, despite its name, a comfortable suite of bright, sizeable rooms, enhanced by access to a private garden with splendid views down the valley. The cell incorporates a chapel, a library, an audience chamber, a dining room and a bedroom and it is graced by a potpourri of religious *objets d'art*. These include several handsome majolica pieces and two unattributed medieval triptychs displayed in the library. These are the *Adoration of the Magi*, a charmingly naive painting in the Flemish style, and an intricate three-panel marble sculpture celebrating the marriage of Pedro II of Aragón (1174–1213), who – if you're after an English connection – came a fatal cropper in a battle with the army of Simon de Montfort outside Toulouse. This degree of luxury – the other cells are of similar proportions – was clearly not what the ascetic St Bruno had in mind when he founded the Carthusian order in the eleventh century. Nevertheless, it's hard to blame the monks at Valldemossa for lightening what must have been a very heavy burden. Bruno's rigorous regime, inspired by his years as a hermit, had his monks in almost continuous isolation, gathering together only for certain church services and to eat in the refectory on Sundays. At other times, lay brothers fed the monks through hatches along the cloister corridors, though this was hardly an onerous task: three days a week the monks had only bread and water, and they never ate meat. The diet and the mountain air, however, seemed to suit them: the longevity of the Valldemossa monks was proverbial.

Along the corridor, **Cell no.2** exhibits miscellaneous curios relating to Chopin and Sand, from portraits and a lock of hair to musical scores and letters; it was in this cell that the composer wrote his "Raindrop" Prelude, but not on the Steinway piano that is here today – that arrived long after the composer's departure. There's more of the same next door in **Cell no.3** and again in **Cell no.4**, where pride of place goes to Chopin's piano, which was finally installed just three weeks before the couple left for Paris after months of unbelievable complications. Considering the hype, these incidental Chopin mementos are something of an anticlimax and neither do things improve much in the ground-floor galleries of the adjacent **Museu Municipal**, which concentrates on local landscape painters and takes a stab at tracing the diligent endeavours of Archduke Ludwig Salvator (see box p.134). But don't give up: the upstairs section of the museum, entitled the **Museu Municipal Art Contemporani**, has a small but outstanding collection of modern art, including work by Picasso, Francis Bacon and Henry Moore. There's also a room full of characteristic squiggles by Joan Miró and a substantial sample of paintings by the Spanish modernist **Juli Ramís** (1909–1990), from geometric abstractions through to forceful, expressionistic paintings like *The Blue Lady* (*Dama Blava*).

Back beside the prior's cell, be sure to take the doorway that leads outside the cloisters and across the courtyard to the **Palau Sancho** (Palace of King Sancho; same times & ticket as the monastery). It's not the original medieval palace – that disappeared long ago – but this fortified mansion is the oldest part of the monastery complex and its imposing walls, mostly dating from the sixteenth century, accommodate a string of appealing period rooms cluttered with faded paintings and other curios. The palace was the first home of the monks, but it has also seen service as the residence of local bigwigs and as a political prison, its most celebrated internee being the liberal reformer Gaspar de Jovellanos, a victim of the royal favourite Manuel de Godoy, who had him locked up here from 1801 to 1802. Nowadays, the palace hosts free and frequent **concerts** of Chopin's piano music. The original entrance to the palace, complete with its fortified towers and eccentric wooden drawbridge linking two internal rooms, is only visible from the narrow side street that runs along the east side of the palace – away from the cloisters.

The rest of Valldemossa

The monastery is very much the main event in Valldemossa, though there are a couple of minor attractions worth seeking out amongst the cobbled lanes and old stone houses of the town centre, which tumbles prettily down the hillside beneath it. First up is the church of **Sant Bartomeu**, an imposing Gothic edifice with a handsome bell tower that lords it over a tiny piazza. Close by, round the back along a narrow alley, at c/Rectoria 5, is the humble birthplace of **Santa Catalina Thomàs**, a sixteenth-century nun revered for her piety. The interior of the house has been turned into a simple little shrine, with a statue of the saint holding a small bird. There's also the awful **Costa Nord visitor centre** (daily 9am–5/6pm; €7.75, Ⓦ www.costanord.com), where – heaven help us – you can, by means of an audio-visual show, "relive the history of Majorca [sic] under the guidance of Michael Douglas". The centre occupies the ugly modern structure on the bypass opposite the tourist office. Opened in 2000, it was Douglas who stumped up the cash to have the centre built, but he sold it to the Balearic government in 2003.

Eating and drinking

The centre of Valldemossa is packed with **restaurants and cafés**. Many are geared up for the day-trippers and offer pretty dire food at inflated prices, but there are exceptions. One sound choice is the pocket-sized, family-run restaurant on the upper floor of the *Hostal Ca'n Mario*, c/Uetam 8 (Ⓣ971 61 21 22; closed Mon), where they serve traditional Mallorcan food at affordable prices with main courses averaging around €14; reservations are advised. A reserve option is the inexpensive *Ca'n Pedro*, Avgda Arxiduc Lluís Salvador s/n (Mon–Fri 1–3.30pm & 8–11pm, Sat 1–4pm & 8–11pm & Sun 1–4pm), a large and traditional café-restaurant serving from an extensive menu; the food isn't exactly memorable and the place can heave with tourists, but it's just about good enough; it's opposite the town's main bus stop. The best restaurant in town is at the *Hotel Valldemossa* (see p.135), where they offer an ambitious menu firmly rooted in island dishes; on the other hand, it is a rather formal place and mains start at a hefty €25.

Around Valldemossa: Port de Valldemossa

The closest spot to Valldemossa for a paddle is **PORT DE VALLDEM-OSSA**, where a handful of seaside villas huddle together in the shadow of the mountains at the mouth of a narrow, craggy cove. There's no public transport, but the drive down to the port, once Valldemossa's gateway to the outside world, is stimulating: head west out of Valldemossa to rejoin the MA-10 and, after about 1.5km, turn right at the sign and follow the twisty side road for 6km down through the mountains. Port de Valldemossa's beach is small and shingly, and tends to get battered by the surf, but the scenery is stunning and the village sports a popular seashore **restaurant**, *Es Port* (daily 11.30am–5.30pm; Ⓣ971 61 61 94), which has a good reputation for its seafood – try the shellfish and lobster paella at just €12 per head; times may vary, so ring ahead to confirm.

12.5km; 674m of ascent; 4hr 30min–5hr. Medium difficulty.

The terrain between **Valldemossa and Deià** is mountainous and wild, abounding in steep cliffs and rocky summits; the lower slopes are wooded but the tops are almost devoid of vegetation, with numerous dramatic viewpoints, many of them overlooking the ocean. The land is rough but, as elsewhere in Mallorca, the mountains are criss-crossed by footpaths first made by charcoal burners, olive growers and hunters. These paths can be stony but this area was also subject to the attentions of the nineteenth-century Austrian archduke **Ludwig Salvator** (see box, p.134), who had some wonderful paths constructed so that he could ride around on horseback admiring the scenery. Today, walkers can still benefit from the archduke's efforts because his estate was acquired in 1967 by ICONA, Mallorca's organization for nature conservation. This **circular walk** – which can be lengthened or shortened to suit – is a classic, showing the area at its best.

The route
From near the monastery on Valldemossa's bypass (Avinguda Palma), proceed along **c/Venerable Sor Aina** past the car park and take the first right up to the school. Climb the **steps** at the left-hand side of the school, then turn right and almost immediately left onto c/Alzines. Go to the end of the street, turn right, ascend slightly, then turn left up a wide path that leads into the woods, entered by a stile over a gate. The stony path twists up quite steeply to reach an opening in the wall at the edge of a wooded plain, the **Pla d'es Pouet**; a shortcut near the top is waymarked but it makes little difference which way you go. From the wall, go straight on across the level ground to reach an old **well** (now polluted) in a large clearing. This well is a vital reference point in a confusing area and it is essential that you take your bearings carefully here.

Take the path bearing slightly right of the well (north east at first, and then north), which leads easily up to the **Coll de S'Estret de Son Gallard**. On the col is a barrier of brushwood set up by hunters who still practise the traditional *caza a coll* method, which you can observe: birds are lured into flying along artificial tunnels created by cutting passages through the trees, then captured in nets.

From the nearby v-shaped stone seats, the path continues uphill to the right. To the south of the main path lies the **Cova de Ermita Guillem**, an interesting hermit's cave, containing icons and candles; this offers excellent shelter if you're unlucky with the weather – look for a branch path on the right and a gap in a wall to the left, which leads to the enclosure in front of the cave. To rejoin the uphill main path, retrace your steps for about 100m and then branch sharply off to the right. The most spectacular part of the walk begins here: it's a wide and easy walkway on the edge of cliffs with a breathtaking view and a good place for picnics.

Southwest to La Granja and Esporles

Heading southwest from Valldemossa, the MA-10 threads a scenic route along the coastal mountains for about 9km until it reaches the 1.5km-long turning for **La Granja** (daily: April–Oct 10am–7pm & Nov–March 10am–6pm; €9.50 or €11.50 at peak periods; ⓦwww.lagranja.net), a grand *hacienda* nestling in a tranquil wooded and terraced valley. The house and its grounds make for a popular package-tourist trip, but, despite the many visitors, the estate just about manages to maintain a languorous air of old patrician comfort. La Granja was occupied until very recently by the Fortuny family, who took possession in the

As you approach the summit of **Caragolí**, you can spy Port de Sóller down on the coast and the mountains Major, Teix and Galatzó rising high above the seashore. Then the path climbs southeast to 944m before descending gently over a sloping, arid plain, the **Pla d'es Aritges** (*aritge* is smilax, a plant with vicious backward-curving thorns). A path junction at an isolated group of pine trees offers a shortcut back to Valldemossa via Fontanelles. To continue on the main route, take the left fork northeast, which brings you over a 935m top and shortly after, to a viewpoint overlooking Deià. After this the path swings southeast and begins to descend to the Teix path junction.

A metre-high **cairn** marks the Teix path junction. Here, branch left (northeast) on a path that scrambles up a little gully and then continues over a sandy plateau towards a high stone wall. Cross this using the ladders provided and walk on to the **Pla de Sa Serp**, a plain where there is a spring – the **Font de Sa Serp**. A well-used path then leads up to the col between the two summits and on to the main west summit of Puig d'es Teix (1062m). From here the views over the Sóller valley and the western summit of Puig Major are especially fine, while the tops of Cornadors, L'Ofre and the Alfàbia ridge form a stunning skyline.

Return to the Teix path junction by the same route (avoid the difficult-to-follow route southwest from Teix towards Sa Bussa) and turn left to follow the main track down the **Cairats valley**. First you'll come to an old "snowhouse" (a deep hole used for storing ice in winter), then a stone mountain refuge and below that a spring and picnic site, the **Font d'es Poll** (Well of the Poplar). The wide track beyond is stony but you'll have no trouble finding the route. On the way down the valley you'll see reconstructions of a *sitja*, a charcoal-worker's shelter. Keep on the main track down the Cairats valley, going over a wall via stone steps to the left of a locked gate. Ignore two branch paths to the left and continue to some iron gates. Go straight on to join c/Xesc Forteza, then bear left into c/Lluis Vives at the end of which is a large old house with a square tower. From here there is a splendid view over the old part of Valldemossa. Continue on down c/Son Gual, turn left into c/Mas, then right onto Avenguda Palma for the centre of Valldemossa.

Extension of the walk to Mirador de Ses Puntes and Veià
1.5km; 116m of ascent; 45min

From the well in the clearing on the Pla d'es Pouet, take the path which leads northwest at first, before zigzagging uphill and swinging west. Fork left shortly after passing an old bread oven to reach the **Mirador de Ses Puntes**. From this superb viewpoint, return to the fork and take the left branch, which rises through the trees to the top of **Pouet** (858m) and, after a little dip, **Veià** (871m). For much of the way, the path is the wide bridleway built by the archduke and from it you can look down on Sa Foradada, a rocky headland near his old house, Son Marroig. From the ruined shelter on Veià the path descends to the **Coll de S'Estret de Son Gallard**, where you rejoin the main path a little up from the well.

mid-fifteenth century; after about the 1920s it seems that modernization simply never crossed their minds.

From the **entrance** in front of the main forecourt, signs direct you up round the back of the house, past an incidental collection of well-weathered farming tackle and on into the tiny formal **gardens**. Next door, a small patio leads to the main **house**, a ramshackle sequence of apartments strewn with domestic clutter – everything from children's games and mannequins, through old costumes, musical instruments and a cabinet of fans, to a fully equipped antique kitchen. There's also a delightful little theatre, where plays were once performed for the household in a manner common amongst Europe's nineteenth-century rural

VALLDEMOSSA TO PUIG D'ES TEIX

▲ Coll de Sóller

KEY TO WALKS:
↟↟ Primary hiking route
↟↟ Extension hiking route
::::: Cart Track

0   1 km

Puig d'es Vent (1004m)
Font de Sa Serp
Teix (1062m)
Cases del Rei Jaume
(887m)
(788m)
Puig de L'Angelet (968m)
Teix (1062m)

Coll d'en Satria
▲ Deià
Es Moli ◉

SERRA DE SON MORAGUES

Caragoli (926m)
Font d'es Poll
(935m)
Pine Trees

Cairats Valley

Son Marroig ▲
Son Rullan
(944m)
Pla d'es Aritges
Fontanelles (874m)

Miramar ●
Mirador de Ses Pites
Coll de S'Estret de Son Gallard
Cova de Ermita Guillem

Veià (871m)
Well
Pla d'es Pouet

Pouet (858m)
Ermita
Mirador de Ses Puntes
Na Torta (737m)

School
Valldemossa

Valldemossa Monastery
▶ Palma

◀ Port de Valldemossa & La Granja
▶ Port de Valldemossa & La Granja

N

landowners. Likewise, the dining room, with its faded paintings and heavy drapes, has a real touch of country elegance, as does the graceful first-floor loggia. Look out also for the finely crafted, green-tinted Mallorcan chandeliers and the beautiful majolica tile-panels that embellish several walls.

Tagged onto the house, a series of **workrooms** recall the days when La Granja was a profitable and almost entirely self-sufficient concern. A wine press, and almond and olive-oil mills prepared the estate's produce for export, whilst plumbers, carpenters, cobblers, weavers and sail makers all kept pace with domestic requirements from their specialized workshops. The Fortunys were one of Mallorca's more enlightened landowning families, and employees were well fed by the kitchen staff, who made cheeses, bread and preserves by hand. The main kitchen is in one of the **cellars**, where you'll also find a grain store and a "torture chamber", an entirely inappropriate addition which holds a harrowing variety of instruments once regularly used by the Inquisition. Moving on, you'll soon reach the family **chapel**, a diminutive affair with kitsch silver-winged angels, and then the expansive **forecourt**, shaded by plane trees and surrounded by antiquated workshops where costumed artisans "practise" traditional crafts such as wood-turning and candle-making. This part of the visit is more than a little bogus, but good fun all the same – and the home-made pastries and doughnuts (*bunyols*) are lip-smacking. Your visit may also coincide with a mildly diverting display of Mallorcan **folk dancing**.

The Palma to Estellencs **bus** stops by the entrance to La Granja eleven times daily Monday through Saturday, three times on Sunday. La Granja is also at the start of a narrow and difficult country road that leads inland to Puigpunyent (see p.146), Galilea (see p.145) and ultimately Capdellà (see p.145), just to the east of Andratx (see p.145).

Esporles

It's a couple of kilometres along the Palma road from La Granja to **ESPORLES**, an amiable, leafy little town whose elongated main street follows the line of an ancient stone watercourse. This is Mallorca away from the tourist throng, and although there's no special reason to stop, you might drop by the town's finest building, its thirteenth-century **church**; a massive, heavily buttressed affair at the top of the town overlooking Plaça Espanya. This certainly wasn't the place to be in 1452, when local landowners finally managed to crush a peasants' revolt that had spread across the island from the Esporles district. The leader of the insurrection, a certain Miquel Forns, was tortured to death on Plaça Espanya and his body was left swinging on a gibbet to ram home the point.

The Palma to Estellencs bus (see above) passes through Esporles.

Onto Banyalbufar

Back on the MA-10, just beyond the turning for La Granja, a narrow side road forks down to the coast at **PORT D'ES CANONGE**. The five-kilometre journey down through thickly forested hills is splendid, but the settlement itself is disappointing, a scrawny, modern *urbanització* flanking a shingle beach. Consequently, you'd do far better to stay on the main coast road for a further 6km, enjoying spectacular views on the way to **BANYALBUFAR**, a drowsy little village whose terraced fields cling gingerly to the coastal cliffs. The land here has been cultivated since Moorish times, with a spring above the village providing a water supply that's still channelled down the hillside along slender watercourses into open storage cisterns, the unlikely looking home for a few carp. The village itself is bisected by its main street, which doubles as the MA-10, with ancient houses and steep cobbled lanes to either side. The cute **main square** perches above the main street, overlooked by a chunky parish **church** dating from the fifteenth century.

Banyalbufar is a fine place to unwind and there's a rough and rocky **beach** fifteen minutes' walk down the hill from the main drag – just follow the signs. The village also has several appealing **places to stay**, the most enticing of which is *Hotel Son Borguny*, just above the main road – and east of the church – at c/Borguny 1 (☎971 14 87 06, ⓦwww.sonborguny.com; ❺). The hotel occupies a sympathetically modernized terrace house that dates back to the fifteenth century and its eight guest rooms are kitted out in pleasant and unfussy modern style; the only drawback is that most of the rooms do not have sea views. A second good choice is the *Hotel Mar i Vent*, in a conspicuous 1940s building on the main street towards the east end of the village (☎971 61 80 00, ⓦwww.hotelmarivent.com; ❺). The decor here is incredibly old-fashioned (and the food very average), but all the better rooms are reasonably large and have sea-facing balconies with fantastic views out along the coast. There's also an outside pool and help for drivers: the staff will park your car for you – a real blessing given the village's steep and narrow lanes. Two more recommendations are the *Sa Coma* (☎971 61 80 34, ⓦwww.hotelsacoma.com; ❹; Feb–Oct), an engaging family-run hotel with great sea views, home cooking and an outside pool down below the village on the way to the beach; and the *Hotel Baronia* (☎971 61 81 46, ⓦwww.hbaronia.com; ❸; closed Nov–March), whose forty plain but perfectly adequate sea-facing rooms are set in a large and much modified old mansion at the west end of the main drag.

Banyalbufar has a middling selection of **cafés and restaurants** strung out along its main drag. Cream of the crop is the *Restaurante Son Tomas*, at the west end of the village (☎971 61 81 49; Wed–Sun 12.30–4pm & 7.30–10.30pm), which has great steaks and a delicious fish of the day (for around €18), as well as an excellent *menú del día* and wide sea views. The busiest place is the café-bar *Pegasón* (Mon–Sat except Thurs 7–11.30pm & Sun 1.30–11.30pm), where they serve up pizzas (from €8) and a limited range of meat and fish dishes (from €12) in two cosy little rooms; it's just below the main street across from the main square.

The Palma to Estellencs **bus** passes through Banyalbufar eleven times daily, three times on Sunday.

Southwest to Estellencs

Pressing on from Banyalbufar, it's about 1.5km to the **Torre del Verger**, a sixteenth-century watchtower built as a sentinel against pirate attack and now providing stunning views along the coast. **ESTELLENCS**, 5km further on, is similar to Banyalbufar, with steep coastal cliffs and tight terraced fields, though if anything it's even prettier; its narrow, winding alleys crimped by old stone houses and a trim, largely eighteenth-century parish **church** – peep inside for a look at the exquisite pinewood reredos. A steep, but driveable, two-kilometre lane leads down from the village, past olive and orange orchards, to **Cala Estellencs**, a rocky, surf-buffeted cove that shelters a shingly beach and summertime bar.

Estellencs has two smashing **hotels**, beginning with the lovely little 🛏 *Hotel Nord*, in a neat and trim old stone building plumb in the middle of the village – and below the main street – at Plaça Triquet 4 (☎971 14 90 06, ⓦwww .hotelruralnord.com; ❺). The hotel's interior has been decorated in a bright and cheerful modern style and the eight bedrooms are similarly appealing. A second – and slightly cheaper – choice is the delightful *Sa Plana Hotel*, c/Eusebi Pascual s/n (℡971 61 86 66, ⓦwww.saplana.com; ⑤), a rusticated, family-run converted finca with plenty of atmosphere at the west end of the village, just south off the main road. Very different is the *Hotel Maristel* (℡971 61 85 50, ⓦwww .hotelmaristel.com; ⑥; closed Nov–Dec), a lumpy modern concrete and glass block beside the main road, but with great views down over the coast; there are fifty-odd rooms here – ask for one with a sea view.

The village possesses two quality **restaurants** and they are next door to each other, overlooking the main street near the church. There's little in it, but the *Montimar* (Tues–Sun noon–3.30pm & 7–10.30pm; ℡971 61 85 76) probably has the gastronomic edge, its menu bristling with Mallorcan favourites like suckling pig and rabbit – and an intriguing rabbit, ham and fig pâté; main courses start at around €11. The *Montimar* occupies antique premises and so does its neighbour, *Son Llarg* (daily except Tues noon–3.30pm & 7–10.30pm; ℡971 61 85 64), where they serve from a slightly wider Mediterranean menu.

The Palma to Estellencs **bus** service terminates here.

Andratx and around

Heading southwest from Estellencs, the **MA-10** threads along the littoral for 6km before slipping through a tunnel and – immediately beyond – passing the stone stairway up to the **Mirador de Ricardo Roca**. At 400m above the sea, this lookout point offers some fine coastal views, and you can wet your whistle at the *Café Es Grau* next door.

Beyond the mirador, the road makes a few final flourishes before turning inland and worming its way up and over forested foothills to **ANDRATX**, a small and unassuming town 19km southwest of Estellencs and just 23km west of Palma. The main event here is the **Wednesday morning market**, a tourist favourite, but otherwise there's not much to detain you, though the old houses and cobbled streets of the upper town do form an harmonious, ochre ensemble, culminating in the fortress-like walls of the thirteenth-century church of **Santa Maria**, built high and strong to deter raiding pirates, its balustraded precincts offering panoramic views down to the coast.

Andratx is well-connected by **bus** with Palma, Sant Elm and Port d'Andratx, but only one bus weekly runs from here to Estellencs and points northeast along the coast to Valldemossa and there are no buses at all east to Galilea.

East of Andratx: Capdellà, Galilea and Puigpunyent

East of Andratx, the MA-1031 squeezes through the foothills of the Serra de Tramuntana in spectacular if nail-biting style bound for the unremarkable settlement of **CAPDELLÀ**, just 9km away. Beyond, there are more auto high jinks as the road – now the MA-1032 – wriggles and worms its way northeast up into the mountains before looping into **GALILEA**, an engaging scattering of whitewashed farmsteads built in sight of a stolid hilltop church. There's a rusty old café-bar beside the church, but the best place to soak up the bucolic atmosphere is the *Café-bar Galilea* (closed Wed), below the church and beside the through road; the views from the terrace are gorgeous and the Mallorcan food is both delicious and inexpensive, with filling snacks from just €5. You can also break your stay here in style at the hillside *Scott's Galilea* (℡971 87 01 00, ⓦwww.scottsgalilea.com; ⑦), the brother to *Scott's Hotel* in Binissalem (see p.196) and with the same high standards – goosedown pillows, all-cotton sheets and so forth. The hotel consists of three cottages and seven studios, all immaculately modern in style and each with a kitchen or kitchenette; breakfast is included in the room rate and there is an outside pool. To get there, just follow the signs.

Pushing on from Galilea, it's a 4km gambol along a benign valley of citrus groves and olive trees to the next settlement, **PUIGPUNYENT**, a workaday farmers' village marginally enhanced by a seventeenth-century church with a squat bell tower. Puigpunyent is, however, home to the *Gran Hotel Son Net* (☎971 14 70 00, ⓦ www.sonnet.es; ⓪), one of the island's grandest hotels, set in a creatively updated pink Renaissance mansion that sits atop the imposing hill in the town centre. This deluxe establishment has wide views, verdant gardens, a whopping pool, excellent international cuisine (with Mediterranean leanings) and attentive service. Beyond Puigpunyent, a narrow and difficult country road hairpins over the mountains and down the valley beyond en route to La Granja (see p.140), about 10km away.

As regards public transport, there is a regular **bus service** from Palma to Puigpunyent and Galilea (2–5 daily), a frequent bus between Calvià and Capdellà, but nothing at all linking Andratx with Capdellà, Galilea and Puigpunyent.

Sant Elm and around

From Andratx, it's 3km west along a handsome country road to the hillside hamlet of **S'Arracó**, which is itself the prelude to a pretty, orchard-covered landscape that buckles up into wooded hills and dipping valleys as it approaches the seashore, another 5km or so away. At the end of the road is the low-key, pocket-sized resort of **SANT ELM**, whose main street strings along the shoreline with a sandy beach at one end and a **harbour** at the other – and, mercifully, no tower blocks in between.

From Sant Elm's minuscule harbour, **passenger boats** (Feb–April & Oct–Nov Mon–Sat 3 daily; May–Sept 4 daily; €10 return; 15min; ☎639 61 75 45

△ Sant Elm beach backdropped by Sa Dragonera

or 696 42 39 33) take a few minutes to shuttle across to the austere offshore islet that comprises the **Parc Natural de Sa Dragonera** (April–Sept daily 10am–5pm, Oct–March daily 10am–3pm; free). This uninhabited hunk of rock, some 4km long and 700m wide, lies at an oblique angle to the coast, with an imposing ridge of seacliffs dominating its northwestern shore. Behind the ridge, a rough track travels the length of the island, linking a pair of craggy capes and their lighthouses. The boat docks at a tiny cove-harbour about halfway up the east shore, which puts both ends of the island within comfortable walking distance, though the excursion north to **Cap de Tramuntana** is both shorter and prettier. There's also a much more challenging trail that clambers up to the **Na Pòpia** lighthouse on the northwest coast. Most people visit for the scenic solitude, but the island is also good for **birdlife** – ospreys, shags, gulls and other seabirds are plentiful, and you may also see several species of raptor. For **sailing times**, call ahead or ask down at the harbour; the tourist office (see below) has both schedules and island maps. Incidentally, be sure to make arrangements for your return boat trip on the outward journey.

The rugged coastal district just to the north of Sant Elm is devoid of development and boasts some enjoyable **hikes**. The most popular are the two-hour return hike to the **Torre de Cala en Bas** watchtower and the slightly longer excursion to the ruinous, nineteenth-century monastery of **La Trapa**. The tourist office will advise on routes and issues free, if rudimentary, hiking maps.

Practicalities

There is a good daily bus service to Sant Elm from Andratx and Port d'Andratx. **Buses** pull in at the south end of the main street, from where it's a couple of minutes' walk to the **tourist office** (May–Oct Mon–Fri 9.30am–3.30pm & Sat 9.30am–2.30pm; ☎971 62 80 19), which has information on local hikes, bus timetables, and the sailing times of the boat to Sa Dragonera (see p.146). The same boat company also operates passenger ferries between Sant Elm and Port d'Andratx (1 daily; €7 one-way).

The resort has two **hotels** and there's a reasonable chance of a vacancy in high season at one of them, the *Hostal Dragonera*, on the main drag at c/Jaume I, 5 (☎971 23 90 86, ℻971 23 90 13; ❸; closed Dec & Jan). This one-star *hostal* occupies a simple modern building with clean and neat rooms, the best of which have balconies with sea views. The other hotel, the *Aquamarín*, at c/ Cala Es Conills 4 (☎971 23 91 05, ℻971 23 91 25; ❸; closed Nov–April) is a package-tour favourite with rarely a spare room in sight. The hotel is a lumpy concrete structure built in the general style of an old watchtower and plonked next to the beach at the south end of the main street.

For such a small place, Sant Elm has a surprisingly wide choice of **cafés and restaurants** dotted along its main street. One good choice is the seafront *Bar-Restaurant Flexas*, which serves delicious and inexpensive snacks and meals, for instance sardines and salad for just €7. Alternatively, the harbourside *Vista Mar* (☎971 23 75 47; closed Tues) has great sea views and does an excellent fish soup as well as fishy main courses from around €15.

Port d'Andratx

In the last decade, the picturesque port and fishing harbour of **PORT D'ANDRATX**, 5km southwest of Andratx, has been transformed by a rash of low-rise shopping complexes and Spanish-style villas. Nevertheless, it's not at all a classic case of overdevelopment: the heart of the **old town**, which slopes up from the south side of the bay, preserves a cramped network of ancient lanes,

Bus stops ▲

ACCOMMODATION
Brismar   A
Catalina Vera   B
Villa Italia   C

RESTAURANTS, CAFÉS & BARS
Galicia   3
La Consigna   1
La Gallega   6
La Piazzetta   2
Mitj & Mitj   5
Rocamar   7
Tim's Bar   4

0   100 m

PORT D'ANDRATX

Andratx

Camp de Mar

C (50m)

and there's no denying the prettiness of the setting, with the port standing at the head of a long and slender inlet flanked by wooded hills. Sunsets show the place to best advantage, casting long shadows up the bay, and it's then that the old town's gaggle of harbourside restaurants crowd with holidaymakers and expatriates, a well-heeled crew, occasionally irritated by raucous teenagers, who come here for the nightlife. Port d'Andratx may be rather sedate, but it's still an enjoyable place to spend a night or two, especially as it possesses several outstanding seafood restaurants and is easy to reach. The one thing it doesn't have is a sandy beach – the nearest one is east over the hills at Camp de Mar (see p.107).

Arrival and information

There are fast and frequent **buses** to Port d'Andratx from Palma, Andratx and all the larger resorts of the Badía de Palma (see p.149) and a reasonably frequent service from Sant Elm. Buses pull in at the back of the bay, a brief walk from both the old town (on the left as you face the sea) and the big, modern marina (on the right). From March to October, there are also once-daily **boats** from Sant Elm; the journey takes 20 minutes and costs €7; for timetable details call ☏639 61 75 45 or 696 42 39 33. There's a **taxi** rank about halfway along the old town harbourfront, or you can call Radio Taxi Andratx on ☏971 13 63 98; the fare to Camp de Mar is about €6, to Sant Elm about €10.

Accommodation

Even in the height of the season, there's a good chance of finding a vacant **room** in Port d'Andratx, but you're much safer booking ahead. The options are, however, limited to an inexpensive *hostal* and two hotels, one a bargain, the other full-blown luxury. All are located on or near the old town's harbourfront.

Hotel Brismar c/Almirante Riera Alemany 6 ☏971 67 16 00. A pleasant, old-fashioned three-star place with fifty spotless, en-suite rooms, the pick of which have port-facing balconies (though avoid these if you're a light sleeper – there's a bar next door). Closed Dec–Feb. **⑤**

Hostal Catalina Vera c/Isaac Peral 63 ☎971 67 19 18. This appealing establishment occupies a neatly shuttered and whitewashed 1950s two-storey house in a quiet location, flanked by a small orchard one block up from the harbourfront. Packed with house plants, the foyer leads to guest rooms that are frugal but well cared for; some with showers, some without. Closed Dec–Feb. ❸

Hotel Villa Italia Cami Sant Carles 13 ☎971 67 40 11, ⊛www.hotelvillaitalia.com. An opulent, 1920s twin-towered Italianate mansion set behind a steeply terraced garden with luxuries such as a rooftop swimming pool, as well as gorgeous views out over the bay. It's located a five-minute stroll west of the old part of town along Camí Sant Carles, an extension of c/Isaac Peral. There are rooms in the old villa and in the more modern annexe. ❻

Eating and drinking

The old town is packed with **cafés and restaurants**, which line up along the harbourfront and crowd the more central portions of c/Isaac Peral, one block up the hill. Generally speaking, standards are high and a local feature is the seafood – good almost everywhere and superb at the town's two Galician places. Eating is the big deal here, but there are several **bars** too, lively little spots that hum till the early hours throughout the summer.

Cafeteria La Consigna Avgda Mateo Bosch 26. Popular and enjoyably modern coffee house-cum-patisserie about a third of the way along the harbourfront with great cakes, croissants and coffees.

Restaurant Galicia c/Isaac Peral 37 ☎971 67 27 05. Highly recommended, bistro-style Galician place serving mouthwatering seafood without the pretensions of some of its rivals down on the harbourfront. Especially strong on shellfish. Has simple, modern decor and very reasonable prices.

Restaurant La Gallega c/Isaac Peral 52 ☎971 67 13 38. Excellent and very popular bistro-style Galician restaurant specializing in seafood, with main courses from about €12.

Mitj & Mitj c/Almirante Riera Alemany 8. The flashiest bar in town, with a wide range of sounds, from house through to jazz, and imaginative decor including art installations on the outside balcony.

Restaurante La Piazzetta Plaça Almirante Oquendo 2. Large, popular restaurant and pizzeria on a pleasant pedestrianized square just up from – and about one-third of the way along – the harbourfront from the head of the bay. Tasty pizzas and pastas from €7 as well as reasonably priced seafood dishes.

Restaurant Rocamar c/Almirante Riera Alemany 27 ☎971 67 12 61. A well-established restaurant at the west end of the harbourfront, away from the crowds and offering delicious seafood; also has a lovely bayside terrace. Daily in summer noon–11pm, restricted hours in winter. Seafood main courses from €15.

Tim's Bar c/Almirante Riera Alemany 10. More subdued than the *Mitj & Mitj* next door, this cosy little bar caters to an older crowd.

Travel details

Buses

For further details, call ☎971 177 777, or check out ⊛tib.caib.es.

Andratx to: Palma (hourly; 1hr); Peguera (every 30min; 20min); Port d'Andratx (every 30min; 10min); Sant Elm (7 daily; 40min); Valldemossa (1 weekly; 1hr 15min).

Banyalbufar to: Andratx (1 weekly; 30min); Esporles (Mon–Sat hourly, 4 on Sun; 20min); Estellencs (Mon–Sat hourly, 3 on Sun; 20min); La Granja (Mon–Sat hourly, 4 on Sun; 15min); Palma (Mon–Sat hourly, 3 on Sun; 1hr); Peguera (1 weekly; 1hr 45min); Valldemossa (1 weekly; 45min).

Bunyola to: Orient (2 daily; 30min, but service by advance reservation only); Palma (Mon–Fri hourly, Sat & Sun every 1–2hr; 20min).

Deià to: Palma (3–5 daily; 45min); Port de Sóller (3–5 daily; 40min); Sóller (3–5 daily; 30min); Valldemossa (3–5 daily; 15min).

Estellencs to: Andratx (1 weekly; 45min); Banyalbufar (Mon–Sat hourly, 3 on Sun; 20min); Esporles (Mon–Sat hourly, 4 on Sun; 40min); La Granja (Mon–Sat hourly, 4 on Sun; 35min); Palma (Mon–Sat hourly, 3 on Sun; 1hr 20min); Peguera (1 weekly; 1hr 30min); Valldemossa (1 weekly; 1hr).

Palma to: Alaró (Mon–Fri 1 daily; 30min); Andratx (hourly; 1hr); Banyalbufar (Mon–Sat hourly, 3 on

Sun; 1hr); Bunyola (Mon–Fri hourly, Sat & Sun every 1–2hr; 20min); Deià (3–5 daily; 45min); Esporles (Mon–Sat hourly, 4 on Sun; 30min); Estellencs (Mon–Sat hourly, 3 on Sun; 1hr 20min); Galilea (2–4 daily; 55min); La Granja (Mon–Sat hourly, 4 on Sun; 35min); Port d'Andratx (hourly; 1hr 15min); Port de Sóller (via the tunnel: Mon–Fri hourly, Sat & Sun every 1–2hr; 35min); via Valldemossa: 3–5 daily; 1hr 30min); Puigpunyent (2–4 daily; 40min); Sóller (via the tunnel: Mon–Fri hourly, Sat & Sun every 1–2hr; 30min; via Valldemossa: 3–5 daily; 1hr 15min); Valldemossa (Mon–Fri every 1–2hr, Sat 6 daily, Sun 4 daily; 30min).

Port d'Andratx to: Andratx (every 30min; 10min); Palma (hourly; 1hr 15min); Peguera (every 30min; 30min); Sant Elm (7 daily; 30min).

Port de Sóller to: Alcúdia (April–Oct 2 daily; 2hr 30min); Ca'n Picafort (April–Oct 2 daily; 3hr); Deià (3–5 daily; 40min); Lluc (April–Oct 2 daily; 1hr 20min); Palma (via the tunnel: Mon–Fri hourly, Sat & Sun every 1–2hr; 35min; via Valldemossa: 3–5 daily; 1hr 30min); Port d'Alcúdia (April–Oct 2 daily; 2hr 35min); Port de Pollença (April–Oct 2 daily; 2hr 10min); Sóller (Mon–Fri hourly, Sat & Sun every 1–2hr; 5min); Valldemossa (3–5 daily; 55min).

Sant Elm to: Andratx (7 daily; 40min); Port d'Andratx (7 daily; 30min).

Sóller to: Alcúdia (April–Oct 2 daily; 2hr 20min); Ca'n Picafort (April–Oct 2 daily; 2hr 50min); Deià (3–5 daily; 30min); Lluc (April–Oct 2 daily; 1hr 10min); Palma (via the tunnel: Mon–Fri hourly, Sat & Sun every 1–2hr; 30min; via Valldemossa: 3–5 daily; 1hr 15min); Port d'Alcúdia (April–Oct 2 daily; 2hr 25min); Port de Pollença (April–Oct 2 daily; 2hr); Port de Sóller (Mon–Fri hourly, Sat & Sun every 1–2hr; 5min); Valldemossa (3–5 daily; 50min).

Valldemossa to: Andratx (1 weekly; 1hr 15min); Banyalbufar (1 weekly; 45min); Deià (3–5 daily; 15min); Estellencs (1 weekly; 1hr); Palma (Mon–Fri every 1–2hr, Sat 6 daily, Sun 4 daily; 30min); Peguera (1 weekly; 1hr 30min); Port de Sóller (3–5 daily; 55min); Sóller (3–5 daily; 50min).

Trains

Palma to: Binissalem (every 30–40min; 30min). For further information, call ☎971 17 77 77, or check out ⊛tib.caib.es.
Palma to: Sóller (7 daily; 1hr). For further information, call ☎971 75 20 51, ⊛www.trendesoller.com.

Northern Mallorca

CHAPTER 3　**Highlights**

* **Lluc** Home to the Balearics' most venerated icon, La Moreneta, this magnificent monastery makes a smashing base for mountain hikes. See p.157

* **The Davallament, Pollença** Held in the beguiling little town of Pollença, the torchlit Lowering of the Cross – the Davallament – is the most evocative of the many events celebrating Easter Holy Week. See p.166

* **Ermita de Nostra Senyora del Puig** A rambling assortment of old stone buildings, this is one of the most appealing of Mallorca's several hilltop monasteries. See p.166

* **Cap de Formentor** This tapered promontory of bleak sea-cliffs and pine-dusted hills offers gorgeous views and is a fruitful area for bird-watching. See p.176

* **Parc Natural de S'Albufera** A small pocket of rare wetland offering the best birdwatching on the island. See p.185

△ Cap de Formentor

Northern Mallorca

The magnificent **Serra de Tramuntana** mountains reach a precipitous climax in the rearing peaks of northern Mallorca, beginning just to the northeast of Sóller. This is the wildest part of the island, long the haunt of brigands and monks, and even today the ruggedness of the terrain forces the main coastal road, the **MA-10**, to duck and weave inland, offering only the occasional glimpse of the sea. A rare exception is the extraordinary side road that snakes down to both overcrowded **Sa Calobra** and the attractive beach at **Cala Tuent**, but it's the lovely monastery of **Lluc** that remains the big draw here – for religious islanders, who venerate an effigy of the Virgin known as La Moreneta, and tourists alike. Pushing on along the coast, the MA-10 emerges from the mountains to reach **Pollença**, a tangle of stone houses clustered around a fine, cypress-lined Way of the Cross. Pollença is one of Mallorca's most appealing towns and it's also within easy reach of both the solitary coastal resort of **Cala Sant Vicenç** and the wild and rocky **Península de Formentor**, the bony, northernmost spur of the Serra de Tramuntana. This peninsula shelters the northern shore of the Badía de Pollença, which is home to the laid-back and low-key resort of **Port de Pollença**, whilst the next bay down holds the more upbeat and flashy **Port d'Alcúdia**. Close by, the old walled town of **Alcúdia** has a clutch of modest historical sights and pocket-sized **Muro** has a splendid main square. Here too is the **Parc Natural de S'Albufera**, which takes the prize as the best birdwatching wetland in Mallorca.

This part of the Serra de Tramuntana offers superb **hiking**. Suggestions for several comparatively easy walks are given in the text, and we have also described in detail one outstanding day-long hike starting at Lluc, another near Alcúdia, and a third, shorter hike beginning in Port de Pollença. The **hiking guide** you want is Editorial Alpina's (@www.editorialalpina.com) "Mallorca Tramuntana Norte", which has trail descriptions and detailed **maps** (1:25,000). To get a copy locally, try the tourist office in Sóller or any large bookshop in Port de Pollença. Northern Mallorca also boasts fine **beaches**, principally in the long, golden strands that stretch round the bays of Pollença and Alcúdia.

As regards **accommodation**, the resorts of northern Mallorca – primarily Port de Pollença, Port d'Alcúdia and Cala Sant Vicenç – muster a veritable phalanx of hotels and *hostals*, but this is predominantly package territory, and from June to early September (and sometimes beyond) independent travellers are well advised to make advance **reservations**. In the shoulder season and in winter things are much easier and cheaper, though many places do close down. More promisingly, the number of inland *hostals* and hotels is on the increase – Pollença, Alcúdia, Sineu and Petra all now have places to stay – and there's

NORTHERN MALLORCA

0 — 5 km

MEDITERRANEAN SEA

Cap de Formentor

Península de Formentor

Platja de Formentor

Talaia d'Albercutx

Mirador Mal Pas

Cala Bòquer

Cala Sant Vicenç

Port de Pollença

Badia de Pollença

Cap des Pinar

Penya Roja (345m)

Ermita de la Victòria

Bonaire

Port d'Alcúdia

Badia d'Alcúdia

Alcúdia

Ca'n Picafort

Ferry to Ciutadella, Menorca

PARC NATURAL DE S'ALBUFERA

Colònia de Sant Pere

Artà

N

MA-12

Santa Margalida

Sa Pobla

Muro

Castell del Rei

Puig de l'Àguila (206m)

Pollença

Ermita de Nostra Senyora del Puig

Coves de Campanet

Campanet

MA-13

MA-2200

MA-10

SERRA DE TRAMUNTANA

Puig Roig (1002m)

Monestir de Lluc

Escorca

Gorg Blau

Puig de Massanella (1365m)

Caimari

Selva

Mancor de la Vall

Inca

MA-13A

Lloseta

MA-13A

MA-13

Consell

Binissalem

Palma

Sa Calobra

Ermita de Sant Llorenç

Puig Major (1436m)

Embassament de Cúber

Castell d'Alaró

Alaró

Cala Tuent

Mirador de Ses Barques

Fornalutx

Biniaraix

Orient

SERRA DE TRAMUNTANA

Bunyola

Jardins d'Alfàbia

Port de Sóller

Sóller

Llucalcari

Deià

Puig d'es Teix (1062m)

Valldemossa

Port de Valldemossa

Cala Deià

Son Marroig

MA-10

MA-11

Palma

Esporles

Port d'Andratx

La Granja

Ferries from Port d'Alcúdia to Menorca

From mid-May to mid-September, Balearia (☎902 16 01 80, ⓦwww.balearia.com) operates a twice daily, fast-ferry **catamaran** service from Port d'Alcúdia to Ciutadella on Menorca (see p.277). The journey time is just one hour and one-way passenger fares start at about €35 (cars from €100). In addition, Iscomar (☎902 11 91 28, ⓦwww.iscomar.com) operates **car ferries** from Port d'Alcúdia to Ciutadella once or twice daily except in the depths of winter; the journey time is two and a half hours, the one-way passenger fare costs about €30, and vehicles up to 4.5m in length are charged around €60. Remember that local car rental firms do not allow their vehicles to leave Mallorca.

not quite the seasonal crush here that there is on the coast. Finally, you could also stay at one of the region's two **monasteries** – at Lluc and just outside Pollença: the rooms are frugal but inexpensive, and there's usually space at any time of the year.

Getting around by public transport is easy enough as even the smaller places have a reasonable **bus** service. Nonetheless, certain buses are seasonal and fairly infrequent – most notably the Sóller–Pollença service – so advance planning is the order of the day; all the area's tourist offices carry bus timetables. Where the bus won't take you, a **taxi** will and rates, especially if you're travelling in a group, are very reasonable; drivers, on the other hand, should be aware that **parking** in all the more populous resorts and towns can be a real pain in the summertime between about 10 or 11am and 5pm.

The northern coast: from Sóller to the Formentor Peninsula

Beyond Sóller, the **MA-10** slips through the highest and harshest section of the Serra de Tramuntana. For the most part, the mountains drop straight into the sea – precipitous and largely unapproachable cliffs with barely a cove in sight. The accessible exceptions are the comely beach at **Cala Tuent** and the horribly commercial hamlet of **Sa Calobra** next door. The best place to break your journey, however, is inland at the monastery and pilgrimage centre of **Lluc**, which offers a diverting museum, top-notch mountain hiking trails and a reliable supply of inexpensive rooms.

There's more low-priced monastery accommodation at the hilltop Ermita de Nostra Senyora del Puig, just outside **Pollença**, a beguiling old town of honey-coloured stone mansions sitting at the foot of a beautiful "calvary" walkway. Nearby, just down at the coast, is **Port de Pollença**, a medium-sized, remarkably amenable resort with a long sandy beach draped around the Badía de Pollença. The resort is a popular summertime retreat for the inhabitants of Palma and abounds in places to stay; it's also within easy striking distance of the dramatic seacliffs of the **Formentor Peninsula** at the northernmost tip of the island.

There are good to excellent **bus services** to and between the towns and resorts stretching along the coast between Ca'n Picafort and Port de Pollença/Pollença. There are also fairly frequent buses from Inca train station to Lluc. However, the coastal bus linking Port de Sóller and Sóller with Lluc, Pollença and Port de

Pollença – as well as Alcúdia and Port d'Alcúdia – only operates between April and October and only twice daily at that. What's more, demand for seats can sometimes outstrip supply, though you will have a better chance of grabbing a seat if you get on board at Port de Sóller rather than waiting at the second stop, Sóller. For the frequencies and journey times of all buses, see p.187.

Gorg Blau

Heading northeast from Sóller, the MA-10 zigzags up into the mountains. After about 5km, the road passes the steep turning down to Fornalutx (see p.118) before offering a last lingering look over the coast from the **Mirador de Ses Barques** vantage point. Thereafter, the road snakes inland and tunnels through the western flanks of **Puig Major** (1436m), the island's highest mountain. Beyond the tunnel is the **Gorg Blau** (Blue Gorge), a bare and bleak ravine that was a well-known beauty spot until a hydroelectric scheme scarred the gorge and its immediate surroundings with a trio of puddle-like reservoirs. The second of the three is the **Embassament de Cúber** (Cúber reservoir), an unappetizing expanse of water redeemed by its abundant birdlife, notably several different types of raptor. For a better look, stop at the lay-by to follow the easy footpath which circumnavigates the reservoir – it only takes a couple of hours to complete. The reservoir is also an obvious starting point for the four-hour hike west to the Barranc de Biniaraix along (part of) the GR221 long-distance footpath.

To the immediate north of the reservoir rear the bare and craggy flanks of **Puig Major**, but the dramatic trail that twists up to the summit from the military base beside the main road remains off-limits on account of its radar station. This makes **Puig de Massanella** (1365m), which looms over the Gorg Blau to the east, the highest mountain that can be climbed on Mallorca – and the climb up it from Lluc is described on p.162.

Cala Tuent

At the far end of Gorg Blau the MA-10 tunnels into the mountains to emerge just short of a left turn leading to Sa Calobra and Cala Tuent. This turn-off makes for an exhilarating, ear-popping detour to the seashore, the well-surfaced road hairpinning its way down the mountain slopes so severely that at one point it actually turns 270 degrees to run under itself.

About 10km down this road, there's a fork: head left over the hills for the four-kilometre journey to the **Ermita de Sant Llorenç**, a tiny medieval church perched high above the coast, and **CALA TUENT**, where a smattering of villas cling to the northern slopes of Puig Major as it tumbles down to the seashore. Ancient orchards temper the harshness of the mountain, and the gravel and sand beach is one of the quietest on the north coast. It's a lovely spot to while away a few hours – if you can wrangle a parking spot (space is extremely limited) – and provided you stay close to the shore, the swimming is safe. There's nowhere to stay, but there is an excellent **restaurant** up on a ridge on the far side of the cove, the *Es Vergeret* (mid-Feb to Oct daily 12.30–4.30pm; ☎971 51 71 05), which offers a wide range of fish and meat dishes from €14, best devoured at the terrace bar in sight of the sea.

Sa Calobra

Heading right back at the fork in the road, it's just 2km to **SA CALOBRA**, a modern resort occupying a pint-sized cove in the shadow of the mountains. The setting itself is gorgeous, but the place is an over-visited disaster: almost every island operator deposits a busload of tourists here every day in summer and the crush is quite unbearable – as is the overpriced and overcooked food at the local cafés. The reason why so many people come here is to visit the impressive box canyon at the mouth of the **Torrent de Pareis** (River of the Twins). It takes about ten minutes to follow the partly tunnelled walkway round the coast from the resort to the mouth of the canyon. Here, with sheer cliffs rising on every side, the milky-green river trickles down to the narrow bank of shingle that bars its final approach to the sea – though the scene is transformed after heavy rainfall, when the river crashes down into the canyon and out into the ocean.

Escorca

Back on the MA-10, about 4km northeast of the Cala Tuent/Sa Calobra turnoff and 26km from Sóller, is **ESCORCA**, a poorly defined scattering of houses that is the starting point for the **descent of the Torrent de Pareis**, a famous though very testing and potentially dangerous hike-cum-climb which requires some basic rock-climbing skills. The river drops from here to Sa Calobra through a formidable, seven-kilometre-long limestone gorge, which takes about five hours to negotiate. The descent is not practicable in winter, spring, or after rainfall, when the river may be waist-high and the rocks dangerously slippery. The descent starts at the **sign** on the main road opposite the conspicuous *Restaurant Escorca*. The gorge is almost always hotter than its surroundings, so it's essential to take lots of water.

The Monestir de Lluc

Tucked away in a remote valley about 35km northeast of Sóller, the austere, high-sided dormitories and orange-flecked roof tiles of the **Monestir de Nostra Senyora de Lluc** (Monastery of Our Lady of Lluc) stand out against the greens and greys of the surrounding mountains. It's a magnificent setting for what has been Mallorca's most important place of pilgrimage since the middle of the thirteenth century, though the religious significance of the place goes back much further: the valley's prehistoric animistic inhabitants deified the local holm-oak woods, and the **Romans** picked up on the theme, naming the place from *lucus*, the Latin for "sacred forest". Thereafter, the **monks** who settled here after the Reconquista were keen both to coin a purely Christian etymology and to enhance their reputation. They invented the story of a shepherd boy named Lluc (Luke) stumbling across a tiny, brightly painted **statue** of the Virgin in the woods. Frightened by his discovery, the lad collared the nearest monk and when the pair returned heavenly music filled their ears, bright lights dazzled their eyes, and celestial voices declared the statue to be an authentically heaven-sent image.

Buses to Lluc from points east and west along the coast, as well as Inca train station, stop in the large car park right outside the monastery, which is itself situated 700m off the MA-10.

The monastery church

The **monastic complex** (daily: April–Sept 10am–11pm; Oct–March 10am–8pm; free) is an imposing and formal-looking affair mostly dating from the eighteenth and early nineteenth centuries. At its centre is the main shrine and architectural highlight, the **Basílica de la Mare de Déu de Lluc**, which is graced by an elegant Baroque facade. To reach it, pass through the monastery's stately double-doored entrance and keep straight on till you reach the second – and final – courtyard, where there's a dreary statue of Bishop Campins, who overhauled

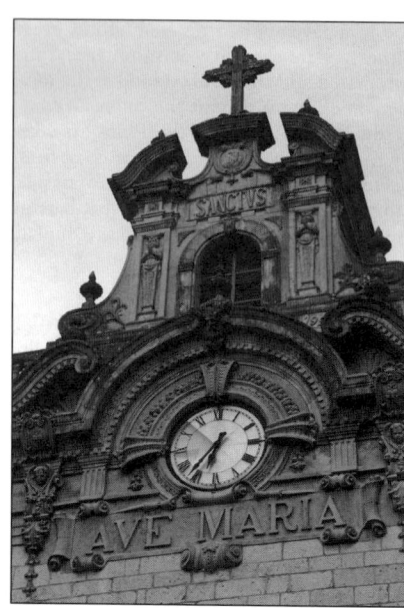
△ Lluc monastery

Lluc in the early part of the last century and is shown kneeling and facing the entrance to the church. Dark and gaudily decorated, the church is dominated by heavy jasper columns, the stolidness of which is partly relieved by a dome over the crossing. On either side of the nave, stone steps extend the aisles round the back of the Baroque high altar to a small chapel. This is the holy of holies, built to display the statue of the Virgin, which has been commonly known as **La Moreneta** ("the Little Dark-Skinned One") ever since the original paintwork peeled off in the fifteenth century to reveal brown stone underneath. Just 61cm high, the Virgin looks innocuous, her face tweaked by a hint of a smile and haloed by a much more modern jewel-encrusted gold crown. In her left arm she cradles a bumptious baby Jesus, who holds the "Book of Life" open to reveal the letters alpha and omega. Every day, the **Escolania de Lluc** boys' choir performs in the basilica during the daily 11am Mass and again at evensong. Founded in the early sixteenth century with the stipulation that it must be "composed of natives of Mallorca, of pure blood, sound in grammar and song", the choir is nicknamed *Els Blauets*, "The Blues", for the colour of their cassocks.

The monastery museum

Just inside and to the right of the basilica's main entrance a small door leads through to a corridor that runs past the stairway up to the enjoyable **Museu de Lluc** (daily: 10am–1.30pm & 2.30–5pm; €3). After the ticket desk, this begins with a modest section devoted to archeological finds from the Talayotic and Roman periods and then it's on into the so-called Sala del Tresor (Treasure Room), packed with all manner of folkloric items brought here to honour La Moreneta, from fancily painted fans, medallions, rosaries and crosses through to walking sticks discarded when the supplicants found they were no longer lame. Beyond, a room of incidental bric-a-brac, featuring examples of traditional island costume, precedes a substantial collection of **majolica** (see box on p.159), glazed earthenware mostly shaped into two-handled drug jars and show dishes or plates. Some two or three hundred pieces are on display, the pick coming from the eighteenth century, when the designs varied in sophistication, from broad and bold dashes of colour to carefully painted naturalistic designs, but the colours remained fairly constant, restricted by the available technology to iron red, copper green, cobalt blue, manganese purple and antimony yellow. There is also a good sample of Balearic and Valencian **lusterware**, brown earthenware with a sheen – or luster – and manufactured between the sixteenth and the eighteenth centuries. The final rooms on this floor are, by comparison, rather

Majolica

The fifteenth century witnessed a vigorous trade in decorative pottery sent from Spain to Italy via Mallorca. The Italians coined the term **"majolica"** to describe this imported Spanish pottery after the medieval name for the island through which it was traded, but thereafter the name came to be applied to all tin-glazed pottery. The process of making majolica began with the mixing and cleaning of clay, after which it was fired and retrieved at the "biscuit" (earthenware) stage. The biscuit was then cooled and dipped in a liquid glaze containing tin and water. The water in the glaze was absorbed, leaving a dry surface ready for decoration. After painting, the pottery was returned to the kiln for a final firing, which fused the glaze and fixed the painting. Additional glazings and firings added extra lustre. Initially, majolica was dominated by greens and purples, but technological advances added blue, yellow and ochre in the fifteenth century. Majolica of one sort or another was produced in Mallorca up until the early twentieth century.

disappointing, devoted to the uninspiring island land- and village-scapes of **José Coll Bardolet** (1912–92).

Upstairs – and this is a bit of a surprise – the museum displays an excellent sample of **Mallorcan art**, either by native artists or artists once resident here. Amongst them, there are the Goya-esque works of Salvador Mayol (1775–1834); the Neoimpressionist canvases of Llorenç Cerdà (1862–1955); the romantic landscapes of Bartomeu Sureda (1769–1851); and the finely observed mountain landscapes of **Antoni Ribas** (1845–1911), arguably the most talented artist on display here.

The rest of the monastery

Back outside the monastery's double-doored entrance, walk a few metres to the west and you'll soon spot the large, rough-hewn column at the start of the **Camí dels Misteris del Rosari** (Way of the Mysteries of the Rosary), a broad pilgrims' footpath that winds its way up the rocky hillside directly behind the monastery. Dating from 1913, the solemn granite stations marking the way are of two types: simple stone pediments and, more intriguingly, rough trilobate columns of Gaudí-like design, each surmounted by a chunky crown and cross. The prettiest part of the walk is round the back of the hill, where the path slips through cool, green woods with rock overhangs on one side and views out over the bowl-shaped **Albarca valley** on the other, with **Puig Roig** (1003m) rearing up beyond. It takes about ten minutes to reach the top of the hill, where a wrought-iron *Modernista* cross stands protected by ugly barbed wire. It's actually possible to stroll down into the Albarca valley on the country road that begins to the left (west) of the monastery's main entrance, but the road fizzles out long before you reach the coast and there's nowhere in particular to aim for. For a longer **hike** into the mountains, see p.162.

On the east side of the monastery are the **Jardí Botanic** (botanical gardens; Mon–Sat 10am–1pm & 3–6pm; free) – they're signed through the conspicuous arches on the right as you face the main building. The gardens are laid out with local plants as well as exotics, plus small ponds and waterfalls, little footbridges and even a windmill. It takes about fifteen minutes to walk through the gardens on a well-defined path.

Practicalities

🚶 **Accommodation** at the monastery (☎971 87 15 25, ℱ971 51 70 96, ℮info@lluc.net; ❶) is highly organized, with simple, self-contained cells for

THE MASSANELLA MASSIF

KEY TO WALKS:

Primary Route
Alternative Ascent
Cart Track

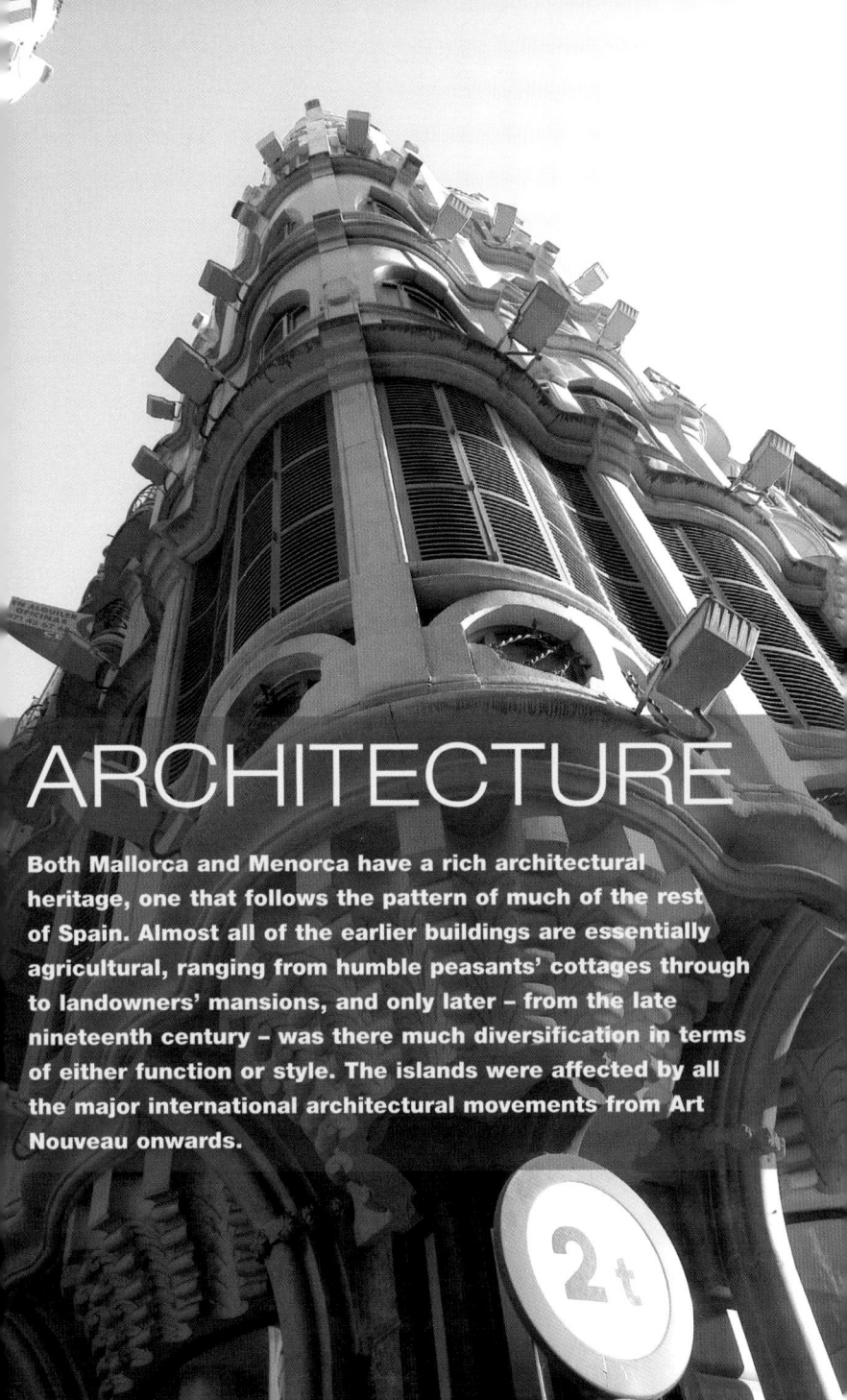

ARCHITECTURE

Both Mallorca and Menorca have a rich architectural
heritage, one that follows the pattern of much of the rest
of Spain. Almost all of the earlier buildings are essentially
agricultural, ranging from humble peasants' cottages through
to landowners' mansions, and only later – from the late
nineteenth century – was there much diversification in terms
of either function or style. The islands were affected by all
the major international architectural movements from Art
Nouveau onwards.

Labour

There's never been any shortage of **stone** on either Mallorca or Menorca and neither – at least until recently – has there been a problem with **labour**: right up until the 1950s, hundreds of farm labourers were desperately keen to supplement their meagre incomes by working on any building project that came along, providing it wasn't forced labour – in the countryside big landowners sometimes had the right to make the local peasantry repair roads without payment.

The combined efforts of generations of island labourers are plain to see across both islands, beginning with the multitude of **dry-stone walls** that both separated one field from another and protected animals and crops. Indeed, on Menorca, where unlike Mallorca there are no mountains to protect the island from the prevailing northerly wind, there were dry-stone structures for just about everything; from ziggurat-shaped shelters for the cattle through to stone wells built around the base of individual olive trees.

Fincas

The main beneficiaries of all this hard graft were the island's landowners, who also had a ready pool of labour when it came to the construction of their stone farmhouses – or **fincas** – which are still a prominent part of the Balearic landscape. Some of these *fincas* – for example La Granja near Valldemossa and Binisues on Menorca – are to all intents and purposes rural palaces (or *haciendas*); others, like Ca's Xorc, are rather more modest country houses. Scores have been modernised for use as holiday homes and hotels but the standard architectural format, of all but the grandest, traditionally comprised a whitewashed, stone or stone-and-rubble exterior, a flagged exterior courtyard, shuttered and grilled rectangular windows, high, wood-beamed ceilings and cellar/basement service quarters. Surrounding these *fincas* were a raft of specialist buildings, from olive presses and workshops through to barns and store houses – many of which have now been turned into restaurants, shops and even hotel bedrooms.

▼ *Hotel Ca's Xorc*

Town houses and mansions

The larger landowners also possessed handsome stone **town houses** and it's these – along with the old stone houses built for the island's merchants – that give the likes of Sóller, Binissalem and Fornalutx their particular charm. In Binissalem, for example, *Scott's Hotel* occupies a sympathetically revamped, eighteenth-century almond grower's house, whilst Lloseta's *Hotel Ca's Comte* is sited in a charming landowner's mansion that dates back to the fifteenth century, if not beyond. It is, however, the patrician mansions of Palma that take the architectural biscuit. Most of medieval Palma was destroyed by fire, so the city's gentry were obliged to rebuild in a hurry in the late seventeenth and early eighteenth centuries – and that's what they did, filling the narrow streets around the cathedral with a wonderful ensemble of mansions built in the fashionable Renaissance style of the time. With their columns and capitals, loggias and arcades hidden away behind outside walls of plain stone, these mansions were surprisingly uniform in layout with an arched gateway giving onto a rectangular courtyard in front of the house. From the courtyard, a stone exterior staircase led up to the main public rooms – with the servants' quarters below and the family's private apartments above.

▲ *Scott's Hotel*, Binissalem

Churches, castles and monasteries

Every single town and village on both Mallorca and Menorca has a church; mostly a large, stern-looking edifice with high stone walls and a capacious single-vaulted nave. The majoriy are essentially Gothic in design, but overlaid with later fiddlings, most notably Baroque side-chapels with unspeakably kitsch furnishings and fittings. Head and shoulders above the rest is **Palma Cathedral**, quite simply the finest building in the Balearics, its soaring buttresses staring out over the Mediterranean. Palma also boasts the islands' best-

◀ Ermita de Nostra Senyora del Puig

preserved medieval castle, the **Castell de Bellver**, whose mighty walls are perched on top of a hill just outside the city centre. There are assorted hilltop castles elsewhere on the islands too, mostly broken down and neglected, like the Castell d'Alaró and Castell Santa Agueda, though Capdepera and Àrta castles are in a much better state of repair. Similarly conspicuous are the hilltop monasteries that dot Mallorca, some of medieval provenance and five now offering some of the quietest and least expensive lodgings on the island – though these pale into insignificance when compared with the island's two largest **monasteries**, Lluc and Valldemossa.

Modernisme and beyond

By the late nineteenth century, many a well-heeled islander felt vaguely embarrassed by the austere stone mansions of yesteryear and was only too pleased to latch onto **Modernisme**, the local version of Art Nouveau, when it came into fashion. Consequently, there are *Modernisme* buildings all over the islands, but the most flamboyant and colourful, with their flowing, organic lines and decorative ceramics, are largely confined to Palma – on and around Plaça Weyler. In its turn, *Modernisme* looked unduly frilly by the 1950s, prompting Joan Miró for one to plump for a straightforward international **Modernist** design, all cubes and angular lines, when he had his studio built in Cala Major. The studio is a good-looking building, no mistake, but it was a false dawn: the hotels that choked much of the Balearic coastline in the 1960s may have espoused modernism in general terms, but too often they were poorly conceived and executed, leaving the islands with a problematic architectural heritage – and one that the newest fad (for sprawling, low-slung villa-villages) has done nothing to resolve.

▲ Palma: *Modernisme* building

▼ Miró's studio

up to four people and slightly more commodious apartments, which offer self-catering but do not provide any utensils. In summer, **phone ahead** if you want to be sure of space; at other times simply book at the monastery's information office on arrival. There's usually an 11pm curfew, except for the apartments, which have their own separate entrance.

For **food**, there's a small general store and several adequate cafés and restaurants in between the monastery and the car park, but the star turn is the monks' former refectory, *Sa Fonda* (Wed–Sun 9am–9pm), a beautifully restored old hall complete with wooden beams, wide stone arches and marble pillars. The food is traditional Spanish, with main courses from around €11; the meat dishes are much better than the fish.

Pollença and around

Founded in the thirteenth century, the pretty little town of **POLLENÇA** nestles among a trio of hillocks 20km northeast of Lluc, where the Serra de Tramuntana fades into coastal flatland. Following standard Mallorcan practice, the town was established a few kilometres from the seashore to militate against sudden pirate attack, with its harbour, **Port de Pollença** (see p.168), left as an unprotected outpost. For once the stratagem worked. Unlike most of Mallorca's old towns, Pollença successfully repelled a string of piratical onslaughts, the last and most threatening of which was in 1550, when the notorious Turkish corsair Dragut came within a hair's breadth of victory. In the festival of **Mare de Déu dels Àngels** on August 2, the townspeople celebrate their escape with enthusiastic street battles, the day's events named after the warning shouted by the hero of the resistance, a certain Joan Más: "Mare de Déu dels Àngels, assistiu-mos!" ("Our Lady of Angels, help us!").

Pollença is also within easy striking distance of **Cala Sant Vicenç**, a small, modern resort on the island's northern shore, and the hiking trail to a medieval castle, the **Castell del Rei**, though at the time of writing access is denied by the landowner.

Arrival and information

Buses to Pollença pull in immediately to the south of the main square, Plaça Major, at the foot of c/Antoni Maura. The town's **tourist office** (Oct–May Mon–Fri 8am–3pm & Sat 10am–1pm; June–Sept Mon–Fri 9am–2pm & 2.30–4pm, Sat 10am–1pm; ☎971 53 50 77, ⓦwww.puertopollensa.com) is metres away in the old cloister wall adjoining Nostra Senyora del Roser. Pollença's tiny centre is best explored on foot, but outlying attractions such as the resort of Cala Sant Vicenç (see p.167) can be reached by bus (for frequencies, see p.187) or taxi. There's a taxi rank in the centre at the corner of Avinguda Pollentia and c/Reina Maria Cristina, or call ☎971 86 62 13. If you're **driving**, you can avoid the baffling one-way streets of the old town by entering Pollença from the south, turning off the main Inca–Port de Pollença road onto Avinguda Pollentia.

Accommodation

Hotel Desbrull c/Marquès Desbrull 7 ☎971 535 055, ⓦwww.desbrull.com. Small hotel with just six fairly sparse but perfectly adequate double rooms kitted out in brisk, modern style. ⑤

Ermita de Nostra Senyora del Puig 2km south of town (see p.166) ☎971 18 41 32. The original monks' quarters have been renovated to provide simple rooms sleeping between two and six guests with shared facilities. A double room costs €20 upstairs, €15 down, otherwise the cost is just €6.50 per person per night. Be warned that it can get cold and windy at night, even in the summer. There's a refectory, but the food is only average. Most guests turn up on spec: to be sure of a room, book ahead. ①

A circular walk from Lluc to Puig de Massanella and the Massanella massif

11km; 795m of ascent; 4hr 30min–5hr round-trip. Medium difficulty.

The large **Massanella massif** has eleven peaks over 1000m and is defended by many crags and steep rocky slopes. Since the construction of a military base put Puig Major out of bounds, **Puig de Massanella**, with its magnificent views, has become the island's best-loved summit. Although quite strenuous, the route is not difficult and deservedly popular, the target being the mountain's twin peaks, the higher of which, at 1367m, is all bare rock. Keep an eye open for black vultures and for the friendly Alpine accentors who often appear on the summit's bare rocks or down by Font de S'Avenc, the spring just below the summit.

The route

The ascent of Massanella can be started at Lluc monastery, but this adds an uninspiring thirty-minute walk to each end of the hike and you are really better off beginning at the **petrol station**, just south of the main coastal highway (the MA-10) on the Inca-Lluc road (the MA-2130); it's usually possible to park here without any problem.

From the petrol station, walk south along the road in the Inca direction. Cross the bridge and turn right through the iron gates onto a wide track. Follow the track for 250m past a spring and water trough. Ignoring the Camí Vell de Lluc, a restored footpath to Caimari that continues straight on, swing sharp right uphill following the red painted waymarks. Continue on the wide track through a gate into the area of the **Comafreda farm**, whose owner may charge €3 at this gate. Pause when you come to a wide opening into a field to look at the impressive **Es Fronto**, a high spur of the Massanella massif with precipitous cliffs. Beyond this, you will see the farmhouse set back on the right and accessed by a track. Ignore this and the track directly in front of you, which passes between gateposts, and instead bear left to take the path on the left hand side of the wall that encloses the fields.

This path is well used and marked with paint signs and cairns. Rising through the woods, it joins a wide cross track at a large **painted boulder** (remember this landmark as it is useful on your descent). Turn left to reach the **Coll de Sa Linea** at 824m, where there is a clearing among the trees and two engraved stones on the right. The main track begins to descend here towards the village of Mancor de la Vall. A possible diversion for strong walkers is to make the ascent of Puig de N'Ali (1035m) by a winding route marked with some cairns and red paint signs; it's not easy to follow, especially at first because of the trees. The top is unusual, with an immense boulder supported in three places to form a sheltered cave with a southern outlook over the plain.

For Puig de Massanella, turn right at **Coll de Sa Linea** up a clearly defined path rising in big swings at first, then twisting and turning to reach a junction where the two paths to the top diverge. At this junction, there's a **stone** engraved with the words "**Puig y Font**" ("Mountain and Spring") on the right-hand side and "Font y Puig" on the left. For the ascent, the route to the right (Puig y Font) is recommended as it is easier to find. It follows an old mule track that was once used to carry ice down from the mountains to the plains. Later on, above the treeline, you'll see the

L'Hostal c/Mercat 18 ☎971 53 52 81, ⓦwww .hostalpollensa.com. Six bright and breezy modern rooms with a/c, just metres from the main square. ❺

 Hotel Juma Plaça Major 9 ☎971 53 50 02, ⓦwww.hoteljuma.com. Enjoyable, small

hotel in an old stone merchant's house that functions rather like a traditional pension with reception on the first floor, a café down below and the a/c rooms up above. The rooms are neat and tidy and the best have balconies with views over the centre. Bang in the middle of town overlooking the main square. ❻ old dry-stone walls of the **Casa de Sa Neu** on the right, where the ice was stored before transportation.

Beyond here the path almost levels out, meandering through boulders and clumps of carritx grass in a shallow valley. Beyond this the Font y Puig path – which you will take on your descent – joins from the left. Continue on heading towards the dip between the **highest peak** of Massanella and the secondary peak to the southwest (1352m), then veer right to the main peak, which is where you are most likely to see a black vulture. Be careful how you go here as there's a pothole some 20m deep close to the summit. On a good day the view from the top encompasses almost the entire island, from the Formentor headland in the northeast to the Bay of Palma. To the north, vertical cliffs plunge 150m to the Coll d'es Prat (1210m), above which lies the northern section of the Massanella massif. Puig Major is readily identified by the radar domes on the summit and the sheer cliffs below.

The descent
To descend, retrace your steps to where the southerly path joins the route up. This southerly path offers an awkward but exhilarating descent over sharp cornered limestone boulders lying at all angles, with deep crevices in between. To go down it, turn right to an **engraved stone**, on the edge of a sloping shelf below the summit. An obvious rocky staircase leads down to a spring, the **Font de S'Avenc**, by which is a red earth platform, conspicuous in the grey rocky landscape. Steps lead down to an upper cave where a table and benches have been cut out of the rock. A further set of steps lead down to a lower chamber with two basins of water (you'll need a torch to see inside the lower cave). The flies that can infest this cavern make it an unlikely picnic spot but it offers shelter from lightning and rain.

The path from the spring contours to the east at first, splitting briefly into two – take either branch. The route is marked, but pay careful attention to where you're going as there are many goat paths and natural ledges to lead you astray. Follow the marked path back into the trees and onto the Puig y Font/Font y Puig engraved stone. Now it's a question of retracing your steps, turning left at the Coll de Sa Linea and right at the painted boulder, before passing through the Comafreda farm and returning to the Inca-Lluc road and the petrol station.

Alternative ascent via Coll d'es Prat
With descent as above, 12km; 795m of ascent; 5hr–5hr 30min round-trip.

An alternative and longer ascent can be made by following the old track from Comafreda up the valley on the north side of Massanella to the high **Coll d'es Prat** (1210m), then descending the **Comellar d'es Prat** valley for about 1km, from where a path climbs up to the 1158m col between Puig de Ses Bassetes (1216m) and Massanella by a short easy scramble. From this col, the direct ascent of the southwest ridge to a secondary peak of Massanella (1352m) is for rock-climbers only, but a walkable path makes its way up a rising traverse, heading east at first, then following the cairns which show the way up the steep and rocky ground. These cairns are difficult to see in the grey rocky wilderness and a descent by this route is not recommended.

Posada de Lluc c/Roser Vell 11 ☏ 971 53 52 20, ⓦ www.posadalluc.com. This small and very comfortable hotel occupies an attractively restored old stone house in the centre of town. The monks from Lluc monastery (see p.157) used to lodge here when they popped into Pollença to pick up supplies – hence the statue of the Madonna over the front door – and many of the original features have been kept, most notably the deep stone arches. There's a small outside pool and each of the a/c guest rooms has been equipped in an appropriate modern version of period style. Closed Dec & Jan. ⑥

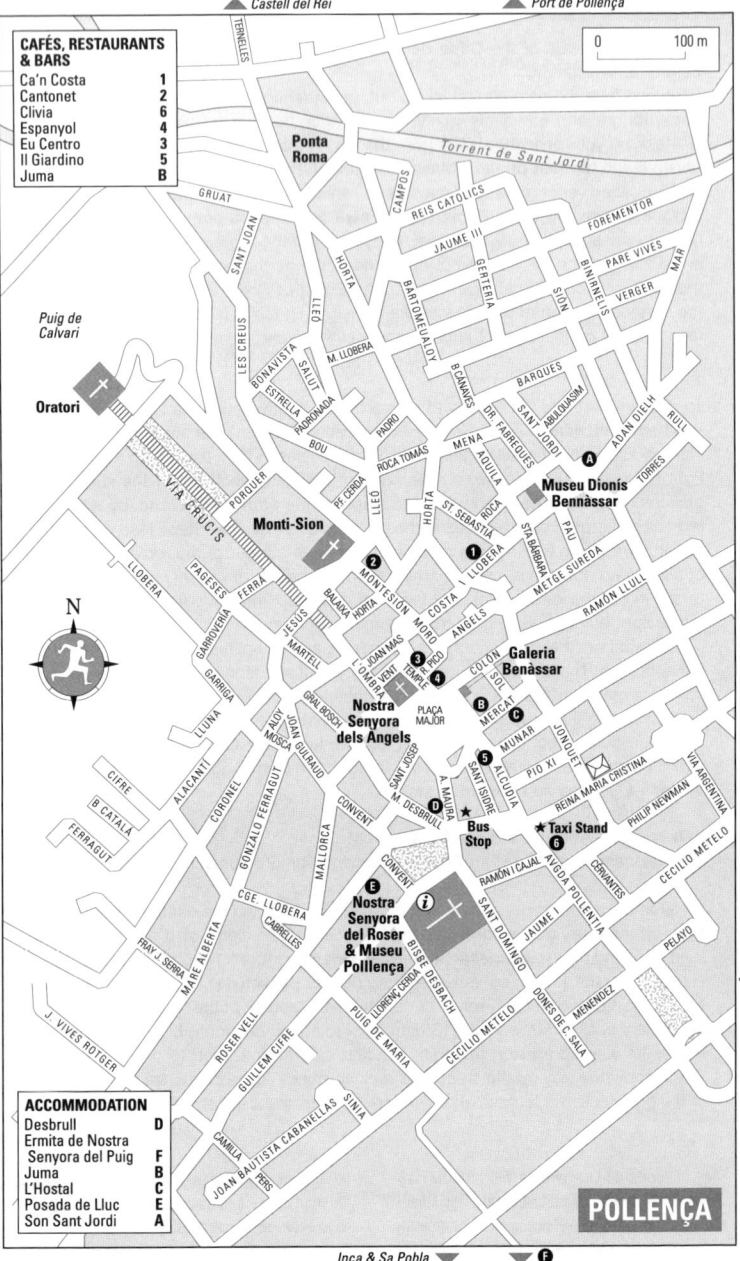

▲ Castell del Rei   ▲ Port de Pollença

CAFÉS, RESTAURANTS & BARS	
Ca'n Costa	1
Cantonet	2
Clivia	6
Espanyol	4
Eu Centro	3
Il Giardino	5
Juma	B

0   100 m

C710 to Lluc

Ponta Roma

Torrent de Sant Jordi

Puig de Calvari

Oratori

Monti-Sion

Museu Dionís Bennàssar

N

Galeria Benàssar

Nostra Senyora dels Angels

PLAÇA MAJOR

Bus Stop   ★ Taxi Stand

Nostra Senyora del Roser & Museu Pollença

POLLENÇA

ACCOMMODATION	
Desbrull	D
Ermita de Nostra Senyora del Puig	F
Juma	B
L'Hostal	C
Posada de Lluc	E
Son Sant Jordi	A

Port de Pollença ▶

Inca & Sa Pobla ▼   ▼ ❻

Hotel Son Sant Jordi c/Sant Jordi 29
☎ 971 53 03 89, ⓦ www.hotel
sonsantjordi.com. In a nineteenth-century town
house beside a mini-piazza, the *Sant Jordi* has
kitted out its bedrooms in a lavish manner with

bunched drapes and four-poster beds. There's
every mod con here, including a/c and a large
garden out the back with a sizeable pool. Handy
location too, just a brief walk from the main
square. ❼

The Town

Although Pollença dodged the piratical attentions of Dragut and his chums, not much of the medieval town has survived, and the austere stone houses that now cramp the twisting lanes of the compact centre mostly date from the seventeenth and eighteenth centuries. The heart of the town is **Plaça Major**, an especially amiable main square, which accommodates a cluster of laid-back cafés and restaurants and is also the site of a lively fruit and veg market on most Sunday mornings. Overlooking the square is the severe facade of the church of **Nostra Senyora dels Àngels**, a sheer cliff-face of sun-bleached stone pierced by a rose window. Dating from the thirteenth century, but extensively remodelled in the Baroque style five centuries later, the church's gloomy interior, with its mighty single-vaulted nave, has a mildly diverting sequence of ceiling and wall paintings, as well as a whopping, tiered and towered high altarpiece. The original church was built for the Knights Templar (for more on whom, see p.81) and passed to another knightly order, the Hospitallers of St John, after the pope suppressed them in 1312. The Hospitallers of St John struggled on until 1802, when the Spanish king appropriated all they owned.

Take c/Antoni Maura from Plaça Major and you soon reach a leafy square, whose greenery surrounds an antique water wheel and a stumpy, much battered watchtower. Behind looms the austere facade of **Nostra Senyora del Roser**, a deconsecrated church with a bright and gaudy Baroque interior that is sometimes used for temporary exhibitions. Otherwise, the church is usually closed, but the adjoining cloisters form part of the **Museu de Pollença** (Tues–Fri 10.30am–1pm, Sat & Sun 11am–1pm, but hours extended during exhibitions; free), which houses a surprisingly good and regularly rotated collection of contemporary paintings, photography and video art, including pieces by winners of the town's annual art competition. There's also a modest assortment of local archeological finds, though these are poorly labelled, and a room of **Mallorcan primitive paintings**, most memorably a warm, tender and exquisitely detailed *Virgin and Musical Angels* by Francesc Comes (1379–1415). In the cloisters, look out for the memorial to Philip Newman (1904–66), the Manchester-born violinist who took a real shine to Pollença in the 1950s, founding and fostering its main musical festival, the **Festival de Pollença**, still held here every year throughout July and August (☎ 971 53 50 77, ⓦ www.festivalpollenca.org).

Warming to this cultural theme, Pollença is dotted with commercial art galleries, the most conspicuous of which is the **Galeria Benàssar**, on Plaça Major (Tues–Sat 10am–1pm & 5–9pm, Sun 11am–1.30pm). The gallery is named after Dionís Benàssar (1904–67), a local artist whose former home, a brief walk northwest of Plaça Major at c/Roça 14, has been turned into the **Museu Dionís Benàssar** (Tues–Sun 11am–1pm; €2). The museum holds a tidy collection of his modernist paintings, brightly coloured canvases amongst which the Mallorcan land- and village- scapes are the most interesting; they also have a lively programme of temporary exhibitions.

If you are roaming out this way, you might keep going north to the old Roman bridge – the **Pont Roma** – which has survived on the edge of town, about 600m away: it's not in itself a remarkable structure, but it has remained intact despite all the historical odds.

Puig de Calvari

Pollença's pride and joy is its **Via Crucis** (Way of the Cross), a long, steep and beautiful stone stairway, graced by ancient cypress trees, which ascends the **Puig de Calvari** (Calvary Hill) to the north of the town centre. At the top, a much-revered thirteenth-century statue of **Mare de Déu del Peu de la Creu** (Mother of God at the Foot of the Cross) is lodged in a simple, courtyarded **oratori** (chapel), whose whitewashed walls sport some of the worst religious paintings imaginable, though the views out over coast and town are sumptuous. On Good Friday, a figure of Jesus is slowly carried by torchlight down from the *oratori* to the church of Nostra Senyora dels Àngels, a procession known as the **Davallament** (Lowering), one of the most moving religious celebrations on the island.

The Ermita de Nostra Senyora del Puig

There are yet more magnificent views from the **Ermita de Nostra Senyora del Puig**, a rambling, mostly eighteenth-century monastery perched on top of the Puig de Maria, a 330-metre-high hump facing the south end of town. The monastic complex, with its fortified walls, courtyard, chapel, refectory and cells, has had a chequered history, alternately abandoned and restored by both monks and nuns. The Benedictines now own the place, but the monks are gone and today a custodian supplements the order's income by renting out cells to tourists (see p.161). There's nothing specific to see, but the setting is extraordinarily serene and beautiful, with the mellow honey-coloured walls of the monastery surrounded by ancient carob and olive trees, a million miles from the tourist resorts clearly visible far below.

It takes around an hour to **walk** to the monastery from the centre of town: head for the main Pollença–Inca road (MA-2200), where a signed turning leads up a steep lane that fizzles out after 1.5km to be replaced by a cobbled footpath winding up to the monastery's entrance. It's possible to drive to the top of the lane, but unless you've got nerves of steel, you're better off parking elsewhere. Note that there have been reports of cars left at the foot of the lane overnight being vandalized; although this is unusual, you might prefer to park in town instead.

Eating and drinking

Pollença does very well for **restaurants**, supported by the villa owners who gather here every evening from the surrounding countryside. The **café and bar** scene is less convincing, but there are several reasonably lively spots on and around Plaça Major. Almost all of the town's cafés and bars serve food of some description, mostly inexpensive *tapas*.

Bar Espanyol Plaça Major 2. Every other place on the main square may heave with the well-heeled and the well-tanned, but the renegades gather here at this old-fashioned, locals' favourite. Drinks are the big deal here, but they also serve filling and inexpensive snacks.

Café-Bar Juma Plaça Major 9. Good range of tasty *tapas* sold in the brisk, modern bar of the *Hotel Juma*. Rapid-fire service and reasonable prices – a standard portion of *tapas* costs about €4. The outside terrace overlooking the main square is particularly pleasant.

Ca'n Costa c/Costa i Llobera 11 ☏971 53 12 76. Beautiful restaurant tucked away in an old mansion

on a picturesque side street, featuring international gourmet cuisine with a Mediterranean slant. Main courses from €17. Mon–Sat from 7pm.

Cantonet c/Monti-Sion 20 ☏971 53 04 29. This fashionable restaurant just north of Plaça Major offers top-notch international/Italian cuisine from a limited menu with main courses starting from as little as €11. In the summer, you can eat out on the terrace of the large church next door. Daily except Tues 7–11pm; closed Nov–Jan.

Clivia Avgda Pollentia 5 ☏971 53 36 35. Very hospitable restaurant, and long-time expatriate favourite, offering an excellent range of Spanish dishes – try the squid in ink. If you choose fish, the waiter brings the uncooked version to the table so you can inspect it, which is really rather refreshing. The decor is traditional Spanish and attracts an older clientele. Mains €15–20. Daily except Wed 1–3pm & 7–10pm.

Eu Centro c/Temple 3. This very central café-restaurant is one of the town's mainstays and popular with locals and tourists alike for its solid Mallorcan fare. Main courses €10–14. Closed Wed.

🏃 **Il Giardino** Plaça Major 11 ☎971 53 43 02. Arguably the best restaurant in town, this smart bistro-style place offers a superb range of Italian dishes from about €14, all prepared with vim and gusto and featuring the best of local ingredients. To be sure of a seat on the terrace – where you will probably want to eat – either come early or book ahead. Great house wines too. Daily from 7pm; closed Nov to mid-March.

Northeast of Pollença: Cala Sant Vicenç

Love or hate the place – and opinions are equally divided – there's no denying that **CALA SANT VICENÇ**, a modern resort 6km northeast of Pollença, boasts an attractive, solitary setting amongst bare rocky outcrops that nudge gingerly out into the ocean. The problem is the resort itself: some visitors like the modern villas that spill over and around the wooded ravine at its heart, others think they are dreary in the extreme, most are agreed on the *Hotel Don Pedro* however, crassly plonked on the minuscule headland separating the resort's two small but sandy **beaches**. If you are staying in the resort, it may be comforting to know that it's easy enough to escape by **hiking north** out onto the wild and wind-licked seashore. The obvious targets are the remote *calas* that punctuate the coastline, but you could also undertake the moderately strenuous hoof up to the top of **Puig de l'Àguila** (206m), from where there are grand views over the surrounding shoreline. This 6km-long hike takes around three

The Castell del Rei

Some 7km north of Pollença stand the battered ruins of the medieval **Castell del Rei** (Castle of the King), glued to an isolated and inhospitable crag which rears high above the seashore. This remote fastness was founded by the Moors and strengthened by Jaume I to guard the northerly approaches to Pollença against pirate attack. In this regard, however, it was something of a failure: the pirates simply ignored it, preferring to land at nearby Cala Sant Vicenç instead. More successfully, it held out for months against the Aragonese invasion of 1285 and was the last fortress to surrender to Pedro of Aragón, the supplanter of the Mallorcan king Jaume III, in 1343. Subsequently, the castle was used as a watchtower, finally being abandoned in 1715.

It takes about two hours to **walk** to the castle from Pollença, an undemanding hike along a country lane and then a forest footpath leading through the pretty **Ternelles valley** – or at least it would do if the local landowner would relent and allow access once again. To check if the circumstances have changed, ask at Pollença tourist office (see p.161) before you set out.

If you have the go-ahead, look for the signposted turning to Ternelles on the MA-10, on the northern edge of Pollença – though the sign is faded and easy to miss: the turning is about 800m to the west of the MA-10/MA-2200. The Ternelles road begins by twisting its way north past attractively renovated old *fincas* and olive and citrus groves. After 1.6km, you'll reach a guarded gate set in the narrow defile at the entrance to the Ternelles valley, where you have to park. An easy-to-follow, rough and dusty track leads to another set of gates, beyond which the path starts to rise, climbing through oak woods to a stretch of mixed woodland dominated by pines. Further on, the trees thin out and the castle ruins can be spied in the distance. About 100m after the start of a fenced-off area on the right-hand side, fork left off the main track – which continues down to the shingly beach at **Cala Castell** – for the climb up to the castle. You can't actually go inside the ruins, but it's worth climbing up for the view.

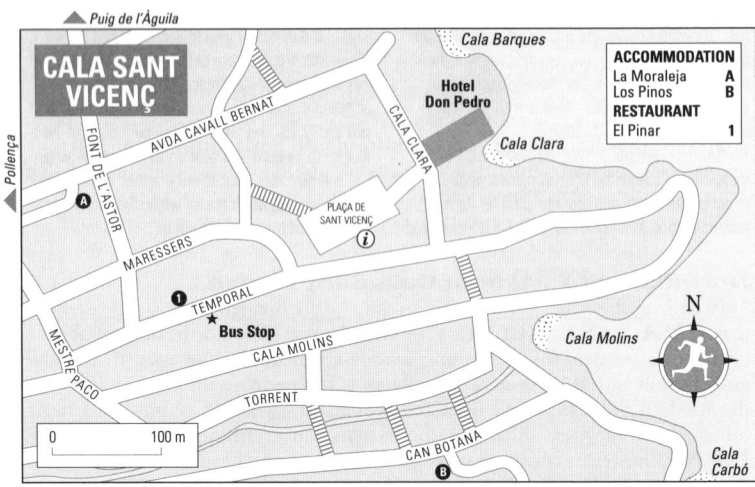

hours; the first part uses a rough stone road, the second follows a well-defined path that leads to the base of Puig de l'Àguila – but you'll still need a proper hiking map to find your way.

Buses to Cala Sant Vicenç stop in the centre of the resort on Avinguda Temporal. From here, it's a short walk northeast to the **tourist office**, on Plaça Sant Vicenç (June–Sept Mon–Fri 10am–2pm & 3–6pm, Sat 10am–2pm; ☎971 53 32 64), and a minute or two more to the resort's two main beaches. This is package territory, so vacant **rooms** are extremely thin on the ground, but you might try the two-star *Hostal Los Pinos*, c/Can Botana s/n (☎971 53 12 10, ⓦ www.hostal-lospinos.com; late April to Oct; ❸), in a traditionally furnished modern villa with a pool, nineteen rooms and a large terrace on the south side of the resort. Cala Sant Vicenç's smartest hotel is the five-star *Hotel La Moraleja*, Avgda Cavall Bernat s/n (☎971 53 40 10, ⓦ www.lamoraleja.net; May–Oct; ❾), in a swish, low-slung modern mansion on the north side of the resort.

Amongst the resort's several **cafés and restaurants**, the pick is *El Pinar*, Avgda Temporal 83 (☎971 53 40 80; closed Wed), which has an extensive menu offering tasty Spanish dishes like stuffed mussels in breadcrumbs and hot spicy prawns; mains begin at around €11.

Port de Pollença and around

With the mountains as a shimmering backdrop, **PORT DE POLLENÇA** is a pleasantly low-key, family-orientated resort that arches through the flatlands behind the Badía de Pollença. The **beach** is the focus of attention here, a narrow, elongated sliver of sand, which is easily long enough to accommodate the crowds, while its sheltered waters are ideal for swimming. A rash of apartment buildings and hotels blights the edge of town, and the noisy main road to Alcúdia cuts through the centre, but there are no high-rises to speak of and the resort is dotted with attractive whitewashed and stone-trimmed villas. Altogether it's quite delightful, especially to the north of the marina, where a portion of the old beachside road – along **Passeig Anglada Camarasa** and **Passeig Voramar** – has been pedestrianised. When – or if – you get bored by the beach, you can also hire a bike and **cycle** out into the surrounding countryside or make the enjoyable **hike** across the neck of the Formentor Peninsula to Cala Bóquer (see p.172).

Port de Pollença has been popular with middle-class Brits for decades – witness Agatha Christie's crime story *Problem at Pollensa Bay* – but the hoi polloi were kept away from the adjoining **Península de Formentor** by an Argentine swank called Adam Diehl. In 1928, Diehl bought the whole peninsula and then built himself the *Hotel Formentor* to cater for his friends and contacts. Since then, Diehl and his heirs have permitted almost no development, and you can now drive to the cape at the end and savour the peninsula's stupendous mountain scenery without a villa in view.

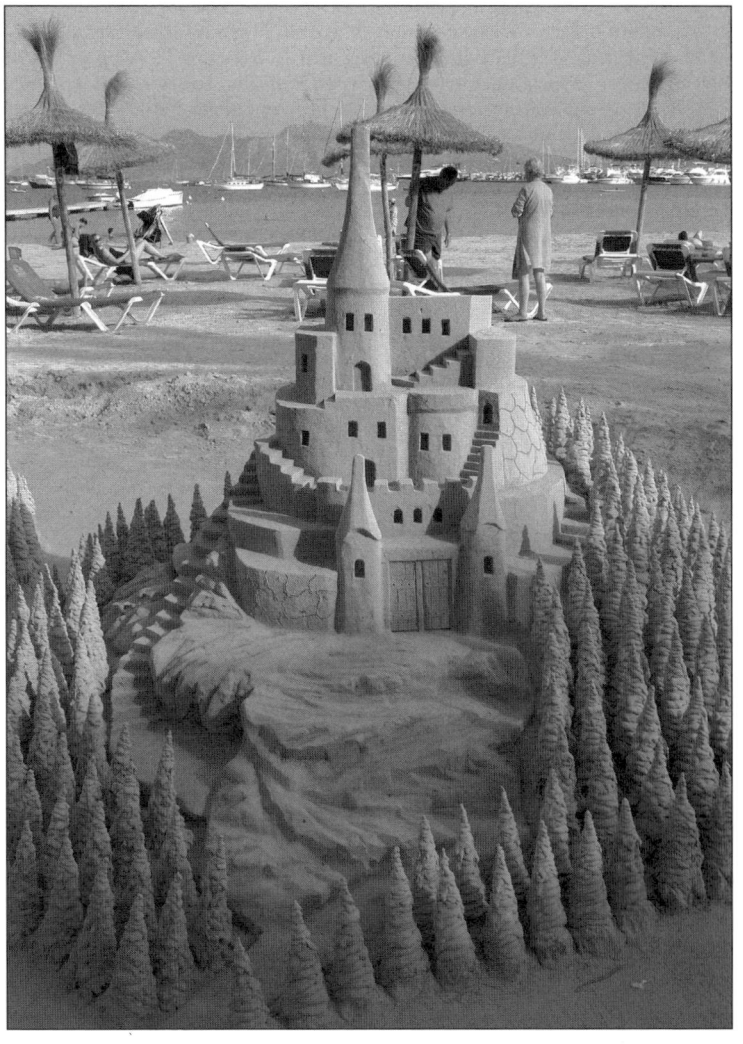

△ Port de Pollença beach

Arrival, information and getting around

Buses to Port de Pollença stop beside the marina bang in the centre of the resort and metres from the **tourist office** (June–Sept Mon–Fri 8am–3pm & 5–7pm, Sat 9am–1pm; Oct–May Mon–Fri 8am–3pm, Sat 9am–1pm; ☎971 86 54 67, ⓦwww.puertopollensa.com), which has loads of local information, including accommodation lists, bus and boat-trip timetables and details of car rental companies.

The rusticated flatlands edging the Badía de Pollença and stretching inland as far as Pollença make for easy, scenic cycling and **mountain bikes** as well as ordinary **bicycles** can be rented from *Rent March*, in the centre of Port de Pollença at c/Joan XXIII, 89 (Mon–Sat 9am–1pm & 4–8pm, Sun 9am–12.30pm; ☎971 86 47 84) – as can mopeds and motorcycles. Ordinary bikes cost in the region of €8 per day or €40 per week. The most obvious **hike** is the delightful jaunt north over to Cala Bóquer, a route that is described in detail on p.172, but for longer excursions contact **Mallorcan Walking Tours – MWT** (☎609 70 08 26, ⓦwww.mallorcanwalkingtours.puertopollensa.com), who operate an outstanding range of day-long hikes during spring and autumn. There is something to suit most levels of fitness and they cover the whole of the Serra de Tramuntana mountains as well as the hilly uplands north of Artà (see p.204). Naturally enough, costs vary depending on the hike but begin at about €25 per person including transport to the trailhead where appropriate, though walkers need to take their own food and water. MWT also do an ambitious week-long traverse of the Serra de Tramuntana from Valldemossa to Pollença and, in the heat of the summer, organize a series of less strenuous island "Discovery Days". Potential hikers need to **book** a minimum of 24 hours beforehand, either direct or preferably at the reception desk of the *Hotel Sis Pins* (see p.172).

Boat trips of various descriptions are extremely popular in Port de Pollença and they all leave from the west side of the marina. There are regular excursions out into the Badía de Pollença (€18.50), to Cap de Formentor (€18.50), and round the coast to Cala Sant Vicenç (€23), but the most popular trip is the quick, twenty-minute hop over to the golden sands of the Platja de Formentor (€9; see p.175).

Accommodation

Port de Pollença has around a dozen **hotels** and not quite as many **hostals**. Needless to say, most of the rooms are block-booked by tour operators, but there's a reasonably good chance of finding a vacancy in the places listed below, especially in the shoulder season. The part of town you want is the pedestrianized Passeig Anglada Camarasa; try to avoid Passeig Saralegui unless you're indifferent to traffic.

Hostal Bahía Passeig Voramar 31 ☎971 86 65 62, ⓦwww.hoposa.es. In a lovely location a few minutes' walk north of the marina along the seashore, this pleasant, unassuming *hostal* offers thirty rooms in one of the port's older villas. Closed Nov–March. ④, ⑤ with sea view.

Hotel Can Llenaire Carretera Llenaire s/n ☎971 53 52 51, ⓦwww.hotelllenaire.com. This imposing Mallorcan manor house sits on the brow of a hill with wide views over the Badía de Pollença. The owner still operates a farm here, with sheep munching away and groves of almond and olive trees, but the house itself has been turned

into a charming country hotel with most of the original features, which date back to the eighteenth century, sympathetically revamped. There are just eleven guest rooms, each decked out in lavish period style. The hotel is clearly signposted down a country lane from the main coastal road just east of the centre of Port de Pollença. ⑧

Hotel Daina c/Atilio Boveri 2 ☎971 86 62 50, ⓦwww.hoposa.es. Straightforward, tower-block hotel with three stars and sixty-odd rooms. The public areas have recently been revamped in pleasant modern style. Great bayshore location beside Passeig Anglada Camarasa. Closed Dec–Feb. ⑥

PORT DE POLLENÇA

Badia de Pollença

N

Marina

Taxi
Stand

Main
Bus Stop

Boats and
ferries

MOLL NOU

Rent
March

Pollença

▲ Cala Bóquer   ▲ Formentor   ▲ Formentor

PASSEIG COLÓN   F

PUBLICA
BÒQUER

0   200 m

ACCOMMODATION
Bahía   E
Can Llenaire   A
Daina   B
Illa d'Or   F
Miramar   C
Sis Pins   D

CAFÉS & RESTAURANTS
IRU   3
Ivy Garden   2
La Balada del
  Agua del Mar   4
Little Italy   5
Los Zarzales   1
Stay   6

▲ (2km) & Alcúdia

Hotel Illa d'Or Passeig Colom 265 ⊕ 971 86 51 00, ⊛ www.hotelillador.com. Well-equipped, four-star hotel by the waterfront on the northern edge of the resort. Set in its own grounds with its own jetty and beach, the hotel is built in traditional Spanish style and dates back to the 1920s, but the interior is ultra modern – pleasant enough but without much character. Closed Dec to mid-Feb. **7**

Hotel Miramar Passeig Anglada Camarasa 39 ⊕ 971 86 64 00, ⊛ www.hotel-miramar.net. Pleasant, three-star hotel in an elegant building – all iron grilles and stone lintels – that dates back to 1912, when it must have been pretty much the only building on the beach. The rooms are standard-issue modern affairs, but it's still worth paying the extra €20 or so for a room with a sea view and a balcony – or you might be plonked at the back looking out over Carretera Formentor. Closed Nov–March. **6**

Hotel Sis Pins Passeig Anglada Camarasa 77 ⊕ 971 86 70 50. Extremely pleasant and immaculately turned out three-star hotel occupying an attractive whitewashed and balconied villa on the waterfront. Two storeys, fifty-one rooms. Owned and operated by the tour company Globespan (⊛ www.flyglobespan.com), the hotel's reception staff take bookings for guided walks and hikes with Mallorcan Walking Tours (see p.24). Closed Nov–March. **6**

Eating and drinking

Port de Pollença heaves with **cafés and restaurants**. Many of them offer run-of-the-mill tourist fodder and there's a plethora of pizza joints, but others serve the freshest of seafood and skillfully blend Catalan and Castilian cuisines. As a

A valley walk from Port de Pollença to Cala Bóquer

6km; 101m of ascent; 2hr return. Easy.

The walk through the sheltered **Vall de Bóquer** is an attractive, easy stroll over gently undulating ground across the neck of the Península de Formentor. The headland at the end of the walk offers splendid views of the severe sea-cliffs that mark the northern coast with the cove and beach below. Return is by the same route, about 3km each way. The walk is suitable for most ages and abilities – though the last leg down to the beach is uneven and can be difficult for young children. The peninsula is also favoured by ornithologists for the variety of resident and migrant **bird life** and by feral goats whose acrobatics can be entertaining.

The route

Start by heading north along the seafront from Port de Pollença's marina and then turn left up **Avinguda Bocchoris**. Continue across the Carretera Formentor into the **Area Publica Bóquer**, a green and leafy space with c/Bóquer to either side – which is where it's easy to park. Proceed up the green area with the seafront behind you to a triple carriageway road. The footpath starts on the opposite side of the roundabout.

On the far side of the roundabout, keep straight along the path with the ridge of the Serra del Cavall Bernat straight ahead. Approximately 300m further on, the path passes through an iron gate. The **Bóquer farmhouse** is ahead on the right, while on the left, before you get to the farmhouse, is an interesting but neglected **terraced garden** shaped like a ship with its prow facing out to sea: the terraces were watered from stone irrigation channels fed from holding tanks, but these are now all dry. There's a splendid view of the Badía de Pollença from here and some fine examples of the *Agave americana*, a succulent whose flower spikes reach heights of three metres.

Beyond the farmhouse, the path turns round to the right, heading north through a small iron gate, then ascends steadily for about 500m, passing between large rocks. Niches in the rocks are occupied by clumps of dwarf fan palms, and you'll probably see the blue rock thrushes that inhabit the area. Here and further along the walk, you may also spot wheatears, black-eared wheatears, black redstarts, rock sparrows and wrynecks, as well as buzzards, peregrines, kestrels, booted eagles, the occasional general rule, competition keeps **prices** down to readily affordable levels, with around €12–18 covering a main course at all but the ritziest establishments.

La Balada del Agua del Mar Passeig Voramar 5 ☎971 86 42 76. Lovely little beachside café-restaurant occupying an old villa whose terrace is shaded by an ancient fig tree. Good salads and seafood. Mains €11–17.

Ivy Garden c/Llevant 14 ☎971 86 62 71. This very competent and cosy restaurant features an inventive modern menu at reasonable prices. Dishes change, but include things like fillet of salmon with spring-onion sauce and duck with orange, honey and soy sauce. Main courses average around €15. March–Dec Tues–Sun 7–11pm.

Little Italy Passeig Voramar 57 ☎971 86 67 49. Amenable and very popular restaurant, where the pizzas are large, authentically Italian and very, *very* good. Pizzas from €10.

Restaurant IRU Passeig Anglada Camarassa 23 ☎971 86 70 02. Bright and breezy seafront restaurant, which outclasses its neighbours – and rivals – with its imaginative cuisine and extrapolations of traditional Mallorcan dishes. Prides itself on its use of local ingredients – and Balearic wine list. Mains from €15. April–Oct daily 12.30–3pm & 7–11pm; Nov–March ring for times.

Restaurant Stay on the Moll Nou jetty ☎971 86 40 13. Recently refitted, this long-established restaurant, with its crisp modern decor and attentive service, is renowned for the quality of its seafood – though the main courses tend towards the small size. Prices are a bit above average, but well worth it for the setting out on the pier; superb desserts and great wine list too. It's a

osprey, Eleonora's falcons in spring and in summer, stonechats and goldfinches. Various warblers pass through this area during migration too, but the big ornithological thrill is the **black vulture**, with a wingspan of around two metres, which glides the air currents of the north coast. There's a fairly good chance of spotting one from the Vall de Bóquer and if you're really lucky you'll get a close view, its large, black body contrasting with a brownish head, beak and ruff.

Beyond the boulders the path descends, becoming less rocky, then passes through a gap in a dry-stone wall before ascending gently for about 150m – a scattering of pine trees 50m to the left offers a shady spot for a picnic. The valley's semi-wild goats have heavily grazed the area, leaving the vegetation sparse and scrubby. The most noticeable plant is *Asphodelus microcarpus*, which grows up to two metres high, bearing tall spikes of white flowers with a reddish brown vein on each petal. Not even the goats like it. Other common shrubs are the *Hypericum balearicum*, a St John's wort whose yellow flowers are at their best in spring and early summer and the narrow-leaved cistus and spurges, whose hemispherical bushes bear bright yellow glands.

At the top of the next incline the path passes through another wall. About 50m off to the right of the junction of wall and path, more or less due south, is a 1.5m high **tunnel**, inside which is a spring. Be careful, however, if you venture in, as it's popular with goats, who like the water and shade. They'll sometimes panic and charge out if they see you coming.

You then pass through a third wall beyond which the **path splits**. At this point you will notice some stone seats with an appearance of carved wood to the right of the path. To descend to the sea take the path which bears to the left and then runs down alongside a dried-up watercourse amidst the cries of sea birds and the whispering of the tall carritx grass. Patches of aromatic blue-flowered rosemary line the path. The **beach** at the end of the walk at **Cala Bóquer** is disappointing, being predominantly shingle and it can also be littered, although the water is clean and is a good place for a swim. Alternatively, take the right fork to reach the headland, from which there are stupendous views of the sea-cliffs and the cove below. Narrow goat tracks will take you to this headland. Look carefully and you will find a picnic bench behind a large rock overlooking the sea. Picnicking goats congregate in this area too.

To return to Port de Pollença retrace your steps along the same route.

very popular spot, so reservations are pretty much essential. Mains from €22. Daily noon–10.30pm.
Los Zarzales c/Jafuda Cresques 11 ☎971 86 51 37. Low-key but popular family restaurant just off the seafront that does a good line in Mallorcan dishes – try the suckling pig or the loin of pork. Competitively priced with mains from €12. Breakfast too. Daily except Tues 8am–11pm.

The Península de Formentor

Heading northeast out of Port de Pollença, Carretera Formentor clears the military zone at the far end of the resort before weaving up into the hills at the start of the twenty-kilometre-long **Península de Formentor**, the final spur of the Serra de Tramuntana. At first, the road (which suffers a surfeit of tourists from mid-morning to mid-afternoon) travels inland, offering grand views back over Pollença, but then, after about 3.5km, it reaches a wonderful viewpoint, the **Mirador de Mal Pas**, where a string of lookout points perch on the edge

△ Serra de Tramuntana

of plunging, north-facing sea-cliffs. There are further stunning views over the southern shore from the **Talaia d'Albercutx** watchtower, but in this case you'll have to brave the wiggly side road that climbs the ridge opposite the Mirador de Mal Pas.

The Platja de Formentor

Beyond the Mirador, the road cuts a handsome route as it threads its way along the coast, somehow negotiating the sheerest of cliffs before slipping down to a fork in the road, where it's straight on for the cape (see p.176) and right for the *Hotel Formentor* (see below). This is also the start of the **Platja de Formentor**, a narrow strip of golden sand that stretches east for about 1km beneath a low, pine-clad ridge. It's a beautiful spot, with views over to the mountains on the far side of the bay, though it can get a tad crowded in the height of the season. Most visitors drive here, using the large car park beside the fork in the road, but it's possible to arrive by **boat** from Port de Pollença (see p.168), or **bus** from Alcúdia and Port de Pollença (May-Oct Mon-Sat 4 daily), which stop at the car park. As you would expect, there is a seashore **café–bar** here, but it really is rather routine and it's well worth stumping up the extra to eat at the beachside *Restaurant Platja Mar* (April-Oct daily 1-3pm; ☎971 89 91 00), an outpost of the *Hotel Formentor*; the restaurant, which occupies a brisk, modern two-storey building, serves up delicious grilled fish and a tasty paella.

Eight hundred metres from the fork is the **Hotel Formentor** itself (☎971 89 91 01, @www.hotelformentor.net; ❾), one of the island's most prestigious, with wonderful terraced gardens that stretch up the hillside behind the beach. Opened in 1930, the hotel was once the haunt of the rich and fashionable – Charlie Chaplin and F. Scott Fitzgerald both stayed here – and although its socialite days are long gone, the hotel preserves an air of understated elegance befitting its hacienda-meets-Art-Deco architecture. The hotel has every facility, and breakfast is taken on the splendid upper-floor loggia with spectacular views over the bay. The rooms are not quite as grand as you might expect, but are still charming; it's worth staying here if you have the cash.

The Cap de Formentor

Beyond the hotel turn-off, the main peninsula road runs along a wooded valley before climbing up to tunnel through Mont Fumat. Afterwards, it emerges on the rocky mass of **Cap de Formentor**, a tapered promontory of bleak sea-cliffs, which offers magnificent views and top-notch **birdwatching**. The silver-domed lighthouse stuck on the cape's windswept tip is out of bounds, but you can gaze at its rocky environs, where the sparse vegetation offers a perfect habitat for lizards and small birds, especially the deep-blue feathered rock thrush and the white-rumped rock dove. From the lighthouse, you can also spy the steep, eastward-facing sea-cliffs which shelter colonies of nesting Eleonora's falcons from April to October, whilst circling overhead there are often ravens, martins and swifts. During the spring and summer migrations, thousands of seabirds fly over the cape, Manx and Cory's shearwaters in particular. For a closer look at the cape, take the steep but clearly marked **footpath** leading along the east coast from the lighthouse to the **Moll des Patronet** viewpoint; allow 15min each way.

If you fancy a snack before heading back from the cape, there's a **coffee bar** next to the lighthouse.

The Badía d'Alcúdia

Moving south from Port de Pollença, it's just 10km round the bay to the pretty little town of **Alcúdia**, whose main claims to fame are its imitation medieval walls and the rubbly remains of the old Roman settlement of Pollentia. The place gets flooded with tourists on market days – Tuesdays and Sundays – but otherwise is really rather restrained and, with its clutch of smart hotels, can make a useful base for exploring this part of the island. The obvious target is the rugged **Alcúdia peninsula** that juts east from the town, its further recesses holding a fine old chapel, the **Ermita de la Victòria**, and some handsome mountain scenery, which is readily explored on the four-hour **hike** we have described on p.180, though you will need a car to get to the trailhead. Just south down the road from Alcúdia lies the mega-resort of **Port d'Alcúdia**, where glistening sky-rises sweep around the glorious sandy beach of the **Badía d'Alcúdia**. In summer the resort is probably best avoided – unless you're into full-on holiday fun – but the shoulder seasons are more relaxing and the beach is comparatively uncrowded. In the wintertime you'll barely see a soul, but then most of the hotels and many of the restaurants are closed.

Port d'Alcúdia's assorted hotels, villas and apartment blocks stretch round the bay to the resort of **Ca'n Picafort**, 10km to the south, almost without interruption. The developers drained the swampland that once extended behind this coastal strip years ago, but one small area of wetland has been protected as the **Parc Natural de S'Albufera**, a real birdwatchers' delight. Further behind the coast lies a tract of fertile farmland dotted with country towns, amongst which **Muro**, with its imposing church and old stone mansions, is the most diverting.

Local **accommodation** is concentrated in Port d'Alcúdia, but in the summertime it's nearly all reserved for package tourists and getting a last-minute room can be problematic, so your best bet is to aim for Alcúdia town or the first-rate *hostal* at the Ermita de la Victòria. Transport connections, particularly from April to October, are very good. Frequent **buses** run along the coast linking Pollença, Port de Pollença, Alcúdia, Port d'Alcúdia and Ca'n Picafort and there are regular buses to all of them from Palma. There is also a useful coastal bus service from Port de Sóller and Sóller to Lluc, Pollença, Port de Pollença, Alcúdia and Port d'Alcúdia, but this only operates twice daily between April and October. There is, however, no bus service east from Alcúdia to the Ermita de la Victòria. Regular **trains** connect Palma and Inca with Muro and Sa Pobla – though Muro train station is a few kilometres out of town – and the rail line will soon be pushed through to Alcúdia. For bus and rail frequencies and journey times, see p.187.

Alcúdia

To pull in the day-trippers, **ALCÚDIA** holds one of the largest open-air **markets** on the island, a sprawling, bustling affair held on Tuesdays and Sundays, its assorted tourist trinkets taking over the whole east end of the old centre. Otherwise, the town's salient feature is the **crenellated wall** that encircles its centre and although this is, in fact, a modern restoration of the original medieval defences, the sixteenth- to eighteenth-century stone houses within are the genuine item. Nowadays, it's all very neat and trim, but Alcúdia has had an especially troubled history. Situated on a neck of land separating two large and sheltered bays, the site's strategic value was first recognized by the Phoenicians, who settled here in around 700 BC and used it as a staging-post for the sea trade between northwest Africa and Spain. A few Phoenician baubles have been unearthed here – including several fine examples of their delicate, coloured-glass jewellery – but their town disappeared when the Romans razed the place and built their island capital, **Pollentia**, on top of the earlier settlement. In 426 AD, Pollentia was, in its turn, destroyed by the Vandals and lay neglected until the Moors built a fortress in about 800 AD, naming it Al Kudia (On the Hill). After the Reconquista, the Christians began again, demolishing much of the Moorish town and establishing Alcúdia as a major trading centre for the western Mediterranean, a role it performed well into the nineteenth century, when the town slipped into a long and gentle decline – until, that is, tourism refloated its economy.

Arrival and information

Buses to Alcúdia stop on the south side of the centre beside the ring road, Avgda del Príncep d'Espanya. The **tourist office** is about five minutes' walk away, bang in the centre of the old town at c/Major 17 (daily except Sat 9.30am–3pm; ☏971 89 71 13, ⊛www.alcudia.net). Alcúdia also has its own spankingly new cultural centre, the **Auditori d'Alcúdia** (☏971 89 71 85), which includes a library, theatre and arts centre; it's just outside – and to the west of – the city wall on Plaça de la Porta de Mallorca.

Accommodation

In the last few years, ever since the old centre was made traffic-free, Alcúdia has sprouted smart, new **hotels**, mostly in tastefully modernized old premises. The catch is that they are all fairly pricey, though the town's oldest, least expensive and plainest *fonda* (guesthouse) has survived for the light of pocket.

Fonda Llabrés Plaça Constitució 6 ☏971 54 50 00, ⊛www.fondallabres.com. The cheapest place in town with a handful of sparse, modern rooms above a café-bar, in a nineteenth-century building on the main square. Rooms both en suite and with shared facilities. ❶

Hotel Ca'n Simó c/Sant Jaume 1 ☏971 54 92 60, ⊛www.cansimo.com. Appealing hotel occupying a substantial, three-storey nineteenth-century stone town house; its seven double bedrooms are kitted out in a modern version of period style. ❻

ALCÚDIA

CAFÉS & RESTAURANTS
Es Convent	B
Mirador de la Victòria	2
Sa Plaça	1

ACCOMMODATION
Ca'n Simó	E
Cas Ferrer Nou	A
Es Convent	B
Llabrés	C
Sant Jaume	D

Ermita de la Victòria & 2 ▲ Port d'Alcúdia ▲

N

FORMENTERA
CREU
MOLINOT
XARA
POLLENTIA
MERCAT
PLAÇA CARLES V
CAMÍ DE RONDA
ROCA
POU NOU
PAU
MOLL
VERDET
SANT VICENÇ
CRISTÒFOL COLOM
PLAÇA CONSTITUCIÓ
QUARTERA
LLEDONER
CASTELLET
L'ASSEMBLEA
Ajuntament
LA CISTERNA
ABELLONS
SANT JAUME
SERRA
RECTORIA
SANTA ANNA
Bus Stop ★
★ Bus Stop
AVINGUDA DELS PRÍNCEPS D'ESPANYA
Teatre Romà ▼
VALENTS
CONVENT
CANYARET
PROGRÉS
MAJOR
BENNÀSSAR
LA PARRA
L'ESGLÉSIA
Museu Monogràfic
Sant Jaume
RONDA
Pollentia
Port d'Alcúdia ▼
PLAÇA PORTA DE MALLORCA
Auditori d' Alcúdia
Pollença & Palma ▼

0   200 m

Hotel Cas Ferrer Nou c/Pou Nou 1 ℡971 89 75 42, ⓦwww.nouhotelet.com. Self-consciously stylish hotel, with just six guest rooms, in a tall and slender former blacksmith's house dating back to the nineteenth century if not beyond. Wood decking and coffee-table books set the tone, minimalist/modern furnishings do the rest. ⑥
Hotel Es Convent c/Progrés 6 ℡971 54 87 16, ⓦwww.esconvent.com. In an immaculately restored old convent, the *Es Convent* comes complete with beamed ceilings, bare stone walls and unfussily modern furnishings and fittings – not to mention a good restaurant. ⑥
Hotel Sant Jaume c/Sant Jaume 1 ℡971 54 94 19, ⓦwww.hotelsantjaume.com. Just like the *Ca'n Simó*, this hotel occupies a nineteenth-century town house, though here the house is a little larger and the modernization has been a good deal gentler, preserving more of its original appearance – down to the attractive, arcaded terrace. ⑥

The town centre

It only takes an hour or so to explore the antique lanes of Alcúdia's compact centre and to check out the town wall and its fortified gates. This pleasant stroll can be extended by a visit to a series of minor sights, which combine to make an enjoyable whole, although none of them is compelling in itself.

Beginning at the old town's eastern entrance, on **Plaça Carles V**, walk through the gateway and keep to the main drag – here c/Moll – and you'll soon reach the slender **Plaça Constitució**, lined with pavement cafés. Just beyond, on c/Major, is Alcúdia's best-looking building, the **Ajuntament** (Town Hall), a handsome, largely seventeenth-century structure with an elegant stone balcony and overhanging eaves. From c/Major, take any of the several sidestreets that lead to the southwest corner of the old town, where you'll find the most diverting of Alcúdia's several sights, the **Museu Monogràfic**, c/Sant Jaume 30 (July–Oct Tues–Fri 10am–3pm, Sat & Sun 10.30am–1pm; Nov–June Tues–Fri 10am–4pm, Sat & Sun 10.30am–1pm; €2, which includes admission to Pollentia – see below). The museum consists of just one large room, but it's stuffed with a satisfying collection of archeological bits and bobs, primarily Roman artefacts from Pollentia, including amulets, miniature devotional objects, tiny oil lamps and some elegant statuettes.

Across the street, dominating this portion of the old town, is the heavyweight and heavily reworked Gothic church of **Sant Jaume**, part of which holds a modest religious museum (May–Oct Tues–Fri 10am–1pm; €1). Amongst the museum's assorted vestments, chalices and crucifixes are a few fine medieval **panel-paintings** illustrative of the Mallorcan Primitives (see p.72, p.78 & p.82). The paintings on display are of unknown provenance, but two sixteenth-century panels stand out – one depicting the Archangel Michael standing on a devil, who is painted red, the second of St John the Baptist, shown – as painterly fashion dictated – with almond-shaped eyes and full lips.

Pollentia and the Teatre Romà

Across the ring road from the church lie the broken pillars and mashed-up walls of Roman **Pollentia** (same times and ticket as the Museu Monogràfic), the disappointingly meagre remains of what was once the island capital. Nearly all the stone was looted by the locals years ago, so you'll need lots of imagination to picture the Roman town, though at least the ruins are clearly labelled.

By comparison, the open-air remains of the **Teatre Romà** (Roman Theatre; open access; free) are much more substantial. Dating from the first century BC, this is the smallest of the twenty Roman theatres to have survived in Spain. Nonetheless, despite its modest proportions, the builders were able to stick to the standard type of layout with eight tiers of seats carved out of the rocky hillside and divided by two gangways, though the stage area, which was constructed of earth and timber, has of course disappeared. It's a pleasant spot, set amidst fruit and olive trees, though you do have to put up with the rumble of the traffic from the main road nearby. **To get there**, just follow the signs down c/Santa Anna, a pleasant country lane lined by old stone walls that runs south from the ring road a couple of hundred metres east of Pollentia; the walk takes about ten minutes.

Eating and drinking

Although Alcúdia has more than its fair share of very average **cafés and restaurants**, there are several first-rate places too, beginning with the slick and smart *Restaurant Sa Plaça*, Plaça Constitució 1 (daily except Wed noon–midnight; ☎971 54 62 78), where they focus on traditional Mallorcan/Catalan cuisine – try the house speciality, salted fish (*bacalao*); main courses average around €19. A second, even flashier and rather more formal choice is the *Restaurant Es Convent*, in the hotel of the same name at c/Progrés 6 (Tues–Sun 1–3pm & 7.30–11pm; ☎971 54 87 16). The menu here is pan-Mediterranean and features the freshest of local ingredients with mains at €20 and counting; note that in wintertime opening hours are curtailed, so ring ahead to check. Finally, if you have your own transport, it's worth considering the 6km jaunt out to the *Restaurant Mirador de la Victòria*, beside the Ermita de la Victòria (see p.181).

A circular walk round part of the Alcúdia peninsula

9 km; 450m of ascent; 4hr round trip, plus 1hr for diversion to Platja des Coll Baix. Moderately difficult.

This walk through the heart of the **Alcúdia peninsula** offers stunning sea views, including a 360-degree panoramic one from the **Talaia d'Alcúdia**, at 445m the peninsula's highest point. The first part of the walk has moderate ascents on tracks, changing to a more strenuous ascent over exposed ground and a rock scramble to reach the Talaia peak. The second half of the walk steadily descends to the **Coll Baix** and returns through pine woods to the starting point. If time permits, a diversion can be made from the Coll Baix to the **Platja des Coll Baix**, a small secluded and unspoilt beach, returning by the same route. There is **parking** at the trailhead.

The route

Leave Alcúdia on the road to El Mal Pas and Bonaire. After about 2km, turn sharp right at the *Bodega del Sol* bar onto **Camí de la Muntanya** and continue straight on until you reach, after another 2km or so, Parque Victoria, a nature reserve administered by ICONA (National Institute for Nature Conservation). Leave your car just inside the park near the **iron gates**. The walk starts at this point. There is a path on the uphill side of the gates. Take this path. It climbs gently upwards and then drops into a shallow valley dotted with pine trees. Walk in the direction of a new white house with columns, which appears on the skyline ahead. Pass by the house, which will be on your left, and descend for about 400m following the path until you reach a T-junction. Turn right at this point to begin your **ascent to Coll de ses Fontanelles**. After 2–3 minutes you will arrive at a stream, the upstream side of which has been dammed with a concrete wall. Do not take the obvious path, which continues ahead of you, but bear right to walk along a narrower track above the dam. Continue along this and wind your way up the stoned path to the valley head (Coll de ses Fontanelles). Beyond the stream crossing point, the valley is largely treeless but is densely vegetated with waist-high shrubs.

The Alcúdia peninsula

East of Alcúdia a steep and rocky promontory, the **Alcúdia peninsula**, pokes a wild finger out into the ocean, its **northern shore** traversed by a country road, which begins at the easternmost intersection of Alcúdia's ring road. After about 2km, this promontory road runs past the turning for the Fundació Yannick i Ben Jakober (see p.183) before weaving its way through the suburban villas of **Bonaire**. Thereafter, the road emerges into more scenic terrain, offering fine views of the Badía de Pollença as it bumps over the steep, pine-clad ridges that fringe the coast. After about 4.5km, the road passes the barracks-like *Albergue de la Victòria* **HI youth hostel** (℡971 54 55 42; ⓦwww.reaj.com; closed Oct–March; reservations advised; ❶), whose inexpensive dorm beds and coastal location attract school parties by the truck load; spare beds are thin on the ground as a consequence.

The Ermita de la Victòria

About 1km further on from the hostel, a signed turning on the right climbs 700m up the wooded hillside to the **Ermita de la Victòria**, a fortress-like church built in the seventeenth century to hold and protect a crude but much-venerated statue of the Virgin. It was a necessary precaution: this part of the coast was especially prone to attack and, even with these defences, pirates

The **Coll de ses Fontanelles** is populated by a stand of trees including a large olive tree. These offer valuable shade on a hot day and make this a good spot to stop, rest, take a drink and get your bearings. Moving on, you should take the path to the left of the olive tree (this runs in a northwesterly direction) and ascend through a boulder strewn area. The path continues to ascend over open, rocky terrain and soon affords excellent sea views. Ahead and above you is the **Talaia** on which you will see a stone building. This ground is now exposed and rocky on what is the most arduous part of the walk. Aim for the left of this stone building as the ridge on which it stands is too steep to tackle. Nevertheless, to gain access to the peak you will still need to negotiate a steep although short rock face. This involves an energetic and exhilarating rock scramble. Once on the top you can climb up to the **Trig Point** (stone column) and be rewarded with a panoramic view of the peninsula with sea views in every direction.

To descend, take the path at the other side of the Trig Point, which drops down to a signpost. Here **turn right for Platja des Coll Baix**. The path bears right again and then sharp left. You will now be walking with a deep valley below to your right. Take care here as the path is subject to falling rocks from the left. Upon reaching the ridge, traverse it straight ahead, noting that there are now two valleys: one left and one right of you. Eventually a large pine tree overlooking the sea looms in front of you and the path ascends to the right. When the path zigzags, descend again and at a sharp right turn look below to see a lovely secluded beach, **Platja des Coll Baix**, tucked in tight against the coastal cliffs. Continue your descent until at the bottom you reach a sparsely wooded area, beyond which are picnic tables, a welcome water fountain and shelter. These are provided by ICONA. The sign for Platja des Coll Baix is also here and if you have time, visit to see its lovely turquoise waters. Be aware, however, that **swimming is not recommended** due to the strong undertows.

Return to Coll Baix by the same route and then follow the easily graded **dirt road** to the walk's starting point by the gates. En route you will pass through pine woods, which have an undergrowth of lentiscs, narrow-leaved cistus, carritx, dwarf fan palms, euphorbias, asphodels and the occasional giant orchid; there are also almond and carob groves.

ALCÚDIA PENINSULA

Badía de Pollença

Sa Penya Roja (345m) ▲

Ermira de la Victoria

es Clot

N

Bonaire

Talaia d' Alcúdia ▲ (445m)

Platja des Coll Baix

Cap de Menorca

Coll Baix

Coll de ses Fontanelles

CAMÍ DE LA MUNTANYA

Badía d' Alcúdia

KEY TO WALKS:
▶▶ ▶▶ Primary Route
→ → Extension Route

Fundació Jakober

0   1 km

still stole the statue twice, though on both occasions the islanders managed to ransom it back. The Virgin is displayed in the simple, single-vaulted **chapel** on the ground floor of the Ermita, but now plays second fiddle to the views out across the bay. Even better, you can stay the night here as the old monastic quarters up above the chapel have been turned into a delightful *hostal*, the ⚒ *Hotatgeria Ermita de la Victòria* (☎971 54 99 12, ⓦ www.lavictoriahotel.com; ❹), which has twelve en-suite guest rooms decorated in a suitably frugal, but highly buffed and polished style. There's a first-rate **restaurant** here too, the ⚒ *Mirador de la Victòria* (reservations advised on ☎971 54 71 73; closed Mon), which offers sweeping sea views from its wide terrace and delicious food. They specialize in traditional Mallorcan dishes – try the snails, the suckling pig or the guinea fowl – and do a good paella; main courses cost €13 and up.

The Ermita is also a popular starting point for **hikes** further along the promontory, whose severe peaks are dotted with ruined defensive installations, including a watchtower and an old gun emplacement. One of the most obvious targets is **Sa Penya Roja** (345m), from the top of which there are more great views. The outward part of the hike, leading up through woods and beneath steep cliffs, is quite strenuous; return is by the same route. Allow thirty to forty-five minutes each way. It begins on the wide and clearly signposted dirt road that climbs up behind the Ermita, but the later sections are on trails that require a proper hiking map.

The Fundació Yannick i Ben Jakober

Doubling back from the Ermita, turn sharp left at the *Bodega del Sol* bar onto **Camí de la Muntanya** and, after a couple of kilometres, continue along the dirt road beyond the trailhead for the circular walk described in the box on pp.180–181. From the trailhead, it's about 2.5km more to the **Fundació Yannick i Ben Jakober** (Tues 9.30am–12.30pm & 2.30–5.30pm; free; ☏971 54 98 80), where the subterranean water cistern of a sprawling mansion has been turned into a bespoke art gallery. Dating from the 1970s, the **house**, Finca Sa Bassa Blanca, has wide views over the ocean and was built in the manner of a Moroccan fortified palace to a design by the Egyptian architect Hassan Fathy. The owners, the eponymous Jakobers, are art-loving sculptors and the house's **gardens** are dotted with large, modern sculptures. The gallery itself is entirely devoted to **children's portraits** dating from the seventeenth to the nineteenth century. It was Yannick who began the collection in the 1970s, when she picked up a striking *Girl with Cherries* by the nineteenth-century Mallorcan artist Joan Mestre i Bosch. None of the artists represented are particularly well known – and neither are the children – but together they provide an intriguing insight into the way the aristocracy of early modern Spain saw their children as miniature adults. Indeed, many of the portraits were hawked around the courts of Europe in search of a suitable bride or groom. Only from the 1750s onwards, do the children seem more childlike, innocent and relaxed.

There are plans to open the gallery more often – ring ahead for the latest news.

Port d'Alcúdia

PORT D'ALCÚDIA, 2km south of Alcúdia, is easily the biggest and busiest of the resorts in the north of the island, a seemingly interminable string of high-rise hotels and apartment buildings serviced by myriad restaurants and café bars. Despite the superficial resemblance, however, Port d'Alcúdia is a world away from the seamy resorts on the Badía de Palma. The tower blocks are relatively well distributed, the streets are neat and tidy and there's a prosperous and easy-going air, with families particularly well catered for. Predictably, the daytime focus is the **beach**, a superb arc of pine-studded golden sand that stretches south for 10km from the jetties of Port d'Alcúdia's combined marina, cruise boat and fishing harbour. About 500m east of the marina along the headland lies the **commercial and ferry port**, Mallorca's largest container terminal after Palma and the departure point for car ferries and catamarans over to Ciutadella, on Menorca (see box, p.155).

Arrival, information and getting around

Port d'Alcúdia acts as northern Mallorca's summertime transport hub, with fast and frequent **buses** up and down the coast between Ca'n Picafort and Formentor as well as regular buses to and from Palma and Port de Sóller. There's no bus station, but instead most local and long-distance buses travel the length of the **Carretera d'Artà**, the main drag, dropping off passengers at clearly signed stops along the way. The main **tourist office** (May–Oct Mon–Fri

Hidropark ▲   ▲ Alcúdia   ▲ Alcúdia

PORT D'ALCÚDIA

Platja d'Alcúdia

Marina

Boat
Cruises

Badía d'Alcúdia

Moll dels
Pescadors

MOLL COMERCIAL

Ferry Port

CAFÉS & RESTAURANTS	
Bodega d'es Port	3
Miramar	2
Pizzeria Steak House Roma	1

ACCOMMODATION	
Condesa de la Bahía	C
Playa Esperanza	B
Vista Alegre	A

0   200 m

▼ Ciutadella (Menorca) & Barcelona

10am–1.30pm & 3–5.30pm, Sat 9am–1pm; ☎971 89 26 15, ⓦwww.alcudia
.net) is at Carretera d'Artà 68, about 2km south round the bay from the marina,
while there's a second, more conveniently located **tourist booth** at the back of
the marina on the Passeig Marítim (May–Oct Mon–Sat 9am–7pm; ☎971 54 72
57). Both have all sorts of information, including useful free maps marked with
all the resort's hotels and apartments.

There's a super-abundance of **car**, **moped and bike rental** companies
strung out along the Carretera d'Artà. Mountain bikes work out at about €12
per day; cars from about €25. Summer **boat trips**, leaving from the marina,
explore the rocky, mountainous coastline of the neighbouring Alcúdia peninsula: the shorter excursions travel as far as its tip, Cap des Pinar, without ventur-
ing into the Badía de Pollença (April–Oct 3 daily; 2hr; €16); the longer versions
continue round this headland and cross the bay to the Platja de Formentor
(April–Oct 1–2 daily; 4hr; €21 or €26).

Accommodation

In season, vacant **rooms** are few and far between, but there's a vague chance
of finding something amongst the budget *hostals* clustered behind the marina
in the oldest – and tattiest – part of the resort. One place to try here is the
all-year *Hostal Vista Alegre*, which occupies a plain modern block on the
seafront at Passeig Marítim 10 (☎971 54 73 47, ⓦwww.hvista-alegre.com;
❶) and has twenty-nine plain rooms, both en suite and with shared facilities. In winter most of the hotels and *hostals* close down, but in the shoulder
seasons it's sometimes possible to get a good deal at one of the plusher chain
hotels, like the whopping, three-star *Hotel Condesa de la Bahía* (☎971 43 13
87, ⓦwww.grupobatle.com; ❺), a huge L-shaped complex beside the beach
about 3km south of the marina. A second beachside choice is the four-star
Playa Esperanza, about 4km south of the marina (☎971 89 05 68, ⓦwww
.esperanzahoteles.com; ❻). Both have a full range of facilities, including outside
swimming pools.

The Town

Port d'Alcúdia marks the beginning of an intensively developed tourist zone built to take advantage of the great swath of pine-studded sandy **beach** stretching around the Badía d'Alcúdia. Some lessons have been learnt from earlier developments – there are more recreational facilities and at least some of the coast has been left unscathed – but first impressions are primarily of concrete and glass. The beach and the sky-rises end on the outskirts of **CA'N PICAFORT**, once an important fishing port; its harbour-marina still preserves vestiges of its earlier function but today the town is an uninteresting suburban sprawl.

From June to September, a tourist "**train**" (on wheels, with clearly marked roadside stops) runs up and down Port d'Alcúdia every hour or so during the daytime, transporting sunbaked bodies from one part of the beach to another. Not that there's very much to distinguish anywhere from anywhere else – the palm-thatched *balnearios* (beach bars) are a great help in actually remembering where you are. A walkway runs along the back of the beach, which is usually more crowded to the north. Just as crowded, and located a kilometre or so inland along Avinguda del Tucán, is the much-hyped **Hidropark**, a gigantic pool complex with all sorts of flumes and chutes (May–Oct daily 10.30am–6pm; ☎971 89 16 72, ⓦwww.hidropark.com; €15 for 12 year olds plus, €8 for 5–11 year olds).

Eating and drinking

There are dozens of **cafés and restaurants** in Port d'Alcúdia, and although many of them are Identikit pizzerias and tourist-style places serving mediocre versions of Spanish food, there are a number of distinctive exceptions.

Bodega d'es Port c/Teodor Canet 8 ☎971 54 96 33. Set on the waterfront, between the marina and the commercial port, and decked out in an appealing version of traditional bodega style with wide windows, wooden chairs and a stone facade. It's a great place for a drink, accompanied by a first-rate selection of *tapas*.

Pizzeria Steakhouse Roma Avgda Pere Mas i Reus 4 ☎971 89 22 27. This is one of the more authentically Italian of Port d'Alcúdia's many pizzerias, with a wide-ranging menu offering pizzas and pastas through to crêpes (which are particularly good) and steaks. It's located just off Carretera d'Artà, across and just up the street from the main tourist office.

Restaurant Miramar Passeig Marítim 2 ☎971 54 52 93. Well-established seafront restaurant serving a fine range of seafood. A full meal with wine will set you back about €40.

The Parc Natural de S'Albufera

Given all the high-rise development along the Badía d'Alcúdia, the pristine wetland that makes up the 2000-acre **Parc Natural de S'Albufera** (daily: April–Sept 9am–6pm; Oct–March 9am–5pm; free), on the west side of Ca'n Picafort, is a welcome relief. Swampland once extended round most of the bay, but large-scale reclamation began in the nineteenth century, when a British company dug a network of channels and installed a steam engine to pump the water out. These endeavours were prompted by a desire to eradicate malaria – then the scourge of the local population – as much as by the need for more farmland. Further drainage schemes accompanied the frantic tourist boom of the 1960s, and only in the last decade has the Balearic government recognized the ecological importance of the wetland and organized a park to protect what little remains.

The **park entrance** is clearly signposted on the MA-12, about 6km round the bay from Port d'Alcúdia's marina. From the entrance, a country lane leads

The Badía d'Alcúdia

just over 1km inland to the **reception** centre, **Sa Roca** (daily 9am–4pm; ☏971 89 22 50), where you can – and should – register your visit and pick up a free map and introductory leaflet; there's also a small wildlife display in the adjacent building. Note that you can't drive down the country lane; the best bet is to **cycle** here or take a **bus** to the entrance and walk – buses from Port d'Alcúdia to Ca'n Picafort and points southeast stop close to the entrance on the MA-12. If you do bring a vehicle, you'll find a small roadside parking area just east of the entrance. Note also that the free map is not especially accurate and, although it's perfectly adequate for short, circular walks, anything more ambitious – say, walking to Can'n Picafort – is not advised.

Footpaths and cycle trails head out from Sa Roca into the reedy, watery tract beyond, where eleven well-appointed hides and observation decks allow excellent **birdwatching** – the best on the island. Over 200 different types of bird have been spotted here, including resident wetland-loving birds from the crake, warbler and tern families; autumn and/or springtime migrants such as grebes, herons, cranes, plovers and godwits; and wintering egrets and sandpipers. Such rich pickings attract birds of prey in their scores, especially kestrels and harriers. The open ground edging the reed beds supports many different **wild flowers**, the most striking of which are the orchids that bloom during April and May.

Muro

From the MA-12 on the west side of Ca'n Picafort, an easy country road heads west across a pancake-flat, windmill-studded hinterland to reach the hilltop town of **MURO**, a sleepy little place dotted with old stone town houses. Muro is at its liveliest on January 16 during the **Revetlla de Sant Antoni Abat** (Eve of St Antony's Day), when locals gather round bonfires to drink and dance, tucking into specialities like sausages and eel pies (*espinagades*), made with eels from the nearby marshes of S'Albufera. Quite what St Antony – an Egyptian hermit and ascetic who spent most of his long life in the desert – would have made of these high jinks it's hard to say, but there again he certainly wouldn't have been overwhelmed by temptation if he had stuck around Muro for the rest of the year.

The Town

Muro's main square, **Plaça Constitució**, is an attractive open area flanked by old stone houses and overseen by the domineering church of **St Joan Baptista**, a real hotchpotch of architectural styles, its monumental Gothic lines uneasily modified by the sweeping sixteenth-century arcades above the aisles. A slender arch connects the church to the adjacent **belfry**, an imposing seven-storey construction partly designed as a watchtower; it's sometimes possible to go to the top, where the views out over the coast are superb. The church's cavernous interior holds a mighty vaulted roof and an immense altarpiece, a flashy extravaganza of columns, parapets and tiers in a folksy rendition of the Baroque.

From the main square, it's a couple of minutes' walk to the **Museu Etnològic**, c/Major 15 (Tues–Sat 10am–3pm & Sun 10am–2pm; €3). This is one of the least-visited museums on the island, and the custodians seem positively amazed when a visitor shows up. It occupies a rambling old mansion and showcases a motley assortment of local bygones, from old agricultural implements, pottery and apothecary jars through to Mallorcan bagpipes and traditional costumes. Amongst the agricultural equipment there's a broken-down example of a mule- or donkey-driven water wheel, a *noria*. Introduced by the Moors, these were common features of the Mallorcan landscape for hundreds of years, though there are few of them left today. Among the pottery, look out for the *siurells*, miniature white-, green- and red-painted figurines created in a naive style. Once given as presents, but now debased as a mass-produced tourist trinket, these are whistles – hence the spout with the hole – shaped in the form of animals, humans and mythological or imaginary figures.

That's just about it for Muro, though on a hot summer's day you'll be glad of a drink at one of the **cafés** around the main square. Best of the bunch is *Los Arcos*, a neat modern little place with a good range of inexpensive *tapas*; it's located at the back of a mini-square, just off Plaça Constitució and across from the church.

Muro has a **train station** with regular connections from Palma and the main towns of the central plain, but it's 4km or so away to the west. **Buses** pull in close to the main square.

Sa Pobla

From Muro, it's just 4km north to the dusty little agricultural town of **SA POBLA**, whose straightforward grid-iron of old streets are at their prettiest in the main square, **Plaça Constitució**, which is also the site of a busy Sunday morning **market**. Also of interest is **Can Planes**, c/Antoni Maura 6, a late-nineteenth-century *Modernista* mansion that has been turned into a cultural centre incorporating a contemporary art gallery and toy museum, the **Museu d'Art Contemporani i Jugeta Antigua** (Tues–Sat 10am–1.30pm & 4–7.30pm, Sun 10am–1.30pm; €3). The mansion is poorly signed and can be hard to find – it's located at the north end of c/Antoni Maura (which runs north–south across the west side of the town centre), close to its intersection with Carretera Inca, the main road to Inca. The gallery's permanent collection features the work of Mallorcan artists and foreign artists resident on the island since the 1970s and there's an ambitious programme of temporary exhibitions too. Upstairs, the toy museum has an assortment of nineteenth- and early-to mid-twentieth-century toys and games – some four thousand exhibits in all, from miniature rocking horses and carousels to baffling board games.

Buses to Sa Pobla pull into the **train station** at the southeast corner of the town centre, about fifteen minutes' walk from Plaça Constitució.

Travel details

Buses

For further details, call ☎971 17 77 77, or check out ⓦtib.caib.es.

Alcúdia to: Cala Sant Vicenç (April–Oct 3 daily; 25min); Ca'n Picafort (May–Oct every 15min; Nov–April hourly; 30min); Lluc (April–Oct 2 daily; 1hr); Palma (Mon–Sat every 30min to 1hr, 5 on Sun; 1hr); Platja de Formentor (May–Oct Mon–Sat 4 daily; 30min); Pollença (April–Oct 3 daily; 20min); Port d'Alcúdia (May–Oct every 15min, Nov–April hourly; 10min); Port de Pollença (May–Oct every 20min, Nov–April hourly; 15min); Port de Sóller (April–Oct 2 daily; 2hr 30min); Sa

Pobla (May–Oct 2 daily; 30min); Sóller (April–Oct 2 daily; 2hr 20min).

Cala Sant Vicenç to: Alcúdia (April–Oct 2 daily; 25min); Lluc (April–Oct 2 daily; 35min); Pollença (April–Oct 2 daily; 15min); Port d'Alcúdia (April–Oct 2 daily; 30min) ; Port de Pollença (April–Oct 2 daily; 20min); Port de Sóller (April–Oct 2 daily; 45min).

Ca'n Picafort to: Alcúdia (May–Oct every 15min, Nov–April hourly; 30min); Cala Sant Vicenç (April–Oct 2 daily; 1hr); Lluc (April–Oct 3 daily; 1hr 45min); Muro (2–6 daily; 10min); Palma (2–4 daily; 1hr 30min); Platja de Formentor (May–Oct Mon–Sat 4 daily; 40min); Port d'Alcúdia (May–Oct every 15min, Nov–April hourly; 25min); Port de Pollença

(May–Oct every 15min, Nov–April hourly; 1hr); Port de Sóller (April–Oct 2 daily; 3hr).

Lluc to: Alcúdia (April–Oct 3 daily; 1hr); Cala Sant Vicenç (April–Oct 2 daily; 35min); Ca'n Picafort (April–Oct 3 daily; 1hr 45min); Palma: bus from Lluc to Inca (Mon–Fri every 1–2 hours, 1 on Sat & Sun; 35min), then train to Palma (see below); Pollença (April–Oct 3 daily; 40min); Port d'Alcúdia (April–Oct 3 daily; 1hr 15min); Port de Pollença (April–Oct 3 daily; 50min); Port de Sóller (April–Oct 2 daily; 1hr 20min); Sóller (April–Oct 2 daily; 1hr).

Muro to: Ca'n Picafort (2–6 daily; 10min); Sa Pobla (2–6 daily; 5min).

Palma to: Alcúdia (Mon–Sat every 30min to 1hr, 5 on Sun; 1hr); Ca'n Picafort (2–4 daily; 1hr 30min); Platja de Formentor (May–Oct Mon–Sat 1 daily; 1hr 30min); Lluc: train to Inca (see below), then bus from Inca to Lluc (Mon–Fri every 1–2 hours, 1 on Sat & Sun; 35min); Pollença (Mon–Fri 5 daily, 3 on Sat, 2 on Sun; 1hr 10min); Port d'Alcúdia (Mon–Sat every 30min to 1hr, 5 on Sun; 1hr 15min); Port de Pollença (Mon–Fri 5 daily, 3 on Sat, 2 on Sun; 1hr 15min).

Platja de Formentor to: Alcúdia (May–Oct Mon–Sat 4 daily; 30min); Inca (May–Oct Mon–Sat 1 daily; 1hr 30min); Palma (May–Oct Mon–Sat 1 daily; 2hr); Port d'Alcúdia (May–Oct Mon–Sat 4 daily; 45min); Port de Pollença (May–Oct Mon–Sat 4 daily; 20min).

Pollença to: Alcúdia (April–Oct 3 daily; 20min); Cala Sant Vicenç (April–Oct 3 daily; 15min); Lluc (April–Oct 3 daily; 40min); Palma (Mon–Fri 5 daily, 3 on Sat, 2 on Sun; 1hr 10min); Port d'Alcúdia (May–Oct 3 daily; 25min); Port de Pollença (May–Oct every 15min to 1hr, Nov–April hourly; 15min); Port de Sóller (May–Oct 2 daily; 1hr 50min); Sa Pobla train station (3–6 daily; 25min); Sóller (May–Oct 2 daily; 1hr 40min).

Port d'Alcúdia to: Alcúdia (May–Oct every 15min, Nov–April hourly; 10min); Cala Sant Vicenç (April–Oct 2 daily; 30min); Ca'n Picafort (May–Oct every 15min, Nov–April hourly; 25min); Lluc (April–Oct 3 daily; 1hr 15min); Palma (Mon–Sat every 30min to 1hr, 5 on Sun; 1hr 15min); Platja de Formentor (May–Oct Mon–Sat 4 daily; 30min); Pollença (May–Oct 3 daily; 25min); Port de Pollença (May–Oct every 15min, Nov–April hourly; 20min); Port de Sóller (April–Oct 2 daily; 2hr 35min); Sa Pobla (May–Oct 2 daily; 40min); Sóller (April–Oct 2 daily; 2hr 25min).

Port de Pollença to: Alcúdia (May–Oct every 15min, Nov–April hourly; 15min); Cala Sant Vicenç (April–Oct 3 daily; 20min); Ca'n Picafort (May–Oct every 15min, Nov–April hourly; 1hr); Palma (Mon–Fri 5 daily, 3 on Sat, 2 on Sun; 1hr 15min); Platja de Formentor (May–Oct 4 daily; 20min); Pollença (May–Oct every 15min to 1hr, Nov–April hourly; 15min); Port d'Alcúdia (May–Oct every 15min, Nov–April hourly; 20min); Port de Sóller (May–Oct 2 daily; 2hr 10min); Sa Pobla train station (3–6 daily; 40min); Sóller (May–Oct 2 daily; 2hr).

Sa Pobla (train station) to: Muro (2–6 daily; 5min); Pollença (3–6 daily; 25min); Port de Pollença (3–6 daily; 40min).

Trains

For further information, call ☎971 17 77 77, or check out ⊛tib.caib.es.

Palma to: Binissalem (every 30–40min; 30min); Inca (every 30–40min; 40min); Lloseta (every 30–40min; 35min); Manacor (hourly; 1hr); Muro (hourly; 50min); Petra (hourly; 55min); Sa Pobla (hourly; 1hr); Sineu (hourly; 50min).

Southern Mallorca

CHAPTER 4 # Highlights

* **Scott's Hotel, Binissalem**
Charming hotel occupying a
sympathetically restored old
almond grower's mansion
in the intriguing town of
Binissalem. See p.196

* **Sineu** The most attractive
of the ancient agricultural
towns of central Mallorca,
home to the island's finest
parish church and a bustling
Wednesday market. See
p.197

* **Artà** Ancient hill-town of
sun-bleached roofs clustered
beneath a castellated chapel-
shrine, while nearby lies the
remarkably intact prehistoric
village of Ses Paisses. See
p.204

* **Cala Rajada** Perched on the
edge of a bumpy headland,
this busy resort is within easy
striking distance of several
excellent, pine-clad sandy
beaches. See p.208

* **Coves del Drac** Perhaps the
finest of eastern Mallorca's
numerous cave systems,
with fantastically shaped
stalactites and stalagmites
and one of the world's largest
subterranean lakes. See p.214

* **Colònia de Sant Jordi**
Charming low-key resort
with several sandy beaches,
smashing seafood restaurants
and easy-going hotels and
hostals. See p.222

* **Cabrera** The fiercely hostile
terrain of this offshore islet
makes for an unusual day's
excursion – and lots of rare
Lilford's wall lizards will help
you with your sandwiches.
See p.225

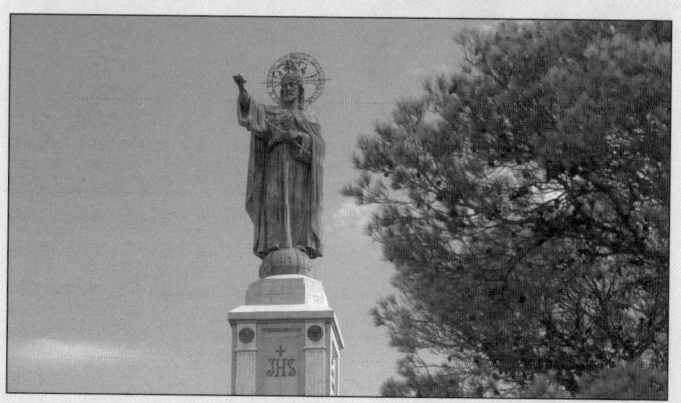

△ Santuari de Sant Salvador

Southern Mallorca

ost of **southern Mallorca** is comprised of the island's central plain, **Es Pla**, a fertile tract bounded to the west by the mountainous Serra de Tramuntana and to the east by the hilly range that shadows the coast, the Serres de Llevant. For many visitors the region is no more than a monotonous interlude between airport and resort, but although it may now seem like a sleepy backwater, it was Es Pla that largely defined Mallorca until the twentieth century: the majority of the island's inhabitants lived here, it produced enough food to meet almost every domestic requirement, and Palma's gentry were reliant on Es Pla estates for their income. Indeed, Mallorca's medieval kings constructed hilltop fortresses along the Serres de Llevant simply to defend the plain from marauding pirates, leaving the eastern shoreline's smattering of insignificant fishing villages and tiny ports unprotected. This situation persisted until the 1960s, when the tourist boom stood everything on its head and the developers simply bypassed Es Pla to focus on the picturesque coves of the east coast.

The towns of Es Pla have largely chosen to ignore the tourist industry and, although things are beginning to change, few put themselves out to attract visitors: accommodation is sketchy, good restaurants are thin on the ground and tourist offices rare. Nevertheless, it's here that you can get the full flavour of an older, agricultural Mallorca, whose softly hued landscapes are patterned with olive orchards, chunky farmhouses and country towns of low, whitewashed houses huddled beneath outsized churches. Admittedly, there's precious little to distinguish one settlement from another, but there are exceptions, most notably wine-growing **Binissalem**, with its streets of handsome old houses; **Sineu**, once the site of a royal palace and now one of the plain's prettiest towns; and **Petra**, with its clutch of sights celebrating the life and times of the eighteenth-century Franciscan monk and explorer Junipero Serra. Other sights worth making a beeline for are the impressive monastery perched on the summit of **Puig Randa** and, in the Serres de Llevant, the hilltop shrine at **Artà** plus the delightful medieval castle at **Capdepera**. All these destinations are readily accessible from either the MA-13, the fast road from Palma to Alcúdia, or the MA-15, which runs the 70km from Palma to Artà, as are the region's two biggest towns, **Manacor**, noted for its artificial pearl factories, and **Inca**, where the big industrial deal is shoes.

The ancient fishing villages of the **east coast** have mostly been swallowed up within mega-resorts, whose endless high-rises and villa complexes blotch the land for miles. There are, however, a couple of enjoyable seaside towns which have avoided the worst excesses of concrete and glass: **Cala Rajada**, a lively holiday spot bordered by fine beaches and a beautiful pine-shrouded coastline,

SOUTHERN MALLORCA

MEDITERRANEAN SEA

N

Badia d'Alcúdia

Port d'Alcúdia

Ca'n Picafort

Colònia de Sant Pere

Ermita de Betlem

Artà

Ses Païses

MASSÍS D'ARTÀ

Cala Agulla

Capdepera

Cala Rajada

Coves d'Artà

Platja de Canyamel

Costa des Pins

Cala Bona

Cala Millor

Son Servera

Sa Coma

S'Illot

Porto Cristo

Coves del Drac

Coves d'es Hams

Cala Magraner

Calas de Mallorca

Cala Murada

Porto Colom

Cala d'Or

Porto Petro

Cala Mondragó

Cala Figuera

Cala Santanyí

Santanyí

Cala Llombards

Cap de Ses Salines

Ses Salines

Santa Margalida

Sa Pobla

Muro

Petra

Manacor

Ermita de Bonany

Villafranca de Bonany

Santuari de Sant Salvador

Felanitx

Castell de Santueri

MA-14

María de la Salut

Sant Joan

Sineu

Els Calderers

Sant Miquel

Ermita de

Montuïri

Porreres

Campos

MA-19

Salines de Llevant

Sa Ràpita

Sés Covetes

Es Trenc

Colònia de Sant Jordi

Lloret de Vista Alegre

Pina

Algaida

Santuari de Cura

Randa

Llucmajor

Gordiola Glassworks

Capocorb Vell

Capocorb

Cap Blanc

Badia de Palma

PALMA

ES PLA

SERRES DE LLEVANT

MONDRAGÓ PARC NATURAL

Cabrera (18km, see inset)

Inca

Binibona

Caimari

Lloseta

Binissalem

Sóller

Lluc

Port d'Alcúdia

MA-13

MA-13A

MA-15

MA-12

MA-440

MA-4023

MA-4014

MA-4012

MA-19A

0   10 km

Colònia de Sant Jordi (18 km)

Cova Blava

Es Port

Boat dock

French Memorial

Sa Plageta

PARC NATIONAL DE CABRERA

0   1 km

and **Cala Figuera**, which surrounds a lovely, steep-sided cove. The former fishing village of **Porto Petro** has also managed to retain much of its original charm, as has the ramshackle old port of **Porto Cristo**. Different again is tiny **Cala Mondragó**, where a slice of coast has been belatedly protected by the creation of a park. The east coast also boasts the cave systems of **Coves d'Artà** and **Coves del Drac**, justifiably famous for their extravagant stalactites and stalagmites.

On the **south coast**, the scenery changes again, with hills and coves giving way to sparse flatlands, whose only star turn is the port-cum-resort of **Colònia de Sant Jordi,** from where boat trips leave for the bleached remoteness of the fauna-rich island of **Cabrera**.

Practicalities

Given the difficulty of finding a room in the coastal package resorts on spec and the general dearth of **accommodation** in the interior, **advance reservations** are a good idea – and pretty much essential in the height of the season. Potential bases, each of which has a healthy supply of non-package hotels and *hostals*, include Artà, Cala Rajada, Porto Cristo and Colònia de Sant Jordi, though towns like Binissalem and Sineu chip in with one excellent hotel each. In addition, three of the region's former **monasteries** offer simple, inexpensive lodgings, and usually have space at any time of year. These are the Santuari de Nostra Senyora de Cura, on Puig Randa near Algaida (see p.201); the Ermita de Nostra Senyora de Bonany, near Petra (see p.199); and the Santuari de Sant Salvador outside Felanitx (see p.216).

Direct **buses** link Palma with almost every resort and town in the region, but services between the towns of Es Pla and along the east coast are patchy. More positively, there are fast and frequent **trains** east from Palma to Binissalem, Lloseta, Inca, Sineu, Petra and Manacor with **connecting bus services** leaving Inca and Manacor train stations for surrounding towns and villages.

Binissalem, Inca, Sineu and Petra

The busiest and fastest road on the island, the **MA-13** motorway, linking Palma with Alcúdia, cuts an ugly swathe through the landscape as it sweeps round the towns on the northern edge of Es Pla, with the old main road, the **MA-13A**, running parallel to it. The key targets here are **Binissalem**, long the centre of Mallorca's prime wine-growing area and a town of some architectural distinction, pint-sized **Lloseta**, and sprawling **Inca**, formerly a grimy industrial town but now a pleasant enough place with a re-energized and revamped old centre. Southeast of Inca, you're into the rural heart of **Es Pla**, whose easy landscapes hold two especially interesting towns: **Sineu**, with its imposing church, and **Petra**, the hometown of the energetic, self-flagellating missionary-monk, Junipero Serra.

Binissalem, Lloseta, Inca, Sineu and Petra are all on the Palma–Manacor **train line** and, with the exception of Inca, each has a very good **hotel**.

Binissalem

BINISSALEM, about 25km east of Palma, may look dull and ugly from the old Palma–Alcúdia road, but the tatty, semi-industrial sprawl that straddles the road camouflages an antique town centre, whose narrow streets contain a proud ensemble of old stone mansions dating from the seventeenth and eighteenth centuries. The Romans settled here, and so did the Moors – Binissalem could be derived from the Arabic "Bani Salaam", meaning Sons of Peace – but the town's commercial heyday began in the sixteenth century, boosted by its vineyards and stone quarries.

The old town zeroes in on its main square, the **Plaça Església**, a pretty, stone-flagged piazza lined with benches where old-timers shoot the breeze in the shade of the plane trees. The northeast side of the square is dominated by the **Església Nostra Senyora de Robines**, the clumpy, medieval nave of which is attached to a soaring neo-Gothic bell tower added in 1908. Inside, the single-vaulted nave is dark and gloomy, its most distinctive features being its glitzy Baroque altarpiece and the grooved stonework that graces the ceilings of the transepts and the apse. This grooved stonework pops up all over town, representing the cockle-shell emblem of **St James the Greater**, one of the apostles. James witnessed the Transfiguration and the capture of Jesus in the Garden of Gethsemane and was the first of the apostles to be martyred, at the hands of Herod in 44 AD. Despite his early demise, however, Spanish legend insists that he visited Spain and preached here; tradition also claims that James's body was brought from Jerusalem to Spain and buried at Santiago de Compostela in the far northwest of Spain. Although these tales verge on the ridiculous, they made St James one of Spain's most venerated saints and transformed Santiago de Compostela into one of the greatest pilgrimage centres of medieval Europe. An especially good time to visit Binissalem is in the third week of July, during the week-long **festivities** that precede the saint's feast day on July 25.

At the southwest corner of Plaça Església is the **Ajuntament** (Town Hall) and from here it's a five-minute walk via c/Concepció to **Can Sabater**, c/Bonaire 25, one of the town's most distinguished patrician mansions. This was once the home of the writer Llorenç Villalonga (1897–1980), whose most successful novel was *The Dolls' Room*, an ambiguous portrait of Mallorca's nineteenth-century landed gentry in moral decline. In his honour, the house has been turned into the **Casa Museu Llorenç Villalonga** (Mon–Sat 10am–2pm; also Tues & Thurs 4–8pm; free), with detailed (Catalan) explanations of his life and times as well as his library and study. The house is typical of its type, with elegant stone arches and high-ceilinged rooms redolent of oligarchic comfort. It also has its own chapel: the island's richer families usually had their own live-in priests.

From the museum, it's a five-minute walk south along c/Bonaire to the MA-13A, which doubles as c/Conquistador, and another five minutes or so west (towards Palma) for the **Bodega José Luis Ferrer**, c/Conquistador 103 (☎971 51 10 50, ⊛www.vinosferrer.com). If you book ahead, you can tour parts of the winery during the working week (Mon–Fri 2 daily; €6), but most visitors are content to visit the **shop** (Mon–Fri 9am–7pm & Sat 10am–2pm), which stocks the full range – and allows limited tastings (€0.90 per glass) – of the company's wines: few would contest the fact that their reds are the best the island produces.

Practicalities

Buses pull in beside the MA-13A (c/Conquistador), a few metres to the west of the foot of c/Bonaire, which leads straight up towards Plaça Església. Binissalem is also on the **train** line from Palma to Manacor, and regular trains from both directions stop at the station on the northern edge of the town centre. From the train station, it's a five- to ten- minute walk to Plaça Església, beside the church on Plaça Església: head straight down c/S'Estació, turn right at the end and then left at the end of this second street. Binissalem has no tourist

SOUTHERN MALLORCA | Binissalem, Inca, Sineu and Petra

BINISSALEM

HOTEL
Scotts Hotel   A
RESTAURANT
Picasso   1

N.S. de Robines

Ajuntament

PLAÇA ESGLÉSIA

Can Sabater

Bodega José Luis Ferrer

★ Bus Stops

0   200 m

N

office as such, but there are sometimes free town **maps** and brochures in the foyer of the Ajuntament, on the corner of Plaça Església and c/Concepció – just help yourself.

Binissalem boasts one of Mallorca's finest **hotels**, ⚑ *Scott's*, right in the centre of town beside the main square at Plaça Església 12 (☎971 87 01 00, ⓦwww .scottshotel.com; ❼). The house was originally owned by an almond grower, and has been immaculately restored, its sweeping stone arches and high ceilings enclosing three suites decorated in elegant, broadly nineteenth-century style. At the back, the old stone outbuildings surround a leafy courtyard and contain more recent rooms, each air-conditioned and decorated in crisp modern style. Breakfast is served on a sunny terrace at the back of the hotel, and there's a non-chlorinated spa pool. The owner, George Scott, is familiar with every nook and cranny of the island and has put his knowledge to good use in his crime novels, including *The Bloody Bokhara* and *The Chewed Caucasian* (see p.334).

There's one excellent **restaurant** in town, ⚑ *Picasso*, c/Pou Bo 20 (Mon–Sat 7–11.30pm; ☎971 87 06 49), where the fusion cuisine is outstanding and reasonably priced with main courses averaging around €20; the decor is idiosyncratic/kitsch, the clientele buffed and polished. The *Picasso* is in an old stone house with beamed ceilings about five minutes' walk from Plaça Església: walk south down c/Bonaire, turn right along c/Reg, left down c/Llorenç Moya and it's on the right at the fork. If you can't be in Binissalem for the July festivities around the day of St James (see p.194), try to aim for the delightful **Festa d'es Vermar** (Festival of the Grape Harvest) in the third week of September, when the cordoned-off streets are lined with trestle tables weighed down with all sorts of local wines and foods, proudly presented by their makers.

Lloseta

The old shoemaking town of **LLOSETA**, about 4km east of Binissalem, is draped over a steep little hill, its pleasant central square, **Plaça Espanya**, decorated by a medieval church surmounted by the most petite of bell towers. Otherwise, Lloseta is really rather humdrum, though it is home to a first-class **hotel**, the *Ca's Comte* (☎971 87 30 77, ⓦwww.cascomte.com; ❻), a family-run establishment with just eight guest rooms. The hotel occupies the Palau Aiamans, a splendid and sympathetically revamped old mansion, where the original fortified tower is attached to the eighteenth-century house with its sweeping balustrades and elegant arcades; it's next to the church on the main square.

Lloseta **train station** is on the south side of town, a ten-minute walk from Plaça Espanya via c/Mestre Antoni Vidal. There's a good **restaurant** here in the shape of the cosy and intimate *Celler Ca'n Carrossa*, c/Nou 28 (Tues–Sun 1–4pm & Tues–Sat 8–11pm; ☎971 51 40 23), which serves up delicious Mallorcan cooking at affordable prices. It's about 200m northeast of Plaça Espanya: take c/Esglesia, turn right onto c/Sant Llorenç and keep going.

Inca

Poor old **INCA**, Mallorca's third city, just 4km east of Lloseta, has long had a bad press as an industrial eyesore. In medieval times, one of the few ways to keep out of the clutches of the island's landowners was to practise a craft and then join the appropriate guild. As early as the fifteenth century, Inca had attracted enough **shoemakers** to become the centre of a flourishing shoemaking industry – and so it remains today with Camper's HQ and main factory-warehouse firmly ensconced here. This may not sound too enticing, but the town centre has recently been spruced up and the **walk** across its pedestrianized core, from the **train station** in the west to Plaça Orient in the east, is an agreeable way to spend an hour or so. Along the way, you'll spy a scattering of immaculate *Modernista* buildings and the town's main church, **Santa Maria la Major**, an imposing sandstone pile with all sorts of Baroque flourishes.

As you might expect, Inca has oodles of cafés and restaurants with one of the best being the long-established *Ca'n Amer*, a wonderfully old-fashioned cellar restaurant a short walk west of the main church at c/Pau 39 (closed June–Oct Sat & Sun & Sun the rest of the year; ☎971 50 12 61).

There's no strong reason to overnight here, but there is a particularly fine finca-**hotel** about 8km north of Inca amidst the foothills of the Serra de Tramuntana near the hamlet of **BINIBONA**. It's ⚐ *Es Castell*, c/Binibona s/n (☎971 87 51 54, ⓦ www.fincaescastell.com; ⓞ), a tastefully restored old stone finca with an outside pool and grand views back down the valley below. They serve first-rate Mediterranean-meets-Mallorcan food here too.

Sineu

SINEU, 13km southeast of Inca, is undoubtedly one of the most interesting of the ancient agricultural towns of Es Pla. Glued to a hill at the geographical centre of the island, the town had obvious strategic advantages for the independent kings of fourteenth-century Mallorca. Jaume II built a royal palace here; his asthmatic successor Sancho liked the place for its upland air; and the last of the dynasty, Jaume III, slept in Sineu the night before he was defeated and killed at the battle of Llucmajor by Pedro of Aragón. The new Aragonese monarchs had no need of the Sineu palace, which disappeared long ago, but former pretensions survive in the severe stone facade of **Nostra Senyora de los Angeles**, the grandest parish church on the island. Built in the thirteenth century, and overlooking the town's main square, Sa Plaça, the church was extensively remodelled three hundred years later, but the majestic simplicity of the original Gothic design is still plain to see. At the side, a single-span arch connects with the colossal freestanding bell tower, and close by, at the top of the steps, a big, modern and aggressive **statue** of a winged lion – the emblem of the town's patron, St Mark – stands guard, courtesy of Franco's cronies.

The best time to visit is on Wednesdays, when the town fizzes with one of Mallorca's liveliest fresh produce and clothes **markets** – it's the only island market still licensed to sell large livestock. It's then that the cafés round the minuscule main square, **Sa Plaça**, are filled to the gunnels, though the best place to **eat** is the *Celler Es Grop*, a few metres away at c/Major 18. This friendly place, whose cavernous interior doubles as a wine vault, hence the wooden barrels, serves first-rate Mallorcan meals, with main courses hovering around €10–14.

From Sineu **train station**, it's about 500m west up the hill to Sa Plaça; there are no signs, you just have to follow your nose. There is no tourist office, but there is one good **hotel**, the ⚐ *Hotel Son Cleda*, Plaça Es Fossar 7 (☎971 52 10 38, ⓦ www.hotelsoncleda.com; ⓞ), which occupies a handsome old mansion about 100m from Sa Plaça. The hotel has just eight bedrooms, each of which is kitted out in an attractive modern version of traditional Spanish style. Alternatively, *Sa Rota d'en Palerm* (☎971 52 11 00, ⓦ www .sa-rota.com; ⓞ), around 6km southeast of Sineu, is a charming and peaceful rural retreat, set in a tastefully restored eighteenth-century country mansion. To reach the hotel from Sineu, take the road towards Lloret de Vista Alegre. About

500m before you reach that village, take the left turn towards Montuïri and after about 800m there's a sign to the hotel on the left; continue for 2.5km to reach the hotel.

Petra and around

Nothing very exciting happens in **PETRA**, 11km southeast of Sineu, but it was the birthplace of **Junipero Serra**, the eighteenth-century Franciscan friar who played an important role in the settlement of Spanish North America. Serra's missionary endeavours began in 1749 when he landed at Veracruz on the Gulf of Mexico. Despite a particularly unpleasant voyage, he and his band of monks promptly walked 500km to Mexico City, thereby completing the first of many mind-boggling treks. For eighteen years, Serra thrashed around the remoter parts of Mexico until, entirely by chance, political machinations back in Europe saved him from obscurity. In 1768, Carlos III claimed the west coast of the North American continent for Spain and, to substantiate his claim, dispatched a small expeditionary force of soldiers and monks north from Mexico. Serra happened to be in the right place at the right time, and was assigned to lead the priests. Even by Serra's standards, the walk from Mexico City to California was pretty daunting, but almost all of them survived to reach the Pacific Ocean somewhere near the present US–Mexico border in early 1769. Over the next decade, Serra and his small band of priests set about converting the Native Americans of coastal California to the Catholic faith, and established a string of nine missions along the Pacific coast, including San Diego, Los Angeles and San Francisco. Pope John Paul II beatified Serra in 1988.

Petra makes a reasonable hand of its connection with Serra. In the upper (southerly) part of town, on c/Major, is the chunky church of **Sant Bernat**, behind which – down a narrow side street – lies a modest sequence of majolica panels honouring Serra's life and missionary work. This simple tribute is backed up by a self-effacing **museum** in a pleasant old house at the end of this same side street (Mon–Fri 9am–7pm; donation requested), with several rooms devoted to Serra's cult: the honours paid to him, the books written about him, and the paintings of him. Another room focuses on Serra's work in California, with photos and models of his foundations. Two doors up the street, at no. 6, is the humble stone **house** where he was born (same hours). The museum and house are sometimes locked, but there are instructions posted outside explaining how to collect the key from the custodian.

Finally, Petra is home to one of the star turns of the Pla i Llevant DO (Denominació d'Origen, see p.37), **Miquel Oliver**, who operates a **bodega** in the centre of town at c/Font 26 (Mon–Fri 9am–1pm & 2.30–6pm; ☎971 56 11 17). Oliver is best known for a dry white, *Muscat Original*, which has garnered a cupboardful of awards.

Practicalities

Petra **train station** is on the northern edge of town, about 700m from the large church at the north end of c/Major – and a further 500m or so from the church of Sant Bernat. There's no tourist office. The best **restaurant** in town is the elegantly old-fashioned *Sa Plaça* at Plaça Ramon Llull 4, where you can eat traditional Mallorcan cuisine either in the antique-filled interior or on the terrace outside; main courses average around €18. The *Sa Plaça* (☎971 56 16 46, ⓦwww.saplacapetra.com; ➎) also doubles as a small **hotel** with three modest double rooms – or you can opt for the Bonany monastery instead (see opposite). Plaça Ramon Llull is the main square and it's located one block east of c/Major – take either c/Ciutat or c/Sol just a couple of blocks south from the church at the north end of c/Major.

From Petra, it's just 10km southeast to Manacor (see p.203).

Ermita de Nostra Senyora de Bonany

The hilltop **Ermita de Nostra Senyora de Bonany**, about 5km southwest of Petra, offers extensive views over Es Pla. To get there, take the Felanitx road out of Petra and look out for the sign on the edge of the village. The monastery is at the end of a bumpy, 4km-long country lane, and takes its name from events in 1609 when desperate locals gathered here at the chapel to pray for rain. Shortly afterwards, the drought broke and the ensuing harvest was a good one – hence *bon any* ("good year"). The prettiest feature of the complex is the **chapel**, which is approached along an avenue of cypress and palm trees and comes complete with a rose window, twin towers and a little cupola. The monastery's conspicuous stone cross was erected in honour of Junipero Serra, who left here bound for the Americas in 1749. There are five simple double **rooms** here (℡971 82 65 68; ❶), one shared bathroom with hot water, and cooking facilities, but you'll have to bring your own food and bedding.

East from Palma to Artà

The fast and busy **MA-15** whizzes through the agricultural landscape due east of Palma past a string of roadside tourist attractions. The most successful of these is the **Can Gordiola glassworks**, which houses a first-rate glassware museum, and **Els Calderers**, a big old country house which is now a museum illustrating *hacienda* life in the nineteenth century. Further east, the highway loops round workaday **Manacor**, the island's second biggest town – albeit a distant rival to Palma with a population of just 28,000 – before proceeding onto pint-sized **Artà**, an attractive little place tucked away amongst the hills of the Serres de Llevant. Artà boasts **Ses Paisses**, one of Mallorca's most complete Talayotic settlements, and is within easy striking distance of the laid-back mini-resort of **Colònia de Sant Pere**, not to mention the assorted coves of the east coast (see pp.207–221). By far the most interesting detour from the MA-15 is south from near the glassworks to the monastery on top of **Puig Randa**, but the road also passes near Sineu (see p.197) and Petra (see p.198), two particularly appealing country towns.

Buses from Palma to Montuïri, Manacor and Artà are fast and frequent and Manacor can also be reached by **train**. As for **accommodation**, Artà has an excellent hotel, and there are monastery rooms on Puig Randa and near Montuïri.

The Gordiola glassworks

Heading east from Palma on the MA-15, it's about 19km to the roadside **Can Gordiola glassworks** (June–Sept Mon–Sat 9am–8pm, Sun 9am–1.30pm; Oct–May Mon–Sat 9am–6.30pm, Sun 9am–1.30pm; free), which occupies a conspicuous castle-like building, whose crenellated walls and clumsy loggias date from the 1960s. Don't be put off by its appearance, however, or by the herd of tourist coaches parked outside, for here you can watch highly skilled **glassblowers** in action, practising their precise art in a gloomy hall designed to resemble a medieval church and illuminated by glowing furnaces. Staff are usually on hand to explain the techniques involved – the fusion of silica, soda and lime at a temperature of 1100°C – though this is really part of a public relations exercise intended to push you towards the adjacent **gift shops**. These hold a massive assortment of glass and ceramic wares, everything from the most abysmal tourist tat to works of great delicacy, notably green-tinted chandeliers of traditional Mallorcan design costing anything up to €2000 – even a single simple goblet fetches about €25.

The gift shops are one thing, but the **Museu del Vidre**, on the top floor, is quite another. The owners of the glassworks, the Gordiola family, have been in business in Mallorca since the early eighteenth century, when the first of the line, Gordiola Rigal, arrived from the Spanish mainland. Since then, successive generations have accumulated an extraordinary collection of glassware, now exhibited in thirty-odd cabinets, each devoted to a particular theme or country, and although the museum is dusty and neglected, there's no gainsaying the quality of the items on display. Unfortunately, the labelling is abysmal and so, to make much sense of what you see, you'll need to invest in a guidebook (€6; on sale at the gift shops).

The earliest Gordiola pieces are transparent jugs, whose frothy consistency – provided by trapped air bubbles – was unwanted. Heated by wood and coal, the original hoop-shaped furnaces had windows through which works in progress could be rotated. With such limited technology, it was impossible to maintain a consistently high temperature, so the glass could not be clarified or cleared of its imperfections. Aware of these deficiencies, the next of the line, Bernardo Gordiola (1720–91), spent years in Venice gaining knowledge from the leading glassmakers of the day, and the results of what he learnt can be seen in the same display case. He greatly improved the quality of the glass and also developed a style of Mallorcan-made jugs decorated with *laticinos*, glass strips wrapped round the object in the Venetian manner. Amongst later Gordiola work, kitchen- and tableware predominate – bottles, vases, jugs and glasses – in a variety of shades, of which green remains the most distinctive. There's also a tendency to extrapolate functional designs into imaginative, ornamental pieces, ranging from hideous fish-shaped receptacles designed for someone's mantelpiece to the most poetic of vases.

Yet Gordiola glassware is just a fraction of the collection. Other cabinets feature pieces from **every corner of the globe**, beginning with finds from Classical Greece, the Nile and the Euphrates. There's also an exquisite sample of early Islamic glassware, Spanish and Chinese opalescents, and superb Venetian vases dating from the seventeenth and eighteenth centuries. More modern items include goblets from Germany and Poland, traditional Caithness crystal from Scotland, and a striking melange of Swedish Art Nouveau glasswork. The museum also exhibits decorative items from cultures where glass was unknown – an eclectic ensemble of pre-Columbian pieces worked in clay, quartz and obsidian, along with the zoomorphic and anthropomorphic basalt figures characteristic of the Sahara.

Algaida and Randa

ALGAIDA, just off the main highway 2km or so east of the glassworks, is typical of the small agricultural towns that dot Mallorca's central plain – low, whitewashed houses fanning out from an old Gothic-Baroque church. There's nothing remarkable about the place, but it's a veritable metropolis compared with some of its neighbours: as late as the 1980s, a young British anthropologist, who was here to research rural communities, spent several months living in the hamlet of **Pina**, just north of Algaida. It was an eye-opener: she was criticized for having her light on late at night (she should have been sleeping) and for wanting to live on the edge of the village (she must have something to hide), but the final straw was the anonymous letters she received suggesting that she was only there to entice a young man back to the UK.

From Algaida it's about 4km south to the turning for **Puig Randa**, at 540m the highest of a slim band of hills that lies between Algaida and Llucmajor. The road to the summit – a well-surfaced but serpentine affair, some 5km long – starts by climbing through **RANDA**, a tiny little place of old stone houses harbouring a comfortable three-star **hotel**, ⚹ *Es Reco de Randa*, at c/Font 21 (☏971 66 09 97, ⓦwww.esrecoderanda.com; ⑤). The hotel has just fourteen guest rooms decorated in traditional Spanish style and comes complete with an outdoor swimming pool on a balustraded terrace that offers panoramic views over the plain below. The hotel is usually booked up months in advance during the summer, but there's often a vacancy out of season, and there's also a delightful **restaurant**, where the specialities include roast lamb and suckling pig; they do **bicycle rental** too.

Puig Randa

The top of **Puig Randa** is flat enough to accommodate a substantial walled complex, the **Santuari de Nostra Senyora de Cura** (Hermitage of Our Lady of Cura), with Cura being the name of the upper part of the mountain. Entry is through a seventeenth-century portal, but most of the buildings beyond are plain and modern, the work of the last incumbents, Franciscan monks who arrived in 1913 after the site had lain abandoned for decades. The scholar and missionary **Ramon Llull** (see p.81 & p.82) founded the original hermitage in the thirteenth century, and it was here that he prepared his acolytes for their missions to Asia and Africa. Succeeding generations of Franciscans turned the site into a centre of religious learning, and the scholastic tradition was maintained by a grammar school, which finally fizzled out in 1826. The Llull connection makes the monastery an important place of pilgrimage, especially for the **Benedicció del Fruita** (Blessing of the Crops), held on the fourth Sunday after Easter.

Nothing remains of Llull's foundation. The oldest surviving building is the quaintly gabled **chapel**, parts of which date from the 1660s. Situated to the right of the entrance, the chapel is homely and familiar, its narrow, truncated nave spanned by a barrel-vaulted roof. Next door, in the old school, there's a modest **museum** (donation requested) with a collection of ecclesiastical bric-a-brac and a few interesting old photos taken by the Franciscans before they rebuilt the place. It only takes a few minutes to look around and you'll soon be moving on to the nearby terrace **café**, which offers average food and superb views out across the island. There are a couple of other belvederes on the hilltop, plus an **information office** by the main entrance where you can get free maps and fix yourself up with a **room** in the guest quarters. These 35 en-suite rooms, which have recently been refurbished in plain but pleasant modern style, occupy a self-contained block. An extra €20 per person per night is charged for one of the four rooms with a balcony. Advance bookings can be made either by phone or online (☏971 12 02 60, ⓦwww.santuariodecura.com; ③).

There are two other, less significant sanctuaries on the lower slopes of Puig Randa. Heading back down the hill, past the radio masts, it's a couple of kilometres to the easily missable sharp left turn for the **Santuari de Sant Honorat**, which comprises a tiny church and a few conventual buildings of medieval provenance. Back on the main summit road, a further 1.2km down the hill, is

△ Monastery at Puig Randa

the more appealing third and final monastery, the **Santuari de Gràcia**, which is approached through a signposted gateway on the left and along a short asphalt road. Founded in the fifteenth century, the whitewashed walls of this tiny sanctuary are tucked underneath a severe cliff face, which throngs with nesting birds. The simple barrel-vaulted church boasts some handsome majolica tiles, but it's the panoramic view of Es Pla's rolling farmland that holds the eye.

Montuïri

Travelling east of Algaida on the MA-15, you'll soon reach the turning for **MONTUÏRI**, a modest country town where a gentle sweep of pastel-shaded stone houses snuggle over a low hill immediately to the north of the main road. The phylloxera aphid that destroyed Mallorca's (and most of Europe's) vineyards at the end of the nineteenth century made many of the island's estates uneconomic, thereby undermining the overweening power of the landed gentry, but here they held on, remaining firmly in the economic and political saddle until as late as the 1940s. Montuïri has just one sight of note, the largely Gothic church of **Sant Bartomeu**, an imposing pile plonked next to the main square and boasting several fine Baroque retables. The town is also a convenient starting point for the short detour north to Sineu (see p.197) and northeast to Petra (see p.198) as well as being just 2km from the hilltop **Ermita de Sant Miquel**, the location of a café-restaurant (☎971 64 63 14; closed Mon) with smashing views over Es Pla; the easiest access to the *ermita* is from the MA-15 – just follow the signs.

Els Calderers

Tucked away at the end of a country lane 2km north of – and clearly signposted from – the MA-15 between Montuïri and Vilafranca de Bonany is **Els Calderers** (daily: April–Oct 10am–6pm; Nov–March 10am–5pm; €9.50). Dating mostly from the eighteenth century, this charming country house bears witness to the wealth and influence once enjoyed by the island's landed gentry – in this case the **Veri family**. The house was the focus of a large estate that produced a mixed bag of agricultural produce: the main cash crop was originally grapes before the phylloxera aphid destroyed the vineyards. The Veris switched to cereals, and at the beginning of the twentieth century were at the forefront of efforts to modernize Mallorcan agriculture, much to the consternation of some of their more stick-in-the-mud neighbours, and to the horror of a workforce used to more traditional methods.

Flanked by a pair of crumpled-looking lions, the entrance to the **house** leads to a sequence of handsome rooms surrounding a cool courtyard with a well. All are kitted out with antique furniture, *objets d'art* and family portraits, and each has a clearly defined function, from the dainty music room to the hunting room, with assorted stuffed animal heads, and the **master's office**, with big armchairs and a polished desk. You can also see the family's tiny chapel (like every land-owning family on the island, the Veris had a live-in priest), and there's more religious material upstairs in the assorted prints which line the walls. They're neither original nor of good quality, but they give the flavour of the mawkish piety that characterized the island's landed class in the late nineteenth century. Attached to, but separate from, the family house are the living quarters of the *missatge* (farm manager), the barn and the farmworkers' kitchen and eating area. To complete your visit, take a stroll round the **animal pens**, though don't expect to see much farmyard activity in the heat of the day. The animals are breeds traditionally used on Mallorcan farms, though they're here to illustrate the past rather than to be of any practical use.

It takes an hour or so to wander round the house and the adjacent animal pens, more if you stop at the simple little **café**, where they serve traditional Mallorcan snacks: the *pa amb oli* (bread rubbed with olive oil) with ham and cheese is delicious.

Manacor

Hometown of the tennis star Rafael Nadal, industrial **MANACOR** declares its business long before you arrive, with vast roadside hoardings promoting its furniture, wrought-iron and artificial pearl factories. On the strength of these, the city has risen to become Mallorca's second urban centre, much smaller than Palma, but large enough to have spawned unappetizing suburbs on all sides. More positively, Manacor's old centre has been attractively restored, the prime target here being the **Església Nostra Senyora Verge dels Dolors** (daily 8.30am–12.30pm & 5.30–8pm; free), a sprawling stone church built on the site of the Moors' main mosque in the thirteenth century, though what you see today is neo-Gothic. The church abuts **Plaça Rector Rubí**, a busy square that is home to the *Palau Café* (closed Sun), at no. 8, where you can sample a local speciality, spicy pork sausage made from black pig (*sobrasada de cerdo negro*). From the square, it's a short walk northwest to Manacor's other principal sight, the **Convent de Sant Vicenç Ferrer** (Mon–Fri 8am–2pm & 5–8pm; free), on Plaça Convent, a classically Baroque complex dating from the late sixteenth century.

Despite these two ecclesiastical attractions, most visitors skip the centre. Instead they stick to the ring road, close to which, on the north side of town on c/Pedro Riche, is the **Perlas Majorica artificial pearl factory**, signposted as the Pearl Centre (Mon–Fri 9–7pm, Sat & Sun 10am–1pm; free), which offers a somewhat perfunctory **free factory tour** and a general insight into the manufacturing process. The core of the imitation pearl is a glass globule onto which are painted many layers of a glutinous liquid primarily composed of fish scales. Artificial pearls last longer than, and are virtually indistinguishable from, the real thing, but are consequently expensive – as you'll discover if you visit the showroom.

Practicalities

Manacor **train and bus station** are located on the northwest edge of the old centre, about 1km from Plaça Rector Rubí. The **tourist office** is about 300m south of Plaça Rector Rubí on Plaça Ramon Llull (☎971 84 72 41); they have a useful selection of local information, including a map marking the town's architectural high points. There's no strong reason to overnight here, but it's just 4km or so north from town to the luxury resort of *La Reserva Rotana* (☎971 84 56 85, ⓦ www.reservarotana.com; ⓽). Facilities include a pool, private nature reserve, golf course and spa. Suites are decorated with unusual antiques and there's also a top-notch restaurant with fresh-flavoured Mediterranean cuisine (count on around €60 a head for a full dinner).

Artà and around

Beyond Manacor, the MA-15 veers northeast to run parallel to the coast, with the flatlands soon left behind for the easy peaks of the **Serres de Llevant**. The top end of this mountain range bunches to fill out Mallorca's eastern corner, providing a dramatic backdrop to **ARTÀ**, an ancient hill-town of sun-bleached roofs clustered beneath a castellated chapel-shrine. It's a delightful scene, even though at close quarters the town is something of an anticlimax, and the cobweb of cramped and twisted alleys doesn't quite match the setting.

Nonetheless, the ten-minute trek up to the **Santuari de Sant Salvador**, the shrine at the top of Artà, is a must. It's almost impossible to get lost – just keep going upwards. At the foot of the town, follow the main street, c/Ciutat, as it slices across the edge of Plaça Conqueridor, and then head straight on up to **Plaça Espanya**, a leafy little piazza that is home to the town hall. Beyond, a short stroll through streets of gently decaying mansions brings you to the gargantuan parish church of **Sant Salvador**. From this unremarkable pile, steep stone steps and cypress trees lead up the **Via Crucis** (Way of the Cross) to the **santuari**, which, in its present form, dates from the early nineteenth century, though the hilltop has been a place of pilgrimage for much longer. During the Reconquista, Catalan soldiers demolished the Moorish fort which stood here and replaced it with a shrine accommodating an image of the Virgin Mary that they had brought with them. This edifice was, in its turn, knocked down in 1820 in a superstitious – and ultimately fruitless – attempt to stop the spread of an epidemic that was decimating the region's population. Built a few years later, the interior of the present chapel is hardly awe-inspiring – the paintings are mediocre and the curious statue of Jesus behind the altar has him smiling as if he has lost his mental marbles – but the views are exquisite, with the picturesque town below and Es Pla stretching away to distant hills.

Arrival and information

Buses to Artà stop beside the MA-15 on the southern edge of the town centre. From the bus stops, it's a couple of hundred metres west to the foot of the short main street, **c/Ciutat**. The town **tourist office** (Mon–Fri 10am–2pm; ☎971 83 69 81) is in the old train station near the bus stops on the south side of the MA-15. They have a useful selection of local information, including a free town map and an illustrated heritage trail leaflet. There's a **market** on Plaça Conqueridor every Tuesday.

Accommodation

Artà has four small, good-quality **hotels**, all of which are in elegant town houses located close to one another – in the old town between Plaça Espanya and Sant Salvador.

Ca'n Moragues Pou Nou 12 ☎971 82 95 09, ⓦwww.canmoragues.com. Decorated in calming shades of yellow and cream, this hotel's eight comfortable rooms oversee a courtyard garden with a small swimming pool and sauna – the two ground-floor rooms give directly onto the garden, the others are upstairs. ⑥

Casal d'Artà c/Rafael Blanes 19 ☎971 82 91 63, ⓦwww.casaldarta.de. Overlooking Plaça Espanya, the Casal d'Artà occupies an immaculately restored, three-storey former grandee's mansion dating from the 1930s. It still has much of the original decor – stained glass, wooden ceilings, decorative ironwork, tiled walls and antique furniture, including several four-poster beds. There is a charming sun terrace on the roof too. ④

S'Abeurador c/Abeurador 21 ☎971 83 52 30. Named after the ancient stone drinking trough just along the road, the S'Abeurador has a lushly planted, multi-level roof garden, its terraces dotted with ponds and arbours. Decorated in both rustic and modern styles, the well-appointed guest rooms are distributed in several different buildings. ④

Sant Salvador, c/Castellet 7 ☎971 82 95 55, ⓦwww.santsalvador.com. Once a grand *Modernista* mansion, the Sant Salvador is now an ultra-modern, luxury hotel with an interior decorated in vibrant Almodóvar colours. Six of the eight rooms – each decorated in a different style and some with Jacuzzis – have balconies. ⑦

Eating and drinking

There are several **café–restaurants** dotted along c/Ciutat, the best being *Café Parisien* (☎971 83 54 40), a chic little place advertising "art/wine/food/things" at no. 18. They have a shaded courtyard garden at the back and their tasty and reasonably priced *tapas*, soups, salads and Italian-influenced dishes are based on what is freshly available in the market. They also offer live music on the weekend and the **shop** upstairs sells clothes, artisan foodstuffs, quality Mallorcan wines and home accessories. The *Ca'n Balaguer* (☎971 83 50 03), on the other side of the street at no. 19, and *Es Passeig* (☎971 82 92 75), at no. 22, are more traditional places where the emphasis is on Mallorcan cooking. Two of the hotels chip in with quality **restaurants** too, the *S'Abeurador*, whose restaurant specializes in fresh food bought daily from the market (daily except Wed 7.30–11pm), and the *Ca'n Epifanio* (daily from 7pm), at the *Hotel Sant Salvador*, which features traditional Mallorcan dishes with a modern twist; you can eat indoors or outside on the terrace overlooking the swimming pool and gardens.

Ses Païsses

On the southern peripheries of Artà, about 800m from the ring road, lie the substantial and elegiacally rustic remains of the Talayotic village of **Ses Païsses** (April–Oct daily 10am–12.30pm & 2.30–6.30pm; Nov–March Mon–Sat 9am–1pm & 2.30–5pm; €1.55). To get there, walk to the bottom of c/Ciutat, turn left along the main through-road and watch for the signposted and well-surfaced country lane on the right. A clear footpath explores every nook and cranny of the site, and its numbered markers are thoroughly explained in the English-language **guidebook** available at the entrance (€2.05).

Tucked away in a grove of olive, carob and holm-oak trees, the prehistoric village is entered through a **monolithic gateway**, whose heavyweight jambs and lintels interrupt the Cyclopean walls that still encircle the site. These outer remains date from the second phase of the Talayotic culture (*c.*1000–800 BC), when the emphasis was on consolidation and defence; in places, the walls still stand at their original size, around 3.5m high and 3m thick. Beside the gate, there's also a modern plinth erected in honour of Miquel Llobera, a local writer who penned romantic verses about the place. Beyond the gateway, the central **talayot** is from the first Talayotic phase (*c.*1300–1000 BC), its shattered ruins flanked by the foundations of several rooms of later date and uncertain purpose. Experts believe the horseshoe-shaped room was used, at least towards the end of the Talayotic period, for cremations, whilst the three rectangular rooms were probably living quarters. In the rooms, archeologists discovered iron objects and ceramics imported from elsewhere in the Mediterranean. Some of them were perhaps brought back from the Punic Wars (264–146 BC) by mercenaries – the skills of Balearic stone slingers were highly prized by the Carthaginians, and it's known that several hundred accompanied Hannibal and his elephants over the Alps in 218 BC.

The Ermita de Betlem

Hidden away in the hills 10km northwest of Artà, the **Ermita de Betlem** is a remote and minuscule hermitage founded in 1805. In itself, the *ermita* is not a major pull, but the scenery hereabouts is lovely. The road to it begins on the north side of Artà beyond Plaça Espanya, but the start is poorly signed and tricky to find: aim for c/Figueretes, go past the *Hotel Sant Salvador* and then follow the signs. The road's rough surface and snaking course also make for a difficult drive, so an alternative is to **walk** – reckon on five or six hours for the return trip. The first portion is an easy stroll up along the wooded valley of the **Torrent des Cocons**, but then – after about 3km – the road squeezes through the narrowest of defiles, with the hills rising steeply on either side. Beyond, the road begins to climb into the hills of the Serra de Llevant – here the **Massís d'Artà** – until, some 3km after the defile, a signposted turn signals the start of the strenuous part of the journey. Here, the track wriggles for 4km up and down the steep hillside before finally reaching the *ermita* at the end of a cypress-lined path.

Amongst the huddle of old stone buildings that comprise the hermitage, the **church** is perhaps the most interesting structure, its ponderous frame holding crude religious paintings on the walls and a poor-quality fresco on the ceiling. The *ermita*'s only facility is a small shop (with uncertain opening hours) that sells religious trinkets and postcards, but there's more than enough compensation in the panoramic views down along the coast and across the Badía d'Alcúdia. A hiking trail leads down from the *ermita* to the bay, ending up on the road just to the east of Colònia de Sant Pere (see below), but this is a difficult hike and you'll need to be properly equipped. Incidentally, if you haven't taken your own picnic, then you can make a pit-stop at the **restaurant** *Sa Tafona de Son Fang* (℡971 82 95 91; closed Wed), just 3km or so out from Artà. In this galleried *finca*, which once housed an ancient oil press (*tafona*), you'll find a good range of Mallorcan dishes – they're particularly proud of their charcoal-grilled specialities.

Colònia de Sant Pere

West of Artà, the **MA-12** ploughs through the hills on its way to Ca'n Picafort and Port d'Alcúdia. On the way, it passes the turning for **COLÒNIA DE SANT PERE**, a downbeat resort and one-time fishing village nestled beside the Badía d'Alcúdia, with the stern escarpments of the Massís d'Artà for a backdrop. Founded in 1881, Colònia de Sant Pere is no more than a few blocks wide, its plain, low-rise modern buildings set behind a pocket-sized sandy beach, and although a flurry of recent building work has festooned the village with villa complexes, at least local planning laws prohibit the construction of houses over two storeys high. It's all very low-key and laid-back – perfect for families with young children – and this, along with the setting, is its charm.

At the time of writing, there are no **hotels** in Colònia de Sant Pere – though the *Hotel Rocamar* is currently under construction – but it is a great place to eat fresh fish at any one of several first-rate **restaurants**. On the seafront, one of the best choices is the *Blau Mari* (☎971 58 94 07; closed Nov–Feb), which specializes in seafood and paellas – and there's even a tank from which you can select your own live lobster. Alternatively, you could go next door to the *Playa* (☎971 58 90 17; closed Dec–March), another quality establishment largely devoted to seafood. Further along the seafront, and with its terrace overlooking the harbour, stands the *Café & Restaurant Club Nautic* (☎971 58 90 09), which serves excellent paellas and *bacalao al ajo confitado* (salt cod with garlic confit), or you can enjoy good-value salads, *tapas* and pizzas at *Es Vivers* (☎971 58 94 78) whilst sitting in the shade of the tamarisks; *Es Vivers* is also *the* place to go in the afternoons to sample their home-made fruit flans (apple, lemon, apricot, strawberry) and cheesecakes.

The east coast

Stretching south for about 60km from Cala Rajada to Cala Santanyí, **Mallorca's east coast** is fretted by narrow coves, the remnants of ancient river valleys created when the level of the Mediterranean was much lower. All of these inlets have accrued at least some development, ranging from a mild scattering of second homes to intensive chains of tower blocks, but everywhere it's tourism – and the tourist economy – that holds sway. An attractive minor road links the resorts, running for the most part a few kilometres inland along the edge of the **Serres de Llevant**, a slim band of grassy hills which rises to over 500m at its two extremities, south outside Felanitx and north around Artà. If you have your own transport, this coastal route enables you to pick and choose destinations with the greatest of ease, dodging the crassest examples of over-development – principally Cala Millor, Calas de Mallorca and Cala d'Or – altogether.

Amongst the larger resorts, boisterous **Cala Rajada** is easily the most enticing, especially as it is within easy reach of excellent sandy beaches, and the lovely medieval fortress of **Capdepera**. South of here, the old port of **Porto Cristo** has a dishevelled charm, which is much more than can be said for the burgeoning bargain-basement resort of nearby **Porto Colom**. By contrast, **Porto Petro** is small and really rather demure, whilst **Cala Figuera** is a lively, medium-sized resort, which possesses some fine restaurants and a top-notch diving centre. At the southern end of the east coast are the relatively untouched beaches of **Cala Mondragó**, now protected as **Mondragó Parc Natural**. The east coast is also famous for its limestone cave systems, with the most impressive formations found at the **Coves d'Artà** in the north, and the **Coves del Drac** at Porto Cristo.

It would be lovely to work your way down the coast, stopping for a couple of nights here and there, but the problem is **accommodation**. In the height of the season, locating a vacant room in one of the more attractive resorts can be a real tribulation – if you do find somewhere reasonable, you'll probably want to stay put. An alternative is to select a less popular spot, primarily Porto Cristo, where there's far more chance of a bed. Things ease up in the shoulder season, but in winter many hotels and *hostals* are closed.

With a bit of patience, you can explore the bulk of the east coast by **bus** from May to October, though in winter you'll need your own transport. There are regular buses from Palma to most of the resorts and one of these services links Felanitx, Cala d'Or and Porto Petro, another the **train station** at Manacor with Artà, Capdepera and Cala Rajada. Otherwise, bus services up and down the coast are sketchy, though there is a reasonably frequent bus connecting Cala d'Or, Porto Petro and Cala Mondragó.

Capdepera

Spied across the valley from the west or south, the crenellated walls dominating **CAPDEPERA**, a tiny village 8km east of Artà and 3km west of Cala Rajada, look too pristine to be true. Yet the triangular fortifications are genuine enough, built in the fourteenth century by the Mallorcan king Sancho to protect the coast from pirates. The village, snuggled below the walls, contains a pleasant medley of old houses, its slender main square, Plaça de L'Orient, acting as a prelude to the steep steps up to the **Castell de Capdepera** (daily: April–Oct 10am–8pm; Nov–March 10am–5pm; €2). The steps are the most pleasant way to reach the castle, but you can also follow the signs and drive up narrow c/Major. Flowering cactuses give the fortress a special allure in late May and June, but it's a beguiling place at any time, with over 400m of walls equipped with a parapet walkway and sheltering attractive terraced gardens. At the top of the fortress, **Nostra Senyora de la Esperança** (Our Lady of Good Hope) is the quaintest of Gothic churches, its aisle-less, vaulted frame furnished with outside steps that lead up behind the bell gable to a flat roof, from where the views are simply superb.

Run-of-the-mill **cafés** line up on Plaça de L'Orient – the best is *Pizzeria L'Orient*, with tasty *tapas* from €5–7. Capdepera also has several excellent **restaurants**. The pick is *La Fragua*, c/Es Pla d'en Coset 3 (℡971 56 50 50; dinner only from 7.30pm, closed Tues), an intimate, romantic spot where they serve delicious Thai meals. It's located just off Plaça de L'Orient, on the way up towards the castle steps. There's nowhere to **stay** in Capdepera, but it's easy enough to visit by bus from Artà and Cala Rajada, or even Palma.

Cala Rajada

Awash with cafés, bars and hotels, vibrant **CALA RAJADA** lies on the southerly side of a stubby headland in the northeast corner of Mallorca. The town centre, an unassuming patchwork of low-rise modern buildings, is hardly prepossessing, but it is neat and trim, and around the town is a wild and rocky coastline, all backed by pine-clad hills and sheltering a series of delightful **beaches**.

Arrival, information and getting around

Most **buses** to Cala Rajada stop in the town centre, near the intersection of c/Juan Sebastian Elcano and c/Castellet. From here, it's a couple of minutes' walk south to the main square, **Plaça dels Pins**, where you'll find the **tourist office** (Mon–Fri 9.30am–1.30pm & 2.30–5.30pm, Sat 9.30am–1.30pm; March–Oct also Sun 10am–1.30pm; ℡971 56 30 33). The office can supply an excellent range of local information including restaurant lists, bus schedules, details of car and bicycle rental firms, and free town maps marked with all accommodation. They also sell a popular, though not very detailed, pamphlet on local **hiking routes**.

The town centre is easy to explore on foot, but for the outlying beaches you'll probably want a **local bus**. Among several summertime services from

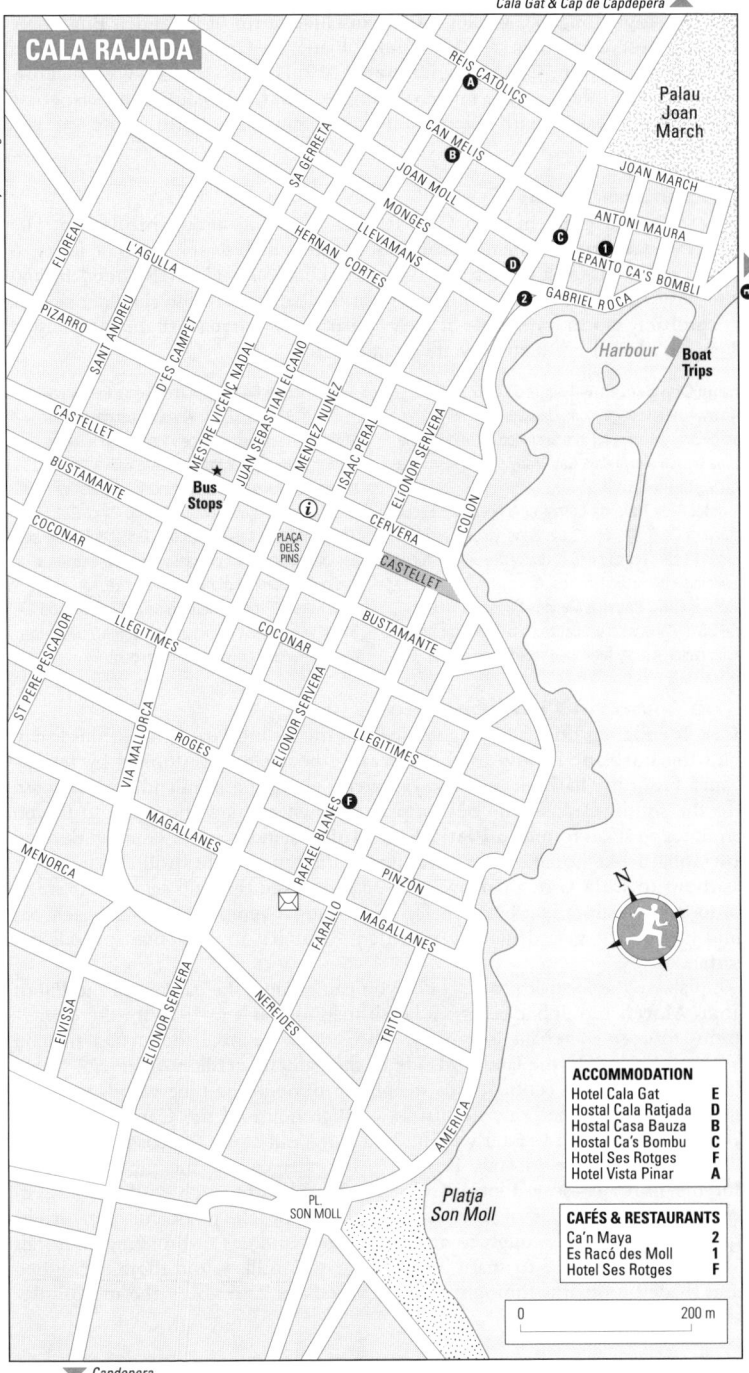

CALA RAJADA

Cala Gat & Cap de Capdepera ▲

Platja Cala Agulla ◄

REIS CATÒLICS

Ⓐ

CAN MELIS

Ⓑ

SA GERRETA

JOAN MOLL

MONGES

LLEVAMANS

HERNAN CORTES

Ⓒ

Ⓓ

Ⓔ

GABRIEL ROCA

LEPANTO CA'S BOMBLI

Ⓐ

Palau
Joan
March

JOAN MARCH

ANTONI MAURA

Harbour

Boat
Trips

FLOREAL

L'AGULLA

PIZARRO

SANT ANDREU

D'ES CAMPET

CASTELLET

BUSTAMANTE

COCONAR

MESTRE VICENÇ NADAL

JUAN SEBASTIAN ELCANO

MENDEZ NUNEZ

ISAAC PERAL

ELIONOR SERVERA

CERVERA

COLON

★
Bus
Stops

ⓘ

PLAÇA
DELS
PINS

CASTELLET

St. PERE PESCADOR

LLEGITIMES

COCONAR

BUSTAMANTE

VIA MALLORCA

ROGES

ELIONOR SERVERA

LLEGITIMES

MAGALLANES

MENORCA

RAFAEL BLANES

Ⓕ

PINZON

FARALLO

MAGALLANES

✉

EIVISSA

ELIONOR SERVERA

NEREIDES

TRITO

AMERICA

N

PL.
SON MOLL

Platja
Son Moll

ACCOMMODATION
Hotel Cala Gat   E
Hostal Cala Ratjada   D
Hostal Casa Bauza   B
Hostal Ca's Bombu   C
Hotel Ses Rotges   F
Hotel Vista Pinar   A

CAFÉS & RESTAURANTS
Ca'n Maya   2
Es Racó des Moll   1
Hotel Ses Rotges   F

0   200 m

▼ Capdepera

the bus stops along c/Castellet, a short distance north of Plaça dels Pins, three of the most useful are to Cala Agulla, Platja de Canyamel and the Coves d'Artà. In addition, **Cruceros Creuers** (☎971 81 06 00, ✉www.cruceros-creuers.com) offers a wide range of summer **boat trips** along the east coast, linking Cala Rajada with several resorts, but principally Porto Cristo (3 daily; €20 return).

Accommodation

The only real problem with Cala Rajada is finding **accommodation**. The town is a favourite German package resort and in high season you'll be lucky to find a room. The best place to try is among the *hostals* and hotels dotted around the busy commercial streets just up from the harbour. In the shoulder season, it's probably worth trying one of the popular seafront hotels. All the places listed here are **closed** between November and March.

Hotel Cala Gat Cala Gat s/n ☎971 56 31 66, ✉www.hotelcalagat.com. Unassuming, fairly traditional small hotel in a secluded location in the pine woods above Cala Gat. Many rooms have sea-facing balconies. ❺

Hostal Cala Ratjada Corner c/Monges at c/Elionor Servera 79 ☎971 56 32 02. Good-value *hostal*, close to the port, set in a characterful white-stucco building with rustic touches. ❷

Hostal Casa Bauza c/Méndez Núñez 61 ☎971 56 38 44, ✉www.casabauza.com. One-star hostal with clean, simply furnished rooms and a pool. ❷

Hostal Ca's Bombu c/Elíonor Servera 86 ☎971 56 32 03, ✉www.casbombu.com. Stylish and appealing place kitted out in a happy version of traditional Spanish style with a pool and terrace restaurant. Breakfast included; great value. ❷

Hotel Ses Rotges c/Rafael Blanes 21 ☎971 56 31 08, ✉www.sesrotges.com. Delightful three-star establishment in an elegantly restored antique villa just out of earshot of the main square. ❺

Hotel Vista Pinar c/Reis Catòlics 11 ☎971 56 37 51, ✉www.hotelvistapinar.com. Large, adequate two-star with its own swimming pool. ❸

The town and its beaches

Cala Rajada was once a fishing village, but there's little evidence of this today, and the **harbour** is now used by pleasure boats and overlooked by restaurants. From the harbour, **walkways** extend along the headland's south coast. To the southwest, past the busiest part of town, it takes about ten to fifteen minutes to stroll round to **Platja Son Moll**, a slender arc of sand overlooked by Goliath-like hotels. More rewarding is the ten-minute stroll east from the harbour to **Cala Gat**, a narrow cove beach tucked tight up against the steep, wooded coastline. The beach is far from undiscovered – there's a beach bar and at times it gets decidedly crowded – but it's an attractive spot all the same.

Up above the footpath to Cala Gat you can glimpse the gardens of the **Palau Joan March** (no public access), a lavish mansion built in 1916 for the eponymous tobacco merchant (see p.75), who was to become the richest man in Franco's Spain. On the landward side of the gardens, c/Elíonor Servera, which begins in the town centre, twists steeply up through the pine woods to reach, after about 1km, the bony headlands and lighthouse of the **Cap de Capdepera**, Mallorca's most easterly point. The views out along the coast are a treat.

Heading north from Cala Rajada, c/L'Agulla crosses the promontory to hit the north coast at **Platja Cala Agulla**. The approach road, some 2km of tourist tackiness, is of little appeal, but the beach, a vast curve of bright golden sand, is big enough to accommodate hundreds of bronzing pectorals with plenty of space to spare. The further you walk – and there are signed and shaded footpaths through the pine woods to assist you – the more isolation you'll get.

Eating

The *Hotel Ses Rotges* (see above) boasts the finest **restaurant** in town, serving from a broadly French menu in immaculate surroundings, but with main courses averaging about €25 it's pricey and there are scores of less expensive rivals serving everything from sauerkraut and sausages through to traditional Spanish cuisine. There are several good spots down at the harbour, most memorably *Es Racó des Moll*, a fashionable little café-restaurant just a few metres back from the water, where they offer a good line in *tapas*. Alternatively, the more upmarket *Ca'n Maya*, just up from the harbour at c/Elíonor Servera 80 (℡ 971 56 40 35), does superb seafood with main courses hovering around €20.

The Coves d'Artà

The succession of coves, caves and beaches notching the seashore between Cala Rajada and Cala Millor begins promisingly with the memorable **Coves d'Artà** (often in Castilian "Cuevas de Artà", as per the website ⓦ www .cuevasdearta.com), reached along the first major turning off the main coastal road (the MA-4040) south of Capdepera. This is the pick of the numerous cave systems of eastern Mallorca, its sequence of cavernous chambers, studded with stalagmites and stalactites, extending 450m into the rock face. Artificial lighting exaggerates the bizarre shapes of the caverns and their accretions, especially in the **Hall of Flags**, where stalactites up to 50m long hang in the shape of partly unfurled flags. Exiting the caves, you're greeted with a stunning view, courtesy of a majestic stairway straight out of a horror movie, which leads up to the yawning hole, beckoning like the mouth of hell high in the cliffs above the bay.

The caves have had a chequered history. During the Reconquista, a thousand Moorish refugees from Artà were literally smoked out of the caves to be slaughtered by Catalan soldiers waiting outside. In the nineteenth century, touring the caves for their scientific interest became fashionable amongst the rich and famous – Jules Verne was particularly impressed – and visits now feature prominently on many a package-tour itinerary. **Tours** of the caves run every half-hour (daily: May–Oct 10am–6pm; Nov–April 10am–5pm; €9) and the guides give a complete geological description in tedious detail and in several languages including English as you wander the illuminated abyss. Allow about an hour for the visit – more if there's a queue, as there sometimes is.

From May to October, Monday through Saturday, there are two **buses** daily to the caves from Cala Rajada and Capdepera; there are also regular **boat trips** here from Cala Rajada (April–Oct 3 daily; €12 including admission).

Platja de Canyamel

PLATJA DE CANYAMEL – not to be confused with the tedious Costa de Canyamel *urbanització* immediately to the south – is a cove resort whose smart modern villas are draped around a pine-backed sandy **beach** in sight of a pair of rocky headlands. It's situated about 1km south of the Coves d'Artà, though there's no connecting road: you have to return to the main coastal road, the MA-4040 running a few kilometres inland, to make the journey. The *platja* makes an agreeable spot for a few hours sunbathing, and there are several inviting **restaurants** plus a number of **hotels**, though they're usually block-booked by German tour operators. Indeed, the only vague chance of a room is at the *Laguna* (℡ 971 84 11 50; ❸; closed Nov–April), an attractive whitewashed hotel plonked right on the beach.

From May to October, local **buses** link Platja de Canyamel with Cala Rajada (Mon–Sat 3–4 daily) as well as Capdepera and Artà (Mon–Sat 1–3 daily).

Cala Millor and around

Continuing south along the main coast road towards Porto Cristo, you'll soon pass the turning for the well-heeled villas of **COSTA DES PINS**, the most northerly and prosperous portion of a gigantic resort conurbation centred on **CALA BONA** and **CALA MILLOR**. This is development gone quite mad, a swathe of apartment buildings, sky-rise hotels and villa-villages overwhelming the contours of the coast as far as the eye can see. The only redeeming feature – and the reason for all this frantic construction in the first place – is the **beach**, a magnificent two-kilometre stretch of sand fringed by what remains of the old pine woods.

To avoid this visual assault, stay on the main coastal road, which remains just inland, cutting a rustic route through vineyards and almond groves as it clips past the turnings for **SA COMA** and **S'ILLOT**, two more sprawling resorts. Thereafter, the main road encounters the multicoloured billboards that announce the cave systems of Porto Cristo.

Porto Cristo

PORTO CRISTO prospered in the early days of the tourist boom, sprouting a string of hotels and *hostals*, but it's fared badly since mega-resorts like Cala Millor and Cala d'Or came on the scene: don't be deceived by the jam of tourist buses clogging the town's streets on their way to the nearby **Coves del Drac** – few of their occupants will actually be staying here. Consequently, this is one of the very few places on the east coast where you're likely to find a room in July and August, and it's not too bad a spot to spend a night either. The **beach** is fine enough for sunbathing – though the swimming isn't great – and is handily located in the centre of town, tucked inside the **harbour**, a narrow V-shaped channel entered between a pair of rocky promontories. Apart from the beach, the harbour accommodates a large marina and meets the oily-green River Es Rivet, which forms the town centre's southern perimeter.

Porto Cristo's origins are uncertain, but it was definitely in existence by the thirteenth century, when it served as the fishing harbour and seaport of Manacor – it boasts one of the most sheltered harbours on the east coast. Nothing remains of the medieval settlement, however, and today the centre, which climbs the hill behind the harbour, consists of high-sided terraced buildings mostly dating from the late nineteenth and early twentieth centuries.

In August 1936, Porto Cristo was the site of a **Republican landing** to try to capture the island from the Falangists. The campaign was a fiasco: the Republicans disembarked over seven thousand men and quickly established a long and deep bridgehead, but their commanders, completely surprised by

Boat trips from Porto Cristo

Cruceros Creuers (☎971 81 06 00, ⊛www.cruceroscreuers.com) organizes a wide range of summer **boat trips** along the east coast, linking Porto Cristo with a string of resorts, including Cala Rajada (3 daily; €20 return). They also offer quick scoots round Porto Cristo harbour in glass-bottomed boats from May to Oct (7 daily; €8 for 30min, €14 for 90min).

their initial success, quite literally didn't know what to do next. The National-ists did: they counterattacked and, supported by the Italian air force, soon had the Republicans dashing back to the coast. Barcelona Radio put on a brave face, announcing, "The heroic Catalan columns have returned from Mallorca after a magnificent action. Not a single man suffered from the effects of the embarkation."

Arrival and information

The main coastal road passes along Porto Cristo's seafront, and a sizeable number of long-distance **buses**, principally from Palma, terminate in the centre close to the harbour and the beach. The **tourist office** is also close to the beach on c/Moll (Mon–Fri 9am–4pm; ☎971 81 51 03, ⓦwww.manacor.org). They can provide useful maps of the town and neighbouring resorts.

Accommodation

Porto Cristo has half-a-dozen **hotels and hostals** and although they're a pretty uninspiring bunch, there's a good chance of a vacancy here at any time of the year. The pick of the bunch is the four-star *Hotel THB Felip*, c/Bordils 41 (T 971 82 07 50, W www.thbhotels.com; ⑤; closed Nov–Jan), which has a great location, in a big old balconied building overlooking the beach. The interior has been revamped in modern style and the rooms are neat and trim – ask for a harbour view. Other, less well-appointed options include the spick-and-span one-star *Hotel Estrella*, c/Curricà 16 (T 971 82 08 33, F 971 82 08 92; ②; closed Nov–April), in a plain postwar three-storey building between the town centre and the caves: to get there, follow the main road south over the river and it's the third turning on the right. Alternatively, the *Sol i Vida* is a small and tidy two-star hotel in a pleasant wooded location on a residential street a few metres from the Coves del Drac caves, at Avgda Joan Servera Camps 11 (T 971 82 10 74, E solivida@wanadoo.es; ②).

The town and the Coves del Drac

Exploring the centre of Porto Cristo is an agreeable way to spend an hour or so, but it won't be long before you're ready to move on and the big attraction hereabouts is the **Coves del Drac** (often signposted in Castilian as "Cuevas del Drac"), across the river, about fifteen minutes' walk south of the centre along the coastal road. Locals had known of the "Dragon's Caves" for hundreds of years, but it was the Austrian archduke Ludwig Salvator (see p.134) who recruited French geologists to explore and map them in 1896. The French discovered four huge chambers that penetrated the coast's limestone cliffs for a distance of around 2km. The eccentric shapes of the myriad **stalactites and stalagmites** adorning each chamber immediately invited comparison with more familiar objects. As the leader of the French team, Edouard Martel, wrote, "On all sides, everywhere, in front and behind, as far as the eye can see, marble cascades, organ pipes, lace draperies, pendants of multi-faceted gems hang suspended from the walls and roof." Since the French exploration, the caves have been thoroughly commercialized. The present complex accommodates a giant car park, ticket office and restaurant, behind which lurk the gardens that lead to the flight of steps down to the caves. You may come to know each step well, as you can wait in line for ages, especially at the weekend. Hour-long **guided tours** of the caves run every hour or ninety minutes (daily: April–Oct 10am–5pm; Nov–March 10.30am–4.30pm; €9.50; W www. cuevasdeldrac.com).

Inside, the innumerable concretions of calcium carbonate, formed by the dissolution of the soft limestone by rainwater, are shrewdly illuminated. Shunting you through the multilingual tour, the guides invite you to gawp and gush at formations such as "the Buddha", "the Pagoda" and "the Snowy Mountain", and magnificent icicle-like stalactites, some of which are snowy white, others picking up hints of orange and red from the rocks they hang off. The *tour de force* is the larger of the two **subterranean lakes** – at 177m long, 40m wide and 30m deep one of the largest underground lakes in the world – whose translucent waters flicker with reflected colours, the mysterious atmosphere further enhanced by a small group of musicians drifting in boats (performances usually begin on the hour). At the end of the tour, some visitors leave on foot, but you can also take a brief boat ride (included in the admission price) across part of the lake.

From the cave complex, it's a short walk across the car park to the well-stocked **Acuàrium** (daily: April–Oct 9.30am–5pm; Nov–March 11am–3pm; €5). Mediterranean creatures lurk on the upper floor, while displays of international ocean life can be found below, where the glass tanks magnify such exotic horrors as electric eels, piranhas and stinging fish.

Coves d'es Hams

There's another cave system situated 2km west of Porto Cristo on the road to Manacor – though you'd hardly want to visit both. The **Coves d'es Hams** (or "Cuevas dels Hams" in Castilian) follow the same format as their rival, with a sequence of somewhat smaller caverns lit to emphasize the beauty of the stalagmites and stalactites. **Guided tours** run every half-hour (daily: April–Oct 10am–5pm; Nov–March 10.45am–noon & 2–3.30pm; €10; ⓦwww.cuevas-hams.com). As at the Coves del Drac, musicians play from boats on an underground lake.

Eating

Although many of Porto Cristo's **restaurants and cafés** are geared up for the passing tourist trade, there are several good places amongst what is generally a pretty mundane scene. Two very recommendable and inexpensive spots are *Sa Carrotja*, a low-key family-run restaurant at the first intersection north from the beach along c/Bordils at Avgda Joan Amer 45 (☎971 82 15 03); and the rather more polished *Siroco* (☎971 82 24 44), whose cosy terrace abuts the harbour a few metres south from the beach on c/Veri. Cream of the crop, however, is the Flamingo, c/Bordils s/n (☎971 82 22 59), which offers enjoyable views over the town and port. The home-made paellas are great, or try the steamed mussels, pizzas (from €6) or the mixed fish grill.

South to Porto Colom

The modern resorts disfiguring the pint-sized coves to the south of Porto Cristo reach their nadir at the **CALAS DE MALLORCA**, the collective name for a band of tourist settlements extending from Cala Magraner to Cala Murada. This part of the shoreline didn't have much charm in the first place – the coves are mostly scrawny and shadeless – and it's even less compelling now. Inland, however, the main coast road – now the **MA-4014** – gives few hints of these scenic disasters as it wends its pastoral way past honey-coloured dry-stone walls and a smattering of ancient farmhouses in the lee of the Serres de Llevant.

The MA-4014 becomes the **MA-4012** at the point where the main road meets the turning for **PORTO COLOM**, a burgeoning resort which straggles round a long and irregular bay some 20km south of Porto Cristo. Originally a fishing village supplying the needs of the neighbouring town of Felanitx, the port boomed throughout most of the nineteenth century from the export trade in wine to France. The good times, however, came to an abrupt end when the phylloxera aphid wiped out the island's vines in the 1870s and the villagers returned to fishing – until, that is, the developers turned up in force during the 1990s. Now, Porto Colom is doomed to accrue villas by the street load.

Felanitx and around

The town of **FELANITX**, located some 13km inland from Porto Colom, is an industrious place, producing wine, ceramics and pearls, and although hardly beautiful, it does have more than a modicum of charm, its tangle of narrow streets lined by handsome old houses mostly dating from the eighteenth and nineteenth centuries. The finest building is the church of **Sant Miquel**, whose mighty, soaring honey-gold facade boasts a dramatic statue of St Michael, shown triumphant with a cringing devil at his feet. The church overlooks one of the town's main squares, **Plaça Sa Font**, where, in an unusual arrangement, a wide and really rather grand flight of stone steps digs down below street level to reach **Font de Santa Margalida**, once the municipal well and now a water fountain. In the last couple of years, the square has also picked up a modern **statue** of a Balearic slinger (see "Contexts" box, p.295), which – no matter what sort of gloss you put on it – is dispiritingly macho: in classical times, the islanders were hired as slingers by any number of armies, but it's almost certain they didn't look like this muscular brute in his loin cloth.

The church stands on a hillock and its easterly supporting wall shadows **c/Major**. Everything looks secure today, but in 1844 the wall collapsed, killing over four hundred people in the worst disaster to hit the town since the days of pirate attack: a **plaque** on c/Major commemorates the dead. The best time to visit Felanitx is on Sunday morning, when a lively fresh produce and craft **market** takes over much of the town centre; there's also a very good covered market, the **mercat municipal** (Tues–Sun), just behind **Sant Miquel** on c/Esglesia. In particular, look out for the capers (Catalan *tapèras*; Castilian *alcaparras*), produced locally and sold by size; the smallest are the most flavoursome, either as *nonpareilles* (up to 7mm) or *surfines* (7–8mm).

Felanitx is on several **bus** routes, including Palma to Porto Colom; buses stop near the main square. There is no tourist office, and neither is there anywhere **to stay** except the nearby Santuari de Sant Salvador.

The Santuari de Sant Salvador

Within easy striking distance of Felanitx is one of the more scenic portions of the Serres de Llevant. The best and most obvious target is the **Santuari de Sant Salvador**, whose assorted buildings stretch along a slender ridge at the top of the 509m-high Puig de Sant Salvador. The drive to the monastery is easy enough and takes about fifteen minutes: head east out of Felanitx on the road to Porto Colom and after about 2km take the signposted, 5km-long side road that weaves its way up the mountain. The Santuari was founded in the fourteenth century in an attempt to stave off a further visitation of the Black Death, which had mauled Felanitx in 1348. It worked, but the original buildings were demolished long ago and the present structure, a strikingly handsome fortress-like complex perched on the edge of the ridge, dates from the early eighteenth century. Inside, beyond the strongly fortified gatehouse, ancient vaulted corridors lead to the **church**, which shelters a much-venerated image of the Virgin Mary. The other end of the ridge is dominated by a gargantuan **statue of Christ the King** stuck on top of a massive plinth. The statue was erected in 1934 and is visible for miles around, though it may well be the island's ugliest landmark. As compensation, the views down across Mallorca from anywhere on the ridge are simply fabulous.

Sant Salvador was the last of Mallorca's monasteries to lose its monks – the last ones moved out in the early 1990s. Thereafter, visitors were initially lodged in the old cells, but a new wing has recently been added and this holds twenty-four really rather comfortable, modern ⚘ **guest rooms** (☎971 82 72 82; ❶), all of which are en suite. The monastery also has a **café**, but confirm its opening times if you're going to arrive hungry. If you've got a car, you could make the sanctuary an unusual and useful base for exploring the locality. It's certainly a very quiet place to stay.

The Castell de Santueri

The custodians at the Santuari de Sant Salvador should be able to point you towards the footpath to the **Castell de Santueri**, about 4km away across the hills to the south. The route is fairly easy to follow and the going isn't difficult, although it's still advisable to have a walking map and stout shoes. The path meanders through a pretty landscape of dry-stone walls, flowering shrubs and copses of almond and carob trees, bringing you to the castle after about an hour and a half. Glued to a rocky hilltop, the battered ramparts date from the fourteenth century, though it was the Moors who built the first stronghold here. Getting inside the ruins is pot luck: sometimes you can (in which case a small entry fee is levied at the main gate), but mostly you can't. If you don't fancy the walk, you can drive to a point below the castle along a five-kilometre country lane, signed off the Felanitx–Santanyí road about 2km south of Felanitx. Curiously enough, one strong local legend insists that Christopher Columbus was conceived here in the castle, the result of a coupling between a local servant girl, one Margalida Colom, and an imprisoned baron, Prince Carl of Viana.

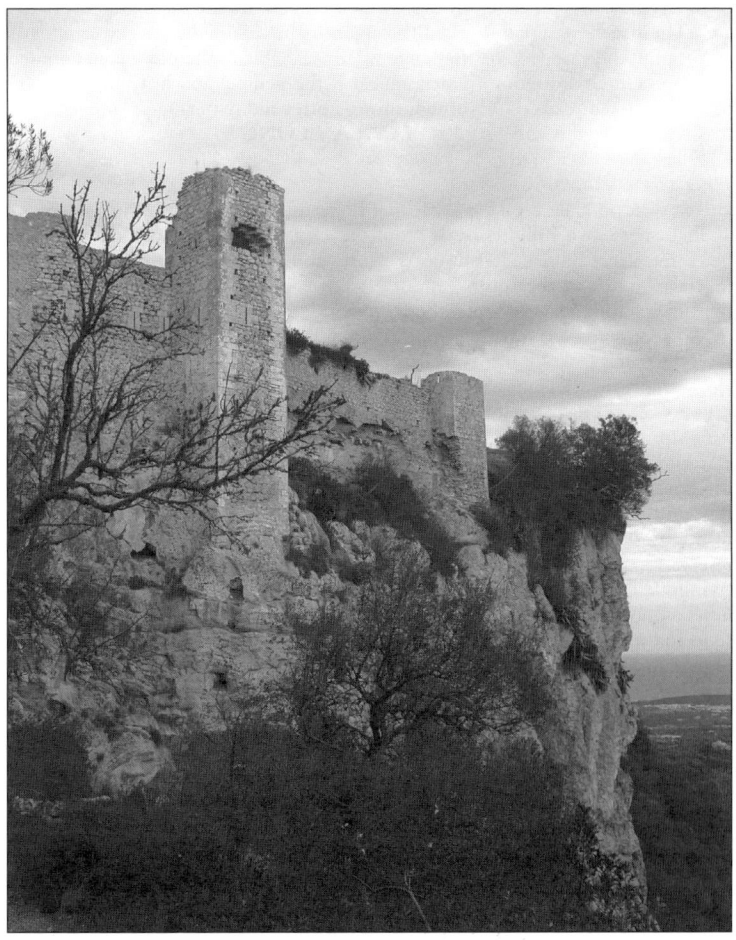

△ Castell de Santueri

Cala d'Or

South along the coast from Porto Colom, the pretty little fishing villages that once studded the quiet coves as far as Porto Petro have been blasted by development. The interconnected resorts that now stand in their place are largely indistinguishable, a homogeneous strip of whitewashed, low-rise villas, hotels, restaurants and bars, mostly designed in a sort of *pueblo* style. Confusingly, this long string of resorts is now usually lumped together under the title "**Cala d'Or**", though this name in fact refers to one particular cove, which is also one of the smallest. The "Cala d'Or" we refer to in this account is the original cove and not the whole development.

To be fair, the pseudo-Andalucian style of the new resorts blends well with the ritzy *haciendas* left by a previous generation of sun-seekers. The latter are largely concentrated on the humpy little headland that separates **CALA D'OR** from its northerly neighbour, **CALA GRAN**. These two fetching little coves, tucked between the cliffs and edged by narrow golden beaches, are the highlights of the area. The beaches are jam-packed throughout the season, but the swimming is perfect and the wooded coastline here is far preferable to the more concentrated development all around. Of equal appeal is the genteel and leafy headland on the south side of Cala d'Or, though this is a brief and flattering preamble to the massive marina and endless villas of **CALA LLONGA**.

Practicalities

Buses stop on Cala d'Or's crowded and charmless main drag, Avinguda Fernando Tarrago, two minutes' walk from the beach. Under various designations, this same street links the main cove resorts, from Cala Esmeralda in the north to Cala Llonga in the south —about a twenty-minute walk from one end to the other. From May to September, a tourist "train" on wheels, the **mini tren** (May–Sept Mon–Sat 6 daily), shuttles along the coast, linking Cala Esmerelda, Cala d'Or and Cala Llonga as well as Porto Petro and Cala Mondragó, stopping along the main street and beside all the beaches.

The Cala d'Or **tourist office** (Mon–Fri 8.30am–2pm; May–Sept also Sat 9am–2pm; ☎971 65 74 63) is situated a few metres up from the Cala Llonga waterside at c/Perico Pomar 10. They can provide resort maps marked with all the hotels and *hostals*, though finding a place **to stay** is well-nigh impossible in the summer – a better bet is to try the *Nereida* in Porto Petro (see below). One of the most appealing options – where you'll almost certainly need an advance reservation – is the four-star *Hotel Cala d'Or*, right above Cala d'Or's beach on Avinguda Bélgica (☎971 65 72 49, ⓦwww.hotelcalador.com; ⑤). The hotel has ninety-odd balconied bedrooms, each furnished in a straightforward modern style and mostly with sea views; the equally engaging public areas include a bar, restaurant and an outside swimming pool. Cala Gran also has one very recommendable hotel, the *Cala Gran-Costa* (☎971 65 71 00, ⓦwww.gavimar.com; ⑥), a bigger and brisker affair at the back of the beach. Most of the modern bedrooms here have balconies and sea views, and there's every convenience, including a swimming pool.

Porto Petro

PORTO PETRO rambles round a twin-pronged cove a couple of kilometres south of Cala Llonga, its old and tiny centre perched on the headland above the marina, with a cluster of whitewashed houses recalling the days before the tourists when it served as Santanyí's seaport. Although it's now all but swallowed up by the Cala d'Or conurbation, Porto Petro still manages to hang onto something of its original character: there's no beach here, so development has been fairly restrained, and although the old fishing harbour has been turned into a marina and villas dot the gentle wooded hillsides edging the coast, it remains a quiet and tranquil spot. Indeed, the only real activity is the promenade round the crystal-watered cove.

Porto Petro can make a pleasant base for exploring this part of the island. **Buses** – from Palma, Felanitx and Cala d'Or – pull in right beside the harbour and an electric *mini-tren* (May–Oct Mon–Sat 6 daily) links it with the resorts to the north and Cala Mondragó to the south. Furthermore, there's a reasonable chance of getting a **room** on spec at the two-star *Hostal Nereida* (ⓣ971 65 72 23, ⓦwww.hostalnereida.com; ❸; closed Nov–April), a comfortable and neat little place, occupying a three-storey modern block just above the main dock; the *hostal* also has its own outside pool, garden and rooftop sun terraces. Porto Petro also has several very good, moderately-priced, harbourside **restaurants**: the *Ca'n Martina* (ⓣ971 65 75 17), by the main dock, serves up a delicious paella (€12 per person) and has a relaxing outside terrace, whilst the *Restaurant Maritimo*, further along the harbour, serves tasty salads and seafood – try the sardines.

From May to October there are once-weekly **boat cruises** from Porto Petro to **Cabrera island** (see p.225), currently on Fridays, departing at 9.30am and returning by 5pm. The cost is €32 per person and reservations should be made ahead of time on ⓣ971 65 70 12.

Mondragó Parc Natural

Beginning about 3km south of Porto Petro, **Mondragó Parc Natural** protects a small but diverse slice of the east coast, around two thousand acres of wetland, farmland, beach, pine and scrub. The park's road signs are a tad confusing, but there are two **car parks** to aim for, both signposted from the MA-19 between Porto Petro and Santanyí. The better target is the **Fonts de n'Alis** car park, 100m from the tiny resort of Cala Mondragó (see below), and this can also be reached direct from Porto Petro along a country road – just follow the signs. The other car park, **S'Amarador**, is on the low-lying headland south across the cove from Cala Mondragó. The park is latticed with footpaths and country lanes, and you can pick up a (rather poor) **map** from the Fonts de n'Alis **visitor centre** (daily 9am–4pm; ⓣ971 18 10 22), at the Fonts de n'Alis car park. This shows the park's four hiking trails: all are easy loops, two of forty minutes, two of thirty. Until the visitor centre sorts itself out with proper hiking maps, the only reliable reference is the billboard map displayed outside.

Cala Mondragó

CALA MONDRAGÓ is one of Mallorca's prettiest resorts. There was some development here before the creation of the park in 1990, but it's all very low key and barely disturbs the cove's beauty, with low, pine-clad cliffs framing a pair of sandy beaches beside crystal-clear waters. Predictably, the cove's "unspoilt" reputation and safe bathing acts as a magnet for sun-lovers from miles around, but you can escape the crowds by staying the night (if there's space) at either of two beachside **hostals**. Choose between the *Hostal Playa Mondragó*, a straightforward, modern block with forty plain but perfectly adequate rooms (ⓣ971 65 77 52, ⓦwww.playamondrago.com; ❸; closed Nov–March); or the slightly more enticing *Hostal Condemar*, about 200m from the beach, where most of the rooms have sea-view balconies and there's an outside pool (☎971 65 77 56, ⓦwww.hostalcondemar.com; ❸; closed Nov–April).

From May to October, there are hourly **buses** to Cala Mondragó from Porto Petro and Cala d'Or; Cala Mondragó is also the southern terminus of the summertime *mini tren* which runs north as far as Cala Esmerelda (May–Oct Mon–Sat 6 daily).

Santanyí and around

Taking its name from a shortened version of 'Santi Annini' (the Lamb of God), the crossroads town of **SANTANYÍ**, about 10km west of Porto Petro, has long guarded the island's southeastern approaches, a role that has cost it dear. Corsairs ransacked the place time and time again, prompting a medieval German traveller to bemoan their fate – "The Saracens constantly arrive in their ships, carry away prisoners, torment them and use them as slaves or sell them for money". In hope, rather more than belief, the townsfolk attempted to protect themselves by fortifying the town on several occasions and, although it didn't do them much good, one of the medieval gates, **Sa Porta**, has survived in good condition. Nonetheless, it's Santanyí's narrow alleys, squeezed between high-sided sandstone houses, that are the town's main appeal along with **Sant Andreu Apòstol**, a bulky, eighteenth-century pile which incorporates a finely worked, early Gothic chapel, the **Capella del Roser**, a thirteenth-century survivor from the first church built on the site.

Santanyí 's main square, Plaça Major, is flanked by **cafés** and bars, amongst which the pick is probably *Sa Font*, at no.27, a groovy little place selling a wide variety of snacks and light meals. While you're here, you could also drop by the chic, German-run jewellery and accessory shop, *Reina Rana*, at Plaça Major 15.

Cala Figuera and Cala Santanyí

Travelling southeast from Santanyí, a 5km-long byroad cuts a pretty, rustic route through to **CALA FIGUERA**, whose antique harbour sits beside a fjord-like inlet below the steepest of coastal cliffs. Local fishermen still land their catches and mend their nets here, but nowadays it's to the accompaniment of scores of photo-snapping tourists. Up above, the pine-covered shoreline heaves with villas, hotels and *hostals*, although the absence of high-rise buildings means the development is never overbearing.

Cala Figuera is extremely popular, and there are precious few vacant **rooms** at its dozen or so hotels and *hostals*, even in the shoulder season. If you do decide to chance your arm, the obvious place to start is on the steep pedestrianized ramp – c/Verge del Carmen – which leads up from the harbour. In this prime location, at no. 50, is the unassuming *Hostal Cala*, with twenty rooms stashed above a restaurant (☎971 64 50 18; ❸; closed Nov–March). Close by at no. 58, the one-star *Ca'n Jordi* has just six simple bedrooms, also over a restaurant (☎971 64 50 35; ❷; closed Nov–March). Moving up a notch, the two-star *Hotel Villa Sirena*, c/Virgen del Carmen 37 (☎971 64 53 03, ⓦwww.hotelvillasirena .com; ❸), is a proficient modern hotel with its own swimming platforms above the water; it's located at the end of the promontory above the end of the cove.

Of Cala Figuera's many **restaurants**, the most distinguished are the seafood places lining c/Verge del Carmen. It's difficult to select – and hard to go wrong – but *Ca'n Jordi* (☎971 64 50 35), at no. 58, is first-rate, with good views, and not too pricey with mains at around €18. In terms of amenities, the resort has car and bike rental outlets, and, down by the harbour, a **diving** school (☎971 64 53 00, ⓦwww.albatros-divers-mallorca.com), which rents out a wide range of gear to experienced divers, and arranges novice courses with three days of tuition going for around €330. What you won't get is a **beach**. The nearest is 4km west at **CALA SANTANYÍ**, a busy little resort with a medium-sized (and frequently crowded) beach at the end of a steep-sided, heavily wooded gulch. To get there, head back towards Santanyí for about 1.5km and follow the signs.

From May to October, there are regular **buses** to Cala Figuera from Palma, Santanyí and Colònia de Sant Jordi.

The south coast

Mallorca's **south coast** – stretching from the Cap de Ses Salines, the island's most southerly point, to the Bay of Palma – has hardly been developed at all, but the reasons for this lack of interest are pretty obvious when you come here: most of the shoreline is unenticingly spartan, a long and low rocky shelf with barely a decent beach in sight. That said, there are moments when the landscape has an eerie sense of desolation – especially at wind-buffeted **Cap de Ses Salines** – and some visitors find this barrenness strangely fascinating. A smattering of modern resorts have gamely made the most of these disheartening surroundings and the pick of them is undoubtedly **Colònia de Sant Jordi**, a curious and most enjoyable amalgamation of tourist settlement and old seaport, which thoroughly deserves an overnight visit. Even better, the resort is also the main departure point for boat trips to the remote islet of **Cabrera**, now a **national park**, and is near a wide skirt of saltflats that attracts birds by the thousand – and backs onto the region's longest beach, **Es Trenc**. Of the other resorts, **Cala Pi**, where a deep ravine frames a sandy beach, is the best-looking and although it doesn't offer much it is close to the substantial remains of prehistoric **Capocorb Vell**. In between Colònia de Sant Jordi and Cala Pi, however, things are pretty dismal with the grim and untidy resorts of Valgornera, S'Estanyol and Sa Ràpita no more than clumps of mundane second homes blotching the treeless shoreline.

Planning an itinerary is straightforward. The best advice is to use the **MA-19** road, which runs from Santanyí northwest to S'Arenal on the Bay of Palma, as your baseline, branching off as you wish. As ever, **accommodation** is at a premium. Throughout the season, your best chance by a long chalk is in Colònia de Sant Jordi, but from November to March nearly everything is closed and you'll almost certainly have to visit on a day trip. **Bus** services are adequate if you're heading somewhere specific from Palma, but are dreadful when you attempt to move between the resorts themselves.

Cap de Ses Salines

Heading southwest from Santanyí (see p.220), a fast and easy country road drifts through a landscape of old dry-stone walls, broken-down windmills, ochre-flecked farmhouses and straggling fields bound for Colònia de Sant Jordi. After about 4km, you pass through tiny **Es Llombards** and shortly afterwards you reach the turning for the **Cap de Ses Salines**, a bleak, brush-covered headland 10km to the south through coastal pine woods. The lighthouse here is closed to the public, but there are fine views out to sea. Thekla larks and stone curlews are often to be seen on the cape, whilst gulls, terns and shearwaters glide about offshore, benefiting from the winds which, when they're up, can make the place intolerable. If the cape takes your fancy, then walk northwest along the seashore to the wide and shallow bay and sandy beach of the **Platja des Caragol**. It's easy walking; allow thirty minutes each way.

Colònia de Sant Jordi

The wide streets of **COLÒNIA DE SANT JORDI**, about 13km west of Santanyí, pattern a substantial and irregularly shaped headland that pokes its knobbly head out into the ocean. The main approach road is **Avinguda Marquès del Palmer**, at the end of which – roughly in the middle of the headland – lies the principal square, the unremarkable **Plaça Constitució**. From here, c/Sa Solta and then Avinguda Primavera lead west to the *Hotel Marquès del Palmer*, which sits tight against the **Platja d'Estanys**, whose gleaming sands curve round a dune-edged cove. South of Avinguda Primavera is the surprisingly pleasant main tourist zone, whose domineering lines of flashy hotels are broken by low-rise villas and landscaped side streets. To the north are the **Salines de S'Avall**, the saltpans which once provided the town with its principal source of income.

East from Plaça Constitució along c/Major, and then left (north) down c/Gabriel Roca, is the old **harbour**, the most diverting part of town. Framed by an attractive, early twentieth-century ensemble of balconied houses, the port makes the most of a handsome, horseshoe-shaped bay. There's nothing special to look at, but it's a relaxing spot with a handful of restaurants, fishing smacks, a marina and a pocket-sized beach, the **Platja Es Port**. Here also is the **kiosk** where you book the boat to Cabrera (see p.225), whose island delights you will be able to sample when the Cabrera island visitor centre, at the north end of the harbour, is completed in 2008.

From the harbour, it's a five-minute walk along the footpath north round the bay to the slender, low-lying headland that accommodates the much more extensive sands of the **Platja d'es Dolç**.

Arrival and information

Buses to Colònia de Sant Jordi stop at several central locations, including the bus stop at the north end of the old harbour beside Plaça Es Dolç and again at the south end on c/Gabriel Roca. During the season, a toy-town **mini-tren** shuttles around town every hour or two, but if all else fails call a **taxi** (℡971 65 52 78).

It's likely to move in the near future, but in the meantime the **tourist office** is on the upper floor of the town hall at c/Doctor Barraquer 5 (Mon–Fri 9am–2pm; ℡971 65 60 73, Ⓦwww.mallorcainfo.com). They issue free town maps, supply a comprehensive list of local accommodation and have information on local **bike rental** shops – cycling in the flatlands around the resort is a popular pastime.

Accommodation

The glossy modern **hotels** at the west end of the resort are very much package territory, but there is a good chance of a spare room on spec amongst the reasonably priced hotels and *hostals* in the vicinity of the old harbour.

Hostal Colonial c/Gabriel Roca 9 ℡971 65 61 82, Ⓦwww.hostal-colonial.com. Very agreeable, family-run, one-star *hostal* with eight frugal but entirely adequate modern rooms, each of which has a small terrace or balcony. Closed Dec–Feb. ❸

Hostal Es Turó Plaça Es Dolç s/n ℡971 65 50 57, Ⓦwww.hostalesturo.com. Unassuming, recently revamped one-star *hostal* in a solid three-storey building plonked right on Es Port beach. There's a rooftop swimming pool and eighteen guest rooms

COLÒNIA DE SANT JORDI

ACCOMMODATION
Hostal Colonial   C
Hostal Es Turó   A
Hotel Lemar   B
Hostal Playa   D
Hotel Villa Chiquita   E

CAFÉS & RESTAURANTS
El Puerto   2
Port Blau   1
Restaurante Hostal
Playa   D

Cabrera
Visitor Centre

Platja Es Port

Harbour

Cabrera
Island Kiosk

GABRIEL ROCA

Bus Stop

ES TAMARELLS
ES JONC
PLAÇA
ES DOLÇ
AUBA
ESTRELLA DEL MAR
BONANÇA
DELFÍN
DR BARRAQUER
CALA GALIOTA

BURGUERA
PORT
SALLOTJA
PESCADORS

PONENT
PLAÇA
SA NA GUARDIA
TORRE
MAJOR
NA PELADA
PUNTASA

CABRERA

GABRIEL ROCA
Bus Stop

Cala Galiota

Sa Puntassa

AVINGUDA MARQUES DEL PALMER

CLAVELL
RAMON Y CAJAL
DE ASIS
CERVANTES
AGUSTINA DE ARAGON
PERLES
ES JONQUET
SAN FRANCISCO
PASSEIG DE LA ROSA
ROADA
ES SALOBRAR

ESTANYS
ES CARRERO
SA SOLTA
PLAÇA
CONSTITUCIÓ
PLAÇA
MARE
DE DEU

MARINA
MAR
SOL
LLUNA
GOYA
PRINCEP
SANTA TERESA DE JESÚS
VELAZQUEZ
SALVADOR DALI
RECO
(DEL
GRECO)
JOAN MIRO
PLAÇA
C. COLON
PUNTA VOLANTINA
L'VILALONGA

Bus Stop
SINIA
BON HUMOR
SOL
PRINCEP
ROMEO Y JULIETA
POU DEN VERVERA
AMISTAD
ALEJANDRO FARNESIO

PLAÇA
EUROPA
AVINGUDA PRIMAVERA

Bus Stop

Salines
de
S'Avall
(saltpans)

Bassa d'es Cabot

PRIMAVERA
AVINGUDA
ROMANI
PINS
CARABELA
ESMERALDA

PLAÇA
MOLI
DE SA SAL

Hotel Marquès
del Palmer

Platja d'Estanys

N

0   100 m

Campos, Santanyi & Es Trenc

Platja d'Es Dolç

– those at the back look out over the beach. Closed Nov–April. ❸

Hotel Lemar c/Bonança 1 ☎971 65 51 78, ⊛www .hotellemar.com. Old but recently re-equipped, high-sided, balconied building overlooking the harbour. Some of the ninety-odd rooms are at the side, down a side street, so specify you want a room at the front. Three stars. Closed Nov to mid-April. ❹

🚶 **Hostal Playa** c/Major 25 ☎971 65 52 56, ⊛www.restauranteplaya.com. About five minutes' walk from the main harbour, this eminently appealing little place has seven double rooms, four of which – and these are the ones you want – look out over the sea as it laps against the beach to the rear of the *hostal*. The rooms are

pretty basic, but they are quite large and each of the sea-facing rooms has a balcony. The public area is delightfully old-fashioned with oodles of wood, old photos and plates stuck on the walls. Breakfast is served on a pretty, sea-facing patio terrace, which doubles as a restaurant (see below). ❸

Hotel Villa Chiquita c/Esmeralda 14 ☎971 65 51 21, ⊛www.hotelvillachiquita.com. This smart and well-tended hotel occupies a rambling, *pueblo*-style modern villa in the tourist zone at the west end of Avinguda Primavera. It has a good-looking garden, with lots of exotic cactuses, and eighteen smartly decorated en-suite guest rooms. Closed Nov to mid-Feb. ❼

Eating

A string of first-rate **restaurants** line up along the harbour and, although they are all geared up for the tourists, everything is pleasantly low-key and small-scale. The big gastronomic deal is the seafood, but here, in a town with its own fishing fleet, portions are substantial and often as not you get the whole fish rather than a slice. Things get busy from around 8pm, but close down early – by about 10.30pm.

🚶 **Port Blau** c/Gabriel Roca 67 ☎971 65 65 55. This smart restaurant lives up to its smashing harbourside location with some of the town's top food, including big, beautifully presented portions of the freshest fish, plus heaped salads and great bread. Mains hover around €25. Closed Tues & Dec & Jan.

El Puerto c/Port 2 ☎971 65 60 47. Down on the harbour, this smart and popular café-restaurant does a good trade in *tapas* and *racions* for €6–10. They also serve up a wide range of full-scale

seafood dishes, including a delicious paella made from fish caught off Cabrera. Daily noon–4.30pm & 7–11pm.

Restaurante Hostal Playa c/Major 25 ☎971 65 52 56. The restaurant of the *Hostal Playa* (see above) may lack a few frills, but there's no complaining about the food – fish and more fish prepared in the traditional Mallorcan manner. The restaurant occupies a very pleasant, sea-facing patio-terrace. Main courses average around €20. Tues–Sun noon–3.30pm & 7.30–11pm, Mon 7.30–11pm.

Around Colònia de Sant Jordi: Es Trenc

One of Colònia de Sant Jordi's attractions is its proximity to **Es Trenc**, a 4km strip of sandy beach that extends as far as the eye can see. It's neither unknown, nor unspoilt, but the crowds are easily absorbed except at the height of the season, and development is virtually non-existent. To drive there, head north from Colònia de Sant Jordi and, about 0.5km out of town, turn left at the roundabout towards Campos; after another 2.8km, take the signed left turn and follow the country lane leading across the salt pans and wetlands to the large car park (€6) at the east end of the beach – a total distance of around 6km. This end of the beach is far more appealing than the other, at **Ses Covetes**, which is blotched by improvised shacks and drinks stalls.

The saltpans backing onto the beach – the **Salines de Llevant** – and the surrounding farm and scrubland support a wide variety of **birdlife**. Residents such as marsh harriers, kestrels, spotted crakes, fan-tailed warblers and hoopoes make a visit enjoyable at any time of year, but the best time to come is in the spring when hundreds of migrants arrive from Africa. Commonly seen in the springtime are avocets, little ringed plovers, little egrets, common sandpipers, little stints, black-tailed godwits, collared pratincoles and black terns. Several

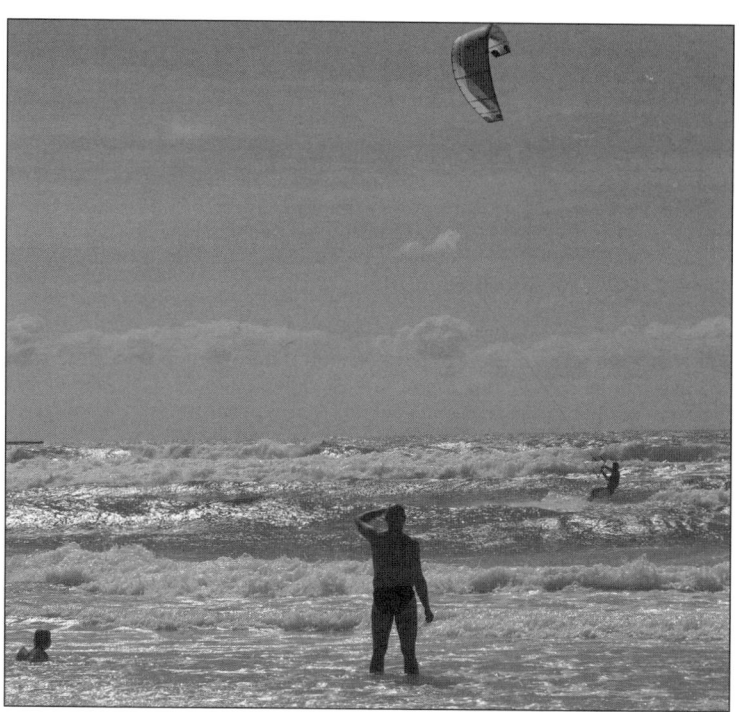

△ Es Trenc beach

footpaths lead from Es Trenc beach into the saltpans, but it's not a good area to explore on foot: the scenery is boring, it's smelly and for much of the year insects are a menace. It's much better to drive or cycle round using the maze-like network of narrow country lanes that traverse the saltpans, stopping anywhere that looks promising.

Cabrera National Park

The **Illa de Cabrera** ("Goat Island") is a bumpy, scrub- and tree-covered chunk of rock lying 18km offshore from Colònia de Sant Jordi. Largely bare, almost entirely uninhabited and no more than 7km wide and 5km long, it is nonetheless easily the largest of a cluster of tiny islets that comprise the Cabrera archipelago. The only significant hint of Cabrera's eventful past is the protective **castle** above its supremely sheltered harbour. Pliny claimed the island to have been the birthplace of Hannibal; medieval pirates hunkered down here to plan future raids; and during the Napoleonic Wars, the Spanish stuck nine thousand French prisoners of war out on the island and promptly forgot about them – two-thirds died from hunger and disease during their four-year captivity. More recently, the island was taken over by Franco's armed forces, and now they've departed the island has been protected as the **Parc National de Cabrera**.

During the summertime, there's a once-weekly boat from Porto Petro to Cabrera (see p.219), but most visitors reach the island from Colònia de Sant

Jordi, where a **harbourfront kiosk** (☎971 64 90 34, ⓦwww.excursionsacabrera .com) has information on, and takes reservations for, Cabrera island **boat trips** (March–Oct 1 daily; 7–8hr; €35). There's nowhere to eat on Cabrera, so you'll either have to take your own food or shell out an extra €7 for the boat company's buffet, with drinks an added extra.

The day trip starts with a sixty-minute voyage to the island. On the final stretch, the boat nudges round a hostile-looking headland to enter the harbour, **Es Port** – a narrow finger of calm water edged by hills and equipped with a tiny jetty. National Park personnel meet the boat to advise about what visitors can do and where – some parts of Cabrera are out of bounds – and there's a small park **information office** by the jetty too. The most popular excursion is the stiff, thirty-minute hoof up the path to the ruins of the fourteenth-century **castle**, which perches high up on Cabrera's west coast. The views from the fortress back to Mallorca are magnificent, and all sorts of **birds** can be seen gliding round the sea-cliffs, including Manx and Cory's shearwaters and the rare Audouin's gulls, as well as peregrine falcons and shags. It is, however, the blue-underbellied **Lilford's wall lizard** that really steals the show: after you've completed the walk to the castle, take time to have a drink down by the jetty, where you can tempt the Lilford's lizards out from the scrub with pieces of fruit.

As an alternative to the castle, it's an easy fifteen-minute walk round the harbour to **Sa Plageta beach**, or you can sign up for a guided tour inland to the sombre **memorial** commemorating the dead French prisoners of war: the path to the memorial begins at Sa Plageta and takes about twenty minutes to walk, but currently you're not allowed to do it without a guide. The excursion includes a visit to a small **museum**, in a former wine cellar and grain ware-house, which traces the history of the island illustrated by a ragbag of archeo-logical finds recovered from the island and its surrounding waters.

On the return journey, the boat bobs across the bay to visit **Sa Cova Blava** (Blue Grotto), sailing right into the cave through the fifty-metre-wide entrance and on into the yawning chamber beyond. The grotto reaches a height of 160m and is suffused by the bluish light, from which it gets its name; you can swim here too.

Campos and Llucmajor

Plonked down amongst the sun-baked flatlands of Es Pla, modest **CAMPOS**, 13km north of Colònia de Sant Jordi, isn't much to look at, but it does have two surprises up its sleeve: it's home to what many consider to be the best **patisserie** on the island, *Pastisserie Pomar*, in the main square at Plaça 20 (☎971 65 06 06); and its church, Sant Julià, holds an especially fine painting of Christ by Bartolomé Esteban Murillo (1617–82), the first Spanish painter to achieve a Europe-wide reputation.

Pushing on, **LLUCMAJOR**, the next settlement to the west, has little to detain you, despite its medieval origins as a market town and its long associa-tion with the island's shoemakers. It was here, just outside the old city walls, that Jaume III, the last of the independent kings of Mallorca, was defeated and killed by Pedro IV of Aragon.

Llucmajor is just 27km from central Palma.

South of Llucmajor: Capocorb Vell and Cala Pi

Travelling south from Llucmajor on the road to Cala Pi, it's about 13km to **Capocorb Vell** (often signposted in Castilian "Capicorp Vey"; Mon–Wed & Fri–Sun 10am–4pm; €2), whose extensive remains date from around 1000 BC. Surrounded by arid scrubland and enclosed within a modern dry-stone wall, this prehistoric village incorporates the battered ruins of five *talayots* and 28 dwellings. A footpath weaves round the haphazard remains, but most of what you see is not very inspiring and gives little idea of how the village was arranged. The most impressive features are the Cyclopean walls, which reach a maximum height of four metres. To make some sense of what you see, pick up the free English leaflet at the entrance.

A short distance further south, just beyond the hamlet of **CAPOCORB**, there's a choice of routes: straight on for **Cap Blanc**, a desultory cape with a lighthouse, or left for the 4km-trip to the resort of **CALA PI**. First impressions of Cala Pi are not encouraging – the bulk of the resort spreads over a bleak headland – but down below is a slender cove that conceals a lovely **beach**, a tiny finger of sand wedged between high, pine-studded cliffs and fringed by ramshackle fishing huts.

Travel details

Buses

Artà to: Cala Rajada (Mon–Sat 4 daily, 2 on Sun; 15min); Capdepera (Mon–Sat 4 daily, 2 on Sun; 10min); Manacor train station (6–8 daily; 30min); Palma (Mon–Sat 4 daily, 2 on Sun; 1hr 20min); Platja de Canyamel (May–Oct Mon–Sat 1–3 daily; 20min).

Cala Figuera to: Palma (Mon–Sat 1–2 daily; 1hr 30min); Santanyí (Mon–Sat 1–2 daily; 15min).

Cala Mondragó to: Cala d'Or (May–Oct 9 daily; 25min); Porto Petro (May–Oct 9 daily; 10min).

Cala Pi to: Palma (1 daily; 1hr 30min).

Cala Rajada to: Artà (Mon–Sat 4 daily, 2 on Sun; 15min); Capdepera (Mon–Sat 4 daily, 2 on Sun; 5min); Coves d'Artà (May–Oct Mon–Sat 2 daily; 30min); Manacor train station (6–8 daily; 50min); Palma (2–6 daily; 1hr 35min); Platja de Canyamel (May–Oct Mon–Sat 2–4 daily; 15min).

Capdepera to: Cala Rajada (Mon–Sat 4 daily, 2 on Sun; 5min); Manacor train station (6–8 daily; 45min); Palma (2–6 daily; 1hr 30min).

Colònia de Sant Jordi to: Manacor (2–3 daily; 1hr); Palma (Mon–Sat 6 daily, 3 on Sun; 1hr); Santanyí (2–3 daily; 10min).

Coves d'Artà to: Cala Rajada (May–Oct Mon–Sat 2 daily; 30min).

Coves del Drac to: Palma (Mon–Sat 4 daily, 1 on Sun; 1hr).

Felanitx to: Palma (Mon–Sat every 1–2hr, 5 on Sun; 1hr); Porto Colom (5–7 daily; 30min); Santanyí (Mon–Sat 2 daily; 1hr).

Manacor to: Colònia de Sant Jordi (2–3 daily; 1hr); Palma (Mon–Sat 10 daily, 5 on Sun; 45min); Santanyí (2–3 daily; 50min).

Manacor train station to: Artà (6–8 daily; 30min); Cala Rajada (6–8 daily; 50min); Capdepera (6–8 daily; 45min); Porto Cristo (6–8 daily; 30min).

Palma to: Algaida (Mon–Sat every 1–2hr, 5 on Sun; 25min); Artà (Mon–Sat 4 daily, 2 on Sun; 1hr 20min); Binissalem (3–6 daily; 20min); Cala d'Or (Mon–Sat 6 daily, 3 on Sun; 1hr 10min); Cala Figuera (Mon–Sat 1–2 daily; 1hr 30min); Cala Millor (Mon–Sat 10 daily, 3 on Sun; 1hr 15min); Cala Rajada (2–6 daily; 1hr 35min); Campos (Mon–Sat 6 daily, 3 on Sun; 35min); Colònia de Sant Jordi (Mon–Sat 6 daily, 3 on Sun; 1hr); Coves del Drac (Mon–Sat 4 daily, 1 on Sun; 1hr); Felanitx (Mon–Sat every 1–2hr, 5 on Sun; 1hr); Inca (Mon–Sat hourly, Sat & Sun 3–5 daily; 30min); Manacor (Mon–Sat 10 daily, 5 on Sun; 45min); Montuiri (Mon–Sat every 1–2hr, 5 on Sun; 35min); Porto Colom (Mon–Sat every 1–2hr, 3 on Sun; 1hr 10min); Porto Cristo (Mon–Sat 9 daily, 3 on Sun; 1hr 10min); Porto Petro (Mon–Sat 6 daily, 3 on Sun; 1hr 35min); Santanyí (Mon–Sat 6 daily, 3 on Sun; 1hr); Sineu (2–4 daily; 1hr).

Porto Colom to: Felanitx (5–7 daily; 30min); Palma (Mon–Sat every 1–2hr, 3 on Sun; 1hr 30min).

Porto Cristo to: Manacor train station (6–8 daily; 30min); Palma (Mon–Sat 9 daily, 3 on Sun; 1hr 10min).

Porto Petro to: Cala d'Or (May–Oct 9 daily; 25min); Cala Mondragó (May–Oct 9 daily; 10min); Santanyí (3–6 daily; 35min).

Santanyí to: Cala Figuera (Mon–Sat 1–2 daily; 15min); Cala Santanyí (May–Oct Mon–Sat 1 daily; 10min); Colònia de Sant Jordi (2–3 daily; 10min); Felanitx (Mon–Sat 2 daily; 1hr); Manacor (2–3 daily; 50min); Palma (Mon–Sat 6 daily, 3 on Sun; 1hr); Porto Petro (3–6 daily; 35min).

Note: For further details, call ☏ 971 17 77 77, or check out ⓦ tib.caib.es.

Trains

Palma to: Binissalem (every 30–40min; 30min); Inca (every 30–40min; 40min); Lloseta (every 30–40min; 35min); Manacor (hourly; 1hr); Petra (hourly; 55min); Sineu (hourly; 50min).

Note: For further information, call ☏ 971 17 77 77, or check out ⓦ tib.caib.es.

Menorca

Mallorca

Menorca

0   20 km

N

CHAPTER 5

Highlights

❉ **Maó** The labyrinthine lanes and alleys of Menorca's engaging capital ramble along the top of a ridge, high above the town marina and its outstanding assortment of restaurants. See p.234

❉ **Talatí de Dalt** The most satisfying of Menorca's many prehistoric remains, in a charming rustic setting just outside Maó. See p.248

❉ **Cap de Faváritx** Wind-stripped headland where a solitary lighthouse shines out over a lunar-like landscape of tightly layered slate. See p.259

❉ **Fornells** This attractive little resort is famous for its *caldereta de llagosta* – lobster stew – which is served up

at a batch of fine seafood restaurants. See p.259

❉ **Monte Toro** Menorca's highest point, offering wonderful vistas of the whole island on a clear day. See p.267

❉ **Ciutadella** The island's prettiest town, its compact centre an inordinately appealing maze of handsome stone buildings culminating in a pocket–sized Gothic cathedral. See p.277

❉ **Cala Turqueta** Menorca has a clutch of unspoilt cove beaches and this is one of the finest: a band of fine white sand set between wooded limestone cliffs and crystal-clear waters. See p.287

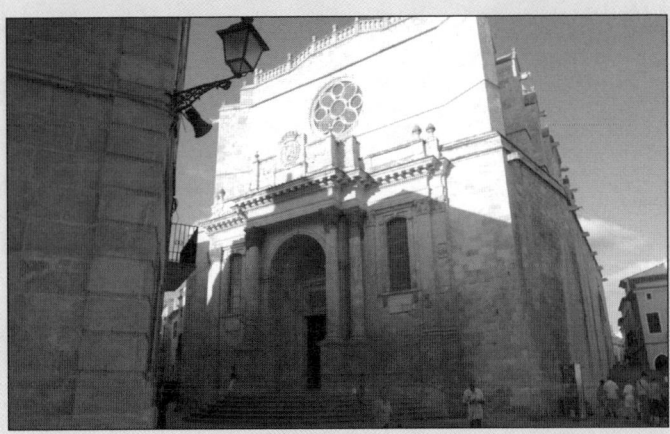

△ Ciutadella Cathedral

5

Menorca

S econd largest of the Balearic islands, boomerang-shaped **MENORCA** stretches west from the enormous natural harbour of **Maó** to the smaller port of **Ciutadella**, a distance of just 45km. Each of these two small towns, which together boast around seventy percent of the population, has preserved much of its eighteenth- and early nineteenth-century appearance, though Ciutadella's labyrinthine centre, with its patrician mansions and Gothic cathedral, has the aesthetic edge over Maó's plainer, more mercantile architecture. Running through the rustic interior between the two, the main **ME-1** highway forms the island's backbone, linking a trio of pocket-sized market towns – **Alaior, Es Mercadal** and **Ferreries** – and succouring what little industry Menorca enjoys, a few shoe factories and cheese-making plants. Branching off the highway, a sequence of asphalted side roads cut along to the **resorts** that notch the north and south coasts. Mercifully, however, the tourist development is largely confined to individual coves and bays, and only amongst the sprawling villa-villages of the southeast and on the west coast has it become overpowering. What's more, there are still many remote cove **beaches** with not a speck of concrete in sight, though access to them is usually along rough and dusty lanes. Neither is the development likely to spread: determined to protect their island from the worst excesses of the tourist industry, the Menorcans have clearly demarcated development zones and have also created a chain of conservation areas that will eventually protect around forty percent of the island, a far-sighted plan that prompted UNESCO to declare Menorca a **Biosphere Reserve** in 1993. The islanders are especially keen to protect their undeveloped beaches, bringing both them and their immediate hinterland into public ownership as speedily as possible. There are even plans to revamp the old mule track that once circled the entire island and turn it into a footpath, but only a small part of this project has been completed at the time of writing.

The ME-1 acts as a rough dividing line between Menorca's two distinct **geological areas**. In the north, sandstone predominates, giving a red tint to the low hills which roll out towards the bare, surf-battered coastline, one of whose many coves and inlets shelters the lovely fishing village and mini-resort of **Fornells**. To the south all is limestone, with low-lying flatlands punctuated by bulging hills and fringed by a cove-studded coastline. Wooded ravines gash the southern zone, becoming deeper and more dramatic as you travel west – especially around **Cala Santa Galdana**, a popular resort set beneath severe, pine-clad seacliffs. Straddling the two zones, **Monte Toro**, Menorca's highest peak and the site of a quaint little church, offers panoramic views that reveal the topography of the island to wonderful effect.

This varied terrain is sprinkled with farmsteads, present witnesses to an **agriculture** that had become, before much of it was killed off by urbanization, highly advanced. A dry-stone wall (*tanca*) protected every field – the island boasts no less than 15,000 kilometres of stone wall – and prevented the **Tramuntana**, the vicious north wind, from tearing away the topsoil. Even olive trees had their roots individually protected in little stone wells, while compact stone ziggurats sheltered cattle from both the wind and the blazing sun. Nowadays, apart from a few acres of rape and corn, many of the fields are barren, but the walls and ziggurats survive, as do many of the old twisted gates made from olive branches. The landscape is further cluttered by scores of **prehistoric stone monuments**, mostly dating from the second millennium BC. Perhaps surprisingly, considering this widespread physical evidence, little is known of the island's early settlers and there has been endless academic debate about exactly what means what. The most common remains are **talayots**, cone-shaped mounds made of stone that may or may not have been watchtowers. It's from these *talayots* that the prehistoric **Talayotic Period** is named, running from 1500 to 123 BC, when the Romans arrived. Three of the finest sites are at **Talatí de Dalt**, just outside Maó, and **Torrellafuda** and the **Naveta d'es Tudons**, near Ciutadella.

In more recent times, Maó's long, deep-water port, the **Port de Maó**, promoted Menorca to an important position in European affairs. The **British** saw its potential as a **naval base** and captured the island in 1708 during the War of the Spanish Succession, confirming their conquest five years later under the terms of the Treaty of Utrecht. Spain regained possession in 1783, but with the threat of Napoleon in the Mediterranean, a new British base was temporarily established under admirals Nelson and Collingwood until Britain finally relinquished all claims to the island in 1802. The British influence on Menorca, especially its architecture, is still manifest: the sash windows so popular in Georgian design are even now sometimes referred to as *winders* and locals often part with a fond *bye-bye*. The British also introduced the art of distilling juniper berries, and Menorcan gin (Xoriguer, Beltran or Nelson) is now world-renowned.

Today, Menorca's economy is dependent on the **tourist industry**, but this is mainly a niche affair focused on holiday homes and package tours with a strong sideline in activity holidays, from walking through to diving. As such, the independent traveller is not especially well catered for and only in Maó, Ciutadella and possibly Fornells is there much chance of finding a **room on spec**. Other peculiarities are the dominance of the British, who account for no less than sixty percent of the island's visitors, and the seasonal nature of the tourist industry: outside of the season, which runs from May to October, many restaurants, cafés and hotels are closed and the bus network is reduced to a skeleton service. Menorca's official **website** is Ⓦwww.e-menorca.org, and most **bus timetables** are available on either Ⓦwww.transportesmenorca.net or Ⓦwww.autofornells.com.

Menorca airport and ferry terminals

Menorca **international airport**, just 5km southwest of Maó, is a smart, compact affair with a handful of car-rental outlets, currency-exchange facilities and a **tourist information desk** (May–Oct Mon–Fri 8am–9pm, Sat 9am–1.30pm; ☏971 15 71 15). The latter has a good selection of free literature, including *Menorca Weekly*, a leaflet detailing forthcoming events, and a general information magazine, *Menorca Welcome*, which has maps of every town on the island as well as all sorts of listings. There are regular buses to Maó from the airport (May–Oct every 30min, Nov–April every 30min to 1hr; €1.50). A taxi will set you back €10–12.

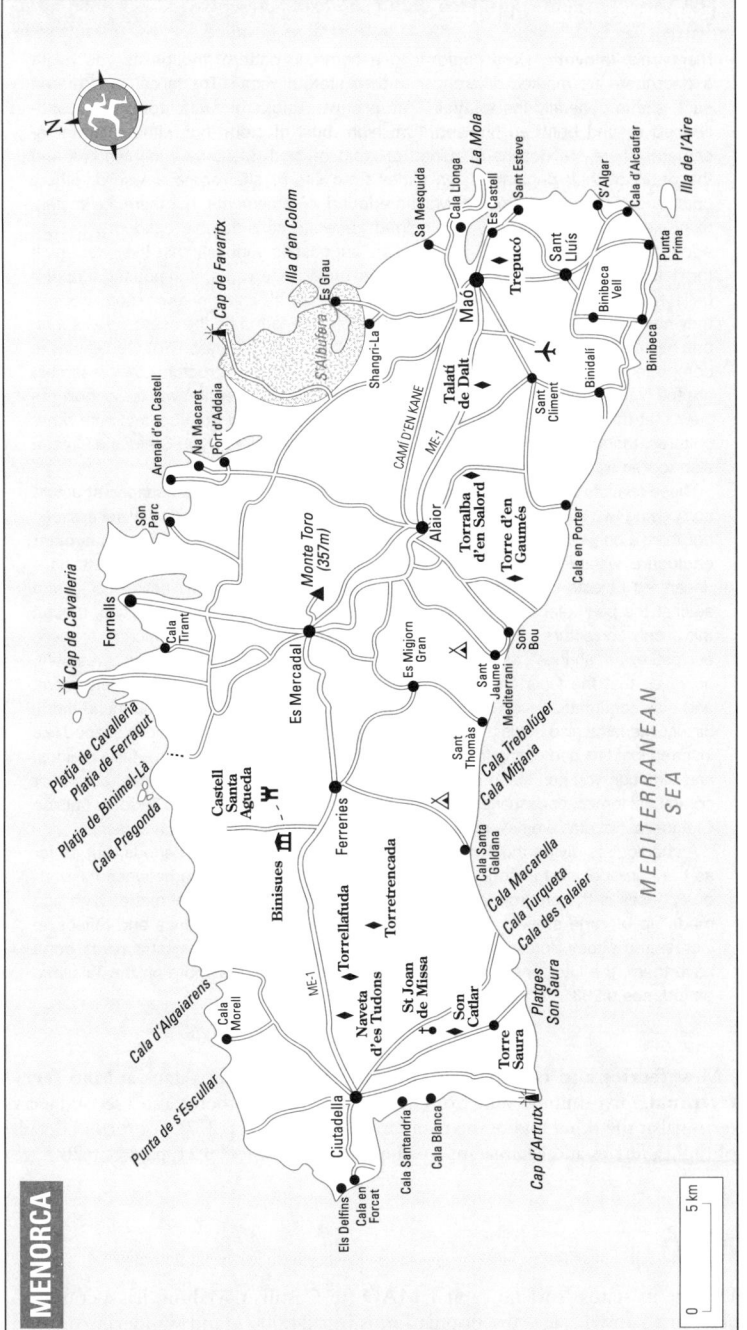

Menorca's Talayotic sites

Menorca's **Talayotic sites** conform to a common pattern, though as you might expect there are marked differences in their state of repair. The tallest structure on each site is generally the **talayot** (from *atalaya*, Arabic for "watchtower"), a cone-shaped mound between 5m and 10m high, built of stone but without mortar or cement. There are dozens of ruined *talayots* on both Mallorca and Menorca and the detail of their original design varies from site to site: some are solid, others contain one or more chambers. Most are found in settlements, but there are solitary examples too. This diversity has helped generate considerable academic debate about their original purpose, with scholars suggesting variously that they were built for defence, as dwellings for chieftains, as burial sites or as storehouses. Popular belief has it that they functioned as watchtowers, but it's a theory few experts accept: they have no interior stairway and only a handful are found on the coast. Even so, no one has come up with a more convincing explanation. The mystery of the *talayots* is compounded by their unusualness. The only Mediterranean structures they resemble are the Nuragh towers found on Sardinia. A Sardinian connection would support the view that this phase in the Balearics' development resulted from contact with other cultures, though Sardinia is but one of several options, with Egypt, Crete and Greece also touted as possible influences.

These *talayots* are often positioned a few metres from a **taula**, a T-shaped structure comprising two huge stones up to 4.5m high. Some sites may contain several *talayots*, but there's only ever one *taula*, and this almost always sits in the middle of a **circular enclosure** whose perimeter is (or was) marked by a low wall. Archeologists have unearthed objects in these enclosures and the remains of firepits have been found against the perimeter wall, both of which seem to imply a religious function, though this is only conjecture – there's certainly insufficient evidence to justify referring to these enclosures as "shrines", as they've sometimes been called. There's general agreement, however, that the *taula* and its enclosure formed the public part of the settlement, and – as confirmation – on many sites the remains of family dwellings surround them. Finally, Menorca also holds a number of **navetas**: stone-slab constructions shaped like inverted loaf tins and dating from between 1400 and 800 BC. Many have false ceilings, and although you can stand up inside, they were clearly not living spaces, but rather communal tombs, or ossuaries. The prime example is the **Naveta d'es Tudons**, outside Ciutadella. Navetas are never found in the same place as the *talayots* and *taulas*.

Archeologists divide the Talayotic period into several different periods, but as far as the non-specialist is concerned, the only significant difference between the various phases is the **encircling wall**, a dry-stone affair often several metres high and made up of large stones. These Cyclopean walls were for defence and reflect an increase in piracy across the western Mediterranean: the earlier settlements don't have them, the later ones – from around 1000 BC – do. For more on the Talayotic period, see p.293.

Most **ferries and catamarans** from Barcelona and Palma dock at **Maó ferry terminal**, a five-minute walk from the town centre, but there's also a second ferry terminal at the other end of the island in Ciutadella (see p.277). For further details of flights, ferries and catamarans to Menorca, see "Basics" p.21, p.22 & p.26.

Maó

Despite its status as island capital, **MAÓ** (in Castilian, Mahón) has a comfortable, small-town feel – the population is just 24,000 – and wandering around the ancient centre, with its long-established cafés and old-fashioned shops, is a relaxing and enjoyable way to pass a few hours. Nowadays, most visitors approach Maó from its landward side, but this gives the wrong impression. Thanks to its position beside the largest natural harbour in the Mediterranean, the town has always been a port and it's only from the water that the logic of the place becomes apparent, its centre crowding the crest of a steep ridge that stands tall against the south side of the harbour. From this angle, Maó is extraordinarily beautiful, its well-worn houses stacked up high on the ridge interrupted by fragments of the old city walls and the occasional church. The town centre possesses two highlights, the Churrigueresque chapel in the church of **St Francesc** and the historical paintings of the **Museu Hernández Sanz, Hernández Mora**, but really it's the general flavour of the place that appeals rather than any individual sight. The icing on the cake is the town's striking and unusual hybrid architecture: tall, monumental Spanish mansions stand cheek-by-jowl with classical Georgian sash-windowed town houses, elegant reminders of the British occupation. Outside the centre, you might also consider visiting the enjoyable **Xoriguer gin distillery**, down on the harbour, where you can sample as many of the island's liquors as you can brave, and two prehistoric sites, **Trepucó** and the more substantial **Talatí de Dalt**.

Port it may be, but there's no seamy side to Maó. **Nightlife** is limited to a few bars and clubs near the ferry terminal, and the harbourfront's main draw is its long string of **restaurants and cafés** which attract tourists in their droves, though few stay the night, preferring the purpose-built resorts close by. As a result, Maó has surprisingly few *hostals* and hotels, which means that you can base yourself here and – if you avoid the waterfront – escape the tourist throngs with the greatest of ease. The lack of places to stay also means that **rooms** are in short supply in July and August, and **reserving** in advance during this period is strongly recommended.

Arrival

There are regular **buses** to Maó from Menorca's international **airport** (see p.232), just 5km southwest of town. These buses run on two different routes, but they all drop by the **bus station**, on Avinguda Josep Anselm Clavé, and travel along the harbourfront via the ferry terminal. All other local and island-wide buses also arrive at – and depart from – the bus station, from where it's a couple of minutes' walk to Mao's main square, Plaça S'Esplanada.

Ferries from Barcelona and Palma sail right up the Port de Maó to Maó harbour, mooring next to the ferry offices, which are located directly beneath the town centre. From the ferry dock, it's a brief walk up the wide stone stairway of Costa de Ses Voltes to Plaça Espanya and the oldest part of town.

Driving through the labyrinthine lanes of central Maó is well-nigh impossible and you're better off **parking** on the periphery. The obvious – and easiest – spot is the underground **car park** (Mon–Sat 8am–midnight) below Plaça S'Esplanada, though this is – at €1.65 per hour – a good deal more expensive than on-street parking (when you can find a place). **On-street parking** is metered during shopping hours (Mon–Fri 9am–2pm & 4.30–7.30pm; mid-June to mid-Sept 5.30–8.30pm, plus Sat 9am–2pm) and there's a maximum stay of two hours (€1.35). At other times, it's free – and there's more chance of a space. Note that if the time you've paid for overlaps into a free period, your ticket will be valid for the time you've got left when the next restricted period begins.

MAÓ

0   100 m

ACCOMMODATION
Hotel del Almirante	G
Hotel Capri	B
Hostal La Isla	D
Hostal Residencia Jume	C
Hotel Mirador d'es Port	A
Posada Orsi	E
Hotel Port-Mahón	F

CAFÉS & CAFÉ-BARS
Café Baixamar	8
Cafeteria La Bombilla	14
Café-bar La Farinera	12
Café Mirador	15
Cristanal Gradinata	9
Varadero	9

RESTAURANTS
L'Arpó	11
Gregal	2
Mesón del Puerto	4
La Minerva	13
Il Porto	1

BARS & CLUBS
Akelarre	6
Berri	5
Mambo	3
Nou Bar	16
Salsa Bar	7

Maó

Naval Base

Illa Pinto

Boat Tours

Museu Sanz & Mora

Claustre del Carme

Església del Carme

PLAÇA MIRANDA

PLAÇA PRINCEP

PLAÇA CARME

Fish Market

Santa Maria

Biblioteca

Ajuntament

Gobierno Militar

PLAÇA CONQUESTA

PLAÇA ESPANYA

PL CONSTITUCIÓ

PLAÇA REIAL

PLAÇA COLON

Teatre Principal

Parc des Freginal

Portal de Sant Roc

PLAÇA BASTIÓ

Xoriguer Gin Distillery

Sant Francesc

Museu de Menorca

Orfila

PLAÇA S'ESPLANADA

Bus Station

Port de Maó

MOLL DE PONENT

COSTA DE SES PIQUES

Trepucó

Sant Lluís

Airport

Bus Station

AV. J.A. CLAVÉ

Information

There is a **tourist information desk** at the airport (see p.232), but the main **tourist office** is down on Maó harbourfront, metres from the ferry terminal at Moll de Llevant 2 (Mon–Fri 8am–8pm, Sat 8am–1pm; ☎971 35 59 52). Both will provide a free map of the island and free leaflets giving the lowdown on almost everything you can think of, from archeological sites and beaches to bus timetables, car rental, taxis, accommodation and banks. They won't help you find accommodation, however. There's also a **public transport information desk** (☎971 36 37 90) at the bus station.

Accommodation

Maó has a limited supply of hotels and *hostals*, but at least none of them is block booked by the tour operators. There are a handful of inexpensive **hostals** close to the town centre and, although they are not especially inspiring, they're reasonable enough and convenient – unlike two of Maó's four classier **hotels**, which are stuck out on the edge of town. **Prices** vary considerably according to season, with rates in July and August about thirty percent more than in winter; **advance reservations** are advised from June to October and are pretty much essential in July and August.

Hostals

Hostal La Isla c/Santa Caterina 4 ☎971 36 64 92. Rooms at this amenable one-star *hostal* may be on the small side, but they are reasonably attractive and comfortable, and all have private bathroom and TV. There's a popular bar and restaurant downstairs. ❷

Hostal Residencia Jume c/Concepció 6 ☎971 36 32 66. Centrally located on a narrow side street, this large, old-fashioned, one-star *hostal* occupies a five-storey modern block and has thirty-five frugal, en-suite rooms. ❷

Posada Orsi c/Infanta 19 ☎971 36 47 51. In a large, old terrace house a couple of minutes' walk from Plaça Reial, this one-star *hostal* has seventeen rooms, nine doubles, three singles and five triples, mostly with shared facilities. The rooms are quite small, but you couldn't possibly complain about the colour scheme – bright pinks, reds, greens and blues throughout. There's a rooftop terrace too. ❷

Hotels

Hotel del Almirante Carretera Maó ☎971 36 27 00, ❺www.hoteldelalmirante.com. Once the residence of British admiral Lord Collingwood, this maroon and cream Georgian house has a delightful lobby, crammed with old bygones, and although the modern bedrooms beyond are quite modest, they are all perfectly adequate. The garden terrace is especially attractive and there's an outside pool. Package-tour operators Thomson use the place, but there are often vacancies. It's located about 2km east of Maó beside the coastal road to Es Castell. To get there from the town centre, take a taxi or the Es Castell bus and ask to be dropped off. Closed Nov–April. ❺

Hotel Capri c/Sant Esteve 8 ☎971 36 14 00, ❺www.rtmhotels.com. Proficient if unexciting three-star hotel in a modern block in the centre of Maó. The rooftop spa and pool is a plus and the breakfasts are good too. The hotel is a brief walk west of Plaça S'Esplanada along Avgda Quadrado. ❺

🏃 **Hotel Mirador d'es Port** c/Dalt Vilanova 1 ☎971 36 00 16, ❺www.hoteles-catalonia.com. This well-equipped chain hotel, with its own pool and gardens, occupies a modern block perched on a hill about ten minutes' walk west of Plaça Bastió. The interior is kitted out in brisk minimalist style and many of the bedrooms have balconies with wide harbour views. ❻

🏃 **Hotel Port Mahón** Avgda Fort de l'Eau 13 ☎971 36 26 00, ❺www.sethotels.es. Elegant, colonial-style, four-star hotel in a superb location with grand views down along the Maó inlet. There's a swimming pool and a chic patio café, plus each of the eighty-odd rooms is kitted out in smart, modern style with air conditioning. Room prices vary enormously, with the top whack a hefty €260. ❼

The Town

With its good-looking mansions and handsome churches, the oldest and most diverting part of **Maó** rolls along the clifftop above the harbour for roughly 1km. Behind, immediately to the south, the predominantly nineteenth-century town clambers upwards, its complicated pattern of tiny squares and short lanes bisected by the principal shopping street and pedestrianized main drag, which goes under various names, with **Costa de Sa Plaça** and **c/Moreres** being the longest individual strips. It takes five to ten minutes to walk from one end of the main street to the other and you emerge at **Plaça S'Esplanada**, the mundane main square.

Plaça Espanya

From behind the ferry terminal, a graceful stone stairway and a narrow, twisting street – the Costa de Ses Voltes – tangle together as they climb up the hill to emerge in the middle of the old town at **Plaça Espanya**. On the north side of the square, a sociable little **fish market** is plonked on top of a sturdy bastion that was originally part of the **Renaissance city wall**. This mighty zigzag of fortifications, bridges and gates once encased the whole city and replaced the city's medieval walls, sections of which also survive. Work on the new Renaissance walls started under the Habsburgs in the middle of the sixteenth century, though the chain of bastions took over one hundred years to complete. On the right-hand side of the fish market a narrow, dead-end alley offers fine views down over the port and is home to the pastel-painted *Mirador Café* (see p.244).

Plaça Carme

Immediately to the east of the fish market, **Plaça Carme** is overshadowed by the massive facade of the eighteenth-century **Església del Carme**, a Carmelite church whose barn-like interior is almost entirely devoid of embellishment. The adjoining cloisters, the **Claustre del Carme**, have, after long service as the municipal courts, been refurbished to house the town's fresh meat, fruit and vegetable **market**, with the stalls set against vaulted arches adorned by religious carvings. The cloisters were taken from the Carmelites in 1837 under the terms of a national edict that confiscated church property, passing vast estates and buildings to the state in what was the largest redistribution of land since the Reconquista. For the liberals, who pushed the edict through, the Church was the acme of reaction, and its monks and priests, who usually opposed progressive reform, the representatives of arcane medievalism. Their legislation was, as might be expected, bitterly resented by the Church, but it caught the popular mood, a volatile mix of anti-clericalism and self-interest, with many small farmers hoping to buy the confiscated land from the state at knock-down prices. The confiscation was just one aspect of the prolonged struggle between conservatives and liberals that destabilized Spain throughout the nineteenth century, but it had permanent effects: later conservative administrations did return some of the ecclesiastical property, but most of the land was lost from the Church for good.

Museu Hernández Sanz, Hernández Mora

In the northeast corner of the Claustre del Carme, one upper floor has been given over to the **Museu Hernández Sanz, Hernández Mora** (Mon–Sat 10am–1pm; free), which comprises an idiosyncratic connoisseur's collection gathered together by the historian Hernández Sanz and gifted to the city by his son, **Joan Hernández Mora** (1902–84). It's not a large collection – it only fills half a dozen small rooms – but it begins smartly enough in the entrance hall with portraits of many of the leading figures from Menorca's history, including **Richard Kane** (see p.264) and two pictures of **Admiral Byng** (see p.302), one plump and bewigged, the other of his execution, by which time he seems to have lost a few pounds. The first room proper holds several sketches of island-ers in traditional costume and then come two rooms stuffed with nineteenth-century paintings, marinescapes for the most part, both oils and watercolours. The highlight here are **Joan Chiesa**'s three historical paintings recording, in precise detail, the comings and goings of the British army, including the final evacuation of Maó in 1802. Little is known of this Chiesa, but he was related to **Giuseppe Chiesa** (1720–89), one-time Spanish governor of the island and himself an artist with a penchant for painting historical scenes. The next room displays some rather dull canvases by one of the Mora family and then it's upstairs for a whole set of island maps. Here also, and this is much more unusual, is a vitriolic British cartoon entitled *The English Lion Dismember'd*: Menorca had been returned to Spain by the Treaty of Amiens in 1802 and this clearly infuri-ated the cartoonist, who shows the English lion with one of his paws chopped off – and the offending paw is shaped like Menorca.

Plaça Conquesta and the Església de Santa Maria

North of Plaça Espanya lies slender **Plaça Conquesta**, whose attractive Geor-gian facades are ill-served by a poorly crafted **statue** of Alfonso III, which was placed here by Franco in a typically nationalist gesture – this was the Aragonese king who expelled the Menorcan Moors. At the far end of the square, turn left along the cobbled lane – c/Alfons III – and you'll soon spy the genteel arcades, bull's-eye upper windows and wrought-iron grilles of the seventeenth-century **Ajuntament** (Town Hall). This was built by the Spanish, but subsequently occupied by the island's first colonial governor, **Sir Richard Kane** (see box on p.264), who donated its distinctive clock. Kane also had portraits of King George III and Queen Charlotte hung in the entrance hall, but these were replaced long ago by portraits of three Spanish kings – Alfonso XIII (1886–1941), Carlos III (1716–88) and Carlos IV (1748–1819), the last two having the flamingo-like noses which centuries of inbreeding accentuated amongst the Spanish Habsburgs.

The Ajuntament is on the northern edge of **Plaça Constitució**, a narrow piazza overshadowed by the **Església de Santa Maria** (7.30am–1pm & 6–8.30pm), a heavy-duty pile founded in 1287 by Alfonso III to celebrate the island's reconquest. Rebuilt in the middle of the eighteenth century and remodelled on several subsequent occasions, the church's exterior is an enjoy-able architectural hybrid, its Gothic features encased within later Neoclassi-cal accretions. Inside, the **nave** is all Catalan Gothic, a hangar-like, aisle-less, single-vaulted construction designed to make the high altar visible to the entire congregation – and indeed there's no missing it, its larger-than-life Baroque excesses featuring the Virgin Triumphant with a flock of helpful cherubs. Unfortunately, the nave is dark and gloomy, as most of the windows are bricked up in flat contradiction to the original design in which kaleidoscopic floods of light would have poured in through soaring, stained-glass windows.

In contrast to the clean lines of the nave, the truncated **transepts** sport intri-cate stuccowork, with loads of cherubs peering out from a swirling, decorative undergrowth, but the church's pride and joy is really its **organ**, a monumental piece of woodwork filling out the elevated gallery above the south entrance. The instrument, with its trumpeting angels, four keyboards and three thousand pipes, was made in Austria in 1810 and lugged across half of Europe at the height of the Napoleonic Wars. Britain's Admiral Collingwood helped with the move, probably as a crafty piece of appeasement: defiance of their new Protestant masters had played a large part in the locals' decision to rebuild the church during the British occupation.

Carrer Isabel II

Running west from Plaça Constitució, long and slim **c/Isabel II** is distinguished by its Georgian architecture, all handsome wooden doors and fancy fanlights, sash windows, bay windows and ornate ironwork. This street was once the heart of the British administration as recalled by today's military governor's house, the eighteenth-century **Gobierno Militar**, about halfway along, with its elaborate paintwork and shaded, colonial-style arcades.

There's a useful – and extremely pleasant – **shortcut** down to the harbour from c/Isabel II: head down **Costa d'es General**, an alley at the foot of c/Rector Mort, which tunnels through the old city wall before snaking its way down the cliff to the waterside below.

The Església de St Francesc

At the end of c/Isabel II, the Baroque facade of the **Església de St Francesc** (daily 10am–12.30pm & 5–7pm; free) appears as a cliff-face of pale golden stone rising above the rounded, Romanesque-style arches of its doorway. The church was a long time in the making, its construction spread over the late seventeenth and eighteenth centuries following the razing of the town by the piratical Barbarossa in 1535. The son of an Ottoman soldier, **Hizir Barbarossa** (*c*.1473–1547) had established a series of fortified bases in today's Algeria and Tunisia by about 1505. He then proceeded to attack Christian shipping, ransoming his prisoners or selling them into slavery, until the protracted struggle for control of the Mediterranean between the Ottomans and the Habsburgs gave him another business opportunity: the Sultan paid him handsomely for lending a helping hand and the sacking of Maó was a prime result. Barbarossa died in 1547, but the war lasted for another twenty-odd years until the Turkish fleet was destroyed at the Battle of Lepanto in 1571.

Inside, the strong lines of the Gothic **nave** are disturbed by some clumsy, concrete panelling round the shallow side chapels, but there's compensation in the superb roof vaulting and the flamboyance of the high altar, whose Virgin Mary is set below grisaille paintings depicting scenes from the life of St Francis designed to edify the (illiterate) congregation. The nave is poorly lit, but it's still easy to pick out the pinkish tint in much of the stone and the unusual spiral decoration of the pillars. In contrast, the **Chapel of the Immaculate Conception**, tucked away off the north side of the nave, is flooded with light – an octagonal wonderland of garlanded vines and roses in the full flourish of the Churrigueresque style. Completed in 1752, the chapel is attributed to Francesc Herrara, the painter, engraver and architect who trained in Rome and worked in Menorca before moving on to Palma in Mallorca.

The Museu de Menorca

The old monastic buildings adjacent to the Església de St Francesc now house the **Museu de Menorca** (April–Oct Tues–Sat 10am–2pm & 6–8.30pm, Sun 10am–2pm; Nov–March Mon–Fri 9.30am–2pm, Sat & Sun 10am–2pm; €2.40), easily the island's largest museum, with multilingual labels to explain many – but unfortunately not all – of the exhibits. The collection is spread over three floors with temporary exhibitions on the ground floor and the permanent collection up above. Entry is through the old Franciscan **cloister**, whose sturdy pillars and vaulted aisles, dating back to the early eighteenth century, illustrate the high point of the Menorcan Baroque.

The **first floor** holds a wide range of prehistoric artefacts, beginning with bits and pieces left by the Neolithic pastoralists who were well established here by about 4000 BC. Then it's on to the **Talayotic period** (1500–123 BC), where the earlier items – household objects and the like – are pretty crude, unlike the later pieces, which exhibit considerable sophistication both in home-made goods and in the use of imported items. In particular, look out for the dainty, rather quizzical-looking bronze bull, probably of fifth-century Phoenician manufacture, found at the Torralba d'en Salord Talayotic site (see p.265). Other imported items include several enormous amphorae, a few pieces of multicoloured Punic jewellery and a small Egyptian bronze of Imhotep found at Torre d'en Gaumés (see p.266). These reflect the final flourishing of Talayotic culture when Menorca became a major port of call for ships sailing through the Mediterranean, particularly between Italy and Spain. The first floor is rounded off by a small sample of Roman pottery.

The collection deteriorates on the **second floor**, where a series of skimpy displays gallop unconvincingly through the Moorish period and continue all the way to 1900. The only item of much interest is the majolica pottery, though you might spare a moment for the whimsical wooden figurines (*vellons*) carved in the likeness of various island notables by two local carpenters, the scurrilous Monjo brothers, in the late nineteenth century.

Plaça Bastió and Parc des Freginal

From the Museu de Menorca, it's a brief walk southeast to **Plaça Bastió**, an attractive square that holds Maó's one remaining medieval gateway, the **Portal de Sant Roc**, a sturdy affair of roughly hewn stone comprising two turrets,

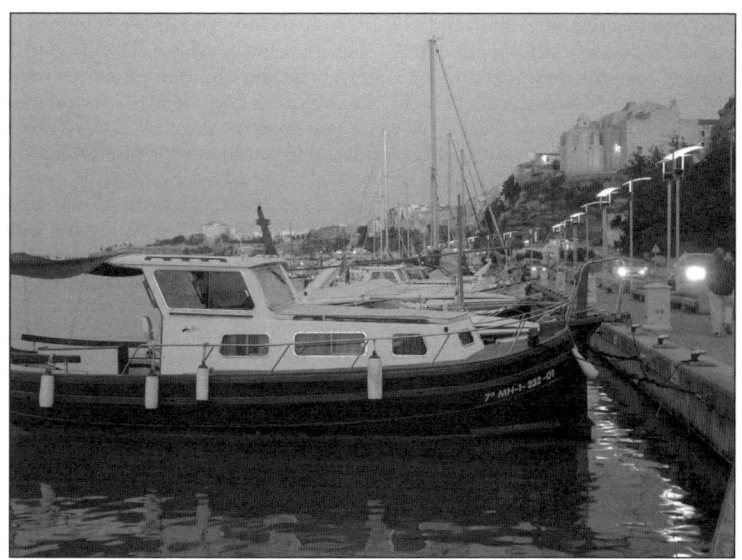

△ Maó harbour

a connecting arch and a projecting parapet. The gateway is named after Saint Roch, a fourteenth-century hermit who was popular hereabouts as a talisman to ward off the plague: Christian legend asserted that he both recovered from a bout of the plague and cured fellow sufferers, a good recommendation at a time when every city in Europe feared an outbreak.

From Plaça Bastió, it's a few paces to the steeply sloping main street, here known as **Costa de Sa Plaça** (also signed as c/Hannover), whose old-fashioned shops and tiny piazzas form the town's commercial centre. From here, it's a few metres east along c/Deià to the town's main park, the **Parc des Freginal**, whose assorted greenery occupies a shallow gorge.

Plaça S'Esplanada

Doubling back to the main drag, there are more shops up the hill along **c/ Moreres** as well as a bust celebrating Maó's **Mateu Josep Orfila** (1787–1853), to all intents and purposes the founder of modern toxicology. Carrer Moreres then brings you to the flowerbeds and benches of the principal square, **Plaça S'Esplanada**, liveliest at weekends, when it fills up with crowds converging on its ice-cream vendors and kiddies' swings. The square is overlooked from the west by an unpleasant reminder of Fascist days in the form of a tall **column** erected to honour those who died for Franco in the Civil War. The column is inscribed with the old fable, "Honor todos los que dieron su vida por Espanya" ("Honour to all those who gave their life for Spain"). Behind the column is a former army barracks and behind that is the bus station.

The quayside

Below the town centre stretches the 3km-long **quayside**, in the middle of which is Maó's ferry terminal. To the west of the terminal, beyond a few bars and restaurants, are the fishing boats and jetties, followed by an industrial area, which extends round the murky waters at the head of the inlet. To the east, it's a couple of hundred metres to the departure point for **boat tours** of Port de Maó (see box opposite) and another short stroll to **Mô**, the pint-sized mermaid statue that has recently appeared here – but no points for originality given that Copenhagen got their harbourside mermaid decades ago. Beyond Mô lies the town's elongated marina, where flashy chrome yachts face a string of restaurants, bars and cafés. By day, the half-hour stroll east along the quayside is tame verging on boring; at night, with tourists converging on the restaurants, it's slightly more animated, but not by much.

There is, however, one enjoyable daytime attraction a couple of minutes' walk west of the ferry terminal. This is the showroom of the **Xoriguer gin distillery** (June–Sept Mon–Fri 8am–7pm, Sat 9am–1pm; Oct–May Mon–Fri 9am–1pm & 4–7pm; free), where you can help yourself to free samples of gin, various liqueurs and other spirits. Multilingual labels give details of all the different types, and there are some pretty obscure examples, such as *calent*, a sweet, brown liqueur with aniseed, wine, saffron and cinnamon; and *palo*, a liquorice-flavoured spirit supposedly of Phoenician provenance. The lime-green *hierbas*, a favourite local tipple, is a sweet and sticky liqueur, partly made from camomile collected on the headlands of La Mola outside Maó (see p.252). In all its guises, it is, however, **gin** which remains the big deal – with *pomada*, a gin cocktail with lemonade, pretty much Menorca's national drink. Gin was first brought to the island by British sailors in the late eighteenth century, but a local businessman, a certain Beltran, obtained the recipe in obscure circumstances and started making the stuff himself. Nowadays, Xoriguer is the most popular island brand, mostly sold in modern versions of the earthenware bottles once used by

Departing from the dock near the foot of Costa de Ses Voltes, various companies run regular boat trips along the **Port de Maó**, with an hour-long scoot down and around the inlet costing €8.50 per person. Frequency depends on the season: in summer there are departures every hour or so, whereas in January there are only a handful of sailings every week, if any at all. Almost all of the boats have glass bottoms for underwater viewing. The three main companies, each of which has a harbourside ticket kiosk, are: Yellow Cats (☎639 67 63 51, ⦿www.yellowcatamarans.com); Pirata Azul (no phone, ⦿www.pirataazul.com); and Don Joan, aka Rutas Marítimas de la Cruz (☎971 35 07 78, ⦿www.rutasmaritimasdelacruz.com).

These Port de Maó boat trips are the only way to get close to the **three islets** that dot the inlet – four if you count tiny **Illa Pinto**, just opposite the dock, which is used by the navy and attached to the north shore by a causeway. The first of the islands after Pinto is the **Illa del Rei**, whose dilapidated buildings once accommodated a military hospital. This was also where Alfonso III landed at the start of his successful invasion of Muslim Menorca in 1287. Next comes pocket-sized **Illa Plana**, a pancake-flat islet that has been used variously as a quarantine station and a naval base. Finally, the larger **Illa del Llatzeret** is the site of a former hospital for infectious diseases, surrounded by imposing walls built of stone retrieved from Fort Sant Felip (see p.250) – the Menorcans were convinced that contagion could be carried into town by the wind, so they built the walls to keep the germs inside. Internal walls separated patients suffering different diseases for precisely the same reason. The hospital remained in service until 1917, since when – oddly enough – it has been used as a holiday retreat for health workers. Llatzeret was only separated from the mainland in 1900 when a canal was cut on its landward side to provide a more sheltered route to the daunting **La Mola** fortress (see p.252).

During the summer, you can also rent boats privately for **longer trips**. The most popular target is Fornells, on the north coast, but you can also venture as far as Ciutadella on the other side of the island with stops for swimming and snorkeling on the way. Half-day trips to, say, Fornells or Cala Galdana, cost around €80 per adult, a full-day trip to Ciutadella €120. One company offering these longer trips is Rutas Marítimas de la Cruz (☎971 35 07 78, ⦿www.rutasmaritimasdelacruz.com), a second is Blue Mediterraneu (☎971 36 44 82, ⦿www.chartermenorca.com).

British sailors and known locally as *canecas*. Here at the showroom, a litre of Xoriguer gin costs about €12.50.

Eating, drinking and nightlife

Maó has a place in culinary history as the birthplace of **mayonnaise** (*mahonesa*). Various legends, all of them involving the French, claim to identify its eighteenth-century inventor: take your pick from the chef of the French commander besieging Maó; a peasant woman dressing a salad for another French general; or a housekeeper disguising rancid meat from the taste buds of a French officer. The French also changed the way the Menorcans bake their bread, while the British started the dairy industry and encouraged the roasting of meat. Traditional Menorcan food is, however, not very much in evidence these days, as most of Maó's **restaurants** specialize in Spanish, Catalan or Italian dishes. These tourist-oriented establishments are mainly spread out along the quayside – the Moll de Ponent west of the main stairway, the Moll de Llevant to the east. There's also a smattering of more economical **cafés** and **café-bars** in the town centre, though there are surprisingly few *tapas* bars.

As far as **opening hours** are concerned, almost all the town's cafés and restaurants open daily during high season, though restaurants usually take a siesta between 4pm and 7pm or 8pm, and things can get eerily quiet on Sundays. Out of season, many places shut completely, while others close early depending on trade.

Nightlife isn't Maó's forte, but there are some fairly lively **bars** dotted along the harbourfront with one cluster just up from the ferry terminal and another towards the east end of the harbour on Moll de Llevant. Places come and go with remarkable speed, so the best advice is to follow the crowds, though we have made a handful of recommendations below. These harbourfront bars open late – some not until midnight – and keep going until well into the small hours, until dawn at weekends, though they sometimes don't open at all in the winter.

Cafés and café-bars

Café Baixamar Moll de Ponent 17. An attractively decorated little café-bar, with old-fashioned mirrors and pastel paintwork, serving tasty traditional Menorcan snacks and *tapas* – island cheese and sausage, for example, costs just €4. Open daily 8am–2am, noon–1am from Nov–April.

Café-bar La Farinera Moll de Llevant 88. Next door to *Restaurant La Minerva* (see below), this spruce and modern café-bar offers tasty snacks, and also has a selection of interesting photographs of old Menorca on the walls. Usually open from 6am till late.

Café Mirador Plaça Espanya 2. Located a few steps from the fish market – just off the top of the main stairway leading from the harbour to the town centre – this appealing little café-bar offers a good range of snacks and tapas, and has great views over the harbour from its terrace. Jazz is the favoured background music. Open Mon–Sat 10am–2am, noon–11pm from Nov–April.

Cafetería La Bombilla c/Sant Roc 31. This pleasant little café, in the town centre on Plaça Bastió, offers a tasty range of *tapas*, averaging about €3 per portion. Has a relaxing outside terrace too. Daily 10am–4pm & 7–11.30pm.

Cristanal y Gradinata c/Isabel II, 1. Chic little café in the midst of the old town with stylish, vaguely Art Nouveau furnishings and fittings plus jazz as the main soundtrack. Mon–Fri 8.30am–3pm & 8–11pm, Sat 10am–3pm.

Varadero Moll de Llevant 4. Close to the ferry terminal – and adjacent to the Yellow Cats dock – this modern place has a restaurant on one side and a café-bar on the other. The café-bar is the place to aim for – a pleasant spot to nurse a drink and sample a small range of *tapas*. Very popular with tourists in the season. Bar open Mon–Sat 9.30am–11pm, evenings only on Sun, and from noon in winter.

Restaurants

L'Arpó Moll de Llevant 124 ☎971 36 98 44. Well-established seafood specialist with a prime selection of fish dishes from €15. Try the paella or the lobster stew (*caldereta de llagosta*). Daily noon–3pm & 7–10pm.

Gregal Moll de Llevant 306 ☎971 36 66 06. The decor may be uninspiring despite the fish tanks, but the food is outstanding, with mouthwatering seafood dishes prepared in all sorts of delicious (and often traditional) ways. Try the John Dory in leek sauce or the sea-anemone fritters. Mains from €18–30. Daily 1–4pm & 8–11pm.

Mesón del Puerto Moll de Ponent 66 ☎971 34 01 75. Just west of the ferry terminal, this old-fashioned bodega-style café-restaurant, with big wooden tables and agricultural bric-a-brac pinned on the walls, has a good, very Spanish-cum-Basque menu – the squid and the cod (both €14) are especially tasty. Daily 1–4pm & 8–11pm.

La Minerva Moll de Llevant 87 ☎971 35 19 95. One of the more polished restaurants in town, with smart furnishings and fittings, a pontoon-terrace, and a menu focused on seafood. The paella is outstanding, and so is the *menú del día*, a relative snip at €16. Save room for the wonderful desserts – the vanilla custard boats in syrup speak (or even shout) for themselves. Reservations well-nigh essential at the height of the season. Daily 12.30–3.30pm & 7–11pm.

Il Porto Moll de Llevant 225 ☎971 35 44 26. An enjoyable place to eat, with a fountain and an arcaded terrace. The cooks perform in full view, turning out tasty fish and meat dishes from a wide-ranging menu that features Italian dishes – the pizzas are particularly good. Popular with families. July & Aug daily 6.30pm–1am; Sept–Nov & Feb–June daily except Wed 1–3.30pm & 7–11.30pm.

Bars and nightclubs

Akelarre Moll de Ponent 41 ℡971 36 85 20. Set down on the waterfront near the ferry terminal, this is probably the best – and certainly the most fashionable – bar in town, occupying an attractively renovated ground-floor vault with stone walls and a miniature garden-cum-terrace at the back, right at the foot of the old city walls. Jazz and smooth modern sounds form the backcloth, with occasional live acts. Daily from 8pm, though sometimes closed in winter.
Berri Costa des General 14. Head up the ramped lane across from the ferry terminal to find this nightclub; there are several other tiny places close by, all of which come to life after midnight and groove on till dawn.

Mambo Moll de Llevant 209.One of the best of the various bars which dot the waterfront east of the ferry terminal, this busy little place occupies creatively converted old premises with stone walls and a beamed ceiling.
Nou Bar c/Nou 1. The ground-floor café here, with its crummy armchairs and gloomy lighting, is a dog-eared old place much favoured by locals. During festivals, it's the place to be, especially on the balcony upstairs.
Salsa Bar Moll de Ponent 29. Tiny, lively, first-floor bar playing mostly Latin sounds.

Listings

Banks Banks and ATMs are dotted along the main street between Plaça Espanya and Plaça S'Esplanada.
Bicycle rental Bike Menorca, out on the ring road to the southeast of the centre at Avgda Francesc Femenies 44 (℡971 35 37 98), rents out ordinary and mountain bikes.
Car rental There are branches of Europcar (℡902 22 25 24) and Centauro (℡971 35 58 88) at the airport. There are also lots of other, smaller downtown companies – the tourist office has the complete list.
Email and Internet access At time of writing, there are no recommendable Internet bars or cafés in Maó, but things are likely to change – the tourist office (see p.237) will have the latest news. Alternatively, there's a free – and freestanding – PC with Internet/email access in the corridor as you approach the Museu Hernández Sanz, in the Claustre del Carme (see p.238); and the public library, the Biblioteca Pública, on Plaça Conquesta, allows visitors one hour's free PC access (Mon–Sat 9.30am–1.30pm & Mon–Fri 5–8.30pm).
Ferries and catamarans Three companies offer car ferry and/or catamaran services between Maó and the Spanish mainland and/or Mallorca. They

are Balearia (℡902 16 01 80, ⊛www.balearia .com); Acciona-Trasmediterranea (℡902 45 46 45, ⊛www.acciona-trasmediterranea.es); and Iscomar (℡902 11 91 28, ⊛www.iscomar.ferries.org). Schedules, tariffs and tickets are available direct from the operators down at the ferry terminal. Note that Menorca's car rental firms do not allow their vehicles to leave the island. For further details of ferry and catamaran routes as well as prices, see "Basics", p.22 & p.26.
Maps & books Llibrería Fundació, facing Plaça Colón at Costa de Sa Plaça 14 (Mon–Fri 9.30am–1.30pm & 5–8pm, Sat 9.30am–1.30pm), stocks a few English-language guidebooks and island bird-watching guides. It also sells Menorca road maps.
Mopeds Moped rental is down by the port at Autos Menorsur, Moll de Llevant 35 (℡971 36 56 66).
Pharmacies Amongst several downtown pharmacies, there's one at c/S'Arravaleta 5 and another at c/Moreres 28.
Post Office The central *correu* is at c/Bonaire 15, just east of Plaça Bastió (Mon–Fri 8.30am–8.30pm & Sat 9.30am–2pm).
Taxis There are taxi ranks on Plaça S'Esplanada and Plaça d'Espanya; alternatively, phone Radio Taxis on ℡971 36 71 11. Advance booking is recommended.

Around Maó: Trepucó and Talatí de Dalt

There are two notable prehistoric sites close to Maó, **Trepucó**, on the southern edge of town near the ring road, and the rather more substantial **Talatí de Dalt**, about 4km to the west of Maó beside the ME-1. If you've ventured out to the latter, you may as well drop by a third site, **Rafal Rubí**, about 2.5km further west on the ME-1. All three sites are signed.

16km; 100m ascent; 4–5hr. Easy.

Starting in the centre of **Maó**, this long but very varied walk winds around the south-eastern corner of the island, initially following the **Port de Maó**, then detouring inland before rejoining the coast to finish at the resort of **Punta Prima**, from where there are regular buses back to Maó during the season (May–Oct Mon–Sat hourly, Sun 6 daily). The coastal scenery is magnificent throughout, while the walk also gives a good impression of the successive layers of fortification that grew up to protect Maó's seaward approaches, as well as more recent tourist development. The going is easy throughout, but be sure to check bus schedules back from Punta Prima before setting out.

Beginning in Maó's **Plaça Espanya**, descend Costa de Ses Voltes and turn right along the waterfront, walking around the headland and the narrow inlet of Cala Figuera to reach, after 1.5km, the *Miramar* and *Rocamar hostals* (both shut-up and abandoned at the time of writing). About 200m past here, shortly before the road turns into a slipway and disappears under water, a flight of steps (arrowed up to "13D") ascends to the right. Climb these and go through the gap in the wall at the top to reach an area of overgrown clifftop scrub, divided into tiny fields by a lattice of stone walls. Follow the clifftop path, from where there are expansive views across the Port de Maó: to the **Illa dei Rei** and its eighteenth-century British hospital buildings in the middle of the channel, with the striking salmon-pink Palladian villa known as the **Golden Farm** (see p.251) perched on a hilltop on the estuary's northern shore behind; ahead in the distance, stacked up above the mouth of the port, are the sombre-looking bastions of **La Mola** (see p.252).

Continue along the cliffs to reach the edge of **Es Castell** (for more on which, see p.250). You should come out at a large, dark-red apartment block. Keep left of this building, then continue straight on down Carrer Stuart for 150m to the junction with Carrer Cala Corb. Turn left here and walk down to the boat-filled *cala*, then up the steep flight of steps on your right. Carry on ahead down Carrer Cales Fonts to Es Castell's attractive main square, **Plaça S'Esplanada**, then continue straight on to rejoin the waterfront above the cove of Cales Fonts. Head right here for 50m, straight past the *Restaurante Irene*, then left onto Carrer Llevant (opposite the *Cafeteria Can Omi*) and follow this road for 300m, straight ahead and over a crossroads, to reach the top of **Cala Padera**. Continue to the *Sol Naciente* restaurant ahead, then turn left along the road (Passeig Marítim) behind it and above the *cala*, passing a block of memorably kitsch pueblo-style development. After 50m, just past a (nameless) *supermercat* and the *pueblo*-style Sunrise Village apartment block, a narrow path heads off along the low clifftops, rounding a line of holiday villas to reach open country – if you reach a second *supermercat* and the *Cafeteria del Este* you've gone too far.

Proceed along the waterfront, passing a walled enclosure containing a Civil War-era bunker. Beyond here, the path zigzags through the scattered outer remains of the **Fort Sant Felip**, the Port de Maó's main defensive emplacement until Carlos III obligingly had it demolished, allowing the British to retake the island in 1798 without a single casualty. Continue 50m along the clifftop until you reach the high perimeter fence of the Sant Felip army camp, then follow the path inland as it makes its way around the fence before bearing right across a field to reach the road leading to the army camp entrance.

Trepucó

It takes about thirty minutes to walk to **Trepucó** (May–Sept Tues–Sat 10am–8pm, Sun & Mon 10am–2.30pm; April & Oct Tues–Sun 10am–2.30pm; Nov–March open access; free) from Plaça S'Esplanada: follow c/Moreres from the eastern corner of the square, take the first right onto c/Cós de Gràcia and

Turn right for 10m, then go left down the road with the dead-end sign for 400m to reach a second dead-end sign, where a track heads off right – the solid-looking cobbles underfoot here are reputedly of Roman provenance, part of a road that once stretched back to Maó. Follow this track down to reach the sequestered inlet of **Cala Sant Esteve**, then rejoin the road and turn right, heading round the *cala* for 300m and past the subterranean entrance to **Fort Marlborough** (see p.251).

When the road ends, head up through a tiny gap in the clump of trees on your left and scramble up to the top, then continue around the clifftop through further decaying military remains and innumerable tumbling dry-stone walls, aiming for the fort's most notable surviving structure, the imposing **Torre d'en Penyat** ("The Hanging Tower"). Built by the British in 1798 at the beginning of their third and final occupation of the island, the tower subsequently acquired a rather lurid reputation as a place in which local miscreants were executed – you can climb a small ladder up into the tower to enjoy its eerily echoing acoustics.

The route now heads inland. From here, go around the right-hand side of the tower, following the small path which heads inland to reach an old donkey trail between high stone walls – the **Camí de Cavalls** – for many centuries a major agricultural thoroughfare which extended around the entire coast of the island, although it now looks distinctly overgrown. Turn left, following the *camí* for 1km, straight over the access road at the entrance to Villa Eugenia, and continue for a further 750m to emerge onto a large track. Turn right here and follow the track as it curves round to the left, ignoring the two tracks which head off right to the farm buildings of the handsome **Binissaida de Damunt** farm (the word *bini,* incidentally, is a Moorish legacy, meaning "sons" in Arabic, and a common component of many place names hereabouts). Some 30m further on you'll reach a fork. Go right here, along the small path signed Camí des Cavalls.

Follow this path for another 750m until you reach the entrance to **Son Vidal** farm. Here the path meets a much larger farm access road. Follow this as it swings right and continue 300m to a T-junction and the gate to **Rafalet Nou** farm. Go left, climbing over the gate (it's usually locked), heading on to the farmhouse a further 750m beyond, then continue straight on through another gate. After 150m there's a gateway (though currently minus its gate), and a small path heads off to the right from here. Follow this path for 200m to a T-junction with a larger track, then turn right, following this new track across a treacherous cattlegird after around 400m then past the drab outlying buildings of **S'Algar** for a further 600m (ignoring all side roads off on the left) until you reach a metalled road. Head straight across for 500m to reach a second road. Turn left, then right, following the signs down to tiny **Xuroy beach**, where there's a bar in summer – you'll probably feel you've earned a drink by now.

Walk to the top of the beach, then go left through the gap in the wall and up around the clifftop, heading to the right of the large **Torre d'Alcaufar Vell**, constructed by the Spanish in 1787 and restored in the 1990s. Conclude by walking a final 2km along the magnificently unspoilt coast to **Punta Prima**, with the prominent lighthouse on the island of Illa de l'Aire just offshore.

Buses back to Maó can be picked up from the top of Carrer des Mestral, which runs uphill directly behind Punta Prima's main section of beach.

then go straight, streaming onto c/Verge de Gràcia just before the ring road. At the ring road, go over the roundabout and follow the twisting lane dead ahead, past the cemetery, and follow the signs. Surrounded by olive trees and dry-stone walls, the tiny site's focal point is a 4.2-metre-high and 2.75-metre-wide **taula**, one of the largest and best-preserved on the island. The *taula* stands

A COASTAL WALK FROM MAÓ TO PUNTA PRIMA

inside a circular compound, which is edged by the remains of several broadly circular buildings. These were thoroughly excavated by a team of archeologists from Cambridge University in the late 1920s, but even they couldn't work out exactly how the complex was structured. There are two cone-shaped **talayots** close by, the larger one accessible, the other not. The shape of the larger *talayot* is, however, not entirely authentic, as the French increased its width to mount their guns on top of it during the invasion of 1781.

Talatí de Dalt and Rafal Rubí

Rather more illuminating than Trepucó and a good deal prettier is **Talatí de Dalt** (May–Oct daily 10am–sunset, €3; Nov–April open access; free), a Talayotic site located 4km from the centre of Maó, just 300m south of the main ME-1 highway. If you're driving, take the short, signposted country lane; by public transport, take any Alaior bus, but check first that the driver is prepared to let you off. Much larger than Trepucó, the site is partly enclosed by a Cyclopean wall and features an imposing *taula* set within a circular precinct. The *taula* here appears to be propped up by a T-shaped pillar, though it's generally agreed that this is the result of an accidental fall, rather than by prehistoric design. Next to the *taula* are the heaped stones of the main *talayot* and just beyond are three **subterranean chambers** with columns and flagstones forming a rough roof. These three chambers, which date from the very end of the Talayotic period, abut an inner courtyard and are much more sophisticated in construction than the earlier prehistoric dwellings that dot the rest of the site. Their exact function is not known, but there's no doubt that the *taula* was the village centrepiece, and probably the focus of religious ceremonies too. The site's rustic setting is also charming – olive and carob trees abound and a tribe of hogs roots around the undergrowth.

Back on the ME-1 and heading west, it's about another 3km to **Rafal Rubí**, where two smallish *navetas* (see box p.234) occupy adjacent fields just north of the main road. Made of large stones and resembling inverted loaf tins, they hardly set the pulse racing, but if you visit on a moonlit night they really are very spooky.

Port de Maó

PORT DE MAÓ, as Menorcans term the whole of the extended inlet that links Maó with the Mediterranean, is one of the finest natural harbours in the world. Over 5km long and up to a kilometre wide, the channel boasts the narrowest of deep-sea entrances, strategic blessings that have long made it an object of nautical desire. The high admiral of the Holy Roman Emperor Charles V quipped that "June, July, August and Mahon are the best ports in the Mediterranean", and after Barbarossa's destruction of Maó in 1535, the emperor finally took the hint and had the harbour fortified. Later, the British eyed up the port as both a forward base for Gibraltar and a lookout against the French naval squadron in Toulon. Using the War of the Spanish Succession as an excuse, they occupied Menorca in 1708 and, give or take the occasional French and Spanish intervention, stayed in control until 1802. They poured vast resources into the harbour defences and, since their departure, the Spaniards have updated and remodelled the fortifications on several occasions.

Both shores – as well as a trio of mid-channel islets (see box, p.243) – are covered in the remains of all this military history and are pockmarked by ruined **fortifications**, thick-walled affairs hugging the contours of the coast. The two highlights of Port de Maó's **south shore** are the unusual subter-ranean fortress of **Fort Marlborough** and **Sant Esteve**, the pretty fishing village where it is located. Of lesser interest is the former garrison town of **Es Castell**, purpose-built by the English in the 1770s. The **north shore** comprises a hilly promontory that nudges out into the ocean, protecting the channel from the insistent northerly wind, the Tramuntana. The promontory's steep terrain has deterred the islanders from settling here, and although recent development has spawned a pair of ritzy suburbs – Sant Antoni and Cala Llonga – the north shore's key feature is the nineteenth-century fortress of **La Mola**, which sprawls over the headland at its very tip, some 7km from Maó. Also of interest are the two dinky little fishing villages that snuggle around rocky coves just over the hills on the island's northeast shore – **Es Murtar** and **Sa Mesquida**, with its wide sandy beach.

To explore either shore thoroughly you'll need your own transport, though there's a frequent **bus** service from Maó to Es Castell. Alternatively, the walk on pp.246–247 offers a good introduction to the southern shore.

Port de Maó's south shore

Tucked in tight against the shore just 3km from Maó, the gridiron streets of **ES CASTELL** (formerly known as Villa Carlos) have a militaristic and very English air. Originally called Georgetown, the town is ranged around **Plaça S'Esplanada**, the old parade ground-cum-plaza, whose Georgian-style town hall, graced by a stumpy, toy-town clock tower, and elongated barracks bear witness to British influence. Elsewhere, sash windows, doors with glass fanlights, and wrought-iron grilles adorn many of the older houses, though nowadays the centre looks somewhat bedraggled. As a garrison town, the fortunes of Es Castell have always been tied to those of the military, and, with Franco gone, the army no longer has the same prestige. This is reflected in the town's general demeanour – and especially on the main square, where two of the barracks stand abandoned and neglected.

Nevertheless, Es Castell is still worth a brief wander, beginning in the Plaça S'Esplanada, where one of the barracks is home to a modest **military museum**, equipped with a motley collection of old rifles and uniforms (Mon–Fri 11am–1pm & first Sun in the month 11am–1pm; €3). From the plaza it's a couple of minutes' walk east down c/Stuart to the harbour, a pleasant spot occupying the thumb-shaped cove of **Calas Fonts**. Stroll north along the waterside from here and you'll pass a string of **restaurants**, one of the best being the *Miramar*, at Calas Fonts 15 (☎971 36 46 43; April–Oct), which serves a tasty range of *tapas*. At the north end of the harbour, a sullen **bastion** is all that remains of the town's fortifications; beyond, c/Bellavista leads south back towards the main square – hang a left at either c/Sant Ignasi or c/Victori.

Buses from Maó stop on c/Gran, just steps away from the main square along c/Victori.

Fort Sant Felip

Beyond Es Castell, the main coastal road continues down towards the mouth of the Port de Maó before veering right for Sant Lluís (see p.253). Keeping straight, you soon pass the turning for Sant Esteve (see below), from where it's a further 300m or so to the gates of a *zona militar*. This restricted military area sprawls over the inlet's final headland, where the Emperor Charles V built an imposing star-shaped fortress in the 1550s, naming it **Fort Sant Felip** (guided tours only: June–Sept Thurs & Sun at 10am; Oct–May Sat at 10am; €3; ☎971 36 21 00) after his son, later Philip II. Once Menorca's greatest stronghold, the fort was adapted by the British, who controlled the seaway from the multitude of subterranean gun batteries they and their predecessors had carved in the soft sandstone. Unfortunately, this irritated the Spanish so much that when Menorca was returned to them in 1782 they promptly destroyed the fort in a fit of pique – a rather misguided move since the lack of defences allowed the British to recapture the island with the greatest of ease just a few years later. Today, nothing survives except the most fragmentary of ruins above ground with several old Spanish and British gun galleries and tunnels down below.

Sant Esteve and Fort Marlborough

Doubling back from Fort Sant Felip, it's a short hop along a narrow country lane to **SANT ESTEVE**, an extraordinarily picturesque little village, whose old fishermen's houses are strung out along a slender cove with a turquoise sea lapping against crumbly cliffs. On the far side of the cove, near the end of the village, a tunnel burrows into the hillside to enter what was once **Fort Marlborough** (May–Sept Tues–Sat 10am–8pm, Sun & Mon 10am–2.30pm; Oct–Dec & April Tues–Sun 10am–2.30pm; closed Jan–March; €3), an intricate, largely subterranean stronghold built to guard the southern approach to Fort Sant Felip by the British between 1710 and 1726. The fort, which was named after one of Britain's most talented generals, Sir John Churchill, the Duke of Marlborough, is a complicated affair, beginning with a long gallery dug into the soft rock with counter-galleries cut at right angles to detect enemy attempts to mine into the fortress. In addition, the main gallery encircles an interior moat – dry now, but once filled with water – and comes complete with gun slits that would have been used to fire on the moat from every angle imaginable. In turn, the moat encircles a small fortified hillock, the most protected part of the fortress and once the site of an artillery battery that had this stretch of the coast in its sights. Fort Marlborough was besieged twice – once by the French in 1756 and once by the Spanish in 1781 – it was captured on both occasions, but only after a prolonged siege. One of the advantages of this type of fortress was that it could tie up a large enemy force for weeks and yet require a minuscule garrison – the British put just sixty men here. The self-guided tour round the fort takes about fifty minutes; note also that the official car park is at the beginning of Sant Esteve, a ten-minute walk from the fort.

Port de Maó's north shore

From the traffic island at the west end of Maó's harbour, a narrow byroad soon leaves the city behind, running past the ugly, modern power station to thread over grassy hills with old stone walls and whitewashed farmhouses to either side. After 2.5km, the road slips past the turning for Sa Mesquida (see p.253) to reach – after another 700m – **Golden Farm** (no public access), a fine old mansion in the British colonial style, perched on the hillside overlooking the Port de Maó. The house is actually seen to best advantage when approached from the east and only then can you spy its grand portico, whose two arcaded galleries dominate the south (Maó) side of the house. The upper gallery – the balcony – is equipped with a delicate balustrade and classical deities decorate the tympanum, a trio of languorous figures in vaguely erotic poses. The mansion may have been **Admiral Nelson**'s headquarters, albeit briefly, during the island's third British occupation (1798–1802), and there's all sorts of folkloric tittle-tattle alluding to romantic trysts here between Nelson and his mistress, Emma Hamilton. In fact, Nelson was much too concerned with events in Naples, where the Hamiltons were ensconced and where he was involved in supporting the Neapolitan king, the Bourbon Ferdinand, against the incursions of the French. Indeed, Nelson did his best to avoid visiting Menorca at all – he only came here once or twice for a couple of days apiece – despite it being crucial for Britain's naval control of the Mediterranean. In July 1799, his superior, Lord Keith, mustered his fleet at Port de Maó to resist a possible French attack and ordered Nelson to join him. Nelson refused point blank, writing to the Admiralty, "I am fully aware of the act I have committed, but, sensible of my loyal intentions, I am prepared for any fate which may await my disobedience." The Admiralty let it go – a good job considering Trafalgar was just round the corner – and Keith ranted and raved in vain.

East to La Mola

Moving on from the Golden Farm, the road skirts the well-heeled suburbs of **Sant Antoni** and **Cala Llonga**, where modern villas tumble down the hillside to the water's edge, and offer fine but fleeting panoramas of the harbour and two of its small islands, **Illa del Rei** and **Illa Quarentena** (see box, p.243). Beyond, the road weaves over a stretch of wind-raked heathland, passing close to the austere stone walls of the **Illa del Llatzeret** (see box, p.243) as it approaches the truncated causeway leading over to **La Mola** (June–Sept daily 10am–8pm; May & Oct daily 10am–6pm & Nov–April Tues–Sun 10am–2pm; €7), one of the most imposing fortresses in the Mediterranean, whose assorted stone walls and gun emplacements dominate the spatulate headland at the end of the promontory. Opened to the public in 2006, visitors can now proceed over the causeway, carrying on for another 600m or so until they reach the car park in sight of the main gate, the **Porta de la Reina** (Queen's Gate), named after **Queen Isabel II** of Spain (1830–1904), during whose turbulent reign the fortress was constructed.

Proclaimed queen on the death of her father, King Fernando VII, when she was just three years old, the first years of Isabel's reign were dogged by civil war between the queen's regents and Fernando VII's brother, Don Carlos – and his Carlist troops – who disputed the (female) succession. The Carlists surrendered in 1839, but there followed another period of chaos as the major power brokers – the army, the Church, the Crown, and two liberal political parties (confusingly, the Moderates and the Progressives) – played a brutal version of musical chairs with the government of the country. Emerging as queen in her own right in 1856, Isabel proved to be dim-witted and quite unable to deal with the competing forces that were destroying her country. The Progressives regarded her attachment to Sor Patrocino, a nun who professed to have received the marks of the stigmata, as inane if not insane, and the conservatives were much offended by both the sexual favours she was thought to have granted to a series of favourites and the conspicuous failure of her marriage (to her cousin). No less a figure than Washington Irving described her as being "rough and somewhat mealy", but it was Isabel's conservatism that did for her, not her appearance: her attempt to run the country by royal decree created an avalanche of opposition, which simply swept her into exile in 1868.

Given all these shenanigans, it seems surprising that anyone had either the time or the money to build La Mola, which was meant to protect Spain's Mediterranean coast from the French and the British. Work began on the fortress in 1850 and continued for 25 years with most of the effort going into the **landward defences**, whose tiers of complementary bastions, ditches and subterranean gun batteries were designed to resist the most intensive of artillery bombardments. The sheer scale of these defences is quite extraordinary and can't help but impress, especially in the sophisticated design of the polygonal salient known as the **Coop**, but in the event it was all a waste of time. La Mola was built on the assumption that naval guns had a limited elevation, but when the British, amongst others, armed their ships with guns that could be elevated (and therefore lob shells over the walls) the fortress was immediately obsolete: consequently no one ever bothered to attack it – and hence its good state of repair. Allow a couple of hours for a thorough exploration.

Es Murtar and Sa Mesquida

Returning from La Mola, take the signposted turning just to the west of the Golden Farm north over the hills for 1.2km to reach the short side road to

ES MURTAR, a tiny fishing village whose whitewashed houses are tucked in between the cliffs and a narrow, sandless cove. It's a pretty spot, though there's nothing specific to see or do.

Back on the byroad, it's a further 600m or so to **SA MESQUIDA**, whose charming whitewashed houses flank a rough and rocky shoreline spiked by miniature pinnacles and bony islets, three of which guard the tiny harbour. Overlooking the scene is the prominent **Torre de Sa Mesquida** (no access), a watchtower of medieval provenance. The tower's battered stonework culminates in a machicolation (projecting parapet), from the apertures of which defenders could dump boiling oil and water and whatever else came to hand on the heads of their attackers. There's nowhere to stay in Sa Mesquida, but there is a first-rate **restaurant**, *Cap Roig* (☎971 18 83 83; closed Mon), which offers tasty seafood – try the grilled sardines – and fine views out to sea from the cliffs at the start of the village.

The road pushes on through the village, swinging up and over the hills to reach, after 800m, the **beach**, a wide arc of pale-brown sand overlooked by bare hills. It's not an especially appetizing spot, but it is the nearest beach to Maó.

Southeast Menorca

Beyond Port de Maó, the **southeast corner** of Menorca, bounded by the road between Maó and Cala en Porter, consists of a low-lying limestone plateau fringed by a rocky shoreline with a string of craggy coves. In recent years this stretch of coast has been extensively developed, and today thousands of villas cover what was once empty scrubland. The result is not pretty and, although many prefer this low-rise architecture to the high-rise hotels of the 1960s, it's difficult to be enthusiastic, especially in **Cala en Porter**, the biggest and perhaps the ugliest *urbanització* of the lot. That said, the coast itself can be beautiful, and the resort of **Cala d'Alcaufar**, one of the earliest developments, fringes a particularly picturesque cove. Inland lies an agricultural landscape criss-crossed by country lanes and dotted with tiny villages, plus one town – mildly diverting **Sant Lluís**.

Most of the district is devoted to villa-style **accommodation** and package-tour operators rule the local roost, so there are only lean pickings for the independent traveller. Nevertheless, there is a reasonable chance of finding a room here and there amongst the southeast's scattering of hotels and *hostals*, with Cala d'Alcaufar being the best bet.

From May to October, getting around by **bus** is fairly straightforward. There are hourly services from Maó to Sant Lluís and Punta Prima, as well as regular services to Cala d'Alcaufar and, from Monday to Saturday, Cala en Porter. In winter, there's a good bus service from Maó to Sant Lluís and Sant Climent, but nothing much else (see p.289 for full details). Bear in mind also that, with the exception of compact Cala d'Alcaufar, all of these resorts spread for miles, and if you've rented a villa you could be facing a very long, hot and confusing trek from the nearest bus stop. You might prefer to ring for a **taxi** from Maó's **Radio Taxis** on ☎971 36 71 11.

Sant Lluís

It's just 4km south from Maó along the ME-8 to **SANT LLUÍS**, a trim, one-square, one-church town of brightly whitewashed terraced houses. As at Es Castell, the town's gridiron street plan betrays its colonial origins: on this occasion, it was a French commander, the Duc de Richelieu, who built Sant Lluís to house his Breton sailors in the 1750s, naming the new settlement after the thirteenth-century King Louis IX, who was beatified for his part in the Crusades. The French connection is further recalled by the three coats of arms carved on the west front of the **church** – those of the royal household and two French governors.

Buses from Maó stop at the north end of town beside Plaça Nova. There's no accommodation in Sant Lluís itself, but it's only 1km or so east along the Es Castell road to the *Biniarroca Rural Hotel*, Camí Vell 57 (☎971 15 00 59, ⓦwww.biniarroca.com; ❼; closed Jan–Feb), which occupies a lavishly renovated old *finca* with plush rooms, a swimming pool and a first-rate 🍴 **restaurant** (reservations required), serving an international menu that features home- and island-grown ingredients; mains from €25.

Southeast to Cala d'Alcaufar

At the south end of Sant Lluís, keep on the main road (the ME-8) and you'll soon reach the turning for Punta Prima (see below) and then the fork that leads to either **S'ALGAR**, where rank upon rank of suburban-looking villas sprawl along the coast, or – a far better option – the pretty little resort of **CALA D'ALCAUFAR**. The development here is restrained, with just a smattering of holiday homes and old fishermen's cottages set beside an inlet of flat-topped cliffs beside a turquoise sea – you can enjoy both the sandy beach and stroll out across the surrounding headlands, one of which has its own Martello tower. The main footpath down to the beach runs through the family-run *Hostal Xuroy* (☎971 15 18 20, ⓦwww.xuroymenorca.com; ❻; closed Nov–April), a pleasant two-star establishment with forty-odd, spick- and- span modern rooms – though most are booked up months in advance by package-tour companies.

Punta Prima

From Sant Lluís, it's 6km south to **PUNTA PRIMA**, a sprawling, standard-issue resort whose villas and supermarkets back onto a wide and windy beach at the island's southeastern tip. Frankly, the place doesn't have much going for it, though at least there are views of the offshore **Illa de l'Aire**, a surly, unin-habited chunk of rock equipped with an automatic lighthouse. Unfortunately, swimming in the choppy channel between the island and the shore can be dangerous – watch for the green or red flags – though there again the wind attracts windsurfers by the truck load; windsurfing equipment is available for rent, as are pedalos and sunbeds.

West from Punta Prima to Sant Climent

Travelling Menorca's south coast from Punta Prima to Binidalí, a distance of around 10km, is a depressing experience. Poorly signposted roads meander across the coastal scrubland, traversing patches of undistinguished tourist devel-opment. On the map, it looks as if there are about half a dozen resorts, but on the ground it's impossible to determine where one settlement ends and another begins. The only vague light in the architectural gloom is a purpose-built settle-ment of second homes at **BINIBECA**, specifically **Binibeca Vell**, where the narrow, whitewashed alleyways, wooden balconies and twisting flights of steps are designed to resemble an old Mediterranean fishing village. At the end of the coastal road is scrawny **BINIDALÍ**, from where (with relief) you can head inland to **SANT CLIMENT**, a tiny village with a minuscule main square and a

The **Cova d'en Xoroi** is the subject of one of the island's best-known folk tales. Legend has it that a shipwrecked Moor named **Xoroi** (literally, "One Ear") hid out here, raiding local farms for food. Bored and lonely, he then kidnapped a local virgin – the so-called "Flower of Alaior" – and imprisoned her in his cave. Eventually, Xoroi's refuge was discovered when locals picked up his tracks back to the cave after a freak snowstorm. Cornered, Xoroi committed suicide by throwing himself into the ocean, while the girl (and her children) were taken back to Alaior, where they lived happily ever after.

dinky little church. The village is also home to the recently revamped *Restaurant Casino* (☎971 15 34 18; closed Wed), where there's live jazz Tuesday evening, of variable styles and quality. Unfortunately for the inhabitants, the village is also within earshot of the airport and is bisected by the busy Maó–Cala en Porter road.

Cala en Porter

From Sant Climent, it's a short haul west to **CALA EN PORTER**, one of the first *calas* (cove beaches) to be developed, and now a sprawling *urbanització* which has all but engulfed a bumpy plateau with hundreds of villas of such similar appearance and proportions that it soon becomes disorientating. Nor is there any focus to the development, which is limited to the south by plunging seacliffs and in the west by a steep bluff that flanks a deep ravine with marshes at the back and a wide sandy beach at the front. Access to the beach is either by road down into the ravine or by flights of steps running down the bluff.

One redeeming feature – and one of the island's most popular attractions – is the **Cova d'en Xoroi** (daily 10.30am–9pm; €5, including one drink), a large cave stuck spectacularly high in the cliff-face above the ocean. A stairway from the entrance on the clifftop winds down to the cave, offering stirring views along the coast. From June to September, the cave turns into a bar and disco from 11pm nightly until around dawn with entry costing a pricey €20 or so, depending on the night.

Fornells and the northeast coast

Between Es Grau and Cap de Cavalleria, Menorca's **northeast coast** holds some of the island's prettiest scenery, its craggy coves, islets and headlands rarely rattled by the developer as the harsh prevailing wind – the Tramuntana – makes life a tad too blustery for sun-seeking packagers. There are developed coves for sure – and four of them contain substantial villa resorts of little immediate appeal – but these are the exception rather than the rule, and for the most part this stretch of coast remains delightfully unspoilt.

Apart from the good-looking village of Sa Mesquida (see p.253), reached from Port de Mao's northern shore most of the northeast coast is approached via the enjoyable, 25km-long minor road linking Maó and Fornells. This runs alongside cultivated fields protected by great stands of trees, with the low hills that form the backbone of the interior bumping away into the distance. At regular intervals you can turn off towards the seashore with the first turning taking you to **Es Grau**, the starting point for a delightful two- to three-hour hike along the coast or a shorter stroll along the marshy shores of **S'Albufera**, a freshwater lake noted for its birdlife. The next major turning – just beyond the Camí d'en Kane (see p.264) – clips north to the windy bleakness of the **Cap de Favàritx**, and the two turnings after that head north again for the four big resorts hereabouts – **Port d'Addaia**, **Na Macaret**, **Arenal d'en Castell** and **Son Parc**. Much more rewarding than this quartet, however, is **Fornells**, whose delightful bayside location and measured development makes it one of the most appealing resorts on the island. Fornells is also renowned for its excellent restaurants, and none of its three *hostals* is block-booked by package-tour operators, so you've a reasonable chance of a room even in the height of the season. There's no **beach** at Fornells itself, apart from a pocket-sized blot of sand, but it makes a good base for visiting some of the more remote cove beaches nearby, such as **Platja de Cavalleria** and **Cala Pregonda**, to name but two.

There's a real shortage of non-package **accommodation** on the northeast coast – only Fornells is likely to have anything, though of course Maó is within easy striking distance too. Public transport between Maó and Fornells is fairly good from May to October, with **buses** running four times daily except on

Es Grau to Sa Torreta

Circular. 9km; 100m ascent; 2hr 30min–3hr. Easy.

This **coastal walk** takes you from the small resort of Es Grau along one of the wildest sections of the Menorcan seaboard, with a detour inland around the S'Albufera lagoon to visit the Talayotic complex of Sa Torreta, one of the remotest prehistoric sites on the island. The going is mainly easy and largely along well-marked tracks, with only one modest ascent towards the highest point of the walk at Sa Torreta farm. There's also a small section of backtracking at the end of the walk, though this is no hardship given the splendour of the coastal scenery.

Starting at the car park (and bus stop) at the entrance to **Es Grau**, walk round the large sandy beach and follow the path on the far side as it climbs up onto the low cliffs. At the top, ignore the well-defined track that heads off left and continue straight on, descending sharply, then follow the path as it bears right until you see a solitary white house ahead.

About 50m before you reach the house, a path branches off uphill to the left. Follow this to the top of the hill, with the low-slung **Illa d'en Colom** off the coast directly ahead, after which the path swings left, giving expansive views of the rugged coast beyond, without a single sign of human habitation to be seen until, about 50m further on, the **lighthouse** on Cap de Favàritx hoves into view. As soon as you see the lighthouse, look for the path that descends to your right. Go down this path, past a curious little stone shelter built into the cliffside, then continue leftwards along the coast, following any of the various paths which cross the scrub hereabouts, a beautifully wild stretch of coastal maquis with low, convoluted clumps of mastic and wild olive dotted with spiky pin-cushions of *Launaea cervicornis* (try not to sit on them). Aim about 45 degrees left of the Martello tower ahead, keeping left of the bare, rocky headland to your right, to reach the small bay of **Fondejador des Llanes**, comprising a tiny, driftwood-covered cove, plus a longer, sandier inlet immediately beyond.

Follow the path directly above the beach to the partially collapsed **fire-warning sign** on the far side (the sign itself has fallen down, though the pole is still clearly visible). Go straight ahead through the gap in the wall here for 20m to reach a small sandy clearing. Bear left at the end of the clearing, following a path for a few more metres to reach a major dirt track (remember this point carefully for later on).

Sunday when there are two, and once daily on four days a week from November to April. There is also a regular Maó to Es Grau bus service, but only from late April to the middle of September.

Es Grau and the Illa d'en Colom

The first right turn off the Maó–Fornells road threads its way up through wooded hills on its way to **ES GRAU**, a neat and trim little village overlooking a horseshoe-shaped bay, where pine trees and sand dunes fringe an unenticing arc of greyish sand. The shallow waters here are, however, ideal for children, and on weekends the handful of **bars and restaurants** that dot the main street are crowded with holidaying Mahonese. The most popular place is the *Bar Es Grau*, whose shaded terrace perches on the water's edge at the start of the village, though you'd be well advised to stick to their salads rather than the pizzas. Alternatively, you could aim for the *Tamarindos* (daily noon–4pm & 7–10.30pm; ☎971 35 94 20), a slightly smarter place just a few metres further into the village along the waterfront, where they serve a good range of seafood with main courses averaging a very reasonable €15.

Turn left and follow the track inland as it climbs up and then downhill through a beautifully secluded valley. After 750m the track gradually swings right and you have your first proper view of **S'Albufera lagoon** (see p.258) to your left, one of Menorca's richest ornithological sites (with binoculars you may be able to see some of its birdlife). The track slaloms right and gradually ascends for a further 1km, climbing steadily uphill (ignore the couple of subsidiary paths which head off to the left). The island's highest point, **Monte Toro**, becomes visible in the distance as you ascend, while near the top to your left there's an overgrown and impassable walled track, typical of many of the island's abandoned donkey trails.

Go through a Menorcan-style gate to reach a T-junction, then go left to arrive at the farmhouse of **Sa Torreta**. Go through another gate, then turn right and walk 100m to a second T-junction. Go left here through a third gate. After 25m you'll pass a large circular threshing floor on your left, with the Sa Torreta's **taula and talayot** now visible ahead. Just past the threshing floor, go through the gap in the wall on your right and cross the field to reach the walled Talayotic enclosure, one of the least-visited prehistoric sites on Menorca, and one of the few on the northern side of the island. The fine four-metre *taula* and partly collapsed *talayot* here are proof of the longevity of Menorca's megalithic culture, postdating the earlier and more famous examples at Trepucó by as much as a thousand years.

You're now at the highest point of the walk, with grand views down to the coast below. Retrace your steps past the threshing floor and back to the (third) gate, then turn left, continuing on along the main track for 1km downhill (ignoring a prominent left turn just before you rejoin the seafront) to reach **Cala Sa Torreta**, a remote, scrub-covered beach littered with dried seaweed and seaborne rubbish – not much good for swimming, though the clump of Aleppo pines behind the beach is a pleasant spot for a picnic and some birdwatching.

The track continues behind the beach to reach a fork. Go left here, past a small stone building, and continue across a small headland back towards the small bay of **Tamarells des Nord** and the Martello tower which you saw earlier. Here the path swings away from the shore. Walk inland for 100m to a rather ill-defined fork. Keep left here and continue for another 150m until you reach the junction just beyond the fire-warning sign you passed earlier. Turn left up the small path here to the sandy clearing and fire-warning sign, then retrace your steps back to Es Grau.

ES GRAU TO SA TORRETA

taula & talayot

Sa torreta
farm

Cala Sa Torreta
stone
building

Martello tower

Es Colomar

fire-warning
sign

Tamarells des Nord

Illa d'en Colom

Fondejador
des Llanes

75m

57m

57m

MEDITERRANEAN
SEA

White
House

N

S'Albufera

Es Grau

Bus Stop

P

- - - Walking Route
0   500 m

From the tiny jetty at the far end of Es Grau's main street, **passenger boats** (May–Sept only) shuttle out to the **Illa d'en Colom** (Pigeon Island) a rocky, one-kilometre-square islet lying just offshore. It's now uninhabited, but in the eighteenth century the British quarantined sick sailors here, and the Spanish followed suit until they built the hospital on the Illa del Llatzeret in Maó harbour (see p.243). The exposed east side of the Illa d'en Colom is bleak and bare, its vegetation stunted by the prevailing winds, but the sheltered west side is a bit more luxuriant and has a couple of **beaches**, the more scenic of which is **S'Arenal d'en Moro**. The boats do not follow a sailing schedule as such, but they leave every hour or so daily throughout the summer from 10am – just wait around at the jetty. You can get off the boat at either beach and the return fare will set you back about €5.

Parc Natural S'Albufera

The scrub-covered dunes behind Es Grau's beach form the eastern periphery of an expanse of dunes encircling the freshwater lagoon of **S'Albufera**. Only 2km from east to west and a couple of hundred metres wide, the lagoon has just one outlet, the faint stream – La Gola – that trickles out into the bay beside Es Grau. The lake was once fished for bass, grey mullet and eels – a real island delicacy – but fishing and hunting have been banned since the creation of the **Parc Natural S'Albufera** in the 1990s. The park boasts a varied terrain, including dunes (which are glued together by a combination of Aleppo pine, marram grass and beach thistle), and wetland, concentrated at the west end of the lake and containing patches of saltworts and rushes. Not surprisingly, therefore, the lagoon and its surroundings are rich in birdlife, attracting thousands of migrant birds in spring and autumn; for more on Menorca's birds, see p.317.

The **access road** into the park begins 2.5km back from Es Grau on the Maó road. Just 1.5km long, it skims past a scattering of villas before terminating at a **car park**, from where clearly marked paths run (in either direction) along the lake's southern shore. It's easy walking and the scenery is gentle on the eye, with the blue of the lake set against the rolling greens and yellows of the dunes.

Birders – both casual and enthusiasts – should aim for **Es Prat**, the large patch of wetland at the west end of the lake, and should be sure to pack binoculars.

Cap de Favàritx

Back on the Maó–Fornells road, heading northwest from the Es Grau turning, it's about 7km to the right turn that weaves its way north to **Cap de Favàritx**. This side road cuts along a slender valley and slips through dumpy little hills to reach, after 6km, an unsigned fork where you veer right for the final leg of the journey. The further you go, the barer the landscape becomes – grass gives way to succulents, but even they can't survive on the wind-stripped cape, where the solitary **lighthouse** shines out over a bare lunar-like landscape of tightly layered, crumbly slate. The lighthouse is closed to the public, but the views out over the coast are dramatic and you can pick your way along the adjacent rocks, though if the wind is up (as it often is) this isn't much fun.

In 1756, Cap de Favàritx witnessed one of the British navy's more embarrassing moments when Admiral **John Byng** (1704–57) anchored his fleet off here for no particular reason. The French had besieged the British garrison at Fort Sant Felip (see p.250) at the start of the Seven Years' War and Byng had been dispatched to Menorca to relieve them. Instead, he dillied and he dallied, allegedly reading and re-reading the Admiralty's instruction book, and managed to get caught with his nautical trousers down when the French fleet turned up off Cap de Favàritx too. The resulting battle was an inconclusive affair, but Byng faint-heartedly withdrew to Gibraltar, abandoning the British garrison to its fate. Back in London, the prime minister, the Duke of Newcastle, fumed: "He shall be tried immediately; he shall be hanged directly" – and proceeded to carry out his threat, if not exactly to the letter. On his return, Byng was court-martialled and shot by firing squad on his own flagship in Portsmouth harbour, an event which famously prompted **Voltaire** to remark in *Candide* that the British needed to shoot an admiral now and again "pour encourager les autres".

Port d'Addaia and Son Parc

"I shall ever think of Adaia, and of the company I enjoyed at that charming little Retirement, with the utmost Complacency and Satisfaction," wrote John Armstrong, an engineer in the British army, in the 1740s. If Armstrong could only see it now. The old **PORT D'ADDAIA**, at the mouth of a long, wooded inlet, has mushroomed dreary holiday homes, supermarkets and a marina, and as if that weren't bad enough, the neighbouring headlands now heave with the villas and apartment buildings of two oversized resorts: low-key **NA MACARET** and **ARENAL D'EN CASTELL**, which at least boasts a wide and sandy beach set within a circular, cliff-edged cove.

The next turning along the Maó–Fornells road leads to **SON PARC**, a work-aday grid of holiday homes and apartment blocks flanking a golf course and overlooking the water. One of the more upmarket resorts, Son Parc is fringed by thick pine woods and has a wide, pink-tinged sandy beach, backed by nice dunes and equipped with a seasonal restaurant and beach bar.

Fornells

FORNELLS may be expanding in some haste, with villas starting to trail over its immediate surroundings, but in essence it remains a low-rise, classically pretty fishing village at the mouth of a long and chubby bay. The place has been popular with tourists for years, above all for its **seafood restaurants**, whose speciality, *caldereta de llagosta* (*langosta* in Castilian), is a fabulously tasty – and often wincingly expensive – lobster stew. Behind the village and across the bay lie rockily austere headlands, where winter storms and ocean spray keep vegetation to a minimum. This bleak terrain envelops various **fortifications** – evidence of the harbour's past importance – of which two are easy to reach: the recently restored remains of **Castell de Sant Antoni**, in Fornells itself, and a circular watchtower, the **Torre de Fornells** (April–Oct Tues–Sat 11am–2pm & 5–8pm, Sun 11am–2pm; €3), peering out over the coast on the headland beyond the village. Fornells picked up its first fortifications in the late seventeenth century against the threat of Arab and Turkish corsairs, but the British went further, constructing a string of mini-forts here, including the Torre de Fornells, and then posting a garrison. In a controversial piece of early tourist development, one of the British commanders also exceeded his military brief, turning a local chapel into a tavern and thereby incurring the disapproval of fellow officer John Armstrong: "In the Temple of Bacchus, no bounds are set to their [the soldiers'] Debauches and such a quantity of Wine is daily swallowed down, as would stagger Credulity itself." Quite – but there again, there wasn't much else for the squaddies to do.

The village's sweeping inlet provides ideal conditions for **scuba diving** and **windsurfing** – you'll see flocks of windsurfers scooting across the calm waters at the southern end of the bay as you approach Fornells. The Diving Center Fornells (℡971 37 64 31, Ⓦwww.divingfornells.com), on the waterfront at the south end of the village, rents out equipment and organizes diving courses for both novice and experienced divers. Advance reservations for courses and equipment are strongly advised, though 24hr is usually enough except in the height of the season. As for windsurfing, Windsurf Fornells (℡971 18 81 50, Ⓦwww.excellence.es/fornells), also situated on the southern edge of the village, offers tuition to both novices and more experienced hands, and teaches **sailing** skills too. Lessons include the use of their wetsuits, boards or boats. Less energetically, there are regular **boat trips** (℡696 10 56 83) round the Fornells inlet throughout the season on the *Brisa II*; trips last about an hour and cost €9. General information about all sorts of water-related activities is available at the Club Náutico de Fornells, in the Ses Salines complex, 1.5km south of the village along the access road (℡971 37 63 28).

Fornells has no **beach** to speak of – apart from a tiny patch of sand just north along the waterfront from the the main square – but there is a long strip of sand 1.5km back down the access road at the **Ses Salines** apartment complex – and other, even more attractive beaches in the area, such as Platja Cavalleria and Cala Pregonda (see p.263).

Arrival and accommodation

Buses to Fornells stop right on the waterfront in front of the main restaurant strip and metres from the minuscule main square, Plaça S'Algaret. There's currently no tourist office, but this is hardly a hindrance as almost all of the amenities are within a few metres of the square, beginning with the village's three reasonably priced and comfortable **hostals**. There's a fair chance of a vacancy in one or other of them even in the high season – but it's best to book ahead just in case.

Hostal Fornells c/Major 17 ℡971 37 66 76, Ⓦwww.hostalfornells.com. Fornells' smartest *hostal*, this pleasant three-star establishment occupies a well-kept two-storey building half a block from the village's central square, Plaça S'Algaret. It has a swimming pool and attractive gardens, and bills itself as a "health eco-resort", with natural herbal treatments and massage available. Avoid the rooms without a view, but plump instead for a balconied room overlooking the pool. Closed Nov–March. ❺

Hostal La Palma Plaça S'Algaret 3 ⓣ 971 37 64 87, ⓦ www.hostallapalma.com. Bang in the centre of Fornells on the main square, this two-star *hostal* is a neat little place, with quaintly authentic local decor and simple but cheerfully bright and colourful rooms. There's also a small swimming pool. Closed Nov–March. ❸

S'Algaret Plaça S'Algaret 7 ⓣ 971 37 65 52, ⓦ www.hostal-salgaret.com. Straightforward two-star hostal with some thirty guest rooms, all en suite and decorated in brisk modern style, plus a small pool. Closed Nov–March. ❹

Eating

With the British garrison long gone, nightlife in Fornells is confined to the **restaurants** that populate the centre of the village to either side of the main square. Such is their reputation that King Juan Carlos has been known to drop by on his yacht, and many people phone up days in advance with their orders.

Es Cranc c/Escoles 31 ⓣ 971 37 64 42. About four minutes' walk north of Plaça S'Algaret, along the pedestrianised main street and just past the church, is this smooth and polished restaurant, which offers a wide variety of fish dishes. The signature *caldereta de llagosta* goes for €60, although the mouth-watering fish soup is a mere €6.75. Closed Wed plus Nov–March.

Es Pla Passeig Es Pla s/n ⓣ 971 37 66 55. Long-time royal favourite, this smart, waterfront restaurant, a short walk south of Plaça S'Algaret, offers a superb lobster paella (minimum two people) for around €60, as well as the traditional lobster stew, weighing in at €70 – that's per person, as well. Suprisingly, they also do a hamburger menu for kids.

Es Port c/Riera 5 ⓣ 971 37 64 03. On the water-front, just south of Plaça S'Algaret, this relaxed and easygoing restaurant concentrates on a magnificent *caldereta de llagosta* (€59).

Sa Nansa c/Vivers 5. Just out of the main restaurant scrum, a short walk north along the waterfront from the main square, this café-restaurant has relatively sensible prices and meals are served on a small terrace facing the village's tiny beach. Try the black paella with squid ink (minimum two people) or the grilled monkfish; mains from €10.

Beyond Fornells

The wild and rocky coastline west of Fornells boasts several **cove beaches** of outstanding beauty, most memorably **Platja de Ferragut**, **Platja de Cavalleria** and **Cala Pregonda**. The developers have barely touched this portion of the island, but nonetheless access to the first two of these three beaches is straightforward with Cala Pregonda requiring a bit more time and effort. All three have sand and solitude in abundance, but no shade or food – take your own. There's also dramatic coastal scenery here at **Cap de Cavalleria**, whose louring seacliffs rise precipitously from the ocean.

Public transport is, as you might expect, non-existent on this stretch of coast and neither is there anywhere to stay.

Cala Tirant

About 3km south of Fornells, the roads from Maó and Es Mercadal meet at a staggered crossroads. From here, a signposted turning leads west down a pretty country lane to pass, after 2km, the clearly marked turning to **Cala Tirant**. This unmade side road offers a fairly rough and dusty two-kilometre drive down to the cove, where a thick arc of ochre-coloured sand lies trapped between bumpy headlands, with grassy dunes and marshland to the rear. It's an attractive spot, but not perfect – there are villa developments on both sides of the cove and the beach is exposed to the Tramuntana wind. In summer, there's a beach bar, loungers, pedalos and windsurfing equipment for hire.

Cap de Cavalleria

West of the Cala Tirant turn-off, the country lane continues through a charming landscape of old stone walls and scattered farmsteads. After about 1km, keep straight on at the intersection and proceed for another 1km or so to the signposted right turning that leads north (along an asphalted byroad) towards **Cap de Cavalleria**. This is easy driving, and 1.9km later, at the bend in the road, there is roadside parking at the start of the 700m-long footpath that leads across the dunes to **Platja de Ferragut**, an arc of sand sheltered to the west by a jutting promontory. Back on the road, it's another 1km to the car park for the delightful **Platja de Cavalleria**, a slightly longer and wider beach next door to the Platja de Ferragut, only on this occasion the walk to the beach only takes a few minutes.

Pushing on, it's about 1km more to the **Ecomuseu Cap de Cavalleria** (daily: April, May, June & Oct 10am–7pm; July, Aug & Sept 10am–8pm; €3), an odd little museum located in an old farmstead perched on a hillock with wide views over the cape beyond. The long and sheltered inlet just below and to the north of the museum, the **Port de Sanitja**, was settled by the Romans in 123 BC, and it was here they built the town and port of **Sanisera** on the ruins of an earlier Phoenician settlement, though almost nothing survives from either period. This ancient history convinced the European Union to fund the Ecomuseu, but it's hard not to think it was more of a job-creation scheme – an impression the museum's paltry if gallant collection of Roman and Talayotic bits and pieces does little to dispel. Archeologists have explored the site of the Roman settlement, which begins about 500m north of the museum turning, and you can spot the scant results of their endeavours beside the road, but the main historical artefact hereabouts is the Martello tower – the **Torre de Sanitja** – built at the very mouth of the inlet by the British at the end of the eighteenth century.

Beyond the museum, the road clips across a bare and rocky plateau nibbled by scores of goats before shelving up towards the **Cap de Cavalleria**, named after the *cavalleries* – baronial estates – into which Menorca was divided after the Reconquista. This is Menorca's northernmost point, a bleak and wind-buffeted hunk of rock with mighty seacliffs, 90m high, and a lonely lighthouse (no access). If you're lucky you'll glimpse some of the puffins that congregate here – an environmental project to restore their habitat has just boosted their numbers.

Platja de Binimel-Là and Cala Pregonda

Back on the country lane at the start of the road to the cape, it's a further 1.7km west to the signposted turning for **Platja de Binimel-Là**. At first, the dirt access road to this beach is wide and fairly easy to negotiate, but, after 1.5km, you take a left and the last bit of road deteriorates – 500m of bone-jangling

---

The Martello tower

Popular with the British military in the late eighteenth and early nineteenth centuries, the design of the **Martello tower**, a combined barracks, gun battery and storehouse, was copied from a Corsican tower (at Martello Point) that had proved particularly troublesome to the Royal Navy when they had tried to capture it. These self-contained, semi-self-sufficient defensive fortifications, equipped with thick walls and a protected entrance, proved so successful and easy to build that they were erected in every corner of the empire, only becoming obsolete in the 1870s with advances in artillery technology.

motoring – so most people spare their cars and park at the turn. It's a shale beach, but the waters are clear and good for swimming and snorkelling, unless, that is, a northerly wind has engulfed it in seaweed and detritus, a perennial problem here.

Binimel-Là is also within comfortable walking distance of several more secluded coves, the key target being the twenty-minute hike west along the coast to **Cala Pregonda**, a splendid, seastack-studded bay with a wide sandy beach. At present, there's no clear path except at the start, but the terrain isn't difficult: climb the whitewashed steps over the wall at the west end of Binimel-Là beach and follow the wide track beyond across the salt flats and round a pebble-strewn cove; then keep straight to clamber over a small headland and you'll see the beach below.

Central Menorca

Central Menorca is the agricultural heart of the island, its rippling hills and rolling plains dotted with scores of whitewashed farmsteads, and although the tourist boom has knocked some of the stuffing out of the island's agriculture – witness the many unkempt fields – it's still surprising, considering Menorca's package popularity, just how traditional things are here. Furthermore, the land still carries the myriad marks of past agrarian endeavours in its dry-stone walls and stone ziggurats (*barraques*), which were built to shelter cattle from wind and sun, and is dotted with scores of **Talayotic sites** in various states of repair and interest. None of the four little towns of the interior – Alaior, Es Mercadal, Ferreries and Es Migjorn Gran – has been much modernized, and each contains a comely ensemble of old houses dating back to the eighteenth century, sometimes further. All four towns are readily reached via the ME-1, which runs the 45km across the island from Maó to Ciutadella.

Heading west from Maó, the **ME-1** begins by traversing a flattish agricultural district before looping past the hilltop town of **Alaior**, which boasts a pretty little centre of mazy cobbled streets. Alaior is also just 3km from one of the island's most extensive prehistoric sites, **Torralba d'en Salord**. Further west, the road slips into the antique village of **Es Mercadal**, overlooked by **Monte Toro**, the island's highest peak, its summit occupied by a cute little church. The road to the mountaintop is excellent and the views superb, revealing the geological make-up of the island: to the north, reddish sandstone hills bump down to a fretted coastline, while to the south the limestone plain is gashed by wooded gorges (*barrancs*). The trip up the mountain is an essential detour – unlike the excursion south to nearby **Son Bou**, a sprawling resort only redeemed by its long sandy beach.

From Es Mercadal, it's a short journey southwest to **Es Migjorn Gran**, a pleasant if unremarkable little town that is the starting point for an excellent two- to three-hour hike down the **Barranc de Binigaus** (see box, pp.270–271), while nearby lurks another big resort, **Sant Tomàs**. Back on the ME-1, you'll soon reach **Ferreries**, the fourth of the towns of the interior and the starting point for another recommended hike (see box on p.274). From Ferreries, it's another short hop west to the **Binisues** manor house and the shattered ruins of the hilltop **Castell de Santa Àgueda**, once an important Moorish stronghold. A short excursion south from Ferreries leads to **Cala Santa Galdana**, an attractive resort of manageable proportions that's within easy hiking distance of several isolated cove beaches.

5

Richard Kane

Born in Ulster in 1666, **Richard Kane** was the quintessential military man. His long career in the British army included service in Canada and campaigns with the Duke of Marlborough. In 1713, following the Treaty of Utrecht, Kane was appointed Lieutenant-Governor of Menorca. He was transferred in 1720 but returned a decade later for a second stint, staying until 1736, the year of his death.

When Kane arrived in Menorca, he found a dispirited and impoverished population, governed from Ciutadella by a reactionary oligarchy. Kane's initial preoccupation was with the island's **food supply**, which was woefully inadequate. He promptly set about draining swampland near Maó and introduced new and improved strains of seed corn. The governor also had livestock imported from England – hence the Friesian cattle that remain the mainstay of the island's cheese-making industry. Meanwhile, a tax on alcohol provided the cash to develop Menorca's infrastructure, resulting in improved port facilities at Maó and the construction of the first **road** right across the island.

These innovations were not at all to the taste of the Menorcan aristocracy, who, holed up in Ciutadella, were further offended when Kane arranged for the capital to be moved to Maó. They bombarded London with complaints, eventually inducing a formal governmental response in an open letter to the islanders entitled 'A Vindication of Colonel Kane'. Most Menorcans, however, seem to have welcomed Kane's benevolent administration, except in **religious matters**, where the governor caused offence by holding Protestant services for his troops in Catholic churches. That apart, there's little doubt that, by the time of his death, Kane was a widely respected figure, whose endeavours were ill served by the colonial indifference of some of his successors.

For part of the way at least, from just north of Maó to Es Mercadal, there is an alternative to the ME-1 – the **Camí d'en Kane**, named after Richard Kane, Menorca's first British governor (see box above), who devoted much time and energy to improving the island's communications. His principal achievement was the construction of a highway between Maó and Ciutadella – funded by a tax on alcohol – and although much of Kane's original road has disappeared beneath the newer road, a healthy portion has survived. A lovely route, this old road follows the agricultural contours of the island, passing ancient *haciendas*, olive groves, pasture and mile after mile of dry-stone wall. To get to the start of it, take the Fornells road out of Maó and, 1.2km after the Es Grau turning, watch for the Camí d'en Kane sign on the left.

There's no public transport along the Camí d'en Kane, but fast and frequent **buses** ply the ME-1, with supplementary summertime services running from Maó to Sant Tomàs and Son Bou, and from Ferreries to Cala Santa Galdana. Es Migjorn Gran is reachable by bus from both Maó and Ciutadella. **Accommodation**, on the other hand, is difficult to come by for independent travellers. The resorts are dominated by the package-tourist industry, though you can, of course, take pot luck. Of the four inland towns, only Es Mercadal and Es Migjorn Gran have recommendable hotels or *hostals* – and even these muster just a couple of places in total.

Alaior

Cheese is as good a reason as any to stop at **ALAIOR**, an old market town 12km from Maó, which has long been a nucleus of the island's dairy industry. There are two major companies, La Payesa and COINGA, both of which have factory shops near to – and signposted from – the old main road as it cuts through the southern periphery of town: to get there from the new ME-1 bypass, which swings round the town to the south, the easiest option is to come off at the easternmost of the three Alaior exits. From this direction, the first – and rather more folksy – shop you reach is **La Payesa**, at c/d'Es Banyer 64 (Mon–Fri 9am–1pm & 4–7pm; T971 37 10 72), while the second is the larger outlet of **COINGA**, c/Es Mercadal 8 (Mon–Fri 9am–2pm & 5–8pm; T971 37 12 27).

Both cheese plants are in the lower and more modern part of Alaior, whereas the tangle of narrow streets and bright-white houses that make up the **old centre** climb up the steep hill behind. It's a quick two-minute drive or a strenuous one-kilometre walk up c/Bassa Rotja to the top, where the imposing parish church of **Santa Eulàlia**, a magnificent edifice of fortress-like proportions built between 1674 and 1690, has recently been restored. The main doorway is a Baroque extravagance, its exuberant scrollwork dripping with fruits and fronds, while the facade above accommodates a rose window and a pair of balustrades. Beyond the church – just up the hill to the northwest along the L-shaped c/Moli de l'Angel – a mini-watchtower is plonked on top of the **Munt de l'Angel**, a hill from where you can look out over the countryside. From the end of c/Moli de l'Angel, it's a few metres north to the old town's main square, **Plaça Nova**, an attractive piazza flanked by pastel-painted civic buildings of considerable age.

If, however, you're here on the second weekend of August, cheese and churches will probably be the last thing on your mind as this is when Alaior lets loose with the **Festa de Sant Llorenç**, a drunken knees-up with displays of horsemanship. As its climax, a procession of horses tears through the packed town square, bucking and rearing, with their riders clinging on for dear life. Although no one seems to get hurt, you might prefer to enjoy the spectacle from the safety of a balcony.

Practicalities

Buses to Alaior pull in on c/St Joan Bautista, from where it's about 350m northwest to Santa Eulàlia. There's nowhere to stay, but Alaior does have a very good **restaurant**, *Cobblers*, set in an intelligently revamped old town house with an arcaded terrace at c/Sant Macari 6 (May–Oct Mon–Sat 6.30–11pm; Nov– April call for times; T971 37 14 00). Combining modern British and Mediterranean cuisines, they do excellent meat dishes here – try the lamb. The restaurant is just to the east of Santa Eulàlia: take c/Pare Diego Saura, turn right onto c/Verge Sa Muntanyeta and it's straight ahead.

Around Alaior: the Torralba d'en Salord

One of the island's more extensive Talayotic settlements, **Torralba d'en Salord** (June–Sept daily 10am–8pm, but closed on the first Sat of every month; Oct–May Mon–Sat 10am–1pm & 3–6pm; €3) lies about 3km southeast of Alaior beside the road to Cala en Porter. The site is muddled by the old (and disused) Cala en Porter road, which slices right through the site, and by the modern stone walls built alongside both the old and new roads. Nevertheless, it doesn't take too long to figure things out. From the car park, signs direct you round the Talayotic remains, beginning with the **taula**, one of the best preserved on the island. The rectangular enclosure surrounding it is also in good condition, and has been the subject of much conjecture by archeologists, who discovered that several of the recesses contained large fire pits, which may well have been used for the ritual slaughter of animals. It was, however, the unearthing of a tiny **bronze bull** (now in Maó's Museu de Menorca, see p.240) that really got the experts going. The theory was that the Menorcans (in common with several other prehistoric Mediterranean peoples) venerated the bull, with the *taula* being a stylized representation of a bull's head. The argument continues to this day. Beyond the *taula*, the signed trail circumnavigates the remainder of the site, which contains a confusion of stone remains, none of them especially revealing. The most noteworthy are the battered remains of a **talayot** just across from the *taula* and, about 30m further to the north, an underground chamber roofed with stone slabs.

From Torralba d'en Salord, it's just 7km to the south coast resort of Cala en Porter (see p.255).

Torre d'en Gaumés, Son Bou and Sant Jaume Mediterrani

On the western edge of Alaior, the ME-1 clips past the Son Bou turning, which leads to both the beaches of the south coast and the rambling Talayotic settlement of **Torre d'en Gaumés** (May–Sept Tues–Sat 10am–8pm, Sun & Mon 10am–2.30pm; April & Oct Tues–Sun 10am–2.30pm, €2.50; Nov–March open access; free). The drive to both is easy enough – for Son Bou (see below) keep straight, for the ruins go left at the signposted fork about 2km south of the ME-1, and follow the asphalted lane for another 2km. The site possesses no fewer than three **talayots**, the largest of which is next to a broken-down **taula** in the centre of a badly ruined circular enclosure. Together, these remains form what is presumed to have been the public part of the village, and it was here in the enclosure that archeologists unearthed a little bronze figure of the Egyptian god of knowledge, **Imhotep** (now in the Museu de Menorca in Maó, see p.240), a discovery which reinforced the theory that these enclosures possessed religious significance. It's impossible to interpret precisely the remains surrounding the outside of the enclosure, as the site was inhabited – and continually modified – well into Roman times. That said, you can pick out the broadly circular outlines of a sequence of private dwellings dating from as early as 1500 BC.

Son Bou and Sant Jaume Mediterrani

At **SON BOU**, 7km south of Alaior, the antiquarian interest is maintained by an extensive **cave complex**, cut into the cliff-face above the final part of the approach road, and the foundations of an early Christian **basilica**, set behind the beach at the east end of the resort. They're hardly popular attractions, however, when compared with the **beach**, a whopping pale-gold strand some 3km long and 40m wide. This is Menorca's longest beach, and behind it has mushroomed a massive tourist complex of skyscraper hotels and villa-villages that spreads west into the twin resort of **SANT JAUME MEDITERRANI**. The sand shelves gently into the sea, but the bathing isn't quite as safe as it appears: ocean currents are hazardous, particularly when the wind picks up, and you should watch for the green and red flags. The beach accommodates several bars, and **watersports** equipment is widely available – everything from jet-skis, snorkels and windsurfing boards to sunloungers and pedalos.

The development is at its crassest – and the crowds at their worst – towards the east end of the beach, where the foreshore is dominated by several huge sky-rise hotels, principally the *Sol Milanos* (T971 37 12 00, Wwww.solmilanospinguinos .solmelia.com; ❼; closed Nov–April) and the *Sol Pinguinos* (same details). These two hotels share facilities, including sun terraces, outside pools, bars and restaurants, and have spruce modern balconied bedrooms. A little to the west, a strip of dune-fringed, marshy scrubland runs behind the beach, providing the shoreline with some much needed protection and pushing the villa developments a kilometre or so inland. As a result, the bathing along this stretch of coast is much more secluded.

This is where you'll also find one of Menorca's two **campsites**, the Son Bou (T971 37 27 27, Wwww.campingsonbou.com; closed mid-Oct to March), which is located 3.5km inland on the main access road linking the ME-1 with Sant Jaume Mediterrani, just west of the Son Bou resort turning. This well-equipped campsite has several hundred pitches, as well as its own swimming pool, tennis courts, laundry, supermarket and restaurant. In high season (July & Aug), adult campers pay €6.60 each, plus €3.70–11.85 per tent, depending on size; cars (€4.45) and tax (7 percent) further add to the bill, and there are small supplementary charges for electrical hook-ups and hot water. Shoulder-season rates are around ten percent less.

Es Mercadal

Nine kilometres northwest of Alaior along the ME-1, **ES MERCADAL** sits amongst the hills at the very centre of the island. Another old market town, it's an amiable little place of whitewashed houses and trim allotments, whose antique centre straddles a quaint watercourse. The minuscule main square, **Sa Plaça**, has a couple of sleepy cafés and from here it's a few paces along c/Major to the Ruritanian **Ajuntament** (Town Hall), at no.16, but that's just about it unless you count the rain-catching, water reservoir – the **Aljub** – at the western end of town, which was built on the orders of Richard Kane (see p.264).

Buses to Es Mercadal pull in beside the ME-1 on the southern edge of town on c/Mestre Gari, a five-minute walk from Sa Plaça. There's no tourist office, but there is somewhere to stay, the one-star *Hostal Jeni*, in a brightly decorated modern building at c/Miranda del Toro 81 (T971 37 50 59, Wwww.hostaljeni. com; ❺). The *hostal* has forty-odd comfortable, en-suite bedrooms and a rooftop pool; to get there, leave the main square – Sa Plaça – along c/Nou, cross the pedestrianised square on the left and go right up c/Miranda del Toro.

Monte Toro

Es Mercadal is the starting point for the ascent of **MONTE TORO**, a steep 3.2km climb along a serpentine but easily driveable road. At 357m, the summit is the island's highest point and offers wonderful views: on a good day you can see almost the whole island, on a bad one, you can still see at least as far as Fornells. From this lofty vantage point, Menorca's geological division becomes apparent: to the north, Devonian rock (mostly reddish sandstone) supports a

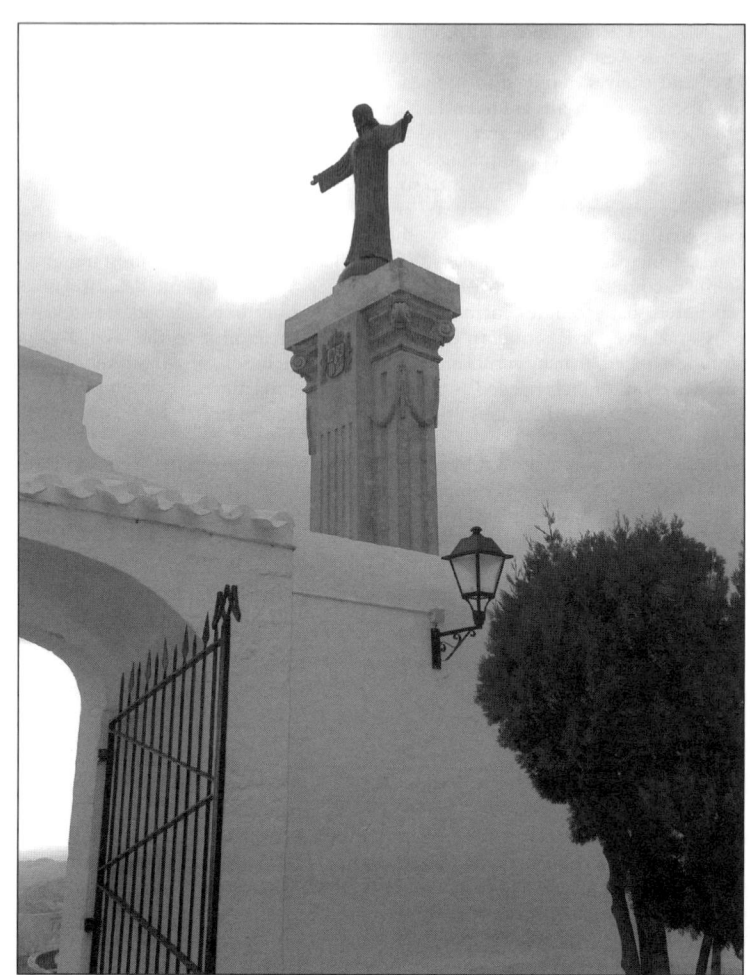

△ Statue of Christ on Monte Toro

rolling, sparsely populated landscape edged by a ragged coastline; to the south, limestone predominates in a rippling, wooded plain that boasts the island's best farmland and, as it approaches the south coast, its deepest valleys.

It's likely that the name of the hill is derived from the Moorish Al Thor ("high point"), but medieval Christians invented an alternative etymology. In predictable fashion, this involves villagers (or monks) spotting a mysterious light on the mountain and, on closer investigation, being confronted by a bull (*toro*) which, lo and behold, obligingly leads them to a miracle-making statue of the Virgin. Whatever the truth, a statue of the Virgin – the Verge del Toro – was installed in a shrine in the thirteenth century and Monte Toro has been a place of pilgrimage ever since. The ceremonial highlight is May 8, when the **Festa de la Verge del Toro** (Festival of the Virgin of the Bull) begins with a special mass at the Monte Toro church and continues with a knees-up down in Es Mercadal.

The Augustinians plonked a monastery on the summit in the seventeenth century, but fearful islanders soon interrupted their monkish reveries by building a small fortress here against the threat of an Ottoman invasion. Bits of both the monastery and the fort survive, the former incorporated within the present **monastery** – though the monks left long ago – the latter in a square stone **tower** that now stands forlorn and neglected. High above both stands a **statue** of Christ erected in honour of those Menorcans who died in a grubby colonial war launched by Spain in Morocco in the 1920s.

The tower and much of the monastery is out of bounds, but the public area, approached across a handsome courtyard with a dinky little well, is still large enough to accommodate a couple of gift shops, a terrace café, a restaurant, and a charming **church**, entered through a low and deep stone porch that is decorated with flowers and shrubs. Inside, the barrel-vaulted nave is a modest, truncated affair dating from 1595, its gloominess partly dispelled by a central dome. The most prominent feature is the gaudy, 1940s high altarpiece, whose fancy woodwork swarms with cherubs and frames the much-venerated **Verge del Toro**, depicting the crowned Virgin holding Jesus in her arms with the enterprising bull of folklore fame at her feet. The statue is typical of the so-called black Catalan Madonnas, made either from black-stained wood or dark stone.

Es Migjorn Gran

Southwest from Es Mercadal, the road weaves a rustic route to **ES MIGJORN GRAN**, a sleepy little town that trails along a low ridge amidst intricate terraced fields. Of the several towns founded on the island in the eighteenth century, this is the only one not to have been laid out by foreigners. Consequently, the gridiron street plans of the likes of Es Castell and Sant Lluís are replaced here by a more organic lay-out, the houses of the old agricultural workers straggling along the elongated main street, **c/Major**, as it curves through town.

Buses pull in beside the bypass on the east side of Es Migjorn Gran, a short walk from c/Major. The village hardly sets the pulse racing, but it is the starting point for an excellent hike (see p.270) and it does have two **places to stay**, the more agreeable of which is *Fonda S'Engolidor*, c/Major 3 (☎971 37 01 93; ❷; closed Nov–April), with four spick-and-span guest rooms in an attractively restored eighteenth-century house towards the west (Ferreries) end

ES MIGJORN GRAN TO THE COAST

Ferreries

Es Migjorn Gran

N

School

Talayots

Cemetery

Talayot

Binigaus Vell

Barranc de Binigaus

Binigaus Nou

104m

Barranc de Binigaus

Cova dels Coloms

64m

MEDITERRANEAN SEA

- - - - Walking Route

0   500 m

Sant Tomàs

Es Migjorn Gran to the coast, via the Barranc de Binigaus

Circular. 8km; 150m ascent; 2hr 30min–3hr. Moderate

Despite its modest dimensions, Menorca packs a surprising diversity into its landscape. One of the island's most unexpected – and best hidden – topographical features is the dramatic limestone gorges, or *barrancs*, which score and scour the southern coast, running from the hills inland down to the sea. Starting in the inland village of Es Migjorn Gran, this walk follows one of these gorges, the **Barranc de Binigaus**, down to the coast near Sant Tomàs, passing through an area rich in *Talayotic* remains and impressive natural limestone formations.

The walk starts on the western edge of **Es Migjorn Gran**: from the main roundabout on Plaça Menorca in the centre of the village, walk for 200m along the road past La Caixa bank and *Sa Branca* restaurant to reach the start of the walk down the unsigned road off on the left, opposite house nos. 26 and 28 and the street sign for Avinguda Binicurdell; there are parking places nearby at the west end of c/Major. The first half of the walk follows this road-cum-track as it meanders slowly downhill to the coast. The road starts by running picturesquely between limestone walls flanked by handsome old Aleppo pines, past a school, an old enclosure housing the substantial remains of two **talayots**, and a cemetery. Some 200m further on you'll pass another *talayot* on your right, followed by an attractive ensemble of white houses and Menorcan-style gates. Continue for a further 1km, passing enclosures littered with limestone boulders, until you reach the attractive old whitewashed farmstead of **Binigaus Vell**.

Just past here you'll have your first sight of the sea, with views over to Mallorca on a clear day. The path continues for a further 750m, with the dramatic limestone formations of the Barranc de Binigaus coming into view on your left. Beyond here, the track passes through an intricate but overgrown system of terraces and enclosures before climbing past a potholed limestone outcrop to reach the brow of the hill. Two more *talayots* are now visible to your left – the land hereabouts holds an incredible jumble of natural, prehistoric and more recent agricultural stoneworking, with the Barranc de Binigaus, issuing into the sea via a narrow defile – your eventual goal – far ahead and below.

---

of town. The second option is the much more ordinary *La Palmera* (☏971 37 00 23; ❷), a simple *hostal*, whose rooms are sited above a café-bar in an oldish three-storey house in the middle of town at c/Major 85. Beneath the *Fonda* is the best **restaurant** in town, the *58 S'Engolidor*, (same number; closed Mon), where the emphasis is on traditional Menorcan cuisine with mains around €15. The restaurant possesses a delightful, summer-only garden terrace with views over a wooded gorge.

Sant Tomàs

South of Es Migjorn Gran, the road shuttles along a wooded ravine that leads down to the south coast – and the crass hotel and apartment buildings of **SANT TOMÀS**. The 3km-long sandy **beach**, however, is superb, very similar to that of Son Bou, a couple of headlands away to the east – though all is not quite as it seems. A thunderous storm stripped the existing sand away in 1989, and what you see today has been imported. The beach looks very inviting as it slopes gently into the ocean, but there are sometimes dangerous undercurrents – look out for green or red flags. The road reaches the shore halfway along the beach, which is called **Platja Sant Adeodat** to the west and **Platja Sant Tomàs** to the east. The latter is easily the more congested, and it's here you'll find the resort's high-rise hotels, among which the air-conditioned,

Descend to the farmhouse of **Binigaus Nou**, a striking baronial-looking structure, and walk round to the left-hand side of the house, where there's an unusual Talayotic **hypostyle chamber** and a fine view of the limestone cliffs of a secondary arm of the *barranc* behind. Beyond here, the path hairpins down into the *barranc* beneath high walls of limestone and then past further wildly overgrown agricultural terracing, until the track reaches the bottom of the hill at a Menorcan-style gate opposite a small path signposted to the Cova dels Coloms.

The route continues along this path to the *cova* (cave). If you want to make the brief detour to the coast, walk through the gate ahead and continue straight on for 150m to reach the sea next to an old gun emplacement buried in the dunes and covered in windswept vegetation. If you're in need of food and drink, head left here and walk along the beach for 750m to reach the resort of **Sant Tomàs**.

Back on the main route, head along the small path signposted to the **Cova dels Coloms**, which gradually ascends back into the *barranc* for 1km through woodland before reaching a large dry stone wall and a fork. Head right here, along the narrowing gorge and beneath increasingly impressive limestone cliffs, scored with caves, until, after a further 750m, you reach a gap in another large wall marked with a splash of red paint. Immediately beyond this is a crossroads. Go left (a red arrow points the way), up a narrow path through thick woodland for another 500m to reach a T-junction. Go right here for 20m to the top of the path, then follow the zigzagging stone terrace up to reach the Cova dels Coloms – a huge natural cave, impressive for its size if nothing else (though the copious graffiti and overpowering smell of guano is less appealing).

Return to the T-junction and now go up the other side of the fork. A few metres beyond here a small path heads off on the left, over a couple of large boulders (there may or may not be a sign here – at the time of writing it had collapsed and was pointing in the wrong direction). Head up this tiny, stony path as it zigzags briskly up out of the gorge, returning you to the original track that you came down on between Binigaus Vell and Binigaus Nou. Thereafter, retrace your steps to Es Migjorn Gran.

ultra-modern *Santo Tomàs* is the most lavish (☎971 37 00 25, ⓦwww .sethotels.com; ⓢ; closed Nov–March), though the substantially less expensive *Sol Menorca* will do just as well (☎971 37 00 50, ⓦwww.solmelia.com; ⓢ; closed Nov–April). Both have pools, restaurants, night-time entertainment and many types of sports facility. Windsurfing boards, jet-skis and pedalos can all be rented on the Platja Sant Tomàs.

Ferreries

The old centre of **FERRERIES**, a modest little town on the ME-1 some 8km from Es Mercadal – and 6km from Es Migjorn Gran – is tucked into a hollow beneath a steep hill, its narrow, sloping streets framed by ancient whitewashed houses. A surprise here is the pagoda-like piece of modern sculpture in the main square, the **Plaça Espanya**, while just up the hill – along c/Fred – stands the neatly shuttered **Ajuntament**, primly facing the old parish church of **Sant Bartomeu**, a largely eighteenth-century edifice with a belfry of 1884 tacked onto the top. The liveliest time to be here is on Saturday morning, when a small fresh produce and crafts **market** is held on Plaça Espanya, but otherwise there's not much to detain you in the town itself, though there are a couple of neighbouring attractions. The more obvious of them is the large **Jaime Mascaró factory shoe and leather shop** (Mon–Sat 9.30am–8.30pm

Son Rubi

Binimel·là

Sant Joan de Serra

Binial-làs

Sant Vicenç

Sant Jaume

Sant Antoni

182m

Son Vives

183m

Mirador (159m)

213m

Rumet

Ruma Vell

Sant Josep

N

Sant Pere

Rumanou

Sant Francesc

208m

- - - - Walking Route

0   500 m

Ferreries

& Sun 10am–2pm), 1km or so east of town along the ME-1, but there's also the **Hort Sant Patrici cheese plant** (May–Oct Mon–Sat 9am–1.30pm & 4.30–8pm; Nov–April Mon–Fri 9am–1pm & 4–6pm, Sat 9am–1pm; Ⓦ www.santpatrici.com; free, but audioguide €6), where you can watch cheese being made, buy it at the shop, stroll the gardens and visit the cheese museum. The plant is just north of Ferreries – you'll pass it on the way to the start of the hike described on p.274.

One definite plus in Ferreries is the *Vimpi* **café-bar**, beside the ME-1 on Plaça Joan Carles, which serves especially tasty *tapas* for €5–7. You wouldn't choose to stay in Ferreries – it's just too quiet – which is just as well because there's no recommendable **accommodation**. **Buses** stop in front of the *Vimpi*, which is itself a four-minute walk from Plaça Espanya, straight up Avinguda Verge del Toro and on the right hand side.

Cala Santa Galdana

South from Ferreries, a fast, eight-kilometre road breezes through a pretty pastoral landscape on its way to the resort of **CALA SANTA GALDANA**. Once a much-loved beauty spot, the bay has experienced a rash of development since the building of the road and is now cluttered with high-rises. But, despite the concrete, there's no denying the beauty of the setting, the curving sandy **beach** framed by wooded, limestone cliffs and flanked by a pint-sized rocky promontory, which is itself next to a narrow river. Early in the morning or out of season is the best time to appreciate the scene – or you can escape the crowds by hiking west or east along the coast to more secluded coves (see p.273). It's possible to hire out all sorts of **watersports** equipment in Cala Santa Galdana, from pedalos and water scooters to windsurfing boards and snorkelling tackle. Small **boats** shuttle out along the south coast to more isolated spots and there are a couple of **car hire** outlets.

The resort has three high-rise **hotels**, easily the pick of which is the four-star ⅍ *Sol Gavilanes* (℡ 971 15 45 45, Ⓦ www.solmelia.com; ❼; closed Nov–March), a large chain hotel built against the cliffs that frame the beach. The hotel has every facility, from air-conditioning, swimming pools to satellite TV, and most of the attractive, modern guest rooms have sea-facing balconies. At the other end of the market, the **S'Atalaia campsite** is located about 3km back down the road towards Ferreries (℡ 971 37 42 32, Ⓦ www.campingsatalaia.com; April

Hiking

It's true that most visitors to Mallorca and Menorca stay firmly glued to the beach, but both islands offer excellent walking, ranging from stiff mountain hikes through to gentle country rambles. What's more, though the islands' footpaths were once poorly signed, things are improving rapidly, making walking easier and safer.

Serra de Tramuntana

As you struggle through Mallorca's massive international airport, it seems incredible that you're just thirty kilometres or so away from some of the Mediterranean's most magnificent mountain scenery. Mallorca may have an unenviable reputation for untrammelled development – and indeed it's true that parts are engulfed by concrete and glass – but the island's northern coast is banded by the wild and wonderful **Serra de Tramuntana** mountains, whose rearing peaks crash down to the sea, interrupted by the occasional rocky cove. This is Mallorca at its scenic best and today the mountains attract hordes of keen walkers, though until the late nineteenth century they were home only to a motley crew of monks and bandits, renegades and peasants, who eked out a living from the thin upland soils. Some locals still tend the olive and almond groves that dot the *serra*, but other mountain tradesmen disappeared long ago, from the hunters and charcoal burners who took meat and charcoal down to the villages of the plain below, through to the ice men, who kept Palma supplied with ice from their subterranean depots until as late as the 1920s.

The trails

Until the early 1990s, the assorted foot, mule and cart tracks that lattice the Serra de Tramuntana were often poorly signed and difficult to navigate. Things aren't perfect yet, but the island's ruling council has begun to take matters in hand and today the mountains boast a dense network of clearly signposted **hiking trails**, offering everything from the easiest strolls to lung-wrenching hauls up to the top of mountain peaks. Several of the most dramatic walks begin near the lovely little town of Sóller and its immediate neighbour Biniaraix, from where an ancient cobbled track ascends a handsome gorge, the Barranc de Biniaraix. There's more fine mountain hiking near the tiny resort of Sant Elm and around the monastery at Lluc, plus smashing coastal hikes in the vicinity of Deià and Valldemossa – and then there's the family-friendly stroll from Pollença to the sea at Cala Bóquer.

Menorca's trails

Very different from its larger neighbour, **Menorca** has no high mountains, but it does possess deep wooded gorges and a wild and windswept northern coast, whose craggy capes and headlands shelter a clutch of beautiful cove beaches. As of yet, the island's hiking trails are not, in general terms at least, as clearly marked as those on Mallorca, but there again the terrain is flatter and the walks much less strenuous.

Hiking essentials

On both Mallorca and Menorca, the prime **hiking seasons** are spring – March, April and May – and autumn, from early October to mid-November. The islands are also warm enough to allow for pleasant hiking in the depths of winter, though there's more rain at this time of year, temperatures can drop dramatically, snow is fairly common on the high peaks, and the number of daylight hours is restricted. In summer, the heat makes all but the shorter hikes unpleasant and very tiring.

Checklist

- A pair of good boots
- A waterproof jacket
- A whistle
- A torch
- Spare warm clothing
- Food and plenty of drinking water
- A compass (on the remoter hikes)
- Insect repellent
- A sunhat
- Sunblock
- Editorial Alpina maps (Ⓦwww .editorialalpina.com) for Serra de Tramuntana or for Menorca, *Menorca Tour & Trail Map* produced by Discovery Walking Guides (Ⓦwww.walking .demon.co.uk).

▲ Waymarker

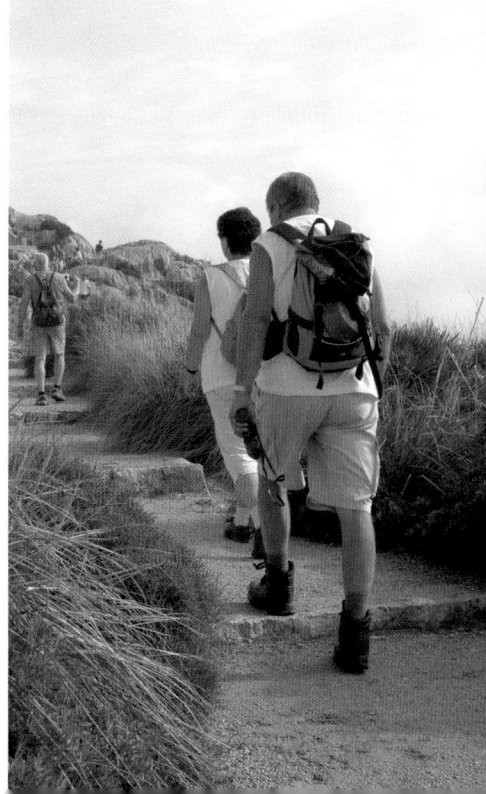

▼ Walkers on Serra de Tramuntana

▲ Walkers in Deià

Nine hikes in Mallorca and Menorca

We have described nine day-hikes in detail in this Guide – five for Mallorca and four on Menorca. They are:

Mallorca:
- ☛ A coastal walk from Deià to Port de Sóller. Linear; 12km; 4hr–4hr 30min. Mostly easy, difficult in parts. See pp.132–133.
- ☛ A circular walk from Valldemossa to Puig d'es Teix by the Archduke's Path. 12.5km; 674m of ascent; 4hr 30min–5hr. Medium difficulty. See pp.140–141.
- ☛ A circular walk from Lluc to Puig de Massanella and the Massanella massif. 11km; 795m of ascent; 4hr 30min –5hr round-trip. Medium difficulty. See pp.162–163.
- ☛ A valley walk from Port de Pollença to Cala Bóquer. Circular; 6km; 101m of ascent; 2hr return. Easy. See pp.172–173.
- ☛ A circular walk round the Alcúdia peninsula. 9 km; 450m of ascent; 4hr round trip, plus 1hr for diversion to Platja des Coll Baix. Moderately difficult. See pp.180–181.

Menorca:
- ☛ A coastal walk from Maó to Punta Prima. Linear; 16km; 100m ascent; 4hr–5hr. See pp.246–247.
- ☛ Es Grau to Sa Torreta. Circular; 9km; 100m ascent; 2hr 30min–3hr. See pp.256–257.
- ☛ Es Migjorn Gran to the coast, via the Barranc de Binigaus. Circular; 8km; 150m ascent; 2hr 30min–3hr. See pp.270–271.
- ☛ An inland walk near Ferreries. Circular; 250m ascent; 3–4hr. See p.274–275.

▶ *Taula* at Sa Torreta, Menorca

to mid-Oct). Pine trees shade much of the site, which has an outdoor swimming pool, a supermarket and a restaurant–bar; it's not a large campsite and it is popular, so advance **reservations** are strongly advised. In high season, a site costs around €6 per adult with extra charges for vehicles (€9), caravans (€7) and electrical hook-up (€4).

There are regular **buses** to Cala Santa Galdana from Ferreries and Ciutadella from May to mid-October; buses stop in the centre of the resort, a brief walk from the beach. There is also a bus stop outside the campsite, but be sure to let the driver know you want to get off here, otherwise you will go whizzing by.

Beaches east of Cala Santa Galdana

There are several exquisite **cove beaches** within easy reach of Cala Santa Galdana, the most obvious choice being **Cala Mitjana**, just 1km to the east. The **footpath** to Cala Mitjana begins at the Plaça Na Gran car park, near the main entrance to the *Hotel Sol Gavilanes* (see p.272): from the resort, proceed back up the main approach road, turn right following the sign for the hotel – the car park is on the left. A gate at the back leads onto an easy-to-follow path, which weaves its way through coastal pine woods to reach Cala Mitjana in about thirty minutes. The **beach** itself is a broad strip of sand at the back of a chubby little cove with wooded cliffs to either side. A favourite sport here is jumping into the crystal-clear water from the surrounding cliffs. It's a lovely spot, though there's sometimes an unpleasant smell of seaweed and the beach can get a little crowded now that a rough dirt road connects it with the Ferreries/Cala Santa Galdana main road; there are no beach facilities, so bring a **picnic**.

Equally appealing, but also afflicted with periodic seaweed and without facilities, is **Cala Trebalúger**, a further 2.5km east of Cala Mitjana and best reached

△ Cala Santa Galdana

An inland walk near Ferreries

Circular. 11km; 250m ascent; 3–4hr. Moderate

This circular inland walk takes you through the miniature hills north of the small town of **Ferreries**, with fine views out over the interior of the island and down to either coast. Most of the walk uses the access tracks of the many farms you'll pass en route, though there are precious few signs of cultivation hereabouts – most of the land is given over to scrub and game enclosures, evidence of the declining state of Menorcan agriculture. Much of the route is across private property (*propiedad privado*), though well-behaved walkers are extremely unlikely to encounter any problems with local landowners. The walk also offers good opportunities to spot Menorca's resident birds of prey, such as the booted eagle or red kite, circling on the thermals overhead, as well as innumerable smaller species which nest in the wind-shaped clumps of wild olive which dot the more elevated sections of the route. If you have your own transport, it's best to start at the farm of Sant Francesc, though at a pinch you could do the walk from Ferreries itself, which is regularly connected by bus to both Ciutadella and Maó; note, however, that this adds around 4km to the total distance, plus a steep climb up to the farmhouse of Sant Francesc at the beginning of the walk.

To reach the start of the walk, first find the roundabout on the eastern edge of Ferreries, by the Meubles allés store. Take the unsigned northern exit off this **round-about** across the industrial estate (*polígon industrial*), past the Lamborghini showroom (displaying tractors, not sport cars), just beyond which the road becomes a country lane. Follow this lane, past the Hort Sant Patrici cheese plant (see p.272), for 1km to a fork at the Camí de Marcona sign, then go right and continue for a further 1km to the top of a steep hill, where you reach the farms of **Sant Pere** and **Sant Francesc** and the beginning of the walk.

Park considerately if you've driven here (there's a convenient layby just beyond the farms), then head through the gate to Sant Francesc and along the ridgetop track, from where there are marvellous views to both the north and south coasts of the island, ahead to the heights of Monte Toro and the coastal village of Fornells, and behind to the neat white cluster of houses at Ferreries.

---

by boat from Cala Santa Galdana (summer 1–2 daily; €16). Cala Trebalúger boasts a beautiful arc of sand flanked by steep cliffs and crossed by a stream that emerges from the gorge behind.

Beaches west of Cala Santa Galdana

The **footpath** leading to the cove beaches west of Cala Santa Galdana begins with a set of wooden steps at the back of the **car park** behind the large and lumpy *Hotel Audax*, which stands near the beach at the west end of the resort. Note, however, that although there are plans to improve the path, at present it can be hard to follow and you'll need a proper hiking map. From the car park, it takes about thirty minutes to reach **Cala Macarella**, whose, severe, partly wooded limestone cliffs surround a band of white sand that shelves gently into the Med. It's a beautiful spot, ideal for swimming – and, unlike the other beaches around Cala Santa Galdana, seaweed is never a problem. There's a touch of development in the form of a summertime beach bar, and sunloungers and pedalos for rent, but it's nothing excessive.

From Cala Macarella, it's another thirty minutes or so to the next major beach along, Cala Turqueta (see p.287).

Follow this track for 750m, then swing left in front of a gate festooned with no-entry signs and the first of innumerable *Coto Privado de Caza* (private game enclosure) notices. Continue for 1km to reach the twin gates for the farms of Rumanou and Sant Josep. Go through the (left-hand) gate to Sant Josep, then continue for a further 300m to reach a second gate for Sant Josep. Go straight on for another 500m, heading around the left side of the farmhouse and climbing over the gate at the far end. Follow the track straight on along the ridgetop for 100m, then veer right through a gap in the wall and continue straight ahead for a further 100m to reach a small walled enclosure-cum-mirador at the highest point of the hill. From here there's a fine view of the ruined fortifications of the **Castell Santa Àgueda** (see below) on the hilltop to your left, and the rocky finger of the Cap de Cavallería stretching out into the sea on the northern coast. Ahead you'll see the farms of **Sant Jaume** and **Sant Vicenç** – your next goal – though the lack of a clear path makes finding a route down to them somewhat difficult. The next 1km is a bit of an unavoidable scramble. Climb over the wall by the *mirador* then bear left down the hill (there are various small tracks hereabouts) aiming for the clearly visible access track of Sant Vicenç, the leftmost of the two farms below, crossing several low stone walls en route – and watching your ankles on the rocky ground.

The remainder of the walk is either on surfaced roads or well-defined paths. Follow the track in front of the Sant Jaume farm straight ahead for 500m to hit a metalled road and turn left, then continue along the road straight ahead over a T-junction. Continue straight on, ignoring the subsequent turn-off to the right (signposted *camino particular*) as the road swings left until the houses of **Son Rubi** appear on the bluff ahead. Continue past the entrance to Son Rubi, after which the road reverts to dirt track.

Keep left at the fork 300m ahead, with Castell Santa Agueda now rearing into view once more on your right. Continue for 500m straight ahead, ignoring the turn-off to the farm of **Sant Joan de Serra**. The path then swings left. Some 250m past the Sant Joan de Serra turn off, pass through the gates to **Sant Antoni de Ruma**. Gird your loins here for the final ascent back up to the ridgetop. Climb up to the farmhouse and make a left turn at the fork just beyond, onto a metalled road, ascending steeply into a narrow wooded valley. Reach the T-junction at the top and turn right for the final kilometre back to your starting point at Sant Francesc.

Binisues and Castell Santa Àgueda

Heading west out of Ferreries along the ME-1, it's about 3km to the (clearly signed) right turn leading to the rural manor house of **Binisues** (May–Oct Mon–Sat 11am–7pm; €5). The house occupies a grand setting, overlooking the valleys and hills of central Menorca, and its elegant symmetries reflect the self-confidence of the island's nineteenth-century landed gentry. The interior, however, is a yawn. Presumably, the intention is to re-create the mansion's old patrician air, but the accumulated knick-knacks look as if they've been thrown in haphazardly. Even worse, if you persevere beyond the family rooms, you'll find an assortment of old agricultural implements on the second floor and a collection of mounted butterflies above – you're much better off sipping coffee at the restaurant and admiring the view.

Returning to the lane below Binisues, it's about 2.2km more to the **deserted schoolhouse** (and parking space) on the right-hand side, which marks the start of the (signed) hour-long path up the rocky and lightly wooded mountainside to the **Castell Santa Àgueda**, whose modest remains perch atop the peak of the same name. Menorca's second highest peak at 268m, the Romans were the first to recognize the hill's strategic value, fortifying the summit in the second century BC, but it was the Moors who developed the stronghold, and it was here that they made their final stand against Alfonso III's invasion in 1287. Fresh from their defeat at Maó, the demoralized Moors didn't put up much of a fight – though they would certainly have been more determined if they had known of their ultimate fate. After the surrender, the Catalans demanded a heavy ransom for every captive. Those who couldn't pay were enslaved and those who weren't fit to work as slaves were shoved onto ships, taken out to sea and thrown overboard. Nowadays, little remains of the Moorish castle, bar a few crumbling turrets and walls, but the views are spectacular.

Torrellafuda and the Naveta d'es Tudons

Travelling west from the Binisues turning on the ME-1, the road soon leaves the central hills behind for the flatlands that precede Ciutadella. These flatlands are dotted with some of the island's more important prehistoric sites, the first one of real significance being **Torrellafuda** (open access; free), which is reached down a clearly signed, 800m-long dirt road. Encircled by the battered remains of its Cyclopean walls, Torrellafuda was once a substantial Talayotic settlement and today its well-preserved *taula* stands in the shadow of olive trees near to a particularly well-preserved *talayot*. The rustic setting is delightful as well – it's a perfect spot for a picnic.

Back on the ME-1, it's almost 3km more from Torrellafuda to the **Naveta d'es Tudons** (May–Sept daily 10am–8pm; Oct Tues–Sun 10am–2.30pm; €2; rest of year open access; free), easily the best-preserved *naveta* on the island. Standing in a field a short stroll from the road, the *naveta* is seven metres high and fourteen long, consisting of massive stone blocks slotted together using a sophisticated dry-stone technique. The narrow entrance on the west side leads into a small antechamber, which was once sealed off by a stone slab; beyond lies the main chamber where the bones of the dead were stashed away after the flesh had been removed. Folkloric memories of the *navetas'* original purpose survived into modern times – Menorcans were loathe to go near these odd-looking and solitary monuments until well into the nineteenth century.

From the *naveta*, it's 5km to Ciutadella.

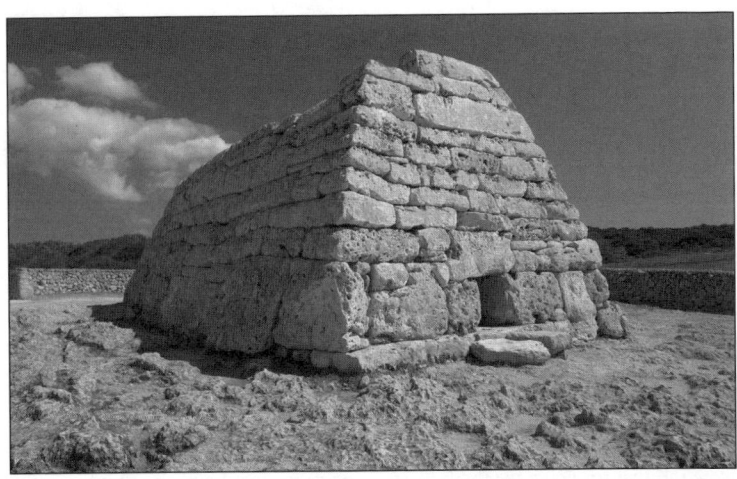

△ Naveta d'es Tudons

Ciutadella

Like Maó, **CIUTADELLA** sits high above its harbour, but here navigation is far more difficult, up a narrow channel too slender for all but the smallest of cargo ships. Nonetheless, despite this nautical inconvenience, Ciutadella was the island's capital until fairly recently: the Romans chose it, the Moors adopted it as Medina Minurka, and the Catalans of the Reconquista flattened the place and began all over again. In the event, the medieval Catalan town didn't last either: in 1558, Turkish corsairs razed the place and carted off three thousand captives – around eighty percent of the population – to the slave markets of Istanbul. As news spread of the disaster, the pope organized a European whip-round, and, with the money in the bag, an intrepid Menorcan doctor, one Marcos Martí, ventured east to Istanbul to buy the slaves back. Martí was remarkably successful – but there again, the Turks were raiding for the money, not to fight a religious war – and the returning hostages, together with the survivors of the assault, determinedly rebuilt Ciutadella in grand style. They re-fortified the town's compact centre and then, reassured, set about adorning it with fine stone churches and sweeping mansions.

Throughout the seventeenth century, Menorca's leading **landowners** hung out in Ciutadella, confident of their position and power. They were, however, in for a shock: for the colonial powers of the eighteenth century, the town's feeble port had no appeal when compared with Maó's magnificent inlet, and the British simply – and abruptly – moved the capital to Maó in 1722. Thereafter, Maó flourished as a trading centre, while Ciutadella stagnated – a long-lasting economic reverie that has, by coincidence, preserved the town's old and beautiful centre as if in aspic.

Despite the loss of its capital status, the bulk of the Menorcan aristocracy decided to stay put. The island's foreign rulers pretty much left them to stew in their own juice – an increasingly redundant, landowning class far from the wheels of mercantile power. Consequently, there's very little British or French influence in Ciutadella's **architecture**: instead, the narrow, cobbled streets boast fine old palaces, hidden away behind high walls, and a set of Baroque and Gothic churches very much in the Spanish tradition. Essentially, it's the whole ensemble, centred on stately **Plaça d'es Born**, that gives Ciutadella its appeal rather than any specific sight, though the mostly Gothic **cathedral** is a delight, as is the eclectic **Museu Diocesà de Menorca**. An ambitious renovation programme has further enhanced the town, restoring most of the old stone facades to their honey-coloured best. Added to this are some excellent **restaurants** and a reasonably adequate supply of *hostals* and **hotels**. It's a lovely place to stay, and nothing else on Menorca rivals the evening *passeig* (promenade), when the townsfolk amble the narrow streets of the centre, dropping in on pavement cafés as the sun sets. Allow at least a couple of days, more if you seek out one of the beguiling **cove beaches** within easy striking distance of town. There are several wonderful spots to choose from, but **Cala Turqueta** and **Cala d'Algairens** are probably the pick of the bunch. Spare time also for the prehistoric sites hereabouts, most pertinently the **Naveta d'es Tudons** (see p.276) and **Son Catlar**.

Arrival

Buses from Maó and points east halt at the bus stops on the south side of Plaça dels Pins, those from the tourist resorts of the west coast stop on the north side. From Plaça dels Pins, it's only a couple of minutes' walk into the town centre.

Car ferries and **catamarans** dock on the north side of the harbour, about five minutes' walk from the town centre in the brand-new terminal building – the port's facilities are being expanded at a rate of knots. For details of bus services to and from Ciutadella, see p.289; principal ferry routes are given on p.26.

If you're **driving** into Ciutadella, there's no missing the ring road, which, under various names – principally Avinguda Jaume I El Conqueridor and Avinguda Capità Negrete – encircles the old town. Approaching from the east, turn left when you hit it at the T-junction and keep going until you reach its conclusion beside the Plaça dels Pins. If you can't find a **parking** spot actually on this square, turn left at the top and drive down Passeig Sant Nicolau, where there's always space.

Information

The main **tourist office** is bang in the middle of the old town, directly opposite the cathedral on Plaça Catedral (May–Oct Mon–Fri 9.30am–8.30pm, Sat 9am–1pm; Nov–April Mon–Fri 9am–1pm & 5–7pm, Sat 9am–1pm; ☎971 38 26 93).

They have a good range of information on Menorca as a whole and Ciutadella in particular, including bus timetables, ferry schedules, lists of *hostals* and hotels, and free maps. They don't, however, help with finding accommodation.

Accommodation

By Menorcan standards at least, Ciutadella has a good supply of non–package **hotels and hostals**, and all of them are either in or within easy walking distance of the old town.

Hostal-residencia Ciutadella c/Sant Eloi 10 ⊤&Ⓕ 971 38 34 62. Unassuming but reasonably comfortable two-star *hostal* in an old terraced house down a narrow side street off Plaça Alfons III. ❸

Hotel Esmeralda Passeig Sant Nicolau 171 ⊤971 38 02 50, ⓦwww.mac-hotels.com. The sweeping curves of this four-storey hotel are a classic example of 1960s design, with a swimming pool and private gardens out front. Most of the bedrooms have wide and expansive balconies and face out to sea – but the bulk are booked up by package-tour operators. Located at the west end of Passeig Sant Nicolau, a fifteen-minute walk from the centre. Closed Dec–March. ❺

Hotel Géminis c/Josepa Rossinyol 4 ⊤971 38 46 44, ⓦwww.hotelgeminismenorca.com. Distinctively painted in pink and white, this well tended, very comfortable two-star hotel has thirty rooms, each decorated in bright modern style. The rooms at the front have Art-Deco-style balconies and overlook a quiet suburban street. To get there on foot, walk a few paces down c/Mossèn J. Salord i Farnés from the ring road and watch for the archway on the right; go through the arch and the hotel's on the right. Closed mid-Dec to Feb. ❸

🏃 **Hotel Hesperia Patricia** Passeig Sant Nicolau 90 ⊤971 38 55 11, ⓦwww .hoteles-hesperia.es. Perhaps the smartest hotel in town, popular with business folk and handy for the centre. The comfortable, modern rooms come with all facilities, the only downer being the lack of a sea view – though the best rooms have rooftop balconies with wide vistas over the town centre. There's also an outside swimming pool. Three stars. ❺

Hotel Madrid c/Madrid 60 ⊤971 38 03 28, ⓦwww.menorcadigital.com. Fourteen quite comfortable rooms in a run-of-the-mill, villa-style building with its own ground-floor café-bar. It's located near the ocean, a fifteen-minute walk west

of the town centre. To get there, follow Passeig Sant Nicolau from the Plaça dels Pins, take the third turning on the left (c/Saragossa) and you'll hit c/Madrid just east of the *hostal* at the first major intersection. There's an outside pool too. Closed Nov–April. ❹

Hostal-residencia Oasis c/Sant Isidre 33 ⊤971 38 21 97. Just a few metres from Plaça Artrutx, this old-fashioned, one-star *hostal* has nine simple rooms next door to a courtyard-restaurant. Closed Oct–March. ❷

Hotel Playa Grande c/Bisbe Juano 2 ⊤971 48 08 64, ⓦwww.grupoandria.com. Straightforward one-star hotel with a brisk modern interior located about ten minutes' walk south of Plaça dels Pins, at the foot of c/Mallorca. At the front, its balconied rooms overlook a narrow cove and a busy road – ask for a room at the back if you're a light sleeper. ❹

Hostal Sa Prensa c/Madrid 70 ⊤971 38 26 98. Recently refurbished, villa-like, one-star *hostal* with seven spartan bedrooms, three of which have balconies and sea views. The *hostal* is above a café-bar, a fifteen-minute walk west of the centre, close to the rocky seashore at the end of c/Madrid. To get there, follow Passeig Sant Nicolau from the Plaça dels Pins, take the fourth turning on the left (c/Joan Ramis i Ramis) and you'll hit c/Madrid just beside the *hostal* at the first major intersection. ❸

🏃 **Hotel Sant Ignasi** Carretera Cala Morell s/n ⊤971 38 55 75, ⓦwww.santignasi. com. This elegant nineteenth-century manor house has been tastefully converted into an immaculate hotel. Each of the twenty bedrooms is individually decorated in a style that blends with the original building, and there are gardens and an outside pool too. It's in the middle of the countryside, though the surrounding farmland is flat and dull. The hotel is about 4km northeast of the centre of Ciutadella, clearly signposted (down a very narrow 1.5km-long lane) from the road to Cala Morell. Closed Nov–Feb. ❻

The Town

All of Ciutadella's key attractions are clustered in the compact **town centre**, a rabbit warren of lanes, fringed by fine old mansions and handsome churches.

Most of the centre is pedestrianized, but it only takes a few minutes to walk from one side to the other, and keeping your bearings is fairly straightforward – the main square and harbour are on the west side of the centre, the ring road to the east.

Plaça d'es Born

Primarily a nineteenth-century creation, **Plaça d'es Born** is easily the finest main square in the Balearic islands. In the middle soars an **obelisk** commemorating the futile defence against the Turks in 1558, a brutal episode that was actually something of an accident. The Ottomans had dispatched 15,000 soldiers and 150 warships west to assist their French allies against the Habsburgs. With no particular place to go, the Turks rolled around the Mediterranean for a few weeks and, after deciding Maó wasn't worth the candle, they happened on Ciutadella, where the garrison numbered just forty. For the locals, the results were cataclysmic. The one-sided siege ended with the destruction of the town and the enslavement of its population – there was so much damage that when the new Spanish governor arrived, he was forced to live in a cave. The obelisk's original Latin inscription, penned by the mid-nineteenth-century politician and historian Josep Quadrado, reads, "Here we fought until death for our religion and our country in the year 1558". Such grandiose nationalism was typical of Quadrado, then the region's most prominent politician and leader of the reactionary Catholic Union, which bombarded Madrid with complaints and petitions whenever central government did anything progressive.

On the western side of the Plaça d'es Born stands the **Ajuntament** (Town Hall), whose early nineteenth-century arches and crenellations mimic Moorish style, purposely recalling the time when the site was occupied by the Wali's *alcázar* (palace). From here, it's a few paces along the north side of the square to the **Teatre d'es Born**, a neat, late nineteenth-century structure built to salvage some municipal pride: the merchants of Maó had just built an opera house and, pricked into cultural action, the oligarchs of Ciutadella promptly followed suit – though they weren't quite as energetic when it came to actually getting people to perform here. The building lay neglected for years, but it has now been restored and is used as both a theatre and cinema.

The northeast corner of the Plaça d'es Born is marked by the sweeping lines of the **Palau Torresaura**, built in the nineteenth century, but looking far older, and the grandest of several aristocratic mansions edging the plaza. Embellished by a handsome loggia, its frontage proclaims the family coat of arms above a large wooden door leading into a spacious coutryard. The antique interior, however, is off limits – like most of its neighbours, the house is still owner-occupied. An exception is the adjacent **Palau Salort** (May–Oct Mon–Sat 10am–2pm; €2.50), which is entered round the corner on c/Major d'es Born, the narrow street that links the square with the cathedral. Dating from 1813, this rambling mansion has seen more illustrious days, but it's still of some mild interest for its sequence of high-ceilinged rooms redolent of nineteenth-century aristocratic life.

Tucked away in the southeast corner of the square, the **Església de St Francesc** is a clean-lined, unpretentious structure, whose hybrid architecture reflects the island's ups and downs. The original church was constructed shortly after the Reconquista and it was here in 1301 that Jaume II met his nobles to parcel up the island into the feudal estates – the *Cavalleries* (from *cavaller*, the Catalan for knight) – that cemented his kingdom. In 1558, the Turks fired the church, but it was rebuilt to the original specifications in the 1590s, with further embellishments added later – the Baroque side door in the eighteenth century, the dome in the nineteenth. Like most of Ciutadella's churches, the Republicans ransacked the interior in the Civil War, but bits and pieces did survive, notably several chintzy carved wood altars and a motley crew of polychromatic saints.

The Cathedral

From beside Palau Salort, c/Major d'es Born leads through to the **cathedral** (daily 9am–1pm & 6–9pm; free), a good-looking structure built by Jaume II at the beginning of the fourteenth century on the site of the chief mosque, but remodelled after the Turkish onslaught of 1558. During the rebuilding, the flying buttresses of the original were partly encased within a thick stone wall to guard against future attack, a modification which gives the cathedral its distinctive appearance. The Gothic **side door** – on the south side of the church – was, however, left intact, its arching columns decorated with strange-looking beasts and the coats of arms of Aragón and Ciutadella, all surmounted by a delicate carving of the Magi honouring the infant Christ. Another survivor was the set of fierce-looking **gargoyles** that decorates the buttresses at roof level. The principal (west) **entrance** was added much later, in 1813, its flashy Neoclassical portico contrasting with the rest of the church and the intricate rose window above.

Inside, light filters through the stained glass of the narrow, lofty windows to bathe the high altar in an ethereal glow. There's also a sequence of glitzy Baroque side chapels and a wonderfully kitsch, pointed high-altar canopy or baldachin. The wall behind the high altar carries a medieval panel painting, *the Purification of the Virgin*, but most of the church's old furnishings and fittings were destroyed in a frenzy of anti-clericalism when the Republicans took control of Menorca during the Civil War. Although the British had made Maó the island's capital in 1722, Ciutadella remained Menorca's ecclesiastical centre and, almost without exception, its resident Catholic hierarchy were rich and reactionary in equal measure. They enthusiastically proclaimed their support for the officers of the Maó garrison when the latter declared for Franco in July 1936, but this turned out to be a major gaffe. The bulk of the garrison stayed loyal to the Republic, and, allied with local left-wing groups, they captured the rebels, shot their leaders and ransacked Ciutadella's main churches as retribution.

The Palau Olivar and Casa Museu Torrent

Directly opposite the cathedral's west entrance is the **Palau Olivar** (no access), whose stern, eighteenth-century facade is partly relieved by a pair of miniature balconies fronted by wrought-iron grilles. In 1707, the house witnessed one of the town's crueller episodes, when a reclusive mother and daughter who worked and lived here were accused of witchcraft. Found guilty on palpably potty charges, the older woman was sent to prison for life, and the younger was executed – by any standard, a heavy price to pay for not joining in the town's social life.

From the Palau Olivar, it's a brief walk north to the **Casa Museu Torrent**, at Sant Rafel 11 (mid-May to Oct Mon–Fri 11am–1pm & 7.30–9.30pm, Sat 11am–1pm & 8–9.30pm & Sun 8–9.30pm; free), which displays around one hundred paintings in the old home of Ciutadella's own **José Roberto Torrent** (1904–90). The son of a cobbler, Torrent is usually regarded as the town's finest painter, a prolific and versatile artist who began with deftly coloured Menorcan landscapes in the Realist tradition. Later, in the 1960s, his paintings became more expressionistic, rendering island scenes in striking colours and shapes, but perhaps his most evocative work was produced in his old age in paintings of infirmity, loneliness and isolation.

The Església del Roser and Museu Diocesà de Menorca

Back on Plaça Catedral, proceed south along c/Roser and you'll soon pass the tiny **Església del Roser** (Mon–Sat 11am–1pm & 6–9pm; free), whose striking Churrigueresque facade, dating from the seventeenth century, boasts a quartet of pillars festooned with intricate tracery. The church was the subject of bitter controversy when the British governor Richard Kane (see p.264) commandeered it for Church of England services, which was not at all to the liking of the Dominican friars who owned the place. Recently deconsecrated, the church's interior has been covered in oodles of cream paint and is now used for temporary exhibitions of contemporary, mostly local, art and crafts.

At the far end of c/Roser, turn left past the palatial, seventeenth-century mansion of **Can Saura**, which is distinguished by its elegant stonework and overhanging eaves, and then left again for c/Seminari and the mildly diverting **Museu Diocesà de Menorca** (Diocesan Museum; Mon–Sat 10am–2pm; €2.50), housed in an old convent and its church, the Església dels Socors. Before you go in, take a look at the convent's elongated perimeter wall, a sober affair interrupted by two doorways – one for the cloisters and the museum, the other for the church, though this is now closed off. This old church doorway is surmounted by the most bizarre of sculpted cameos, depicting the **Virgin Mary**, armed with a cudgel and standing menacingly over a cringing, cat-like dragon-devil.

Inside, the **museum** collection is distributed amongst the tiny rooms that flank the immaculately preserved Baroque **cloister**, whose vaulted aisles sport coats of arms and religious motifs. The first two rooms – to either side of the entrance – hold a hotchpotch of Talayotic and early classical archeological finds, notably a superbly crafted, miniature bull and a similarly exquisite little mermaid (*sirena*), almost certainly Greek bronzes dating from the fifth century BC. On the left-hand side of the cloister is the domed and single-aisled **Església dels Socors**, whose standard-issue Baroque decoration culminates in an extraordinarily artless high altar. Beyond that is a **vestment room**, stuffed with ecclesiastical tackle, from monstrances and communion cups to reliquaries, crosiers and fancy capes. Moving on, the old, vaulted **refectory** displays some dreadful religious paintings, mostly dating from the eighteenth century, and then there is a room devoted to the artist **Pere Daura** (1896–1976), one-time Communist and Republican soldier, who fled Spain after Franco seized power. Both before and after his exile, Daura spent most of his time abroad, mostly in France or the USA, and although he was born in Ciutadella, this was more by accident than design – his family were travelling through here when he arrived. As for the paintings themselves, Daura is strongest when it comes to still lifes, done very much in the Impressionist manner, though his village scenes and landscapes can be engaging too.

The market to the Estatua des Be

Immediately north of the museum along c/Seminari, turn right down c/Socors to make the quick detour east to the **market** (*mercat*; Mon–Sat mornings), which rambles over two miniature squares, Plaça Francesc Netto and Plaça Llibertat. This is another delightful corner of the old town, where fresh fruit, vegetable, meat and fish stalls mingle with lively and inexpensive cafés selling the freshest of *ensaimadas*. The fish stalls occupy a dinky little structure of 1895; the rest fill out a slender arcaded gallery that was constructed thirty years before as part of a municipal drive to clean up the town's food supply.

Doubling back to c/Seminari, turn right to pass the savings bank which occupies part of the **Palau Saura**, built in grand style by the British for a

Menorcan aristocrat, one Joan Miquel Saura, in return for his help in planning their successful invasion of 1708. Just north along the street is the flamboyant facade of the **Capella del Sant Crist**, a Baroque extravaganza with garlands of fruit and a pair of gargoyle-like faces. Inside, the intimate nave supports an octagonal stone dome and is also home to an unattributed medieval panel painting depicting three saints of local significance. The skeletal crucified Christ above the high altar is supposed to have dripped with sweat in 1661 and remains a popular object of devotion.

From the chapel, it's a few metres north to the narrow, pedestrianized main street that runs through the old town – here c/J. M. Quadrado. Look to the left and you'll spy a perky bronze lamb – the **Estatua des Be** – stuck on a column. The lamb, symbolizing the Lamb of God and carrying a flag bearing the cross of St John the Baptist, is a reminder of Ciutadella's biggest shindig, the Festa de Sant Joan (see p.40).

East from c/Seminari to Plaça Alfons III

From the top of c/Seminari, the pedestrianized main street of the old town runs east as **c/J.M. Quadrado**. The first stretch is crimped by a block of whitewashed, vaulted arches, **Ses Voltes**, distinctly Moorish in inspiration and a suitable setting for a string of busy shops and cafés. Just beyond is **Plaça Nova**, an attractive little square edged by some of the most popular pavement cafés in town. Just off the square along c/Sant Antoni, a narrow archway cuts through what was once the town wall, which explains the name of the alley beyond, "Qui No Passa" ("The one that doesn't go through"). Returning to Plaça Nova, c/Maó leads east to leave the cramped alleys of the old town at **Plaça Alfons III**, a traffic-choked square that was once the site of Ciutadella's east gate. The big old windmill here, the **Moli d'es Comte**, looks as if it should be in the countryside, its forlorn appearance not helped by its partial conversion into a bar.

Santa Clara

Directly opposite the top of c/Seminari, a long, straight street – c/Santa Clara – shoots off north, hemmed in by the walls of old aristocratic palaces. At the top is the convent of **Santa Clara**, a mundanely modern incarnation of a centuries-old foundation. In 1749, this was the site of a scandal that had tongues clacking from Ciutadella to Maó. During the night, three young women hopped over the convent wall and placed themselves under the protection of their British boyfriends. Even worse, as far as the local clergy were concerned, they wanted to turn Protestant and marry their men. In this delicate situation, Governor Blakeney had the room where the women were staying sealed up by a priest every night. But he refused to send them back to the convent and allowed the weddings to go ahead, thereby compounding a religious animosity – Catholic subject against Protestant master – which had begun in the days of Richard Kane.

The Museu Municipal

Beyond Santa Clara, at the end of c/Portal de Sa Font, the **Museu Municipal** (Tues–Sat 10am–2pm & 6–9pm; €2.20) occupies part of the old municipal fortifications, a massive bastion overlooking a slender ravine that once had, until it was redirected, a river running along its base and on into the harbour. Inside the museum, a long vaulted chamber is given over to a wide range of archeological artefacts, primarily a substantial collection of Talayotic remains, featuring finds garnered from all over the island and covering the several phases of Talayotic civilization. The earlier pieces, dating from around 1500 to 700

> **The Rissaga**
>
> Almost all of the time, Ciutadella's long and slender harbour is as flat as a mill-pond, but every so often, for reasons that remain obscure, it is subjected to a violent disturbance, the **Rissaga**. This begins with sudden changes to the water level and is followed by a dramatic rush of water into the harbour before normality returns. The last great Rissaga of 1984 submerged the harbourside beneath two metres of water, giving everyone down there a horrid shock.

BC, include many examples of crudely crafted beakers and tumblers as well as a set of five skulls, which appear to have been subjected to some form of brain surgery, though no one is sure quite how or why. Later work – from around 700 BC – reveals a far greater degree of sophistication, both in terms of kitchenware, with bowls and tumblers particularly common, and bronze weaponry. From this later period, which ended with the arrival of the Romans in 123 BC, comes most of the (imported) jewellery, whose fine detail and miniature size suggests a Carthaginian origin. A leaflet detailing the exhibits in English is available free at reception. Temporary exhibitions take place downstairs.

From the Museu Municipal, it's a five-minute walk back to Plaça d'es Born along **c/Sa Muradeta** with pleasant views down the ravine to the harbour. As you near Plaça d'es Born, a wide flight of steps – the **Baixada Capllonc** – cuts down to the harbour, where yachts and fishing smacks bob up and down in front of a series of waterside restaurants, with the old town walls forming a scenic background.

The Castell de Sant Nicolau

Running west from the top of Plaça dels Pins, Passeig Sant Nicolau cuts a dead-straight course to reach, after about 800m, the headland **Castell de Sant Nicolau** (Tues–Sat 11am–1pm & 6–8pm; free), a dinky little seventeenth-century watchtower equipped with a drawbridge, oil holes and turrets – all stuck on unwelcoming rocks. The interior, however, is disappointingly bare unless, that is, there is an art exhibition being held here, but even then most people venture out to the *castell* to watch the sun set out beyond Mallorca.

Beside the castle is a statue honouring **David Glasgow Farragut**, who is shown with telescope in hand and wind in his hair. The son of a Ciutadellan who emigrated to America in 1776, Farragut entered the US navy in 1810, the start of a long naval career distinguished by several audacious attacks on Confederate strongholds in the Civil War. Most famously, Farragut forced the surrender of New Orleans in 1862 and as a result of this and other actions was made an admiral of the US fleet four years later. He visited Menorca in 1867 and was greeted by cheering crowds everywhere he went – in Ciutadella, the throng was so dense that he had to abandon his carriage and walk to his lodgings near the cathedral. At church the next day, as his secretary wrote approvingly, "hundreds of eyes were riveted upon the pleasant countenance of the unappalled admiral".

Eating, drinking and nightlife

For an early **breakfast** the best place to go is the market (*mercat*) on Plaça Llibertat, where a couple of simple cafés serve coffee and fresh pastries. Later in the day, around **lunchtime**, aim for c/J.M. Quadrado, Plaça Nova and Plaça Alfons III, which together hold a good selection of inexpensive café-bars, offering *tapas* and light meals. In the **evening**, most tourists make a beeline for the **restaurants** that string along the harbourside, but – with the odd exception – you're actually better off seeking out the better-value establishments amongst the side streets near Plaça d'es Born. As regards **opening hours**, most cafés and bars open daily from approximately 9am to 9pm, whilst restaurants usually open from noon to 11pm with a siesta between 3/4pm and 7/8pm. Restaurants are more likely to close for one day a week and those down on the harbour mostly close altogether during the wintertime. Note also, that although almost all the harbourside restaurants have an outside terrace, when the ferries arrive and depart the noise can be deafening and private boats are often moored uncomfortably close.

People don't come to Ciutadella for the **nightlife**, but there is a small complement of late-night bars dotted round the old town with the liveliest places in the ravine at the head of the port, on Es Pla de Sant Joan. Places come and go with remarkable speed, so although we have mentioned a couple of late-night bars below, your best bet is to wander along Es Pla de Sant Joan until somewhere takes your fancy. Finally, Ciutadella is one of the few places you can still enjoy the evening *paseo* (promenade), with families wandering up and down the main street taking the evening air as they have done for generations – though it's a dying custom in much of the rest of Spain.

Cafés and café-bars

Café-bar Aurora Plaça Alfons III, 3. This café is situation next to the ring road on the eastern edge of the old town. Open all day for both *tapas* (€3–6) and full meals, with the emphasis on Menorcan standards. Daily from 10am–10pm.

Café-bar Ulises Plaça Llibertat. This amenable, low-key café-bar next to the market is a locals' favourite. Their *ensaimadas*, a snip at €1.30 each, are some of the best in town. Mon–Sat from 8am.

Ca'n Nito Plaça d'es Born 11. Specializing in *tapas*, this modern café-bar is one of the liveliest spots in town and its tiny terrace, on the main

square, is a popular place for a drink. Daily 1–4pm & 7pm–12.30am.

Sa Xarxa c/Sebastià 1. Agreeable café serving a good line in *tapas* and snacks at inexpensive prices. Its terrace is just set off the main drag, which means it's a good place to watch the evening *paseo*. Daily 10am–10pm.

La Torre de Papel Camí de Maó 46. The most urbane coffee house in town with a bookshop at the front and a tiny, vaguely New Age terrace café at the back. Tues–Sat 10am–2pm & 6–9pm.

Restaurants

La Guitarra c/Nostra Senyora dels Dolors 1 ☎971 38 13 55. Located a short walk from the cathedral, this is arguably the best restaurant in town, a family-run affair featuring the very best of Menorcan cuisine with main courses – anything from seafood to lamb – averaging a very reasonable €12–18. They also do a particularly delicious lobster

stew for €35. The restaurant occupies an old cellar, whose stone walls sport a scattering of agricultural antiques. Mon–Sat 12.30–3.30pm & 7.30–11pm.

El Horno c/Forn 12 ☎971 38 07 67. French-style basement restaurant near the northeast corner of Plaça d'es Born, with good and reasonably priced food. Mains hover around €12. Daily 7–11pm.

Bakeries

Ciutadella has several first-rate **bakeries**. One of the best is the *Pastisseria Mol*, across the square from the cathedral at c/Roser 2 (Mon–Sat 9.30am–5pm), which sells excellent takeaway pizza slices, filled bread rolls and mouthwatering cakes. Alternatively, *Pastelería Montaner*, near the cathedral at c/Bisbe 11 (Mon–Sat 9.30am–5pm), is the oldest pastry shop in town and sells what many locals believe to be the tastiest *ensaimadas* on the island baked in its ancient ovens.

Restaurant Café Balear Es Pla de Sant Joan 15 ☏ 971 38 00 05. Justifiably popular, this attractively decorated restaurant sits at the back of the harbour by the bridge – at a safe distance from the ferries and the moored boats. The terrace is the best place to eat, but there are tables inside too. The food is first rate with shellfish and fish the big deals; main courses average around €20. Open Mon–Sat noon–4pm & 7.30–11.30pm, but may operate more restricted hours in winter.

Bars and clubs

Cactus Bar Baixada Capllonc s/n. At the foot of the steps leading down from the old town to the harbour, this large bar has an outside terrace and a cavernous interior, inside the old city walls. The best cocktails in town. Starts to hop at about 11pm. **Café-bar Es Molí** Camí de Maó 1. Housed in the Moli d'es Comte, the old windmill across the street from Plaça Alfons III, this is a noisy and gritty café-bar, with a (very) young Menorcan crowd at night, old timers during the day. Open till 1am. **Gabanna** Plaça de Sant Joan 3. Groovy bar-cum-club with a chill-out terrace and alternative jazz, house, rock and world music scene. Open from 10pm to 4am.

Listings

Banks ATMs are dotted all over the centre and there's one at the Banca March, Plaça d'es Born 10.
Bicycle and moped rental Velos Joan, c/Sant Isidre 32, off Plaça Artrutx (Mon–Fri 8am–1.30pm & 3.30–8.30pm, Sat 9am–1.15pm & 7–8pm & Sun 10–11.30am; ☏ 971 38 15 76).
Boat hire Menorca Boats, down on the harbour near the bridge, rent out all manner of speed boats (☏ 971 38 03 49, ☒ www.menorcaboats.com). Prices begin at a hefty €320 per day.
Car rental The most centrally located major car rental company is Betacar, on the ring road at Avinguda Jaume I El Conqueridor 59 (☏ 971 38 29 98, ☒ www.betacar.biz).
Diving Menorcatech, Pla de Sant Joan 10 (☏ 971 38 60 30, ☒ www.menorcatech.com) organize a wide range of deep-sea diving trips out along the west coast.
Email and Internet access Café Internet, Plaça dels Pins 37 (Mon–Sat 9am–11pm).
Ferries and catamarans Three companies offer car ferry and/or catamaran services between Ciutadella and the Spanish mainland and/or Mallorca. They are Balearia (☏ 902 16 01 80, ☒ www.balearia.com); Acciona-Trasmediterranea (☏ 902 45 46 45, ☒ www.acciona -trasmediterranea.es); and Iscomar (☏ 902 11 91 28, ☒ www.iscomar.ferries.org). Schedules, tariffs and tickets are available direct from the operators down at the harbour. Note that Menorca's car rental firms do not allow their vehicles to leave the island. For further details of ferry and catamaran routes as well as prices, see "Basics", p.22 & p.26.
Maps and books Libreria d'es Racó, c/J.M. Quadrado 40, stocks an excellent range of island road maps and a reasonably good selection of travel books.
Pharmacies Amongst several downtown options, there's a pharmacy at Plaça Nova 2.
Post Office The main *correu* is handily located at Plaça d'es Born 8 (Mon–Fri 8.30am–8.30pm, Sat 9.30am–1pm).
Taxis Taxis leave from Plaça dels Pins and Avinguda Constitució, round the corner from Plaça Alfons III, ☏ 971 38 11 97.

Around Ciutadella

The diverse attractions of **west Menorca** are all within easy striking distance of Ciutadella, beginning with the pristine cove **beaches** that notch the island's southern shore just a few kilometres away. There are several delightful beaches to choose from, including the appealing **Cala des Talaier** and beautiful **Cala Turqueta**, and now that the island's ruling council has bought the rights from local landowners, access is free. On the other side of Ciutadella, the north coast is wild and almost completely undeveloped, but there is one resort here, the smart villa-village of **Cala Morell**, which occupies a bleak and barren cove with a gritty beach. Remember also that Ciutadella is only a few kilometres from two of the island's finest prehistoric sites, the **Naveta d'es Tudons** (see p.276) and Torrellafuda (see p.276).

Entirely different is the intensively developed **west coast**, where long lines of villas carpet the flat and treeless seashore to either side of Ciutadella, from **Cales Piques** in the north to **Cap d'Artrutx**, 15km away to the south. By and large, this is all pretty dreadful, a remorseless suburban sprawl that is ugly and dull in equal measure, though, here and there, the villas bunch round narrow coves to form reasonably pleasant resorts, the pick of these being **Cala Santandria**.

From May to October, there are regular **buses** from Ciutadella's Plaça dels Pins to the tourist settlements of the west coast and Cala Morell; there are, however, no buses to the beaches southeast of town, including Cala Turqueta. All buses between Maó and Ciutadella pass by the Naveta d'es Tudons (see p.276), but check the driver is prepared to let you off at the site before you embark.

Southeast of Ciutadella

Beginning at the traffic island on c/Alfons V, the cross-country **Camí de Sant Joan de Missa** runs southeast from Ciutadella to the undeveloped coves of the south coast. After about 3km, you reach the farmhouse of **Son Vivó**, where the road branches into two, with each (signposted) **fork** leading to several south-coast beaches, the nearest of which are about 10km away from town. Both roads are in good condition, the signs are easy to follow, and, whichever beach you choose, you'll end up in a parking lot a five- to ten-minute walk from the seashore. Incidentally, if you've rented a moped be prepared for a bumpy ride and watch out for the dust and muck churned up by passing cars. There's only one place to stay hereabouts, the *Hotel Rural Morvedrà Nou*, a sympathetically converted stone farmhouse with seventeen air-conditioned guest rooms and a pool on the Camí Sant Joan de Misa, 7km from Ciutadella (April–Oct; ☎971 35 95 21, Ⓦwww.morvedranou.es; ❼).

South to Cala Turqueta and Cala des Talaier

Taking the more easterly road from the Son Vivó fork, it's about 1.5km more to the **Ermita de St Joan de Missa**, a squat, brightly whitewashed church with a dinky little bell tower. There's a fork here too, but the signposting is clear and you keep straight, with the road slicing across the countryside, before you swerve round the **Marjal Vella farmhouse**. Shortly afterwards, about 4.3km from the church, you turn at the sign, going through the gateway to reach the car park for **Cala Turqueta**, a lovely cove flanked by wooded limestone cliffs. The beach consists of a sheltered horseshoe of white sand sloping gently into the sea, making it ideal for bathing, and because there are limited facilities it's unusual to find a crowd.

From Cala Turqueta, it's about 1km west to the next cove along, **Cala des Talaier**, where a tiny strip of pale sand is backed by pine trees and overlooked by a ruined watchtower. With no handy parking, this beach is even quieter than Turqueta – and, again, there are no facilities.

Son Catlar and Platges Son Saura

Back at the Son Vivó fork, it's 3km along the more westerly road to **Son Catlar** (open access; free), the largest prehistoric settlement on Menorca and one which was still expanding when the Romans arrived in force in 123 BC. The most impressive feature of this sprawling Talayotic village is its extraordinary stone wall, originally three metres high and made of massive blocks – the square towers were added later. Inside the walls, however, all is confusion. The widely scattered remains are largely incomprehensible and only the *taula* compound and the five battered *talayots* make much sense.

Pushing on south, the asphalt peters out about 1.5km further down the road when you reach the ornate gateway of the **Torre Saura farmhouse**. To the left of the gateway, a 2km-long dirt road bumps its way down to a parking lot behind a wide horseshoe-shaped cove that shelters two beaches, the **Platges Son Saura**. The west side of the cove is more exposed and is often sticky with seaweed, so aim for the more sheltered eastern side, where a wide arc of white sand is fringed by pines. There are more facilities here than at most of its neighbours, including a summer beach bar.

Northeast of Ciutadella

Signposted from the ME-1 on the outskirts of Ciutadella, a well-surfaced country lane carves northeast across a pastoral landscape bound for the smallish tourist settlement of **CALA MORELL**, just 8km from town. This is one of the island's more refined *urbanitzacions*, its *pueblo*-style villas – on streets named in Latin after the constellations – hugging a steep and rocky, dog-legged bay. There's swimming off the gritty beach here and you can also visit some of the old **caves** for which Cala Morell is noted, visible beside the road as you drive down into the resort. Dating from the late Bronze and Iron Ages, the caves form one of the largest prehistoric necropolises known in Europe, and are surprisingly sophisticated, with central pillars supporting the roofs, and, in some instances, windows cut into the rock and classical designs carved in relief. No one owns the caves, so there's unlimited access – just scramble up from the road. The sight of one or two is sufficient for most visitors, but if you're after more than a glimpse, bring a torch. From the car park at the end of the main access road, a rough footpath leads north out along the bare and rocky promontory that protects the west side of the bay, but only the truly adventurous will attempt the very difficult hike west to the **Punta de S'Escullar** headland, the site of one of the largest colonies of Cory's shearwaters in the western Mediterranean with thousands of birds returning to their cliffside burrows in the late afternoon throughout the summer.

Doubling back along the Cala Morell road, it's about 3km to a signed intersection, where you turn along a narrow, country lane to reach – after another 3.5km – **Cala d'Algaiarens**, whose two sandy cove beaches, backed by dunes and pine woods, offer excellent swimming in sheltered waters. At the time of writing, the landowner still levies a charge for using "his" beach, but the island council is about to buy access rights, making a visit free.

South to Cap d'Artrutx

Heading south from Ciutadella along the main coastal road, you're soon amongst the interminable villa complexes that extend almost without interruption as far as **Cap d'Artrutx**, at the southwest tip of the island. This is all rather depressing, but, amidst the aesthetic gloom, the resort of **CALA SANTANDRIA** does at least possess a modicum of charm, its low limestone seacliffs framing a narrow cove and a small sandy beach. The swimming is safe and the beach has all the usual resort facilities, including a bar and water-ski-, lounger- and pedalo-rental.

Travel details

Note: For further information, call TMSA on ☎ 971 36 04 75, or check out ⊕ www .transportesmenorca.net – with the exception of routes to and from Fornells, where the operator is Autos Fornells (☎ 686 93 92 46, ⊕ www .autosfornells.com), and buses out from Ciutadella to the resorts of the west coast, which are operated by Torres (⊕ www.e-torres.net).

Buses (May–Oct)

Ciutadella to: Alaior (Mon–Fri hourly, Sat & Sun 6 daily; 40min); Cala en Blanes (hourly; 10min); Cala Santandria (hourly; 10min); Es Mercadal (Mon–Fri hourly, Sat & Sun 6 daily; 30min); Ferreries (Mon–Fri hourly, Sat & Sun 6 daily; 20min); Maó (Mon–Fri hourly, Sat & Sun 6 daily; 50min); Sant Tomàs (Mon–Sat 4 daily; 45min).
Es Mercadal to: Fornells (Mon–Sat 2 daily; 20min); Maó (Mon–Fri hourly, Sat & Sun 6 daily; 30min).
Es Migjorn Grand to: Ferreries (4 daily; 10min); Maó (4 daily; 30min).
Ferreries to: Alaior (Mon–Fri hourly, Sat & Sun 6 daily; 20min); Cala Santa Galdana (hourly; 20min); Ciutadella (Mon–Fri hourly, Sat & Sun 6 daily; 20min); Es Mercadal (Mon–Fri hourly, Sat & Sun 6 daily; 10min); Es Migjorn Gran (4 daily; 10min); Maó (Mon–Fri hourly, Sat & Sun 6 daily; 40min).
Fornells to: Es Mercadal (Mon–Sat 2 daily; 20min); Maó (2–4 daily; 35min).
Maó to: Alaior (Mon–Fri hourly, Sat & Sun 6 daily; 20min); Arenal d'en Castell (Mon–Sat 7 daily, Sun 2 daily; 20min); Cala Santa Galdana (2 daily; 50min); Ciutadella (Mon–Fri hourly, Sat & Sun 6 daily; 50min); Es Mercadal (Mon–Fri hourly, Sat & Sun 6 daily; 30min); Es Castell (hourly; 10min); Es Migjorn Gran (4 daily; 30min); Ferreries (Mon–Fri hourly, Sat & Sun 6 daily; 40min); Fornells (2–4 daily; 35min); Punta Prima (hourly; 20min); Son Bou (5–7 daily; 40min); Son Parc (Mon–Sat 4 daily, Sun 2 daily; 40min).

Buses (Nov–April)

Ciutadella to: Alaior (Mon–Fri hourly, Sat & Sun 6 daily; 40min); Es Mercadal (Mon–Fri hourly, Sat & Sun 6 daily; 30min); Ferreries (Mon–Fri hourly, Sat & Sun 6 daily; 20min); Maó (Mon–Fri hourly, Sat & Sun 6 daily; 50min).
Es Mercadal to: Ciutadella (Mon–Fri hourly, Sat & Sun 6 daily; 30min); Fornells (Mon–Sat 2 daily; 20min); Maó (Mon–Fri hourly, Sat & Sun 6 daily; 30min).
Es Migjorn Grand to: Ferreries (Mon–Sat 1 daily; 10min); Maó (Mon–Sat 1 daily; 30min).
Ferreries to: Alaior (Mon–Fri hourly, Sat & Sun 6 daily; 20min); Ciutadella (Mon–Fri hourly, Sat & Sun 6 daily; 20min); Es Mercadal (Mon–Fri hourly, Sat & Sun 6 daily; 10min); Es Migjorn Gran (Mon–Sat 1 daily; 10min); Maó (Mon–Fri hourly, Sat & Sun 6 daily; 40min).
Fornells to: Es Mercadal (Mon–Sat 2 daily; 20min); Maó (2–4 daily; 35min).
Maó to: Alaior (Mon–Fri hourly, Sat & Sun 6 daily; 20min); Ciutadella (Mon–Fri hourly, Sat & Sun 6 daily; 50min); Es Castell (hourly; 10min); Es Mercadal (Mon–Fri hourly, Sat & Sun 6 daily; 30min); Es Migjorn Gran (Mon–Sat 1 daily; 30min); Ferreries (Mon–Fri hourly, Sat & Sun 6 daily; 40min); Fornells (2–4 daily; 35min).

MENORCA | Travel details

Contexts

Contexts

History

T he earliest inhabitants of the Balearics seem to have reached the islands from the Iberian peninsula, and carbon-dating of remains indicates that human occupation was well established by 4000 BC. The discovery of pottery, flints and animal horns fashioned into tools suggests that these early people were **Neolithic pastoralists**, who supplemented their food supplies by hunting, particularly the *Myotragus balearicus*, a species of mountain goat now extinct. Hundreds of these animals' skulls have been discovered and several are exhibited in the islands' larger museums. The frequency of these finds has encouraged some experts to assert that the *Myotragus* was domesticated, the principal evidence being the supposed remains of crude corrals on the coast of Mallorca near Valldemossa; this assertion is, however, strongly contested.

Why, or how, these Neolithic peoples moved to the Balearic islands is unknown. Indeed, the first landfall may have been accidental, made by early seafarers travelling along the shores of the Mediterranean –and part of a great wave of migration that is known to have taken place in the Neolithic period. Many of the oldest archeological finds have been discovered in natural **caves**, where it seems likely that these early settlers first sought shelter. Later, cave complexes were dug out of the soft limestone that occurs on both islands, comprising living quarters, usually circular and sometimes with a domed ceiling, as well as longer, straighter funerary chambers. These complexes represent the flourishing of what is commonly called the **Balearic cave culture** – one good (and readily accessible) example is at the resort of **Cala Morell**, on Menorca (see p.288).

The archeological evidence indicates that Balearic cave dwellers soon came into regular contact with other cultures: the Mediterranean, with its relatively calm and tide-free waters, has always acted as a conduit of civilization. The discovery of Beaker ware at Deià indicates one of the earliest of these outside influences to have been the **Beaker people**, whose artefacts have been found right across Western Europe; they are named after their practice of burying their dead with pottery beakers. The Beaker people had knowledge of the use of bronze, an alloy of copper and tin, and they exported their bronze-working skills into the Balearics in around 1500 BC. This technological revolution marked the end of the cave culture and the beginning of the Talayotic period.

The Talayotic period

The megalithic remains of the **Talayotic period**, which lasts until the arrival of the Romans in 123 BC, are strewn all over Mallorca and Menorca – though, surprisingly, there's no evidence of them on Ibiza. The structure that gives its name to the period is the **talayot**, a cone-shaped tower with a circular base, between five and ten metres in height. Although the purpose of these *talayots* remains unknown, it is clear that by 1000 BC a relatively sophisticated, largely pastoral society had developed on both Mallorca and Menorca, with at least some of the islanders occupying the walled settlements that still dot the interior: the three best examples are **Capocorb Vell** (see p.227), south of Llucmajor on Mallorca, where you can still inspect four *talayots* and the remains of up to thirty houses; **Ses Païsses** (see p.205), a settlement of comparable proportions outside Artà; and Menorca's **Son Catlar** (see p.287), not far from Ciutadella. All three were occupied well into the Roman period.

Talayotic culture reached dizzying heights on Menorca, and it's here you'll find the most enigmatic remains of the period. These are the **taulas** ("tables" in Catalan), T-shaped structures standing as high as four metres and consisting of two massive dressed stones. Their purpose is unknown, though many theories have been advanced. One early nineteenth-century writer believed that they were altars used for human sacrifice, but the height of most *taulas* makes this very unlikely – unless the islanders were on stilts. More intriguingly, some academics have argued that the "T" was a **stylized head of a bull**, an animal that was much venerated in many parts of the ancient Mediterranean, most notably in Minoan Crete. True or not, it is certainly the case that the enclosures which surround every *taula* do seem to have had religious significance. This was confirmed during excavations at **Torralba d'en Salord** (see p.265), where archeologists discovered animal remains and pottery in side recesses of fireplaces, and concluded that these must have been ritual offerings. They also found a bronze sculpture of a bull, suggesting that cattle were, indeed, worshipped. Torralba d'en Salord is one of the many places where *taulas* and *talayots* stand cheek by jowl. Often the remains are too broken down to be of much interest, but two other good spots are **Torrellafuda** (see p.276) and **Talatí de Dalt** (see p.248), which incorporates a *talayot*, a *taula* and several columned chambers or **hypostyles**. Partly dug out of the ground and roofed with massive slabs of stone, these hypostyles must have taken considerable effort to build, and may have been used for important gatherings, possibly of communal leaders.

The other distinctive structure to be found on Menorca is the **naveta**, made of roughly dressed dry-stone blocks and looking like an inverted bread tin. Dating from the beginning of the Talayotic period, the **Naveta d'es Tudons**, near Ciutadella (see p.276), is the finest example, but there are around thirty-five others sprinkled across the island. They were collective tombs, or, more correctly, ossuaries, where, after the flesh had been removed, the bones of the dead were placed along with some personal possessions such as jewellery, pottery and bone buttons.

Phoenicians, Greeks and Carthaginians

Fearful of attack from the sea, the Talayotic people built their walled settlements a few kilometres inland. This pattern was, however, modified from around 900 BC, when the Balearics became a staging post for the **Phoenicians**, maritime traders from the eastern Mediterranean whose long voyages reached as far as Cornwall in southwest England. According to the Roman historian Pliny, the Phoenicians established a large settlement at **Sanisera** on Menorca's north coast (see p.262) and archeologists have also discovered Phoenician artefacts at **Alcúdia** on Mallorca (see p.177). In general, however, very few Phoenician remains have been found on the Balearics – just a handful of bronze items, jewellery and pieces of coloured glass.

The **Greeks** displaced the Phoenicians around 800 BC, as several city-states explored the western Mediterranean in search of trade and potential colonies. Like the Phoenicians, the Greeks appear to have used the Balearics primarily as a staging post, for no Greek buildings have survived on either Mallorca or Menorca. The absence of metal apparently made the islands unsuitable for long-term colonization, and the belligerence of the native population may have played a part too: the Greeks coined the islands' name, the "**Balearics**", which they derived from *ballein*, meaning "to throw from a sling". The islanders were adept at this form of warfare, and many early visitors were repelled with showers

Balearic Slingers

Quintus Metellus, the Roman commander who invaded Mallorca in 123 BC, had a healthy respect for the warlike qualities of the islanders in general and their skill with the **stone-throwing sling** in the particular. He had good reason. The Carthaginians had been using Balearic mercenaries for many decades and the islanders had inflicted heavy casualties on the Roman legions throughout the Punic Wars. Consequently, Metellus went to great trouble to protect his men by erecting mammoth shields of hide along the decks of all his ships – a stratagem which worked extremely well.

Male islanders were trained to use the sling in childhood and they could propel a stone with great accuracy and force sufficient to crush a shield or helmet. The slinger had three slings of different lengths, one held in his hand, another wrapped round his stomach and a third tied round his head. According to the historian **Diodorus Siculus** (90–30 BC) these slingers were not a particularly pleasant bunch. They often went naked, covering their bodies in a mixture of pig fat and olive oil; were inordinately fond of wine; were keen on female slaves; and rounded off their weddings with all the male guests having congress with the bride in descending order of age – before passing her over to the groom.

of polished sling-stones – though some historians dispute this theory, claiming rather that the name comes from the Baleri tribe of Sardinia.

The Greeks were also discouraged from colonization by the growth of the **Carthaginian Empire** across the western Mediterranean. The Phoenicians had established Carthage, on the North African coast in 814 BC, and from this base they gradually extended their authority across the western Mediterranean. They began to colonize the Balearics in the seventh century BC and the islands were firmly under their control by the beginning of the third century BC, if not earlier. Little is known of the Carthaginian occupation except that they established several new settlements. It is also claimed that the Carthaginian general, **Hannibal**, was born on Cabrera island off Mallorca, though Ibiza and Malta claim this honour too.

In the third century BC, the expansion of the Carthaginian Empire up into the Iberian Peninsula triggered two **Punic Wars** with Rome. In both of these wars the Balearics proved extremely valuable, first as stepping stones from the North African coast to the European mainland and second as a source of mercenaries. **Balearic slingers** (see box above) were highly valued and accompanied Hannibal and his elephants across the Alps in the Second Punic War, when (for reasons that remain obscure) the islanders refused gold and demanded payment in wine and women instead. After Hannibal's defeat by the Romans at the battle of Zama in 202 BC, Carthaginian power began to wane and they withdrew from Mallorca and Menorca, although they continued to have some influence over Ibiza for at least another seventy years.

Romans, Vandals and Byzantines

As the Carthaginians retreated so the **Romans** advanced, incorporating Ibiza within their empire after the final victory over Carthage in 146 BC. On Mallorca and Menorca, the islanders took advantage of the prolonged military chaos to profit from piracy, until finally, in 123 BC, the Romans, led by the consul Quintus Metellus, restored maritime order by occupying both islands. These victories earned Metellus the title "Balearico" from the Roman senate and two of the islands were given new names, Balearis Major (Mallorca) and Balearis Minor (Menorca).

For the next five hundred years all of the Balearics islands were part of the **Roman Empire**. Amongst many developments, Roman colonists introduced viticulture, turning the Balearics into a wine-exporting area, and initiated olive-oil production from newly planted groves. As was their custom, the Romans consolidated their control of the islands by building roads and establishing towns. On Mallorca, they founded Pollentia (Alcúdia) in the north and Palmaria on the south coast, near the site of modern Palma, whilst on Menorca they developed Port Magonum (Maó) as an administrative centre with Sanisera – previously the site of a Phoenician trading post – becoming an important port. Initially, the Balearics were part of the Roman province of Tarraconensis (Tarra-gona), but in 404 AD the islands became a province in their own right with the name **Balearica**.

By this time, however, the Roman Empire was in decline, its defences unable to resist the westward-moving tribes of central Asia. One of these tribes, the **Vandals**, swept right across the Balearics in around 425 AD, thereby ending Roman rule. So thoroughgoing was the destruction they wrought that very few signs of the Romans have survived – the only significant remains are those of Pollentia at **Alcúdia** (see p.177).

The Vandals had been Christianized long before they reached the Mediterra-nean, but they were followers of the **Arian** sect. This interpretation of Christi-anity, founded by Arius, an Alexandrian priest, insisted that Christ the Son and God the Father were two distinct figures, not elements of the Trinity. To ortho-dox Christians, this seemed dangerously close to the pagan belief in a multiplic-ity of gods and, by the end of the fourth century AD, Arianism had been forcibly extirpated within the Roman Empire. However, the sect continued to flourish amongst the Germanic peoples of the Rhine, including the Vandals, who, armed with their "heretical" beliefs, had no religious truck with their new Balearic subjects, persecuting them and destroying their churches. As a conse-quence, only a handful of Christian remains from this period have survived, primarily the ruins of the basilica at **Son Bou** (see p.266).

In 533 the Vandals were defeated in North Africa by the Byzantine general Count Belisarius (who was the subject of a novel by one of Mallorca's adopted sons, Robert Graves). This brought the Balearics under **Byzantine** rule and, for a time, restored prosperity and stability. Nonetheless, the islands were too far removed from Constantinople to be of much imperial importance and, when the empire was threatened from the east at the end of the seventh century, they were abandoned in all but name.

The Moors

As the influence of Byzantium receded, so militarized Islam moved in from the south and east to fill the vacuum. In 707–8 the **Moors** of North Africa conducted an extended raid against Mallorca, destroying its entire fleet and carrying away slaves and booty, and by 716 the Balearics' position had become even more vulnerable with the completion of the Moorish conquest of Spain. In 798 the Balearics were again sacked by the Moors – who were still more interested in plunder than settlement – and in desperation the islanders appealed for help to **Charlemagne**, the Frankish Holy Roman Emperor. As emperor, Charlemagne was the military leader of Western Christendom (the pope was the spiritual leader), so the appeal signified the final severance of the Balearics' links with Byzantium and the East.

Charlemagne's attempt to protect the islands from the Moors met with some success, but the respite was only temporary. By the middle of the ninth century, the Christian position had deteriorated so badly that the Balearics were compelled to enter a non-aggression pact with the Moors, and, to add to the islanders' woes, the Balearics suffered a full-scale **Viking** raid in 859. Finally, at the beginning of the tenth century, the **emir of Córdoba** conquered both Menorca and Mallorca. Moorish rule lasted over three hundred years, though internal political divisions among the Muslims meant that the islands experienced several different regimes. In the early eleventh century, the emirate of Córdoba collapsed and control passed to the *wali* (governor) of Denia, on the Spanish mainland. This administration allowed the Christians – who were known as **Mozarabs** – to practise their faith, and the islands prospered from their position at the heart of the trade routes between North Africa and Islamic Spain.

In 1085 the Balearics became an independent emirate with a new dynasty of *walis*, from **Amortadha** in North Africa. They pursued a more aggressive foreign and domestic policy, raiding the towns of the mainland and persecuting their Christian citizens. These actions blighted trade and thereby enraged the emergent city-states of Italy at a time when Christendom was fired by crusading zeal. Anticipating retaliation, the Amortadhas fortified Palma, which was known at this time as Medina Mayurka, and several mountain strongholds. The Christian attack came in 1114 when a grand Italian fleet – led by the ships of Pisa and supported by the pope as a mini-crusade – landed an army of 70,000 Catalan and Italian soldiers on Ibiza. The island was soon captured, but Mallorca, the crusaders' next target, proved a much more difficult proposition. Palma's coastal defences proved impregnable, so the Christians assaulted the landward defences instead, the concentric lines of the fortifications forcing them into a long series of bloody engagements. When the city finally fell, the invaders took a bitter revenge, slaughtering most of the surviving Muslim population. Yet, despite their victory, the christians had neither the will nor the resources to consolidate their position and, loading their vessels with freed slaves and loot, they returned home.

It took the Moors just two years to re-establish themselves on the islands, this time under the leadership of the **Almoravides**, a North African Berber tribe who had previously controlled southern Spain. The Almoravides proved to be tolerant and progressive rulers, and the Balearics prospered under them: agriculture improved, particularly through the development of irrigation, and trade expanded as commercial agreements were struck with the Italian cities of Genoa and Pisa. The Pisans – crusaders earlier in the century – defied a papal ban on trade with Muslims to finalize the deal; consciences could, it seems, be flexible even in the "devout" Middle Ages when access to the precious goods of the east (silks, carpets and spices) was the prize.

Jaume I and the Reconquista

In 1203 the Almoravides were supplanted by the **Almohad** dynasty, who forcibly converted the islands' Christian population to Islam and started raiding the mainland. This was an extraordinary miscalculation, as the kingdoms of Aragón and Catalunya had recently been united, thereby strengthening the Christian position in this part of Spain. The unification was a major step in the changing balance of power: with their forces combined, the Christians were able to launch the **Reconquista**, which was eventually to drive the Moors from the entire peninsula. Part of the Christian jigsaw was the Balearics and, in 1228, the emir of Mallorca imprudently antagonized the young **King Jaume I** of Aragón and Catalunya by seizing a couple of his ships. The king's advisers, with their eyes firmly fixed on the islands' wealth, determined to capitalize on the offence.

C

They organized the first Balearic publicity evening, a feast at which the king was presented with a multitude of island delicacies and Catalan sailors told of the archipelago's prosperity. And so, insulted by the emir and persuaded by his nobility, Jaume I committed himself to a full-scale invasion.

Jaume's expedition of 150 ships, 16,000 men and 1500 horses set sail for Mallorca in September 1229. The king had originally planned to land at Pollença, in the northeast, but adverse weather conditions forced the fleet further south, and it eventually anchored off Sant Elm, where it must have given the one shepherd who lived there a terrible shock. The following day, the Catalans defeated the Moorish forces sent to oppose the landing and Jaume promptly pushed east, laying siege to Medina Mayurka. It took three months to breach the walls, but on December 31 the city finally fell and Jaume was hailed as "**El Conqueridor**".

The cost of launching an invasion on this scale placed an enormous strain on the resources of a medieval monarch. With this in mind, Jaume subcontracted the capture of Ibiza, entering into an agreement in 1231 with the Crown Prince of Portugal, Don Pedro, and the count of Roussillon. In return for the capture of the island, the count and the prince were to be allowed to divide Ibiza between themselves, provided they acknowledged the suzerainty of Jaume. This project initially faltered, but was revived with the addition of the archbishop of Tarragona. The three allies captured Ibiza in 1235 and divided the spoils, although Don Pedro waived his rights and his share passed to Jaume.

In the meantime, Jaume had acquired the overlordship of Menorca. Unable to afford another full-scale invasion, the king devised a cunning ruse. In 1232 he returned to Mallorca with just three galleys, which he dispatched to Menorca carrying envoys, while he camped out in the mountains above Capdepera on Mallorca. As night fell and his envoys negotiated with the enemy, Jaume ordered the lighting of as many bonfires as possible to illuminate the sky and give the impression of a vast army. The stratagem worked and the next day, mindful of the bloodbath following the invasion of Mallorca, the Menorcan Moors capitulated. According to the king's own account, they informed his envoys that "they gave great thanks to God and to me for the message I had sent them for they knew well they could not long defend themselves against me". The terms of submission were generous: the Moors handed over Ciutadella, their principal settlement, and a number of other strongpoints, but Jaume acknowledged the Muslims as his subjects and appointed one of their leaders as his *rais* (governor).

The retention of Moorish government in Menorca, albeit under the suzerainty of the king, was in marked contrast to events on Mallorca. Here, the land was divided into eight blocs, with four passing to the king and the rest to his most trusted followers, who leased their holdings in the feudal fashion, granting land to tenants in return for military service. In 1230 Jaume consolidated his position by issuing the **Carta de Població** (People's Charter), guaranteeing equality before the law, an extremely progressive precept for the period. Furthermore, Mallorca was exempted from taxation to encourage Catalan immigration, and special rights were given to Jews resident on the island, a measure designed to stimulate trade. Twenty years later, Jaume also initiated a distinctive form of government for Mallorca, with a governing body of six **jurats** (adjudicators) – one from the nobility, two knights, two merchants and one peasant. At the end of each year the *jurats* elected their successors. This form of government remained in place until the sixteenth century.

Jaume I died at Valencia in 1276. In his will he divided his kingdom between his two sons: **Pedro** received Catalunya, Aragón and Valencia, whilst **Jaume II** was bequeathed Montpellier, Roussillon and the Balearics. Jaume II was crowned in Mallorca on September 12, 1276.

The Balearic Kingdom

Jaume I's division of his kingdom infuriated **Pedro**, as the Balearics stood astride the shipping route between Barcelona and Sicily, where his wife was queen. He forced his brother to become his vassal, but in response Jaume II secretly schemed with the French. Predictably enough, Pedro soon discovered his brother's treachery and promptly set about planning a full-blooded invasion. However, Pedro died before the assault could begin and it was left to his son, **Alfonso III**, to carry out his father's plans. Late in 1285, Alfonso's army captured Palma without too much trouble, which was just as well for its inhabitants: wherever Alfonso met with resistance – as he did later in the campaign at the castle of Alaró – he extracted a brutal revenge. Indeed, even by the standards of thirteenth-century Spain, Alfonso was considered excessively violent and the pope excommunicated him for his atrocities – but not for long.

With Mallorca secured and Jaume deposed, Alfonso turned his attention to Menorca, where he suspected the loyalty of the Moorish governor – the *rais* was allegedly in conspiratorial contact with the Moors of North Africa. Alfonso's army landed on Menorca in January 1287 and decisively defeated the Moors just outside Maó. The Moors retreated to the hilltop fortress of Santa Agueda, but their resistance didn't amount to much and the whole island was Alfonso's within a few days. The king's treatment of the vanquished islanders was savage: those Muslims who were unable to buy their freedom were enslaved, and those who couldn't work as slaves – the old, the sick and the very young – were taken to sea and thrown overboard. Alfonso rewarded the nobles who had accompanied him with grants of land and brought in hundreds of Catalan settlers. The capital, Medina Minurka, was renamed **Ciutadella**, and the island's mosques were temporarily converted to Christian usage, before being demolished and replaced.

Alfonso's violent career was cut short by his death in 1291 at the age of 25. His successor was his brother, Jaume, also the king of Sicily. A more temperate man, Jaume conducted negotiations through the papacy that eventually led, in 1298, to the restoration of the partition envisaged by Jaume I: he himself presided over Catalunya, Aragón and Valencia, while his exiled uncle, **Jaume II**, ruled as king of Mallorca and Menorca. Restored to the Crown, Jaume II devoted a great deal of time to improving the commerce and administration of the Balearics. To stimulate trade, he established a weekly market in Palma, reissued the currency in gold and silver, and founded a string of inland towns, including Manacor, Felanitx, Llucmajor and Binissalem on Mallorca and Alaior and Es Mercadal on Menorca. Jaume II attended to God as well as Mammon, and his reign saw the building of many churches and monasteries. In the same vein, the king also patronized **Ramon Llull** (see p.81 & p.82), the Mallorcan poet, scholar and Franciscan friar, providing him with the finance to establish a monastic school near Valldemossa. Perhaps his most important act, though, was to grant Menorca its own **Carta de Població**, which bestowed the same legal rights as the Mallorcans enjoyed.

On his death in 1311, Jaume was succeeded by his asthmatic son, **Sancho**, who spent most of his time in his palace at Valldemossa, where the mountain air was to his liking. Nonetheless, Sancho did his job well, continuing the successful economic policies of his father and strengthening his fleet to protect his territories from North African pirates. Mallorca and Menorca boomed. Mallorca in particular had long served as the entrepôt between North Africa and Europe, its warehouses crammed with iron, figs, salt, oil and slaves, but in the early fourteenth century its industries also flourished, primarily shipbuilding and textiles. In 1325, the traveller Ramón Muntaner praised Palma as an "honoured city of greater wealth than any with the most businesslike inhabitants ... of any city in the world". He may have been exaggerating, but not by much, and Palma's merchants were certainly inventive: spotting a gap in the market they went into **crossbow–making** and by 1380 they were exporting them by the boat load.

Internationally, Sancho worked hard to avoid entanglement in the growing antagonism between Aragón and France, but the islands' future still looked decidedly shaky when he died without issue in 1324. Theoretically, the islands should have passed to Aragón, but the local nobility moved fast to crown Sancho's ten-year-old nephew as **Jaume III**. Hoping to forestall Aragonese hostility, they then had him betrothed to the king of Aragón's five-year-old daughter, though in the long term this marriage did the new king little good. After he came of age, Jaume III's relations with his brother-in-law, **Pedro IV of Aragón**, quickly deteriorated, and Pedro successfully invaded the Balearics in response to an alleged plot against him. Jaume fled to his mainland possessions and sold Montpellier to the French to raise money for an invasion. He landed on Mallorca in 1349, but was no match for Pedro, who defeated and killed him on the outskirts of Llucmajor. His son, the uncrowned **Jaume IV**, was also captured and although he eventually escaped, he was never able to drum up sufficient support to threaten the Aragonese.

Unification with Spain

For a diversity of reasons the **unification** of the Balearics with Aragón – and their subsequent incorporation within Spain – proved a disaster for the islanders. In particular, the mainland connection meant that the islands' nobility soon gravitated towards the Aragonese court, regarding their local estates as little more than sources of income to sustain their expensive lifestyles. More fundamentally, general economic trends moved firmly against the Balearics. After the fall of Constantinople to the Turks in 1453, the lucrative overland trade routes from the eastern Mediterranean to the Far East were blocked and, just as bad, it

The Jews in Mallorcan history

For several centuries, Mallorca's large Jewish community, concentrated in Palma and Inca, played a crucial part in maintaining the island's money supply and sustaining trade with North Africa. In return, they were treated in that strangely contradictory manner which was common across much of medieval Europe, alternately courted and discriminated against. They were, for instance, expected to live in their own ghettos and wear a distinctive type of dress, but were allowed (unlike their Christian neighbours) to divorce and re-marry. Predictably, they were often blamed for things over which they had no control, from famine to plague, and were intermittently subjected to pogroms like the ones in Palma in 1391 and again in 1435 (see p.80). They were also subject to the attentions of the **Holy Office of the Inquisition**, which set up shop in Palma in 1484 determined to impose orthodoxy on all of the island's citizenry. The Inquisitors bore down on the Jews, most of whom either left or chose the course of least resistance and converted to Christianity, though a small percentage were burnt to death. As late as the 1970s, the descendants of these converts still formed a distinct group of Palma gold- and silversmiths, but no such enclave exists today.

was the Portuguese who discovered the way around the Cape of Good Hope to the Indies. In 1479, **Fernando V of Aragón** married **Isabella I of Castile**, thereby uniting the two largest kingdoms in Spain, but yet again this was bad news for the islanders. The union brought mainland preoccupations and a centralized bureaucracy, which rendered the islands a provincial backwater – even more so when, following Columbus's reaching the Americas in 1492, the focus of European trade moved from the Mediterranean to the Atlantic seaboard almost at a stroke. The last commercial straw was the royal decree that forbade Catalunya and the Balearics from trading with the New World. By the start of the sixteenth century, the Balearics were starved of foreign currency, and the islands' merchants had begun to leave, signalling a period of long-term economic decline.

Sixteenth-century decline

Political and economic difficulties destabilized the islands' social structures throughout the sixteenth century. The **Jews**, as useful scapegoats, focused some of the swirling antagonisms that perturbed the islands, but there were many other signs of discontent. The aristocracy was divided into warring factions, the country districts were set against the towns, and perhaps most destabilizing of all were high taxes and an unreliable grain supply. In Mallorca, this turbulence coalesced in an **armed uprising** of peasants and artisans in 1521. Organized in a *Germania*, or armed brotherhood, the insurrectionists seized control of Palma, whose nobles beat a hasty retreat to the safety of either Palma's Castell de Bellver or the Alcúdia citadel – those who didn't move fast enough were slaughtered in the streets. The rebels soon captured the Bellver, and polished off the blue-bloods who had sought protection there, but Alcúdia held out until relieved. It was a long wait: only in 1523 did the forces of authority return under the command of **Emperor Charles V**, king of Spain, Habsburg Holy Roman Emperor and the grandson of Fernando and Isabella. Charles negotiated generous terms for the surrender of Palma, but once in possession of the city, promptly broke the agreement and ordered the execution of five hundred of the rebels, who were duly hung, drawn and quartered.

The Balearics witnessed other sixteenth-century horrors with the renewal of large-scale **naval raids** from North Africa. This upsurge of piratical activity was partly stimulated by the final expulsion of the Moors from Spain in 1492, and partly by the emergence of the Ottoman Turks as a Mediterranean superpower. Amongst many attacks, Muslim raiders ransacked Pollença (1531 and 1550), Alcúdia (1551), Valldemossa (1552), Andratx (1553) and Sóller (1561), whilst **Hizir Barbarossa** ravaged Menorca's Maó after a three-day siege in 1535. Hundreds of Menorcans were enslaved and carted off, prompting Charles V to construct the fort of Sant Felip to guard Maó harbour. Two decades later, the Turks returned and sacked Ciutadella, taking a further three thousand prisoners – about eighty percent of the city's population. Muslim incursions continued until the seventeenth century, but declined in frequency and intensity after a combined Italian and Spanish force destroyed the Turkish fleet at **Lepanto** in 1571.

British and French occupation

The Balearics' woes continued throughout the seventeenth century. Trade remained stagnant and the population declined, a sorry state of affairs that was exacerbated by continued internal tensions. Palma, in particular, was plagued by

vendettas between its aristocratic families, with the Canavall and Canavant factions regularly involved in street battles and assassinations, whilst the (often absentee) landowners failed to invest in their estates. By the 1630s the population problem had become so critical that Philip IV exempted the islands from the levies that raised men for Spain's armies – though this gain was offset by the loss of 15,000 Mallorcans to the **plague** in 1652.

A new development was the regular appearance of **British** vessels in the Mediterranean, a corollary of Britain's increasing share of the region's seaborne trade and the Royal Navy's commitment to protect its merchantmen from Algerian pirates. The British didn't have much use for Mallorca, and largely ignored it, but they were impressed by Maó's splendid harbour, a secure and sheltered deep-water anchorage where they first put in to take on water in 1621. Forty years later, Charles II of England formalized matters by instructing his ambassador to Spain to "request immediate permission for British ships to use Balearic ports and particularly Port Mahon". The Spanish king granted the request, and the advantages were noted by a poetic British seaman, a certain John Baltharpe:

Good this same is upon Minork

For shipping very useful 'gainst the Turk.

The King of Spain doth to our King it lend,

As in the line above to that same end.

For a time the British were simply content to "borrow" Maó, but their expanding commercial interests prompted a yearning for a more permanent arrangement. It was the dynastic **War of the Spanish Succession** (1701–14), fought over the vacant throne of Spain, which gave them their opportunity. A British force **invaded Menorca** in 1708 and, meeting tepid resistance, captured the island in a fortnight. Apart from the benefits of Maó harbour, Menorca was also an ideal spot from which to blockade the French naval base at Toulon, thereby preventing the union of the French Atlantic and Mediterranean fleets. Indeed, so useful was Menorca to the British that they negotiated its retention at the **Treaty of Utrecht**, which rounded off the war.

Menorca's first British governor, **Sir Richard Kane**, was an energetic and capable man who strengthened the island as a military base, and worked hard at improving its administration, civilian facilities and economy. He built the first **road** across the island from Maó to Ciutadella and introduced improved strains of seed and livestock. During the first forty years of British occupation, the production of wine, vegetables and chickens increased by five hundred per cent. Relations between the occupying power and the islanders were generally good – though the Catholic clergy no doubt found it difficult to stomach the instruction to "pray for His Britannic Majesty".

The first phase of British domination ended when the **French** captured Menorca in 1756 at the start of the **Seven Years War**. Admiral Byng was dispatched to assist the beleaguered British force, but, after a lacklustre encounter with a French squadron, he withdrew, leaving the British garrison with no option but to surrender. Byng's indifferent performance cost him his life: he was court-martialled and executed for cowardice, prompting Voltaire's famous aphorism that the English shoot their admirals "pour encourager les autres". The new French governor built the township of **Sant Lluís** (see p.253) to house his Breton sailors and, once again, the Menorcans adjusted to the occupying power without too much difficulty. In 1763, Britain regained Menorca in exchange for the Philippines and Cuba, which it had captured from France during the Seven Years War.

The **second period of British occupation** proved far less successful than the first. The governor from 1763 to 1782, General Johnston, was an authoritarian and unpopular figure, who undermined the Menorcans' trust in the British. The crunch came in 1781, when, with Britain at war with both Spain and France, the Duc de Crillon landed on the island with eight thousand soldiers. In command of a much smaller force, the new British governor, General John Murray, withdrew to the fort of Sant Felip, where he was besieged for eight months. Succoured by the Menorcans, the Franco–Spanish army finally starved the British into submission; Murray's men were badly stricken with scurvy, and only 1120 survived. With the British vanquished, Menorca temporarily reverted to Spain.

The **third and final period of British rule over Menorca** ran from 1798 to 1802, when the island was occupied for its value as a naval base in the Napoleonic Wars. Landing at Port d'Addaia, the British took just nine days – and suffered no casualties – in recapturing the island, helped in no small measure by the foolhardy destruction of Fort Sant Felip by the Spaniards in the mid-1780s. It seems that the Spanish high command did not believe they could defend the fortress, so they simply flattened it, thereby denying it to any colonial power – and, of course, making the island vulnerable in the process. The British finally relinquished all claims to Menorca in favour of Spain under the terms of the Treaty of Amiens in 1802.

Meanwhile **Mallorca**, lacking a harbour of any strategic significance, was having a much quieter time, though the islanders did choose the wrong side in the War of the Spanish Succession. Most of Spain favoured the French candidate, Philip of Anjou, but Catalunya and Mallorca preferred the Austrian Habsburg Charles III, who was supported by Britain and the Netherlands. Philip won, and promptly proceeded to strip the island of its title of kingdom and remove many of its historic rights. Otherwise, Mallorca was left pretty much untouched by the European conflicts that rippled around it during the early eighteenth century, but even so it did not prosper. Instead, it turned in on itself, becoming a caste- and priest-ridden backwater preoccupied with its own internal feuds. By the 1740s, however, this reactionary introspection was ruffled by more progressive elements, who, influenced by the **Enlightenment**, introduced liberal and rationalist ideas into island society. Oddly enough, the ideological conflict between Conservatives and Liberals focused on Ramón Llull (see p.82) with the former keen to have him beatified, the latter eager to denigrate his complex mysticism. The traditionalists won, but the bitterness of the dispute combined with its length (1749–77) divided the middle class into hostile camps

One other major change was Madrid's edict pronouncing **Castilian** as the official language of the Balearics in place of the local dialect of Catalan.

The nineteenth century

For both Mallorca and Menorca, the nineteenth century brought difficult times. Neglected and impoverished outposts, they were subject to droughts, famines and epidemics of cholera, bubonic plague and yellow fever. Consequently, the islanders became preoccupied with the art of survival rather than politics, and generally stayed out of the **Carlist** wars between the Liberals and the Conservatives, which so bitterly divided the Spanish mainland. Many islanders emigrated, some to Algeria after it was acquired by the French in 1830, others to Florida and California. The leading political figure of the period was the historian **Josep Quadrado**, who led the reactionary Catholic Union, which bombarded Madrid with petitions and greeted every Conservative success with enthusiastic demonstrations.

Matters began to improve towards the end of the nineteenth century, when agriculture, particularly almond cultivation, revived. Modern services, like gas and electricity, began to be installed and a regular steam-packet link was established between Mallorca and the mainland. Menorca also developed a thriving export industry in footwear thanks to the entrepreneurial Don Jeronimo Cabrisas, a Menorcan who had made his fortune in Cuba, and later supplied many of the boots worn by the troops in World War I. Around this time too, a **revival of Catalan culture**, led by the middle classes of Barcelona, stirred the Balearic bourgeoisie. In Palma in particular, Catalunyan novelists and poets were lauded, Catalan political groupings were formed, and the town was adorned with a series of splendid *Modernista* buildings.

Much less positively, Balearic politics became polarized between Conservative and Liberal groupings. This failure to create a political discourse between rival factions mirrored developments in the rest of Spain, and both here and on the mainland chronic instability was to be the harbinger of the military coup that ushered in the right-wing dictatorship of General Primo de Rivera in 1923.

The Spanish Civil War

During the **Spanish Civil War** (1936–39), Mallorca and Menorca supported opposing sides. General Goded made Mallorca an important base for the Fascists, but when General Bosch attempted to do the same on Menorca, his NCOs and men mutinied and, with the support of the civilian population, declared their support for the Republic. In the event – apart from a few bombing raids and an attempted Republican landing at Porto Cristo (see p.212) – the Balearics saw very little fighting. Nevertheless, the Menorcans were dangerously exposed towards the end of the war, when they were marooned as the last Republican stronghold. A peaceful conclusion was reached largely through the intervention of the British, who brokered the surrender of the island aboard *HMS Devonshire*. Franco's troops occupied Menorca in April 1939 and the *Devonshire* left with 450 Menorcan refugees.

1945 to 1995

The rich and famous discovered Mallorca's charms in the late nineteenth century – Jules Vernes, for one, liked to visit and both Edward VII and the German Kaiser regularly cruised its waters. The high-water mark of this elitist tourist trade was reached in the 1930s when the Argentinian poet Adan Diehl opened the *Hotel Formentor* (see p.175). Never knowingly outdone, Diehl advertised the hotel in lights on the Eiffel Tower and attracted guests such as Edward VIII, the Aga Khan and Winston Churchill – no mean guest list by any standard.

From such small and privileged beginnings, the Balearics' **tourist industry** mushroomed at an extraordinary rate after World War II. In 1950, Mallorca had just one hundred registered hotels and boarding houses, but by 1972 the total had risen to over 1600, and similarly the number of visitors to Menorca rose from 1500 in 1961 to half a million in 1973. It was an extraordinary phenomenon and the prodigious pace of development accelerated after the **death of Franco** in 1975, thereby further strengthening the local economy. One twist, however, was the relative price of real estate: traditionally, island landowners with coastal estates had given their younger children the poorer agricultural land near the seashore, but it was this land the developers wanted – and so younger siblings found their prospects transformed almost at a stroke. In more general terms, the burgeoning tourist economy pumped huge quantities of money into the Balearics and, by the 1990s, the archipelago had one of the highest per capita incomes in Spain, four times that of Extremadura for instance, and well above the EU average.

The Balearics also benefited from the political restructuring of Spain following the death of Franco. In 1978, the Spanish parliament, the Cortes, passed a new **constitution**, which reorganized the country on a more federal basis and allowed for the establishment of regional Autonomous Communities. In practice, the demarcation of responsibilities between central and regional governments has proved immensely problematic, leading to intense wrangling that continues unabated to this day, not least because the Madrid government has often been reliant for its majority in the Cortes on the support of the regionalists (primarily the Basques and the Catalans). Nonetheless, the Balearics, constituted as the **Comunidad Autónoma de las Islas Baleares** in 1983, have used their new-found independence to assert the primacy of their native Catalan language – now the main language of education – and to exercise a tighter local control of their economy.

1996 to present

After fourteen years in power, the Socialist PSOE was defeated in the Spanish **general election of 1996**, but the new Conservative regime, led by **José Maria Aznar**, was, despite its centralizing credentials, also reliant on the regionalists. Consequently, the trend towards **decentralization** continued with most government expenditure now coming under the control of the Autonomous Communities. In particular, the Balearic administration used these regionalized resources to upgrade a string of holiday resorts and modernize much of the archipelago's infrastructure. In part, this reflected a particular concern with Ibiza and Mallorca's somewhat tacky image and was accompanied by the imposition of stricter building controls, a number of environmental schemes and the spending of millions of pesetas on refurbishing the older, historical parts of Palma. On Menorca, the money also paid for the creation of a Parc Natural protecting the wetlands of S'Albufera d'es Grau and the adjacent coastline.

In addition, the Conservative-led Balearic administration made moves to curb tourist development, but in this they failed to keep pace with public sentiment – as exemplified by a string of large-scale **demonstrations** during 1998 and 1999. The demonstrations focused on four primary and inter-related concerns: the spiralling cost of real estate, foreign ownership of land (some twenty percent of Mallorca is now in foreign hands), untrammelled development and loutish behaviour in the budget resorts. This failure to keep abreast of popular feeling resulted in the defeat of the Conservatives in the **1999 regional elections** and their replacement by an unwieldy alliance of regionalists, socialists and greens committed to halting further tourist development in its tracks. As one of its spokesmen expressed it: "We need to dignify the tourist sector, not promote it as the cheapest in Europe with the idea that you can come here and do whatever you like." Faced with an annual influx of around eleven million holidaymakers, few islanders disagreed, and the coalition made significant progress, though they came unstuck when the tourist industry hit (comparatively) hard times in 2002 with an eight percent drop in the number of visitors.

The main reason for the decline was the economic travails of Germany, but Balearic anxieties focused on the so-called **tourist tax** imposed by the regional government in May 2002. The idea was to impose a modest tax on every visitor over twelve years of age and spend the money – potentially about thirty million euros a year – on environmental improvements. However, the tourist industry created a huge hullabaloo that undermined the Balearic administration, and the Conservatives, who had pledged to rescind the tax, were returned to office in the **regional elections of 2003**. This was a major setback for the environmentalist cause at a time when Spain's regionalists were already losing ground to Madrid – Aznar had won a second **general election in 2000**, but this time with an overall majority in the Cortes, thus firmly sidelining the regionalists.

Since 2003, the new Balearic administration has been remarkably gung-ho when it comes to **development**, ignoring environmental concerns by embarking, for example, on a large-scale road-building programme in the belief that more roads will create better motoring – never mind the disfiguring of agricultural land that this has involved. They have even become quite evangelical in their desire for development, most notably supporting a mass demonstration in favour of the expansion of port facilities at Ciutadella – an expansion that Menorca's PSOE-led council strongly opposes. Frankly, this is all very depressing, the only hope being that the Conservatives running the Balearics will ultimately become more conciliatory following the defeat of Aznar and his Conservatives in the 2004 Spanish general election. Other than that, regional elections loom in 2007.

A chronology of Spanish history

C11th–5th BC ▶	Phoenicians, Greeks and Celts invade Spain and inter-mingle with the native (Iberian) population.
C3rd BC ▶	Carthaginians conquer southeast Spain, incorporating the region within their Mediterranean empire.
C3rd–2nd BC ▶	Carthage and Rome wrestle for control of the Iberian Peninsula in three Punic Wars. Rome wins all three and their final act is the destruction of Carthage (in present-day Tunisia) in 146 BC.
C2nd BC ▶	Spain becomes part of the Roman Empire, its administrative capital established at Córdoba in 151 BC. The region's mines and granaries bring unprecedented prosperity, and roads, bridges and aqueducts are built to network the peninsula.
C1st AD ▶	Christianity makes rapid progress across Roman Spain.
264–76 ▶	Barbarian tribes, the Franks and the Suevi, ravage the peninsula.
414 ▶	The Visigoths reach Spain and become the dominant military force, with their capital at Toledo.
711 ▶	Islamic Moors (Arabs and Berbers from North Africa) invade and conquer the Visigoths' kingdom in a whirlwind campaign that lasts just seven years. However a Christian victory at the battle of Covadonga (722) halts the Moorish advance and leads to the creation of the kingdom of the Asturias – a Christian toehold on the northwest corner of the Iberian peninsula.
756 ▶	Abd ar-Rahman I proclaims the Emirate of Córdoba, confirming Moorish control over almost all of Spain.
778 ▶	The Holy Roman Emperor Charlemagne invades Spain from France, but is defeated. In the dash back across the Pyrenees, the Christian rearguard – led by Roland – is hacked to pieces at Roncesvalles, inspiring the epic poem the *Chanson de Roland*. Charlemagne's subsequent endeavours meet with more success and undermine Moorish control of Navarra and Catalunya.
C9th ▶	The Christian kingdoms of Catalunya and Navarra are founded.
C10th–early 11th ▶	The Emirate of Córdoba flourishes, its capital becoming the most prosperous and civilized city in Europe. Abd ar-Rahman III breaks with Baghdad to declare himself caliph of an independent western Islamic empire.

C11th ▶	The caliphate disintegrates into squabbling *taifas*, or petty fiefdoms. A local chieftain, El Cid, leads Christian forces against the Moors of Valencia, but his victories have no lasting effect. Independent Catalunya expands.
1037 ▶	Fernando I unites the kingdoms of Castile and León-Asturias.
1162 ▶	Alfonso II unites the kingdoms of Aragón and Catalunya.
C13th ▶	The pace of the Christian Reconquista accelerates after the kings of Navarra, Castile and Aragón combine to defeat the Muslims at the crucial battle of Las Navas de Tolosa in 1212. Subsequent Christian victories include the capture of Mallorca (1229), Córdoba (1236), Valencia (1238) and Seville (1248). The reconquered territories are mostly distributed amongst the Christian nobility in great estates, the *latifundia*. Men from the ranks also receive land, forming a lower, larger landowning class, the *hidalgos*.
1479 ▶	Castile and Aragón, the two pre-eminent Christian kingdoms, are united under Isabella I and Fernando V, the so-called Catholic Monarchs (Los Reyes Católicos). Spain subsequently emerges as a single political entity, with the Inquisition acting as a unifying force. The Inquisitors concentrate their attention on the Jews, expelling around 400,000 from Spain for refusing Christian baptism.
1492 ▶	The fall of Granada, the last Moorish kingdom. Columbus reaches the Americas.
1494 ▶	At the Treaty of Tordesillas, drawn up under the approving eye of the pope, Spain and Portugal divide the New World between them. Portugal gets Brazil and Spain takes the rest of modern-day Latin America.
1516–56 ▶	On the death of Fernando, his grandson Carlos I succeeds to the Spanish throne. Three years later Carlos also becomes Holy Roman Emperor – as Charles V – adding Germany, Austria and the Low Countries to his kingdom. Throughout his reign, he wages almost incessant war against his many enemies, principally the French, the Protestants and the Muslims of North Africa. He funds his campaigns with the gold and silver bullion that is pouring into Spain from the New World, where Spanish adventurers have conquered, colonized and exploited a vast new empire.
1519 ▶	Cortés lands in Mexico, seizing its capital two years later.
1532 ▶	Pizarro "discovers" Peru, capturing Cuzco the next year.
1539 ▶	Hernando de Soto stakes out Florida.

1541 ▷	Pedro de Valdivia founds Santiago, Chile.
1555 ▷	Charles V finally accepts he is unable to suppress the German Reformation and agrees to a compromise peace with the Protestants at the Treaty of Augsburg.
1556 ▷	Charles V abdicates. His son, Felipe II (Philip II), becomes king of Spain and its colonies, Naples, Milan and the Low Countries. His brother, Ferdinand I, becomes Holy Roman Emperor, ruling Germany and Austria. An ardent and autocratic Catholic, Felipe continues the militaristic policy of his father, but concentrates his efforts against the Protestants.
1567 ▷	The Protestants of the Low Countries rise against Felipe II, beginning a protracted conflict that will drain Spanish resources and exhaust the Low Countries.
1571 ▷	Spain wins control of the Mediterranean after defeating the Turkish fleet at Lepanto.
1581 ▷	Spain annexes Portugal.
1588 ▷	The English defeat Felipe II's Armada, eliminating Spain as a major sea power.
1598 ▷	Felipe II dies. His legacy is an enormous but bankrupt empire: Spain's great wealth, so ruthlessly extracted from its colonies, has been squandered in over seventy years of continuous warfare.
C17th ▷	The decline. Spain's international credibility is undermined by the loss of Portugal (1640) and the Netherlands (1648), emphasizing the country's military deterioration. Domestically, the poverty and suffering of the mass of the population – as compared with the opulence of the royal court – fuels regional discontent and insurrection. Cervantes publishes *Don Quixote* in 1605.
1701–14 ▷	Europe's nation states slug it out in the War of the Spanish Succession. The Bourbon (French) claimant – as opposed to that of the Holy Roman Emperor – wins out to become Felipe V. The British pick up Gibraltar and Menorca. As Spain declines, so it moves into the French sphere of influence.
1804 ▷	Napoleon crowned Emperor of France. Spain assists him in his war against England.
1805 ▷	The British navy, under Nelson, destroys the Franco-Spanish fleet at the Battle of Trafalgar.
1808 ▷	Napoleon arrests the Spanish king and replaces him with his brother, Joseph. This starts the War of Independence (otherwise known as the Peninsular War) in which the Spaniards fight the French army of occupation with the help of their new-found allies, the British.

1811 onwards ▶	The South American colonies take advantage of the situation to assert their independence, detaching themselves from Spain one by one.
1815 ▶	The end of the Napoleonic Wars.
C19th ▶	Further Spanish decline. The nineteenth century is dominated by the struggle between the forces of monarchist reaction and those of liberal constitutional reform. There are three bitter Carlist wars, named after one of the claimants to the throne (Don Carlos). The progressives finally triumph in the 1870s, but the new government's authority is brittle and Spanish society remains deeply divided. Elsewhere, Puerto Rico, the Philippines and Cuba shake off Spanish control with the help of the USA. Spain's American empire is at an end.
1900–31 ▶	Liberals and Conservatives fail to reach a secure constitutional consensus, keeping the country on a knife edge. Working-class political movements – of anarchist, Marxist and socialist inclination – grow in strength and stir industrial and political discontent. Spain stays neutral in World War I, but the success of the Russian Bolsheviks terrifies King Alfonso XIII and the bourgeoisie, who support the right-wing military coup engineered by General Primo de Rivera in 1923. Rivera dies in 1930 and the king abdicates in 1931 when anti-monarchist parties win the municipal elections.
1932–36 ▶	The new Republican government introduces radical left-of-centre reforms, but separatists (in Catalunya, Galicia and the Basque country), revolutionaries and rightists undermine its authority. Spain polarizes to the political left and right. Chaos and confusion prevail.
1936–39 ▶	The Spanish Civil War. General Francisco Franco leads a right-wing military rebellion against the Republican government. His Nationalists receive substantial support from Hitler and Mussolini. The Republicans get sporadic help from the Soviet Union and attract thousands of volunteers, organized in the International Brigades. The Civil War is vicious and bloody, ending in 1939 with a Fascist victory. Franco becomes head of state and bloody reprisals follow. Pope Pius XII congratulates the dictator on his "Catholic victory".
1939–75 ▶	Franco establishes a one-party state, backed up by stringent censorship and a vigorous secret police. By staying neutral during World War II, he survives the fall of Nazi Germany. In 1969, Franco nominates the grandson of Alfonso XIII, Juan Carlos, as his successor, but retains his vice-like grip on the country until his death in 1975.

Juan Carlos recognizes the need for political reform and helps steer the country towards a parliamentary system. He reinforces his democratic credentials by opposing the attempted coup of 1981, when Colonel Tejero leads a group of Guardia Civil officers loyal to Franco's memory in the storming of the Cortes (parliament). The coup fails.

In 1982, Felipe González's Socialist Workers' Party – the PSOE – is elected to office with the votes of nearly ten million Spaniards. It's an electoral landslide and the PSOE, buoyed up by the optimism of the times, promises change and progress. But González finds it hard to deliver and loses the enthusiasm of the left, his electoral power base. The left feels that González has followed a semi-monetarist policy, putting economic efficiency above social policies and rating the control of inflation as more urgent than the reduction of unemployment. Nevertheless, Spain's economy grows dramatically, the country becomes a respected member of the EU, and the PSOE attempts to deal with Spain's deep-seated separatist tendencies by permitting a large degree of regional autonomy. No effort is made to hunt down Franco's thugs – part of an accommodation between left and right designed to stop Spain from degenerating into a cycle of political revenge.

At the 1996 general election, the Conservative Popular Party led by José Aznar becomes the largest party in the Cortes, but does not get an overall majority. Aznar enlists the support of Catalan and Basque nationalist deputies to form an administration. The price is more powers to the regions. In government, Aznar moves his right-wing party to the political centre, mixing gestures to the unemployed (Spain's unemployment rate is one of the highest in the EU) and substantial investment in the country's infrastructure with privatization (of the national airline, Iberia, for one) and cuts in income tax. His measures are sufficiently well received for Aznar to win a second general election in March 2000 – and this time the Conservatives have an overall majority in the Cortes.

Aznar announces on the day after his election victory that he will seek to govern in conjunction with the regionalists, seeking alliances wherever he can and indicating that he is keen not to threaten the delicate consensus which has developed since the death of Franco. Aznar even acknowledges the role of the rival PSOE in modernizing Spain and pledges himself to keep to the political centre. In 2002, Aznar steers

Spain into the single-currency euro zone to general approval. Less encouragingly, Aznar fails to reach a rapprochement with the nationalists (and separatists) of the Basque region, and controversially sends troops to support the American occupation of Iraq in 2003. Meanwhile, José Luis Rodríguez Zapatero becomes leader of the PSOE.

The 2004 election ▶ At the start of 2004, the opinion polls show solid public support for the Aznar administration, suggesting that the general election scheduled for March will deliver a comfortable victory for the ruling PP and its new leader, Mariano Rajoy. Then, on March 11, three days before polling day, a series of bombs explode on Madrid's commuter trains, killing 192 people and injuring almost two thousand more. Rashly, the PP leadership immediately blame the Basque terrorist group ETA for the explosions, believing, so it would seem, that this false accusation will deflect attention away from the real reason for the attack – Spain's support for the Iraq war (ninety percent of Spaniards had been against it) – just long enough for the votes to be counted. It doesn't wash and by the time the polls open, many have come to believe – as was subsequently proved to be the case – that Islamic terrorists had blown the trains. The voters vent their political spleen against the PP, giving Zapatero and the PSOE an unexpected victory and the new premier's first act is to announce the immediate withdrawal of Spanish troops from Iraq.

2004 to today ▶ Since the election, Zapatero's record has been competent if unspectacular and he – like all of his immediate predecessors – has struggled to deal with the demands of the Basque and Catalan regionalists, both of whom are determined to further distance themselves from Spain as a whole. Already one of the most decentralized nations in Europe – the seventeen autonomous regional governments control three-quarters of all public expenditure – it is difficult to see where this tug-of-war will end, particularly when Spain's founding 1978 Constitution both recognizes the right of the "regions and nationalities" to autonomy but also declares "the indissoluble unity of the Spanish nation".

Flora and fauna

Despite their reputation as overdeveloped, package-holiday hotspots, Menorca and more especially Mallorca have much to offer birders and botanists alike. Separated from the Iberian Peninsula some fifty million years ago, the Balearic archipelago has evolved (at least in part) its own distinctive flora and fauna, with further variations between each of the islands. Among the wildlife, it's the raptors inhabiting the mountains of northwest Mallorca – particularly the black vulture – which attract much of the attention, but there are other pleasures too, especially the migratory birds which gather on the islands' saltpans and marshes in April and May and from mid-September to early October. The islands are also justifiably famous for their fabulous range of wild flowers and flowering shrubs.

Some of the islands' most important habitats have, however, been threatened by the developers. This has spawned an influential conservation group, **GOB** (Grup Balear d'Ornitologia i Defensa de la Naturalesa; ⓦwww.gobmallorca .com), which has launched several successful campaigns in recent years. It helped save the S'Albufera wetlands from further development; played a leading role in the black vulture re-establishment programme; successfully lobbied to increase the penalties for shooting protected birds; and won its fight to protect and preserve Cabrera island.

The account below of the islands' flora and fauna serves as a general introduction, and includes mention of several important birding sites, cross-referenced to the descriptions given throughout the book. For more specialist information, some recommended **field guides** are listed on p.335.

Habitats

The Balearic islands are a continuation of the Andalucian mountains of the Iberian Peninsula, from which they are separated by a submarine trench never less than 80km wide and up to 1500m deep. **Mallorca** comprises three distinct geographical areas with two ranges of predominantly limestone hills falling either side of a central plain, **Es Pla**. Mallorca's northwest coast is dominated by the **Serra de Tramuntana**, a slim, ninety-kilometre-long range of wooded hills and rocky peaks, which is fringed by tiny coves and precipitous sea-cliffs; it reaches its highest point at Puig Major (1447m). Also edged by sea-cliffs is the **Serres de Llevante**, a range of more modest hills that runs parallel to the island's east shore and rises to 509m at the Santuari de Sant Salvador.

Menorca has less topographical diversity, dividing into two distinct but not dramatically different zones. The **northern half** of the island comprises rolling sandstone uplands punctuated by wide, shallow valleys and occasional peaks, the highest of which is Monte Toro at 357m. To the **south** lie undulating limestone lowlands and deeper valleys. Steep sea-cliffs and scores of rocky coves trim the island's north and south shores.

Mallorca and Menorca share a temperate Mediterranean **climate**, with winter frosts a rarity, but there are significant differences between the two. The Serra de Tramuntana protects the rest of Mallorca from the prevailing winds that blow from the north and also catches most of the rain. Menorca, on the other hand, has no mountain barrier to protect it from the cold dry wind (the Tramuntana) which buffets the island from the north, giving much of the island's vegetation a wind-blown look, and obliging farmers to protect their crops with stone walls.

Mallorcan flora

The characteristic terrain of Mallorca up to around 700m is **garrigue**, partly forested open scrubland where the island's native trees – Aleppo pines, wild olives, holm oaks, carobs and dwarf palms – intermingle with imported species like ash, elm and poplar. Between 700m and 950m, the *garrigue* gives way to **maquis**, a scrubland of rosemary, laurel, myrtle and broom interspersed with swaths of bracken. Higher still is a rocky terrain that can only support the sparsest of vegetation, such as an assortment of hardy grasses and low-growth rosemary.

Across much of the island, this indigenous vegetation has been destroyed by cultivation. However, the **Aleppo pine** and the evergreen **holm oak** – which traditionally supplied acorns for pigs, wood for charcoal and bark for tanning – are still common, as is the **carob tree**, which prefers the hottest and driest parts of the island. Arguably the archipelago's most handsome tree, the carob boasts leaves of varying greenness and bears conspicuous fruits – large pods which start green, but ripen to black-brown. The **dwarf palm**, with its sharp lance-like foliage, is concentrated around Pollença, Alcúdia and Andratx. The **wild olive** is comparatively rare (and may not be indigenous), but the cultivated variety, which boasts silver-grey foliage and can grow up to 10m in height, is endemic and has long been a mainstay of the local economy. There are also **orange** and **lemon** orchards around Sóller and innumerable **almond** trees, whose pink and white blossom adorns much of the island in late January and early February.

Mallorca has a wonderful variety of **flowering shrubs**. There are too many to list here in any detail, but look out for the deep blue flowers of the **rosemary**; the reddish bloom of the **lentisk** (or mastic tree); the bright yellow **broom** which begins blossoming in March; the many types of **tree heather**; and the autumn-flowering **strawberry tree**, found especially around Ca'n Picafort. **Rockroses** are also widely distributed, the most common members of the group being the spring-flowering, grey-leafed cistus, with its velvety leaves and pink flowers, and the narrow-leafed cistus whose bloom is white.

In spring and autumn the fields, verges, woods and cliffs of Mallorca brim with **wild flowers**. There are several hundred species and only in the depths of winter – from November to January – are all of them dormant. Well-known flowers include marigolds, daisies, violets, yellow primroses, gladioli, poppies, hyacinths, several kinds of cyclamen, the resinous St John's wort with its crinkled deep-green leaves and, abundant in the pine woods near the sea and in the mountains, many types of orchid. Two common mountain plants are the pampas-like grass **Ampelodesmos mauritanica**, giant clumps of which cover the hillsides, and a local variety of the sarsaparilla, **Smilax balearica**, which flourishes in limestone crevices where its sharp thorns are something of a hazard for walkers. Other common and prominent plants are the giant-sized **agave** (century plant), an imported amaryllid with huge spear-shaped, leathery leaves of blue-grey coloration, which produces a massive flower spike every ten years (just before it dies). There's also the distinctive **asphodel**, whose tall spikes sport clusters of pink or white flowers from April to June. The asphodel grows on overgrazed or infertile land and its starch-rich tubers were once used by shoemakers to make glue. Another common sight is the **prickly pear**, traditionally grown behind peasants' houses as a windbreak and toilet wall. A versatile plant, the smell of the prickly pear deflects insects (hence its use round toilets) and its fruit is easy to make into pig food or jam.

Finally, many islanders maintain splendid **gardens** and here you'll see species that flourish throughout the Mediterranean, most famously bougainvilleas, oleanders, geraniums and hibiscus.

Mallorcan birds

Mallorca's diverse **birdlife** has attracted ornithologists for decades. The island boasts a whole batch of resident Mediterranean specialists and these are supplemented by migrating flocks of North European birds that descend on the island in their thousands during the spring and autumn.

The limestone **Serra de Tramuntana** mountains crimping the northwest coast are a haven for birds of prey. The massive black vulture is the real star here. This rare and impressive raptor, with its near three-metre wingspan, breeds in small numbers, but its size and residency means there's a reasonable chance of a sighting. The Puig Roig area (see p.159) is an excellent place to see this vulture, but note that during late spring and summer there are sometimes access restrictions to the bird's active sea-cliff nesting areas. The booted eagle is another mountain highlight, and there's a supporting cast of ospreys, red kites, Eleonora's falcons, kestrels and peregrines.

The **Embassament de Cúber** (Cúber Reservoir; see p.156), just west of Lluc, provides a natural amphitheatre from where up to ten species of bird of prey can be seen, including ospreys and red-footed falcons hunting over the water itself. The colourful rock thrush breeds in the quarry just west of the reservoir dam and on the nearby crags. The **sea-cliffs** of the western coast are the breeding grounds of shearwaters, Mediterranean shag, storm petrels and Audouin's gulls. The most impressive seabird colonies are on the **Illa Dragonera**, off Sant Elm (see p.147), which is home to all these birds as well as over 75 pairs of Eleonora's falcons. The district's seabirds may also be viewed from **La Trapa**, a small headland nature reserve of pristine coastal *garrigue* that is owned and operated by GOB. The reserve is about an hour's walk north of Sant Elm, but the going is fairly tough. A similarly good spot for seabirds is **Cap de Formentor** (see p.176), at the other end of the island, and birds from here wander the bays of Pollença and Alcúdia.

Characteristic birds of the island's **scrubland** can also be found around the Embalse de Cúber, including a variety of warblers and small songbirds, such as nightingales, larks, pipits and colourful chats. Another area of rich scrubland is the **Vall de Bóquer** (see p.172), near Pollença. Thoughtless development has harmed the olive groves and almond orchards at the base of the valley, but the Bóquer remains a migration hotspot, its pine avenues and denser wooded slopes hosting firecrests and crossbills among more familiar woodland birds like tits and woodpigeons. If you venture to the north end of the valley, you should be rewarded with the colourful delights of Marmora's warbler and the blue rock thrush. In spring, hundreds of bee-eaters can be heard and seen in and around the valley, as these stunning birds move through to breed elsewhere in the Mediterranean.

Wetlands are a magnet for birds in the arid climate of the Mediterranean. Mallorca boasts the most important birdwatching spot in the whole of the Balearics in the marshes of the **Parc Natural de S'Albufera** (see p.185). Here, resident species are augmented by hundreds of migrating birds, who visit to find fresh water after their long journey north or south. Amongst scores of species, the shorter grasses shelter moorhens, coots, crakes and the recently re-introduced purple gallinule, while the reeds hide healthy numbers of several species of heron, bittern and egret as well as the occasional flamingo. A wide variety of small wading birds visit the marsh too, including the distinctively long-legged black-winged stilt and the abundant Kentish plover. The open water is popular with ducks and in spring large numbers of terns may be seen. In winter the variety of duck species increases and kingfishers are common. This rich diversity of birdlife attracts birds of prey and this is as good a place as any to see ospreys and marsh harriers. In addition, over one hundred Eleonora's falcons have been seen together over the marsh in spring. Among the smaller birds, the spring dusk and dawn choruses provided by wetland warblers such as Cetti's, moustached and great reed are unforgettable. Neither is the sound of birds restricted to the daytime. At night, listen for the plaintive single note of the scops owl against a backdrop of warblers, crakes and crickets.

The scops owl can also be heard in the south of the island, usually preferring almond groves and olive clumps. Generally speaking, the south is not as rich in birdlife as other parts of the island, the main exception being the **saltpan** habitat of the **Salines de Llevant**, near Colònia de Sant Jordi (see p.224). Here, a wide variety of migrant wading birds, wintering duck and small flocks of wintering flamingoes and cranes can be seen. The site also has a breeding flock of over a hundred black-winged stilts in summer and the abundance of prey attracts raptors, most frequently marsh harriers, kestrels and ospreys. The pans also host terns and Audouin's gulls: this red-billed gull is a Mediterranean specialist and can be chanced upon at many coastal spots but the southern saltpans are favoured.

The country lanes that lattice Mallorca's **central plain**, Es Pla, also have their own distinctive birdlife. In spring and summer, the calls and songs of small birds like serins, corn buntings and Sardinian warblers and the ubiquitous fan-tailed warbler create a busy backdrop to hot, lazy afternoons. Nightingales seem to be everywhere and their rich song leaves a lasting impression. In the shade of the abundant olive groves, the subtly plumaged wryneck can be found all year, often sharing this ancient landscape with the striking hoopoe.

Other Mallorcan fauna

Mallorca's surviving **mammals** are an uninspiring bunch. The wild boar and red fox were eliminated early in the twentieth century, leaving a motley crew of mountain goats, wild sheep, pine martens, genets, weasels and feral cats, as well as commonplace smaller mammals such as hedgehogs, rabbits, hares and shrews.

As far as **reptiles** go, there are four types of snake – all hard to come by – and two species of gecko (or broad-toed lizard): the lowland-living wall gecko and the mountain-dwelling disc-fingered version. With any luck, you'll spot them as they heat up in the sun, but they move fast since warm gecko is a tasty morsel for many a bird. Off the south coast of Mallorca, the desolate island of Cabrera (see p.225) has a large concentration of the rare, blue-bellied **Lilford's wall lizard**.

Among **amphibians**, Mallorca has a healthy frog population, concentrated in its marshlands but also surviving in its mountain pools (up to around 800m). There are also three types of toad, of which the **Mallorcan midwife toad**, hanging on in the northern corner of the island, is the rarest. With no natural predators, its evolution involved a reduction in fecundity (it produces only a quarter of the number of eggs laid by its mainland relative) and the loss of its poison glands. This was fair enough until someone introduced the viperine snake to the island and, in the ensuing slaughter, the midwife toads were all but wiped out – only about five hundred pairs remain.

Common **insects** include grasshoppers and cicadas, whose summertime chirping is so evocative of warm Mediterranean nights, as well as over two hundred species of moth and around thirty types of **butterfly**. Some of the more striking butterflies are red admirals, which are seen in winter, and the clouded yellows and painted ladies of spring. One of the more unusual species is the two-tailed pasha, a splendidly marked gold-and-bronze butterfly that flits around the coast in spring and late summer, especially in the vicinity of strawberry trees.

Menorcan flora

Far flatter than its neighbour, Menorca's indigenous vegetation is almost all **garrigue**, though intensive cultivation has reduced the original forest cover to a fraction of its former size – nowadays only about fifteen percent of the island is wooded. Native trees are the holm oak, the dwarf palm, the carob and, commonest of all, the **Aleppo pine**, which has bright green spines, silvery twigs and ruddy-brown cones. Olive trees are endemic and illustrate the effects of the prevailing Tramuntana, with grove upon grove almost bent double under the weight of the wind.

Menorca's soils nourish a superb range of **flowering shrubs** and **wild flowers**. There is less variety than on Mallorca, but the islands have many species in common. In addition, Menorca boasts a handful of species entirely to itself, the most distinguished of them being the dwarf shrub **Daphne rodriquezii**, a purple-flowering evergreen, present on the cliffs of the northeast coast. In addition, the cliffs of much of the coast have a flora uniquely adapted to the combination of limestone yet saline soils. Here, **aromatic inula**, a shrubby perennial with clusters of yellow flowers, grows beside the **common caper**, with its red pods and purple seeds, and the **sea aster**.

Menorcan birds

The varied **birdlife** of Menorca includes birds of prey, wetland specialists, seabirds, waders and characteristic Mediterranean warblers, larks and pipits, but perhaps the most striking feature is the tameness of many of the birds – presumably because there is less **shooting** here than in almost any other part of the Mediterranean.

There are several ornithological hotspots, but wherever you are birds of prey should be evident. Of these, the Egyptian vulture is the most impressive; there are around a hundred of them, the only resident population in Europe. Red kites, booted eagles and ospreys can also be seen year round, and they are joined by marsh and hen harriers in winter. Peregrines, kestrels and, in winter, sparrowhawks complete the more reliable raptors, although in spring and autumn several others – such as the honey buzzard and black kite – may appear. **Monte Toro** (see p.267), the highest point on Menorca, is as good a vantage point for birds of prey as any.

The island's best birdwatching spot is the marshland, reeds and *garigue* (partly forested scrubland) fringing the lake of **S'Albufera**, near Es Grau (see p.258), which is itself part of the larger Parc Natural S'Albufera that extends north to Cap de Favaritx. The lake and its environs are popular with herons and egrets, the most elegant of wetland birds. Over a year, little and cattle egrets, purple, grey, night and squacco herons will all be seen, too. Booted eagles are also common, flying over the area, and the muddy parts of the marsh attract many smaller waders in spring, the leggy black-winged stilt in summer. The lake itself hosts several thousand ducks in winter. The nearby pine woodland, next to the beach at Es Grau, is used by night herons that rest high in the trees by day and then move onto the marsh at dusk. Also at dusk, listen out for the plaintive single note of the scops owl against a backdrop of warblers, crakes and crickets;

The list below describes many of the most distinctive **birds** to be found on Mallorca and/or Menorca. We have given the English name, followed in italics by the Latin, a useful cross-reference for those without a British field guide.

Serin (*Serinus serinus*). Menorca. Winter visitor. Tiny, green-and-yellow canary-like bird of the finch family, with characteristically buoyant flight. Appears in virtually any habitat.

Fan-tailed warbler (*Cisticola juncidis*). Mallorca and Menorca. Very common breeding resident. Typical small brown bird, but with very distinctive "zit-zit-zit" song, usually uttered in flight. Prefers wetland areas.

Nightingale (*Luscinia megarhynchos*) Mallorca and Menorca. Common breeding summer visitor. Rich-brown-coloured robin-like bird with astonishingly rich, vigorous and varied song. Prefers to sing from small bushes, often deep inside and out of sight.

Wryneck (*Jynx torquilla*). Mallorca and Menorca. Mallorca: breeding resident. Menorca: spring, autumn and winter visitor. Medium-sized bird with a complex pattern of brown, grey and lilac plumage. A member of the woodpecker family. Favours olive groves.

Hoopoe (*Upupa epops*). Mallorca and Menorca. Common breeding resident. Pigeon-sized, pinky-brown bird with black head-crest. It is named after its distinctive "upupu upupu" call. Its wings sport a complex black and white barring, creating a striking sight when in flight. Favours open areas with some trees nearby for nesting.

Black vulture (*Aegypius monachus*). Mallorca. Breeding resident only in the northern mountains. Massive, dark, powerful and solitary raptor with a wingspan approaching three metres. The most distinctive of the islands' birds. Probably fewer than fifty remain.

Booted eagle (*Hieraaetus pennatus*). Mallorca and Menorca. Resident breeder. A small and very agile eagle, similar in size to a buzzard. Prefers the mountains, but happily hunts over scrub and grasslands.

Eleonora's falcon (*Falco eleonorae*); Mallorca and Menorca: Mallorca: fairly common breeding summer visitor. Menorca: spring and autumn migrant. Dark, slim, elegant falcon. Hunts small birds and large insects with fantastic speed and agility. Often seen hunting insects near water.

Rock thrush (*Monticola saxatilis*). Mallorca and Menorca. Mallorca: breeding summer visitor. Menorca: spring and autumn migrant. Beautifully coloured rock- and quarry-loving thrush. Males have a pale blue head and orangey-red breast and tail. Females are a less distinctive brown and cream.

Blue rock thrush (*Monticola solitarius*) Mallorca and Menorca. Common breeding resident. Blue-coloured thrush, recalling a deep-blue starling. Can be found in any rugged, rocky areas at any time of year.

Firecrest (*Regulus ignicapillus*). Mallorca and Menorca. Common breeding resident. The smallest bird on the islands. This tiny pale green bird is named after its vivid orange and yellow crown. Abundant in any woodland.

Crossbill (*Loxia curvirostra*). Mallorca. Abundant breeding resident. The vivid red males and the lemon-green females of this bulky finch have an unusual crossed bill and a distinctive parrot-like appearance. The bill is adapted to extract seeds from pine cones.

Marmora's warbler (*Sylvia sarda*). Mallorca. Common breeding resident. A small blue-ish grey warbler with a long, often-upright tail and distinctive red eye-ring. Prefers the bushy cover of the coastal lowlands.

Purple gallinule (*Porphyrio porphyrio*). Mallorca. Breeding resident only at Mallorca's S'Albufera. This purple-blue oddity was re-introduced to its marshland habitat at S'Albufera in 1991. It is now well established. Its incredibly long feet and swollen red bill make this hen-like bird very distinctive.

Little egret (*Egretta garzetta*). Mallorca and Menorca. Mallorca: breeding resident. Menorca: spring and autumn migrant. Long-legged, elegant white wading bird. In summer has beautiful long white plumes trailing from the back of its head. Breeds at S'Albufera only. A wetland specialist, though well adapted to treetop life.

Little bittern (*Ixobrychus minutes*). Menorca. Spring and autumn visitor. Secretive wetland specialist. This is the smallest member of the heron family breeding in Europe, measuring little more than 30cm tall. The male is an attractive pink-cream colour with contrasting black wings and cap. Males advertise themselves with a far-carrying gruff basal note, repeated regularly.

Purple heron (*Ardea purpurea*). Mallorca. Breeding summer visitor. Large, slender heron fond of reed beds. The male plumage has beautiful purple and rich-brown tones. Despite its size it can be rather elusive, hiding deep inside the reeds.

Black-winged stilt (*Himantopus himantopus*). Mallorca and Menorca. Mallorca: common breeding resident; Menorca: summer visitor. Incredibly long-legged black-and-white wader. Its medium size is somewhat extended by its long, straight, fine, red bill. Can appear anywhere there is mud, but particularly common on saltpans.

Kentish plover (*Charadrius alexandrinus*). Mallorca and Menorca. Mallorca: common breeding resident. Menorca: spring and autumn visitor. Small, delicate wader of saltpans and marshes. Its pale-brown upper body contrasts with its gleaming white head-collar and underparts.

Cetti's warbler (*Cettia cetti*). Mallorca and Menorca. Very common breeding resident. This rather nondescript, chunky, wren-like warbler prefers dense thickets close to water. It possesses an astonishingly loud explosive song: "chet-chet-chet-chetchetchet".

Great reed warbler (*Acrocephalus arundinaceus*). Mallorca and Menorca. Breeding summer visitor. This large, unstreaked, brown warbler can be found in significant numbers where there is reed and marsh vegetation. Its song is a loud and harsh mixture of unusual grating, croaking and creaking noises.

Scops owl (*Otus scops*). Mallorca and Menorca. Common breeding resident. This tiny owl (only 20cm tall) is stubbornly nocturnal. At night, its plaintive "tyoo" note is repeated every few seconds often for long (monotonous) periods. Groves, plantations, small clumps of trees, conifer woodland and even gardens can host this bird.

Greater flamingo (*Phoenicopterus ruber*). Mallorca and Menorca. Winter/spring visitor in small numbers. The unmistakable silhouette of this leggy wader with roseate wings, bill and legs can be seen on any wetland in spring. In winter, it's confined to the southern reaches of Mallorca – and especially the S'Albufera wetland.

Great white egret (*Egretta alba*). Mallorca and Menorca. Winter visitor. This marshland specialist is really just a large version of the commoner Little Egret – an all-white, tall, elegant heron.

Audouin's gull (*Larus audouinii*). Mallorca and Menorca. Resident breeder. This rare gull favours the rocky coastline of both islands. It's the size and light-grey colour of a typical "seagull" but boasts a rather splendid red bill. Unfortunately it takes three years for birds to reach this adult plumage and prior to this they are much less distinctive.

Bee-eater (*Merops apiaster*). Mallorca and Menorca. Mallorca: common spring visitor, rare summer breeder. Menorca: breeding summer visitor. A brightly coloured, medium-sized bird, with a slim body, long pointed wings and slightly de-curved bill. As if the iridescent green, orange, yellow and blue of this bird aren't distinctive enough, its bubbling "pruuk" call is instantly recognizable. It prefers open, relatively flat, rugged countryside.

Egyptian vulture (*Neophron percnopterus*). Mallorca and Menorca. Mallorca: rare migrant. Menorca: breeding resident. Medium-sized raptor with small, rather pointed protruding head and featherless face. Wings held flat when soaring.

Cattle egret (*Bubulcus ibis*). Mallorca and Menorca. Mainly winter visitor. This small heron-like wader is a regular winter visitor to the larger Balearic marshes. In winter it is white, but is distinguished from the Little Egret by its stubby all-yellow bill and stockier gait.

Night heron (*Nycticorax nycticorax*). Mallorca and Menorca. Mallorca: small resident population, increasing in summer with migrants. Menorca: spring and autumn migrant. Adults of this stocky, medium-sized heron are an attractive combination of black, grey and white. In contrast, younger birds up to three years old are a rather nondescript brown with cream speckling. This water bird is most active at night or dawn and dusk. By day they roost in the tree canopy or large bushes.

Stone curlew (*Burhinus oedicnemus*). Mallorca and Menorca. Resident breeder, more common in summer. Thick-set wader that prefers dry rolling countryside to mud. Has a large, yellow, almost reptilian eye. Largely dull brown with some darker streaking, but with relatively distinctive long yellow legs. When in flight, its strikingly black and white wings become apparent.

Cory's shearwater (*Calonectris diomedea*). Mallorca and Menorca. Common breeder on offshore islands, but seen regularly all along the coast from March to August. Fairly large seabird. Like all the shearwaters, this bird flies close to the sea's surface with stiff outstretched wings. This pattern of flight as well as its size (nearly half a metre long with a wing span of more than a metre) are its most distinctive features as its plumage is rather boring. At sea it appears dark-backed and dirty-white below. A close view should reveal some yellow on the bill and a white eye ring. Thousands breed on offshore islands across the Balearics and at sea they will often mix with the smaller pale brown Mediterranean shearwater.

and, most strikingly, the rich-toned song of the nightingale. The tiny firecrest is common in the woodland, and in the spring this whole area comes alive with hundreds of migrants.

There are smaller marshes elsewhere on the island and those at Cala Tirant in the north and Son Bou in the south are very good for birds. The wetland at **Son Bou** (see p.266) holds the island's largest reed-bed and the characteristic species of such a rich habitat are the noisy great reed warbler, moustached warbler and Cetti's warbler. The wetland at **Cala Tirant** (see p.261) can be just as prolific and the sandy area just inland of the beach is a first-rate place to see the spectacular bee-eater, which breeds in several small colonies on the island. Nearby, the **Cap de Cavalleria** (see p.262), at the northern tip of the island, attracts the curious-looking stone curlew, several larks and pipits; and ospreys can often be seen fishing in the cape's **Port de Sanitja** (see p.262). Another special Balearic bird is the distinctive red-billed Audouin's gull, one of the world's rarest. A good place to see these is just off the coast by the lighthouse at the end of Cap de Cavalleria, where Mediterranean shags and shearwaters are also regularly seen. Audouin's gulls can also be seen in and around Maó.

The lush vegetation in the bottom of the Algendar Gorge, just inland of **Cala Santa Galdana** (see p.272), is a magnet for small birds and a perfect setting to hear nightingales and the short explosive song of Cetti's warbler. Above the gorge, booted eagles, Egyptian vultures and Alpine swifts nest. The ravine also attracts a wonderful array of butterflies.

Finally, although the barren, stony landscape of the northwest coast may seem an unpromising environment, **Punta de S'Escullar** is the site of one of the largest colonies of Cory's shearwaters in the western Mediterranean. Thousands return to their cliffside burrows in the late afternoon throughout the summer. This rugged terrain also hosts the attractive blue rock thrush and migrant chats, wheatears and black redstarts. Pallid swifts and crag martins also breed on the cliffs.

Other Menorcan fauna

Menorca's **mammals** are a low-key bunch, an undistinguished assortment of weasels, feral cats, hedgehogs, rabbits, hares, mice and shrews. The one highlight is the island's **reptiles**. Of the four species of Balearic lizard, Menorca has three. There are two types of wall lizard – Lilford's, a green, black and blue version, and the olive-green and black-striped Italian lizard – as well as the Moroccan rock lizard, with olive skin or reticulated blue-green coloration.

Common **insects** include grasshoppers and cicadas as well as over a hundred species of moth and around thirty types of **butterfly**. Three of the more striking butterflies are red admirals, which are seen in winter, and the clouded yellows and painted ladies, seen in spring.

Writers on Mallorca

Mallorca and Menorca have produced few writers of note, but Mallorca has been the subject of many foreign jottings, beginning with the well-heeled travellers who nosed around the island in the nineteenth century. The most distinguished of these was **George Sand**, the partner of Frédéric Chopin, who wintered here in 1838–39. More recently, Mallorca has been used as a backdrop in the works of several English-language thriller writers, with Agatha Christie setting one of her short stories here, and has also produced **Tomás Graves**, who was born and raised on the island and is fluent in its language and culture.

George Sand

George Sand (1804–76) was the pen name of the French aristocrat Armandine Lucile Aurore Dupin, the Baroness Dudevant. She married the eponymous baron in 1822, and left him nine years later for the literary life of Paris, where she embraced the Republican cause. A prolific author, dramatist and journalist, Sand campaigned against conservatism in its many forms and became a well-known figure in French political circles. She travelled occasionally and one of her excursions, in the company of her partner, the pianist and composer Frédéric Chopin, was in 1838 to the then backward and remote island of Mallorca (for more on their visit, see p.136). This extract is from Sand's memoir of the time, A Winter in Majorca.

A visit to Valldemossa

It is three leagues from Palma to Valldemossa, but three Majorcan leagues, which can't be covered driving fast in under three hours. The road rises imperceptibly for the first two. During the third it enters the mountains and leads up a well-paved slope (possibly a former work of the Carthusian monks), but very narrow, horribly steep, and more dangerous than the rest of the way.

There one has one's first chance to admire the Alpine part of Majorca. But it is not enough that the mountains rise up on either side of the gorge, and that the torrent leaps from rock to rock; only in the heart of winter do these regions take on the wild, untamed aspect that the Majorcans attribute to them. In the month of December, and in spite of recent rains, the torrent was still a delightful stream, which glided along among tufts of grass and clusters of flowers; the mountain was in a smiling mood, and the valley in which Valldemossa nestled opened before us like a garden in spring.

To reach the Cartuja you have to leave the coach, for it is impossible for any vehicle to clamber up the stony track that leads to it. It is a fascinating approach with its sudden twists and bends among magnificent trees, and with wonderful views that are unfolded at every step, and increase in beauty the higher one rises. I have seen nothing more pleasing; nor at the same time more melancholy than these prospects where the green holm oak, the carob tree, the pine, the olive, the poplar and the cypress mix their various hues in dense masses of foliage, veritable abysses of verdure amongst which the torrent pursues its course through thickets of gorgeous richness and inimitable attraction. I will never forget a certain bend in the defile from where, turning round, one can see high up on a mountain one of those pretty Arabic-type cottages, half-hidden among the leaves of the prickly pears, and, projecting its silhouette into the air, a great palm tree leaning over the chasm. When the mud and fog of Paris overwhelm me with depression, I shut my eyes and see again, as in a dream, that mountain full of greenery, those bare rocks, and that solitary palm, alone in a rose-coloured sky.

The Valldemossa cordillera rises up in a series of plateaux, becoming narrower and narrower until they form a kind of funnel, surrounded by high mountains and shut in on the north by the slope of the last plateau, at the entrance to which stands the monastery.

The Carthusian monks, through the work of years, have modified the ruggedness of this romantic spot. At the head of the valley where it reaches the hillside, they have made a vast garden, surrounded by walls that do not block the view, and to which a belt of cypress trees, in pyramidal form and disposed irregularly in pairs, give an appearance appropriate to a stage-set graveyard.

This garden, with palm and almond trees, occupied the whole inclined background of the valley, and rises in a succession of wide terraces on the lower slopes of the mountain. By moonlight, and when its irregularity is masked by the darkness, it could be taken for an amphitheatre carved out for the battles of giants. In the centre and under a group of lovely palms, a stone-built reservoir collects the water from the mountain springs, and distributes it to the lower terraces by means of paved channels, similar to those which irrigate the environs of Barcelona. These works are on too great a scale and too ingenious not to have been the creation of the Moors. They are spread over the whole interior of the island, and the channels that start at the garden of the Carthusian monks, skirt the bed of the torrent and take running water to Palma at all seasons.

The Cartuja, situated at the highest point of this gorge, looks on the north side over an extensive valley, which widens out and rises in a gentle slope to the coastal cliffs, whose base is battered and eroded by the sea. One arm of the cordillera points towards Spain, and the others towards the Orient. From this picturesque Carthusian monastery therefore, the sea can be glimpsed or sensed on two sides. Whilst its roar is audible to the north, it can be descried to the south like a fine, brilliant line beyond the descending mountain slopes and the immense plain which is revealed to the eye. It is a surpassing picture, framed in the foreground by dark, pine-covered crags; beyond that by the sharply outlined profiles of mountains set off by superb trees; and in the background by the rounded humps of hills, which the setting sun gilds with the warmest shades, and on whose crests one can still distinguish, from a distance of a league, the microscopic outlines of the trees, as fine as the antennae of butterflies, as black and distinct as a trace of Chinese ink on a backdrop of sparkling gold. …

In accordance with the Carthusian rule, thirteen monks, including the superior, lived in the Cartuja in Valldemosa. It had escaped the decree which in 1836 ordered the demolition of monasteries occupied by less than a dozen persons conjointly; but, like all the others, they [the monks] had been dispersed and the convent suppressed, to be considered, as it were, the property of the State. The Majorcan government, not knowing what to do with these immense buildings, had decided to let the cells to persons who would care to occupy them, in the expectation that time and negligence would cause the place to decay and fall down. In spite of the rents being extremely moderate, the villagers in Valldemossa had not chosen to take advantage of the offer, possibly because of their extreme piety and the affection they had felt for the monks, and perhaps also through superstitious fear; this did not prevent them going there to dance on carnival nights, although they did not cease to look very much askance at our irreverent presence among those venerable walls.

Nevertheless, the Cartuja was inhabited during the summer months by middle-class people from Palma who, at that altitude and under the monastery's thick arches, undoubtedly found the air fresher than on the plain or in the city. But with the approach of winter, the cold drove them away, and when we lived in it, the Cartuja had as its only inhabitants, besides myself and my family, the apothecary, the sacristan, and Maria Antonia.

Maria Antonia was a kind of housekeeper who had come from the mainland I believe to get away from squalor and poverty, and she had rented a cell in order to exploit the transient occupants of the Cartuja. Her cell was located next to ours and we made use of it as a kitchen, while she declared herself to be our factotum and help. She had been good-looking and was elegant, clean in appearance and pleasant. She said she came from a good family, had delightful manners, a nice voice, and an ingratiating demeanour. She exercised a very curious sort of hospitality; she would offer her services to the new arrivals and refuse, with an offended air and almost turning pale at the idea, any kind of recompense for her attentions. She did it, she asserted, for the love of God, to be of assistance, and with the sole object of winning the friendship of her neighbours. Her entire furniture consisted of a small folding bed, a foot-warmer, two wicker chairs, a crucifix, and some earthenware crockery, all of which she put at our disposal with great generosity, allowing us to accommodate our new servant, and store our pots and pans, in her dwelling.

But she would immediately take charge of all your belongings, and reserve for herself the best of your finery and food. I have never seen a godly person so fond of her stomach, nor fingers so quick to dip down into a boiling pot without getting burnt, nor a throstle [thrush] so supple to swallow the coffee and sugar of her dear lodgers, stealthily, whilst she hummed a popular air or a bolero. It would have been interesting and amusing, if one had been completely disinterested in the matter, to see the good Antonia, Catalina the queer witch-like Valldemossa woman who was our maid, and the *niña* (little girl), a small dishevelled monstrosity who acted as our errand girl, quarrelling among themselves over our food. It was the hour of the Angelus and the three never failed to recite it. The two elders, praying in unison, put their hands into every dish, and the small one, as she answered *Amen*, succeeded in palming some chop or candied fruit with unequalled dexterity. It was quite something to watch and worthwhile pretending not to notice; but when the rains cut communication with Palma and our provisions diminished, the "assistance" of Maria Antonia and her party became less pleasing; and my children and I found ourselves in the role of sentinel and relieving each other, in order to keep a watch on our food stores. I remember once hiding under the head-board of my bed a few packets of biscuits which were earmarked for breakfast the next day; and on another occasion, I had to keep a vulture's eye on some plates of fish in our cooking-stove, so as to scare away those birds of prey who would have left us only the bones.

The sacristan was a lusty young fellow who had possibly served at mass with the Carthusian monks since his childhood; he was now the keeper of the keys of the monastery. There was a scandalous story about him. He was once convicted of and confessed to having seduced a *señorita* who had stayed some months in the Cartuja with her parents. He excused himself on the grounds that the State had only entrusted him with the guardianship of the virgins in the pictures. He was not a good type by any standard, but he put on very pretentious airs. Instead of the semi-Arabic attire used by people of his class, he wore European trousers with braces, which certainly dazzled the girls of the district. His sister was the most beautiful Majorcan girl that I've seen. They didn't live in the monastery. They were rich and proud and had a house in the village; but they made a daily round of the Cartuja and were often in Maria Antonia's cell, who invited them to partake of our provender when she had no appetite herself.

The apothecary was a Carthusian who used to shut himself in his cell, put on his former white robe, and recite his office all alone. As soon as anyone knocked on his door to ask him for some marsh-mallow or couch-grass root (the only specific remedies he possessed), he would quickly hide his habit under his bed and appear in black breeches, stockings and a short pea jacket, the same as worn by the male ballet dancers in Molière's interludes. He was a very mistrustful person who never ceased complaining, and who perhaps prayed for the triumph of Don Carlos [a pretender to the Spanish throne supported by the far right] and the return of the Holy Inquisition; but he meant no harm to anybody. He sold us his herbs at the price of gold, and consoled himself with these small gains, having been released from his vow of poverty. His cell was a fairly long way from ours, being situated at the entrance to the monastery in a hidden corner, whose door was camouflaged by castor-oil bushes and other medicinal plants of pleasing aspect.

Tomás Graves

Born in 1953, Tomás Graves, the son of Robert Graves (see p.129), lives on Mallorca, where he works as a guitarist, printer and author. His knowledge of – and enthusiasm for – the island and its people permeates every page of Bread and Oil, *a diverse and intriguing book, first published in Catalan in 1998, that describes many aspects of Mallorcan life via its gastronomy.*

Olive cultivation

The vegetation on Majorca's terraced hillsides hardly changes colour with the seasons. There are several shades of evergreen: the dark holm-oak forest, the vivid pines which sprout on any untended terraces, the grey-green olive groves which flash silver when the strong winds turn up the undersides of their leaves; and among the olives, the occasional broad-leaved carob tree.

Our olive groves have drifted into the realms of what some Majorcan farmers derisively call *hobby farming*. We've reached this point because it's not worth a peasant's while to become a registered olive-grower and pay the corresponding social security if he and his family are only going to gather a few sacks of olives in the best of years. It's hardly worth it even to pick up a few subsidies to repair any of the centuries-old stone terraces that collapse. What really subsidizes the continuing existence of the olive groves is our seasonal tourism. Most Majorcans from the *serra* who work in the hotels and restaurants, sign on the dole in November and have all winter to spend looking after their olive groves and go hunting, as well as doing a little moonlighting on the side. If the harvest were in summer, all the olives would rot on the ground.

Spain's olive groves produce forty per cent of the world's olive oil and represent 146,000 permanent jobs as well as temporary labour to the tune of 46 million day's wages a year. Economically speaking, Majorca's share of the oil business is negligible. Not only does the size of the small-holdings make them unprofitable – property is usually divided up *ad absurdum* between heirs – but the local topography limits the kind of mechanization that you see in parts of Andalucia. There's no way you could get a tractor with a tree-shaking attachment up the Moorish steps of the Barranc de Biniaraix, nor could you manoeuvre a crop-dusting plane between those crags. Throughout the Mediterranean, the olive is a crop which, in spite of mechanization, gives work to entire families and is responsible for preserving the social fabric of the mountainous regions, culturally as well as economically. If the olive groves were to disappear, the rural exodus would be catastrophic because no other crop can be cultivated in the mountainous areas. At least, for the moment, no *legal* crop.

Olive cultivation in the *possessions* or large estates was based first on a slave economy, later on serfdom, and then (until the tourist boom) on the exploitation of the fact that an island's work force can't afford to look for work elsewhere. After a couple of decades of plunging olive oil prices (due to bad press and cheap imported sunflower and soya oil) they began to steadily rise in the 1980s, and today a litre of Majorcan oil fetches double what is paid in Andalucia, due to the demand for local produce. But even so, it doesn't begin to pay for the labour-intensive work of picking olives, maintaining the drystone terraces, ploughing and pruning the trees in the high groves which are accessible only by foot or donkey.

Olive picking

"The degree of acidity is set by the olive, there's no part of the process at the oil-press that can affect it," explains professional oil-taster Gaspar, shouting over the noise of the newly-imported Italian machinery at the Sóller Co-op oil-mill. "Olive oil must be one of the few products which has absolutely no additives. You can't mix anything in with it. Every year it's different; some years the acidity is higher, nobody knows exactly why. The weather may have been exactly the same as the year before, the trees are pruned the same way, given the same fertilizer, but the oil is different from one season to the next."

"Here on the island, ninety per cent of the olives are picked off the ground. No other fruit is harvested off the floor, it's always better straight from the tree. On the mainland they pull the olives straight off the branches; they're a little greener and the oil they produce has a fruitier smell, a bitterer taste. It's a bit spicy and has a lower acid content; this is the extra virgin oil, the best there is. The green olive – in fact it's neither green nor black but mottled – produces less oil but the quality is better. It's best to beat or comb the tree; you can do it mechanically or with hand-held rakes which don't damage the branches."

It seems that the habit of picking green originated in the northern Mediterranean where the olives had to be harvested before the frost set in. In southern Italy they tend to gather ripe olives from the ground, while in the north they pick them green. Many Majorcan inventors have come up with contraptions to gather olives off the ground, yet whether the principle is suction, a brushing action, or a spiked roller, no mechanical picker seems to be able to distinguish this year's juicy olives from last year's shrivelled ones ... or from sheep's droppings.

"The Majorcans are used to an oil which can reach four or five degrees of acidity and that's what they're after because it's tasty, but it's the musty taste of an olive that's been on the damp ground too long. We're telling the members of our co-op to put their olives in crates instead of in sacks where the air doesn't get to them, where there are bacteria. That's when the olive gets spoiled, it ferments and the acidity increases."

In medieval times when strong olive oil was set aside for preserving food, recipe books would recommend adding honey to counteract the excess acidity. In this [the twentieth] century, in the postwar years when even the sharpest oil was better than none, a bit of sugar on your *pa amb oli* would stop the oil grating at the back of your throat.

"Here people pick olives the same way they did a hundred years ago. You could say that if Majorcan oil hasn't the quality of the mainland oil it's partly because here the problem is the terrain; it's not easy to get the olives to the press quickly."

Gathering olives off the ground can be, for someone unaccustomed to this work and to the damp winter climate of the *serra*, an ordeal for the knees and kidneys. Every basketful of four kilos of olives renders a scant litre of oil; not much to show for an hour's work poking about between damp shrubs and under thistles. Many of us who still go for gathering from the ground have found we can save a lot of time by using a strimmer to clear the grass under the trees a week or so before the olives change colour. To go olive picking as a family outing or in order to spend the weekend with friends is a profitable way to commune with nature, each according to his humour. You can work in a group chatting away, but it is equally conducive to solitary meditation.

Why don't we follow the rational northern method of knocking the olives down as soon as they begin to turn colour and thus only have to pick once instead of our weekly pass under the same tree? Well, a Majorcan would say that the only way of ensuring the olive is ripe is to wait for it to fall to the ground… but the hidden argument is that beating or combing the trees not only gives you a crick in the neck, it's also harder work than gathering off the ground. Besides, we've always done it this way and, as they say in the southern US, "if it ain't broke, don't fix it".

The *tafona*, or oil press

The first operation of the traditional oil press, after sifting out any leaves and stones, is to crush the olives on the *jaç*, a flat circular bed about a metre high and three across, fashioned out of a single piece of local stone. A contrivance consisting of a wooden funnel connected to a conical millstone rotates on a vertical axle set in the centre of the stone bed, driven by a blinkered donkey or mule which walks round and round the *jaç*. The sorted olives are tipped into the funnel, the *tremuja*, which feeds them, a few at a time, into the path of the rumbling *trull*. As the olives are crushed to a paste, the *trull* pushes the dark sludge outwards into the gutter which runs around the rim of the *jaç*. From here the virgin oil seeps out of the paste and trickles into a vat.

"The olive contains more water than oil. What flows from the *trull* is pure olive juice, the true virgin olive oil, a mixture of oil and water. When I was a little girl I used to go to school in Estellencs," remembers Maria Riera, "and there was a *tafona* in the village where they'd make oil. The *tafoners* would let the schoolmistress know the day before a *trullada*, and we'd all troop in with our slices of bread, and they'd toast them over the coals. Then they'd take the toasted bread with a pair of tongs and dip it in the oil which had just come out, and it was so good… it was delicious just like that, you didn't even have to put salt on."

Antoni Pinya explains that "in the *possessions*, at the end of the working day when the olives had been crushed and were ready for the hot pressing the next morning, a bottle of virgin oil would be collected from the *trull* for the *Senyors* of the estate. After the token bottle had been given to the landowner, all the paste left on the *trull* would be shovelled into a stone vat, the *esportinador*. Then the *madona* – the overseer's wife – would roll up her sleeve, make a fist and stick it into the paste up to her forearm. As she took out her arm it would leave a good sump-hole in the olive paste, into which more virgin oil would seep overnight. The next morning, the *tafoners* would toast their bread and dunk it into the oil that had gathered in the sump. This was the *tafoner*'s breakfast, the rien-ne-va-plus, the Number One in the world of bread and oil, known as *pa amb oli de tafona*."

After the 'cold pressing' comes the hot or 'scalded' pressing. In a traditional *tafona* this is done under the weight of an enormous wooden beam, weighing well over a ton: one end of the beam rests on the ground while the other end is raised and then lowered – by means of a vertical wooden screw, turned by arms of the *tafoners* – onto the tall stack of circular esparto mats, *esportins*, spread with olive paste. As the beam is lowered, one *tafoner* 'scalds' the paste by ladling hot water onto the pile; it seeps down through the mats, drawing the oil out of the paste. Some people still refer to hot-pressed oil as *oli de bigues*, 'beam oil'.

Having pressed the paste under a beam until it will yield no more liquid, the process is still not over. The dry paste is scooped out of the *esportins* and thrown back into the *esportinador* where it is beaten with more hot water. The mats are again spread with this rehydrated paste and submitted once more to the heavy pressure treatment, doused with a continuous flow of boiling water to extract that little bit more. The oil obtained by this pressing is known as 'seconds': the quality is lower than the first hot pressing because the continuous heat destroys the vitamin E content as well as part of the flavour and bouquet.

The traditional way of pressing olives produced several qualities of oil, from the virgin pressing for the immediate use of the landowner's family, right down to the 'thick' oil from the second or third pressing, which was used for making soap, lubricating cart axles and for treating woodwork.

Extract from Bread and Oil: Majorcan Culture's Last Stand, © *2000, Tomás Graves*. Bread and Oil *is published by Grub Street, London, England*.

Books

Most of the following books should be readily available in bookshops or online (ⓦ www.amazon.com or ⓦ www.abebooks.co.uk). That said, you may have a little more difficulty in tracking down those few titles we mention which are currently out of print, signified o/p, as well as those titles published locally either in Mallorca or Menorca, though in these cases we've given the name of the publisher. If you do have difficulty finding any title, one excellent specialist source for books about Spain – new, used, and out of print – is Paul Orssich, 2 St Stephen's Terrace, London SW8 1DH (☎ 020/7787 0030, ⓦ www.orssich.com). Titles marked with the 🏃 symbol are especially recommended.

Impressions and travelogues

Sir John Carr *Descriptive Travels in the Southern and Eastern Parts of Spain and the Balearic Islands.* Sharp comments and witty asides as Sir John noses his way around the islands at the beginning of the nineteenth century.

Tom Crichton *Our Man in Majorca* o/p. The American sailor, adventurer and journalist Tom Crichton was briefly a package-tour representative on Mallorca in the early 1960s. With the encouragement of Robert Graves, he published this account of a comical, disaster-filled fortnight. A book for the sunlounger.

John Hooper *The New Spaniards.* This excellent, authoritative portrait of post-Franco Spain was written by *The Guardian's* former Spanish correspondent in the 1980s and published in a revised edition – now in need of a further update – in 1995. It is still one of the best possible introductions to contemporary Spain.

Lucy McCauley (ed) *Spain: Travelers' Tales.* It would be hard to better this anthology of writing on Spain, which gathers its stories and journalism predominantly from the last fifteen years. Featured authors include Gabriel García Márquez, Colm Tóibín and Louis de Bernières, whose "Seeing Red", on the tomato-throwing festival of Buñol, is worth the purchase price alone, and there's also the striking "In a Majorcan Garden" by Jill Burberry.

🏃 **George Sand** *A Winter in Majorca.* Accompanied by her lover, Frédéric Chopin, Sand spent the winter of 1838–39 on Mallorca, holed up in the monastery of Valldemossa. These are her recollections, often barbed and sharp-tongued – and very critical of the islanders. Readily available in Valldemossa and Mallorca's better bookshops. Read an extract on p.322.

🏃 **Giles Tremlett** *Ghosts of Spain.* Tremlett (the Madrid correspondent of *The Guardian*) digs into the untold story of Spain's Civil War dead and the collective conspiracy of silence surrounding the war's terrors, and goes on to peel away the layers of the post-Franco era to present an enthralling and often disturbing study of contemporary Spain.

Gordon West *Jogging Round Majorca.* This gentle, humorous account of an extended journey round Mallorca by Gordon and Mary West in the 1920s vividly portrays the island's pre-tourist life and times. The trip had nothing to do with running, but rather "jogging" as in a leisurely progress. West's book lay forgotten for decades until a BBC radio presenter, Leonard Pearcey, stumbled across it in a secondhand bookshop and subsequently read extracts on air. The programmes were very well received, and the book was reprinted in 1994.

Charles W. Wood *Letters from Majorca*. Worrying Wood recorded his assorted observations in Mallorca in the 1880s, when everyone knew the Brits were best.

James Woodall *In Search of the Fire-dance: Spain through Flamenco*. This is a terrific history and exploration of flamenco, and as the subtitle suggests it is never satisfied with "just the music" in getting to the heart of the culture.

General background

Mossèn Antoni Alcover *Folk Tales of Mallorca*. The nineteenth-century priest and academic Mossèn Alcover spent decades collecting Mallorcan folk tales and this is a wide selection of them, running to almost 400 pages. They range from the intensely religious through to parable and proverb, but many reveal an unpleasant edge to rural island life, both vindictive and mean-spirited. Makes for intriguing background material, but unfortunately particular places on the island are never mentioned or described.

Phil Ball *Morbo – The Story of Spanish Football* (When Saturday Comes Books, UK). Excellent account of the history of Spanish football from its nineteenth-century beginnings with the British workers at the mines of Río Tinto in Huelva to the golden years of Real Madrid and the dark days of Franco. Ever-present as a backdrop is the ferocious rivalry or *morbo* – political, historical, regional and linguistic – which has driven the Spanish game since its birth. Essential reading for every football aficionado visiting Spain.

Vicky Bennison *The Taste of a Place – Mallorca*. Enjoyable, well-illustrated book giving the low down on Mallorcan food and wine – not so much where to eat it, but more what it is like and where to buy it. Recipes too.

Anthony Bonner (ed.) *Doctor Illuminatus: A Ramon Llull Reader*. A selection from the lengthy and heavy-going treatises on mysticism and Christian zeal written by Llull, the thirteenth-century Mallorcan scholar and philosopher (see p.82). Llull's works were some of the first to be written in Catalan, but are not for the faint-hearted. More manageable is *Romancing God: Contemplating the Beloved*, edited by Henry Carrigan Jnr, a 120-page introduction to Llull.

Barbara Catoir *Miró on Mallorca*. Lavishly illustrated, if somewhat dated book covering Miró's lengthy residence in Cala Major, just outside Palma. There's discussion of the work Miró produced in this period and of his thoughts on the island as a whole. Too hagiographical for some tastes, however.

Carrie B. Douglass *Bulls, Bullfighting and Spanish Identities*. Anthropologist Douglass delves into the symbolism of the bull in the Spanish national psyche, and then goes on to examine the bullfight's role in some of the thousands of fiestas country-wide that support it.

Tomás Graves *Bread & Oil: Majorcan Culture's Last Stand*. Written by a son of Robert Graves, this intriguing and entertaining book explores Mallorca via its palate, with sections on what the islanders eat and how the ingredients end up where they do. See p.325 for an extract. Adopting a similar approach, but with music in mind, is the same author's *Tuning up at Dawn: A Memoir of Music and Majorca*.

William Graves *Wild Olives: Life in Mallorca with Robert Graves.* Another son of Robert Graves, William was born in 1940 and spent much of his childhood in Palma and Deià, sufficient inspiration for these mildly diverting accounts of his Mallorcan contemporaries. The book's real focus, however, is his troubled family life and his difficult relationship with his father.

Gijs van Hensbergen *Gaudí: the Biography.* At last, a worthy biography of one of the world's most distinctive architects. Van Hensbergen puts substantial flesh on the man while placing his work firmly in context.

Robert Hughes *Goya.* No, there aren't any *Goyas* on public display in Mallorca or Menorca, but he was one of Spain's greatest painters and Hughes is arguably the world's finest writer on art − so we can't resist mentioning this book here. Hughes has written a simply fabulous biography, a gripping account of Goya's life and work, placed within the context of turbulent eighteenth- and early nineteenth-century Spain.

Arthur Koestler *Dialogue with Death* o/p. Koestler was reporting the Civil War in 1937 when he was captured and imprisoned by Franco's troops − and this is essentially his prison diary.

Janis Mink *Miró.* Beautifully illustrated book that tracks through the artist's life and times. The text is rather ponderous, but there are lots of interesting quotations and, at 96 pages, you're not drowned in detail.

George Orwell *Homage to Catalonia.* Stirring account of Orwell's participation in, and early enthusiasm for, leftist revolution in Barcelona, followed by his growing disillusionment with the factional fighting that divided the Republican forces during the Civil War.

Jan Read *Guide to the Wines of Spain.* Encyclopedic (yet pocketable) guide to the classic and emerging wines of Spain by a leading authority. Includes maps, vintages and vineyards.

Miranda Seymour *Robert Graves: Life on the Edge.* Lengthy account of Robert Graves's personal life with lacklustre commentary on his poetry and novels. Includes much detail on Graves's residence in Deià.

History

David Abulafia *A Mediterranean Emporium: the Catalan Kingdom of Majorca.* Detailed, serious-minded study of medieval Mallorca that is something of a specialist read − the same author's *The Western Mediterranean Kingdoms: The Struggle for Dominion 1200–1500* may be of more general appeal, though both are expensive.

Michael Baigent and Richard Leigh *The Inquisition.* Trenchant trawl through the history of this infamous institution from medieval beginnings to gradual collapse. Particularly good on the Inquisition's relationship with the papacy.

Antony Beevor *The Spanish Civil War.* Long before Beevor hit the headlines with *Stalingrad*, he was ploughing an historical furrow − and this competent synopsis of the Civil War, running to just over 300 pages, was first published in 1982.

Raymond Carr *The Spanish Tragedy: the Civil War in Perspective; and Modern Spain 1875–1980.* Over the years, Carr has worked his way through Spain's convoluted history, producing a series of classic texts. These are two of the best, especially as both of them − unlike some of Carr's books − are relatively short and readily absorbed.

Carr also edited and compiled the nine essays that comprise the much-praised *Spain: A History.*

Roger Collins *The Arab Conquest of Spain 710–97.* Much lauded, enjoyably concise study documenting the Moorish invasion of Spain and the significant influence that the conquered Visigoths had on early Muslim rule. Collins's earlier *Early Medieval Spain 400–1000* takes a broader overview of the same subject.

🏃 **J.H. Elliott** *Imperial Spain 1469–1716.* The best introduction to Spain's "golden age" – academically respected as well as being a gripping yarn. Also see his erudite *The Revolt of the Catalans: A Study in the Decline of Spain 1598–1640*, though this comes in at a whopping 640 pages and is only in hardback.

Desmond Gregory *Minorca, the Illusory Prize: History of the British Occupation of Minorca between 1708 and 1802* o/p. Exhaustive, scholarly and well-composed narrative detailing the British colonial involvement with Menorca. It's only published in hardback, however, and is therefore expensive.

David Howarth *The Voyage of the Armada.* An account from the Spanish perspective of the personalities, from king to sailors, involved in the Armada.

🏃 **Henry Kamen** *The Spanish Inquisition: An Historical Revision.* A highly respected examination of the Inquisition and the long shadow it cast across Spanish history. Kamen's *Philip of Spain* is the first full biography of Felipe II, the ruler most closely associated with the Inquisition.

Bruce Laurie *Life of Richard Kane: Britain's First Lieutenant Governor of Minorca.* Detailed (290-page) historical biography providing an intriguing insight into eighteenth-century Menorca. Only available in hardback – and consequently very pricey.

🏃 **Geoffrey Parker** *The Army of Flanders and the Spanish Road (1567–1659).* Sounds dry and academic, but this fascinating book gives a marvellous insight into the morals, manners and organization of the Spanish army, then the most feared in Europe.

🏃 **Paul Preston** *Franco* and *The Spanish Civil War.* A penetrating – and monumental – biography of Franco and his regime, which provides as clear a picture as any of how he won the Civil War and survived in power so long. *Civil War* is a compelling introduction to the subject and is also more accessible for the general reader than Hugh Thomas's work (see below).

Hugh Thomas *The Spanish Civil War.* Exhaustively researched, brilliantly detailed account of the war and the complex political manoeuvrings surrounding it, with a small section on Mallorca. First published in 1961, it remains the best book on the subject.

Justin Wintle *The Rough Guide History of Spain.* A very readable – and extremely competent – skip through Spanish history, covering all the bases from prehistoric times till 2003. If the subject is unfamiliar, this is the best place to start.

Fiction

Arturo Barea *The Forging of a Rebel.* Autobiographical trilogy, taking in the Spanish war in Morocco in the 1920s and Barea's own part in the Civil War. Sometimes reprinted in its component titles: *The Forge, The Track* and *The Clash.*

Agatha Christie *Problem at Pollensa Bay* Amongst her many attributes, Agatha Christie (1890–1976) was a pioneering world traveller, who spent long periods of time in the Middle East working on archeological digs alongside her husband Max Mallowan. Christie visited Mallorca on several occasions and the eponymous tale that gives this collection of short stories its title is redolent of the days when only the well-heeled few could visit the island.

Juan Goytisolo *Marks of Identity, Count Julian, Juan the Landless, The Virtues of the Solitary Bird* and *Makbara*. Born in Barcelona in 1931, Goytisolo became a bitter enemy of the Franco regime and has spent most of his life in exile in Paris and Morocco. Widely acclaimed as one of Spain's leading modern novelists, his most celebrated works (the first three titles listed above) confront ambivalent ideas of Spain and Spanishness. The fourth of the five titles above (from 1988) is a deep and powerful study of pain and repression, the fifth (from 1980) explores the Arab culture of North Africa in sharp and perceptive style. Goytisolo has also written an autobiography, *Forbidden Territory*.

Lucia Graves *A Woman Unknown: Voices from a Spanish Life*. Robert Graves's children seem determined to make a literary name for themselves. This effort by his daughter Lucia is a thoughtful recollection of life in Mallorca in particular and Spain as a whole – lucid and interesting in equal measure.

Ernest Hemingway *The Sun Also Rises* and *For Whom the Bell Tolls*. Hemingway remains a big part of the American myth of Spain – *The Sun Also Rises* contains some lyrically beautiful writing, while the latter

– set in the Civil War – is a good deal more laboured. Hemingway also published two books on bullfighting: the enthusiastic and not very good *Death in the Afternoon* (1932) and *Dangerous Summer* (1959), an overheated account of the contest between Dominguín and Antonio Ordóñez for the title of top-dog matador.

Roderic Jeffries *An Enigmatic Disappearance*. Jeffries has turned out a number of murder mysteries set in Mallorca with Inspector Alvarez as his protagonist cop. The author is a Londoner by birth, but is now resident on the island. Other novels in the Alvarez series are *An Artistic Way to Go* and *A Maze of Murders*.

Norman Lewis *Voices of the Old Sea*. Lewis lived in Catalunya from 1948 to 1952, just as tourism was starting to arrive. This book is an ingenious blend of novel and social record, charting the breakdown of the old ways in the face of the "new revolution".

Sian Mackay *Rafael's Wings* Mackay knows contemporary Mallorca like the back of her hand and, although the drama at the centre of the book doesn't work too well, there's all sorts of interesting stuff on the island, its customs and predicaments.

Javier Marias *Tomorrow in the Battle Think on Me*. There are many who rate Marias as Spain's finest contemporary novelist – and the evidence is here in this searching, psychological thriller, with its study of the human capacity for concealment and confession. Two other Marias novels, *A Heart So White* and *All Souls*, are also available in English translation.

Ana María Matute *School of the Sun*. The loss of childhood innocence on the Balearics, where old enmities are redefined during the Civil War.

🏃 **Manuel Vázquez Montalbán** *Murder in the Central Committee, An Olympic Death, The Angst-ridden Executive, Off Side.* Original and wonderfully entertaining tales by the man who was, until his untimely death in 2003, Spain's most popular crime thriller writer. A long-time member of the Communist Party, Montalbán became a well-known journalist in post-Franco Spain and was a resident of Barcelona. His great creation was the gourmand private detective Pepe Carvalho. If this trio of titles whets your appetite, move on to *Southern Seas* and a world of disillusioned Communists, tawdry sex and nouvelle cuisine – Montalbán's trademark ingredients – but don't bother with his very disappointing *The Man of My Life.*

Rafael Reig *Blood on the Saddle.* Witty, surprising and extraordinarily original novel set in a futuristic Madrid, which has been partly submerged by water. Stars the melancholic private eye Carlos Clot and his odd-ball accomplices. Reig hails from Asturias, in northern Spain.

Arturo Pérez Reverte *The Seville Communion, The Queen of the South.* Pérez Reverte is one of Spain's leading writers and *Seville Communion* is an entertaining crime yarn played out against the colourfully described backdrop of Sevilla. His latest book in translation, *Queen of the South*, was another Spanish bestseller and relates the story of a woman drug trafficker running narcotics between Morocco and Cádiz.

George Scott *The Bloody Bokhara.* Detective thriller set in modern-day Mallorca, which served as a literary debut for an American who also runs a hotel on the island. It's a fairly good yarn, if a bit ponderously written, and is excellent for background information – as is Scott's second novel, *The Chewed Caucasian.*

Llorenç Villalonga *The Dolls' Room* o/p. Subtle if somewhat laboured portrait of nobility in decline in nineteenth-century Mallorca. Villalonga (1897–1980) was Mallorca's most prominent writer for several decades, but although several of his books are still in print, none are currently available in English. The author's old house in Binissalem is now a museum (see p.194).

Specialist guidebooks

David & Rosamund Brawn The Brawns produce regularly updated hiking books and maps of both islands: even better, directions are almost always easy to follow and each slim booklet detailing the hikes comes with a 1:25,000 or 1:40,000 map; they're inexpensive too. Current offerings include *Walk! Mallorca West* (2005) and *Walk! Menorca* (2005) plus there's also *Mallorca North and Mountains Tour and Trail Map* (from 2004). Brawn publications are, however, almost impossible to find on Mallorca or Menorca, so get them beforehand from a major supplier or direct from Discovery UK (ⓦwww.walking.demon.co.uk). For recommended **hiking maps**, see "Basics" p.50.

Herbert Heinrich *Twelve Classic Hikes through Mallorca* (Editorial Moll, Mallorca). Heinrich has published a number of Mallorcan hiking guides in German. This was his first (and best) English volume, a compilation of some of the most enjoyable and less demanding one-day hikes in the Serra de Tramuntana mountains. The descriptions are a bit patchy, but the topographical sketches are extremely helpful. Widely available in Mallorca.

Gaspar Martí *Walking Tours Around the Historical Centre of Palma* (Ajuntament de Palma, Mallorca). Detailed and enjoyable exploration of Palma's historical nooks and crannies. Quality sketches illuminate the text. Published by Palma city council and available in most leading bookshops in the city.

June Parker *Walking in Mallorca*. Refreshed in 2006, this popular hiking guide is easily the most detailed book on its subject currently on the market. Published by Cicerone – and up to their usual high standard.

Flora and fauna

Christopher Grey-Wilson, et al. *Wild Flowers of the Mediterranean*. Excellent, comprehensive field guide.

Graham Hearl *A Birdwatching Guide to Mallorca* and *A Birdwatching Guide to Menorca, Ibiza and Formentera*. First-rate descriptions of where to see what bird in every part of every Balearic island. There is a handy bird checklist at the back of both books and the text is sprinkled with useful local maps. The sketches of various birds are, however, not very illuminating – and you'll still need a field guide.

Lars Jonsson *Birds of Europe*. As good a field guide as the Collins guide by Mullarney et al., but more specialized.

Killian Mullarney, et al. *Collins Bird Guide: The Most Complete Guide to the Birds of Britain and Europe*. Excellent field guide to birds – nothing better.

Oleg Polunin, et al. *Flowers of Europe: A Field Guide*. First-rate field guide.

Enric Ramos *The Birds of Menorca* o/p. Specialist handbook describing all the species of bird recorded in Menorca. It's well illustrated, but you'll still need a field guide.

Ken Stoba *Birdwatching in Mallorca* o/p. First published in 1990, this slim book is a competent introduction to Mallorca's birdlife and major birdwatching sites.

Language

Language

Language

ost of the inhabitants of Mallorca and Menorca are bilingual, speaking **Castilian** (Spanish) and their local dialect of the **Catalan** language – *Mallorquín* or *Menorquín* – with equal facility. *Català* (Catalan) has been the islanders' everyday language since the absorption of the Balearics into the medieval Kingdom of Aragón and Catalunya in the thirteenth century; Castilian, on the other hand, was imposed much later as the official language of government and business at the instigation of Madrid – and with special rigour by Franco. Almost inevitably, therefore, Spain's recent move towards regional autonomy has been accompanied by the islanders' re-assertion of Catalan as their official language. The most obvious sign of this has been the change of all the old Castilian town and street names into their Catalan equivalents.

On paper, **Catalan** looks like a cross between French and Spanish and is generally easy to understand if you know those two languages, although when it is spoken it has a very harsh sound and is surprisingly hard to come to grips with.

Numerous **Spanish phrasebooks and dictionaries** are available with the most user-friendly being Rough Guide's *Spanish Dictionary Phrasebook*. No **English–Catalan phrasebook** is currently in print and there's only one **dictionary**, published by Routledge.

Some background

When **Franco** came to power in 1939, *Català* publishing houses, bookshops and libraries were raided and their books destroyed. Furthermore, throughout his dictatorship Franco excluded Catalan from the radio, TV, daily press and, most importantly, the schools, which is why many older people cannot read or write *Català* even if they speak it all the time. More recently, the islands' linguistic jigsaw has been further complicated by the emigration of thousands of mainland Spaniards to the islands, and nowadays it's estimated that Castilian is the dominant language in around forty percent of Balearic households.

Català is spoken by over six million people in the Balearics, Catalunya, part of Aragón, most of Valencia, Andorra and parts of the French Pyrenees; it is thus much more widely spoken than several better-known languages such as Danish, Finnish and Norwegian. It is a Romance language, stemming from Latin and more directly from medieval Provençal. Spaniards in the rest of the country often belittle it by saying that to get a *Català* word you just cut a Castilian one in half (which is often true), but in fact the grammar is much more complicated than Castilian and there are eight vowel sounds, three more than in Castilian.

Getting by in Mallorca and Menorca

Although Catalan is the preferred **language** of most islanders, you'll almost always get by perfectly well if you speak Castilian (Spanish), as long as you're aware of the use of Catalan in timetables and so forth. Once you get into it, Castilian is one of the easiest languages there is, the rules of pronunciation pretty straightforward and strictly observed. You'll find some basic pronunciation rules below for both Catalan and Castilian, and a selection of words and phrases in both languages. Castilian is certainly easier to pronounce, but don't be afraid to try Catalan, especially in the more out-of-the-way places – you'll generally get a good reception if you at least try communicating in the local language.

Castilian (Spanish): a few rules

Unless there's an accent, words ending in d, l, r, and z are **stressed** on the last syllable, all others on the second to last. All **vowels** are pure and short; combinations have predictable results.

A somewhere between back and father.

E as in get.

I as in police.

O as in hot.

U as in rule.

C is lisped before E and I, hard otherwise: cerca is pronounced "thairka".

CH is pronounced as in English.

G is a guttural H sound (like the ch in loch) before E or I, a hard G elsewhere: gigante is pronounced "higante".

H is always silent.

J is the same sound as a guttural G: jamón is pronounced "hamon".

LL sounds like an English Y: tortilla is pronounced "torteeya".

N as in English, unless it has a tilde (ñ) over it, when it becomes NY: mañana sounds like "man-yaana".

QU is pronounced like an English K.

R is rolled, RR doubly so.

V sounds more like B, vino becoming "beano".

X has an S sound before consonants, a KS sound before vowels.

Z is the same as a soft C, so cerveza is pronounced "thairvaitha".

Catalan: a few rules

With *Català*, don't be tempted to use the few rules of Castilian pronunciation you may know – in particular the soft Spanish Z and C don't apply, so unlike in the rest of Spain it's not "Barthelona" but "Barcelona", as in English.

A as in hat if stressed, as in alone when unstressed.

E varies, but usually as in get.

I as in police.

IG sounds like the "tch" in the English scratch: lleig (ugly) is pronounced "yeah-tch".

O varies, but usually as in hot.

U lies somewhere between put and rule.

Ç sounds like an English S: plaça is pronounced "plassa".

C followed by an E or I is soft; otherwise hard.

G followed by E or I is like the "zh" in Zhivago; otherwise hard.

H is always silent.

J as in the French "Jean".

LL sounds like an English Y or LY, like the "yuh" sound in "million".

N as in English, though before F or V it sometimes sounds like an M.

NY replaces the Castilian Ñ.

QU before E or I sounds like K; before A or O as in "quit".

R is rolled, but only at the start of a word; at the end it's often silent.

T is pronounced as in English, though sometimes it sounds like a D, as in viatge or dotze.

TX is like the English CH.

V at the start of a word sounds like B; in all other positions it's a soft F sound.

W is pronounced like a B/V.

X is like SH in most words, though in some, like exit, it sounds like an X.

Z is like the English Z.

Useful words and phrases

Basics

English	Castilian	Catalan
Yes, No, OK	Sí, No, Vale	Si, No, Val
Please, Thank you	Por favor, Gracias	Per favor, Gràcies
Where, When	Dónde, Cuándo	On, Quan
What, How much	Qué, Cuánto	Què, Quant
Here, There	Aquí, Allí, Allá	Aquí, Allí, Allà
This, That	Esto, Eso	Això, Allò
Now, Later	Ahora, Más tarde	Ara, Més tard
Open, Closed	Abierto/a, Cerrado/a	Obert, Tancat
With, Without	Con, Sin	Amb, Sense
Good, Bad	Buen(o)/a, Mal(o)/a	Bo(na), Dolent(a)
Big, Small	Gran(de), Pequeño/a	Gran, Petit(a)
Cheap, Expensive	Barato/a, Caro/a	Barat(a), Car(a)
Hot, Cold	Caliente, Frío/a	Calent(a), Fred(a)
More, Less	Más, Menos	Més, Menys
Today, Tomorrow	Hoy, Mañana	Avui, Demà
Yesterday	Ayer	Ahir
Day before yesterday	Anteayer	Abans-d'ahir
Next week	La semana que viene	La setmana que ve
Next month	El mes que viene	El mes que ve

Greetings and responses

English	Castilian	Catalan
Hello, Goodbye	Hola, Adiós	Hola, Adéu
Good morning	Buenos días	Bon dia
Good afternoon/night	Buenas tardes/noches	Bona tarda/nit
See you later	Hasta luego	Fins després
Sorry	Lo siento/discúlpeme	Ho sento
Excuse me	Con permiso/perdón	Perdoni
How are you?	¿Cómo está (usted)?	Com va?
I (don't) understand	(No) Entiendo	(No) Ho entenc
Not at all/You're welcome	De nada	De res
Do you speak English?	¿Habla (usted) inglés?	Parla anglès?
I (don't) speak	(No) Hablo Español	(No) Parlo Català

My name is...	Me llamo...	Em dic...
What's your name?	¿Cómo se llama usted?	Com es diu?
I am English	Soy inglés/esa	Sóc anglès/esa
Scottish	escocés/esa	escocès/esa
Australian	australiano/a	australià/ana
Canadian	canadiense/a	canadenc(a)
American	americano/a	americà/ana
Irish	irlandés/esa	irlandès/esa
Welsh	galés/esa	gallès/esa

Hotels and transport

English	Castilian	Catalan
I want	Quiero	Vull (pronounced "fwee")
I'd like	Quisiera	Voldria
Do you know...?	¿Sabe...?	Vostès saben…?
I don't know	No sé	No sé
There is (is there?)	(¿)Hay(?)	Hi ha(?)
Give me...	Deme...	Doneu-me…
Do you have...?	¿Tiene...?	Té...?
...the time	...la hora	...l'hora
...a room	...una habitación	...alguna habitació
...with two beds/	...con dos camas/	...amb dos llits/
double bed	cama matrimonial	llit per dues persones
...with shower/bath	...con ducha/baño	...amb dutxa/bany
for one person	para una persona	per a una persona
(two people)	(dos personas)	(dues persones)
for one night	para una noche	per una nit
(one week)	(una semana)	(una setmana)
It's fine, how much is it?	Está bien, ¿cuánto es?	Esta bé, quant és?
It's too expensive	Es demasiado caro	És massa car
Don't you have anything cheaper?	¿No tiene algo más barato?	En té de més bon preu?
Can one...?	¿Se puede...?	Es pot...?
...camp (near) here?	¿...acampar aquí (cerca)?	...acampar a la vora?
Is there a hostel nearby?	¿Hay un hostal aquí cerca?	Hi ha un hostal a la vora?
It's not very far	No es muy lejos	No és gaire lluny
How do I get to...?	¿Por dónde se va a...?	Per anar a...?
Left, right, straight on	Izquierda, derecha, todo recto	A l'esquerra, a la dreta,tot recte
Where is...?	¿Dónde está...?	On és...?
...the bus station	...la estación de autobuses	...l'estació de autobuses
...the bus stop	...la parada	...la parada
...the railway station	...la estación de ferrocarril	...l'estació
...the nearest bank	...el banco más cercano	...el banc més a prop
...the post office	...el correo/ la oficina de correos	...l'oficina de correus
...the toilet	...el baño/aseo/servicio	...la toaleta

English	Castilian	Catalan
Where does the bus to... leave from?	¿De dónde sale el autobús para...?	De on surt el auto bús a…?
Is this the train for Barcelona?	¿Es este el tren para Barcelona?	Aquest tren va a Barcelona?
I'd like a (return) ticket to...	Quisiera un billete (de ida y vuelta) para...	Voldria un bitllet (d'anar i tornar) a...
What time does it leave (arrive in...)?	¿A qué hora sale (llega a...)?	A quina hora surt (arriba a...)?
What is there to eat?	¿Qué hay para comer?	Què hi ha per menjar?
What's that?	¿Qué es eso?	Què és això?

Days of the week

English	Castilian	Catalan
Monday	lunes	dilluns
Tuesday	martes	dimarts
Wednesday	miércoles	dimecres
Thursday	jueves	dijous
Friday	viernes	divendres
Saturday	sábado	dissabte
Sunday	domingo	diumenge

Numbers

English	Castilian	Catalan
1	un/uno/una	un(a)
2	dos	dos (dues)
3	tres	tres
4	cuatro	quatre
5	cinco	cinc
6	seis	sis
7	siete	set
8	ocho	vuit
9	nueve	nou
10	diez	deu
11	once	onze
12	doce	dotze
13	trece	tretze
14	catorce	catorze
15	quince	quinze
16	dieciséis	setze
17	diecisiete	disset
18	dieciocho	divuit
19	diecinueve	dinou
20	veinte	vint
21	veintiuno	vint-i-un
30	treinta	trenta

	Castilian	Catalan
40	cuarenta	quaranta
50	cincuenta	cinquanta
60	sesenta	seixanta
70	setenta	setanta
80	ochenta	vuitanta
90	noventa	novanta
100	cien(to)	cent
101	ciento uno	cent un
102	ciento dos	cent dos (dues)
200	doscientos	dos-cents (dues-centes)
500	quinientos	cinc-cents
1000	mil	mil
2000	dos mil	dos mil

Food and drink

Although we've provided a reasonably extensive **Castilian and Catalan food and drink glossary** below, most restaurants, cafés and bars have **multilingual menus**, with English, Catalan and Castilian almost always three of the options. The main exceptions are out in the countryside, where there may only be a Catalan menu or maybe no menu at all, in which case the waiter will rattle off the day's dishes in Catalan or sometimes Castilian.

Basics

English	Castilian	Catalan
Bread	Pan	Pa
Butter	Mantequilla	Mantega
Cheese	Queso	Formatge
Eggs	Huevos	Ous
Fruit	Fruta	Fruita
Garlic	Ajo	All
Oil	Aceite	Oli
Pepper	Pimienta	Pebre
Rice	Arroz	Arròs
Salt	Sal	Sal
Sugar	Azúcar	Sucre
Vinegar	Vinagre	Vinagre
Vegetables	Verduras/Legumbres	Verdures/Llegumes
To have breakfast	Desayunar	Esmorzar
To have lunch	Almorzar	Dinar
To have dinner	Sopar	Cenar
Menu	Carta	Menú
Bottle	Botella	Ampolla
Glass	Vaso	Got
Fork	Tenedor	Forquilla

Knife	Cuchillo	Ganivet
Spoon	Cuchara	Cullera
Table	Mesa	Taula
The bill/check	La cuenta	El compte
Grilled	A la brasa	A la planxa
Fried	Frit	Fregit
Stuffed/rolled	Relleno	Farcit
Casserole	Guisado	Guisat
Roast	Asado	Rostit

Fruit (fruita) and vegetables (verdures/llegumes)

English	Castilian	Catalan
Apple	Manzana	Poma
Asparagus	Espárragos	Espàrrecs
Aubergine/eggplant	Berenjenas	Albergínies
Banana	Plátano	Plàtan
Carrots	Zanahorias	Pastanagues
Cucumber	Pepino	Concombre
Grapes	Uvas	Raïm
Melon	Melón	Meló
Mushrooms	Champiñones	Xampinyons (also bolets, setes)
Onions	Cebollas	Cebes
Orange	Naranja	Taronja
Peach	Melocotón	Préssec
Pear	Pera	Pera
Peas	Arvejas	Pèsols
Pineapple	Piña	Pinya
Potatoes	Patatas	Patates
Strawberries	Fresas	Maduixes
Tomatoes	Tomates	Tomàquets

Bocadillos fillings

English	Castilian	Catalan
Catalan sausage	Butifarra	Butifarra
Cheese	Queso	Formatge
Cooked ham	Jamón York	Cuixot dolç
Cured ham	Jamón serrano	Pernil salat
Loin of pork	Lomo	Llom
Omelette	Tortilla	Truita
Salami	Salami	Salami
Sausage	Salchichón	Salxitxó
Spicy sausage	Chorizo	Xoriç
Tuna	Atún	Tonyina

Tapas and racions

English	Castilian	Catalan
Anchovies	Boquerones	Anxoves
Stew	Cocido	Bollit
Squid, usually deep-fried in rings	Calamares	Calamars
Squid in ink	Calamares en su tinta	Calamars amb tinta
Snails, often served in a spicy/curry sauce	Caracoles	Cargols
Cockles (shellfish)	Berberechos	Cargols de mar
Whole baby squid	Chipirones	Calamarins
Meat in tomato sauce	Carne en salsa	Carn amb salsa
Fish or chicken croquette	Croqueta	Croqueta
Fish or meat pasty	Empanadilla	Empanada petita
Russian salad (diced vegetables in mayonnaise)	Ensaladilla	Ensalada russa
Aubergine (eggplant) and pepper salad	Escalibada	Escalibada
Broad beans	Habas	Faves
Beans with ham	Habas con jamón	Faves amb cuixot
Liver	Hígado	Fetge
Prawns	Gambas	Gambes
Mussels (either steamed, or served with diced tomatoes and onion)	Mejillones	Musclos
Razor clams	Navajas	Navallas
Olives	Aceitunas	Olives
Hard-boiled egg	Huevo cocido	Ou bollit
Bread, rubbed with tomato and oil	Pan con tomate	Pa amb tomàquet
Potatoes in garlic mayonnaise	Patatas alioli	Patates amb all i oli
Fried potato cubes with spicy sauce and mayonnaise	Patatas bravas	Patates cohentes
Meatballs, usually in sauce	Albóndigas	Pilotes
Kebab	Pincho moruno	Pinxo
Octopus	Pulpo	Pop
Sweet (bell) peppers	Pimientos	Prebes
Kidneys in sherry	Riñones al jerez	Ronyons amb xeres
Sardines	Sardinas	Sardines
Cuttlefish	Sepia	Sípia
Tripe	Callos	Tripa
Potato omelette	Tortilla española	Truita espanyola

Plain omelette	Tortilla francesa	Truita francesa
Pepper, potato, pumpkin and aubergine (eggplant) stew with tomato purée	Tumbet	Tumbet
Mushrooms, usually fried in garlic	Champiñones	Xampinyons
Spicy sausage	Chorizo	Xoriç

Selected Balearic dishes and specialities

Many of the specialities that follow come from the Balearics' shared history with Catalunya. The more elaborate fish and meat dishes are usually limited to the fancier restaurants.

Sauces

Salsa mahonesa	Mayonnaise
Allioli	Garlic mayonnaise
Salsa romesco	Spicy tomato and wine sauce to accompany fish (from Tarragona)

Soups (sopa), starters and salads (amanida)

Amanida catalana	Salad with sliced meat and cheese
Carn d'olla	Mixed meat soup
Entremesos	Starter of mixed meat and cheese
Escalivada	Aubergine/eggplant, pepper and onion salad
Escudella	Mixed vegetable soup
Espinacs a la Catalana	Spinach with raisins and pine nuts
Esqueixada	Dried cod salad with peppers, tomatoes, onions and olives
Fideus a la cassola	Baked vermicelli with meat
Llenties guisades	Stewed lentils
Pa amb oli	Bread rubbed with olive oil, eaten with ham, cheese or fruit
Samfaina	Ratatouille-like stew of onions, peppers, aubergine/eggplant and tomato
Sopa d'all	Garlic soup
Sopas mallorquinas	Vegetable soup, sometimes with meat and chickpeas (garbanzos)

Truita (d'alls tendres; de xampinyons; de patates)	Omelette/tortilla (with garlic; with mushrooms; with potato). Be sure you're ordering omelette (tortilla), not trout (truita).

Rice dishes

Arròs a banda	Rice with seafood, the rice served separately
Arròs a la marinera	Paella: rice with seafood and saffron
Arròs negre	"Black rice", cooked with squid ink
Paella a la Catalana	Mixed meat and seafood paella, sometime distinguished from a seafood paella by being called Paella a Valencia

Meat (carn)

Alberginies en es forn	Aubergines/eggplants stuffed with grilled meat
Botifarra amb mongetes	Spicy blood sausage with white beans
Conill (all i oli)	Rabbit (with garlic mayonnaise)
Escaldum	Chicken and potato stew in an almond sauce
Estofat de vedella	Veal stew
Fetge	Liver
Fricandó	Veal casserole
Frito mallorquín	Pigs' offal, potatoes and onions cooked with oil
Mandonguilles	Meatballs, usually in a sauce with peas

347

Perdius a la vinagreta	Partridge in vinegar gravy
Pollastre (farcit; amb gambas; al cava)	Chicken (stuffed; with prawns; cooked in sparkling wine)
Porc (rostit)	Pork (roast)
Sobrasada	Finely minced pork sausage, flavoured with paprika

Fish (peix) and shellfish (marisc)

Bacallà (amb samfaina)	Dried cod (with ratatouille)
Caldereta de llagosta	Lobster stew
Cloïsses	Clams, often steamed
Espinagada de Sa Pobla	Turnover filled with spinach and eel
Greixonera de peix	Menorcan fish stew, cooked in an earthenware casserole
Guisat de peix	Fish and shellfish stew
Llagosta (amb pollastre)	Lobster (with chicken in a rich sauce)
Lluç	Hake, either fried or grilled
Musclos al vapor	Steamed mussels

Pop	Octopus
Rap a l'all cremat	Monkfish with creamed garlic sauce
Sarsuela	Fish and shellfish stew
Suquet	Fish casserole
Truita	Trout (sometimes stuffed with ham, a la Navarre)

Desserts (postres) and pastries (pastas)

Cocaroll	Pastry containing vegetables and fish
Crema Catalana	Crème caramel, with caramelized sugar topping
Ensaimada	Flaky spiral pastry, often with fillings such as cabello de ángel (sweetened citron rind)
Mel i mató	Curd cheese and honey
Postres de músic	Cake of dried fruit and nuts
Turrón	Almond fudge
Xurros	Deep-fried doughnut sticks (served with hot chocolate)

Drinking

English	Castilian	Catalan
Water	Agua	Aigua
Mineral water	Agua mineral	Aigua mineral
(sparkling)	(con gas)	(amb gas)
(still)	(sin gas)	(sense gas)
Milk	Leche	Llet
Juice	Zumo	Suc
Tiger nut drink	Horchata	Orxata
Coffee	Café	Café
Espresso	Café solo	Café sol
White coffee	Café con leche	Café amb llet
Decaff	Descafeinado	Descafeinat
Tea	Té	Te
Drinking chocolate	Chocolate	Xocolata
Beer	Cerveza	Cervesa
Wine	Vino	Vi
Champagne/Sparkling wine	Champán/Cava	Xampan/Cava

Glossary

Glossary of Catalan terms

Ajuntament Town Hall

Albufera Lagoon (and surrounding wetlands)

Altar major High altar

Aparcament Parking

Avinguda (Avgda) Avenue

Badía Bay

Barranc Ravine

Barroc Baroque

Basílica Catholic church with honorific privileges

Cala Small bay, cove

Camí Way or road

Ca'n At the house of (contraction of casa and en)

Capella Chapel

Carrer (c/) Street

Carretera Road, highway

Castell Castle

Celler Cellar, or a bar in a cellar

Claustre Cloister

Coll Col, mountain pass

Convent Convent, nunnery or monastery

Correu Post office

Coves Caves

Església Church

Estany Small lake

Festa Festival

Finca Estate or farmhouse

Font Water fountain or spring

Gòtic Gothic

Illa Island

Jardí Garden

Llac Lake

Mercat Market

Mirador Watchtower or viewpoint

Modernisme Literally "modernism", the Catalan form of Art Nouveau, whose most famous exponent was Antoni Gaudí; adjective "modernista".

Monestir Monastery

Mozarabe A Christian subject of a medieval Moorish ruler; hence **Mozarabic**, a colourful building style that reveals both Christian and Moorish influences.

Mudéjar A Moorish subject of a medieval Christian ruler. Also a style of architecture developed by Moorish craftsmen working for Christians, characterized by painted woodwork with strong colours and complex geometrical patterns; revived between the 1890s and 1930s and blended with Art Nouveau forms.

Museu Museum

Nostra Senyora The Virgin Mary ("Our Lady")

Oficina d'Informació Turística Tourist office

Palau Palace, mansion or manor house

Parc Park

Passeig Boulevard; the evening stroll along it

Pic Summit

Plaça Square

Platja Beach

Pont Bridge

Port Harbour, port

Porta Door, gate

Puig Hill, mountain

Rambla Avenue or boulevard

Reconquista The Christian Reconquest

of Spain from the Moors beginning in the ninth century and culminating in the capture of Granada in 1492.

Rei King

Reial Royal

Reina Queen

Reixa Iron screen or grille, usually in front of a window

Renaixença Rebirth, often used to describe the Catalan cultural revival at the end of the nineteenth and beginning of the twentieth centuries. Architecturally, this was expressed as modernisme.

Retaule Retable or reredos, a wooden ornamental panel behind an altar

Riu River

Romeria Pilgrimage or gathering at a shrine

Salinas Saltpans

Santuari Sanctuary

Sant/a Saint

Serra Mountain range

Talayot Cone-shaped prehistoric tower

Taula T-shaped prehistoric megalithic structure

Torrent Stream or river (usually dry in summer)

Urbanització Modern estate development

Vall Valley

Glossary of English art and architectural terms

Ambulatory Interior covered passage around the outer edge of the choir in the chancel of a church.

Apse Semicircular protrusion (usually) at the east end of a church.

Art Deco Geometrical style of art and architecture popular in the 1930s.

Art Nouveau Style of art, architecture and design based on highly stylised vegetal forms. Popular in the early part of the twentieth century. (See also **Modernisme** in the colour section on *Architecture*).

Balustrade An ornamental rail, running, almost invariably, along the top of a building.

Baroque The art and architecture of the Counter-Reformation, dating from around 1600 onwards. Distinguished by its ornate exuberance and (at its best) complex but harmonious spatial arrangement of interiors. Some elements – particularly its gaudiness – remained popular in the Balearics well into the twentieth century.

Caryatid A sculptured female figure used as a column.

Chancel The eastern part of a church, often separated from the nave by a screen; contains the choir and ambulatory.

Churrigueresque Fancifully ornate form of Baroque named after its leading exponents, the Spaniard José Churriguera (1650–1723) and his extended family.

Classical Architectural style incorporating Greek and Roman elements – pillars, domes, colonnades, and so on – at its height in the seventeenth century and revived, as Neoclassical, in the nineteenth.

Clerestory Upper storey of a church, incorporating the windows.

Cyclopean Prehistoric style of dry-stone masonry comprising boulders of irregular form.

Fresco wall painting – durable through application to wet plaster.

Gothic Architectural style of the thirteenth to sixteenth centuries, characterized by pointed arches, rib vaulting, flying buttresses and a general emphasis on verticality.

Majolica See p.159.

Nave Main body of a church.

Neoclassical Architectural style derived from Greek and Roman elements – pillars, domes, colonnades, and so on – that was popular in the nineteenth century.

Plateresque Elaborately decorative Renaissance architectural style, named for its resemblance to silversmiths' work (*platería*).

Renaissance That period of European history - beginning in Italy in the fourteenth century – that marks the end of the medieval and the beginning of the early modern era. It is defined, amongst many criteria, by an increase in classical scholarship, geographical discovery, the rise of secular values and the growth of individualism; the term is also applied to the art and architecture of the period.

Retable Altarpiece.

Romanesque Early medieval architecture distinguished by squat forms, rounded arches and naive sculpture.

Rood screen Decorative screen separating the nave from the chancel; a rood loft is the gallery (or space) on top of it.

Stucco Marble-based plaster used to embellish ceilings, etc.

Transept Arms of a cross-shaped church, placed at ninety degrees to nave and chancel.

Triptych Carved or painted work on three panels.

Tympanum Sculpted, usually recessed, panel above a door.

Vault An arched ceiling or roof.

L

LANGUAGE | Glossary

Travel store

Available from all good bookstores

Kenya
Marrakesh **D**
Morocco
South Africa, Lesotho
  & Swaziland
Syria
Tanzania
Tunisia
West Africa
Zanzibar

Travel Specials

First-Time Africa
First-Time Around
  the World
First-Time Asia
First-Time Europe
First-Time Latin
  America
Travel Health
Travel Online
Travel Survival
Walks in London
  & SE England
Women Travel
World Party

Maps

Algarve
Amsterdam
Andalucia
  & Costa del Sol
Argentina
Athens
Australia
Barcelona
Berlin
Boston & Cambridge
Brittany
Brussels
California
Chicago
Chile
Corsica
Costa Rica
  & Panama
Crete
Croatia
Cuba
Cyprus
Czech Republic
Dominican Republic
Dubai & UAE
Dublin

Egypt
Florence & Siena
Florida
France
Frankfurt
Germany
Greece
Guatemala & Belize
Iceland
India
Ireland
Italy
Kenya & Northern
  Tanzania
Lisbon
London
Los Angeles
Madrid
Malaysia
Mallorca
Marrakesh
Mexico
Miami & Key West
Morocco
New England
New York City
New Zealand
Northern Spain
Paris
Peru
Portugal
Prague
Pyrenees & Andorra
Rome
San Francisco
Sicily
South Africa
South India
Spain & Portugal
Sri Lanka
Tenerife
Thailand
Toronto
Trinidad & Tobago
Tunisia
Turkey
Tuscany
Venice
Vietnam, Laos
  & Cambodia
Washington DC
Yucatán Peninsula

**Dictionary
Phrasebooks**

Croatian
Czech
Dutch
Egyptian Arabic
French
German
Greek
Hindi & Urdu
Italian
Japanese
Latin American
  Spanish
Mandarin Chinese
Mexican Spanish
Polish
Portuguese
Russian
Spanish
Swahili
Thai
Turkish
Vietnamese

Computers

Blogging
eBay
iPods, iTunes
  & music online
The Internet
Macs & OS X
MySpace
PCs and Windows
PlayStation Portable
Website Directory

Film & TV

American
  Independent Film
British Cult Comedy
Chick Flicks
Comedy Movies
Cult Movies
Film Musicals
Film Noir
Gangster Movies
Horror Movies
Kids' Movies
Sci-Fi Movies
Westerns

Lifestyle

Babies
Ethical Living
Pregnancy & Birth

Music Guides

The Beatles
Blues
Bob Dylan
Book of Playlists
Classical Music
Elvis
Frank Sinatra
Heavy Metal
Hip-Hop
Jazz
Opera
Pink Floyd
Punk
Reggae
Rock
The Rolling Stones
Soul and R&B
World Music
  (2 vols)

Popular Culture

Books for Teenagers
Children's Books,
  5-11
Conspiracy Theories
Crime Fiction
Cult Fiction
The Da Vinci Code
Lord of the Rings
Shakespeare
Superheroes
Unexplained
  Phenomena

Science

The Brain
Climate Change
The Earth
Genes & Cloning
The Universe
Weather

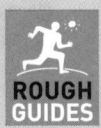

For more information go to www.roughguides.com

Small print and

Index

A Rough Guide to Rough Guides

Published in 1982, the first Rough Guide – to Greece – was a student scheme that became a publishing phenomenon. Mark Ellingham, a recent graduate in English from Bristol University, had been travelling in Greece the previous summer and couldn't find the right guidebook. With a small group of friends he wrote his own guide, combining a highly contemporary, journalistic style with a thoroughly practical approach to travellers' needs.

The immediate success of the book spawned a series that rapidly covered dozens of destinations. And, in addition to impecunious backpackers, Rough Guides soon acquired a much broader and older readership that relished the guides' wit and inquisitiveness as much as their enthusiastic, critical approach and value for-money ethos.

SMALL PRINT

These days, Rough Guides include recommendations from shoestring to luxury and cover more than 200 destinations around the globe, including almost every country in the Americas and Europe, more than half of Africa and most of Asia and Australasia. Our ever-growing team of authors and photographers is spread all over the world, particularly in Europe, the USA and Australia.

In the early 1990s, Rough Guides branched out of travel, with the publication of Rough Guides to World Music, Classical Music and the Internet. All three have become benchmark titles in their fields, spearheading the publication of a wide range of books under the Rough Guide name.

Including the travel series, Rough Guides now number more than 350 titles, covering: phrasebooks, waterproof maps, music guides from Opera to Heavy Metal, reference works as diverse as Conspiracy Theories and Shakespeare, and popular culture books from iPods to Poker. Rough Guides also produce a series of more than 120 World Music CDs in partnership with World Music Network.

Visit www.roughguides.com to see our latest publications.

Rough Guide travel images are available for commercial licensing at www.roughguidespictures.com

Rough Guide credits

Text editor: Nikki Birrell
Layout: Umesh Aggarwal
Cartography: Jasbir Sandhu
Picture editor: Siobhan Donoghue
Production: Aimee Hampson
Proofreader: Anna Leggett
Cover design: Chloë Roberts
Photographer: Simon Bracken
Editorial: **London** Kate Berens, Claire
Saunders, Joanna Kirby, Ruth Blackmore, Polly
Thomas, Richard Lim, Alison Murchie, Karoline
Densley, Andy Turner, Keith Drew, Edward
Aves, Alice Park, Sarah Eno, Lucy White,
David Paul, James Smart, Sam Cook, Joe
Staines, Duncan Clark, Peter Buckley, Matthew
Milton, Tracy Hopkins, Ruth Tidball; **New York**
Andrew Rosenberg, Steven Horak, April Isaacs,
AnneLise Sorensen, Amy Hegarty, Ella Steim,
Anna Owens, Joseph Petta, Sean Mahoney
Design & Pictures: **London** Scott Stickland,
Dan May, Diana Jarvis, Mark Thomas, Jj Luck,
Harriet Mills, Nicole Newman; **Delhi** Madhavi
Singh, Ajay Verma, Jessica Subramanian,

Ankur Guha, Pradeep Thapliyal, Sachin Tanwar,
Anita Singh
Production: Lauren Britton, Katherine Owers
Cartography: **London** Maxine Repath, Ed
Wright, Katie Lloyd-Jones; **Delhi** Jai Prakash
Mishra, Rajesh Chhibber, Ashutosh Bharti,
Animesh Pathak, Rajesh Mishra, Karobi Gogoi,
Amod Singh, Alakananda Bhattacharya,
Athokpam Jotinkumar
Online: **New York** Jennifer Gold, Kristin
Mingrone; **Delhi** Manik Chauhan, Narender
Kumar, Rakesh Kumar, Amit Verma, Amit Kumar,
Rahul Kumar, Ganesh Sharma, Debojit Borah
Marketing & Publicity: **London** Niki Hanmer,
Louise Maher, Anna Paynton, Jess Carter, Libby
Jellie; **New York** Geoff Colquitt, Megan Kennedy,
Katy Ball; **Delhi** Reem Khokhar
Special projects editor: Philippa Hopkins
Manager India: Punita Singh
Series editor: Mark Ellingham
Reference Director: Andrew Lockett
Publishing Coordinator: Megan McIntyre
Publishing Director: Martin Dunford

SMALL PRINT

Publishing information

This fourth edition published March 2007 by
Rough Guides Ltd,
80 Strand, London WC2R 0RL
345 Hudson St, 4th Floor,
New York, NY 10014, USA
14 Local Shopping Centre, Panchsheel Park,
New Delhi 110017, India
Distributed by the Penguin Group
Penguin Books Ltd,
80 Strand, London WC2R 0RL
Penguin Putnam, Inc.
375 Hudson Street, NY 10014, USA
Penguin Group (Australia)
250 Camberwell Road, Camberwell,
Victoria 3124, Australia
Penguin Books Canada Ltd,
10 Alcorn Avenue, Toronto, Ontario,
Canada M4V 1E4
Penguin Group (NZ)
67 Apollo Drive, Mairangi Bay, Auckland 1310,
New Zealand
Cover concept by Peter Dyer.

Typeset in Bembo and Helvetica to an original
design by Henry Iles.
Printed and bound in China
© Phil Lee

368pp includes index
A catalogue record for this book is available from
the British Library
ISBN 978-1-84353-796-0

Help us update

We've gone to a lot of effort to ensure that the
fourth edition of **The Rough Guide to Mallorca
& Menorca** is accurate and up-to-date. However,
things change – places get "discovered", opening
hours are notoriously fickle, restaurants and
rooms raise prices or lower standards. If you
feel we've got it wrong or left something out,
we'd like to know, and if you can remember the
address, the price, the time, the phone number,
so much the better.

   We'll credit all contributions, and send a copy
of the next edition (or any other Rough Guide

if you prefer) for the best letters. Everyone who
writes to us and isn't already a subscriber will
receive a copy of our full-colour thrice-yearly
newsletter. Please mark letters: "**Rough Guide
Mallorca & Menorca Update**" and send to:
Rough Guides, 80 Strand, London WC2R 0RL,
or Rough Guides, 4th Floor, 345 Hudson St,
New York, NY 10014. Or send an email to **mail@
roughguides.com**

   Have your questions answered and tell others
about your trip at
www.roughguides.atinfopop.com

Acknowledgements

Phil Lee would like to thank his editor, Nikki Birrell, for her patient and diligent work on this new edition of Mallorca & Menorca – it was much appreciated. Special thanks also to Gareth Rees, Jan Ogden, and Gavin Thomas for their help with the day hikes; Maria Peterson for all sorts of fact finding; Yvonne McFarlane for her insightful contributions; Ilse Bock for her hospitality and advice; and George Scott for his help – and wit.

Readers' letters

Thanks to all the readers who have taken the time to write in with comments and suggestions (and apologies if we've inadvertently omitted anyone's name):

Jim Abercrombie; Jenny Aldous; Frances Allen; David Anderson; Dinah Anderton; Marcene Ansterberry; Marek Antoszewski; Jenny Atton; Billy Averall; Ann Bamforth; John Banfield; Jim Barrell; Bridget Beck; Miguel Bonet; Michael & Frances Bowerman; Mike Braide; Lynette Brucks; Derek Bryce; Stuart Bull; Philip Burnard; Rebecca & Natasha Burnham; Sarah Callan; Val Carlill; John and Midge Cassetton; Angela and Matt Chapman; Chris Coakes; Sue Coats; V. A. Cooke; I. A. Cowie; Darrall Cozens; Jane Crawford-Baker; Damon Crawshaw; Anita Creed; Robert Crouch; Paul Davis; Mike Dean; Mark Dorrington; Kathryn Drewitt; Tove Elander; Alison Ewington; Graeme Falconer; John Fanshawe; Bettina Hartas Geary; Eri Gideon; John and Valerie Given; Anne Goodchild; Nick Gool; Annekatrin Grafton; Steven Graham; Mel Greig; Steve Hale; Nick Halsted; Nicola Hambridge; Roberta Heneage; Liz Heron; Karin von Herrath; Simon Hillyard; Nina Holmes; David Ireland; Pam and John Ireland; Malcolm Jackson; Tim Jenkins; Stuart Johnson; Lynn Tipper Jones; Hugh Josty; Susan Jurczyk; Hugh Kearney; Solna, Roger, J A Ketley; Elizabeth and Geoff Key; John Kop; Paul Lampard; John Landau; David Lee; Peter Lloyd; Roger Loxley; B. R. Lumby; Janet Macdonald; Yvonne McFarlane; Claire McGregor; Sian Mackay; Barbara McKiernan; Mary Marshall; Robbie Martzen; David Mather; Nicola and Ian Maunders; Phil Minshull; Andy Mitter; Clare and Richard Morgan; Lisa Nellis; David & Christine Neville; Hilary Nicol; Clive Paul; Chris Peake; Joan Pozzoli; Ann Roberts; Tony Robinson; Eric and Sally Rowland; Carol Saddington; H. H. Saffery; Helen Sandelands; George Scott; Judith de Serra; Jean Sinclair; David Sloan; Debbie Smith; Roxane Smith; Pat Stafford; Edward Staines; Wendy Stock; Zelda Tolley; Jan Trapmore; Barry Turner; Ann Viera; David Wallington; Christine Watson; Stephanie Webb; Wolfgang Weiss; M. Welch; John Weldon; E. Werenowska; Selina Westbury; Tom Whitehall; Clive Wilkin; Stephen Withers; Jean Woods; Claire Woodward-Nutt; Leesa Yeo.

Photo credits

All photos copyright Rough Guides except the following:

Introduction
Sunbathers and sunshades © Alamy

Things not to miss
07 Cabrera Island, Mallorca© Oriol Alamany Delimont /Corbis
02 Valldemossa, © Walter Bibikow /Alamy

Index

Map entries are in colour.

I

INDEX

INDEX

I

Map symbols

maps are listed in the full index using coloured text

------	Chapter division boundary	ᶸᵛᵁᵛ	Cliff
▬▬▬	Motorway	⩔	Spring
═══	Main road	⊤	Gardens
──	Minor road	⩔	Viewpoint
▬▬▬	Pedestrianized road	⋏	Campsite
- - - - -	Footpath	◉	Accommodation
⅏⅏⅏⅏	Steps	▣	Restaurant
─■──	Railway	ⓘ	Information office
┼─┼─┼	Tram line	⊠	Post office
─ ─ ─	Ferry route	@	Internet access
───	Waterway	★	Bus stop/taxi stand
■■■■■	Wall	🅿	Parking
◆	Place of interest	⛽	Petrol station
✈	Airport	⊞	Hospital
⊥	Church/Cathedral	⋂	Arch
⛪	Monastery	▬	Building
♛	Castle	⊞	Church (town maps)
▮	Tower	⬭	Stadium
∴	Ruins	▢	Market
⌒	Cave	▦	Park
▲	Mountain peak	▦	Beach
☀	Lighthouse	⊠	Restricted area
⛫	Stately home	⬡	Saltpan

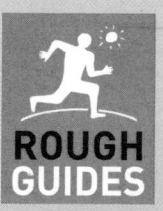